Powell's Recollections of a New York Chief of

OP/14.98   NDJ (H)

Americana & Regional Studies   103971

RECOLLECTIONS

OF A

NEW YORK CHIEF OF POLICE

PATTERSON SMITH REPRINT SERIES IN
CRIMINOLOGY, LAW ENFORCEMENT, AND SOCIAL PROBLEMS

A listing of publications in the SERIES *will be found at rear of volume*

Publication No. 133: Patterson Smith Reprint Series in
Criminology, Law Enforcement, and Social Problems

Recollections of a New York Chief of Police

by

GEORGE W. WALLING

with a Supplement on the Denver Police

by

A. KAUFMANN

Reprinted with the addition of
a new Introduction by James F. Richardson
and an Index

Illustrated

Montclair, New Jersey
Patterson Smith
1972

Recollections of a New York Chief of Police
first published 1887 by the Caxton Book Concern

Republished 1890 with the addition of
Historic Supplement of the Denver Police

Reprinted 1972 by Patterson Smith Publishing Corporation
Montclair, New Jersey 07042

New material copyright © 1972 by
Patterson Smith Publishing Corporation

Library of Congress Cataloging in Publication Data

Walling, George Washington, 1823–1891.
    Recollections of a New York chief of police.
    (Patterson Smith reprint series in criminology, law enforcement, and social problems. Publication no. 133)
    Reprint of the 1890 ed. with a new introduction and index.
    1. New York (City)—Police. 2. Crime and criminals—New York (City). I. Title.
HV8148.N5W3   1972   363.2'097471   70-129311
ISBN 0-87585-133-9

This book is printed on
permanent/durable paper

INTRODUCTION TO THE REPRINT EDITION

GEORGE WALLING'S *Recollections of a New York Chief of Police* first appeared in 1887, two years after his retirement as superintendent of the New York Police Department. In 1890 a second edition was published, consisting of the original text with the addition of A. Kaufmann's "Historic Supplement of the Denver Police." This reprinting also contains both the Walling and the Kaufmann material.

Arthur Schlesinger, in his *The Rise of the City,* asserted that the 1880s marked the emergence of the city as the major force in American life and the time when Americans came to realize that theirs was to be an urban future. Recognition of the United States as a society dominated by its cities may have come a decade or two earlier, but certainly the 1880s saw a spate of books acclaiming urban growth or lamenting urban pathology. In the latter category were such classics as Josiah Strong's *Our Country,* which features urbanization and its consequences and in which most of the chapter-titles begin with the word "Perils"; and *The American Commonwealth* by James Bryce, the perceptive Englishman who observed that municipal government was the one conspicuous failure of American society.

Crime and the police occupied an important position in the literature on the city, from lurid exposés of the "sins of the great city," which could serve as guides to where the action was, to sober discussions of how urban politics could be restored to the control of gentlemen and made respectable again. Journalists supplied magazines and Sunday newspapers with accounts of famous crimes and successful detectives, while moralists called for police crusades against gambling-houses, brothels, and saloons open on Sunday. Both romantics and reformers wrote on the police.

From 1885 to 1887, at least three books were published on or by members of the New York Police Department in addition to Walling's *Recollections*. Augustine E. Costello's *Our Police Protectors* appeared in 1885, Inspector Thomas F. Byrnes's *Professional Criminals of America* in 1886, and a little book entitled *Our Police,* published anonymously by Andrea Kornmann, the wife of Patrolman Frederick Kornmann, in 1887. Like Kaufmann, the author of the Denver section of this volume, Costello was a journalist who announced his intention to devote part of the proceeds of his book to his local police benevolent fund. Byrnes in 1886 was Chief of Detectives of the New York department; his title of Chief Inspector had been created for him by the state legislature. He may well have been the most famous policeman in the country, and he knew how to exploit the public's interest in crime and detection to enhance his own status and prestige. Mrs. Kornmann published her book herself, and found the market somewhat saturated, especially as she did not receive any assistance from the authorities in selling it.

All these books are in the romantic tradition. They stress famous crimes and criminals and heroic or exceptionally shrewd police exploits. Walling, for example, devotes much space to the murder of the wealthy broker Benjamin Nathan, the *modus operandi* of the noted fence Mother Mandelbaum, and such bizarre cases as the harassment of the eminent Episcopal divine, Morgan Dix, by Eugene Fairfax Williamson. (W. A. Swanberg recently published a small book on this incident, entitled *The Rector and the Rogue*.) In the last chapter, however, Walling establishes his credentials in the reform camp by making recommendations for improving the state of public order and morality and the quality of municipal government.

For the most part Walling's recommendations reflect the standard "good government" approach of the Gilded Age. New York City suffered from an extremely high tax-rate and grossly inadequate public services because, according to Walling, "we have a government by the politician, of the politician, and for the politician" (p. 598). His solution was to throw the rascals out and get gentlemen back into political participation and public office. An elected judiciary and prosecutor had been disastrous for the effective administration of criminal justice, since these officials were "elected and controlled in a great measure by the very elements they are called upon to punish and keep in check" (p. 599). Universal suffrage had proved a failure in great cities, although Walling specifically ruled out a property qualification for the franchise. He often alluded to the potent combination of politics and the police, and presented the usual Mugwump conception of the necessity of separating the two in order to provide disinterested public service and clean municipal government.

For modern readers Walling provides more than a short course in respectable late nineteenth-century political thought. He demonstrates that much of what we now know as the urban crisis, including crime in the streets and the breakdown of morality, has been with us for a long time. His accounts of murders, bank robberies, forgeries, the "social evil," and urban riots remind us that we are not the first generation to feel threatened by an overwhelming tide of crime, vice, and disorder, and he tells us much that is useful about the social patterns of crime and criminals in the last century.

The author also provides important insights into the outlook of the police and their role in society. He strongly defends, for example, his order that pickpockets be arrested on sight on public holidays and at parades. He recounts his battle with A. Oakey Hall, former district attorney and mayor, when the police held men allegedly responsible for robbing the Adams Express Company without taking them before a magistrate as required by law. Although the commissioners fined Walling ten days' pay for holding the men, he maintains that he was morally right even if technically wrong. On another occasion he forced an emetic down the throat of a swindler who had swallowed a counterfeit bill, to make him cough up the evidence. He notes without objection that the police habitually made arrests on suspicion; those detained would spend the night in the station-house lockup, only to be released by a police justice in the morning for lack of evidence. He contrasts the freedom of action of the New York police in breaking up crowds and making arrests on suspicion with the constraints under which the London force operated, and Walling's sympathies are all with the New York system. To him civil liberties, claims for justice at the hands of power, are hindrances to the police, who could not do their jobs if hemmed in by procedural limitations. Like many of his contemporaries and successors, Walling believed that the policeman was justified in stretching the law for the sake of keeping the peace and dealing adequately with criminals.

At the end of the book, he comments on the bad relations between civilians and the police and the extent of community hostility, but he never considers whether the police's view that they were above the law might have had something to do with these problems. To be fair, policemen in his day and in ours have been pressed to show results, to give civilians a feeling that their lives, property, and sense of order are being protected. If achieving these goals requires extraordinary methods, so be it, says Walling, as long as the police do not make the mistake of applying tactics suitable to the "dangerous classes" (to use a nineteenth-century expression) on respectable and powerful members of society. In short, it is not what the police do that counts, but to whom they do it. As a result the relations between the police and the poor and the alienated have never been good: Walling reminds us that this situation is not new.

The public view of the police, then as now, also suffered from the fact that the department was traditionally charged with preventing or suppressing behavior which many people thought harmless. In the case of consensual crimes, crimes without victims (such as gambling), any attempt to enforce the law engendered strong opposition. The statutes proclaimed that the saloons had to remain closed on Sundays; but the moral values of the majority of the urban population and of most policemen sanctioned a few beers on a Sunday afternoon. If the police did attempt to enforce the law, they were charged with "rigid" and "harsh" conduct and often subjected to political reprisal; if they did not, they could be attacked by the supporters of morals legislation for violating their trust and ignoring their obligations. They found themselves in the middle of a tug-of-war between social groups with conflicting conceptions of licit behavior. Police performance that satisfied one group had to outrage another, and it was impossible for the force to arrive at a satisfactory and lasting understanding with all the elements of its diverse constituency.

Walling does not relate the police problems over gambling and prostitution to competing value-systems, but rather to the department's internal structure, its chain of command. He served as superintendent, the leading position within the department, from 1874 to 1885; but the actual executive power lay with the Board of Commissioners, which at that time consisted of four civilians appointed by the mayor for terms of six years each. Walling objected that he was in the worst of all positions: he had responsibility without power. For example, the superintendent could do nothing about gambling and prostitution; only the captain of each precinct could possibly close faro parlors and brothels.

Early in Walling's term of office the commissioners weakened whatever control the superintendent had had over the captains, or precinct commanders, by decreeing that all orders and reports between superintendent and captains must go through the inspectors. Before this ruling, the four inspectors had served as a staff for the superintendent; now the commissioners grouped the precincts into four inspection districts, each under the command of an inspector. Walling protested that the new arrangement denied him any effective supervisory power. He could issue an order, but it was up to the inspectors and captains to execute it, and if they saw fit to ignore or circumvent him, his only recourse was to prefer charges against them before the commissioners. If the commissioners saw fit not to act, the superintendent was helpless.

Time and time again have I attempted, one way or another, to have fuller power placed in my hands, but for the last four years during which I was superintendent, my position was that of a mere figure-head. What I claim is, that a man who is held responsible for the actions of certain subordinates in any public department, should have absolute control over those under him as to assignment and transfer. (p. 578)

Walling naturally wanted the superintendent to have effective powers of discipline, transfer, and assignment, but such an arrangement conflicted with the political role of the department and its Board of Commissioners. From 1864 until 1901 the four men on the board were usually divided equally, by custom if not by law, between the major political parties. In 1895, after the famous investigation conducted by the Lexow Committee, the legislature made this pattern mandatory in order to curb Tammany Hall: the bipartisan board supposedly ensured that each party would receive a reasonable share of police patronage—appointments, desirable assignments, and promotions. Turning these powers over to the superintendent would have given one party or faction a monopoly, if the superintendent were partisan; if he were not, the party organizations would have been completely frozen out. Neither alternative was acceptable to the politicians, and Walling, as superintendent, remained in an anomalous position throughout his career. Theoretically, he was chief executive officer of the department, but the real decision-making power lay with the board.

The commissioners did not function as autonomous bureaucrats; rather they represented and protected the interests of the party or faction which had appointed them. Thus they decided questions of discipline and assignment on the basis of the balance of political power in the city, and sometimes in the state, not the professional and organizational needs of an independent agency. Policemen and politicians constantly sought favorable assignments for themselves or their supporters, and every promotion, every transfer, and every disciplinary action could evoke heavy political pressure. If a policeman made a mistake, such as arresting a saloonkeeper with influence, he could be transferred or otherwise reminded that he had used his authority unwisely. (The Kaufmann supplement indicates that the Denver police also had to operate with a sharp eye to political realities—each new mayor there brought in a new chief of police.)

Almost every subsequent head of the New York Police Department has chafed at his inability to establish effective control over the force. Theodore Roosevelt, the most famous and colorful of New York's nineteenth-century police commissioners, wrote of the statute making a bipartisan board mandatory: "a more foolish or vicious law was never enacted by any legislative body.

It modelled the government of the police force somewhat on the lines of the Polish parliament, and it was avowedly designed to make it difficult to get effective action."

In 1901, the legislature abolished the police board in favor of a single commissioner. Those interested in improving the performance of the police had supported a single-commissioner system since the 1880s, and Walling endorsed the proposal in his final chapter. Recent history, however, indicates that the institution of a single commissioner has not eliminated the administrative problem. No commissioner has ever been able to suppress corruption and abuse of authority among his subordinates completely. Nor have many commissioners been willing, or if willing able, to move the department in new directions, to replace tradition with innovation as the mainspring of police activity.

Ironically, his adherence to tradition was the one criticism the *New York Times* made of Walling's performance as superintendent. On the occasion of his retirement, the *Times* wrote: "The only complaint that can be fairly made of Superintendent Walling is that he has fallen too much into the routine and the traditions of the force, and that the traditions are not good traditions." It would seem in fact that Walling, however responsible his position might have appeared to the public, was a powerless and altogether unwilling victim of the traditions that fettered the police superintendent's authority.

Supervisors from that day to this have expressed similar grievances. Running through the *New York Times'* interview with former Commissioner Howard R. Leary published on June 8, 1970, is the theme that it is much easier for the commissioner to identify problem areas and concerns than it is for him to mount the resources to deal with them effectively. The commissioner's responsibilities are far-ranging indeed; his power to meet these responsibilities, including that of controlling his own subordinates, is distinctly limited.

In the nineteenth century, the party organizations hampered the superintendent's leadership. In the twentieth century, state and city agencies have offset some evils of the past by giving policemen job security and making appointments and promotions to the level of captain subject to civil-service procedures. These changes have in many ways increased the strength of the bureaucracy; organizations such as the Patrolmen's Benevolent Association have acquired power beyond anything conceived of in the nineteenth century. To a considerable extent the police have themselves become active and potent participants in the political process, rather than simply instruments of the political parties. The political power of these bodies and the nature of police work itself make the control of his own department the commissioner's most difficult task.

Perhaps the most disappointing feature of Walling's work as a source for the contemporary student is his reticence about the precise nature of the relationships between police, politicians, and the underworld. He speaks only in general terms, not in specifics. Nor does he provide the information necessary to understand the political context in which the police of his time operated. Walling spent almost 38 years with the New York Police, from 1847 to 1885, and the department's administrative structure during that time was anything but static. When he joined the force, policemen were appointed by the Council members of their wards for terms of only two years. In 1849 the legislature lengthened the term to four years, and from 1853 onwards policemen served for good behavior—that is, they could be removed only for cause. Before 1853, men appointed when one party had control of the ward would probably not be reappointed when their terms expired if the opposition had come to power in the meantime. Walling himself met this problem: he had to move from the Third to the Eighteenth Ward in order to continue his police career.

The 1853 law, backed by the newly formed City Reform party led by Peter Cooper among others, made other substantial changes in police organization. Each of the city's wards had previously constituted a police patrol district, and the alderman of the ward controlled the appointments of captain and men for that precinct. There was a Chief of Police with an office in the basement of City Hall, but he lacked any effective supervisory power. The early police were, as Walling notes, not uniformed, and there were no limitations on age or requirements as to physical condition; the department thus had a number of "old and feeble" members. The 1853 law attempted to remedy some of these defects by entrusting the management of the police to a Board of Commissioners consisting of the mayor, the recorder (a judicial official), and the city judge. These board members would, it was hoped, be more respectable and less parochial than the aldermen elected from the various wards. The creation of the board paralleled contemporary moves in other cities, as city councils all over the country were losing control over increasingly complex administrative functions. The new commissioners instituted a uniform for the force, over some strenuous objections, and raised the level of discipline and morale; boards also ensured that no one man or officer would have full power over the police. Americans feared political power and believed that the only way to prevent power from becoming despotism was to keep it limited and divided.

Walling tells us that the board worked well at first, but that under Fernando Wood the police became "used for political purposes." The board, he continues, "failed to give satisfaction and was ridiculed and condemned" (p. 54). He then baldly states that the state legislature took control of the New York Police Department by creating a Metropolitan Police under commissioners appointed by the governor. The story is more interesting and more involved than this. Wood was elected mayor in November, 1854, and on taking office in January, 1855, he stressed his intention to reform city government in general and the police force in particular. His campaign had won him sufficient support from many leading merchants, editors, and political figures to beat back an attempt, mounted by opponents of the New York City Democratic party in the state legislature in March, 1855, to transfer control of the police from city to state officials.

Wood later lost much of this support. He instructed the police to pay no attention to a law passed by the legislature in April, 1855, forbidding the sale of alcohol for other than medicinal or sacramental purposes. The courts declared it unconstitutional the following year, but, even before that, it was never enforced in New York City. Moreover, Wood did use the police to advance his own political career. He appointed his supporters to the force, systematically collected from the police for his 1856 campaign fund, and sent a good many policemen on furlough to canvass for his reelection rather than patrol the streets. He won a second term as mayor, but his opponents secured a majority in the state legislature.

Early in the session of 1857, they introduced a bill transferring control of the police to commissioners appointed by the governor. This change would increase Republican patronage in the Police Department, make it more difficult for the Democrats to control elections, increase the level of enforcement of the Sunday closing laws, and reduce the political influence of the Democratic saloonkeepers. Originally, the law applied only to New York City, but the legislature enlarged the police district to include some of the suburban counties—in order to bypass a provision of the state constitution of 1846 that employees of local governments had to be elected by the voters or appointed by the officials of the local government in question. As a new district, created specially by the legislature, however, the Metropolitan Police district did not come under this provision; and the courts upheld the governor's power to appoint commissioners.

Walling's account of the conflict between the two police forces—the minority who accepted the new commissioners and the majority who remained faithful to Mayor Wood in defying the Metropolitan Police law—is one of the most valuable sections of the book. His "verbatim" conversations concerning the City Hall riot of June 16, 1857, must be treated with skepticism; these events had taken place thirty years before. But he is accurate in all of the particulars in which he can be checked, such as the number of policemen on each side, and even the extent of the damages awarded against Wood in favor of those Metropolitans injured in the riot (pp. 54-61).

As one of the minority of captains who supported the Metropolitan commissioners, Walling played an important role in the new department. He served as head of detectives, and later as commander of the Twentieth Precinct, and in 1866 he was promoted from captain to inspector to fill the vacancy caused by the death of Daniel Carpenter. It was just at this time that the scope and authority of the Metropolitan Police were being increased by the state legislature, because the Republicans there found this a convenient and effective way of increasing party power in predominantly Democratic New York City.

During these years, however, William Tweed was consolidating his hold over the city and later over the state Democratic party as well; by 1869, he had succeeded in electing a Democratic governor and a Democratic majority in the legislature. The following year Tweed beat back factional challenges within the party and guided a new charter for New York City through the legislature. (He later admitted that he spent $600,000 to accomplish this goal.) The Tweed charter returned control of the police to municipal authorities; commissioners, instead of being chosen by governor or legislature, would henceforth be appointed by the mayor, with the consent of the Board of Aldermen, for six-year terms. Walling mentions the resignation of John A. Kennedy in 1870, after ten years as superintendent of police, but he does not discuss the restoration of municipal, and therefore Democratic, control which preceded Kennedy's resignation. Walling himself became superintendent in 1874.

He is equally uninformative about the circumstances surrounding his own retirement on June 9, 1885. He gives us the date but not much more. According to the *New York Times,* the commissioners had asked Walling to resign two years earlier, but he had refused. In 1885 the legislature made retirement mandatory at the age of sixty, for all ranks in the Police Department. It was widely understood that Walling was the target of this law: he was sixty-two at the time. He retired when the commissioners made known their determination to force him out if need be. This of course then made possible promotions down the chain of command from superintendent to sergeant. It is difficult to say whether his age or the weakness of his political position constituted Walling's greater handicap.

George Walling returned to his native New Jersey and died there on December 31, 1891. By devoting his last years to writing these *Recollections* he ensured that his service to the public did not come to an end with his retirement.

JAMES F. RICHARDSON.

University of Akron
December, 1971

George W. Walling

RECOLLECTIONS

OF A

NEW YORK

CHIEF OF POLICE,

BY

GEORGE W. WALLING.

AN OFFICIAL RECORD OF THIRTY-EIGHT YEARS
AS
PATROLMAN, DETECTIVE, CAPTAIN, INSPECTOR
AND
CHIEF OF THE NEW YORK POLICE.

ILLUSTRATED FROM ORIGINAL DRAWINGS
AND PHOTOGRAPHS.

———•·•·•———

NEW YORK:
CAXTON BOOK CONCERN, LIMITED.
1888.

[*title page of the 1888 printing*]

INTRODUCTION.

In penning this volume of police history, together with that of criminals and prominent men, I have much to say that will please, instruct, and, I trust, better its readers.

In many instances the facts given will be told for the first time. No lurid pen was needed, for no fiction could be so rich in sensational incident as the true record of the lives of great criminals. The tale of the professional law-breaker in the glory of his success, the homage paid him by the lesser lights of the profession, contrasted with his downfall, and the misery that, sooner or later, surely visits him, forms a more startling and deeper warning than comes from any pulpit.

My work is not confined to either sex, but treats of male and female unfortunates alike. If, now and then, these facts seemingly trench upon personalities, in the business, social, political and criminal life of the city of New York, during the period over which my connection with, and control of the police force extends, mine is not the blame nor responsibility. Full well do I know the power of that mighty combination—Politics and Police. I attempted to make a stand against it, but the result was most disastrous to myself, and will be found recorded in the concluding chapters. So long as this combination is allowed to exist, just so long will delay and corruption have a grasp upon that which should uphold the honor, integrity and well-being of our citizens.

The incidents narrated in this volume are those which came under my personal observation, and although they may differ somewhat from reports published at the time of the occurrences, or generally accepted traditions, yet the official records will bear me out, and be a complete vindication of my truthfulness.

In writing this book, no private ends nor aims are sought to be served. My endeavor, throughout, has been to lay before the public a plain, unvarnished statement of indisputable facts which have not before been accessible to the public.

GEO. W. WALLING.

CONTENTS.

CHAPTER I.

EARLY YEARS.—REMOVAL TO KEYPORT, N. J.—THE "CHINGARORA." —"THE LONG, LOW, BLACK SCHOONER."—A REGULAR SCARE. —ON THE "SPENCER."—THE MURDER OF HELEN JEWETT.— THE COLT TRAGEDY.—DID THE MURDERER COMMIT SUICIDE?— THE PRETTY CIGAR GIRL.—EDGAR A. POE AS AN AMATEUR DETECTIVE.—THE STADT HUYS.—BELL-AND-RATTLE WATCH.—THE WHIPPING-POST.—CREMATION WITH A VENGEANCE.—"LEATHERHEADS."—WASHINGTON IRVING'S PRACTICAL JOKE......PP. 23–32.

CHAPTER II.

I BECOME A POLICEMAN.—"BUTTER-CAKE DICK."—"YOU MUST NEVER DO THAT AGAIN."—THE "BUTTON" CASE.—A SHARP PIECE OF DETECTIVE WORK.—HOW I SAVED TOM HYER FROM YANKEE SULLIVAN'S GANG.—"THE FORTY-NINERS."....PP. 33–42.

CHAPTER III.

ASTOR-PLACE RIOTS.—FORREST AND MACREADY.—"SI" SHAY AND "BUTT" ALLEN.—RIOTERS STORM THE OPERA HOUSE.—FEARFUL LOSS OF LIFE.—AUTHORSHIP OF INFLAMMATORY HANDBILLS.—THE "HONEYMOON" GANG.—ENGLISH ROW AND IRISH ROW.—ATTACK ON N. P. WILLIS.—"STAND BACK, GENTLEMEN."—JENNY LIND.—BILL POOL AND LEW BAKER.—DELIBERATE MURDER.—GRAND FUNERAL.—AN OCEAN CHASE.—CAPTURE OF THE ASSASSIN.—"I DIE A TRUE AMERICAN."—THE SWORD-CANE.—BOND STREET TRAGEDY.—THE BOGUS BABY.
PP. 43–53.

CHAPTER IV.

CHANGES IN POLICE DISCIPLINE.—POLITICAL INFLUENCE.—FERNANDO WOOD'S BATTLE.—WARRANT FOR THE ARREST OF THE MAYOR.—HE DEFIES MY AUTHORITY.—ANOTHER ATTEMPT.—THE SEVENTH REGIMENT APPEARS ON THE SCENE.—RELUCTANT SURRENDER.—$50,000 WORTH OF DIAMONDS.—HICKS, THE PIRATE.—A FLOATING SLAUGHTER-HOUSE.—A COSTLY BANQUET.—FLOORS WASHED WITH WINE.—VISIT OF THE PRINCE OF WALES.—EXECUTION OF CAPTAIN GORDON.—MARRIED TO HER FATHER'S COACHMAN.—MURDER IN THE "LIBRARY."—A JUSTIFIABLE DEED.—THE PANIC.—RUN ON THE BANKS.
PP. 54–67.

CHAPTER V.

THE POLICE AND SECESSIONISTS.—AN ANTE-BELLUM EPISODE.—PLOT TO ASSASSINATE PRESIDENT LINCOLN.—DOWN IN DIXIE.—THE SOUTHERN VOLUNTEERS.—A PERILOUS POSITION AND A MYSTERIOUS GUIDE.—ON THE TRAIN.—A JUMP FOR LIFE.—BRAVE TIM WEBSTER AND HIS SAD FATE—THE MAN WITH THE FUR CAP ....PP. 68–77.

CHAPTER VI.

IN WAR TIME.—THE DRAFT RIOTS.—HEROISM OF THE POLICE.—THE BATTLE OF THE BARRICADES.—THE SHARP-SHOOTER ON THE ROOF.—WITH A BULLET IN HIS BRAIN ....PP. 78–86.

CHAPTER VII.

CAPTURING HACKENSACK.—MYSTERIOUS VISITS TO NEW YORK.—AT THE SHOP WINDOW.—THE FATEFUL RING.—RECEIVING THE RUSSIANS.—TRYING TO BURN THE CITY.—THE BLACK BAGS.—THE "BOGUS" PROCLAMATION.—BURNING OF BARNUM'S MUSEUM.—AN UNHAPPY "HAPPY FAMILY."—STRUGGLE OF THE EAGLE AND

SERPENT.—EMBEZZLING $250,000 TO SATISFY BLACKMAILERS.
—A POLICEMAN MURDERED.....................PP. 87–100.

CHAPTER VIII.

ALBERT D. RICHARDSON'S MURDER.—THE DYING MAN'S RECOGNITION.—TRIALS OF A YOUNG WIFE.—THE LOVER'S PROMISE.—THE MURDERER FREE.—VAN EETEN FORGERIES.—A STERN CHASE BUT A SUCCESSFUL ONE.—RE-ARRESTED WHEN LIBERTY WAS SECURED.—BEFORE THE LAST JUDGE OF ALL..PP. 101–112.

CHAPTER IX.

THE NATHAN MURDER.—A TERRIBLE NIGHT.—THE TWO BROTHERS.—A GHASTLY SCENE.—TWELVE BLOWS WHICH TOOK A LIFE.—BLOODY FINGER-MARKS ON THE WALL.—FINDING OF THE IRON "DOG."—MERCILESS SUSPICIONS.—THE HOUSEKEEPER'S SON.—"HIS CLOTHES DON'T FIT HIM."—CLEANSING THE ROOM.—AN UNSOLVED MYSTERY...............................PP. 113–125.

CHAPTER X.

THE "SAWDUST" SWINDLE.—A BROKER DUPED.—THE BOGUS DETECTIVE.—MOCK AUCTIONS.—FLANNEL AND HOT WATER.—WITH A BIBLE IN HIS HAND.—A HORSEY GO-BETWEEN..PP. 126–137.

CHAPTER XI.

THE THIEVES OF THE RIVER.—MURDER ON THE "WATSON."—KILLED FOR TWELVE CENTS.—THE HARBOR POLICE.—SCENE IN A BROOKLYN HORSE-CAR.—"SOCCO, THE BRACER'S" END.—THE HOOK GANG.—GONE TO BROOKLYN AND JERSEY CITY....PP. 138–152.

CHAPTER XII.

ON DUTY ON STATEN ISLAND.—APPOINTED INSPECTOR.—THE "CAR HOOK" MURDER.—THE ORANGE RIOTS.—A GOOD STORY ABOUT

JIM FISKE.—HIS DEATH.—STEVE GORDON AND THE $1000 BILL.—"BOSS" TWEED AND HIS RING.—HOW WINANS WAS BRIBED.
PP. 153–163.

CHAPTER XIII.

SURPRISED BY NIGHT.—HOW THEY WERE TO "DO IT."—BROCKWAY, THE COUNTERFEITER.—THE PEDLER.—WOMAN'S LOVE OF FINERY.—A MILLION-DOLLAR SWINDLE.—ABOARD THE "THURINGIA."—TWO IMPERFECT BILLS.—SENTENCED FOR LIFE.—A SWINDLER'S CAREER.—AN UNSUSPECTING CATTLE DROVER.—AFTER TIFFANY'S DIAMONDS..................PP. 164–177.

CHAPTER XIV.

DISPUTE WITH THE POLICE COMMISSIONERS.—CRANKS WHO WRITE LETTERS.—EXPECTING COUNTERFEIT NOTES AND GETTING SAWDUST.—A LITTLE BY-PLAY ON BROADWAY.—"THE THIRD DEGREE."—THE MAN WHO PULLED OUT HIS WHISKERS.—FACTS ABOUT THE FINEST FORCE..................PP. 178–197.

CHAPTER XV.

KIDNAPPING OF CHARLEY ROSS.—MYSTERIOUS LETTERS.—ON THE TRACK OF THE CRIMINALS.—SEARCHING LAND AND WATER.—A TREACHEROUS AIDE.—THE BURGLARY AT VAN BRUNT'S HOUSE.—DEATH OF THE ABDUCTORS..............PP. 198–208.

CHAPTER XVI.

BURGLARS.—HOW THEY WORK.—PRETTY SERVANT GIRLS.—A LITTLE PIECE OF SCARLET RIBBON.—THIEVES ON THE ROOF.—A LEAP IN THE DARK.—"STUTTERING JOHN" ASHORE IN JERSEY.—HOW PICKPOCKETS OPERATE.—A MAN WHO KNEW IT ALL.—ARRESTED AT SIGHT.—HOW I WAS FINED.—THIEVES WHO TALKED FROM THEIR CELL DOORS...............PP. 209–223.

CHAPTER XVII.

THE COMPLETE STORY OF THE ROBBERY OF A. T. STEWART'S GRAVE.—WORK OF THE GHOULS.—CONCEALMENT OF THE BODY.—DEMAND FOR A RANSOM.—MRS. STEWART'S DISTRESS—JUDGE HILTON'S REFUSAL TO PAY THE ROBBERS.—FINAL NEGOTIATIONS.—THE BONES OF THE MILLIONAIRE EXCHANGED FOR MONEY UPON A HILL IN WESTCHESTER COUNTY.—RESTORED AND BORNE TO THE CATHEDRAL VAULT.—THE GOBLIN BELLS...PP. 224–235.

CHAPTER XVIII.

BANK BURGLARIES. — KINGS AMONG THIEVES. — "FOUR-FINGERED JACK."—THE SATCHEL IN THE HALL.—MAKING THE CASHIER UNLOCK A BANK VAULT.—"RED" LEARY'S BRAVADO.—"IF THE FUNDS HAVE GOT TO GO, I WILL GO WITH THEM."—A HEROIC CASHIER.—A TERRIBLE DISCOVERY.—UNJUST SUSPICIONS.—THE HOLE UNDER THE PRESIDENT'S CHAIR.—THE SCHEME THAT WAS HATCHED IN A BROADWAY BILLIARD PARLOR.—SMOULDERING BAGS OF GOLD.—THE LITTLE BLACK TRUNK ON ELIZABETH STREET.—BARON SHINDELL.—BUGGINS, THE BANK MESSENGER............................PP. 236–260.

CHAPTER XIX.

ROBBING THE MANHATTAN BANK.—A SYNDICATE OF BURGLARS.—A NARROW ESCAPE.—THE DUMMY MISLEADING.—QUICK WORK.— LOADED WITH WEALTH. — A LOQUACIOUS POLICEMAN. — NABBED.—A GENIUS AS A BANK BURGLAR.—THE DECOMPOSING BODY.—A MISTAKE AT NORRISTOWN.—A YOUTHFUL BRIDE.—THE SOUTH KENSINGTON BANK.—A WIFE'S DISCOVERY.—THE LAST TIME ALIVE.—PROBABLY THE MURDERER......PP. 261–278.

CHAPTER XX.

MOTHER MANDELBAUM, THE QUEEN OF FENCES.—THE OLD WOMAN'S WORD NEVER DOUBTED.—THE HOUSE IN CLINTON

STREET.—A PATRON OF CRIMINALS.—THE FIRST MISTAKE.—A DETERMINED DISTRICT ATTORNEY.—DETECTED.—OFF FOR CANADA.—A MOTHER AND HER DEAD DAUGHTER........PP. 279–291.

CHAPTER XXI.

ESCAPES FROM PRISON.—THE STRANGE WOMAN IN BLACK WHO WALKED OUT OF THE TOMBS.—THE BANK BURGLAR'S SWEETHEART.—" YOUR TICKET, PLEASE."—THE MAN WHO SOAPED HIS BODY AND WRIGGLED THROUGH A HOLE.—DESPERATE FIGHT IN A BOWERY BEER SALOON.—A BOLD LEAP FOR LIBERTY.—THE STRANGE MAN ON DE KALB AVENUE WITH TWO COATS.—THE WAX IMPRESSION FOUND IN "LONG MARY'S" ROOM.—" RED LEARY'S ESCAPED !".................PP. 292–305.

CHAPTER XXII.

PERSECUTING THE RECTOR OF TRINITY CHURCH.—ONSLAUGHT OF THE CHILDREN OF ISRAEL.—NOT AN EPILEPTIC FIT.—UNWELCOME LIQUOR BILLS.—A " HERALD " PERSONAL.—AN INDIGNANT HUSBAND.—TRACING THE HANDWRITING.—FOUND IN BALTIMORE.—" GENTLEMAN JOE'S " DEATH........PP. 306–320.

CHAPTER XXIII.

A LAW-BREAKER AS KNOWN BY HIS FAMILY.—SOME MISCONCEPTIONS.—NOT AN AGENT OF THE ASSOCIATED PRESS.—PHILIP SCHUYLER OR JOHN SPICER ?—A FIFTY-YEAR-OLD SON WHO DIDN'T KNOW HIS FATHER.—A SOMEWHAT COMPLICATED WILL CASE.—ISAAC M. SINGER AND HIS MANY WIVES.—FIRST A STROLLING PLAYER AND THEN A MILLIONAIRE.—CHARACTERISTICS OF CRIMINALS.—WHAT MAKES A LAW BREAKER.—THE FIRST STEP IN EVIL-DOING.—THE HARRIS FAMILY·.................PP. 321–334

CHAPTER XXIV.

FORGERS AND FORGING.—THE ARISTOCRATIC AND WEALTHY MEXICAN DOCTOR.—" A MOST CONSUMMATE VILLAIN."—THE SUN-

DAY-SCHOOL TEACHER WHO FORGED CHECKS FOR $250,000.—THREE MEN WHO CAME FROM A HOUSE IN ALLEN STREET ON A DARK WINTER'S NIGHT.—HOW JAMES A. GARFIELD WAS NEARLY DEFEATED.—THE FORGER WITH BLACK EYES AND RAVEN HAIR. —LORD ASHBURTON AND HIS ROMANTIC CAREER.—ROCKY MOUNTAIN BLACKMAILERS.—THE UNION BANK OF LONDON FORGERIES... ....PP. 335–349.

CHAPTER XXV.

SWINDLERS AND BLACKMAILERS.—"HE CAN'T BEAT ME PLAYIN' POKER."—A SWINDLER SWINDLED.—DIVORCES PROCURED BY WHOLESALE.—SWINDLING A GREAT DRY GOODS HOUSE.—A BANK BILL.—HOW TO PUNISH A BLACKMAILER.—"I CAME IN HERE TO KILL YOU."..........................PP. 350–361.

CHAPTER XXVI.

A PLOT OF NIHILISTS.—THREATENING LETTERS.—LITTLE ROSA STRASBURGER.—A CAUTIOUS RABBI.—DETECTIVE CAMPBELL'S WATCH.—"I'LL BLOW YOUR BRAINS OUT."—A BLACKMAILER'S DEATH.—LETTERS TO JAY GOULD.—INTERESTED IN "SALVATION."—WATCHING THE MAILING-BOXES.—THE MYSTERY SOLVED..............................PP. 362–372.

CHAPTER XXVII.

PRIZE-FIGHTING AND FIGHTERS.—THE LAW ON THE SUBJECT.—EARLY HEROES IN THE "RING."—AN ADVENTURE WITH "BILL" HARRINGTON.—JOHN MORRISSEY.—HIS ARRIVAL IN NEW YORK.—JOHN L. SULLIVAN.—HIS LIFE.—FARO.—"EDE" NORRIS AND HIS VISITORS.—LEGAL ASPECT OF GAMBLING.—WHY IT IS NOT SUPPRESSED.—A REMEDY.—PLAYING ON A SYSTEM.—A SUCCESSFUL GAMBLER.—POLICY, KENO AND POKER.—MATTHIAS DANSER'S MONEY.—CUTTING COUPONS BY CANDLE LIGHT.—$8000 UNDER SEWING-MACHINE PLATES.—A GAMBLER'S FORTUNE GIVEN TO THE CHURCH.....................PP. 373–386.

CHAPTER XXVIII.

A GLIMPSE OF PRISONS.—A NIGHT IN A STATION-HOUSE CELL.—SOBBING BOYS AND CURSING WOMEN.—SHRIEKS OF TERROR THROUGH THE CORRIDORS.—LUXURIOUS LIVING IN LUDLOW STREET JAIL.—WARD'S DINNER-PARTIES.—BECKY JONES' GOAT-RACE WITH JAMES D. FISH.—LIFE IN THE TOMBS. PP. 387–398.

CHAPTER XXIX.

MURDERS AND MURDERERS.—THE BLOODY AFFRAY IN "SHANG" DRAPER'S SALOQN.—RUNNING INTO THE ARMS OF A DETECTIVE.—PROSTRATE ON THE FLOOR IN A POOL OF BLOOD.—THE SNOW ON TWELFTH STREET DEFILED WITH GORE.—THE SKELETON IN THE CELLAR.—KNOCKED DOWN AND KILLED AT EARLY DAWN.—THE MURDERER OF MRS. HULL CAUGHT BY A REPORTER...PP. 399–417.

CHAPTER XXX.

THE CHINESE QUARTER.—HAUNTS OF CHINESE VICE.—A SUNDAY'S VISIT.—IN AN OPIUM JOINT.—THE GAME OF POLICY.—AT THE FONG TONG TABLE. — THE SOCIAL EVIL. — DEGRADATION OF WHITE WOMEN.—THE EVIL OF THE LAUNDRIES.—CHINESE AND AMERICAN MARRIAGES.—BEFORE THE GREAT JOSS. PP. 418–433.

CHAPTER XXXI.

ABORTIONISTS.—MADAM RESTELL'S PALACE OF WICKEDNESS.—A RAID BY ANTHONY COMSTOCK.—SUICIDE IN A BATH TUB.—THE NAKED CORPSE FOUND IN A TRUNK.—A SHRIEK WHICH STARTLED THE COURT.—" FOR GOD'S SAKE, SPARE MY POOR FRANK."..PP. 434–442.

CHAPTER XXXII.

FRAUDS ON INSURANCE COMPANIES.—A NOTABLE INSTANCE.—ERNST ULING AND HIS CLEVER SCHEMES.—CONVULSIONS AND SOAP.—A LIVELY CORPSE.—WHAT THE COFFIN CONTAINED.—THE LAST SAD RITES OVER NINETEEN BRICKS.—HID UNDER THE BED.—A FULL CONFESSION.—FINK, THE UNDERTAKER.—STATE'S PRISON FOR BOTH.. PP. 443–448.

CHAPTER XXXIII.

BEGGARS.—THE DUDE MENDICANT.—FROM BEGGING TO THIEVING.—TILL TAPPERS.—SNEAK THIEVES ROBBING RUFUS LORD.—SHOPLIFTING.—HOW THE "CONFIDENCE" GAME IS WORKED.—CATCHING A TARTAR.—THE USE OF DRUGS BY THIEVES.—A MISTAKEN IDEA................................PP. 449–466.

CHAPTER XXXIV.

A POT POURRI OF CRIMES.—A BLOODY ASSASSINATION IN FRONT OF SUTHERLAND'S RESTAURANT.—THE MUFFLED GROAN OF "MURDER!"—HIGHWAY ROBBERIES IN A THIRD AVENUE CAR.—GARROTED IN THE FOURTH AVENUE TUNNEL.—A THIEF TRIPPED UP BY A SERVANT GIRL.—THE RICH MAN'S SON WHO SHOT A LAWYER.—GRADY, THE MASCULINE RIVAL OF MADAME MANDELBAUM.—A RASCALLY THEOLOGIAN..........PP. 467–478.

CHAPTER XXXV.

THE DIVES OF NEW YORK.—FROM THE HAYMARKET TO THE MORGUE—IN THE CREMORNE.—TOM GOULD'S DIVE.—HARRY HILL'S THEATRE.—AT THE AMERICAN MABILLE.—VICE IN THE BLACK-AND-TAN.—THE CAN-CAN IN ITS GLORY.—BILLY M'GLORY'S SYSTEM,

—THE WRECK OF A WOMAN.—THE SAILORS' DIVES.—A FRENCH BALL..PP. 479-496.

CHAPTER XXXVI.

BUTCHER-CART THIEVES.—STARVING CHILDREN IN "THE SHEPHERD'S FOLD."—GARFIELD'S MURDERER AT POLICE HEADQUARTERS.—THE WOMAN WHO THOUGHT SHE WAS SHADOWED.—THE NOTORIOUS FLORENTINE FORGERS.—A VISIT TO EUROPE.—HOW THE EXCISE LAWS ARE EVADED....PP. 497-516.

CHAPTER XXXVII.

THE DETECTIVE OF ROMANCE.—SOME POPULAR ERRORS CORRECTED. LOST CHILDREN.—MYSTERIOUS DISAPPEARANCES.—MISSING MR. SMITH.—HOW I FOUND HIM.—STEPPING OVER THE COUNTY LINE.—LIVINGSTONE THE FORGER.—A CHASE AS FAR AS CHICAGO.—AN ACCOMPLISHED PENMAN.—MORTGAGING A DEAD MAN'S PROPERTY.—CLEVER TRICK ON A LAWYER.—THE STORY OF A WATCH.
PP. 517-530.

CHAPTER XXXVIII.

TRAIN ROBBERS IN HOBOKEN, N. J.—THE CASHIER'S SATCHEL.—A BALKY HORSE.—CLEVERLY CAPTURED.—EX-POLICEMAN NUGENT'S EXPLOIT.—THE CHARLTON STREET GANG OF PIRATES.—SILK STEALING ON A STORMY NIGHT.—BANK BURGLARS FOILED.—HOW MR. ALEXANDER'S PLAN MISCARRIED.—POTS OF "JAM."—THE CONSPIRACY FOILED.—"JOHNNY" ROWE AND HIS CLUB-HOUSE.—HOW THE PLUMBER WAS ROPED IN.—HIS REVENGE.
PP. 531-542.

CHAPTER XXXIX.

REMARKABLE CRIMES IN BROOKLYN.—SUPT. CAMPBELL AS A DETECTIVE.—THE HEAD THAT WAS FOUND IN A LUMBER YARD.—A

HORRIBLE SMELL.—THE DETECTIVES' DISCOVERY.—WHAT WAS BOILING IN THE POT.—AN INHUMAN DEED.—THE GOODRICH MURDER.—LOOKING FOR KATE STODDARD.—A FEMALE DETECTIVE AND HER PROVIDENTIAL MEETING WITH THE MURDERESS.—ONLY A LOCKET.—CRUMBS OF CONGEALED BLOOD.—SEARCHING EVERY HOUSE IN BROOKLYN.—SUCCESS AT LAST.

PP. 543-551.

CHAPTER XL.

CHIEF STEWART OF THE PHILADELPHIA POLICE.—STORY OF A CRANK.—SAVED FROM HIS ENEMIES.—CHIEF KELLY, OF THE PHILADELPHIA DETECTIVES.—POOR KIRBY, AND HOW HE WAS KILLED BY POLITENESS.—CLEVERLY LAID PLANS MISCARRY.—A PLOT TO STEAL $11,000,000.—COPPER INSTEAD OF GOLD.—DISAPPOINTMENT AND DEATH.—"GOPHER BILL," THE CUNNING COUNTERFEITER.—HIS CAREER AND HOW HE WAS CAPTURED.—WALTER SHERIDAN.—A CURIOUS HISTORY.—A CASE OF SHANGHAI.—THE "BUNDLE" GAME.—PRINTED DESCRIPTIONS OF THIEVES.—SOME CURIOUS SPECIMENS.—A BRUTAL MURDER IN PENNSYLVANIA.—ROBBERY OF THE PHILADELPHIA MINT.—A BAR OF SILVER THAT WASN'T MISSED.................PP. 552-571.

CHAPTER XLI.

JUSTICE'S JUSTICE IN NEW YORK.—HOW THE WHEELS ARE "COGGED."—AN INADEQUATE JUDICIARY.—EVASION OF PUNISHMENT.—SEVERAL INSTANCES.—"BUNCO" MEN AND SWINDLERS.—WHY THEY ARE NOT BROUGHT TO TRIAL.—ROUGH ON THE COMPLAINANT.—SEVENTEEN WEEKS IN THE HOUSE OF DETENTION.—"FINE WORK."—SOMETHING ABOUT GAMBLERS.—NOT A SINGLE HONEST ONE.—WALL STREET'S INSATIABLE MAW.—SOLITARY MR. SMITH, OF RHODE ISLAND.—WHERE ALL THE MONEY GOES.—POLICE CAPTAINS SHOULD BE MADE RESPONSIBLE FOR THE EXISTENCE OF "HELLS."—BLACKMAIL LEVIED ON GAMBLING HOUSES.—REMEDIES SUGGESTED.........................PP. 572-578.

CHAPTER XLII.

THE "SOCIAL EVIL" AGAIN. — HOW TO CLEAR A RESPECTABLE NEIGHBORHOOD.—A NOVEL PLAN.—CAPTAINS NOT UNAWARE OF ILLEGAL RESORTS IN THEIR PRECINCTS.—"FIXED UP" REPORTS. — MISREPRESENTATIONS WHICH HAVE OCCURRED. — BLACKMAILING BY DETECTIVES. — HOW I CAUGHT THE OFFENDERS. — A STORY WITH AN INTERESTING SEQUEL. — "PLIN" WHITE'S WONDERFUL CAREER.—HOW HE WENT HOME TO DIE,..PP. 579-588.

CHAPTER XLIII.

INFORMATION TO REPORTERS.—ABUSES WHICH CREEP IN.—A CASE IN POINT.—BLISSFUL IGNORANCE OF THE PUBLIC.—PUNISHMENT NOT THE SOLE PURPOSE OF A COURT OF JUSTICE.—ITS REAL END AND AIM.—FULL PUBLICATION DESIRABLE UNDER CERTAIN RESTRICTIONS.—A PARALLEL CASE WITH THAT OF MR. COMMISSIONER SQUIRE. — HOW MR. DISBECKER BECAME A POLICE COMMISSIONER.—WHY HE DID NOT RESIGN.—PERSONAL APPEARANCE OF THE "FINEST."—HOW IT CAN BE IMPROVED.— A PROPOSED "SCHOOL OF DEPORTMENT."—THE ART OF WEARING CLOTHES.—MR. E. BERRY WALL AS AN INSTRUCTOR.—A POLICEMAN WITH A PERFECT MENTAL EQUILIBRIUM.— WHAT A VICTORY!—EFFECT OF POLITENESS ON THE LOWER CLASSES.—A POWERFUL OBJECT LESSON.........................PP. 589-595.

CHAPTER XLIV.

TWO MAIN CAUSES OF CRIME.—MUNICIPAL GOVERNMENT IN NEW YORK.—"POLITICS" SYNONYMOUS WITH POWER AND PLUNDER. —THE PREDOMINANT IDEA IN A POLITICAL CAMPAIGN.—ALL THE SNEAKS ARE REPUBLICANS, AND ALL THE ROUGHS ARE DEMOCRATS.—NEW YORK RULED BY THE WORST ELEMENTS IN THE COMMUNITY.—WHY THE BETTER CLASSES DO NOT ATTEND THE PRIMARIES.—RESULTS OF OUR FORM OF GOVERNMENT.—

EXCESSIVE TAXATION. — SHAMEFUL STREETS. — DISGRACEFUL DOCKS.—INSUFFICIENT SCHOOL ACCOMMODATION.—THE JUDICIARY.—NOT AN EDIFYING SIGHT.—HOW JUSTICE IS PERVERTED.—WHY JAY GOULD COULD DEFY THE LAW.—PERSECUTING A PROSECUTOR.—OUR LIBERTIES CURTAILED.—ONE LAW FOR THE RICH AND ANOTHER FOR THE POOR.—THE EXCISE LAWS.—SOME SUGGESTIONS.—THE SOCIAL EVIL AND HOW TO DEAL WITH IT.—THE COMMISSIONER OF JURORS. — UNIVERSAL SUFFRAGE A FAILURE.—DIFFICULTIES IN THE PATH OF REFORM.—THE ROOT OF THE EVIL.—REMEDIES.—THE LAST PAGE.

PP. 596–608.

SUPPLEMENT ON THE DENVER POLICE...PP. 609–678

INDEX TO BOTH WORKS ....PP. 681–698

ILLUSTRATIONS.

The illustrations of this work are from original drawings by the following well-known artists: Baron C. DeGrimm, (by permission of Mr. James Gordon Bennett), Valerian Gribayédoff, James A. Wales of "Puck," Wm. E. Mc Dougall and Geo. Folsom, Philip G. Cusachs, Chas. Broughton, A. Meyer, H. E. Patterson, Louis Dalrymple, Jno. A. McDougall, Jr., C. Beecher, A. B. Shults and J. F. J. Tresch.

PAGE		DRAWN BY
	GEO. W. WALLING...............	*Frontispiece.*
25.	HELEN JEWETT...........................	*Wm. E. McDougall.*
26.	RICHARD P. ROBINSON........	"
27.	COLT TRAGEDY—THE DISCOVERY.............	*McDougall and Folsom.*
28.	MARY ROGERS' RESTING-PLACE................	"
30.	THE DUCKING STOOL........................	*C. Beecher.*
31.	THE PILLORY AND WHIPPING POST............	"
37.	OLD BOWERY THEATRE	*Geo. Folsom.*
41.	TOM HYER.................................	*" V. G."*
42.	YANKEE SULLIVAN..........................	"
45.	ASTOR PLACE RIOT	*Phil. G. Cusachs.*
49.	BILL POOLE...............................	*"V. G."*
50.	MURDER OF BILL POOLE—STANWIX HALL	*H. E. Patterson.*
57.	MAYOR FERNANDO WOOD......................	*J. F. J. Tresch.*
59.	FIGHT BETWEEN THE METROPOLITAN AND MUNICIPAL POLICE..........................	*Valerian Gribayédoff.*
63.	PRINCE OF WALES' BALL....................	*James A. Wales.*
65.	HANGING OF GORDON THE SLAVE TRADER......	*Phil. G. Cusachs.*
70.	DETECTIVE THOMAS SAMPSON.................	
73.	WILLARD'S HOTEL, WASHINGTON, D. C........	*McDougall and Folsom.*
76.	THE LEAP FOR LIFE........................	"
81.	BATTLE OF THE BARRICADES.................	*J. F. J. Tresch.*
83.	AT THE CHURCH............................	"
90.	THE WIDOW AT WORK........................	*Louis Dalrymple.*
92.	"THIS WOMAN IS A THIEF"..................	*H. E. Patterson.*
95.	BURNING OF BARNUM'S MUSEUM...............	*McDougall and Folsom.*
102.	THE DEATH-BED RECOGNITION................	"
109.	THE FORGED CHECK.....	*A. Meyer.*
116.	AN UNSOLVED MYSTERY......................	*Chas. Broughton.*
123.	SUPT. JOHN JOURDAN.......................	
129.	A BITER BITTEN...........	*Phil. G. Cusachs.*

PAGE		DRAWN BY
136.	A Horsey Go-Between	*Phil. G. Cusachs.*
140.	Police and River Pirates	"
147.	Wharf Rats at Work	"
155.	Car Hook Murder	*J. A. McDougall, Jr.*
157.	Orange Parade	*Phil. G. Cusachs.*
158.	James Fiske, Jr.	
168.	The Pedlar at the Door	*H. E. Patterson.*
170.	The Counterfeiters' Den	*A. Meyer.*
174.	A Warm Welcome	*H. E. Patterson.*
179.	Supt Walling's Badge	
181.	Police Headquarters, Mulberry Street	*Geo. Folsom.*
183.	Supt. Walling's Office	*McDougall and Folsom.*
185.	Rogues' Gallery and Mementoes	"
186.	The Cell Corridor	*Geo. Folsom.*
187.	The Museum—Burglars' Tools	*McDougall and Folsom.*
188.	" " —Relics of Crime	"
190.	Inspector Byrnes' Office	"
191.	Private Rooms, Central Office	"
192.	Chas. Williams (No. 843)	"V. G."
195.	Police Parade, Broadway	*McDougall and Folsom.*
199.	Charley Ross	"V. G."
207.	Death of the Abductors	*McDougall and Folsom.*
211.	Inspector Henry V. Steers	"V. G."
213.	Ashore in Jersey	*A. B. Shults.*
221.	Adams Express Robbery	"
225.	A. T. Stewart's House and Store	*McDougall and Folsom.*
227.	St. Mary's Church—Stealing Stewart's Remains	"
234.	The Meeting	"
240.	Bank Burglars' Outfit	"
248.	Interior of Bank Vault	
255.	Dan Noble	"V. G."
257.	Fac Simile of a Requisition	
262.	Pete Emerson, *alias* Banjo Pete	"
265.	The Manhattan Bank	*McDougall and Folsom.*
267.	John Hope	"V. G."
275.	Billy Porter	"
276.	Edward Gearing, *alias* Eddie Goodie, Butcher-cart Thief	"
280.	Mother Mandelbaum	"
282.	"Big" Frank McCoy	"
284.	Mandelbaum Store and House	*Geo. Folsom.*
285.	Michael Kurtz, *alias* Sheeney Mike	"V. G."
288.	Geo. Mason, *alias* Oscar Decker, Burglar	"
290.	"Marm" Mandelbaum's Dinner Party	*Valerian Gribayédoff.*
293.	Wm. J. Sharkey	"
295.	Escape of Sharkey	*H. E. Patterson.*

ILLUSTRATIONS.

PAGE		DRAWN BY
303.	"Red" Leary............................	"V. G."
310.	Dr. Dix's Visitors.........................	C. DeGrimm.
342.	Wm. E. Brockway.........................	"V. G."
352.	"Hungry Joe's" Poker Game..............	Phil. G. Cusachs.
376.	John Morrissey............................	"V. G."
377.	John Lawrence Sullivan...................	
381.	Jimmy Elliott.............................	"V. G."
393.	The Tombs—Exterior......................	
394.	The Tombs—Courtyard....................	
395.	The Tombs—Interior......................	
396.	Blackwell's Island........................	
397.	The "Black Maria".......................	
400.	John Walsh...............................	"V. G."
401.	Capt. Alex. S. Williams, 29th Precinct......	"
403.	Surprised at Work........................	A. Meyer.
416.	At the Prayer-meeting.....................	Phil. G. Cusachs.
435.	Madam Restell............................	"V. G."
437.	Suicide of Madam Restell.................	Phil. G. Cusachs.
439.	Dr. Rosenzweig...........................	"V. G."
440.	Alice Augusta Bowlsby.....................	"
450.	Capt. Anthony J. Allaire.................	"V. G."
454.	Spencer Pettis............................	"
457.	"Tip" Little..............................	"
460.	Jimmy Price..............................	"
464.	Theo. Bishop.............................	"
474.	Jim Brady's Jump.........................	A. Meyer.
486.	A Bowery Dive............................	
490.	Owney Geogeghan.........................	"V. G."
493.	French Ball...............................	H. E. Patterson.
503.	The Shepherd's Flock......................	Phil. G. Cusachs.
544.	A Brooklyn Chief..........................	
553.	A Philadelphia Chief......................	
559.	A Chief of Detectives.....................	

RECOLLECTIONS

OF A

NEW YORK CHIEF OF POLICE.

CHAPTER I.

EARLY YEARS.—REMOVAL TO KEYPORT, N. J.—THE "CHINGA-RORA."—"THE LONG, LOW, BLACK SCHOONER."—A REGULAR SCARE.—ON THE "SPENCER."—THE MURDER OF HELEN JEWETT.—THE COLT TRAGEDY.—DID THE MURDERER COMMIT SUICIDE?—THE PRETTY CIGAR GIRL.—EDGAR A. POE AS AN AMATEUR DETECTIVE.—THE STADT HUYS.—BELL AND RATTLE WATCH.—THE WHIPPING POST.—CREMATION WITH A VENGEANCE.—"LEATHERHEADS."—WASHINGTON IRVING'S PRACTICAL JOKE.

I WAS born on the first of May, 1823, in Middletown township, Monmouth county, New Jersey, some two miles from Keyport. The original Walling stock was Welsh; a Walling settled in New Jersey at the close of the seventeenth century. My grandfather, Daniel Walling, served in the Revolutionary army, and afterwards received a pension from the United States. My mother's maiden name was Catharine Aumack; her ancestors came from Denmark. My father, Leonard Walling, was a civil engineer and surveyor; he kept a country store, and had been a member of the State Legislature.

I was sent to a school in the village, where I received most of my early instruction. My father, who had ambitious views for me, was desirous of preparing me for college; to which, be it said, I never went. When not at school I acted as clerk in my father's store. Sometimes I would accompany him on his frequent trips to

New York, to purchase goods. The journey was made on a sloop or packet, and sometimes took an entire day. These excursions were my delight, for I was an open-air boy, fond of athletic exercises, proficient in rowing, swimming and running, and capable of sailing a boat.

In 1832, when I was nine years old, my father removed to Keyport and opened a store there; but, to my delight, he soon after gave up store-keeping and built a schooner of about a hundred tons, which he named the "Chingarora." He had taught himself navigation and made several trips on the vessel as her master. The schooner brought pine wood and oysters from Virginia, and naval stores from North Carolina, and carried back miscellaneous freights to Southern ports. I made several trips to Virginia before I was fourteen years old, and so learned something about sea life.

This "Chingarora" deserves more than passing mention, for she wrote history to the extent of a slang phrase. Even now you will hear the expression, "long, low, black schooner;" fifty years ago it was in everybody's mouth and quite the vogue. I will tell you what gave birth to it. Father was bound to New York with a load of Virginia oysters; a little off the Hook he met the old Liverpool liner, "Susquehanna," outward bound. The captain hailed father and asked him what he had to sell. "Virginia oysters," he replied, and forthwith went aboard and made a sale. It was dusk, and some inward-bound vessels sighted father's boat alongside the packet. The "Chingarora" was painted black, with the exception of a narrow red streak below the bulwarks. She had no cabin windows and her masts were tall and rakish. The next day the news was reported that a pirate had boarded a large ship off Sandy Hook; newspapers printed columns about the mysterious "long, low, black schooner," and accounts of the ferocious pirate went broadcast over the country, while official reports were furnished to all the ports. Meanwhile, of course, the "Susquehanna" went silently to sea.

Father came up innocently to New York, sold his oysters, loaded up again and proceeded peacefully to Baltimore, where he was immediately taken into custody as a bold buccaneer. Of course his papers were in order and his identity was easily established. The scare about pirates went out in a roar of laughter and "long, low, black schooner" became the fashion in speech.

Poor old "Chingarora." We had to sell her when my good father ended his sturdy life, but the sea knowledge I gained on her stood me in good stead. I adopted the sea as my profession, and worked on several of the steam-boats then plying up the North River and the Sound. I was one of the hands on the old "Columbus" and the "Neptune" of those days.

In 1845 I went on the revenue steamer "Spencer" and remained with her a few months. I remember a great fire in New York in 1845, at which the crew of the "Spencer," and a squad of marines from the Brooklyn navy-yard assisted as guardians of property. This was really my first service as a keeper of the peace.

Growing tired of marine life, I left the "Spencer" and took up my residence in New York. I went into business, and sold market produce brought to Washington Market by the river craft. In spring, summer and fall I was kept busy, but during the winter months I had but little to do.

I had not thought of police work then, but recollect all the great crimes that startled the country, and particularly one of the most remarkable and atrocious which had been committed. This was the murder of the notorious courtesan, Helen Jewett, by, as was alleged, her quondam lover, Richard P. Robinson, on the night of April 11, 1836. Helen, whose real name was Dorcas Doyan, was but twenty-three years old. She possessed rare beauty of person and intelligence.

HELEN JEWETT.
(From a Photograph.)

The story of her career need not be repeated here. It may be simply related that Robinson remained her lover for a considerable time, and, eventually, upon her solicitation, agreed to go through the form of a marriage. At the time of her murder, Helen was an inmate of Mrs. Townsend's house on Thomas Street, and there, on the night of April 11, 1836, she was visited by Robinson. After that she was never seen alive.

At about three o'clock the next morning, when Mrs. Townsend entered the room, she was met by a dense volume of smoke which almost overpowered her. The chamber was on fire, and there, on the floor, lay the body of the ill fated Helen, her transparent forehead half divided by a gaping wound, and her body half consumed by fire. Robinson was arrested a few hours later, but was acquitted of the charge of murder. There is almost conclusive evidence that he escaped the gallows through the bribery of one of the jurors.

RICHARD P. ROBINSON.
(From a Photograph.)

Another fearful tragedy, which occurred on September 17, 1841, was the horrible murder of Samuel Adams, a printer, by John C. Colt, book-keeper and teacher of ornamental penmanship, in an office at the corner of Broadway and Chambers Street. After braining Adams with a hatchet, Colt cut up the body and salted it down in a box. He then had it conveyed by a teamster to a vessel bound for New Orleans, lying at the foot of Maiden Lane. This vessel was to have departed immediately, but she was delayed a week. A horrible stench came from the hold, and the order was given by the captain to "break cargo." The result was the discovery of the box containing all that remained of Adams. Colt was arrested, and shortly afterwards confessed his crime, stating, however, that there had been a fight between him and his victim. He was sentenced to be hanged, but committed suicide by stabbing himself to the heart with a knife. This has been generally accepted as true by the public, but I have heard it declared over and over again, by those in a position to know, that Colt did not commit suicide; that the body found in his cell when the Tombs caught fire was only a corpse prepared for the purpose, and that he escaped in the confusion. The coroner, it is said, was aware of the deception, and the jurymen were selected for their ignorance of Colt's personal appearance. Persons who knew Colt well are positive they have seen him since the time of his alleged suicide in both California and Texas.

The mysterious murder of Mary Rogers, the "pretty cigar girl," occurred in 1842. For some years previously Mary was employed to sell cigars in the store of John Anderson, the famous snuff manufacturer. She was a very handsome girl, and her fame extended far and wide among the swells of that period, who were constant customers at the store. In the early part of 1842 she relinquished her position in the cigar store, and henceforward assisted her mother, who kept a boarding-house at No. 126 Nassau Street. One Sunday in July, 1842, Mary left her home, telling Daniel Payn, a young man to whom she was to be married, that she was going to church, and that if she were not home to supper he was to call at a female friend's house for her. There was a heavy thunder storm that evening, and Payn, thinking his betrothed would stay over night with her friend, did not call for her. He never saw

COLT TRAGEDY.—THE DISCOVERY.

her again in this world. The next morning her body was found floating in the water near what was then known as the "Sybil's Cave," in the vicinity of the Elysian Fields, on the Jersey side of the Hudson. It bore the marks of the most horrible and nameless maltreatment. Subsequently, some articles of wearing apparel, which were recognized as having belonged to the murdered girl, were found in a thicket of the Elysian Fields, where the crime was undoubtedly committed, the body being afterwards thrown into the water. Several persons were arrested on suspicion of having committed the crime, including a rejected suitor for the victim's hand, but no evidence was forthcoming, and the suspected persons were all discharged.

The excitement following the murder of Mary Rogers was conspicuously felt by the prominent New Yorkers of the day. Such men as Gen. James Watson Webb, Gen. Scott, M. M. Noah, James Gordon Bennett, Fenimore Cooper, Washington Irving, N. P. Willis and Edgar A. Poe, were acquainted with the dainty figure and pretty face where they bought their cigars. Edgar A. Poe possessed, or thought he possessed, high ability as a detective; and his ingenuity in this ghastly groping is shown in "The Gold

MARY ROGERS' RESTING-PLACE.

Bug," "Murder on the Rue Morgue," and "The Mystery of Marie Roget."

In the latter story he endeavors to account for the disappearance of the pretty cigar girl. He slightly disguises her name, substitutes the Rue Morgue for Broadway, the Seine for the Hudson, the Bois de Boulogne for the Hackensack Wood, etc. He follows all her acquaintances, analyzes their characters, and examines their relation to her, coming to the conclusion that a well-known officer in the United States Navy was her murderer. The best authorities of that time do not agree with Poe's finding, but the tragic romance is full of painful interest.

But leaving these records of crime for a time to deal directly with the ancient police force of the city, which exerted itself to detect criminals, I will write of the old watchmen who found their headquarters in the City Hall.

The first of these buildings of which New York could boast was built in 1642, on Pearl Street, close to the Battery. It was called the "Stadt Huys," and was five years old when old Peter Stuyvesant, with his wooden leg, took his seat in the governor's chair, and commenced his vigorous crusade against the liquor saloons in the interests of temperance. Nine years later, the first police force was organized. It was called "the rattle watch," and consisted of just half a dozen men. They marched about the streets at night, sounding the rattles with which they were equipped, and yelling: "By the grace of God, two o'clock in peace!"

The records show that boys in those days were as noisy and mischievous as they are now, for we are gravely told that "two boys were arrested for shouting after Indians in Pearl Street." And Pearl Street, by the way, is one of the few city thoroughfares which has held its name from the very first.

Street lighting came into fashion some ten or fifteen years later, an ordinance being passed commanding that "every seventh house in all the streets shall, in the dark of the moon, cause a lantern and candle to be hung out on a pole, the charge to be defrayed equally by the inhabitants of the said seven houses." In 1673 a decree was promulgated looking to the banishment of the droves of hogs with which the streets were infested. The reason given for this decree was "because the hogs which are kept within this city in multitudes have from time to time committed great damage to the fortifications."

Twenty years later, the first uniformed policeman of the city appeared in its streets. He was armed with a bell and a long and formidable looking axe. His uniform was "a coat of ye citty livery, with a badge of ye citty armes, shoes and stockings." The cost of all this paraphernalia was charged "to ye account of ye citty." For the punishment of offenders there were erected on the wharf at Whitehall, a gallows, a pillory, a cage, whipping-post and ducking-stool. The mayor in person was the public administrator of all forms of punishment.

A new City Hall was built in 1700, its site being where the Sub-Treasury now stands, on Wall Street, near the corner of Nassau, then commonly spoken of as "the road that runs by the pie-woman's." What is now the City Hall Park, with its fountain, neat walks and well kept green sward, was known as the Common in those days. Here it was that those persons convicted of heinous crimes were burnt alive! Ah, those were "good old days," were they not! Why, even as late as 1712, a poor old slave, known as "Tom," suffered this awful penalty. He

THE DUCKING-STOOL.

belonged to Nicholas Roosevelt, and the sentence passed upon him read this wise: "That you be carryed from hence to the place whence you came, and from thence to the place of execution; and there be burned with a slow fire, that you may continue in torment for eight or ten hours, and continue burning in the said fire until you be dead and consumed to ashes." In these days such punishment would be deemed barbarous, inhuman, or worse; yet the majority of people who were then living were loud-professing, earnest and fervent Christians. New York was very religious then, far more so than it has ever been since, with all her costly churches and wide-spreading missionary efforts. For twenty years the whipping-post stood on Broad Street, and its site is at present flanked by D. O. Mills' colossal building, where the great banking house of Henry Clews & Co. is now located. Down through this thoroughfare ran a canal, crossed by bridges. Wall Street was the northern boundary of the city, and along it, dividing it from the country beyond, was a high wall.

But about the whipping-post. Why, one of the newspapers of that time disposes of a case of whipping in this manner, as if it

THE PILLORY AND WHIPPING-POST.

were quite a common occurrence: "A woman was whipped at the whipping-post on the 3d, and afforded much amusement to the spectators by her resistance." The pillory was not idle, either, for "James Gain, pursuant to sentence, stood in the pillory near the City Hall, and was most severely pelted by great numbers of spectators; a lad was also branded in the hand."

The old night-watchmen of the city were required to announce not only the hour, but the state of the weather at the time, ringing their bell and chanting lustily something like this: " Past four o'clock, and a dark and cloudy morning." The highest wages paid to policemen in New York, up to the close of the Revolutionary war, was $5.25 a week.

During the first half of the present century the police were known as "Leatherheads," a nickname which arose from the fact that they wore leather hats, something like an old-fashioned fireman's helmet, with a broad brim behind. Twice a year these hats received a thick coat of varnish, and after a time they became almost as hard and heavy as iron. These old "Leatherheads" were subject to very little discipline, and were anything but imposing or athletic. Should one attempt to make an arrest, he was either very roughly handled, or led a long and fruitless chase, in the course of which he was sure to meet with many and ludicrous mishaps. He was, in fact, unable to protect himself, let alone guarding and protecting citizens and property. The young bloods of those days took liberties with this official which no youth of our time, if he valued his head and health, would dare take with "One of the Finest." Youthful and exuberant New Yorkers considered that an evening out was not spent in the orthodox manner unless they played some rough practical jokes on the poor, old, inoffensive "Leatherheads." It is recorded of such a staid young man as Washington Irving, even, that he was in the habit of upsetting watch-boxes if he caught a "Leatherhead" asleep inside; and on one occasion, so it is said, he lassoed the box with a stout rope, and with the aid of companions dragged it down Broadway, while the watchman inside yelled loudly for help. The only insignia of office which these old fellows had, besides the leather helmet, was a big cloak and a club; at night they also carried a lantern.

CHAPTER II.

I BECOME A POLICEMAN.—" BUTTER-CAKE DICK."—" YOU MUST NEVER DO THAT AGAIN."—THE " BUTTON " CASE.—A SHARP PIECE OF DETECTIVE WORK.—HOW I SAVED TOM HYER FROM YANKEE SULLIVAN'S GANG.—" THE 'FORTY-NINERS."

ONE day, late in 1847, I was hunting quail in New Jersey, when a friend accosted me and asked whether I would like to take his position on the New York police force. He was about to resign, and the alderman and assistant-alderman of his ward had given him the privilege of naming his successor.

In those days aldermen and assistant-aldermen nominated, subject to the mayor's approval, which was rarely refused. The term of service of each appointee was two years.

I certainly never had the slightest idea of becoming a policeman, but the proposition did not displease me. I had no particular business at the time and decided that I might as well carry a club till something better turned up. I accepted my friend's offer. Little did I think then that I was to pass my life on police duty.

My friend sent in his resignation and I was nominated by Alderman Egbert Benson and Assistant-Alderman Thomas McElrath, the latter well known as one of the original proprietors of the *Tribune*, with the illustrious Horace Greeley. The mayor, Mr. Wm. V. Brady, approved and swore me in on the twenty-second day of December, 1847.

My *début* was made as one of the force of the Third Ward. I received no special instructions as to what were to be my duties, but was ordered to report to Captain Tobias Boudinot, who was then in charge of the Third Ward station, situated on Robinson Street, west of College Place. The station was a small frame building, with a stoop; there was a door below opening into the basement, where the cells were.

It is amusing to me to recall the ease with which my appointment was secured. The men at that time owed their appointments entirely to political preferences; there were no surgeons' inspections, nor any civil-service examinations, in fact no attention whatever was paid to the physique or mental acquirements of the applicant. The salary was $600 a year, the pay days were twice a month. The sergeants then, the roundsmen of to-day, visited the various posts to see that the men were on duty.

The merely physical work, to a young man like myself, accustomed to walk all day with a gun on my shoulders, shooting birds in the Jersey fields, was not at all onerous. As far as covering my post went, I had no trouble about that; nor did an exact obedience to the rules present much difficulty. But I must confess that once I fell from grace.

Just at the beginning of my official career there came a bitterly cold night. I had been on post for a number of hours, and if there was anything on this earth that I yearned for it was a cup of hot coffee. Now, in those days one Richard Marshall, better known as "Butter-cake Dick," kept a coffee-and-cake saloon under the then *Tribune* building. I could look from my post across the Park and see the genial light of this haven of refuge, the windows deliciously frosted with congealed coffee-steam. O, how I wanted coffee!

Well, I was young, and I found my feet instinctively crossing the Park and irresistibly carrying me to "something hot." I entered the shop, and to my amazement *it was filled with policemen!* "Butter-cake Dick" himself, as if it were the most natural thing in the world, brought me refreshments, and, speechless, I swallowed my coffee as quickly as I could, gobbled my butter-cakes and flew back to my post. But, to my horror, Nemesis, in the rotund person of Sergeant Hervey, was there, and apparently looking for me.

"Where have you been, sir?" said he.

"To 'Butter-cake Dick's,' sir," I replied, quaking.

"You must never do that again," said he, very sharply.

But he was a kind-hearted sergeant, and I suppose he saw my dismay, for he went on to say that in *very* severe weather, if I were *very* cold, and if coffee was *very* necessary, I could wait till I saw him, ask his permission, and he would patrol my post till I returned. He wound up by telling me that as I was a new hand he would not report me for this first offence, but if it ever happened again he would have to send my name up.

It never did!

But I could not help wondering how the other policemen I had seen in the coffee-shop managed it. And here, at this late day, I am informing on them.

In 1848, when Mr. George W. Matsell was chief of police, complaints were frequently made to him of Sunday robberies among the wholesale and retail houses about Maiden Lane and John Street. These depredations were sources of as great annoyance to Mr. Matsell as to the members of the force. One morning the chief of police sent for Theodore Shadbolt, John Reed, John Wade and me, and said: "Boys, I have sent for you to help me. Every Monday morning when I come down to the office I have complaints of burglaries committed in Maiden Lane or John Street, and if you do not catch the thieves I shall have to jump off the dock."

Of course we all looked exceedingly vigilant and wide awake, but we had to wait further developments.

One Monday morning Mr. Matsell sent for us. The chief was not in a good humor. There had been enough to ruffle him. He began at us at once with: "There has been another burglary in Maiden Lane. I want you to go there and investigate, and see what you can do!"

Accompanied by Reed and Shadbolt, I went at once to the store in Maiden Lane and made a thorough examination. We found that the burglars had entered the store by breaking through a small window opening on an alley. The thieves had stolen some very choice cutlery and costly suspenders. In counting the stock, about the exact quantity of cutlery was determined; and upon examining the loss of suspenders, three pairs were found missing. It was a fair suspicion that three burglars had been at work, and that each man had helped himself to a pair of suspenders. Examining every nook and corner of the place, we found a number of bits of newspaper, and in sorting them out carefully, we came across a single button. This button would be now classed as an ordinary one, but thirty odd years ago it was a button not in common use. Sack coats had just then come into fashion and were novelties.

This button was covered with the same material as the cloth of the coat. The button had been, therefore, part and parcel of one of these new-fashioned garments. The question arose whether any one in the store wore a sack coat, or had lost a button? The clerks were brought before us, of course not aware why their clothes were examined so particularly; but none of them wore a sack. How, then, did the button come there? It did not look as if it had been pulled off suddenly. I came to the conclusion that the owner of the button, when it became loose, had put it in his pocket, intending to have it sewed on again. When he was filling his pockets with the cutlery, to make room for the fine knives, he had turned out the paper in his pocket with the other contents, and the button had fallen on the floor. A button was a very insignificant clue, but it was all we had. We returned to Mr. Matsell and reported our investigation. We said there were three burglars, and one of them had lost a button. I do not know whether the chief of police was very well satisfied. We held a consultation with the officers of the force. We were all of the opinion that we must find a man wearing a sack coat, minus a button or buttons which would match the one in our possession. We all studied, very carefully, the configuration of that little disc, and, if I may so express it, got it by heart.

We now visited all the places wherein we fancied thieves would congregate, but no buttonless rascals were visible. We began to be quite despondent; but nevertheless, that button kept passing around.

About a month and a half had elapsed, when, one very cold night, I was on duty at the old Chatham Street Theatre, just above Pearl Street. Officer Shadbolt came to me and said:

"There are three young men going up stairs. I know them to be thieves. I will give you the cue so that you can distinguish them, and then you watch them. As the men know me by sight, I mustn't show."

"All right, Mr. Shadbolt," I replied, "I will keep my eye on them."

Presently three men came up to one of the upper galleries. Shadbolt signalled to me, and I knew my men. I took a theatre bill, and was apparently very much interested in the performance. Being in plain clothing, I took a seat directly behind the men. Always having that button on the brain, the first thing I did was to scan their coats. There was not a button wanting. I scrutinized the make of all their buttons. Could I believe my eyes? Yes! one of them displayed buttons precisely like the one we had treasured. More than that, this same man with the suspicious buttons had one button on his coat of a slightly different pattern.

There was no doubt about the matter; we had the thief, perhaps the thieves. I hurried down the stairs of the theatre at once, and saw Shadbolt. "Those are the fellows we are looking for," I said. "We will watch them. As they will come out with the crowd, we might lose them. You keep in the shade, somewhere in the house, and follow them out. I will go on the opposite side of the street. When you are on their track, lift your hat, and then I will take the trail and follow them. When you see me in their wake, station yourself in front of the Bowery Theatre and do not

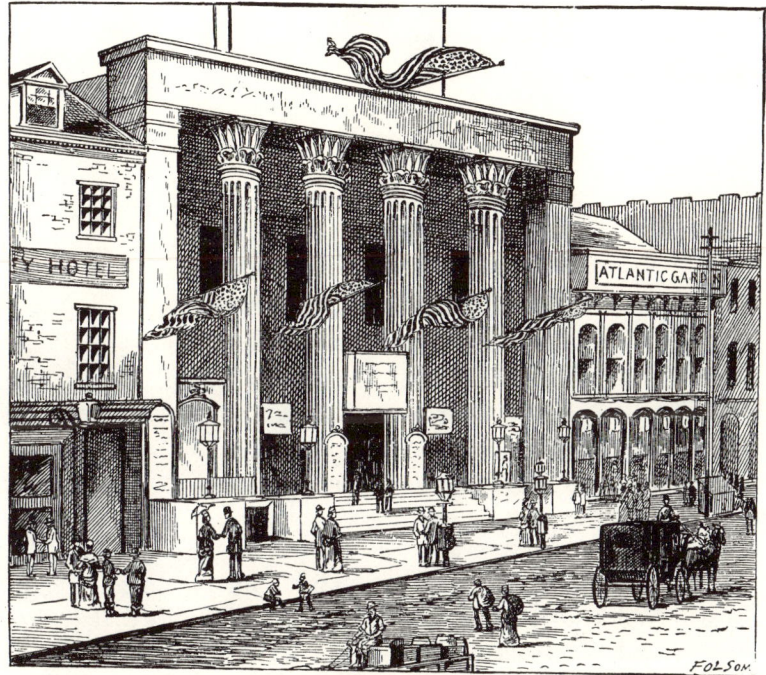

OLD BOWERY THEATRE.

leave it until you hear from me. Then perhaps Mr. Matsell will not jump off the dock."

Shadbolt agreed to the plan, and at midnight, when the theatre was closed, I was on the track, following the three men.

They went into an eating-house in Chatham Street, and had some supper; came out, and then went on their way to the east side of the street. The house they went into had a light in the door-way. I waited for a long time, and made up my mind that the men had gone to bed. The house was probably a lodging-place. It was bitterly cold, and I had hidden myself in a doorway on the opposite side of the street. After having run the men to earth, it would never have done to lose them. I must not leave my place of observation.

At about half-past two o'clock in the morning I saw a man come along. I slipped out of the door-way. The man was apparently alarmed and started across the street. I halted him and assured him that there was no cause for fear. "Do not be frightened," I said, "I am an officer." I took out my star and showed it to him. I asked him in what direction he was going. It so happened that on his way to his house he would have to pass the Bowery Theatre. I begged him to notify the officer he would find in front of the theatre where I was and to come to me at once.

The man left. After a while down came Mr. Shadbolt. I quickly explained to him the condition of affairs, and told him that the men were in the house opposite and asleep. I begged him to go at once to the Tenth Ward police station and to send Reed and Wade to meet me where I then was, at five o'clock in the morning.

Promptly on time, Reed and Wade were there. We went to the house, knocked and were admitted by the man in charge. I told him: "You have three men in bed in this house, and we want them." I advised him what to do, so that we might get into the room where they were, in order that we could catch them all at once.

It was arranged that the lodging-house keeper should tell them to open their door so that he could get their candle. The man went to the room, knocked, awoke the sleepers and the door was opened. No sooner was the door ajar than I went in, followed by Reed and Wade. I put my foot in the door so that it could not be closed. It looked as if our visit was no surprise, for one of the men said to the others, "Get up—the 'cops' are here for us." The men made no resistance and were taken to Mr. Matsell's office and locked up in the cells. In searching them we found that every man of them had on a pair of suspenders of the best quality. We sent at once to the house in Maiden Lane, reporting the finding of the suspenders.

The Maiden Lane merchant examined the suspenders, and declared that they were exactly like those which had been stolen, but unfortunately he had sold a great many and could not of course swear that these were the stolen ones. Here then came the chance that, after all our trouble, nothing could be proved against the men. The button was good for nothing in court; other evidence against the thieves was necessary.

I thought the problem out, and made up my mind that Shadbolt, because he knew the thieves, would be of use to us. It should be remembered that, so far, the three men had no knowledge that Shadbolt had had anything to do with this arrest. A little comedy was agreed upon by Mr. Matsell, Shadbolt and myself, and the play was managed in this way:

I took the three men before Mr. Matsell, and they were left with him for a little while. Then Mr. Shadbolt came in and asked Mr. Matsell for permission to leave the city. Mr. Matsell was to be apparently very much engaged, so as not to pay immediate attention to Shadbolt's request. Seeing the three men, Shadbolt expressed surprise, and inquired: " What are you doing here? "

Then I came in, apparently in a towering rage. "What!" I cried, "Mr. Matsell, is this the way business is carried on in this office, sir? When I have prisoners, can another officer come in and talk to them? This is an injustice which I will not permit."

Then Mr. Matsell turned on Shadbolt, and said: " Mr. Shadbolt, this is contrary to every rule. You have no right to talk to these prisoners. If ever anything of this kind occurs again I shall bring charges against you."

I turned quickly on Shadbolt, and told him he had no business at all in the office. I ended by insisting "that his room was better than his company." Then I took the prisoners and put them in a passage-way and left them again, apparently, for a moment. Shadbolt then returned to where they were. One of the men called him to them.

Shadbolt looked around with suspicion, and said: " Is Walling gone?" The men replied, "Yes." Shadbolt said: " I can talk with you for a minute. Talk quickly, however, for it is more than my place is worth for me to be seen talking with you. What are you here for, anyhow?"

The men said they did not know. Shadbolt told them that he would find out. Then Shadbolt went away, came back after a while and informed them that it was in regard to stealing suspenders and cutlery, and that they had better confess their guilt, and get off with a short imprisonment. This they consented to do. They confessed the theft. Then Shadbolt advised them to tell Mr. Matsell what they had done with the property. I was given charge of the men and took them before Mr. Matsell. The men informed us that they had sold their goods to a man in Centre Street.

Mr. Matsell despatched me to Centre Street at once. I said to the man: "You have been buying goods from three thieves. We have got the men fast. Now you had better tell me where the cutlery and other things are." The man positively denied that he had bought any stolen goods. "Then," I said, "I will search the place," and I did so.

In one corner of the room, stowed away behind some boxes, I found the cutlery. No sooner had I put my hands on the knives than I said: "Here is evidence enough to send you to the State prison."

I sent for a truck and carried to Mr. Matsell's office a whole load of plunder. Among the goods we found the stock of a tailor, who had been robbed in Brooklyn some time before. The "fence" was tried, convicted and sent to State's prison. As for the thieves, they pleaded guilty on three charges, and were convicted.

A coat button lost by a thief, the finding of it by a policeman, the element of luck entering to some slight degree in the matter, led to the discovery of the burglars, the taking of the receiver and the capture of property worth a great deal of money, the result of seven burglaries. I suppose a certain tenacity of purpose in detective work is always necessary. If the clew is worthless to-day, it may be valuable to-morrow. In following up a rascal an endless number of small things, apparently insignificant, must be always borne in mind.

Political feeling ran high during the year 1848. The excitement, in fact, was intense, and fights were more than frequent between the members of the various factions. I was on duty on Broadway the night that Tom Hyer thrashed Yankee Sullivan. It was about twelve o'clock when, just as I was passing an oyster saloon at Park Place and Broadway, I heard the sound of disputing going on within. The doors were wide open and the place was brilliantly lighted. I paused for a few minutes on the sidewalk, and then, as the noise suddenly ceased, I proceeded to patrol my beat, going down Broadway towards Cortlandt Street. Barely was the latter thoroughfare reached before I heard the rap of a policeman's club. Hurriedly retracing my steps, I found the officer who had signalled me standing in front of the oyster saloon which I had just left.

"There's a fight going on down there," he said, "somebody's going to be killed."

I tried the doors and found they were locked and bolted. Evidently there was a row going on, and a lively one, judging from the noise. Presently one of the waiters came running out of the saloon through a side entrance on Park Place, and I immediately captured him. He showed me the door through which he had come, and I entered the place, telling the other police-officer to keep close to me. But he didn't; when I got inside he was not there.

There stood Tom Hyer, whom I knew well by sight and reputation, placing a percussion-cap upon the nipple of a pistol which he held in his hand. In one of the boxes was Yankee Sullivan, who looked as if he had been roughly handled. I took in the situation at once.

"Put up that pistol," I said to Hyer, who looked calm and collected enough, and with no trace on his person of having been engaged in a fight.

"Who the devil are you?" he asked, in a gruff voice.

"I'm an officer," I replied, exhibiting my star.

"They're going to bring the gang here," said Hyer, in a calm voice; "and I'm not going to let them murder me without a pretty tough fight for my life."

TOM HYER.
(From a Photograph.)

"Come, get out of this. Come along with me," I said, and Hyer, taking hold of my arm, we left the saloon. Just as soon as we reached the street, Hyer said he thought he would go to the Empire Club, and, bidding me good-night, crossed Broadway.

No sooner was he out of sight than a howling mob of Sullivan's friends came rushing toward me. They had heard of Sullivan's discomfiture, and were in search of Hyer, who, if they had caught him, would most assuredly have been murdered. Some of the crowd asked me where Sullivan was, and when I told them where I had last seen him they made a rush for the oyster saloon. I could plainly hear their yells of rage when they found their friend. Hyer had not left the place a moment too early.

I frequently met Hyer after that, but he never referred to his narrow escape on that night,—neither did I. Concerning Hyer, I may say that with associates of his own class, who were all fighting men, the word and the blow would follow each other closely; but with those physically his inferiors he was never inclined to pick a quarrel. The same, I am sorry to say, cannot be said of the pugilists of to-day.

The year 1849 opened with the excitement resulting from the discovery of gold in California. This craze, for such it was, exceeded anything of the kind ever experienced in this

YANKEE SULLIVAN.
(From a Photograph.)

country. From this city there went merchants, professional men and men of every grade of wage-workers. Among them was Sam Ward, the epicure and prince of dinner-givers. He was then a member of the firm of Prime, Ward & King, but he subsequently became the best known lobbyist in the country. In the same emigration went three sons of Robert Emmett, S. S. Osgood, the artist, and others. I well remember the sailing of the bark "Joseph" for San Francisco. She was purchased and equipped by young men from the Seventh Ward. The number of expeditions fitted out was very large, parties coming from Utica, Buffalo, Hudson, Oswego, Albany and other parts of New York State.

CHAPTER III.

ASTOR PLACE RIOTS.—FORREST AND MACREADY.—" SI " SHAY AND " BUTT " ALLEN.—RIOTERS STORM THE OPERA HOUSE.—FEARFUL LOSS OF LIFE.—AUTHORSHIP OF INFLAMMATORY HANDBILLS.—THE " HONEYMOON " GANG.—ENGLISH ROW AND IRISH ROW.—ATTACK ON N. P. WILLIS.—" STAND BACK, GENTLEMEN."—JENNY LIND.—BILL POOLE AND LEW BAKER.—DELIBERATE MURDER.—GRAND FUNERAL.—AN OCEAN CHASE.—CAPTURE OF THE ASSASSIN.—" I DIE A TRUE AMERICAN."—THE SWORD-CANE.—BOND-STREET TRAGEDY.—THE BOGUS BABY.

The Astor Place riots—the outcome of jealousy between the two great actors, Forrest and Macready—occurred during the latter part of 1849, two years after my appointment as a police officer. In this, therefore, was gained my first experience in the concerted action of the force to quell a disturbance.

Upon the night of the riot Macready was to appear at the Astor Place Opera House. Long before the hour for the performance to begin a large and excited crowd assembled near the theatre. The first two acts of the play were proceeded with in comparative quiet, though there was some groaning and hissing heard. Being on duty within the theatre I saw everything that occurred. In the upper galleries was a crowd of disorderly persons, many of whom I knew. Two of the leaders in the disturbance were " Si " Shay and " Butt " Allen. They were yelling and inciting others to do the same. I went towards them with the intention of ordering them to desist. As I neared them Allen picked up a heavy chair and was about to throw it at Mr. Macready, who was then on the stage. I caught hold of it. At the same instant, several young ruffians, friendly to Allen, attacked me, and a rough-and-tumble fight ensued. Allen managed to wrench the chair from my grasp, and taking careful aim, threw it at Macready. It struck within two feet of him, but he never flinched. He simply looked up and went on with his lines. A few moments afterwards a shower of stones from the mob outside shattered nearly every window in the theatre. This stopped the performance for that night, and Mr. Macready announced it to be his intention not to appear again in this city. Many prominent persons waited upon him in a body, however, and insisted that he should give a second performance, promising him ample protection. He reluctantly consented, and the result was one of the most serious disturbances which has ever occurred in New York.

A sewer was being constructed on Fourth Avenue, and the pavements, in consequence, had been torn up. At Macready's next performance the cobble-stones became effective weapons in the hands of the mob. Where the Bible House now stands was a stone-yard. The stone clippings which the rioters found there furnished sufficient ammunition to pelt the military and police. The main attack came from Fourth Avenue, the police being stationed there, as well as on Astor Place, Broadway, Eighth Street and Lafayette Place. I was in charge of the amphitheatre entrance to the theatre, on Astor Place. There were six men under me. The stones came from the mob in volleys. Several soldiers were struck down, one or two of them being seriously injured. I carried them within the theatre. There the scene was one of terror and confusion. Shower after shower of paving-stones was hurled against the windows. The stones, however, fell in the midst of the frightened audience, which became positively terror-stricken.

When the military appeared the rioters became still more demonstrative. Mr. Frederick A. Talmage, the recorder, ordered the rioters to disperse, but their only reply was another volley of stones. General Hall was in command of the military, and very reluctantly gave the order to—

"Fire!"

The first volley was aimed over the heads of the crowd. Many of the bullets struck the wall of Mrs. Langdon's house, at Lafayette and Astor places, and many innocent persons, taking no part in the riotous proceedings and standing far from the fighting, fell to the ground, wounded by the spent bullets. The scene was now one of the wildest excitement, and the fury of the mob became uncontrollable. Immediately after the first firing some of the rioters shouted :

"Don't run ; they're only firing blank cartridges. Damn 'em, they daren't shoot anybody."

It was apparent that unless the militia acted in a decisive manner they would be driven from their position. A brief pause, and then, amid the din and discord of that awful scene, was heard the command:

"Fire!"

There was a flash, a deafening roar, and then were heard the cries of the wounded and the groans of the dying. The effect of that volley was awful. Scores lay upon the ground, writhing with pain. Terror-stricken, the cowardly rioters rushed from the scene, trampling upon the prostrate forms of those who had fallen. In twenty seconds there was not a person to be seen on the street who was capable of moving.

Edward Z. C. Judson, otherwise known as "Ned Buntline," took a very active part in leading the mob. He was arrested on the spot, and subsequently sentenced to one year's imprisonment and a fine of $250.

The police, at this time, were not uniformed. They were commended by all peaceful persons for their bravery. So far as I was able to learn, not a single man showed the white feather.

A careful inquiry was made after the riot as to its cause. Mr. Matsell, the chief of police, was satisfied that there had been premeditation on the part of some of the rioters, and placed clews in my possession to be followed.

My experience has satisfied me that the concerted actions of a mob have rarely anything spontaneous about them. In most cases the so-called "uprising" has much premeditation in its composition. In order to bring about the Astor Place riot, handbills were distributed, and an endeavor had been made to set two elements of our foreign population against each other—the English and the Irish. Some of these handbills bore an appeal to the Irish, headed, "Will you allow Englishmen to rule this country?" Others were addressed to Englishmen, calling upon them to "sustain their countrymen." The latter were circulated among the English sailors. Both handbills were pasted side by side upon walls, boxes and all available places. Astor Place was designated as the rendezvous for both factions.

Mr. Matsell furnished me with copies of both handbills, and I at once sought the printer. The first place I visited was a job office in the old *Tribune* Building. There the proprietor informed me that from some peculiarity in the type he suspected they were printed at an office in Ann Street. Thither I went, and at once asked, as if I were sure of the whole matter :

" For whom did you print these handbills ? "

" I don't know ; I can't tell you," was the reply. " A man called with the copy, gave me instructions to print the bills, paid me in advance and ordered me to deliver them, with the copy, at No. 25 Park Row."

" All right," I replied.

Now, I knew that the Empire Club occupied rooms at the address mentioned. I also knew that it was the headquarters of the " Native American " party, as it was then called. There was a saloon there, kept by William Miner ; it was frequented by members of the Empire Club. I went to Miner, and questioned him about the mysterious package of handbills.

" Yes," he said ; " there was such a package left here. Somebody came and took it away, but I don't know who it was."

That was as far as I could trace the handbills. I never discovered who wrote the copy, or who had the bills printed and circulated. But for all that I had my suspicions.

Some months after the riot, while I was standing in front of Chief Matsell's office, Isaiah Rynders came along. I immediately began a conversation about the Astor Place riot, and suddenly made this remark, in a sharp tone of voice :

" The man who got up those handbills ought to have been shot, instead of so many innocent persons."

Rynders turned upon me, and in an angry manner said : " Well, maybe you ought to have been shot instead of me."

" I haven't accused you of it yet, Mr. Rynders," I replied. " But if the shoe fits, you are welcome to wear it."

My last remark seemed to put Rynders in a greater passion. He ripped out in a savage manner :

" It was a big red-headed Irishman of about your size who did it."

I had no direct evidence that Rynders had taken any part in the distribution of the bills, but I shall always believe that he was one of those who incited the trouble.

In 1849 my first two years of service expired, and owing to political differences with the aldermen who appointed me was refused a re-appointment. I removed, however, to Ward Eighteen, lived there for a short time, and was once more nominated for a position on the force, this time by Alderman Jonas Conkling. This appointment, under the existing laws, was for the term of four years; but in 1853 an act was passed by the Legislature empowering policemen to retain their position during good conduct. This, I believe, was the first time that appointments on the force were made for merit only. The same year I was promoted to be captain of police in the Eighteenth Ward. The station was on Twenty-ninth Street, between Madison and Fourth avenues. "Squatters" were plentiful in this locality. Fights were of frequent occurrence, and the precinct was by no means as orderly as it is now. There was one especially notorious party of ruffians, known as the "Honeymoon Gang." It was named after its leader. For a long time the members of this "gang" had everything their own way, and I determined to clear them out of the ward. Taking five or six of my best men, all in citizen's dress, I began hunting the ruffians, and in a few weeks, by dint of some pretty hard "licks," judiciously administered, the ward was cleared. At this time there was no regular surgeon attached to the force to care for prisoners, and we had to frequently call upon one who lived near the station to dress their wounds. His fee was $1.00 for attending to a single cut. Not infrequently one head would be worth as much as $5.00 to him.

On Twenty-second Street, between Second and Third avenues, there were two rows of tenements, known as the "English" and "Irish." They were on either side of the street, and the occupants were rarely at a loss for an excuse to come to blows. I have known them to indulge in as many as a dozen fights in one evening. After dusk the life of a policeman who patrolled this beat alone was not worth much. But by a severe course of discipline the neighborhood was soon made safe.

It was in June, 1850, that Edwin Forrest assaulted Nathaniel P. Willis, the poet. This encounter occurred in Washington Square, Forrest striking Willis from behind and knocking him down. While the latter was on the ground, Forrest beat him unmercifully with a gutta-percha cane. Willis shouted loudly for help, but the bystanders who attempted to interfere were warned off by Forrest, who exclaimed:

"Stand back, gentlemen; he has interfered in my domestic affairs."

After a few more blows, Forrest allowed Willis to make his escape, badly bruised. This encounter, I have every reason to know, was an outcome of the famous Forrest divorce case.

The arrival of Jenny Lind in this country on September 1, 1850, by the steamship "Atlantic," was the occasion of a great assembly in the vicinity of the Canal-Street pier, where a triumphal arch had been erected. From thirty to forty thousand persons were packed upon the wharf and vicinity. Five or six of them were pushed into the water in the mad struggle to obtain a glimpse of the famous songstress. Her first concert was given in Castle Garden. She received $1000 a night for her services. Genin, the hatter, paid $225 for the first choice of a seat. The receipts for the first concert were $24,753.

BILL POOLE.
(From a Photograph.)

During the years 1854–55 violence and ruffianism, resulting from the "Know Nothing" excitement, was rampant. It was in the early part of 1855 that "Bill" Poole, the famous pugilist, was murdered by Lewis Baker. Between these men there had been much "bad blood," and it was foretold by those who knew both men that their differences could only be settled by the death of one. On the night of February 24, 1855, Poole was shot by Baker in Stanwix Hall, opposite the Metropolitan Hotel, in Broadway. "Lew" Baker, James Turner, and a man named McLaughlin, *alias* "Paudeen," followed each other into Stanwix Hotel at about midnight. Poole was standing in front of the bar, drinking with some of his friends. "Paudeen," who was the last to enter, remarked to him as he locked the door:

"What are you looking at, you black-muzzled ———?"

MURDER OF BILL POOLE.—STANWIX HALL.

Poole, who must have known something serious was to happen, was very cool. Even when "Paudeen" had spit in his face several times and challenged him to fight, Poole simply took a hundred dollars in gold from his pocket and offered to bet that amount upon his ability to thrash any one of his opponents. He treated "Paudeen" with disdain, saying he was beneath his notice. Suddenly, Turner took off his cloak, and swinging a large revolver once round his head, fired at Poole, using the hollow of his left arm as a rest. From some cause or other the bullet entered Turner's arm and he fell to the floor, but not before he had fired a second shot. This time Poole was wounded in the leg. He staggered toward Baker, who drew his revolver and fired two shots into Poole as he lay on the floor. He then escaped from the saloon. Notwithstanding that one of the bullets penetrated Poole's heart, he was taken to his home and actually lived fourteen days afterwards. Poole was a brawny man, proud of the fact that he was an American. In those days such men were in politics. Upon his death-bed his last words were: "I die a true American."

The excitement following the tragedy was great, and Poole's funeral was one of the most extraordinary I ever remember to have seen. It was attended by an immense assembly of "sports" and "toughs," together with thousands of respectable men who belonged to the "Native American" party, and Broadway was completely lined with spectators from Bleecker Street to Whitehall. The coffin was wrapped in the American flag, and plays were produced at various theatres in the city, in which the hero, encircling his limbs with the star-spangled banner, departed this life to slow music and red fire, exclaiming: "I die a true American!"

Baker boarded a brig bound for the Canary Islands, but the clipper yacht "Grapeshot" was sent in pursuit, arriving at the port of Teneriffe two hours before the vessel in which the murderer had taken passage, and Baker was brought back to New York. He was indicted with a number of others, and tried three times for the murder. The jury, however, disagreed in each case, and he was finally discharged on bail.

There has been only one funeral of such character since then which approached that of Poole's. This was that of Joseph Elliott, killed by "Jerry" Dunn, in Chicago, in 1884, and buried from New York. His funeral came the nearest in magnitude to that of

Poole's, and was attended by "toughs," "blacklegs," gamblers, and "sports" of all grades.

Perhaps the last recorded case of the use of the sword-cane was at the St. Nicholas Hotel, now demolished, but well known to travellers. Dr. R. H. Graham, of New Orleans, at the dead of night, intoxicated, noisy, and being unable to find his room, was accosted by a fellow-guest, Colonel Charles Loring, of California, whose slumbers had been disturbed, and who arose from his bed. Graham, enraged at the interference, drew a sword which the cane enclosed, and without warning plunged it into the body of the Colonel, whose cries aroused the entire hotel. The Colonel died.

I continued captain of the Eighteenth Ward until the close of 1856. It was in the following year that what was known as "the Bond-Street tragedy" occurred. At about half-past ten o'clock on the night of Friday, January 3, 1857, many persons residing on Bond Street were startled from their sleep by the shrill cry of "murder!" Then followed silence, and those who had been aroused turned over and went to sleep again. The next morning it was discovered that Dr. Harvey Burdell, a dental surgeon, of No. 31 Bond Street, had been murdered in the night. When his room was entered by a boy to light a fire, a terrible scene was disclosed. The life-blood of Dr. Burdell had smeared the whole apartment with its crimson stains. It had splashed against the door to a height of five feet. There was blood on the stairs, in the hallway and on the front door. Blood was also on the stairway leading to the attic, and on the floor of the attic itself. An examination disclosed fifteen wounds on the body, any one of which would have been sufficient to cause death. In addition, there was the mark of a cord around the neck, as though an attempt had been made to strangle the dentist. That the murdered man had fought desperately against his unknown assailant there could be no doubt, the furniture of the room being scattered.

The ostensible landlady of the house was a Mrs. Cunningham, the house, owned by Dr. Burdell, being leased to her. Mrs. Cunningham, it was said, was very much in love with the doctor, and, as she subsequently asserted, had married him on the 28th of October, the previous year. This fact was denied by the relatives of the murdered man; but there is little doubt that on the date mentioned Mrs. Cunningham was married to somebody. If she was in fact Mrs. Burdell, at the doctor's death she would be entitled to her share of his property, and he was quite a wealthy man.

There also lived in the house a Mr. John J. Eckel, who, it was reported, was a lover of Mrs. Cunningham. Both were arrested, but Mrs. Cunningham alone was tried. She was acquitted after a three days' hearing.

And now comes the sequel. If, as Mrs. Cunningham asserted, she had been married to Dr. Burdell, she would, after his death, be entitled to one-third of his property. As the mother of a child by him she would secure control of the whole of it. This absolute possession was what she wanted, but in order to have her desire satisfied it would be necessary to secure a child. She went about the business in a most methodical manner, "making up," as time went on, after the most artistic fashion. Unfortunately, however, for the ultimate success of her plan, she made a confidant of Dr. Uhl. He informed District Attorney Hall, and between the two it was decided to let Mrs. Cunningham have all the freedom she wanted. She asked the doctor to assist her in her subterfuge, and he promised to aid her. The time set for the consummation of the scheme drew near. At length the child was "born" again, one having been obtained from Bellevue Hospital, through the connivance of the District Attorney.

Mrs. Cunningham was happy. But not for long. She made her claim on the estate, and was at once confronted with the most damning proofs of her intended fraud. What became of her is not known, but I think she went to California, and afterwards wandered from place to place. A year or two ago she appeared in this city again, under an assumed name, in a "dispossession" case, before the First District Civil Court. She was, however, so old and poor as to be almost unrecognizable.

Eckel turned out badly, serving a term of imprisonment for defrauding the Government.

CHAPTER IV.

CHANGES IN POLICE DISCIPLINE.—POLITICAL INFLUENCE.—FERNANDO WOOD'S BATTLE.—WARRANT FOR THE ARREST OF THE MAYOR.—HE DEFIES MY AUTHORITY.—ANOTHER ATTEMPT.—THE SEVENTH REGIMENT APPEARS ON THE SCENE.—RELUCTANT SURRENDER.—$50,000 WORTH OF DIAMONDS.—HICKS, THE PIRATE.—A FLOATING SLAUGHTER-HOUSE.—A COSTLY BANQUET.—FLOORS WASHED WITH WINE.—VISIT OF THE PRINCE OF WALES.—EXECUTION OF CAPTAIN GORDON.—MARRIED TO HER FATHER'S COACHMAN.—MURDER IN THE "LIBRARY."—A JUSTIFIABLE DEED.—THE PANIC.—RUN ON THE BANKS.

FROM 1853 to 1857 the police force was controlled by a commission composed of the mayor, recorder and city judge. At the commencement, all officers were selected and promoted for efficiency. This continued until Fernando Wood became mayor, when he assumed full control of the force, which resulted in its being used for political purposes. It failed to give satisfaction and was ridiculed and condemned.

In 1857 the Legislature declared that the great city was too corrupt to govern itself, and the control of the police was transferred from the city to the State. The new police district comprised New York, Kings, Westchester and Richmond counties, and was managed by a board of five commissioners appointed by the Governor. These men appointed the chief, who under this act was given the title of superintendent of police and controlled the whole force. Under him were two deputy superintendents, five surgeons, inspectors and captains (not to exceed forty), sergeants (not more than one hundred and fifty), the rest being called "patrolmen."

Of course the change created a tremendous excitement in the force, and there was much talk of resistance among the old members, encouraged by the mayor, Fernando Wood. In May the new law was declared constitutional by the Supreme Court. That settled the matter in my mind. But fifteen captains and between seven and eight hundred policemen refused to obey the commis-

FAC SIMILE OF BADGE PRESENTED TO ME ON OCTOBER THIRTEENTH, 1853.

On the reverse is this inscription:

GEORGE W. WALLING,
Eighteenth Patrol District.

Presented to George W. Walling, on his promotion to the office of Captain of the Eighteenth Ward Patrol District, by the officers attached to the office of the Chief of Police, and other friends, as a token of respect and esteem.

sioners. When called upon to vote on the question as to which side they would serve (the Municipal or the Metropolitan), the old or the new, only about 300 out of 1100 voted at roll-call to support and respect the authority of the State board. The others were tried for insubordination and dismissed; but they defied dismissal and remained on duty and in charge of the police stations. The Metropolitans rented headquarters in White Street.

So the Mayor filled the places of the 300 absentees in the Municipal force. Subsequently the Metropolitan board filled the 800 vacancies in the State force. Thus there were two complete sets of policemen on duty, covering the same beats throughout the city. Collisions were frequent.

When Deputy Superintendent Matsell refused to obey the order of the Metropolitan board to furnish men to go to Quarantine and guard the public hospitals he was dismissed and I was sent. I took charge, and came up to the city jail to report at police headquarters. On the sixteenth of June, when I arrived at headquarters, in the hallway I met Jas. W. Nye, one of the police commissioners appointed by the Governor, and afterwards a senator from Nevada. He hailed me.

As I went in at the door, he said: "Here's just the man we want."

Turning toward me, he added: "Come in the room."

He took me into the room before the other commissioners, and said:

"Here's a warrant for the arrest of Fernando Wood."

I said: "Very well, give it to me. Shall I arrest him now?"

"Yes, this minute," answered Nye. "How many men do you want?"

"None."

Nye smiled grimly, and handed me the warrant. I found the City Hall the scene of great excitement. It was filled with hundreds of the Mayor's police.

I stepped to the anteroom of the Mayor's office, and sent in my name. I was requested to wait till the Mayor was at leisure, and after five or ten minutes the man at the door said:

"The Mayor will see you now."

As I went in the Mayor inquired: "Well, sir, what will you have?"

"I have a warrant for your arrest," I answered, exhibiting the paper.

"I do not recognize you as an officer," he said; "I dismissed you from the department."

"I am an officer," I retorted; "a member of the Metropolitan police."

"I do not recognize the legality of the service or the existence of the Metropolitan police," he answered. "I will not submit to arrest, or go with you, or concede that you are an officer at all."

I remarked: "Well, sir, as we don't agree on that point, I shall be obliged to do as I always did when I served warrants under your authority; I shall have to take you out forcibly if you resist."

"I will not be taken! You may consider that answer resistance if you please."

"No, sir, that is not resistance," I replied. "That is only refusal."

FERNANDO WOOD.
(From a Photograph.)

I went around the desk to take hold of him; he ordered me away and struck his office bell. It brought Captain Ackerman, of the Municipals, who had adhered to the Mayor's usurpation. He rushed in with several of his men. He and his men grabbed hold of me at Wood's order and forcibly ejected me from the office.

I would have been put out of the building, except that I was well known to the men in the corridors, having served with them. So I came and went at pleasure. One of the Municipals, a stranger, stopped me, but others shouted to him:

"Here! What are you about? Let go of him! He's all right."

I reported to the recorder, James M. Smith, who had issued the warrant; and he immediately wrote a letter addressed to

Sheriff Westervelt, directing him to furnish me with a posse for the execution of the warrant. This I delivered to the sheriff, who requested me to wait till he could consult his counsel, Mr. Brown, of the firm of Brown, Hall & Vanderpoel.

While I was waiting, I was surprised to see a body of fifty Metropolitan policemen marching from Chambers Street, apparently under the command of Coroner Perry and Captain Jacob Seabring, of the Ninth Ward.

D. D. Conover, who claimed to be street commissioner, had obtained an order of arrest against the Mayor and Sheriff from Judge Hoffman, in a suit for damages for having been forcibly ejected from the office which he claimed.

As the patrolmen came up the steps there was a collision. The place was garrisoned by some 800 or 900 Municipals, who attacked the approaching force, about one-fifteenth of their number. There was a fierce battle between the "preservers of the peace." The Metropolitans were attacked front, flank and rear, and terribly beaten. Many were badly hurt, and a few, including Patrolman Crofut, of the Seventeenth Precinct, were almost killed. The seriously wounded were carried over to Recorder Smith's rooms. There doctors dressed their injuries. The affair was a disgrace and dishonor to the Mayor, and from it his reputation never recovered.

About this time Mr. Brown, the lawyer, came into the sheriff's office, and, after a short consultation, said:

"Sheriff Westervelt, it is clearly your duty to get the necessary force and execute this warrant at all hazards."

The sheriff answered: "Come with me, you and Walling, and we'll execute the warrant."

I returned to the Mayor's office with them, where Mr. Brown said: "Mr. Mayor, here is an order for your arrest. It is in the hands of the sheriff of this county. I warn you that it is your duty as a law-abiding citizen to quietly submit to arrest."

Mayor Wood stood up behind his desk, seized his staff of office, jammed it down defiantly and angrily on the floor, and exclaimed: "I will never submit! You are invading the city's precincts and violating the law. I will never submit. You only want to humiliate me! I will never let you arrest me."

Mr. Brown then added: "Mr. Mayor, a battle has been fought before this building, and a number of men have been nearly killed

FIGHT BETWEEN THE METROPOLITAN AND MUNICIPAL POLICE.

on account of your obstinacy in resisting the execution of a process. Your duty is to submit to arrest by the officers of the law, and if you refuse, and further blood is shed, the consequences will be on your head."

Just at this moment George W. Matsell, who had continued to act as Chief of Police under Wood, entered the door and said, exultingly: "Mr. Mayor, the Metropolitans came and we've beat them off."

The Mayor refused to allow himself to be arrested, and we, desiring to avoid another combat, retired and consulted. Soon after, the Seventh Regiment was seen gayly marching down Broadway to take the boat for Boston, where it was to have a grand reception. The Police Board called upon General Sanford for assistance. The regiment was halted, the trumpets were stilled, and the regiment marched into the Park. It formed in line in front of the City Hall, facing the Mayor's window.

Matsell and his men looked out at the exhibition, and said to one another: "Well, our game is up."

Their conclusion seemed to be correct, for General Sanford walked into the City Hall by the side of Street Commissioner Conover, and the writ was read to the obstinate mayor.

Wood saw that further resistance would be not only futile but wicked, and he submitted to arrest. The conflict between the State and the city was over. The Metropolitans had won. By an arrangement the Municipals held their places for a month after that, during which both the "old" and the "new" were on duty, saluting each other on their beats. But it was observed by all men that in this conflict of authority and the anomalous conditions which accompanied it, the city had become demoralized. The repression of crime had been neglected, thieving had become rampant, and law-breakers had ceased to respect or fear the officers of the law. The succeeding troubles followed as a matter of course.

One thing I should mention in connection with this conflict of authorities. Those officers of the Metropolitan police who had been wounded in the affray sued Mayor Wood for their injuries, and employed Mr. David Dudley Field as their counsel. Mr. Charles O'Connor was retained for the defendant, against whom a verdict was rendered for each of the plaintiffs for $250, together with the total costs, amounting to about $13,000. The defendant never paid the money. It was finally put in the tax levy by the Legislature, and the city eventually paid both damages and costs.

A great crowd thronged old St. Patrick's Cathedral in Mott Street early on the morning of October 13, 1859, to witness the marriage of Miss Frances Amelia Bartlett, daughter of Lieutenant W. A. Bartlett, of No. 59 West Fourteenth Street, and Don Esteban Sancta Cruz de Oviedo, a very wealthy Cuban planter. The ceremony took place at noon, and was performed by Archbishop Hughes. The reception following this wedding was so thronged that detectives were sent to watch the house. The jewels, ordered from Tiffany's, cost $50,000; the bride's wardrobe was valued at $15,000. A few days after the wedding Mr. Edmund Clarence Stedman published a satirical poem on the humorous features of the event. This he entitled "The Diamond Wedding." The poem angered Lieutenant Bartlett, and he sent a challenge to Mr. Stedman. The poet refused to apologize, and Mr. Bartlett withdrew his challenge.

The trial of Hicks, the pirate, occurred in 1860. He was one of the crew of the oyster sloop "E. A. Johnson," which left this port on March 16, for Deep Creek, Virginia. The crew of the sloop consisted of Captain Burr, Oliver and Smith Watts (boys), and a man who had shipped under the name of William Johnson. He afterwards turned out to be Hicks. Five days after the sloop left New York she was picked up at sea and towed to Fulton Market slip. There was no one on board, and everything was in confusion. The cabin floor and furniture, as well as the bedding, were spattered and stained with blood. The scene was a ghastly one. The day previous to the finding of the sloop, Johnson, it was afterwards discovered, had returned to his home in New York, with a large amount of money in his possession. He had immediately started for Providence, R. I., with his wife and child. He was followed and arrested, but denied that he had ever been on the sloop, or that his name was Johnson. A watch belonging to Captain Burr, and a photograph given to Oliver Watts by a young lady, were found on him, however, and his identity was also established in many other ways. His name, he said, was Albert E. Hicks.

Notwithstanding his protestations of innocence, he was found guilty of the murders, and sentenced to be hanged on Bedloe's Island, where the statue of Liberty Enlightening the World has been erected. While in the Tombs after trial and conviction, Hicks made a confession of his guilt. He was hanged on July 13, 1860, and maintained his coolness and bravado to the very last. The scaffold was erected only a short distance from the shore, and the execution was witnessed by a large number of persons.

The same year that this horrible crime was committed, the first embassy from Japan visited New York. This was on the 16th of June, and the arrival of the Japanese was made an excuse for festivities of the most elaborate character. The members of the embassy arrived on the steamer "Alida," and enormous crowds assembled at the Battery where they landed. Their journey up town was a continuous ovation. More than six thousand soldiers were in line. One of the notable incidents of the visit was the "matinee" given by Mrs. James Gordon Bennett in honor of the two Japanese princes at Fort Washington. Three thousand invitations were issued, and Delmonico was told to spare no expense in preparing the collation. A grand ball was given by the Municipal authorities at the Metropolitan Hotel, the tickets of admission to which commanded a premium of $30. The hotel and Niblo's Garden were profusely decorated with flowers. The supper rooms were opened at 10 P. M. Ten thousand bottles of champagne were drunk. The crush was terrible, and before morning the floors were literally washed with wine. This was one of the most costly banquets ever given by the city of New York. It was estimated that the festivities cost between $90,000 and $100,000.

It was on Thursday, at 2 P. M., October 11, 1860, that the Prince of Wales landed at Castle Garden, and was escorted to the Fifth Avenue Hotel by the military and police. The Prince rode in a barouche drawn by six horses. Broadway made a beautiful display of bunting, and the Prince was continually greeted with cheers. A grand serenade was given him at midnight. A splendid ball, which I attended, was given in the evening of the second day at the Academy of Music. The Prince arrived at 10 P. M., and shortly after, to the great dismay of the enormous crowd, the ball-room floor gave way, and the police had hard work to keep the crowd back. The Prince folded his hands and looked on without emotion. After repairs had been made the Prince opened the ball with Mrs. Governor Morgan.

At this ball, as at all others tendered him in various parts of the country, partners were assigned the Prince who were evidently not to his taste. As a general rule, ladies very estimable in every re-

PRINCE OF WALES' BALL

spect, but advanced in years, were forced upon his notice and company. The result was that it was only towards the close of the ball that this scion of royalty was free to exercise his own fancy in the matter of selecting partners from among the youthful beauties present.

Toward the close of 1860 I was placed in command of the Twentieth Ward. The trial of Captain Nathaniel Gordon, the slave trader, occurred the following year and excited a great deal of public attention. Gordon was master of the ship "Erie," and sailed from Havana for the west coast of Africa, having on board everything considered necessary for carrying on the slave trade. Near the mouth of the Congo River he shipped nine hundred negroes, male and female, who were packed in the hold without ventilation. He then set sail for Cuba, but when about fifty miles from his journey's end he was captured by the United States man-of-war "Michigan," and conveyed, together with such of his human freight as had survived that awful passage, to Monravia. Upon his second trial—the jury having failed to agree upon a verdict in the first instance—he was convicted, and sentence of death was passed upon him by Judge Shipman. "Remember," said the Judge, "that you showed mercy to none—carrying off, as you did, not only those of your own sex, but women and helpless children. Do not flatter yourself that, because they belonged to a different race from yourself, your guilt is therefore lessened. Rather fear that it is increased. Do not imagine that, because others shared in the guilt of this enterprise, yours is thereby diminished; but remember the awful admonition of the Bible: 'Though hand join in hand, the wicked shall not go unpunished.'" His execution was fixed for February 7, 1862, and the most strenuous exertions were made by Gordon's relatives and friends, particularly his devoted wife and mother, to save the man from the gallows. They even went to Washington together in the hope of obtaining a pardon from the President. Their efforts were in vain, but a respite of two weeks was granted. On the evening previous to the day set for his execution, Gordon took a most affecting farewell of his family. Mrs. Gordon, together with the prisoner's aged mother, called at the prison about six o'clock in the evening and remained an hour or more. He received them in a most affectionate manner and talked most tenderly of his little son, who was absent. He appeared to

HANGING OF GORDON, THE SLAVE TRADER.

trouble himself very little about his own fate, but was very anxious concerning the future of his wife and only child. At about three o'clock the next morning the keepers who occupied the same cell with Gordon were considerably surprised to see him seized with convulsions. A physician was summoned, and it was found that Gordon was suffering from the effects of poison. How he obtained it no one could tell. The man was evidently dying, but by means of the stomach-pump and the use of brandy he was brought back to consciousness. He then begged the doctors to let him die by his own hand rather than suffer the disgrace of a public execution. But to no avail. Gordon walked, or rather tottered, to the scaffold in the City Prison like a drunken man, and while the rope was being adjusted he had to be supported by two of the deputy-marshals.

It has been so much the fashion of late years for young ladies to marry coachmen, that I cannot help recalling almost the first noted instance. It occurred in 1857, when Miss Mary Ann Baker, the daughter of Mr. John E. Baker, a well-known importer at No. 93 Front Street, married John Dean, her father's coachman. When Mr. Baker heard of the marriage, he locked his daughter in a back room, informing her friends that she was of unsound mind. Dean procured a writ of *habeas corpus*, but Mr. Baker threatened to shoot the officer who went to execute it. The house was watched until after the departure of the European steamer by which, it was said, Mr. Baker intended to smuggle his daughter out of the country. A commission *de lunatico inquirendo* was appointed, and their report was that Mrs. Dean was perfectly sane. An order was accordingly made by the court for her restoration to her husband.

In 1857 the "Library," a saloon at No. 480 Broadway, was a noted resort. Theodore S. Nims, formerly city librarian, was leaning against the bar one evening in August, conversing with a party of friends, when a Tombs "shyster" lawyer, named Henry J. Wagstaff, entered the place. He walked up to the party and suddenly struck Nims two stunning blows in the face. Nims took refuge behind a table, but being closely followed by his assailant, drew a double-barrelled pistol and fired two shots. Wagstaff fell dead. An inquest was held, and the coroner, addressing Nims, who had been arrested on a charge of murder, said: "In my opinion this deed was committed in self-defence, and upon my own responsibility I shall discharge you from custody." Wagstaff was a notorious character about the city, and no one appeared to regret his death.

The climax of the great financial panic of 1857 was reached on October 13th. The excitement on Wall Street was intense. Tremendous "runs" occurred on all the banks in the city, and tens of thousands of people thronged the streets. Suspensions were the rule with scarcely an exception. Large forces of police guarded the banks and great trouble was feared, but the impending storm blew over.

CHAPTER V.

THE POLICE AND SECESSIONISTS.—AN ANTE-BELLUM EPISODE.—PLOT TO ASSASSINATE PRESIDENT LINCOLN.—DOWN IN DIXIE.—THE SOUTHERN VOLUNTEERS.—A PERILOUS POSITION AND A MYSTERIOUS GUIDE.—ON THE TRAIN.—A JUMP FOR LIFE.—BRAVE TIM WEBSTER AND HIS SAD FATE.—THE MAN WITH THE FUR CAP.

To the young men of to-day the war is a thing of the past—a page of history. I, who belong to the generation that is passing, recall with a shudder the years of bloody fight, and that time yet more dismal that preceded open hostilities, when all was foreboding, trembling with uncertainty; when, if I may so express it, the volcano was smoking, but not yet ablaze.

One day, early in January, 1861, Superintendent Kennedy ordered me, by telegraph, to report immediately at headquarters. I did so, but he had gone, leaving word for me to proceed to his house. I went at once, and found his wife awaiting me with the message that he was at Cortlandt Street ferry, and I was to meet him there. I found him deep in consultation with certain officials. He said to me:

"Buy two tickets for Washington; you are to go with me. I will explain later."

I bought the tickets. In fifteen minutes we were on our way to Washington by the fast express.

During the journey the superintendent told me of the condition of affairs. He was alarmed at the state of public feeling in Maryland, especially in Baltimore, through which Mr. Lincoln was to pass on his way to Washington to assume office. Riots were feared, and there were sinister rumors of threatened attempts to assassinate the President-elect. I learned from the superintendent that the Washington authorities were uneasy. They had requested that some of the most trustworthy officers of the New York police should be detailed for service in Baltimore to ascertain what grounds there were for such suspicions.

Upon reaching Washington we were instantly admitted to consultation with a Government officer, high in position, whose nervousness was proof of the gravity of the crisis. With secret instructions from this gentleman we went to Baltimore.

Mr. Kennedy's duty was a very delicate one. We were soon satisfied that Baltimore was bitterly irritated, but whether the feeling against Mr. Lincoln was personal enough to make his passage through the city dangerous was hard to determine. Such evidence as we could hastily collect we sifted; and though we found that many of the rumors current in New York were not trustworthy, there was enough bad feeling to give cause for alarm. The situation demanded closer investigation, and Mr. Kennedy, with whom I entirely agreed, instructed me to return at once to New York and send on two of the best officers of the detective corps. So back to New York I went.

I carefully considered the selection of proper detectives for this delicate affair, and after anxious thought I chose Messrs. Sampson and De Voe. They were instructed to go to Baltimore, look over the ground and ingratiate themselves with disaffected persons. In other words, to use their own discretion and find out all they could.

It may be that Superintendent Kennedy was thoroughly informed as to the exact situation in Baltimore at that time, though this is open to doubt. I will say, however, that I was not. Matters were bad enough, I knew, but I was not aware what terrible risks the two officers were to run. As this ended my personal connection with the affair, I have thought it proper to give Mr. Sampson's own graphic version of his adventures:

"I was selected by Captain Walling, with Mr. De Voe as my partner, under Superintendent Kennedy's orders, to go to Baltimore. Our instructions were to investigate the situation there and to see Mr. Lincoln safely through.

"As soon as we reached our destination we assumed the rôle of Southern sympathizers and mixed freely with the secessionists. I had been at Augusta and knew some persons there, so I called myself 'Anderson' and hailed from Augusta. De Voe dubbed himself 'Davis' from Mobile, because he had lived there for some time.

"We were well supplied with money, very swaggering and loud-mouthed, and soon made friends with a certain class of Southern-

THOMAS SAMPSON.
(Detective Municipal and Metropolitan Police. U. S. Marshal and Chief of Police U. S. Sub-Treasury.)

ers whose talk was 'fight to kill.' We stayed at the Fountain Inn and for some weeks had a good time.

"By degrees we worked our way into the confidence of our new friends. We had to be cautious, though, for, as is well known to-day, defection was common enough in the Government bureaus at Washington, and the South was kept well posted of all movements made North. There were in consequence plenty of persons watching the movements of Kennedy and the New York police.

"For a time things went on smoothly. De Voe and I became members of a military company that met regularly in a kind of barracks. Our presiding officer and military instructor was a Texan, Captain Hays by name, and a picturesque Texan he was, with great flashing eyes and long floating hair, topped with a huge white sombrero. We had no muskets, but that was nothing to the inventive Texan. He put us through the manual of arms with laths. Sometimes there was a squad of forty men at drill. Our company was known as the 'Southern Volunteers.'

"All this time we were communicating with New York by telegraph. It would not have been safe to send messages from Baltimore, so we forwarded them from Cockeysville, a suburb of the city.

"But suddenly I discovered that we were suspected. It was no laughing matter. The 'Volunteers' were loud in their threats against traitors. The desperadoes of the company were in the majority. All carried revolvers, and De Voe and I stood a first-rate chance of being killed on sight. There was even a detail whose duty it was to 'do away' with suspected persons.

"I do not know how the intimation of danger came to me, but I was positive that we were watched. I had been asked searching questions as to the identity of 'Davis' (De Voe). His wife had been indiscreet enough to write him a letter, addressed in his assumed name, and bearing the New York post-mark. It had been in some way seen by one of the 'Volunteers.' Now a letter from the North for 'Davis' did not dove-tail with 'Davis's' account of himself. I may here remark that to act an imaginary story or identity straightly is one of the most difficult bits of work a detective has to do.

"I was at once asked many questions in regard to the letter—where it came from and what it was about. I had to turn it off as well as I could. I am afraid that my explanation was not at all complimentary to good Mrs. De Voe, but that unconscious victim was revenged; my explanation was accepted dubiously. It looked as if we, the shadowers, were about to become the shadowed. A telegram of inquiry to Augusta or Mobile would make it very hot for us. I thought it was time to go, and we went.

"How we got to Washington in safety I do not recollect. We were in too tight a place for comfort and had no time to spare. We left all our wardrobe in Baltimore and assumed another guise. I remember that I had worn a heavy cloth cap with a band of fur around it. I gave it away, and donned a soft slouch hat.

"Whew! let me stop a moment. A good many years have passed, but even now I cannot understand why we were not murdered in Baltimore, unless, perhaps, the conspirators thought something more was to be had by letting us go on to Washington.

"Well, we went to Willard's and registered as Anderson and Davis. It happened that our signatures were written on the last half of the page. As I wrote I noticed the peculiar scrawl of Horace Greeley and remarked to De Voe that we were in good company. We went to our rooms and talked matters over. We made up our minds that we were in a bad box. How much did we know of these 'Southern Volunteers'? They numbered many hundreds, perhaps thousands, and we were acquainted with but a few. We felt certain that they were on the watch for us.

"We could not stand being caged in our rooms. We went down the stairs, and looking carefully around, examined the main hall. There, sure enough, we recognized several of our genial friends, the 'Southern Volunteers,' who were critically examining the hotel register. I watched them breathlessly. When Mr. Greeley's signature was reached they stopped at that for an instant. Then one of them ran his finger down the column and stopped again while he read our assumed names. I cursed my stupidity in not having thought to change my alias. The man turned and whispered to his associates, and they all went slowly out.

"'What on earth shall we do?' asked De Voe.

"'Do?' said I, 'I don't know. About the best thing is to get some supper.'

"We went slowly down the stairs. I knew we were watched. Some of the party might be outside. 'Our only chance,' I whispered to De Voe, 'is that in the crowd and confusion here, our new get-up may throw them off the track for the moment. But that won't be for long.'

"When we entered the hall, De Voe leaned on the cigar-stand, and I cast my eyes toward the billiard-room. I don't want to disguise matters; I was afraid, and cudgelling my brains how to get out of the mess we were in. I did not move for a few instants, when a man in a long overcoat lounged along and got his back directly toward me. Then he suddenly spoke to me—in a very low tone—so that I could just hear his words:

WILLARD'S HOTEL, WASHINGTON, D. C.

"'For God's sake, Tom, come out of this.'

"He spoke just above his breath and did not move. I was startled, but had wits enough about me to understand that I was not to show, in any way, that I knew the speaker. I certainly did not, nor could I see his face. His low voice sounded strange and sepulchral. Mind, I was using all my wits just then, every nerve and muscle at full strain.

"I replied, also without budging: 'I do not recognize you.'

"The man's hand just faintly moved behind him, as though bidding me to follow. What was I to do? Was he friend or foe? It was just as pleasant to be killed inside the house as out of it.

"The man went deliberately out of the hotel. I followed very close to him, my steps almost locking his. I carried a self-cocking pistol, and I knew how to use it. I made up my mind that at the first suspicious movement I would shoot. As we stepped on the avenue the man exclaimed, still very low:

"'My God! where is Wash. Walling?'

"I asked: 'What Wash. Walling?'

"'Why, Tom, Captain Walling,' was the reply.

"This time I did not answer. Alert with suspicion I fancied that Captain Walling might be in Washington; that it was supposed I knew where he was. The man was seeking him. Walling, perhaps, was to be killed.

"My companion had on a great, rough coat, with the collar turned up to his nose. A heavy cap was drawn over his eyes. We walked silently along Pennsylvania Avenue. I was on the side toward the street, near the gas-lamps. 'If he is an enemy,' I thought, 'he has put me where he can the better see me.'

"We had walked on a little way, I with my hand on my pistol, when the man said: 'Tom, for God's sake tell me who is with you, and where is your fur cap?'

"This made me start. The man knew I had exchanged my cap for a soft hat. He must have followed me from Baltimore. I could stand the suspense no longer. I caught him suddenly by the arm, spun him around with my left hand, while with my right I still gripped the pistol. The violence of the movement flung open his coat and shifted his cap, so that his face was revealed. He made no movement but looked calmly at me. Then slowly, very slowly, his face came back to me.

"'Is that you, Tim?' I cried, overjoyed.

"'You did not know Tim Webster, Tom?' he asked.

"'You will never know, Tim,' said I, 'how near you came to being killed. For the last five minutes my finger has been on the trigger of my pistol.'

"Sure enough it was Tim Webster, whom I had not seen for many years. Now Tim was one of Captain Walling's and my best friends. He had been on the force with us in former years and I knew him to be a man of exceptional honesty and courage.

"'It was not a question of killing me, Tom,' said Tim Webster, rapidly, 'but it is to save you from death that I have followed you. Your life is not worth a cent. I swear to you there are twenty men after you this very instant. Even now I expect we are being watched. I may not be suspected, for I am with them, but they shan't kill my old friend if I can help it. But you clear out of this just as fast as you can, Tom; it is more serious than you think. The chances are you will not get through safely unless you use every precaution. Quickness of movement is everything now.'

"Perhaps he thought I looked incredulous. I didn't feel so. He went on—

"'Tom, it's so close a shave that at this moment if there's anything particular you'd like to say to your wife you'd better say it to me for her.'

"This was pleasant indeed. 'But, Tim,' said I, 'I can't leave De Voe in the lurch.'

"'He will have to take care of himself. You're a dead man if you go back after him.'

"I insisted, however, on going back for De Voe, and Tim reluctantly consented to help me. We slipped around to the hotel by a back way, and Tim told me briefly that he was in detective work himself and had been affiliated with the most desperate branch of the Secession party; that he was one of the leading spirits, and that it was his special duty to kill De Voe and me on sight.

"I managed by no end of manœuvring to get De Voe out of Willard's and explain matters to him.

"Said Tim, 'If you go to the railroad depot you will both be dead men. You will have to walk around Washington some fifteen miles and take the train there. I will start with you and put you on the track. It is your only chance of escape, for every other exit is guarded.'

"Tim led us out of the city, and we got to a barn, where he left us. There we slept, and early in the morning took the first train to Baltimore. Bad luck still pursued us. As we stepped in our car we saw three of the 'Southern Volunteers,' our quondam friends; men we had drilled with.

"'There they are,' I whispered to De Voe. 'If they are only three we can hold our own, I suppose.' Presently, from another car, three more walked in. They knew we were in the car. One of them, with a grin, pointed his thumb backward toward us. We were in the rear end. They were deliberating what to do and how to do it. Then they all sat down. Evidently they were going to wait till we got out at Baltimore, when history would know De Voe and me no more.

"An idea—an inspiration—came to my aid. 'De Voe,' said I, 'let us take a jump for life.' De Voe understood in a moment. 'Done,' he replied.

"We were going at a rapid rate, but it was certain death to stay on that train; there was a chance for life if we jumped. We sauntered out on the platform, closed the door, and took the leap. De Voe fell with a yell, he had sprained his ankle badly. I was much cut and bruised, but not seriously hurt. The train sped on. We had escaped.

THE LEAP FOR LIFE.

"It was agony for De Voe to walk, but he had to, and I helped him all I could. We made the circuit of Baltimore and reached the side opposite Washington. We hailed a horse-car, and I helped De Voe on. Along we went, and, said I, 'At last we are safe.'

"But where should that confounded car pull up but exactly in front of our old drill-room. 'Car stops here!' sung out the conductor. Of all places in the world what a terminus! We had to alight. I reconnoitred the house. I dreaded to see the flashing eyes, the floating hair, the huge sombrero of our Texan teacher.

Thank heaven! neither he nor any other 'Southern Volunteer' was visible. Poor De Voe was almost fainting with the agony of his sprain, and could walk no more. I looked down the street and discovered a hack with a negro driver. I went up to him. 'Engaged, sah,' says Sambo. 'How much do you expect from your fare?' I asked. 'One dollar, boss.'

"'I will give you five,' I returned.

"The look of joy that spread over that darkey's face was soon reflected on mine. The driver deserted his customer (I hope he was a 'Volunteer'); we bundled De Voe in and rattled merrily away to the Philadelphia depot. We caught the train for the North and our troubles were over. After we had started, a member of the Philadelphia detective force, whom I knew, came up and spoke to me. 'Why, Mr. Sampson,' said he, 'we were positive that De Voe and you had been murdered somewhere in Maryland. Where is your fur cap?'

"And so we should have been murdered but for the good head and great heart of Tim Webster, the bravest, coolest man, I think, that ever lived. Poor fellow, his fate was a sad one. He was executed as a spy at Richmond. After the war they brought his body North for Christian burial, and I followed to the grave the remains of him to whose skill and courage I owe it that I am alive to-day to tell this tale.

"Upon our return to New York we received the thanks of Superintendent Kennedy and Captain Walling.

"There were some rather laughable stories brought to headquarters about a man in Baltimore distinguished by a renowned fur cap, who was reported as a very dangerous person, furiously Southern in his sentiments, breathing nothing but blood and murder. Putting this and that together I am inclined to believe that I am the individual.

"In conclusion, let me say that the change made by Mr. Lincoln as to the date of his arrival in Washington, prior to his taking the oath of office, and his escape from insult, were in no small measure due to the unwearied efforts of Superintendent Kennedy and Captain Walling."

CHAPTER VI.

IN WAR TIME.—THE DRAFT RIOTS.—HEROISM OF THE POLICE.—THE BATTLE OF THE BARRICADES.—THE SHARP-SHOOTER ON THE ROOF.—WITH A BULLET IN HIS BRAIN.

AFFAIRS progressed very quietly in the Twentieth Ward, of which I was still captain, until 1863, when the draft riots occurred. We did not lack warnings of these troubles. Handbills had been circulated and meetings held, protesting against the draft. Mr. John A. Kennedy, then superintendent, did not believe that these mutterings of discontent would grow into riot, and did not prepare for danger. Even on that Monday morning in June, when the first mob assembled and showed its aggressiveness, the "off-platoon" had not been called on duty. The only reserve ready in an emergency was one section of police in each of the stations. These sections were immediately ordered to the scene of disturbance. Having different routes, they did not arrive at the same time, and were beaten by the mob in detail. The only effective way would have been for the various sections to have had a common rendezvous, and then, when a sufficient number of men had arrived, marched on the rioters. The police would have asserted their power and the mob would have been broken.

For my part, I had for several days noticed with great uneasiness the growing discontent among certain classes. Things, I thought, were coming to a head, and so I remained at the precinct station Sunday night. Early on Monday morning I went to my house, took breakfast and proceeded to headquarters to make my customary report. At Third Avenue and Nineteenth Street I learned, for the first time, that rioting was in progress. I was told that the mob had attacked an enrolling office in Third Avenue, driven off the police and set fire to the building. My station was in Thirty-fifth Street, between Eighth and Ninth avenues. I immediately started back again on the "dead run," believing the whole force would be called out. I was not mistaken. In a short time orders were sent from headquarters directing me to collect my "off-platoon." Messengers were despatched, and soon all the men reported for duty.

Information was received that the rioters were on their way to the Colored Orphan Asylum, on Fifth Avenue, between Forty-third and Forty-fourth streets, in which were about two hundred colored children, besides the matron and attendants. Then came the news that the institution had been attacked by a mob three thousand strong, pillaged and burned to the ground, the inmates making their escape as best they could. All were brought to my station, the small upon the backs of the larger, and were made as comfortable as possible, remaining with me a week. The poor creatures were almost crazed with terror, and were glad enough when, after the riots were over, arrangements were made to convey them to a temporary place of refuge on Blackwell's Island. Just as the negroes were coming into the station I received orders to report at police headquarters. No cars or stages were running, and in order to get to Mulberry Street as quickly as possible I hired stages, in which I placed all my available force, leaving in the station a sergeant, two doormen and a few partially disabled patrolmen who were on the sick-list. We arrived safely at headquarters. Meantime a body of rioters had attacked and burned another enrolling office in Broadway, near Twenty-sixth Street.

That evening we were stationed in the City Hall, as threats had been made to destroy the *Tribune* and other newspaper offices. Some time during the next morning one of my men came to me and said:

"Captain Walling, I've seen a big, rough-looking fellow peeping through the window. He's done it three or four times."

"Ah!" I remarked; "perhaps it will be just as well to keep a watch on him. Next time he peeps in call my attention to it."

"There he is again," said the man, presently. And sure enough, the dim outline of a man's face could be seen pressed against the window pane. I opened the door cautiously, and slipping out quietly grabbed him by the collar.

"Good heavens!" I exclaimed, as I looked at his features. "What are you doing here, Leonard?" for it was no other than my brother, who was a ship-carpenter.

He told me his fellow workmen had struck and wouldn't let him work. "Well, if you can't work, can you fight?" I asked him.

"Try me," he replied.

I immediately had him sworn in, gave him a club and had no occasion to feel ashamed of my unexpected recruit. He served under me the whole of the week, and took an active part in all that occurred, on one occasion narrowly escaping death.

That day I was directed to proceed with my men—one hundred in number—to certain buildings in the Twentieth and Twenty-second wards which were to be protected. We marched up Broadway, being supported by a company of regulars from the Invalid Corps. Thirty-second Street was reached without any exciting incident; but on arriving there I was informed that a mob was about to attack the Sixth Avenue car stables. This was not exactly true, the mob having designs on Dr. Ward's and other private residences in the neighborhood of Forty-sixth Street and Fifth Avenue. We marched up to Forty-fifth Street, and through it to Fifth Avenue. We were confronted by a howling mob of men and women, numbering over 2000. A large number were armed with bludgeons. There was but one thing to do, and that was done quickly. I shouted out at the top of my voice, so that the rioters could hear me:

"Kill every man who has a club. Double quick. Charge!"

And at them we went with our clubs. The rioters dropped their bludgeons, tumbling over each other, and took to their heels.

We took no prisoners, but left the rioters where they fell. The number of broken heads was large. The mob dispersed in all directions, despite the frenzied cries of the women for the men to "stand up and give the police ———."

This scrimmage, however, was nothing compared with what was to follow.

Early the next day, Wednesday, at the request of General Sanford, I conveyed a large number of colored persons, who had taken refuge in the Arsenal, to my station. This was crowded already, but I managed to stow them away somehow, the officers and men giving up their rooms. Barricades had been erected by the mob on Ninth Avenue, at certain intervals, all the way from Twenty-sixth to Forty-second Street. These obstructions were constructed of carts, bricks, wagons, etc., the vehicles being lashed together with telegraph wires, or anything else that came to hand. Many of the rioters had fire-arms. They could be seen not only behind the barricades, but on the house-tops.

BATTLE OF THE BARRICADES.

My instructions were simply to "clear the streets," and a company of Zouaves having been sent to support us, we proceeded to obey orders. We advanced towards the first barricade at the "double quick" with the soldiers in our rear. When within a short distance of it we were greeted by a sharp volley of pistol shots, with an occasional bullet from a musket by way of variety. Fortunately most of the balls passed over our heads, but it was warm work. The barricade could not be carried by the police alone, so we deployed to the right and left, thus allowing the soldiers space in which to manœuvre and return the fire of the mob. This they did, and the rioters retreated.

Barricade No. 1 was won.

The police then went to the front, but were again greeted with a volley from the mob, while the Zouaves, in skirmishing order, occupied the sidewalks, getting a shot at the rioters whenever they exposed themselves.

Even after so many years one or two tragical incidents come to my mind in connection with this sad affair as distinctly as though they happened yesterday. One was that of a rioter who had stationed himself with a musket at the corner of an intersecting street, and was firing at us as fast as he could load, simply poking the muzzle of his gun round, he being protected by the angle of the house. One of the Zouaves saw this trick, and, watching his opportunity, fired completely through the wooden house, killing the man instantly.

Another fellow on top of a house made himself very conspicuous during the conflict by taking a shot at either the police or the soldiers, and then dodging behind one of the chimneys. He tried this once too often. Suddenly, while I was watching him, he threw up his arms and fell headlong to the street with a rifle ball through the very centre of his forehead.

Every inch of ground was disputed by the now desperate rioters, but slowly and surely we advanced. One by one we captured the remaining barricades with the aid of the soldiers, until our task was accomplished.

We marched back to the station only to find that our duties for that day were by no means ended. At night, word was brought that the mob had attacked a church in Twenty-seventh Street belonging to a colored congregation, and that we must disperse the rioters.

AT THE CHURCH.

No time was lost in getting to the scene of action, but the rioters were well prepared to give us a warm reception. They had thrown out a line of pickets to warn them of our approach. It happened that several fire-engines were passing through the street at the time, and mixing with the party of firemen we approached close to the church without attracting much attention. The building was occupied by the rioters, and no sooner was our presence made known than we were greeted with a sharp fusillade from pistols, muskets, shotguns, etc. My men returned the fire with their revolvers, and this was the first time during the day that the police under my command had recourse to fire-arms. But now they did use them they proved most effective, as the following incident will show:

One of the rioters had straddled the ridge-pole of the church, and was hacking away at the timbers with an axe. The outline of his form stood out boldly against the sky, and he was in full view of the crowd. His actions were watched with great interest, and I kept my eye on him, as did everybody else. Presently the arm of one of my men was slowly raised to the proper level, there was a flash and a report, and the man on the roof disappeared from sight. Next day his body was found at the rear of the church. The bullet had lodged in his skull, and death must have been instantaneous.

That shot was followed by a howl of rage from the rioters, who attacked us in a savage and determined manner. We also set to work with a will, clubbing our opponents most unmercifully. The neighborhood was cleared in short order.

Before this a tragic occurrence was added to my day's experience. I was standing on Eighth Avenue, at Thirty-fifth Street, late in the afternoon, when six or eight burly-looking fellows, armed with clubs, marched up the street. In the middle of the block was a hardware store kept by a man named Heiser, and there it was that the party of ruffians stopped. The one who was evidently the leader was flourishing a heavy cart rung, with which he attempted to smash in the door. Heiser dealt in guns and pistols among other things, and if these men succeeded in getting into the store they would arm themselves and their comrades. I was alone, and there was no time to waste in seeking assistance. The fellow with the cart rung plied his weapon with such energy and strength that at the third or fourth blow he split the door in two.

It so happened that his club stuck in the crack, and while he was endeavoring to pull it out I rushed forward and struck him a terrible blow on the head with my locust. He fell to the pavement as if he had been shot. His companions, who made no attempt to attack me, put him in a wagon and hauled him away. A doctor was afterwards sent for to attend him, but his only remark on seeing the patient was:

"He doesn't want a doctor. He needs an undertaker."

The man was dead!

I am entirely aware that resistance to the draft was the first incentive to these disturbances; but in New York, as in all large centres of population, where any set of men makes a demonstration to ventilate its grievances, there will always be grouped around this party of malcontents the very worst elements of society. Aside from the strictly criminal classes—always ready to take advantage of any local troubles in order to carry on their peculiar vocations—there is a large body of idle persons, with no interests at stake, who amalgamate with the thieves for the purpose of sharing in the plunder. At times, when the utmost license has been rampant, this class has formed a most dangerous element. I really know of no instance of a riot occurring in New York, or in any other large city, during which robbery did not play a prominent part. A riot, or disturbance, is the thief's opportunity, and he is sure to take advantage of it. For more than a year after the draft-riots various articles, stolen during the disturbances from the houses of well-to-do citizens, were discovered by the police in different parts of the city. Furniture, carpets, china and other articles of a domestic character were carried off, and in some instances tapestry carpets, valuable rugs and rich hangings were found decorating some of the most squalid and poverty-stricken shanties on Manhattan Island.

One circumstance more in connection with these riots will bring my reminiscences of them to a close. On Wednesday afternoon, after the Battle of the Barricades on Ninth Avenue, the police under my command, together with the Zouaves, returned to the station. While there, waiting for orders, the Governor (Horatio Seymour), accompanied by Alderman John Hardy, came up and I accosted them. Alderman Hardy said to me:

"The Governor and myself have been over on Ninth Avenue,

and found a number of persons there killed in the fight. It's too bad."

"I can't help that," was my reply. "They were there behind their barricades, and we had orders to clear the street. If there were any innocent persons there, I regret it very much. But such persons had no business there; they should have got out of the way when ordered to disperse. It's certain they were there, and gave encouragement to the rioters by their presence. If they come back," I added, after a pause, "I shall attack them again and serve them in the same way."

Turning to the Governor, I asked him:

"Have you anything to say, sir; or any orders to give?"

The Governor's reply was: "Take your orders from your official superiors."

Both then walked away.

The draft-riot was certainly the most serious uprising that has ever occurred in New York, both in the area over which the disturbances extended and in the number of persons engaged in it. The forces of the police at the beginning of the trouble were not of sufficient strength to cope with the rioters at all points at once; but whenever the police and the mob came in contact the former were invariably the victors. No sooner, however, had the conflict ended in one part of the city than it began in another. That the struggle would have been prolonged and more disastrous had it not been for the aid of the military, there is no doubt; but I believe the police would have subdued the mob eventually.

Whenever there are the slightest premonitions of a riot, an ounce of prevention is worth more than a ton of cure in the shape of clubs or bullets. At the beginning of such a conflict a mob has no organization, and can be readily broken up.

CHAPTER VII.

CAPTURING HACKENSACK.—MYSTERIOUS VISITS TO NEW YORK.—AT THE SHOP WINDOW.—THE FATEFUL RING.—RECEIVING THE RUSSIANS.—TRYING TO BURN THE CITY.—THE BLACK BAGS.—THE "BOGUS" PROCLAMATION.—BURNING OF BARNUM'S MUSEUM.—AN UNHAPPY "HAPPY FAMILY."—STRUGGLE OF THE EAGLE AND SERPENT.—EMBEZZLING $250,000 TO SATISFY BLACKMAILERS.—A POLICEMAN MURDERED.

SHORTLY after the stirring events of the early part of 1863, the adventures of a woman known as Mrs. Klineschmidt caused society to take a quickened interest in the criminal classes. To that part of the world which did not know her, Mrs. Klineschmidt was a lady. She dressed like one, looked like one, and spoke like a woman of education and refined tastes. Her acquaintance was cast, as much as possible, among severely respectable persons.*

She was young when she first became known to the police. Her beauty was of the full-blown, blowzy sort, if you please, but it was effective with all men and many women. She made her physical attractions pay her a heavy royalty all the time. Not satisfied with that, she became one of the most adroit thieves ever known in New York. For some years, about the time of the war, she travelled between New York and Chicago, sometimes stopping in Canada, and smuggling by wholesale. She was arrested several times, and so became a person of note on the police records. She had a husband in the early part of her career, but he subsequently disappeared.

Finally she disappeared, too. Nobody knew what had become of her. It was afterwards discovered, however, that she was living in the village of Hackensack, New Jersey. There in the latter part of 1862, from the proceeds of her theft and economy, she built a stylish mansion. The Mandelbaums, some of whom are known to the detective police of America, lived across the street in good style. The two households resolved to "capture Hackensack."

---

* This incident did not come under my personal observation.

Mrs. Klineschmidt was eager for the fray. Her social ambition demanded that she should "shine in society." She was anxious to test upon persons of established respectability the powers that had won her such success in her own circle. She furnished her house after the most luxurious fashion. In the rooms were high-priced couches, lounges, ottomans and easy chairs, dressing-cases, Wilton carpets and portières of heavy satin. The walls were hung with tapestry. Valuable pictures were on the walls, and statuary was among the decorations of hall and drawing-room. On the front lawn a fountain played. Her carriage was a magnificent vehicle—perhaps a trifle too magnificent—the wheels and tongue red, and the body green. The upholstery was of brilliant yellow satin. The coachman's livery was of blue and silver, and the harness of the white horses was mounted with gold. She dressed in the latest fashion, and her beauty was a theme of never-failing comment among the male population of the town. Some persons to whom she was a mystery declared that she was the daughter of a rich old sea-captain who had just died in Nantucket; some that she had bought Harlem at a lucky moment on a tip from Commodore Vanderbilt; others that she had got rich in cotton, by the connivance of General Banks; still others that she had been the housekeeper for a miserly Californian who had just died and left her rich.

When she had succeeded in arousing the curiosity of the whole town, she coyly confessed to the veterinary surgeon, who called to attend her lap-dog, and who said he had seen service in Calcutta, that she was the grandchild of an Indian merchant who had left her a colossal fortune, which he had made in the spice-trade. The man spread the news.

Ladies began to call on her. Some were shy and still inquired. The men were not incredulous; they admired her from the first. She returned the calls, and did her utmost to ingratiate herself. The suspicion of the people gradually disappeared. As the winter passed she gave a ball at her residence, and was gratified with a general response. She took a conspicuous pew in church. She became the queen of Hackensack.

There were three or four families who did not welcome her, and on these she vainly tried all her arts. The men surrendered, but the women refused to associate with the Klineschmidt. This she resented, and resolved to punish. One young man, Blank, whose wife was thus placed under her ban, she secretly encouraged until he was completely infatuated with her. He was a tall, handsome, alert, and wealthy young fellow, and he became dazzled by her vulgar splendor, and by the preference for him which she manifested.

Mrs. Blank was not long in learning that her husband's affections were being estranged. She told him her fears and reproached him. The secret of the transfer of his affection soon became the property of the public, for the foolish fellow spent evening after evening at Mrs. K's. There was one thing which confused and puzzled him. She spent two nights and days of every week in New York; and when he asked her why, he received an answer which silenced, while it did not satisfy him. He became madly jealous, and resolved to find out whether she had another *amour* in the great city.

His suspicion was wrong. The fact was, that being the social arbiter of Hackensack cost considerable money, and her treasury needed constant replenishing. Blank, however, determined to find out what these mysterious disappearances meant; and the next time she crossed to New York he followed her. He watched her go to a house on Thirty-fourth Street, waited till he was certain that she would remain there, then took the number for future investigation, and slipped back home. He was unconscious of being followed by a tall and graceful boy. But his wife had thus disguised herself to make certain of the whereabouts of the inconstant Blank.

The next morning Mrs. Blank expressed a desire to visit her mother, in New York, for a day or two. He assented, and she immediately crossed the river, took a school-friend into her confidence, and together they watched the house on Thirty-fourth Street. While they were watching, Mrs. Klineschmidt came in after a predatory excursion to Broadway. Storing her booty, she again sallied forth.

"There she is, the hussy! Quick, or we shall lose her!" exclaimed Mrs. Blank to her friend.

"Hush! She may notice us."

"No fear of that. Our own mothers wouldn't know us; and I am not certain that she has ever seen either of us."

"How she is muffled up—for disguise, I suppose."

"There! she has stopped to see those people by that shop window. Let's dodge in this door-way."

THE WIDOW AT WORK.

"There! There! See, Kate, see!"

"Heavens! She is a thief. How skilfully she works!"

"What shall we do? How shall we trap her?"

The ladies talked the matter over, and then consulted the nearest captain of police. Mrs. Blank did not wish the woman arrested,—"not yet."

"Ah!" observed the astute officer, "you want her to steal something from you, so that you can hold it over her?"

"That was it," said she.

"Very well; go out to-morrow, or any day when you can find her. Dress in your best, so as to attract her. When you are in her vicinity and feel yourselves inspected, let your friend hand you a roll of bills. Put them in your purse and put the purse in your pocket. Have in it, also, some odd ring, or other piece of jewellery that you can identify. I will have a detective there to witness the theft."

The scheme worked to a charm the next day. Her purse was taken, and the thief made off.

The next week Mrs. Klineschmidt gave a grand ball at her house in Hackensack. Everybody went: even Mrs. Blank accompanied her husband, to his great surprise. Mrs. Klineschmidt met them at the door of her drawing-room with an air of triumph. Mrs. Blank's appearance created a sensation. All eyes turned on her; but they were astonished to see that she was arrayed in plain walking attire. She turned one look on the obsequious figure of her would-be hostess, and then to the astounded guests said:

"I am sorry to disturb you, but this woman is a thief!"

"A thief!" they exclaimed in amazed chorus.

"Yes, she picked my pocket in Broadway. There is my emerald ring on her finger now. The one your neighbors gave me for selling the most tickets at the bazaar."

Mrs. Klineschmidt drew her hand convulsively within her dress folds, and shouted in desperation: "You're a liar!"

"Here is an old acquaintance of yours who saw you do it. Walk in, Mr. Officer."

The detective stepped into the room. Soon all the guests stepped out.

"Well," laughed Mrs. Klineschmidt, "I've had a good time, and fooled all these stupid asses. Going over to-night?"

"Yes," answered the officer.

"THIS WOMAN IS A THIEF!"

And the queen of Hackensack was dethroned.

Late in the autumn of the year when Klineschmidt was run to earth (1863), Admiral Lessoffsky, with a Russian squadron, arrived in New York waters. This was the signal for a grand military reception, a municipal banquet, and a ball at the Academy of Music, on the evening of the fifth of November. This ball was the finest and most elaborate ever seen in New York. Irving Hall was used for a supper room. Some 6000 persons assembled about the Academy to see the guests arrive. Besides Admiral Lessoffsky, the guests included Baron Stoeckel, General Dix and Admiral Farragut.

The following year was made memorable by the discovery of a plot to burn New York. The police had received information concerning this dastardly scheme, but they refused at first to believe it. The intention of the conspirators was to start fires up and down town at the same time, and while the firemen were thus engaged to fire the hotels in the centre of the city.

The first fire was discovered at 8.43 o'clock on the evening of November 25th, at the St. James Hotel. At the same time Barnum's Museum was found to be in flames. In quick succession, alarms came from the St. Nicholas Hotel, the United States Hotel, the Lafarge House, the Metropolitan, the New England Hotel and Lovejoy's. At midnight an attempt was made to burn the shipping in the North River, and from that time until daylight, the Belmont, Fifth Avenue, Howard and Hanford hotels, the Astor House and Tammany Hall were found to be on fire. Lumber yards in various parts of the city were also in flames. Fortunately, all these schemes miscarried, and the fires were extinguished in time to prevent a general conflagration. Bags of black canvas were discovered in the rooms set on fire at the different hotels and were taken to police headquarters. Each contained a quantity of paper, about a pound and a half of rosin, a bottle of turpentine and one or two bottles containing phosphorus in water. The fires were started by piling the bedding in the middle of the room and saturating it with turpentine, setting it on fire and then locking the door. The hotel-keepers offered a reward of $20,000 for the detection of the criminals, but they all escaped. The terror in the city on the night of the fire and some weeks after was very great.

A somewhat amusing, yet withal an important incident connected with war times in New York, was the publication on May

18, 1864, of what purported to be a proclamation from the President, recommending a Fast-day, and calling for 400,000 troops. The document was printed in the *World* and the *Journal of Commerce*. It was soon discovered that the proclamation was bogus.

A large mob collected about the office of the *Journal of Commerce*, in Wall Street, and demanded that the report should be contradicted forthwith. The Government at once suppressed both papers, and the Associated Press offered a reward of $1000 for the conviction of the author. In due time it was discovered that "Joe" Howard, Jr., wrote the proclamation. He was arrested and sent to Fort Lafayette.

Although an attempt to burn Barnum's Museum had been made in the "Black Bag" conspiracy, it was not until July 1, 1865, that it was destroyed by fire. With it was consumed almost the entire block bounded by Fulton, Ann and Nassau streets and Broadway. The fire originated in the upper story of the Museum, and gradually worked its way down, at the same time spreading to the adjoining buildings. The entire loss reached $2,000,000. During the progress of the fire a large force of policemen was kept busy in looking after the thieves and pickpockets with whom the city fairly swarmed at that time. Several stores were pillaged. One of the places broken into was Knox's hat store, the hats being offered for sale in the most barefaced manner within sight of the shop from which they were stolen. They found a ready sale, so many head-coverings having been lost in the trampling and crush of the vast crowd.

Although I witnessed the conflagration, I prefer to describe it in the words of an account which appeared in the New York *Tribune* of the following day, which created a great sensation:

> Soon after the breaking out of the conflagration, strange and terrible howls and moans proceeding from the large apartment in the third floor of the Museum, startled the throngs who had collected in front of the burning building, and who were at first under the impression that the sounds must proceed from human beings unable to effect their escape. Their anxiety was somewhat relieved on this score, but their consternation was by no means decreased upon learning that the room was the principal chamber of the menagerie connected with the Museum, and that there was imminent danger of the release of the animals there confined, by the action of the flames. Our reporter fortunately occupied a room. the windows of which looked immediately into this apartment. Luckily the windows of the Museum were unclosed, and he had a perfect view

BURNING OF BARNUM'S MUSEUM.

of almost the entire interior of the apartment. The following is his statement of what followed, in his own language:

"Protecting myself from the intense heat as well as I could, by taking the mattress from the bed and erecting it as a bulwark before the window, with only enough space reserved on the top so as to look out, I anxiously observed the animals in the opposite room. Immediately opposite the window through which I gazed was a large cage containing a lion and lioness. To the right hand was the three-story cage, containing monkeys at the top, two kangaroos in the second story, and a happy family of cats, rats, adders, rabbits, etc., in the lower apartment. To the left of the lion's cage was the tank containing the two vast alligators, and still further to the left, partially hidden from my sight, was the grand tank containing the great white whale, which has created such a furore in our sight-seeing midst for the past few weeks. Upon the floor were caged the boa-constrictor, anacondas and rattlesnakes, whose heads would now and then rise menacingly through the top of the cage. In the extreme right was the cage, entirely shut from my view at first, containing the Bengal tiger and the Polar bear, whose terrific growls could be distinctly heard from behind the partition. With a simultaneous bound the lion and his mate sprang against the bars, which gave way and came down with a great crash, releasing the beasts, which for a moment, apparently amazed at their sudden liberty, stood in the middle of the floor lashing their sides with their tails and roaring dolefully.

"Almost at the same moment the upper part of the three-story cage, consumed by the flames, fell forward, letting the rods drop to the floor, and many other animals were set free. Just at this time the door fell through and the flames and smoke rolled in like a whirlwind from the Hadean river Cocytus. A horrible scene in the right-hand corner of the room, a yell of indescribable agony, and a crashing, grating sound, indicated that the tiger and Polar bear were stirred up to the highest pitch of excitement. Then there came a great crash, as of the giving way of the bars of their cage. The flames and smoke momentarily rolled back, and for a few seconds the interior of the room was visible in the lurid light of the flames, which revealed the tiger and the lion locked together in close combat.

"The monkeys were perched around the windows shivering with dread, and afraid to jump out. The snakes were writhing about, crippled and blistered by the heat, darting out their forked tongues, and expressing their rage and fear in the most sibilant of hisses. The 'Happy Family' was experiencing an amount of beatitude which was evidently too cordial for philosophical enjoyment. A long tongue of flame had crept under the cage, completely singeing every hair from the cat's body. The felicitous adder was slowly burning in two and busily engaged in impregnating his organic system with his own venom. The joyful rat had lost his tail by a falling bar of iron; and the beatific rabbit, perforated by a red-hot nail, looked as if nothing would be more grateful than a cool corner in some Esquimaux farm-yard. The members of the delectated convocation were all huddled together in the bottom of their cage, which suddenly gave way, precipitating them out of view in the depths below, which by this time were also blazing like the fabled Tophet.

"At this moment the flames rolled again into the room, and then again retired. The whale and alligators were by this time suffering dreadful torments. The water in which they swam was literally boiling. The alligators dashed fiercely about, endeavoring to escape, and opening and shutting their great jaws in ferocious torture; but the poor whale, almost boiled, with great ulcers bursting from his blubbery sides, could only feebly swim about, though blowing excessively, and every now and then sending up great fountains of spray. At length, crack went the glass sides of the great cases, and whale and alligators rolled out on the floor with the rushing and steaming water. The whale died easily, having been pretty well used up before. A few great gasps and a convulsive flap or two of his mighty flukes were his expiring spasm. One of the alligators was killed almost immediately by falling across a great fragment of shattered glass, which cut open his stomach and let out the greater part of his entrails to the light of day. The remaining alligator became involved in a controversy with an anaconda, and joined in the *mêlée* in the centre of the flaming apartment.

"A number of birds which were caged in the upper part of the building were set free by some charitably inclined person at the first alarm of fire, and at intervals they flew out. There were many valuable tropical birds, parrots, cockatoos, mocking birds, humming-birds, etc., as well as some vultures and eagles, and one condor. Great excitement existed among the swaying crowds in the streets below as they took wing. There were confined in the same room a few serpents, which also obtained their liberty; and soon after the rising and devouring flames began to enwrap the entire building, a splendid and emblematic sight was presented to the wondering and upgazing throngs. Bursting through the central casement, with flap of wings and lashing coils, appeared an eagle and a serpent wreathed in fight. For a moment they hung poised in mid-air, presenting a novel and terrible conflict. It was the earth and air (or their respective representatives) at war for mastery; the base and the lofty, the groveller and the soarer, were engaged in deadly battle. At length the flat head of the serpent sank; his writhing, sinuous form grew still; and wafted upward by the cheers of the gazing multitude, the eagle, with a scream of triumph, and bearing his prey in his iron talons, soared towards the sun. Several monkeys escaped from the burning building to the neighboring roofs and streets; and considerable excitement was caused by the attempts to secure them. One of the most amusing incidents in this respect, was in connection with Mr. James Gordon Bennett. The veteran editor of the *Herald* was sitting in his private office with his back to the open window, calmly discussing with a friend the chances that the *Herald* establishment would escape the conflagration, which at that time was threateningly advancing up Ann Street, towards Nassau Street. In the course of his conversation, Mr. Bennett observed: 'Although I have usually had good luck in cases of fire, they say that the devil is ever at one's shoulder, and—' Here an exclamation from his friend interrupted him, and turning quickly he was considerably taken aback at seeing the devil himself or something like him, at his very shoulder as he spoke. Recovering his equanimity, with the ease and suavity which is usual with him in all company, Mr. Bennett was about to address the intruder when he perceived that what he had taken for the gentleman in black was nothing more than a frightened orang-outang. The poor creature, but recently released from captivity, and doubtless thinking that he might fill some vacancy in the editorial corps of the paper in question, had descended by the water-pipe and instinctively taken refuge in the inner sanctum of the establishment. Although the editor—perhaps from the fact that he saw nothing peculiarly strange in the visitation—soon regained his composure, it was far otherwise with his friend, who immediately gave the alarm. Mr. Hudson rushed in and boldly attacked the monkey, grasping him by the throat. The book-editor next came in, obtaining a clutch upon the brute by the ears; the musical critic followed, and seized the tail with both hands, and a number of reporters, armed with inkstands and sharpened pencils, came next, followed by a dozen policemen with brandished clubs; at the same time, the engineer in the basement received the preconcerted signal and got ready his hose, wherewith to pour boiling hot water upon the heads of those in the streets, in case it should prove a regular systematized attack by gorillas, Brazil apes and chimpanzees. Opposed to this formidable combination, the rash intruder fared badly, and was soon in durance vile.

"We believe that all the human curiosities were saved; but the giant girl, Anna Swan, was only rescued with the utmost difficulty. There was not a door through which her bulky frame could obtain a passage. It was likewise feared that the stairs would break down, even if she should reach them. Her best friend, the living skeleton, stood by her as long as he dared, but then deserted her, while, as the heat grew in intensity, the perspiration rolled from her face in little brooks and rivulets, which pattered musically upon the floor. At length, as a last resort, the employees of the place procured a lofty derrick which fortunately happened to be standing near, and erected it alongside the Museum. A portion of the wall was then broken off on each side of the window, the strong tackle was got in readiness, the tall woman was made fast to one end and swung over the heads of the people in the street, with eighteen men grasping the other extremity of the line, and lowered down from the third story amid enthusiastic applause. A carriage of extraordinary capacity was in readiness, and, entering this, the young lady was driven to a hotel.

"When the surviving serpents, that were released by the partial burning of the box in which they were contained, crept along on the floor to the balcony of the Museum and dropped on the sidewalk, the crowd, seized with St. Patrick's aversion to the reptiles, fled with such precipitate haste that they knocked each other down and trampled on one another in the most reckless and damaging manner.

"Hats were lost, coats torn, boots burst and pantaloons dropped with magnificent miscellaneousness, and dozens of those who rose from the miry streets into which they had been thrown, looked like the disembodied spirits of a mud bank. The snakes crawled on the sidewalk and into Broadway, where some of them died from injuries received, and others were despatched by the excited populace. Several of the serpents of the copper-head species escaped the fury of the tumultuous masses, and, true to their instincts, sought shelter in the *World* and *News* offices. A large black bear escaped from the burning Museum into Ann Street, and then made his way into Nassau, and down that thoroughfare into Wall, where his appearance caused a sensation. Some superstitious persons believed him the spirit of a departed Ursa Major, and others of his fraternity welcomed the animal as a favorable omen. The bear walked quietly along to the Custom House, ascended the steps of the building, and became bewildered, as many a biped bear has done before him. He seemed to lose his sense of vision, and no doubt, endeavoring to operate for a fall, walked over the side of the steps and broke his neck. He succeeded in his object, but it cost him dearly. The appearance of Bruin in the street sensibly affected the stock market, and shares fell rapidly; but when he lost his life in the careless manner we have described, shares advanced again, and the Bulls triumphed once more.

"After the fire several high-art epicures groping among the ruins, found choice morsels of boiled whale, roasted kangaroo and fricasseed crocodile, which, it is said, they relished; though the many would have failed to appreciate such rare edibles. Probably the recherché epicures will declare the only true way to prepare those meats is to cook them in a museum wrapped in flames, in the same manner that the Chinese, according to Charles Lamb, first discovered roast pig in a burning house, and ever afterward set a house on fire with a pig inside, when they wanted that particular food."

Very early on the morning of August 10th, 1865, Patrolman McCarty, of the Twenty-ninth Precinct, arrested Henry B. Jenkins, cashier of the Phœnix Bank, one of the wealthiest institutions on Wall Street. Jenkins was charged with embezzling $250,000. He had been in the employ of the bank for twenty years. He admitted his guilt, and asserted that five or six other persons were implicated in the crime. Excitement ran high, and a number of arrests were made at once.

It soon became known that Jenkins was the victim of an infamous case of blackmailing. Having become the dupe of a woman whose acquaintance he made in a concert saloon, he was forced to support her and her "lover" in richly furnished apartments in Bleecker Street. One of the men implicated was James H. Earl, a clerk in an office on Wall Street. He admitted having received $100,000 in stolen bonds from Jenkins. He was arrested and taken to a cell in the police station, in Twenty-ninth Street, near Fourth Avenue. There he immediately committed suicide with a small pen-knife, which he had concealed. "Vieve Brower," the mistress of Jenkins, and Charles Brower, her paramour, were also arrested. Vieve was the leech who bled Jenkins, sometimes getting from him as much as $1000. She discovered Jenkins' dishonest practices, and used the secret as a threat so that she and her associates could obtain money.

She told other persons of her suspicions, and soon Jenkins found himself surrounded by rowdies, pimps, and ex-bounty jumpers, who demanded large loans of money, which he was afraid to refuse.

Soon after the detection of this crime the city was shocked by the murder of Patrolman Thomas Walker. While Walker and a fellow-officer, named Rork, were patrolling West Seventeenth Street, about two o'clock on Tuesday morning, August 15, 1865, they heard the screams of a woman coming from a carpenter's shop near by. Drawing their revolvers, they entered the place where they found twelve or fifteen men.

"You devilish scoundrels, what are you doing here?" cried Officer Rork.

The reply was a volley of shots from the room. A ball struck Walker on the head, over the right ear, passing through the brain. He instantly fell dead, and was found lying on his back with his pistol in the hand that was stretched across his breast.

The men in the carpenter shop fled, but Rork pursued them, capturing one named John Ward. Before daybreak the police had succeeded in arresting twelve of the gang. The funeral of Walker was attended by the police force of the city.

CHAPTER VIII.

ALBERT D. RICHARDSON'S MURDER.—THE DYING MAN'S RECOGNITION.—TRIALS OF A YOUNG WIFE.—THE LOVER'S PROMISE.—THE MURDERER FREE.—VAN EETEN FORGERIES.—A STERN CHASE BUT A SUCCESSFUL ONE.—RE-ARRESTED WHEN LIBERTY WAS SECURED.—BEFORE THE LAST JUDGE OF ALL.

IN the latter part of 1869, New York gossip fairly hummed with the details of the murder of Albert D. Richardson, a prominent journalist. At five o'clock on the afternoon of November 25, 1869, Richardson opened the door of the *Tribune* office which led from Spruce Street, and walking to a desk at one end of the counter, asked if there was any mail for him. No sooner had the words left his mouth than from behind the counter sprang a man with a revolver in his hand. He leaned forward, took hasty aim and fired. Richardson, mortally shot, held on to the edge of the counter a moment for support, then staggered to the fourth floor where the editorial rooms were, and threw himself upon a sofa. There he lay in terrible agony. The murderer, seeing that his purpose was accomplished, leaped over the counter behind which he had been concealed, and with the still smoking weapon clutched to his breast, vanished in the crowd. George M. King, a clerk, stood within a few feet of him, and yet so sudden was the shooting that he did not realize what had happened until it was over. Neither did the other clerks, nor the men who were going in and out of the office, nor the passing throng on the sidewalk. The murderer, unknown, unrecognized, had disappeared, leaving no trace.

In room No. 31 at the Westmoreland Hotel that night was a man who was unknown to the proprietors, or to any of the guests in the house. He had registered in the afternoon with a trembling hand, and had left orders not to be disturbed. At ten o'clock Captain Allaire, of the Fourth Precinct, knocked at the door of that room. He opened it and found himself in the presence of the murderer, Daniel McFarland, an assistant assessor in the city government.

THE DEATH-BED RECOGNITION.

When told that he was under arrest for shooting Albert Richardson, his limbs jerked spasmodically and his features were distorted, as he cried out in hoarse tones:

"My God, it must have been me—No!—It was not—Yes, it must have been me!" The man seemed dazed.

There was another scene before the day closed on this tragedy. It occurred a half hour later, and was placed in the Astor House, room No. 115. The wounded journalist was there with his life slowly ebbing away. He had been brought across the square from the *Tribune* building. Dr. Swan had probed for the fatal ball and was trying to make his patient comfortable. Suddenly two men entered—one in uniform. They approached the bed on which Richardson lay. The murderer and his victim were face to face. The stricken man looked feebly up, let his eyes fall for a second on the captain's companion, and in a thrilling whisper said:

"That is the man."

There was a woman in the case, of course; else gossiping tongues wouldn't have wagged. This woman was the wife of Daniel McFarland. Her maiden name was Abby Sage, and her childhood had been spent in Manchester, N. H. Here McFarland found her—a girl in her teens, bright, beautiful and talented. He was an Irishman, born in the old country, left at twelve years of age without parents and obliged to cut his own way through the world. He came to this country, worked hard for an education and received a degree from Dartmouth College. When Abby Sage met him he had been admitted to the practice of the law seven years. According to her sworn testimony he had represented himself to be enjoying a good practice in Madison, Wisconsin, to own property worth $20,000 or $30,000, and a man of excellent morals. So they were married in 1857.

They went to Madison to live, but after a few weeks returned to New York. The young wife ascertained that her husband's property was in Wisconsin lands, and little money could be realized on them. Within three months from the time of the marriage her jewels were in the hands of New York pawnbrokers and the bride was sent home to visit her father. McFarland visited her there, and, according to her own story, she got to know him better. She found out that he was passionate in disposition, profane, and intemperate. In the following year they took a house in Brooklyn, and at Christmas time a child was born—born to die within a few months.

Domestic harmony after this was often interrupted. Mrs. McFarland several times left her husband on account of his alleged brutality and went home to her father's. In April, 1860, the second child, Percy, was born. The mother paid her physician's bill out of the proceeds of a public reading which she gave for that purpose—for she had no small talent as an elocutionist. In the spring of 1861 the little family moved back to Madison for a year, and then returned to New York. They went to Mrs. Oliver's to board, at No. 58 Varick Street.

And now this young woman of Puritan stock, who had beauty and charms and talent, but an uncongenial and ill-tempered husband, began to prepare herself for going on the stage. She took lessons of Mr. and Mrs. George Vanderhoff, and gave numerous dramatic readings, thereby earning enough money to support both her husband and herself. But McFarland continued to treat her cruelly. She told afterward, how one morning, after he had been out all night on a drunken orgie and had risen from their bed in one of his worst tempers, she approached him as he stood by the mirror finishing his toilet and tried to soothe him. In reply he turned around fiercely and struck the woman he had married across the face, sending her reeling backward. She said that sometimes he would extend his hands, with his fingers bent like claws, as if he were about to clutch her throat, and cry out: " How I should like—*like* to strangle you !" She told Mrs. John F. Cleveland (a sister of Mr. Greeley) about the blow she had received, and won that lady's sympathy.

About this time and later, Mrs. McFarland, through her readings, made the acquaintance of a number of persons who were openly designated in the courts afterward as Free-lovers, Fourierites, Mormons and the like. They were for the most part persons of more or less social prominence in the city, and professed the most affectionate interest in the young dramatic reader. They encouraged her plans for going on the stage, and were the confidants of her trials and misfortunes. The weak young wife's heart easily softened towards them under such genial rays of affection. Mrs. McFarland's enemies afterward accused these persons with being the instruments of her destruction. They openly charged them with having conspired to tear her from her legal husband,

and join her with him for whom they thought her soul had an "affinity." But Mrs. McFarland, to the last, denied the existence of any such conspiracy. Under the influence of their acquaintanceship, however, or on account of further harsh treatment from her husband, the breach between Mr. and Mrs. McFarland grew wider.

Albert D. Richardson, whom Daniel McFarland shot in a fit of jealousy, was born in 1833. He chose a literary occupation, and during the war became correspondent of the New York *Tribune*. He was taken prisoner by the Confederate army and remained in jail for some time. After the war he came to New York, continued his connection with the *Tribune*, and won considerable fame as a newspaper writer and as the author of several books. Among his more intimate friends in New York were Mr. and Mrs. Samuel Sinclair and Mrs. L. G. Calhoun. He was a frequent visitor at their homes. Mrs. Sinclair and Mrs. Calhoun, it chanced, were also Mrs. McFarland's most intimate friends. They were attracted by her charms and talents, and all three being persons of literary tastes found congenial companions in each other. "There are just three persons who are much to me in the flesh," wrote Mrs. Calhoun to Mrs. McFarland, " you—and you can guess the other two."

Mrs. McFarland's introduction to such society had given her a taste of the sweet poison which was to ruin her. She longed for wealth and refinement and love. Her home relations became repulsive to her. Perhaps she considered them the irksome ties which prevented her from occupying the sphere in life which she thought belonged to one of her talents. She had won some notice as a writer in the *Independent*, in the *Riverside Magazine*, and had written a little book called "Percy's Year of Rhymes" for children. But this success only tickled her vanity. She was led by her friends to believe that she could shine on the stage, and to win public applause behind the foot-lights became her sole ambition.

She first met Mrs. Calhoun in the winter of 1866. Mrs. Calhoun interested herself in getting Mrs. McFarland a theatrical engagement. Her efforts were successful, and the dramatic reader secured a position in the Winter Garden Theatre, which was controlled by Edwin Booth. Her salary was $20 a week, and on November 28, 1866, she made her *début* as Nerissa, in the "Merchant of Venice."

In January, 1867, Mr. and Mrs. McFarland moved to No. 72 Amity Street, and took the back parlor and extension room. The rooms were rented from a Mrs. Mason. The two had not been there a month when Richardson, who had been boarding at No. 61 Amity Street, came to see about engaging rooms. This, Mrs. McFarland said, was the first time he had called upon her. Richardson secured a room, and after that, Mrs. McFarland said in a written statement, "I saw him often, and he did me many kindnesses. I knew very well he pitied me, because he thought I was overworked and not very happy. . . . He called sometimes at my room, which was next his, but from its situation, and the fact that it was my sleeping-room, parlor and dining-room in one, made it in no sense a private room."

On the evening of February 19, Mr. McFarland entered the house and saw his wife standing at Richardson's door. The husband thought it was time to expostulate, and he did. But this was his wife's reply: "I did not go into Mr. Richardson's room and I am not in the habit of going there. Even if I was, it is not a private room, but an office in the day time." But Mr. McFarland was not satisfied. That night he raged and tore around. "Did Richardson ever kiss you?" he shouted to his wife. "Have you ever been in his room alone with him?"

The partition between McFarland's room and Richardson's was so thin that the latter heard all this conversation. The next day McFarland spent at home, and had the pleasure of seeing his wife's lover open the door and hurriedly retreat as soon as he discovered the husband's presence. McFarland left the house for a while, and when he returned his wife had fled and the boy Percy was on his way to Boston. Mrs. McFarland had gone to the Sinclairs, where she had seen Richardson, and he had assisted in taking her and her boy from the husband and father. Three days later, in the presence of Mr. and Mrs. Oliver Johnson, Mr. Sinclair and Mr. Sage, Mrs. McFarland told her husband that she had determined to leave him forever. His answer was brief:

"I bow to it, and submit to it."

That evening Richardson was at the Sinclair house. As he was about to leave, Mrs. McFarland followed him to the door. As they stood alone in the hallway, the woman murmured:

"You have been *very*, VERY good to me. I cannot repay you, but God will bless you for it." She spoke with great emotion.

"How do you feel about facing the world with two babies?" he asked.

"It looks hard for a woman, but I am sure I can get on better without that man than with him," was her answer.

All this while Richardson held her hand. Now he leaned over and in a low tone said: "I wish you to remember, my child, that any responsibility you choose to give me in any possible future, I shall be very glad to take."

Two nights later he called again, and proposed marriage.

The relations between the two thereafter are a matter of dispute, and I do not pretend to decide which side was right. It should be mentioned, however, that on the night of March 13, of this year, while Richardson was returning from the theatre with Mrs. McFarland, Mr. McFarland came up behind them and fired several shots, one of them wounding Richardson in the thigh. Finally, in 1868, Mrs. McFarland went to Indiana to get a legal divorce from her husband. On October 31, 1869, she returned to her mother's house a free woman. She saw Richardson on Thanksgiving Day. Then he went back to New York, and a week later she heard that he had been mortally wounded by her former husband.

This was the story of a woman's trials and temptations which resulted in the *Tribune* office tragedy. Shocked as the woman undoubtedly was by the intelligence which sped to her over the wire, she was not frightened. Her part in this sad play was not yet ended. Nothing but hate filled her heart toward her lover's murderer; nothing but pity and affection had she for the dying victim. She came to him at once, and by his bedside in the Astor House watched until he died. But three days before death came, Albert D. Richardson and Abby Sage McFarland were lawfully married. The ceremony was performed by the Rev. Henry Ward Beecher and the Rev. O. B. Frothingham. It was a tender and touching marriage. Then came death, on the night of December 2. Five persons watched the spirit take its flight. These were Junius Henri Browne, Col. T. H. Knox, Mrs. Sage and the two doctors, Carter and Swan.

The trial of the murderer began on April 4, 1870. His case was represented by Col. Charles S. Spencer, John Graham, and Elbridge T. Gerry. For the prosecution were District Attorney Garvin, his assistant, Mr. Fellows, and Noah Davis. The hearing was before Recorder Hackett. The court room was crowded. Prominent men were dragged in as witnesses. Horace Greeley was in the box; so were Whitelaw Reid, Amos J. Cummings, Junius Henri Browne, Fitz-Hugh Ludlow, William Stuart, manager of the Winter Garden Theatre; F. B. Carpenter, the artist; Samuel Sinclair, the publisher of the *Tribune*, and Oliver Johnson. The speeches of the counsel were florid and eloquent. Public curiosity looked eagerly for the verdict. After the jury had been out two hours, it came: "Not guilty." Daniel McFarland wiped the perspiration from his brow, and walked out of the court room to breathe a purer and freer air.

One of the most expert forgers in the country made a very clever attempt at swindling in 1871, and, when discovered, led one of the detectives in the office on a chase which included thousands of miles and covered half a continent. The circumstances were these:

In October of that year, a man named John R. Livingstone was introduced to Mr. Cyrus G. Clark, a broker, of No. 3 Exchange Place, by Mr. George W. Chadwick, a dealer in real estate. The three men talked together, and finally Mr. Clark promised to buy for Livingstone $100,000 worth of bonds from Mr. Goddard, the treasurer of Wells, Fargo & Co. Livingstone paid for the bonds by a check on Hallgarten & Co. for $77,500. He took them to the Commercial Warehouse Co., and deposited them as security for two checks of $25,000 each.

Having endorsed the checks, Livingstone handed them over to Mr. Chadwick, asking him to go to Caldwell & Co., at No. 77 Wall Street, and get them cashed. Chadwick willingly assented. It so happened that at the very instant Chadwick entered the office and presented the checks, a Mr. Gilman, president of a railroad in Alabama, who was there conversing with Mr. Caldwell, was telling the latter how nearly he had escaped being swindled by a rascal named Livingstone.

"Why!" exclaimed Mr. Caldwell, "here are checks payable to the very John R. Livingstone that you are talking about!"

The thought naturally occurred to both men that the checks were forgeries. A messenger was despatched to make inquiries, but it was found there was nothing wrong about the checks themselves. Still Mr. Caldwell hesitated to cash them, and put Chadwick off with some trivial excuse, telling him to call on the next

THE FORGED CHECK.

day, when he should receive for the checks $30,000 in Government bonds and $20,000 in currency.

At the appointed time Chadwick was there. The bonds and the bills were counted out and he started to put the money in his pocket. Just then a messenger, almost breathless, rushed into Mr. Caldwell's office with the astounding information that Livingstone was a forger. Mr. Caldwell started as if shot. Mr. Gilman looked as if he wanted to say "I told you so," and the real estate dealer scarcely knew what to make of it. Chadwick was compelled, however, to give up the money, and immediately disappeared from the office.

It was singular how the forgery had been discovered. On the morning that Chadwick was to receive the cash for the two checks, the officers of the Park Bank discovered that Hallgarten & Co. had overdrawn their account. The attention of the firm was called to the fact and the members were naturally very much surprised. The check for $77,500, given by Livingstone to Mr. Goddard, came to light. No one knew anything about it, but the work upon it was of so skilful a character that the firm hesitated at first to say that the check was a forgery. Nevertheless it was. The bonds purchased with it were found at the office of the Warehouse Company, and Mr. Caldwell's office was reached in the nick of time to prevent the payment of the money to Chadwick.

Now efforts were directed to catch the forger, and the assistance of the police was asked. Detective Thomas Sampson was assigned to work up the case. Sampson went to work with a will, and quickly discovered that Livingstone was none other than Louis W. Van Eeten, already notorious in this department of crime.

Chadwick was arrested by Sampson just as the former was making arrangements for a trip to Europe. From him it was learned that upon the discovery of the forgery he had gone to Van Eeten and informed him of the state of affairs. Van Eeten swore that Chadwick had played him false, put a pistol to the latter's head and forced him to give up $1000, which was all the money he had. Van Eeten took flight.

Then began a long and remarkable chase after the forger. Sampson first heard that he was in San Francisco. There Van Eeten obtained from the Bank of California the value of a $10,000 United States registered bond, which had been stolen from Señor B. Castillo. In San Francisco Van Eeten assumed the name of

Van Tassell, but embarked for the Isthmus of Panama under the name of Phillips. Sampson was close upon his heels, but did not arrive until the day after the steamer sailed. At Panama Van Eeten struck out at once for Central America. Sampson still tracked his footsteps. Van Eeten then tried to make his way to Mexico, but gave it up as useless, and went to St. Thomas; thence to Havana, and from there to New Orleans. He put up at the St. Charles Hotel and remained there for several days. By the lavish manner in which he spent his money at the bar, and by his interesting conversational powers, he made many friends. He knew, however, that as long as he remained on American soil he was liable to arrest, should he be recognized. He therefore settled upon Tampico as his next abiding place. He announced his intention one evening to leave the hotel on the next morning, and was busily engaged in his room, packing his trunk, when a stranger entered the hotel and looked over the register.

"Is Mr. Phillips in his room?" he asked.

"He is," replied the clerk, and at the same time directed a call-boy to conduct the stranger to Mr. Phillips's apartment.

Arrived at the door, the boy knocked, and a voice replied:

"Come in."

The stranger entered. The occupant's back was towards the door. He turned his head to greet his visitor, and then, in a terrified manner, jumped to his feet.

"Why! Captain—" he gasped. "I never expected to see you."

"I don't suppose you did," was the reply of Detective Sampson, for the stranger was none other than he, while Mr. Phillips was Louis M. Van Eeten.

This ended the chase. Van Eeten practically admitted his guilt when brought back to New York and tried. He was sentenced to ten years' imprisonment in Sing Sing, and while there invented an automatic arrangement by which a keeper could sit in his chair at one end of a corridor and have certain knowledge whether convicts were in their cells or not.

One Sunday morning, some eight years afterwards, immediately upon his release from prison—for he earned a commutation of his sentence by good conduct—Van Eeten called at Detective Sampson's house. The call was merely a friendly one, Van Eeten only wishing to show Sampson that he entertained no ill feeling towards him for performing his duty. Still pursuing the line of duty, however, Sampson telegraphed to the Bank of California the fact that Van Eeten was at liberty, and the next day there came an order for his arrest upon a charge of stealing the $10,000 United States registered bond in San Francisco. Van Eeten's capture was easily effected, and Sampson, with another officer, took him to Trenton, N. J., there to await the arrival of the requisite documents from California. Van Eeten took his re-arrest very much to heart, and seemed completely broken down.

"Never mind," said Sampson to him, "you'll have an easy judge in 'Frisco, and you will get off with a light sentence."

"That's all very well," Van Eeten replied, "but before morning I shall go before the best judge of all."

And he did. The officers slept in the same room with him, but somehow he managed to swallow a dose of laudanum. Where he obtained the drug is a mystery. Despite the efforts of several medical men who were called in, the unfortunate man never regained his senses and died before the sun had risen.

CHAPTER IX.

THE NATHAN MURDER.—A TERRIBLE NIGHT.—THE TWO BROTHERS. —A GHASTLY SCENE.—TWELVE BLOWS WHICH TOOK A LIFE.— BLOODY FINGER-MARKS ON THE WALL.—FINDING OF THE IRON "DOG."—MERCILESS SUSPICIONS.—THE HOUSEKEEPER'S SON.— "HIS CLOTHES DON'T FIT HIM."—CLEANSING THE ROOM.—AN UNSOLVED MYSTERY.

THE month of July, 1870, is remembered as being one of the most glorious months of that most enjoyable summer. The days were warm with a seasonable warmth, and the nights were cooled by showers and eastern breezes. Just previous to Independence Day, Mr. Benjamin Nathan had left his business affairs on Wall Street, where he was a broker and private banker of great fortune and repute, to go to his country-seat at Morristown, New Jersey. His luxuriously furnished town house at No. 12 West Twenty-third Street had been given over to upholsterers and decorators, to be refitted for the autumn. Once or twice a week it was Mr. Nathan's habit to visit his office, confer with his confidential clerk about the light financial operations of the summer, call at his mansion to see how the alterations were progressing and then to return to his retreat.

On July 29 he made one of his trips to the city. He planned to pass the night at his up-town house. Chief of his objects in doing this was to make a fast day of the succeeding one, the anniversary of his mother's death. He intended to pass the morning in prayer at the synagogue to which he belonged. He found his house the scene of disorder. Not a room was prepared to receive him, as Mrs. Kelly, the housekeeper, was not aware of his intention to remain. But his sons, Frederick, his favorite, and Washington, who was something of a scapegrace, were in town and he expected to meet them. The former was a broker of repute like his father; the latter was simply a man of pleasure, whose pastimes were a source of much anxiety to his venerable father. But Mr. Nathan's patience with "Wash," as he was called was proof against any but the gravest misdeeds, and on the night of the anniversary of his mother's death the old man decided once more to warn his erring child.

Early in the evening the skies in the west began to darken, and prospects of a storm increased as the night progressed. It was cool, and a right sort of time for the charms of retrospection to seize upon an elderly man. In a little hall bedroom on the second floor Mr. Nathan kept his family papers, and as the sentiment of the anniversary he was about to celebrate grew upon him, he decided to look over these familiar archives after he had settled the housekeeping bills of the month. So he directed Mrs. Kelly to arrange a bed of mattresses upon the floor of the reception-room immediately adjoining his little office room, and there he thought he would sleep after he had concluded his work. The old gentleman, after his bed had been prepared, passed several hours in his little office engaged with his affairs. There were mutterings of thunder without, but no heed was paid to the approaching storm. As the hours passed footsteps sounded less frequently upon the pavements, and then the old man began to wonder why his sons did not return. Fred was making some calls among those of his friends who were still in the city; Wash was clinking glasses with men of questionable repute and women of the *demi monde*.

The growling of the storm grew more distinct. Lightning flashed, but yet no rain fell. The anniversary of his mother's death grew nearer, and after gazing affectionately at the features of his beloved parent, which were disclosed from the case of a miniature, Mr. Nathan replaced the case in a small safe which stood in the corner of the little room, locked the iron door, dropped the keys into his pocket and prepared for rest. Within an hour after he had retired, or just before midnight, Fred Nathan entered the house. Passing the reception-room he entered and, finding his father still awake, chatted with him for a time about "Wash," who was still away from home, and then kissing his father upon the forehead, wished him good-night and retired to his bedroom. Mr. Nathan watched his son leave the room with the eagerness of a parent who is sure of his child's love. A half-hour afterwards, it is said, "Wash" Nathan entered the house, and observing, as he afterwards declared, his father sleeping peacefully upon his bed of mattresses went to his room on an upper floor.

At midnight the storm broke. It was one of those awful manifestations of nature's power which frequently occur in the tropics, but seldom in our temperate climate. The rain fell in sheets with a persistency which made it almost impossible for a pedestrian to withstand their force. The lightning was extremely vivid, and the thunder followed the flashes with sharp reports that resembled the volleys of musketry upon a battle field. Patrolman John Mangam, of the Twenty-ninth Precinct, had that night the post on which the Nathan mansion was situated, and was struggling bravely against the storm. He saw a light flash for a moment in the windows of the splendid house of the banker millionaire, and then all was dark.

The day dawned bright and glorious. The terrible storm of the night had passed. The sky was of that vivid blue which our northern heavens assume after a storm. Mangam passed along Twenty-third Street, toward Sixth Avenue, thinking of his relief at six o'clock and of those at home. It lacked but a few minutes of that hour when he was walking slowly along on the last turn of his beat. But, hark! A voice, even at a distance vibrant with terror, calls to him.

"Officer! Officer! For God's sake, hurry!"

Mangam turned right about. Away up the street toward Fifth Avenue, on the brown-stone steps of their home, in their night-clothing, stood Washington and Fred Nathan, the latter intensely excited, and the former pale but calm. They shouted again while Mangam was going towards them, so excitedly that he began to run, and went up the steps at a dash. While he was uttering: "What's the matter, gents?" Fred exclaimed:

"Officer, quick! My father's been murdered!"

Washington chimed in, like an echo:

"Father's lying murdered up stairs."

Mangam threw down his water-proof, went to the street railing and struck a vigorous rap on the sidewalk. Without waiting to see if this summons for assistance was answered, he rushed up stairs, after inquiring of the "boys" if they suspected anybody— if the murderer was in the house. He was told where the murdered man was. Going into the reception-room and turning the pile of mattresses aside, he saw one of the most ghastly spectacles that ever met the eye of a policeman.

Lying with its feet on the threshold of the little hall bedroom

AN UNSOLVED MYSTERY.

and its head to the east was the body of Benjamin Nathan. It was lying on its back, with the left leg bent up, the right arm extended straight above the head, and the left arm by the side, so covered with blood that the corpse resembled a red Irish setter dog asleep more than a human being. Mangam rushed to Mr. Nathan's side, knelt down beside him, put his hand on his breast and exclaimed to Fred, who had followed him up stairs:

"Why, he can't be dead! There's life here yet."

"What shall I do?" asked Fred.

"Send for a doctor, quick!" was Mangam's reply.

Patrolman Theodore Rowland had by this time answered the alarm rap. He was despatched to the Fifth Avenue Hotel for a physician. One came in a few minutes. But before his arrival Mangam had discovered that in his agitation he had made a mistake. Mr. Nathan's body was quite cold, and when the doctor entered he told him the man was dead. There was in fact every indication that the murdered man had been dead for three hours or more. Little blood remained that was not coagulated or entirely dry.

As soon as the doctor arrived, Mangam went to the front door and told the Nathan boys that while he regretted it very much it was his duty, under the circumstances, to take complete charge of the house and not permit any one to leave the premises. He then despatched Patrolman Rowland to the Twenty-ninth Precinct Station with a request that Captain Henry Burden should visit the scene of the murder. This the latter did within half an hour. He commended Mangam for what he had done, and remarked that he seemed to know his duty so well that he might remain in charge of the house for the remainder of the day. Captain Burden set the machinery of justice in operation by placing his ward detectives on the case and notifying Superintendent John Jourdan and Chief Detective James J. Kelso.

After the news of the murder had been telegraphed to police headquarters detectives arrived in a short time. They had seen the results of many bloody quarrels and self-inflicted injuries, but had never witnessed a bloodier scene, or greater evidences of a terrible and determined struggle for life on the part of a victim. Hardly had they regained their self-possession when Chief Jourdan and Captain of Detectives Kelso entered the room, and they, too, were appalled at what they saw—Jourdan especially so. He looked at the body, cast a glance round the room, gazed upon the crimson evidences of the struggle and became as white as a marble statue. His voice faltered as he called out to Kelso, "Come here," and the two retired to a corner of the room to discuss the tragedy.

On Mr. Nathan's body were the marks of eleven or twelve distinct blows, evidently inflicted with an instrument, and that a blunt one. There were four wounds on the head, two of which were each sufficient to cause immediate death. It is certain that Benjamin Nathan was not conscious after he received the first of them. Upon his right hand were the marks of two crushing blows, sufficient to break three of the fingers and fracture the knuckles. There were five other marks of the instrument used upon his arms, breast and back.

The body lay in a pool of blood, three by four feet in extent, surrounded by blotches and smaller pools. Everything pointed to a struggle having taken place in the doorway, between the room in which he had laid down to rest and the little hall bedroom, or office. The most desperate struggle evidently occurred in the angle formed by the west and front walls. Here, covering a space of four by three feet, were gouts, blotches and smears of blood, and the imprint of bloody fingers. One set of these finger-marks was as distinct as though the person whose hand had touched the wall had purposely dipped his hand in blood and placed it there. The other set differed greatly from the hand of the murdered man, and was long and lady-like, with well-kept fingers—in short, that of a gentleman.

Where the fatal blow was struck was clearly and accurately defined. There was a smear on the wall, as if, when struggling hand-to-hand with his assailant, old Mr. Nathan received a crushing blow and pitched headlong to the floor.

He could have been safely left there by the murderer, but whoever he may have been, he evidently did not think so. This is proved by the fact of the body being found a distance of four feet from the smear on the wall alluded to. It was evident that another blow was dealt, apparently with a view of making sure of the old man's death and thus avoiding the possibility of the story of the crime ever coming from his lips.

A thorough examination of the room revealed little or nothing that was of value to the police. It was apparent that whoever killed old Mr. Nathan also committed robbery, either to make it appear that the crime was the work of a thief, or to secure enough money with which to leave the city. The murdered man's keys had been taken from his pocket, whether before or after his death is, of course, not known. The safe in the private office had been unlocked. This was a somewhat peculiar circumstance, as the safe was so situated that even an expert burglar, if a stranger, could hardly have discovered its existence. From it had been taken a wooden receptacle, or trunk, which contained several rare old gold, silver and copper coins, of value only to collectors. When the murder was discovered the wooden receptacle in question was on the pile of mattresses, and the coins missing. The safe itself had been rifled. In it Mr. Nathan generally kept the money for housekeeping purposes. This never amounted to less than $100, and often reached as high as $600 or $700. There were also missing some cherished family trinkets, valuable to a thief only as old gold. Upon the desk in the office was a partly written check, which, it was afterwards explained, was to have been drawn in payment of a stock transaction. In the room where the body lay, the murderer secured a Jurgensen watch and chain, worth about $600, and three diamond studs. That these studs were taken after the murder was committed is indisputable, as bloody finger-marks were found on Mr. Nathan's shirt. In the basin in the bath-room was found bloody water, as if the murderer had washed his hands before leaving the house. The assassin had not apparently explored any other part of the dwelling, or even ventured into the passage leading to the apartment of the housekeeper, Mrs. Kelly.

While Patrolman Mangam was waiting at the street door for the arrival of Captain Burden, young Fred Nathan, who was with him, suddenly stooped, exclaiming:

"Here's something."

The "something" proved to be an iron bar, about twenty inches long. It was smeared with blood, and there were a few gray hairs on it. That this was the instrument with which the awful deed was committed there could be no doubt. It was what is known among ship-carpenters and lumbermen as a "dog," a bar of one-inch wrought iron with the two ends turned up.

The whole community was startled by the news of the tragedy. The excitement was not confined to New York. The press of the entire country commented upon it, and with one voice called on the authorities to discover the perpetrator of the crime.

When the real work of the detectives began they were confronted by a great many obstacles. The first and greatest was the intense interest manifested in it by the Hebrew community. Foremost among those who looked after the interests of the late Mr. Nathan and his family were ex-Judge Cardozo and Mr. Emanuel B. Hart. It is unfortunate for Mr. Nathan's children that the mystery enshrouding the crime has never been cleared up, because suspicion—justly or unjustly—still attaches to one of the members of his family. Possibly those who sought to divert this suspicion knew how in some cases circumstantial evidence might err, and were unwilling that the slightest misfortune, neglect, or false evidence should put the neck of the suspected individual in jeopardy. The first care of the detectives was to inform themselves as to the movements, habits and character of the persons who slept in the house the night of the murder; those who knew its ins and outs, or who had the slightest motive for killing Mr. Nathan. In this they were at first merciless. It was generally known that Mr. Nathan did not regard Washington as he did his other sons. "Wash" had been rebellious, dissipated, heedless, and had fallen so much under the ban of his father's displeasure that when the old gentleman's will was read it was found to be particularly harsh in his regard. It practically disinherited him.

When Patrolman Mangam first saw the two brothers on the stoop, he noticed that Fred's shirt-front and socks were bloody. This was easily explained. Finding his father dead, he had thrown himself on the body, after wading in the blood which surrounded it. Washington Nathan had exhibited no such emotion, and in addition some one interested in the family had taken precautions which afterwards increased the suspicion against him. His demeanor was not that of a dutiful son suddenly and terribly bereaved. For a whole week after the murder he wore a handkerchief, so arranged as to conceal his neck. The stories told of his life and associates were such as to cause the police, if not to put him in the position of a prisoner, to place him under the surveillance of friends, who pledged themselves to produce him at the inquest.

Stress has been laid on the fact that on the night before the murder Washington Nathan was not in proper company, but this is worthy of but slight consideration. Still, it is true he was at a resort in Fourteenth Street, near Fourth Avenue, from an early hour Thursday evening up to the time when he started to walk home. His companion that evening was a fallen woman, of great beauty, who afterwards went the way of all such unfortunates. The inquest held by Coroner Rollins shortly afterwards released Washington Nathan, and for the time held back the tide of suspicion against him.

The police were encouraged in every way to discover the murderer. Rewards were offered by the Stock Exchange, the municipality, the Israelites of the city and friends of the dead man—aggregating more than $45,000. As usual in such cases, the police were hampered by cranks and that class of practical jokers who appear, in such an emergency, to take delight in leading the detectives astray. Why, within the three weeks succeeding the murder Superintendent Jourdan received at least 500 letters from all parts of the country, proffering advice, venting suspicions and giving "clews."

When the inquest was over, the action of those in authority on the police force was strongly commented upon. They appeared to have failed utterly in making one step towards lifting the veil which concealed the identity of the criminal. Half-a-dozen arrests were made, and all sorts of plans were adopted to establish a reasonable theory. Some of the able detectives engaged on the case insisted that it was what is known as an "inside job," without the slightest reference to the possibility of a member of Mr. Nathan's family having committed the crime. Others said it was a "stow-away"; the instrument used was that of a "duffer"; no professional criminal, they argued, would have carried such a tool into a house, and, as a matter of fact, such an instrument would have been useless to break open a drawer in a mahogany cabinet. Still others came to the conclusion that it was a first-class, professional, "second story job," marks on the pillars of the portico being pointed out as proof.

Those who held to the theory that it was an "inside job," pointed at William Kelly, the son of the housekeeper, as the guilty man. The adherents of the "stow-away" theory had a long, weary, and fruitless hunt among the seven thousand or more professional and unprofessional bummers of New York, each of whom was capable of committing the crime, supposing, as was not the case, that the front door had been left open.

My own personal belief is that William Kelly, the son of the housekeeper, admitted confederates into the house with a view of robbing the safe; that they succeeded in getting the key and opening it, and in doing so aroused Mr. Nathan, who engaged in a struggle which ended in his death. He must have recognized young Kelly, and this made it necessary, in order to insure the safety of the party, to close the old man's mouth forever. This explains the many unnecessary blows inflicted on the body. Since the murder it has been shown that Kelly was the associate of thieves, and he has never satisfactorily explained his whereabouts on that eventful night.

Among those arrested on suspicion was George Ellis, a burglar, who was brought down from Sing Sing on the supposition that he was possessed of valuable secrets in regard to a man who had been "named" by the police as having committed the murder. Ellis was kept under guard in the Sixth Precinct Station for more than three months, a man being detailed to watch him day and night. One of these men was Detective Patrick Dolan, of the Central Office, to whom Ellis remarked one day:

"Pat, Jourdan (the superintendent) is going to die, and I'm a goin' back to State's Prison. Isn't it too bad?"

"How do you know that?" Dolan inquired.

"Well—his clothes don't fit him."

That was Ellis's gauge of Superintendent Jourdan, who did, in fact, die shortly afterwards. From the day after the Nathan tragedy Jourdan seemed to pine away, and never, apparently, regained his old familiar air. Was he in possession of an awful secret?

There were other persons arrested, namely, Hayes, John T. Irving (who "confessed" in order to be brought from San Francisco to New York free of charge), and Robert Kipling. Each arrest furnished a certain amount of news for the papers and that was all that came of it. There was much ado made concerning the disposition made of the room in which Mr. Nathan died, shortly after the discovery of the crime; also concerning "Wash" Nathan's clothing. The story told concerning the latter was that a mysterious bundle of bloody articles was smuggled out of the house before noon on the day of the murder. Yet with more than $45,000 ready to be given to them in case of their success, and at their disposal to trace the crime, the detectives were unable to cajole or frighten the washerwoman who received the bundle into disclosing its contents. The story of the disposition of the room is startling. Before dusk on the day of the murder, and shortly after Benjamin Nathan's mutilated body had been laid out in state in the handsome parlor of his residence, the carpet of the reception-room was on its way to a cleaner's establishment and every blood-stain on the walls was removed.

JOHN JOURDAN.

The story of the Nathan murder remains the greatest mystery of the age. "Murder will out," they say. If this be true, the query, "Who killed Benjamin Nathan?" will one day be answered. Men yet living, who were young and vigorous when it occurred, have never lost sight of it, and will never give up the search so long as they are capable of continuing it.

Some day the police may "revive" the murder; they have come near doing it more than once. They should "revive" it in justice to Benjamin Nathan's memory and to his suspected son. They came near doing it not very long ago.

Washington Nathan did not reform when his father died. His associations became worse instead of better. He not only associated with gamblers, but was a companion of one of the most notorious of this city—"Philo" Fields—on West Twenty-second Street, between Seventh and Eighth avenues. His liaisons became public and disgraceful. By one woman with whom he associated his life was threatened in a fit of jealousy, and he was afterwards shot at by her in the Coleman House. A curious experiment might have been tried on Mr. Washington Nathan at this time. His injuries by the bullets were such as to make a certain operation almost inevitable. Had such an operation been performed it is possible that a well-known physician of this city would have been taken into consultation. He has declared that in such an event it would have been necessary to employ an anæsthetic. One would have been used which would first have placed the patient in a state of stupor, then in a condition of anæsthetic inebriety, and lastly in a state of coma. In returning to consciousness the patient would have passed into the inebriate stage again. The physician in question, an expert in anæsthetics, knew, as all first-class practitioners do, that in this inebriate condition the patient is incapable of retaining a secret. The physician, had he been called in, would have determined to either clear Washington Nathan, for whose family he had the greatest regard, or satisfy himself of his guilt. He proposed, when the patient should be in the inebriate stage, to question him in such a deft manner as to rapidly ascertain whether he slew his father, or was innocent. He would have repeated the questions at the second inebriate stage; and he would have left the chamber of the patient convinced one way or the other.

The operation was not performed, and the opportunity was not afforded the physician of making the desired test.

Mr. Nathan, in later years, married the daughter of Colonel J. H. Mapleson, a widow of high social standing. The last heard of "Wash" was that he was seriously ill in Europe.

Was the secret of the Nathan murder too awful a one for such a man as John Jourdan to keep? From the day of Nathan's death,

Jourdan failed. He never made a step in advance, and died a few months afterwards.

The "dog" with which the crime was committed disappeared during Mr. Kelso's administration; and the one among the relics of crime at the Central Office is only a *fac simile*.

CHAPTER X.

THE "SAWDUST" SWINDLE.—A BROKER DUPED.—THE BOGUS DETECTIVE.—MOCK AUCTIONS.—FLANNEL AND HOT WATER.—WITH A BIBLE IN HIS HAND.—A HORSEY GO-BETWEEN.

THE " Sawdust" swindle is so termed because the victim gets a box filled with sawdust, instead of the counterfeit money he expected. A large number of printed circulars are sent throughout the country by the swindler. Sometimes he advertises his wares, addressing "country merchants in trouble," and inviting them to write to him, as he can give "assistance to those financially embarrassed, on the most favorable terms." Of course he gets many answers, and is thus provided with an excellent list of names to use in his operations. He informs his prospective victim that he has a large quantity of "green goods" (counterfeit money) of different denominations, which he will sell at a great discount. He invites a visit to the city for inspection. In one of the many circulars which fell into my hands, $3000 in "green goods" was offered for $200 in good cash; $5000 for $300, $8000 for $400, $15,000 for $600, and so on in proportion. Of course the person addressed, if he be dishonest, concludes that he has a good chance to make money, and has an interview with his correspondent. He is shown what are said to be specimens of the counterfeits, but which, in reality, have just been obtained from the bank. If he has any doubts about being able to pass this money, he and the "operator" take some of it and purchase articles at a neighboring store. It is accepted without a word, and the countryman is satisfied. He concludes to take a certain amount. The counterfeits are to be sent by express, "as it would be dangerous for him to carry so much of the stuff on his person." The victim goes away perfectly satisfied, with bright pictures of the manner in which he will enjoy himself when he gets home. A box arrives, "C. O. D." He pays the charges and carries it to a quiet corner in the hay-loft, where, away from other eyes than his own, he opens the box and finds it filled usually with sawdust. Sometimes a little green paper is thrown in by way of variety. The farmer feels like kicking himself all round the cow-yard, while the swindler and his confederates in the city are asking: "What are you going to do about it?" The answer is, "Nothing." The would-be swindler has been swindled. He must bear with it, or else risk the exposure which would result if he complained.

The Davis-Holland murder case, in which the former was shot, furnishes a good illustration of the way in which the "sawdust swindle" is operated, though with some slight variations in the procedure.

A clever trick is the "gold brick" swindle. Some wealthy business man is selected by the swindlers, who approach him with a plausible story concerning a solid brick of gold which they have in their possession, and which they will part with for a very small sum, for certain reasons they don't care to have known. They give the impression that they have come by it in an underhand manner. The usual tests of the gold are made with satisfactory results, and a bargain is struck. The money is paid, and then the victim discovers that the supposed gold brick is made of brass. A corner has been chipped off the baser metal and pure gold substituted. This is what is tested, and the wealthy business man is "out" the amount he paid for the brick.

Of the innumerable cases of fraud which have come under my observation, I do not recall any more cleverly arranged and carried out than the one I now relate. A man visited a broker's office on Chatham Street, and showed several ounces of gold dust as a sample. He offered it for sale, representing that it was only a small part of a large quantity which he had. As it came into his possession in a somewhat peculiar manner, he did not care to sell it all at once. He was not only willing, but anxious to have the sample assayed without any delay, so that its real value should be determined. If it proved to be all right, a price was to be named for the remainder. To this the broker agreed, and his caller left.

A few minutes later the broker noticed a small handbill upon the floor of his office, in which a reward of $1000 was offered for the recovery of a large quantity of gold dust which had been stolen. The man who had just left him, the broker thought, was the thief, or, at any rate, knew where the stolen dust was. Being a man of considerable reputation he would not be suspected of complicity, even if he bought it. He could get the gold at his own price; the man would not dare say a word for fear of being arrested. But was the sample genuine gold? An assayer was visited and his report was favorable—the dust was gold, indeed.

A day or two passed, and the owner of the dust again visited the broker's office. This time he was greeted in a pleasant manner, and the broker signified his willingness to take all the dust that he had, provided they could agree upon the price. The broker offered $10 an ounce. His visitor laughed and said:

"Fifteen; not a cent less."

"Nonsense, my dear fellow. Look here. That dust of yours was stolen and I know it. Why, here is the very handbill offering a reward of $1000 for the recovery of that gold dust (holding up the piece of paper which he had found on the floor of his office). However, I won't be hard on you. I'll give you $12 an ounce and you can take that or nothing."

The visitor was very naturally much alarmed at the turn affairs had taken, and managed to say:

"All right. You can have the stuff, but I won't bring it here. Meet me at ———," naming a retired spot up town.

Provided with a pair of small steelyards, gauged for weighing sixteen ounces to the pound, the broker went to the appointed place. His unknown visitor was there, and produced a quantity of the gold dust. In the shadow of a dimly-lighted alley-way the broker produced his steelyard, the dust was weighed and the money paid.

If the broker had been a little less intent upon the business in hand, and had glanced across the street, he might have noticed a short, thick-set man who was watching the whole transaction with considerable interest. But the broker didn't look in that direction, and so didn't see this third person. Steelyards and gold dust were securely in his possession, his coat was buttoned, and he had turned to leave the alley-way, the individual from whom he had made the purchase having left in a hurry.

At this moment, the watcher from over the way stepped up to the broker, and accosted him with the information that he was an officer. The broker's knees trembled under him.

"You are just the man I've wanted for a long time. That gold you have is stolen, and a reward of $1000 has been offered for its recovery. I must arrest you."

A BITER BITTEN.

"For God's sake, don't expose me," cried the now thoroughly frightened broker. "I shall be ruined if you do. Come with me to my office, and see if we can't arrange this thing."

"Can't do it," was the short, stern reply of his captor. "You'll have to go with me."

The broker pleaded hard, and the detective finally relented, and accompanied him to his office, where $1000 was paid to the latter, on condition that the matter should be allowed to drop. It was a heavy blow to the broker, who had congratulated himself upon having made a remarkably good bargain. But he consoled himself with the thought that he still had the gold dust, sixteen ounces to the pound, whereas he could sell it at twelve ounces.

He sent the gold to an assayer, but imagine his rage and consternation when it was reported to him that it was not gold at all— simply very fine brass filings, some of which were covered with a thin wash of the precious metal.

I was in charge of the detective force at the time, and the discomfited broker called upon me. He had, he said, a very serious complaint to make. He had purchased a large quantity of gold dust, and on sending it to an assayer it turned out to be brass. During my long experience with brokers I had always found them to be extremely shrewd and careful in their transactions, and it struck me as very strange that he should not have ascertained whether the dust was genuine or not before purchasing. Of course I listened attentively to his story, and by close questioning succeeded in getting from him a pretty full description of the man from whom he had bought the dust. It tallied with that of a well-known confidence man, and I had him arrested.

The story he told was very different from that of the broker. He admitted being the individual who had played the trick on the broker, and that he had dropped the bogus handbill on the floor of the office for the purpose of misleading him. The detective who had arrested the broker was no detective at all. He was a confederate. The police justice before whom the case was tried had no alternative but to discharge the sharper. The broker, I afterwards discovered, was a thorough-paced rascal, who only got his deserts.

In my time I have been acquainted with many brokers, and my relations with them, as a whole, have been very pleasant. It is not unusual for them to be asked for quotations on bonds or other securities which have been stolen. In such cases, an honest broker loses no time in informing the police. But sharp and suspicious as some brokers are, they are occasionally swindled by a method differing very little from the "sawdust" game. A man goes to a broker, and pulling out of his pocket a bundle of what are apparently bonds, takes one from the package and asks the broker to name its value. The broker examines it carefully, finds it is genuine and mentions the price.

"Well," says the visitor, "I have fifteen or twenty just like that. They belong to a friend of mine, and I think he would be inclined to sell them at a bargain—something under the regular price. I'll see him about it, and call again in a day or two."

This is only a way of finding out whether the broker is honest or not. If he is not he may be caught in the trap, for the man is sure to make a second call, and an arrangement is made to have the transfer of the money and the bonds take place in the streets. And a sorry transfer it is for the broker. The "bonds" turn out to be nothing more than nicely folded sheets of tissue paper.

I have often wondered how such an obvious fraud can blind any one's eyes. One can have little sympathy for such men, and while human nature remains what it is, there will be always those who are eager to take advantage of what appears to be a weakness of their fellows.

The "mock auction" dodge is another of the tricks played on rustics, though of late years it has been pretty well suppressed. A store is rented, usually on some frequented thoroughfare, and fitted with a stock of goods—cigars, for instance. These are seemingly sold at public auction, but the crowd generally assembled around the auctioneer consists of confederates in the swindle. A stranger enters, and bids on a box of cigars; they are low in price, and are finally "knocked down" to him. He steps up to the cashier to settle his bill and is informed he has bought a dozen or more boxes. He remonstrates, but after some haggling he pays the amount demanded, and orders the goods sent to his address, only to discover that they are not worth smoking.

Another trick of auction-dealers, so called, which cannot be strictly termed a swindle, is the fitting up of a house with furniture, and representing it as being second-hand, sold out to close an estate, or something of that sort. It is an old belief that women in search of bargains will pay more for a second-hand article than they will for a new one; and the dealers thus set the nets to catch the unwary. I know of one house on Twenty-third Street where the red flag has been flapping in the breeze for nearly twenty years; the auctioneer has held a "peremptory sale" once a week during that period.

A curious swindle which was successful for a season in New York was known as the "hot water" scheme. A natty, fashionably dressed little fellow, innocent looking, fluent in conversation, with a delicate blonde mustache, calculated to disarm suspicion, went about the city, from house to house, pulling door-bells and inquiring for the lady of the house. He had a partiality for flats. Entering the main hall of the building, he asked the elevator boy who lived in the right hand flat on the second floor.

"Mrs. Stevens," the boy would reply.

"Yes, that's the name. I wish to see her. Take me up, please."

When her bell had been answered he would say in the blandest manner possible:

"I have come to fix the piano."

The servant would show him into the drawing-room, and he would note the name of the maker before the mistress of the house appeared. As she entered he would bow gracefully, saying:—

"Mrs. Stevens, I presume."

"Yes," the lady would reply. "The girl tells me you have come to fix my piano."

"Yes, madam. Mr. Steinway sent me up. He said Mr. Stevens called a day or two ago and wished some one to be sent to examine the piano. He thought it needed a little tuning. I see you have a beautiful Steinway. Do you play?"

"Well, yes, I play some for my own amusement. I hadn't discovered that there was anything the matter with the piano."

"I can soon tell," replied the swindler going to the instrument and deftly running his fingers up and down the key-board.

"It is a little 'off pitch,' as we say, in the higher notes. No wonder, in this dreadful climate of ours and in the steam-heated rooms of flats. Steam heat is so bad for pianos, madam."

By this time Mrs. Stevens ceases to think about the strangeness of her husband's actions in relation to her piano. He was never before known to have sent a tuner to the house. But men are such strange creatures! She becomes absorbed in the work and conversation of the agreeable man. He opens a little hand satchel, takes out a tuning key, raises the lid of the piano and begins to tighten the high strings.

"I suppose you might as well have your piano put at concert pitch," he says. "That will do no harm, for there is sure to be a lowering of tone in a little while."

So he turns this staple and that, and keeps up a vigorous pounding on the instrument, striking single notes and chords.

"Ah!" he declares at last, elevating his eyebrows, and listening with keen attention. "Here is a note which needs special treatment. May I trouble you to get me a piece of flannel and a dish of boiling hot water."

"Certainly, if you will wait a few moments," is the reply, and Mrs. Stevens darts out of the room and finds a servant, or flies to the kitchen herself. She is gone a considerable time, for flannel and boiling hot water are not to be brought on the instant. The fire is poked, and drawers are ransacked for flannel.

The "bogus" piano-tuner smiles serenely. He keeps up a strumming of the piano and looks about the room for any little valuable trinket he can pocket. He usually sees one and steals it.

Ultimately the hot water and flannel arrive, and after an elaborate operation he declares the work of tuning completed.

"How much do I owe you?" the lady asks.

As she has taken him at his word without any suspicions, he modestly replies:

"Five dollars. And the next time you play you will get much better effects than ever before."

Finally the husband comes home to his seven o'clock dinner.

"Whatever made you think of sending a piano-tuner up to the house?" she asks.

"A piano-tuner! What do you mean? I haven't seen any piano-tuner."

"Well, but didn't you stop at Steinway's a few days ago and ask them to send a man to fix our piano?"

"No, of course not. Why should I? What do I know about pianos?"

"But a man came here, and said he was sent by you."

"Well?"

"And he tuned the piano."

"Well?"

"And I paid him five dollars."

"Swindled! An impostor! A humbug! Nobody sent him. I suppose if a man came and said Redfern had sent him, you'd give him your $600 dress to be fixed. A button off, or a stitch broken."

"You frighten me. Why, it is perfectly dreadful! He may have stolen something from the parlor!"

"Most likely he did," replies the husband.

She rushes about and finds her pocket-book and watch missing, which were in the next room; also a rare bronze ornament which stood on the parlor chimney-piece, and a costly Japanese embroidered scarf which hung over a picture.

The next morning, on his way down town, Mr. Stevens steps into Steinway's to ascertain if they did ask a tuner to call at his house.

"We know nothing of the matter," is the reply. "Half a dozen persons have been here within a week, to ask questions about the same fellow. He's no tuner at all, but a piano destroyer! One day he claims to be from this house; the next day he is from Chickering's, or some other establishment. He always plays the hot water and flannel dodge, to give himself a chance to rob while the lady of the house is away."

Complaints have been made to me very often by farmers from New Jersey, Long Island and other places of having been swindled by a person who travels about in the garb of a clergyman. He enters a farm-house, and declaring that he is an agent of the New York Bible Society, says that he needs a meal. After having eaten as much as he can, he inquires the cost, and is usually informed that there is no charge. He insists upon leaving twenty-five cents in the hands of his host, remarking that the Bible Society will not allow him to receive any charity. But the Society is very strict about the production of vouchers or receipts for money paid by its agents.

"Please sign this voucher," says the agent. "It is a mere matter of form, you know."

And the farmer signs, and forgets all about it in an hour. But the incident is brought to his mind in a forcible manner, ninety days afterwards, when he receives a letter from the county bank asking him to settle a note for $146.25, signed by him, which the bank had discounted in good faith. The next clerical-looking individual who calls at that farmer's house is treated with suspicion, if nothing else.

The sheriff of Monroe County, New York, was a very shrewd man. He declared that he had not been constable of Irondequoit, and a policeman in Rochester, for nothing. He had learned all there was to learn about "sharpers." So when he was on a train going to the metropolis one morning to buy a horse, harness and various trappings, he bought a paper and looked over the news. He informed himself, and then he turned sleepily to the column of "horses at auction" and read the advertisements—among others this:—

"FOR SALE AT IMMENSE SACRIFICE!—Owing to death in the family, a widow is compelled to sell for what they will bring, her entire stock of horses, carriages, harness, etc. Among these are some young and handsome Hambletonians of the following pedigree—[here follows alleged pedigree.] Apply at stable corner Morton and Ashby streets, and ask for coachman, John."

"I'll call and look at those," said the shrewd sheriff to himself.

After going to the Bull's Head the next morning and looking over the stock, he answered the attractive advertisement. John was present, exercising the animals in the yard. The sheriff cast a critical glance at their fetlocks, and the horse-talk began. The examination continued. Presently in came another customer. The coachman slyly questioned him and found that he was a dealer, looking for stock for omnibuses. This fact was revealed just as a bargain was making for two strong-looking horses at $450. The coachman suddenly exclaimed:

"No use talking any longer. You can't have any of these horses at any price. I suspected you was a dealer at first, and now you want 'em for omnibuses. No, sir! My mistress instructed me positively not to sell any of 'em 'cept to private parties, who would feed 'em well and treat 'em kindly. So no use for you to talk."

The buyer expostulated, but the coachman was firm, and the dealer reluctantly went away.

"I wouldn't sell them two horses to him for $1000!" John exclaimed when he and the sheriff were alone. "Omnibus horses! Jim and Nancy, who never knew anything harder than to toddle around with the old lady or the girls, and live on the fat of the land. I'd sell 'em for private use cheaper than I charged him."

The sheriff inquired and found that he could get them for $400.

A HORSEY GO-BETWEEN.

But he knew something about horse-flesh, and thought he saw evidences of their having been doctored and "fixed up" to sell. So he declined with thanks and withdrew, thinking, "Now, if I could buy them for $400 and sell them to the other fellow for $450!"

He had not gone a block before he met the disappointed searcher after horses, who bowed to him and asked, "Did you buy 'em?"

"No," replied the sheriff, "but I could. In fact, I thought of buying them for you."

"Why didn't you?"

"Well, hang it! I can't take any risks. I'd no idea I should ever see you again."

"The fact is," said the other, "I sort of stayed around here to see if I couldn't get the horses somehow. I shall hire somebody to buy them for me, some respectable-looking man like yourself."

"B' George!" exclaimed the sheriff, "I'll get 'em for you. You say $450 for 'em?"

"Yes, $450 it is, and blamed glad I shall be. They're worth $600 if a cent. I've seen 'em on the road."

The sheriff went back, bought the steeds for $400, and led them through the double doors to the street, with the halters which John had generously "thrown in." He led them around the corner to where the anxious purchaser was ten minutes ago, but, alas! was no longer. He had vanished.

The sheriff climbed on one of the horses and waited for the owner. When dusk came he thoughtfully took the horses back to the stable.

"Of course," John said, "I know nothing about the other gentleman. Never saw him before."

Sadly the sheriff led his hungry purchase to the Bull's Head, and inquired how much they were worth.

"Them?" said a good-natured expert; "them? Well, hides, $2.50; shoes—there're only five—fifty cents; hoofs and so forth, fifty cents more—Well, them horses may be worth four dollars, if you sell 'em quick!"

Leaving them as temporary boarders, he hurried back to Morton Street with a sturdy policeman, but the darkey had shifted his quarters and was seen no more.

CHAPTER XI.

THE THIEVES OF THE RIVER.—MURDER ON THE "WATSON."—KILLED FOR TWELVE CENTS.—THE HARBOR POLICE.—SCENE IN A BROOKLYN HORSE-CAR.—"SOCCO, THE BRACER'S" END.—THE HOOK GANG.—GONE TO BROOKLYN AND JERSEY CITY.

ON a dark night in August, 1852, three men in a small boat pushed out into the East River from the neighborhood of James Slip, and with oars muffled rowed stealthily for a few rods to where the ship "William Watson" was moored. It was just the night for a crime. The black river rushed on its course as though afraid to stop and see what was doing on its surface. Heavy clouds hung overhead. The air was hot and oppressive, and the atmosphere was thick with mist. The small boat neared the larger vessel. In a moment they joined. Two men rose from their seats and climbed nimbly over the ship's side to her deck. Neither man was more than twenty years old. The lights from the great city, which now and then shone on their faces, revealed features marked with crime. They worked quietly about the deck, stealing whatever they could, until they were discovered by the watchman. But what was he to men who lived on crime? One of them whipped out his revolver, fired, and in a second Charles Baxter's body was inanimate. Nicholas Howlett and William Saul, two notorious river thieves, were his murderers. William Johnson, their confederate, whom they had left in the small boat, stupidly drunk, was no unwilling witness of the tragedy.

The pistol shot which killed the watchman of the "Watson" was not loud, but it was heard by a policeman on shore, and the results of the investigation which followed aroused the police authorities of New York to face a new and prolific source of crime. I was put at the head of an able corps of detectives to ferret out the murderers. Our task was not an easy one, but suspicion centred on the right persons, and they were arrested. Johnson turned State's evidence. He was committed to imprisonment for life, but Saul and Howlett were hanged on January 28, 1853.

My investigations in this murder opened to me a chapter in the annals of crime, of the full horrors of which I never dreamed. If they could be told exactly as they occurred, they would make a tale of human depravity unparalleled in history. Citizens were thrilled with wonder as they realized for the first time what human monsters prowled around our river fronts. The police found that there were organized bands of harbor thieves, who thought no more of the life of a man than that of a chicken. If they had been merely thieves, the revelations would not have caused the sensation they did; but these men, or boys rather, looked on murder merely as a means to enable them to steal without molestation. Perhaps a more hopeless maze of crime was never laid bare in the city of New York. No way appeared at first for checking it. Detective skill had been successful in nearly every kind of crime on shore, but here it was baffled by natural disadvantages. The main part of the island was bounded by piers and slips, which were in turn fringed on one side by grog shops, rum holes, and all kinds of iniquitous dens, breeding crimes as rapidly as mosquitoes are bred in a swamp. Along the piers ran the swiftly flowing rivers, a constant source of escape by day or night. Down the North River fronts and up the East River docks criminals formed the greater part of the population. They went in gangs. Each gang had its leaders and its rough rules of discipline. Its members lived in the vilest dens. Carousing or scheming all day, prowling, marauding and thieving all night—these were their occupations.

The criminal operations of these men were not confined to the water. They stole, and robbed, and murdered on land as well. Woe to the pedestrian who happened to be seen alone at night in the dark places along the river! It is dangerous enough now, but then it was a thousand times worse. These fiends infested every place where men were likely to spend money. Here they watched their prey, tracked them out-of-doors, waylaid and robbed them. Abandoned women were confederates of the thieves. They promenaded on the fashionable streets, and lured victims into the haunts of their companions in crime. To rob was the consuming motive; a murder was an amusement. There must have been at least one every month. The criminal records include thousands. How many more occurred is known only to the waters that eddy round Manhattan Island and then hurry out to sea. With no

POLICE AND RIVER PIRATES.

police supervision on the water there was little danger that a murder would out. It was an easy thing to stun a man in some dark corner, rifle his pockets and toss the body into the river. The splash was the only sound likely to betray the awful crime.

It made no difference apparently to these criminals how little money or how few valuables their intended victim had about him. A few pennies were sufficient reward for a dastardly crime. A German immigrant, poorer in appearance than themselves, and nothing but a wanderer, without even a home, was found at midnight walking on the Battery. A single blow with a slung-shot ended his life. His assailants secured twelve cents as the result of their conscienceless crime, and threw the body into the water. It was winter, and the river was frozen. This body did not drift out to sea with other victims of these midnight monsters; it remained upon the ice, and those who passed along the Battery wall early the next morning saw glaring at them the fixed eyes of a frozen corpse. There was still a worse case. Three sailors, being rowed out to their ship in the North River, were overtaken by four of these river pirates, robbed of their trunks and thrown overboard to drown. The wretches who did the crime went coolly to the shore with the captured boat.

A somewhat similar case, though not attended with murder, happened on the North River in broad daylight. It was an achievement of the gang known as the "Daybreak Boys." They were mere boys in years, but were patriarchs in villany. They were called the "Daybreak Boys" because they nearly always chose for their depredations that hour of dawn when men sleep soundest. In this instance, however, they were out of their dens in the daytime. As they rowed leisurely along, they discovered three boys at a distance, out for a pleasure sail. The boys were sons of respectable parents, and in an innocent way were enjoying their sport to the utmost. In a moment the young thieves were alongside the sail-boat. Grabbing the edge of the boat and holding it fast, they flourished some ugly knives in the air and began to climb into it. The frightened boys attempted to resist, but in vain. Resistance wounded the pride of these tyrants. They flourished their knives with more bravado, and let forth a volley of oaths that would have made a hardened reprobate quiver. The boys gave in. They let themselves be robbed of their pocket knives, their money and the silver watch which one of them had, and then were obliged to row their captors ashore. Fortunately, there was a detective on the shore, and the thieves were arrested and afterwards imprisoned.

Two classes of thieves infest the river front and ply their nefarious trade on the waters surrounding Manhattan Island, Long Island and Staten Island. The first are the "wharf rats," as they are called. These, as a rule, confine their operations to the piers and docks, and conduct them during the day. They are the "sneaks" of the profession, and are for the most part boys and young men. The other and more dangerous class is composed of those who know no short lengths in crime—men who plunge their knives up to the hilt in the bodies of defenceless victims, in order that their lust for money or valuables may be gratified—men who know no resistance, scarce even the mighty power of the law. To them the cutting of a throat is no worse a crime than the stealing of a bag of coffee. If they can get the coffee without interruption, well and good. But woe to him who interferes.

The thousands of vessels which load and unload in New York harbor are the sources from which these river pirates get their stolen property. There is nothing extraordinary in the mere thefts of these men; it is the way they commit them and the means they use, together with their audacious boldness and hardness. When the blackness of night hangs over the harbor, then the pirates dart out from the shore in their small boats to the ship they wish to ransack. They watch for a moment when well out, to see that they are not observed. By ropes they climb nimbly up the vessel's sides and soon are looking for things to steal. The sailors on the ship sleep soundly, familiar with the crime which lurks on all sides of them, but made reckless by their very familiarity with it. Usually the prowlers meet with no opposition. They go through the vessel like hungry men through a pantry. Nothing is too small for them to carry away. A rope's-end, a pulley, anything they can afterward dispose of. Sometimes the vessel is loaded with rice, or sugar, or coffee. If there are any stray bags they seize them, drop them gently over into their boat, and when well laden pull back to their dives. It is almost impossible to convict them if captured, for they tear the wrappings from the stolen articles, and it is hard to prove that the sugar, or rice, or coffee, or what not in their possession, is the same as that missed from the vessel. Sergeant Edwin O'Brien in one year made fifty-seven arrests, and yet secured only three convictions. The stolen property is taken to police headquarters and placed under the charge of the property clerk. Sometimes the owners think they recognize it as theirs, but they dare not swear so; so the thieves go free and get their goods besides.

When I was superintendent, however, it occasionally happened that we caught and convicted the thieves by a shrewd move which took them completely by surprise. We would let the charge of larceny go by, detain the thieves, and send for the customs officers, who held them for smuggling. The rascals could not demonstrate, of course, that they had paid duty on the goods which they asserted had come into their possession by lawful means, and so were obliged to surrender their plunder and boats to the United States Government. Another happy thought on the part of the police was to prosecute the offenders for violating the quarantine laws, in boarding vessels which were under surveillance by the State authorities. The neighborhood of Quarantine was at that time thickly infested with harbor thieves, and efforts to secure their conviction when caught, on the charge of larceny, failed, as in many other cases. But this new scheme reached them nearly every time, and so many convictions were secured that the thieves were gradually scattered to other parts of the river and harbor.

The stolen property of the river pirates is disposed of at the shops of the junk dealers. These line the river fronts almost as thickly as rum shops, and are quite as fruitful in fostering crime. The junk dealers are in most cases the equals in iniquity with their piratical business friends. They are the "fences." It is in their shops often that foul murders are plotted. It is there that choice fields for robbers' work are made known and talked over. To get their stolen goods to these places the pirates have to call into play all their cunning, and the junk dealers in turn have to exert all their shrewdness in getting rid of the property before the police discover it. It has been said that junk dealers will receive almost anything save hot-house flowers or an iceberg.

When Saul and Howlett were hanged for that foul murder committed on the night of the 25th of August, 1852, it had a wholesome effect for a time upon this kind of villany. The thieves had hitherto prospered undisturbed. Now public attention and police attention were fixed upon them. They stood in little awe of both, it is true, but nevertheless Crime stalked not quite so triumphantly as it had. The establishment of a corps of harbor police was the first step to wipe out this evil. The captain in charge of this corps had fifty-seven men under his command. The rules to which the force was subjected were essentially the same as those which governed the land force. There was a station-house on shore. There were six boats constantly on patrol and, well manned, they worked their way up and down the two rivers at regular hours of the day. These did not protect the entire water-front of the city, but they frightened somewhat these demons who before had shown no signs of fear. Yet robberies and murders went on.

During the first year of its organization the new force signalized itself by practically breaking up the old gang of which Saul and Howlett were the leaders. Twelve pirates had been shot; " Bill " Lowrie, a famous thief, had been sent to prison for fifteen years; " Sam " McCarthy had been driven from the river, and the rest of the mob had been dispersed. The good work was kept up, and soon the harbor police became an indispensable auxiliary to the land force. Instead of the row-boats with which they at first patrolled the river, they were supplied with a fast little steamer of one hundred and fifteen tons, called the " Seneca," and thus they were enabled to make their work still more efficient.

The tragedy which was the final one during my term of office of superintendent of police, and which directly concerned the harbor squad, was that which occurred on Sunday, August 31, 1884. The lads and young girls employed in a laundry in West Houston Street determined to indulge themselves in an outing, after their long summer of excessively enervating work. They had formed an association among themselves, and after chartering a tug and two barges they invited all their friends and set out for a jolly excursion up the Hudson River. Their destination was Linden Grove, where there was much fun to be obtained from the double swings, merry-go-rounds and the dancing platform. These working persons were most respectable. But in their distribution of tickets they did not make judicious selections.

On all well regulated New York excursions there is a luncheon counter on one of the decks of the barges. That on the laundry's pleasure trip had been rented by a quiet German, named Kopf. Near him was a bar for the sale of beer. The trip up the river was made pleasantly, save for the disorderly actions of a party of five or six men who attempted to swindle the bar-keeper out of his beer. These men were partly intoxicated when the excursion left Linden Grove. They drank more liquor, however, and became exceedingly obnoxious to the women on board the barge. They singled out Mrs. Kopf from the rest and insulted her. She paid no attention to them and they went away.

Mrs. Kopf had several of her young children with her on the excursion, and as they played about her and gazed, open-eyed, at the sweep of the majestic highlands, the mother was unmindful of the unpleasant adventure of a little time before. Luncheon from the stand down stairs was eaten, and Mrs. Kopf was already counting the prospective profits of the day. But suddenly she heard a rush made on the lower deck. Then came the loud protestations of a man and a volley of curses from a crowd. Another rush was made; women who were seated near her shrieked and fainted, but Mrs. Kopf was a sturdy German matron whose nerves were seldom shaken. Then there was the sound of crashing glass, a groan and a shout:

"Beat them back—they've killed the Dutchman!"

Mrs. Kopf thought the fight was becoming interesting, so she drew her children about her and went towards the stairway to watch it. She went half way down stairs. She saw a form lying upon the deck with ugly red blotches of blood about it. She looked at the face. It was but a glance.

"Oh, my God! Oh, my children, they have killed him—they have murdered your father!"

Kopf was dead. The ruffians had made an attack on his counter with the intention of raiding it, but the courageous German stood his ground and defended his sandwiches. His defence cost him his life. One of the ruffians caught up a heavy beer-glass and struck Kopf on the head, driving a piece of the skull into the brain. Death was almost instantaneous. The fight continued until the barges reached New York, and before the boats were moored the men who had killed the German leaped to the pier and escaped. Then the harbor police appeared, but it was too late; the murderers had fled. The barges were towed to Staten Island and there an arrest was made, but the prisoner was discharged on some legal technicality. Kopf's murderers never paid the penalty of their crime.

One morning the passengers in a Brooklyn street-car were astonished and horrified by a man who, with blood streaming down his garments, jumped aboard, and, sinking into a seat, exclaimed :

"I am a watchman at Harbeck's stores. My name is Thomas Hayes. Ned Perry shot me!"

The man spoke and then was dead. The passengers on that car never forgot that tragic scene. Perry, who was a junkman, was arrested and tried. It was proved that Hayes was shot in order that a certain robbery might be committed—a deliberately planned murder—yet Perry escaped hanging and was sentenced for life.

Several years passed with no unusual occurrence, the routine work being carried on with great efficiency. However, as the old thieves were "settled" in various ways, the younger ones became more ambitious, committing many bold and daring robberies. In May, 1873, Joseph Gayles, alias "Socco, the Bracer," "Bum" Mahoney, and "Billy" Woods, all expert river thieves, the latter a murderer, stole a boat, and muffling their oars rowed out to the brig "Margaret" at Pier 27. They boarded her and were engaged in rifling the captain's trunk, when both the captain and mate were awakened. Thereupon the thieves, for a wonder, took to their boat, but not until an alarm had been sounded which brought two officers on the scene. The night was very dark. The policemen looked at first in vain for any signs of the missing thieves. The waters danced to a mournful song, and seemed grimly to rejoice that they were sheltering criminals. The fog, too combatted the blue-coated messengers of justice. One of the policemen brought out his dark-lantern. The flash from the bull's-eye lit up the surface of the river, yet revealed no shadowy figures floating off with the tide. Again the water was scanned, and with no better result. Had the river itself opened to receive at last the fiends who had filled it with victims? But now! What do these policemen see? The rays of the lantern have lit up that blackest space beneath the pier, and there, crouching in the darkness, are three men in a boat, one at the oars, the other two standing with drawn revolvers. Without a word being spoken on either side Policeman Musgrave's pistol breaks the silence. As it echoes across the river, "Socco, the Bracer," falls, mortally wounded, to the bottom of the boat. A fusillade of shots follow, but the pirates are too alert. Down the stream they urge their boat. Socco, the Bracer's, body becomes too heavy a weight to carry for those who are trying to escape from brave and determined men, so overboard it goes,

WHARF RATS AT WORK.

and is picked up four days later at the foot of Stanton Street. Socco was the only one who met his punishment; his companions escaped from their pursuers.

Shortly after this, another brig, lying off the Battery, was boarded by a gang of thieves, masked and heavily armed. They abused the captain in a shocking manner, assaulted his wife and departed with everything of value on board. Two well-known river thieves were arrested for this crime, tried and sentenced to twenty years' imprisonment. While they confessed that they were river pirates and had been such for years, they denied any knowledge of this crime, and years afterward the police discovered that they really were innocent, and that the outrage had been committed by a gang under the lead of "Denny" Brady, "Larry" Griffen and "Patsey" Conroy, who had also committed many depredations in suburban villages.

In the same year, Engleman, another famous Fourth Ward river thief, robbed the bark "Zouma." Being discovered, he jumped overboard and clung to the rudder of a schooner. A rope was thrown him but he exclaimed: "Go to h—— with your rope," and dove under the vessel. Swimming from dock to dock, he evaded for three hours six policemen in row boats, but was finally captured and afterward convicted and sentenced.

Not long after this an attempt was made to steal some merchandise from Pier 8, North River, but the watchman gave an alarm which brought the police. A shot in the dark after the thieves' retreating boat was answered with the cry, "Oh, I'm shot!" But if a man was shot no one ever knew it. No body of a dead or wounded thief was afterward found. Perhaps the cry was a ruse; perhaps the North River really did claim another body.

The pirates of the day of Saul and Howlett probably had their successors in the "Hook Gang," which had its headquarters at the foot of Stanton Street, and operated anywhere between the Battery and Fourteenth Street. It was one of the boldest of the gangs. The leaders were Merricks, a desperate thief; James Coffee, who had served one term in State's prison; Preslin, a fearless robber; Le Strange and Lewis, professionals in all sorts of crime; "Sam" McCracken, John Gallagher and "Tommy" Bonner. At one o'clock on the night of December 20th, the three last mentioned members of this gang climbed to the deck of the canal boat "Thomas H. Birch," which was lying off Fourteenth

Street, in the East River, and marched with pistols in their hands to where the captain lay asleep.

"Gag him!" whispered "Tommy" Bonner.

They set to work to do it. The captain refused to be gagged. He struggled, and, in spite of their desperate efforts to prevent him, yelled. The sound of his voice aroused Officer Booz and Captain M. J. Murphy, who came to his assistance. When they got there the thieves had got the best of the boat captain, and he lay bound hands and feet and unable to speak. The policemen cornered the robbers, covered them with their revolvers, and made them prisoners. The three thieves were afterward sent to the Auburn prison.

Among the places where thieves assembled and discussed their trade was Slaughter House Point, a low rum hole at Water Street and James Slip. At one time "Bill" Lowrie and "Slobbery Jim" were the leaders of the gang which had its headquarters here. Captain Thorne, then of the Fourth Ward, thought it was time to close up the den after seven murders had been committed there. But closing the gin mill did not break up the gang. "The Rising States," kept by Lowrie and "Moll" Maher, the woman who passed as his wife, was opened near by in Water Street. Another place, then well known to the police, was "One-armed Charley's" grog shop, called the "Hole in the Wall," where "Patsey, the Barber," was killed by "Slobbery Jim."

"Denny" Brady, who figured as a leader among the harbor thieves, was connected in his day with almost every great robbery which took place in this country. He was engaged in the Kensington Bank robbery, where he took $100,000 from the safe. Other chief spirits in this kind of crime were often participants in robberies of a greater magnitude.

Few depredations of the harbor thieves were more daring than the outrage on board the brig "Mattan." Early on the morning of November 30th, 1873, the brig had been loaded with petroleum, and on the Sunday previous to the time of the crime had dropped down the river from an up-town pier and anchored off the Battery. Her captain and owner, T. H. Connauton, was expecting to take his crew aboard on the following day and then to embark for Liverpool. Unexpectedly his voyage was delayed. The very night on which he brought his vessel to anchor near Castle Garden, a gang of river thieves was watching his movements and laying plans for robbing him. These plans were carried out with audaciousness and brutality.

The quiet of the stillest part of the night—2 A.M.—hung over the harbor and the city, as a boatload of seven men pushed out from a dark retreat on the river front, and slowly and cautiously made its way to the "Mattan." Just before reaching the brig, the seven men adjusted the masks which concealed their features, and scanned the surrounding waters for a moment. Then they came close to the vessel and climbed upon her decks. Unfortunately for them they made considerable noise. The first mate went forward to see what was the matter, and the gang at once seized and gagged him. The second mate was treated in the same way, and when the steward ventured to show his head above the hatchway he, too, was bound, and prevented from using his voice.

In the cabin, asleep, were the captain, his wife and three children. They had no consciousness of the presence of strangers aboard the vessel until the two mates and the steward had been bound and gagged. Then Captain Connauton cried out:

"Who's there?"

"The harbor police," came the reply, as the gang rushed toward the half-open stateroom door. The captain quickly closed the aperture and braced himself against the door. One of the marauders fired a heavy navy revolver. The ball passed through the panel and wounded Connauton in the lower part of the leg. The door finally gave way to their repeated blows, and with pistols raised and cocked they demanded that the captain should give them the $4000 which they said he had on Saturday, and all the jewellery there was on board.

The captain did not lose his coolness in this emergency. He tried to parley with his assailants, but they were in no mood for that. When he hesitated to comply with their demands they seized him and dragged him about the narrow cabin. The wound in the captain's leg was causing him great agony, and at last he became submissive; for one of the gang had hold of Mrs. Connauton, and with the barrel of a pistol against her head was threatening to blow her brains out if she and her husband did not facilitate the thieves' search for valuables. The pirates, however, secured only $45 in money, a diamond ring, two watches, three chains, a ruby ring, and several silk dresses. They were on the brig just an hour, and after cautioning those whom they had robbed and maltreated not to give an alarm, on penalty of future injuries at the hands of the gang, they made their departure and escaped. Within twenty-four hours the police of the Twenty-fourth Precinct, under direction of Captain Siebert, had arrested two of the seven marauders. Their names were William Carroll, a boatman, aged twenty-one years, and William Dagan, a bar-tender, aged twenty-three.

From year to year, improvements of more or less importance were made in the harbor police system. The wisdom of forming such an organization had been abundantly shown, and the work which it did was generally recognized. Those respectable persons whose duties obliged them to be in the neighborhood where such wretched crimes had been committed, breathed far more freely. They were no longer in constant fear as they walked out at night lest some devilish assassin should leap out from a dark corner and deal out a death-blow. The public looked back with horror at the state of things as they had existed in the fifties and early sixties. The commissioners of police were liberal in their expenditures for this purpose.

The steam-boat squad, which was organized in 1876 and put under the command of Captain G. W. Gastlin, still further improved the police protection on the waters. It succeeded especially in freeing the river front, the steam-boats, the ferries, and Castle Garden from that more refined class of criminals known as confidence men. Swindlers had taken the place largely of the abandoned thieves and murderers who were their predecessors in crime. This class of operators is numerous enough at present, but poor immigrants and unsuspecting travellers ten years ago were "fleeced" much more frequently than now. There were two sharpers, I remember, who passed themselves off for priests, and so easily won the confidence of foreigners who arrived at Castle Garden. One morning Mazin, one of the "priests," got into conversation with an Italian, named Mono, who was about returning home, and told him he was going to Italy and needed an interpreter. Mono accepted the position and gave the alleged priest his money for safe keeping. The clerical impostor then sent his newly employed interpreter to get some cigars. When the latter returned, Mazin was gone, together with his confrère, Michell. Both were arrested afterwards and sent to State's prison.

A short time after this occurrence, Hilza Von Zauen, alias Le Marquis O'Neil de Lassantas, was employed as a waiter in Newport. In the evening he was in the habit of dressing himself as a woman, in which guise he became the rage among the young "bloods." Afterward he came to New York and was employed as a waiter in a Fifth Avenue house, which he robbed and then fled. Captain Gastlin arrested him as he was about leaving the city, on a boat for Boston. The prisoner was sent to Sing Sing.

The work of the harbor police is most difficult. They are obliged to be out in all kinds of weather, and in winter the inconveniences are almost unbearable. Captain William Schultz took charge of the force in 1876. The "Seneca" was then in need of repairs, which she received. In 1880 the little steamer burned in some unknown manner. Then the "Moses Taylor" was used, but she was good for nothing. Then came the "Tiger Lily"; then the "Florence," a fair boat. In 1882, the "Patrol" was built at a cost of $60,000. She served not only as a headquarters for the harbor police, but is well supplied with powerful engines and pumps throwing ten or twelve streams. Large boats are of no use for the best purposes of the harbor police, for to do effective work in chasing thieves in and out of and around wharves and piers, boats of small size are necessary, and small steam-launches would overcome many failings of the service. In 1877, the captain of the "Seneca" discovered some thieves making away with plunder in a small boat. With his spy-glass he could see that the boat was loaded with merchandise, but as soon as the "Seneca" was upon the thieves, lo! there was no load in the boat at all. The thieves had thrown it overboard when they saw the police were after them, and they denied having had a load. This is a trick frequently practised. Sometimes, especially when the thieves have aboard a cargo of iron or other booty which is heavy and is not likely to be injured by the water, they do not throw the cargo overboard, but sink the boat and all into the river. In this way they prevent their enemies from confiscating either the stolen goods or the boat.

The harbor is not yet free from pirates, but they have left the New York river fronts largely, and have sought the less exposed and less protected piers of Jersey City and Brooklyn. Crime is still committed there and relics of the old criminal gangs are still to be found. They have opportunities in their present quarters which they cannot get now in New York, and unless checked in time may yet grow bold enough again to terrorize the harbor.

CHAPTER XII.

ON DUTY AT STATEN ISLAND.—APPOINTED INSPECTOR.—THE "CAR HOOK MURDER."—THE ORANGE RIOTS.—A GOOD STORY ABOUT JIM FISKE.—HIS DEATH.—STEVE GORDON AND THE $1000 BILL. —" BOSS " TWEED AND HIS RING.—HOW WINANS WAS BRIBED.

WHILE still in command of the Twentieth Precinct, where I remained for nearly six years, I was detailed for duty at Seguin's Point, Staten Island. The old Garibaldi candle-factory buildings there were being arranged for hospital purposes by the quarantine commissioners, and the villagers energetically objected to these proceedings. They protested against the establishment of hospitals anywhere on the island. Indignation meetings were held, mobs assembled near the old candle factory and threats were made to burn the buildings. I was sent with one hundred men to protect this property. Although the situation at times appeared to be rather serious, no important disturbance occurred. I remained until the buildings were nearly completed, when the plan of establishing a hospital there was abandoned.

It must not be regarded as egotistical if I say that by this time I had become familiar with all the administrative requirements of the police force, and when Inspector Daniel Carpenter died I was appointed to fill the vacancy. My two colleagues were James Leonard and George Dilks, the latter being office inspector. Every other night Inspector Leonard or I was required to be on duty from 6 P. M. to 8 A. M. We had the city divided into districts, Broadway being the dividing line. It was our duty to visit the various precincts at irregular intervals, to inspect the police stations, see that the books were properly kept and that the captains, sergeants and others performed their duties. Each month we had to make a report of our inspections to the superintendent. Having no one to assist us, it is no wonder we found the work arduous, requiring, as it did, constant personal watchfulness.

During the year 1870 several important changes occurred in the police force. In April, Mr. John A. Kennedy, the superintendent, resigned, and the vacancy was filled by the appointment of Captain John Jourdan, of the Sixth Precinct. Upon his death, in October of the same year, he was succeeded by James J. Kelso, captain of the detective force.

What is known as the "car-hook murder" occurred on the night of April 26, 1871. The victim was Avery D. Putnam; his assailant was William Foster, a horse-car conductor. In company with Madame Duval and her daughter, Mr. Putnam was riding up town on a Broadway car. Foster, who was not on duty, and had been on a protracted debauch, was standing upon the front platform. Miss Duval, happening to look through the front window, Foster pressed his face closely against the glass and made an insulting grimace. The ladies took no notice of him. He then opened the door. Mr. Putnam remonstrated with him, and Foster replied:

"I'm going as far as you, and before you get out I'll give you hell."

The ladies and their escort stopped the car at Forty-sixth Street. Putnam had one foot on the rear platform, when Foster, stepping behind him, dealt him a crushing blow on the head with the car-hook, felling him to the ground and fracturing his skull. Madame Duval shrieked for help, but the driver of the car whipped up his horses and drove rapidly away. Foster was at liberty only until three o'clock the next morning. The jury before whom he was tried found him guilty of murder in the first degree, and he was sentenced to death on May 25, one month after the murder. A reprieve was granted, but the sentence of the court was eventually satisfied on March 21, 1873. His execution was witnessed by about three hundred persons.

Shortly after this murder, on July 12, 1871, the famous Orange riots occurred. They happened just eight years after the terrible scenes during the draft. They resulted from the well-known antipathy between Roman Catholic and Protestant Irishmen. The twelfth of July is the anniversary of the Battle of the Boyne, and on that day it was customary with the Orange societies to turn out in large numbers and march in procession. When the "twelfth" came in 1871, Mr. A. Oakey Hall was Mayor, and at his instigation Superintendent Kelso issued an order forbidding the parade. This at once caused a great outcry; the newspapers were filled with arguments *pro* and *con*, and finally the matter was

CAR-HOOK MURDER.

brought officially to the attention of Governor Hoffman. He immediately issued a proclamation countermanding Mayor Hall's instructions to the police, assuring the Orangemen that they should have ample police and military protection. Public feeling, of course, ran high. Irish Protestants and Roman Catholics were pitted against each other, and it was very evident that little would be needed to cause a serious disturbance.

The day for the parade arrived. Wise because of the lessons taught during the draft riots, Superintendent Kelso massed the whole of the police force on Eighth Avenue, near Lamertine Hall, whence the procession was to start. The Ninth, Sixth, and Eighty-fourth regiments were also assembled here under command of General Varien, to aid the police, should it become necessary. The sidewalks on both sides of the avenue were crowded with a yelling mob, and before the procession started several futile attempts were made to break through the lines.

Superintendent Kelso placed me in command of the police at this point, with Inspector Jamieson (appointed on the death of Leonard) to assist me. Dividing the force under me into two battalions, I directed Jamieson to cover the left or rear of the procession, while I assumed command of the right. And here, let me say, there were probably as many policemen as Orangemen. As an advance guard, we threw out a body of mounted men under Captain Wilson.

The line of march was down town, and beyond some shouting and hissing nothing of any moment occurred until Twenty-sixth Street was reached. There a dense crowd, including many women, had collected. It was with the greatest difficulty that my men could clear the way for the Orangemen, who were obliged to come to a halt. At Twenty-fifth Street, Captain Joseph Petty found it necessary to order the men under him to charge the rioters, driving them towards Seventh Avenue. Stones and other missiles were now thrown from the housetops, not a few of which struck members of the Ninth Regiment, who were in position at Eighth Avenue and Twenty-fifth Street.

Suddenly a shot was fired from a window near the corner of Twenty-fourth Street. Other accounts say that the shot came from one of the soldier's rifles, which was accidentally discharged. However that may be, that shot was most certainly the signal for the horrible scene which immediately followed.

ORANGE PARADE.

In an instant the Eighty-fourth Regiment, without waiting for orders, fired upon the crowd. Then came volleys from both the Sixth and Ninth Regiments. The sight which was disclosed when the smoke cleared away was heart-rending and terrible in the extreme. Dozens of bodies—men, women, and children even—lay upon the ground; the shrieks and groans of the wounded rang out above the noise caused by the feet of the vast mob, now madly trampling upon the weaker of the fugitives in the wild rush to reach a place of safety. In consequence of this reckless, wholesale

JAMES FISKE, JR.
(From a Photograph.)

shooting on the part of the military, no less than one hundred and twenty-eight persons were either killed or injured, including a policeman and a soldier.

Colonel "Jim" Fiske, who was in command of his regiment, did not cover himself with unqualified glory upon this occasion. He was on horseback, and as soon as the first volley was fired he dismounted with considerable alacrity and ran into a saloon on Eighth Avenue. After scaling a back-yard fence he at length found shelter in a house on Twenty-third Street. There he rid himself of his uniform, replacing it with citizens' clothing, and made rapid time to the North River, where he got aboard a tug. The next heard of him was that he was at Long Branch, but how he got there was a secret which he would never disclose. Neither did he ever give any explicit explanation of the causes which led to his precipitate flight from the scene of the disturbance. After the military had fired upon the crowd, and the dead and wounded had been removed to the hospitals, there was no further trouble. The procession marched to the Cooper Institute in comparative silence and disbanded.

Poor Fiske! Little he thought then that within six months he would be shot down on the stairway of the Grand Central Hotel by his rival, Stokes. This, however, occurred on the afternoon of January 6, 1872.

There is an incident connected with the trial of Stokes which has hitherto escaped publication. One of the men on the jury was named James D. Centre. He was formerly a member of the police force, and is now, I believe, a private detective. Grave suspicions were entertained that Centre had been bribed by the "jury fixers," and there were certainly good grounds for these suspicions. So much so, in fact, that he was arrested on a bench-warrant for contempt of court, having boasted at Harry Hill's place that he would save Stokes from the gallows, at the same time displaying a large sum of money. For this, after the trial, he was sentenced to a short term of imprisonment.

Some few weeks subsequent to his release, Centre visited a liquor saloon in Jersey City. He had been drinking freely, and taking a $1000 bill out of his pocket, said he could beat any man in the room at wrestling. After some little talk, a man named Steve Gordon (nicknamed "Pirate") offered to try conclusions with him. The stakes were the drinks. Centre put the $1000 bill back in his vest pocket and prepared for the struggle. A space was cleared and the two went at it. Gordon, though an expert wrestler, was advanced in years, and was easily thrown by Centre. As though ashamed of his defeat, Gordon quickly left the saloon. In a few minutes Centre discovered that he had lost his $1000 bill, and at once had the "Pirate" arrested. No proof, however, was forthcoming at the examination and Gordon was discharged.

The matter subsequently came to my ears, and meeting Gordon one day as I was walking along West Street, I said :

"Hullo, Steve; they tell me you can't wrestle now."

"O yes, I can, a little," was Gordon's reply.

"But I understand Centre threw you, though," I rejoined.

"Yes," said he; "Centre throwed me; *but I won his money.*"

While Mr. A. Oakey Hall was Mayor of New York he was intimate with Tweed, Sweeney and Connolly of the Tammany "Ring," whose bare-faced robberies and corruptions in administering municipal affairs left such a stain upon the city's history. The "Ring" controlled the Board of Audit, and millions of dollars found their way into the pockets of Tweed and his followers, by means of fraudulent vouchers.

Among the many who asserted that the city treasury was indebted to them was Mr. James O'Brien, formerly a sheriff. He presented a bill of $200,000 for unpaid fees due him, and the Board of Audit refused to approve it. He repeatedly demanded payment, but always with the same result—he could get nothing. In some way O'Brien managed to secure copies of the fraudulent vouchers in the comptroller's office, and handed them to the New York *Times*. That paper made a thorough investigation, and published a most startling array of facts and figures, all tending to prove the existence of a most gigantic robbery. The conspirators were with few exceptions punished.

Certain matters in connection with what is known as the "Irving week" of 1871 which came to my knowledge will be of interest. It was in the winter of that year. The Democrats had sixty-five votes in the Assembly and seventeen in the Senate. The twenty-one assemblymen from New York City were all bound to support Tweed's measures. They had obtained fat offices, and if they did not vote as he ordered them, their monthly visits to the paymaster's office would become things of the past. Affairs went on very smoothly until "Jim" Irving assaulted Smith Weed by striking him in the face, and was obliged to resign from the Assembly. Previous to this the Democrats had been able to pass any measures they pleased, having just the requisite majority in both branches. But when Irving resigned there came a dead-lock. Whenever an attempt was made to pass a bill the vote stood: Democrats, 64; Republicans, 63.

Bad feeling began to show itself, and so bitter was the strife that Republicans and Democrats would not affiliate. When asked what he thought about the situation, Sweeney simply remarked:

"We have been in worse snaps than this, and got out of them all right."

The Republicans held a caucus, and decided to force a vote in the Assembly on certain measures upon which they knew Tweed had set his heart. One of the Albany evening newspapers published the resolutions passed by the Republicans at their caucus, signed by every one of the sixty-three.

The next day the Assembly Chamber was filled to overflowing. Four bills, which would decide Tweed's fate, were called up for consideration. A motion was made to suspend the usual order of business. This was carried, and before the spectators had recovered from their surprise the first of the bills was read a third time, and the call of the roll began. As the first name was called, Tweed walked into the gallery and pushed his way to the front. With his small gray eyes glittering maliciously, and his arms folded across his chest, he stood looking down upon the Assembly. Not a movement on the floor escaped his notice. As name after name was called his head was thrust forward and inclined on one side, the more easily to hear the response.

When the "B's" were reached, he rested his hands on the rail and leaned over. The "B" who had been expected to vote in favor of the bill cast a decided "No." A faint flush, as of disappointment, swept over the face of the "Boss," and a word, which sounded very much like "damnation," came from between his lips. He was calm again in an instant and resumed his former position. Finally came the name of "Winans." Throughout the session, Winans had been the most exacting of Republicans. He had never failed to add a bitter word to every discussion, denouncing the rough-shod methods of the Democrats. He now voted "Aye," and made a short speech explaining his reasons for voting with the Democrats. The effect upon those in the Chamber was electrical. Those in the galleries cheered loudly and the Democrats on the floor jumped to their feet in a body. The Republicans were completely dumbfounded, and remained motionless in their seats like statues.

Truly it was a sad day for the Republicans; but what of the author of their defeat—Winans? He became an outcast; everyone—Democrats and Republicans alike—avoided him as though he had been a leper. Previous to uttering that blighting "Aye" he had been popular with all persons he came in contact with. The morning after the vote Winans was a changed man; he had aged in a single night, and acted during the remainder of the session as though he were suffering from a horrible nightmare.

Was Winans bribed? He always denied that he was, but admitted that Gould and Fiske had compelled him to act as he did. He held a position under them on the Erie Railroad, he said, and was threatened with discharge if he failed to obey their behests.

The amount which Winans's vote cost has never been made public, but a little circumstance which occurred the night before the memorable scene doubtless had something to do with binding him so closely to the interests of Tweed. That "little circumstance" was this: About four o'clock in the morning a covered sleigh was driven up near the railroad track adjoining the Delavan House at Albany, there being no depot there then. A man got into this sleigh and was driven down the road which leads along the canal to Troy. There was a negro on the box, and alongside of him, wearing an overcoat with its collar nearly hiding his head, was a New York assemblyman who shall be nameless. Before the strange man entered the sleigh at the Delavan House there were two others in it. One was "Tom" Fields and the other a well-known lobbyist.

The sleigh was driven down the dark road for a short distance, and then came to a stop in one of the side streets. Here the New York assemblyman alighted. An hour later he was in his room. It was during the drive that the bribery was consummated. Some say the assemblyman was paid $100,000 in small bills for his work, but the amount was generally believed to be $75,000. The negro driver never uttered a word on the subject; but "Tom" Fields was questioned about it by a police official who had seen the assemblyman get out of the sleigh and had caught a glimpse of Fields's face at the same time. Fields replied with a laugh:

"Why, I'm subject to rheumatism, and when I drink a good deal of champagne I always take a ride before going to bed—my doctor told me to take one."

Who that doctor was can easily be imagined. It was William M. Tweed. Years afterwards "Jim" Fiske once remarked to a well-known newspaper writer:

"Winans was too good a fellow to be killed off the way he was at Albany; but when you're in a tight place there's nothing one won't risk to get out of it. The only trouble with Winans was that he had to do something everybody knew about. Fellows in that Legislature who did worse than he did are now respected citizens. But they didn't happen to be found out."

CHAPTER XIII.

SURPRISED BY NIGHT.—HOW THEY WERE TO "DO IT."—BROCKWAY, THE COUNTERFEITER.—THE PEDLER.—WOMAN'S LOVE OF FINERY.—A MILLION-DOLLAR SWINDLE.—ABOARD THE "THURINGIA."—TWO IMPERFECT BILLS.—SENTENCED FOR LIFE.—A SWINDLER'S CAREER.—AN UNSUSPECTING CATTLE DROVER.—AFTER TIFFANY'S DIAMONDS.

WHILE I was in charge of the detective force, a curious and somewhat startling incident occurred. Sauntering along Broadway one day, a detective happened to see a man named Cartwright, whom he knew to be a counterfeiter. Cartwright had assured us some time before that he had "retired from business," but it nevertheless occurred to the detective that it might be worth while to find out for himself if the fellow was still engaged in his unlawful occupation.

Following him across the Harlem River into Westchester County, the officer reached a spot near the Harlem Railroad company's tracks where there were but few dwellings. Cartwright there entered a frame house. This meeting and its result were reported to me. There was nothing particularly suspicious in Cartwright's proceedings; still I deemed it advisable to watch the house, and so sent two or three men to remain near it for several nights. After waiting patiently for a week, they saw enough to convince them that "work" was carried on at the place.

I then joined the party of watchers, and determined to force an entrance into the house. Dividing my men into two parties, I stationed one in the rear and the other in front of the building. We waited until the lights were extinguished.

We had been able to locate the occupants of the house by assuming that they slept in the rooms where we last saw the lights.

Detective Sampson and I then advanced to the rear door, while the two other detectives were at the front. At a signal a rush was made for the doors. Sampson and I easily burst open the rear one, as it was not very strongly fastened, and, lanterns in hand, made for a room on the left of the hall. The door was open and our sudden entrance awoke the occupant. Without a moment's hesitation he reached out his hand towards a pistol which lay on a stand near his bed. Before he could grasp it we both sprang upon him, while Sampson, pressing the cold muzzle of a revolver against the fellow's head, ordered him to give up his weapon and lie quietly. He did; and after securing him we went up stairs to the room in which we had last noticed a light. Here we found another man.

"Hullo!" he shouted, apparently guessing our errand; "I'm only a visitor here."

"Can't help that," was my unconsoling reply; "you're my prisoner."

Somewhat crestfallen, he remarked: "Well, anyhow, you'll allow me to put on a clean shirt." With that he stepped to a bureau which stood against one side of the room, took out a snowy white garment and put it on.

Bureaus, under certain circumstances, have a strong fascination for me. This one had, so giving in to the feeling I searched it. Five other shirts were carefully folded in a drawer. Under them I got what I wanted: a plate for making counterfeit money.

In the mean time I had been closely watching the gentleman with the clean shirt, and noticed that he kept glancing at the fireplace every now and then in a furtive manner. In fact, it seemed to have a very peculiar attraction for him. Consequently it interested me so greatly that I determined on a closer examination. A quantity of burnt paper on the hearth looked like business. Brushing the ashes carefully away I discovered a number of partly consumed counterfeit ten-dollar bills representing those of the Ogdensburg Bank. Evidently they had not been satisfactory impressions, and so had been destroyed. Searching further we secured a large quantity of excellent specimens of these ten-dollar bills which were finished, including the signature. At the foot of a small pear tree in the garden we found another plate.

The counterfeiters were tried and convicted shortly afterwards, before Judge Robertson at White Plains.

I had a conversation with the men after their conviction, and they informed me of the unique and ingenious device with which they had expected to "work off" the counterfeit bills. A big prize fight was just about to occur, and they intended to bet $20,000 on each of the contestants. Of course, whatever might have been the result of the fight, the counterfeiters would have obtained $20,000 in good money.

At this time a number of complaints were made to me regarding counterfeit gold dollar and two-dollar-and-a-half coins which were circulating. Some specimens were shown me. They showed great skill in their making. They were so well finished indeed that it was not at all surprising that so many persons were deceived.

Now it is by no means easy to trace counterfeit money to its source. In the first place it is necessary to discover whether its circulation is restricted to one locality. The coin or bill may pass through a great many hands before its spurious character is discovered, and even then no one is quite willing to bear the loss and so tries to pass it on. This is human nature. Then again a man may take a counterfeit coin from a customer who has received it in good faith, and who has perhaps handled large amounts of money. The latter, of course, if the character of the coin be pointed out, will probably insist that the coin given is genuine. Long and tedious research is necessary to find out how innocent each man is in these transactions and who may or may not be the counterfeiter. The one who first passed the false coin of course uses every precaution to conceal his identity.

In these coin counterfeiting cases I finally came to the conclusion that the locality where the work was carried on was on the east side of the city. Many of the coins were found in the omnibuses, and the dollar pieces were frequently passed by the drivers in making change. Cautious detective work was begun and ultimately success began to crown our efforts.

We found a man nick-named "Tom Hyer," who seemed to have some knowledge of the matter. Hyer intimated to some of the officers that he had an idea where the "stuff" could be bought.

After questioning him I secured his services, undertaking to pay his expenses and for his time. For two days I saw nothing of him. At the end of that time he reported to me that for $30 he could buy $100 worth of the counterfeits we were after. "A man," he said, "has agreed to meet me at a certain place near Chatham Square. I must have $30. He will have the $100 of his money and will make an exchange in the street, at two o'clock to-morrow."

"All right," I said, "you shall have the money."

With the $30 in his pocket Hyer left the office. I had him

"shadowed" to his home. Next day he was seen by my detectives to go to Chatham Square, where, they informed me, a short, dark-complexioned man met Hyer and the exchange of coin took place. Officer John McCord subsequently followed the man who had passed the counterfeits. Again Hyer came to the office and reported the matter to me, saying:

"I've got the money."

Whoever Hyer was or whatever might be his character, his version of the story agreed with that of the detective.

Two days afterwards McCord said to me: "I witnessed the exchange and then followed the man the rest of the afternoon. There was nothing suspicious about his actions that day. At ten o'clock at night he went into a house in the Fifth Ward, and as he did not come out again I suppose he slept there. I followed him the next day. He walked down Beekman Street and went into a store where sheet-metal is sold, then he crossed Fulton Ferry to Brooklyn and got on a Myrtle Avenue car. I went to a hackman and hired his carriage; the driver got inside, while I took off my coat, rolled up my sleeves, jumped on the box and followed that car. After awhile the man got out and went into a drug store, and then took another car. I drove after him for about a mile, when he left the car and proceeded on foot. I dismissed the hack, and kept my man in view as he went towards a house on the outskirts of Brooklyn. I cut across the open fields, and, approaching the dwelling, hid behind a fence and waited, but I saw no more of him after that. I left this morning to report the state of affairs."

Officer McCord asked for help, so two men were sent to him. For four days the detectives watched, but nothing remarkable occurred. The man who sold the counterfeit coin would go to New York and return again. While he was absent the time was spent in studying the house and its inmates, and so was not wasted. For instance, we discovered that the house was protected with many locks, bolts and bars. The butcher, baker, grocer and milkman came with the usual supplies, but were not admitted. The stores were taken in at the basement by a woman who used a great deal of precaution. These tradespeople would knock, and the door, which had a sliding chain, would be cautiously opened.

As the chase was now becoming interesting I joined the party, and we discussed the best means of effecting an entrance. We were satisfied that the counterfeit coin was being made in the house. We, of course, must arrest the "gang" with their tools. They must not be allowed to carry off their machinery, nor must they have the opportunity of concealing their dies. My desire was to break up the concern, root and branch. To employ brute force was entirely out of the question. What then was the best method of accomplishing the object? The fact that the doorkeeper was of the gentler sex was something in our favor. Could no persuasive means be used to induce her to admit us? I remembered that Walpole is reported to have said, with regard to political bribes, that he never saw but one woman who refused gold; and diamonds captured her. Acting in a measure upon the above suggestion, we attired Mr. Thomas Sampson as a pedler. He was dressed in a long black coat, and was provided with a capacious blue paper box. Neatly packed in it were such articles as were calculated to excite feminine cupidity. The property-clerk at headquarters furnished Sampson with his stock in trade. And it may be as well to say that a police property-clerk in New York can produce any description of outfit on very short notice, from a needle to an anchor.

Thus disguised, Sampson knocked at the basement door. It was opened a little way, the chain still remaining up. The pale face of a woman was visible.

"What is it?" she asked, sharply and suspiciously.

"Oh! mine tear madam, I vas a trafflin merchant, a pedler. I haf some beautiful tings vot I vill sold you, mine tear," at the same time Sampson flourished an embroidered handkerchief before the woman's eyes.

She looked longingly at the article, but answered, "No," and was about to close the door in his face.

"Don't go for to shut the door, mine tear. I haf here a real beauty," said Sampson, now producing a very handsome cream-colored crêpe shawl, elaborately embroidered. "See how vresh and nize it vas, my tear. It vas vorth a huntred tollars. I vill sold it to you—only to you, for feefty. Dirt sheep, mine tear, dirt sheep. Shoost look at eet."

The woman stretched out her hand to touch the delicate fabric.

"Dry it on, my tear. If I vas to go round I might get sometings vat it was vorth. Say twenty-five tollars!"

The bait was too much for the woman. She loosed the chain,

THE PEDLER AT THE DOOR.

made one step outside the door, and Sampson was inside the house before she realized the situation.

Two of the officers at once rushed from their concealment and ran to the rear of the house. I joined Sampson, who with pistol in hand was ready for any emergency. Running through to the back of the house I let in the two other men, and with this force admitted everything was in our hands. There was no show of fight. The prisoners were as docile as lambs. Criminals know that when fairly caught, to fight only makes matters worse.

We found four persons engaged in making this false money, Brockway, Thomas, another man and the woman who coveted the crêpe shawl. A press complete in every particular was found in the basement. Brockway was cool about the matter. Going to a bureau he took out of a drawer a thousand dollars in good bank bills, and offering them to me, said :

"If you will let me off I'll give you a thousand dollars more."

He had the assurance to produce his bank book, showing there was something more than that amount to his credit.

"Let one of your men go to the savings bank and draw out the money," he remarked. "I will give you that provided you make no search."

I, of course, refused, and we were about to ransack the premises, when Brockway remarked: "Very well, I will save you a great deal of trouble."

He went to another bureau and exhibited a quantity of counterfeit one-dollar and two-dollar-and-a-half gold pieces. Then from a secret drawer he produced the dies. We took nothing for granted, however. Long strips of metal were found in the cellar from which the blanks had been punched. By counting these holes we were satisfied that Brockway had manufactured not less than a hundred thousand dollars in spurious coin. We took possession of everything, and carried prisoners and machinery to headquarters. We found the silver imitations were poor, only a few spurious half-dollars were among them ; the gold coins, however, were works of art.

The prisoners were tried in the United States court. We had no evidence against one of the men, and he was released ; but the others were sentenced and sent to prison. The woman pretended to be Brockway's wife, and claimed that she acted as a counterfeiter under compulsion; but she could not prove it, and was put

THE COUNTERFEITERS' DEN.

on trial. Brockway was more than fifty years of age, and was tall and slim. With the exception of Marcus Cicero Stanly, no one seems to have been personally acquainted with him.

I had the dies put in a neat velvet case and took them to Washington, where they are to be found to-day among the curiosities of counterfeiting. The Government of the United States, it might be thought, would have paid the expenses incurred in arresting the Brockway party, but such was not the case. The cost was defrayed by the New York Police Department. It was rumored that the woman was a confirmed opium-eater, but this had not apparently blunted her appreciation of what was really a superb china crêpe shawl.

George MacDonnell was the most expert and persistent forger and confidence man that ever exercised his cunning on unsuspecting humanity in this country and in Europe. Detection, capture, and even imprisonment were no restraining influences on the development of this man's knavish propensities. To paraphrase Shakespeare's phrase, he was a rascal, take him all in all; I ne'er shall look upon his like again. Failure goaded him to new endeavors; success nerved him. That he was shrewd, cautious, determined and bold goes without saying. It was a long while before eager justice got a tight grip upon this polished villain, but when once it did there was no letting up, and MacDonnell was doomed to pass the remainder of his life in prison stripes. His last crime was his greatest, for it was no other than swindling the Bank of England out of one million dollars.

Gray clouds were hanging over New York harbor one summer's morning in 1873. The sun was just making his appearance over the bastions of Fort Hamilton, and his first rays shone full in the face of a man who was slowly pacing up and down the dock in front of the health officer's house at Quarantine. Something was evidently preying on the man's mind. A close observer would have noticed lines of care on his forehead. Every now and then his eyes glanced furtively from beneath his brow and took in the scope of the harbor. They rested for a moment upon the huge ocean steamships with their black hulls that lay anchored a dozen rods or so from shore; they scanned the waters reaching down into the lower bay, and noticed in the distance the little cloud of black smoke which betokened the approach of another ocean racer. Then they turned quickly in the direction of the health officer's house, which sat prettily among the trees of the neighboring bluff. Suddenly the man's expression brightened, as from above he heard a sound of feet and beheld the deputy health officer walking down the path. A few minutes later a steam tug left the dock and puffed rapidly out to the steamships which lay at rest in the stream. The strange man on the dock and the deputy health officer were the tug's only passengers. They boarded the different steamers, and while the Government officer examined critically for signs of disease among the incoming passengers, his companion was busily studying their faces.

"Did you find your man?" the deputy asked, as the two returned to the tug and were taken back to shore.

"No," answered the detective, for such he was. "He isn't on those vessels."

Other steamers came into port during the day, and this inspection was repeated. The sun reached its zenith, sank slowly in the west, and was finally gilding Fort Hamilton from over in the Jersey marshes.

At this time another steamer came through the Narrows and anchored off Quarantine. Again the deputy health officer and the detective went out to board her. She was the "Thuringia." The passengers were called up for examination, and among the number was one who answered the description of George MacDonnell, the object of the detective's search.

"You are my prisoner," said the detective, quietly.

The man started back, and then in apparent indignation demanded, "What do you mean, sir? I want to know the meaning of this insult."

MacDonnell, the forger, was tall, well-built and very handsome. His voice was gentle, except when he was angry, and he possessed a ready vocabulary. He had a delicately fair skin, and wore a dark brown beard. He was not the man you would have picked out for a criminal. But the detective's experience had taught him to be no respecter of appearances, and even when his distinguished prisoner professed to be greatly insulted, and threatened in loud tones to make the officer "pay bitterly for this outrage," as he called it, the detective had no idea of letting him go. MacDonnell was taken to jail as soon as the "Thuringia" landed at her pier, and was held for examination.

The clever bit of forgery of which he was accused was accom-

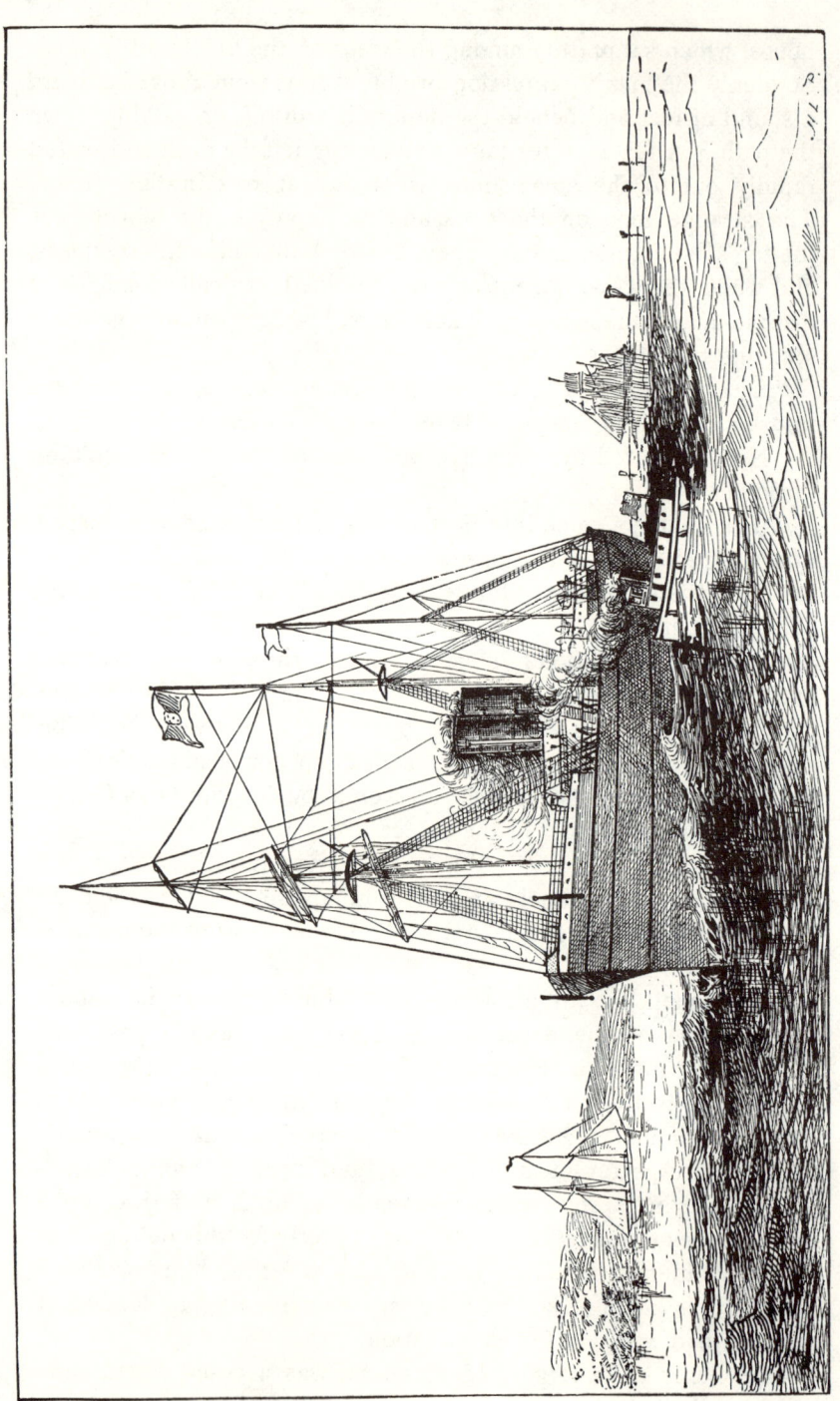
A WARM WELCOME.

plished in this manner: After having prospered for years in their devices for swindling, MacDonnell and three associates, Austin and Biron Bidwell, brothers, and Edwin Noyes, conceived the gigantic scheme of defrauding the Bank of England out of many hundred thousands of dollars. The reputation of the bank for conservatism and shrewdness in management did not warn them. They knew that untold millions were there to steal, and they boldly matched their wits against those of the bank officers. Their plans were well laid. They went at their task deliberately and cautiously. They established an office in London, and put a large amount of money in their business. The firm's name was "MacDonnell & Co.," and they deposited English gold in the vaults of the Bank of England. They were in no hurry to reap the rewards of their iniquitous conspiracy. They carried on a legitimate business for months, and made a reputation for honesty and fair dealing. George MacDonnell opened an account with the western branch of the bank, and waited patiently for an opportunity to execute his forgeries. When the conspirators thought the time had come, they set to work to manufacture the forged bills. This required great ingenuity and labor. It was necessary to copy exactly, water marks and all, the particular kind of paper used by the various firms upon which they intended to draw the bills. This was done so carefully and perfectly, that when the forgeries were at last discovered it was not because the genuineness of the bills was questioned. They were payable in three months, and the forgers had no difficulty in discounting them. But by a very careless blunder, MacDonnell and his associates forgot to put the date of acceptance on two of the bills which they presented at the bank, and the firms whose names were upon the paper were asked by the bank officers to rectify the supposed mistake. Then of course the bills were pronounced forgeries.

It was too late, however, to capture the forgers. They had taken alarm and fled with nearly a million dollars, the earnings of their conspiracy. MacDonnell was supposed to have gone to New York, and a minute description of him was cabled thither. It was for the man of this description that the detective at Quarantine searched all incoming vessels, and at last found him on the "Thuringia." MacDonnell's associates were afterwards discovered in this country, and all four were taken to London. On August 26, 1873, in the Old Bailey Court, they were convicted and sentenced to hard labor for life. By good fortune the bank officers recovered the bulk of the stolen money.

MacDonnell was well known to the police of this country. Previous to this, his last crime, he had performed many daring swindling operations on this side the water. Once, while on his way to New York from the West, he made the acquaintance of a good-natured cattle drover. MacDonnell called into play his most fascinating manners, talked brilliantly, and made a deep impression on the Westerner. Both drank frequently from the flask of excellent brandy which the forger carried with him, and soon the cattleman was sound asleep. It was a very easy matter then for MacDonnell to take his companion's pocket-book. This he did, and was richer by $2600. He placed the money in some newspapers he had with him, and addressing them to a fictitious name in this city posted them at the next station.

By the time the drover awoke the train was at a junction, and he invited MacDonnell to take luncheon with him. The two ate, and when they had finished the drover took out his pocket-book to pay the bill. He found to his astonishment that it was empty. He turned to his companion and said :

"I had $2600 in that pocket-book ; where is it?"

"Do you accuse me of taking it?" asked MacDonnell indignantly, and then insisted upon being searched. This was done, but nothing of course was found. The cattleman was greatly humbled, and naturally ashamed of himself for his suspicions. During the rest of his journey he treated MacDonnell with the greatest courtesy, and apologized over and over again for his rudeness. At Buffalo they parted the best of friends. MacDonnell came to New York, secured the papers with the money inclosed, and enjoyed the profits of his ill-gotten gains.

In the autumn of 1867 MacDonnell was in New York. He answered the advertisement of Dr. James W. Barnard, a well known physician on Fifth Avenue, who wished to rent the front parlor and adjoining rooms of his house. Calling at the house and presenting a card on which was the name of Henry B. Livingston, he represented himself as an English traveller who was tired of hotel life. After inspecting the rooms he agreed to take them. The rent was high, but he professed no objection, and paid part of it in advance. During his call he was accompanied by a valet, whom he addressed as Clarence.

Later on the same day he went to Tiffany's and asked to look at diamonds. He chose a brooch with seven stones, a solitaire ring, two diamond ear drops, and two large unset diamonds. The value of all was about $2500. He gave his name to the salesman as W. H. Barnard, and said that he had not sufficient money with him to pay for the diamonds, but would go down town and see his father. Pretty soon he returned and said that his father was out, but that he had left word to have the money left at his residence on Fifth Avenue. His carriage was outside, he said, and he invited the salesman to take the diamonds and ride with him to his house, where he would be paid. The salesman assented, and they were driven off by a coachman whom MacDonnell called "Charles." They stopped at Dr. Barnard's residence, and went in the parlor. MacDonnell asked Clarence, who was there, where his father was. Clarence replied that he had just stepped out, mentioning where he had gone. Then MacDonnell told his valet to go after him and get the money for the diamonds. Clarence did so, and returned with a check drawn for the proper amount upon a prominent bank, and signed by Jas. W. Barnard. This was given to the salesman, and he departed with the worthless check. MacDonnell and Clarence, who was no less than one of the Bidwells, left the city at once. Charles, the coachman, had been in the conspiracy, but his companions had "shelved" him at the last moment, and he, through spite, divulged the fraud. MacDonnell was found by detectives in Portland, Maine, and brought back to New York, where he was sentenced to prison for three years. Bidwell escaped.

CHAPTER XIV.

DISPUTE WITH THE POLICE COMMISSIONERS.—CRANKS WHO WRITE LETTERS.—EXPECTING COUNTERFEIT NOTES AND GETTING SAWDUST.—A LITTLE BY-PLAY ON BROADWAY.—"THE THIRD DEGREE."—THE MAN WHO PULLED OUT HIS WHISKERS.—FACTS ABOUT THE FINEST FORCE.

I was appointed superintendent of police on July 23, 1874. At that time the force consisted of four inspectors, thirty-six captains, one hundred and thirty-five sergeants, two thousand two hundred and seventy-two patrolmen and eighty doormen—making a total of 2521.

In a strictly legal sense, the superintendent of the New York police is the executive officer of the department; but during the eleven years I occupied the position my powers were considerably curtailed, with the exception of the short period when Mr. Matsell was president of the Police Board. At the time I was appointed superintendent, the Board of Police had authority under a special act of the Legislature to remove me when they pleased. This arbitrary power they held until the Consolidation Act was passed in 1882. It will be at once manifest that if, under the old act, the superintendent attempted to carry out the promptings of his own judgment, and his actions happened to be at variance with the ideas of any member of the Police Board, that member in all probability became his enemy. Under such circumstances it can readily be seen that the removal of the superintendent would not be a very difficult thing to bring about.

As a general rule, the subjects of dispute between the police commissioners and myself were not of major importance. There was one point, however, on which we never could agree, and that was in regard to the duties of the inspectors. Prior to my assuming the position, captains were responsible to the superintendent personally; they were under his immediate control and not under that of the inspectors. By more recent regulations, the inspectors received the reports of the captains. They thus came between me and the latter. The inspectors were four in number, and when Inspector Byrnes was appointed he was given command of the detective force, which had heretofore been under my control. His duties differed materially from those of the others. The captains of the various precincts, therefore, did not feel under any special responsibility to him, as no analogy exists between the work of the detectives and that of the general patrol force. Under the new rule, captains soon came to consider that the inspector of their

district was the officer to whom their allegiance was directly due, and whose instructions they should follow. With such a divided responsibility and authority, a great many matters occurred in the city which might be classed among lesser misdemeanors, and which did not come under the immediate notice of the superintendent, and only reached his ears after some lapse of time. Orders, too, emanating from the superintendent and addressed to the captains through the medium of the inspectors, were imparted by the latter in a half-hearted manner. In fact, it rested wholly with the inspectors themselves whether the superintendent's wishes should be supported or practically ignored. I have every reason to believe that because the inspectors failed to give me the aid which they should have given the laws in regard to gambling, lotteries and policy playing were not enforced. Had the old and intimate relations which heretofore existed between the superintendent and captains continued, I am certain I could have suppressed many of the evils to which I have alluded.

Mr. Hawley, who was chief clerk, co-operated most heartily with me in the endeavor to effect a change in these rules relative to inspectors. Our efforts were in vain; but I am pleased to know that Mr. Murray, my successor, who, as inspector and with the other inspectors opposed the change, has now urged the very identical changes which I had tried to obtain for so many years, and that his "requests" have been complied with.

To explain in detail the varied work which falls to the lot of the police superintendent in New York would occupy many pages, and I can give only a brief sketch of his complex duties. The hours of the day, even when re-enforced by those of the night, are barely sufficient to meet all the requirements of the situation. It was my habit to be at the office promptly at eight o'clock in the morning, and, with the exception of a brief interval for luncheon, to remain there until six o'clock at night. Sunday was never a day of rest to me. I was always prepared for night work, and was frequently called upon at the most unexpected hours. It was also my duty to be present at all riots, serious fires, etc. Anything like regular hours or an established routine of work was altogether impossible.

The daily mail of a New York superintendent of police is very large. Everybody in the United States seems to want to write to him; and besides the letters from this country, he gets communications from all over the world. Everybody with a grievance of any kind addresses him; and in addition to a great deal of trivial matter, no small amount of important business reaches his busy hands. The bulk of his correspondence comes from people who complain of having been "swindled." In most cases of this kind even a cursory examination of the letters shows that the "swindled" are not above suspicion themselves. The grievances are many. Some say they have sent good money, expecting to receive counterfeit notes in return, and got nothing but blank paper or sawdust. Others expected to obtain a $250 piano for $5; a $60 sewing machine for $2; or a $10 washer and wringer for fifty cents. And because their expectations were

POLICE HEADQUARTERS, MULBERRY STREET.

not realized they get angry, denounce the "swindler" to the superintendent, and demand justice. To such I paid no attention. But whenever it was clear that a fraud or swindle had been perpetrated, I always did the best I could to make it "warm" for those who were carrying on the crooked business.

With letters of this kind there come to the superintendent inquiries demanding his closest attention. Many of these are of a strictly private, or family, character. A man is paying attention to a woman who lives a thousand miles from New York, and has told her that he formerly resided in this city; that he is unmarried, in independent circumstances and of fair repute. "There is something," says the writer, "which is not quite plain in regard to the gentleman who sues for the lady's hand. Will the superintendent kindly find out all he can?" Why, if the superintendent's office were the General Intelligence Bureau of the Continent of North America it would not suffice for the numerous and preposterous demands made upon its time and patience. Some people seem to have the impression that the superintendent is at the head of a commercial agency, and it is not unusual to find in the correspondence requests that the financial standing, probity and so on, of such and such a firm shall be investigated and revealed. If it were possible to give such information as is requested by anxious parents, lovers, and creditors, the superintendent would be perfectly willing to impart all he knows; but in most cases he is helpless.

On every day in the year the office of the superintendent is in communication with the leading cities of the United States in regard to business which is particularly within his province: the whereabouts and conduct of criminals. A robbery is committed, and the perpetrator is supposed to have fled to New York. A description of him is immediately sent to the New York police. Or perhaps a burglary has occurred in this city, and the criminal is stealthily making his way to some other place; if we have a photograph of the supposed culprit, a number of his pictures are immediately struck off and forwarded, together with printed particulars of the robbery and the articles stolen, to all parts of the country.

Foreign letters are frequent. Germans, Frenchmen, Italians, Swedes, Norwegians, English, Irish, Scotch and persons of all other nationalities who have sons or daughters in the United

States (and in South America even, sometimes), write to the superintendent to learn of their children's whereabouts. Whenever possible, inquiries of this nature are given attention.

A considerable portion of the superintendent's time is taken up by callers, and many valuable hours are lost through the thoughtlessness of persons who come on all kinds of matters which are utterly foreign to police business. Everybody, however, must be listened to attentively, for now and then a genuine grievance

SUPERINTENDENT WALLING'S OFFICE.

comes to light, requiring prompt action. The "routine" work of the superintendent alone requires a great deal of time and attention, no matter how commonplace it may seem.

All parades and public meetings come under the supervision of the superintendent. In such cases, notice of the time and place and route is sent to headquarters. If a procession is likely to be large, the superintendent studies the route, and instructions concerning the disposition of the force are sent to the police captains. During the close presidential contest of 1884 the police force was taxed to its utmost, and from the superintendent down to the patrolmen not one had scarcely a moment's rest for three weeks.

And let me say here that the good sense and temper of the community were never more conspicuous than on those occasions. The tens of thousands of excited people who congregated on the streets were easily managed.

The superintendent has no leisure. His position is no sinecure or bed of roses; and with the rapid growth of New York and the country of which it is the commercial mart, his responsibilities are rapidly increasing.

The reader will be interested in the actual circumstances usually attendant upon the arrest of a criminal by a Central Office detective, and I cannot do better than narrate an incident which occurred some time ago. In company with a Western friend interested in police matters, I was walking on Broadway one afternoon in the vicinity of the Fifth Avenue Hotel, when I caught sight of a little by-play which was going on unnoticed by the large number of persons on the street. An exceedingly well-dressed individual, wearing modest but expensive jewellery, was engaged in apparently friendly conversation with another man, about whom there was nothing to attract observation, unless it was his efforts to escape it.

"Do you see that?" I asked of my friend, pointing out the two men.

"Yes," he replied; "but what about them?"

"Well, one of them is a detective, and the other is a forger whom he is arresting."

"Tell me all about it," said my friend. "I've long wanted to know the *modus operandi* of such a capture—the conversation and so on between the detective and his prisoner."

"That detective is 'Phil' ——, and his prisoner is John ——. I think I can guess at the conversation between them. I'll wager it's something after this fashion:

"'How are you, John?'

"'O, first-rate, thank you, Phil,' answers the fellow, knowing well that Phil's inquiry bodes him no good.

"'John, the old man [that's me] wants to see you.'

"'All right. I'll go along.'

"'Well, look here, no skipping. I'm fixed, and there might be a little accident if you tried to go as you please here. Understand?'

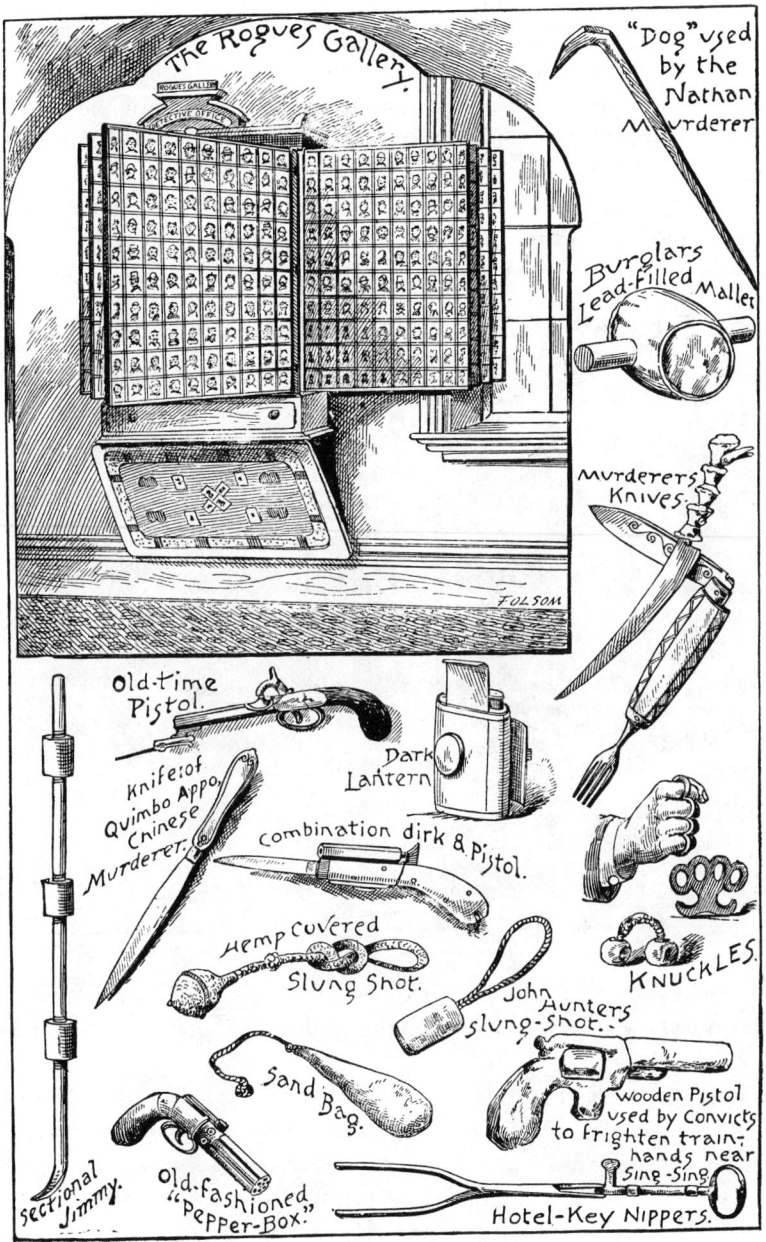

ROGUES' GALLERY AND MEMENTOES.

"'Why, certainly, Phil. Don't suppose I'm going to give you the slip, do you?'"

The detective and his prisoner now walked along the street, and we followed. The pair had the appearance of being old friends, just going to take a drink. There was no exhibition of revolver or "billy," nippers or handcuffs. John knew well that even if he made a bolt and escaped the bullets from Phil's pistol, his re-arrest would quickly follow, and an exhibition of his ability as a pedestrian would be accepted as an evidence of his guilt.

THE CELL CORRIDOR.

"John," I informed my friend, "is a notorious 'layer down' of checks, who has given the community and the police a great deal of trouble."

The two jumped aboard a car and alighted at Bleecker Street. We followed, and my Western acquaintance could not avoid remarking that Phil walked along as if he didn't know of any such place as police headquarters. Turning into Mott Street, Phil and his charge approached the rear of the Central Office, went down a flight of stairs, and entered a corridor just outside of what is used as an office by the boiler inspectors and policemen detailed to enforce the health ordinances. Phil was anxious that his chief should know what he had achieved, while John, knowing too well who had him in custody, was aware that the sooner he got in a cell the sooner he would have a little comfort.

So far, no sign of a prison has met the eye. But the detective and his man now reach a door fitted with heavy springs, on which might be written, "All hope abandon ye who enter here." This door gives entrance to a gloomy-looking arched passage-way, on

THE MUSEUM.—BURGLARS' TOOLS.

either side of which are yards paved with stone slabs. There is no chance for escape. The walls surrounding the yards rise to the level of the fifth story, and are unscalable. To the left is a huge chamber barred with iron windows and fitted with iron doors, and used for the safe confinement of large numbers of prisoners, as in times of riot. To the right are two sets of casemates, arranged with cells, out of which nobody, even if left alone and possessed of the most improved tools, could escape. Hurrying his prisoner along, Phil turns sharply to the right, to a yard under the "Bridge of Sighs," as it is called, the connecting link between the office of the superintendent and the Detective Bureau. A ring at the wooden door brings Turnkey Birney to view. He is bearded and has a martial and business-like air, and his eyes are as piercing as a gimlet. He appreciates the situation at a glance, opens wide the door, and when his visitors have passed through

THE MUSEUM.—RELICS OF CRIME.

closes it with a resounding slam. Birney follows the officer and his prisoner past the "day room" of the detectives, where they pass the time while waiting for orders in writing "baby letters" and playing dominoes. The prisoner is then conducted up one of the worst corkscrew staircases that ever a builder constructed. The landing on the top leads directly into the main office of the Detective Bureau—an ample, lofty apartment, railed off at the east end. Outside the railing is a measuring-stand and a subordinate rogues' gallery. Behind is venerable "Deacon" Sergeant Isaac Bird, spare, angular, always exceedingly neat, particular, white-bearded, amiable, business-like and gentlemanly. He is of course busy when Phil and his charge enter, but he leaves his mysterious occupation to reach for the "blotter," while he says:

"What's the case?"

"Forgery," replies Phil, in a mechanical tone of voice.

The "Deacon" dips his pen in the ink, searches for the proper line, and then, addressing the prisoner, says:

"What's your name?"

"John Jones."

The "Deacon" glances at Jones, and then makes an entry of the single letter "W." This signifies "white."

"Your age?"

"Thirty-five."

"Born?"

"United States."

"Married or single?"

"Married."

"Occupation?"

"Speculator."

Then the "Deacon," without consulting the prisoner, and as if holding communion with himself alone, murmurs:

"Forgery," and enters it.

"Complainant?" he then inquires.

"Phil Riley. Guess the chief wants to see this man." (This means chief of detectives, not the superintendent of police.)

"Well, wait a second, I'll see." Saying which the "Deacon" disappears through a doorway, only to reappear after a brief absence and hold up his finger. This indicates that the prisoner is going to pass a bad quarter of an hour, or what is known in police slang as "getting the third degree."

Phil accordingly hurries his charge into the presence of Inspector Byrnes, who is fully prepared to receive his visitors. He has struck a meditative attitude behind his low but simple desk, crossed his legs, and begins operations by casting a short, sharp glance at unfortunate John Jones. John knows the inspector, so he makes a humble salutation. If the interview is likely to be a prolonged one he is waved to a seat. Not so with Phil; if it lasted all day he must stand.

John Jones enters the presence of Mr. Byrnes, determined to do the best he can for himself. The inspector is perfectly well aware of John's intention and proceeds to upset it. Of course Jones has certain secrets connected with his nefarious profession; but the inspector soon shows him that the possession of such secrets is a joint stock affair. All that Jones has done, or nearly all, for months, appears to be as familiar to the inspector as to the prisoner himself. He begins to forget an original intention of keep-

INSPECTOR BYRNES'S OFFICE.

ing "mum," is entrapped into making admissions and contradictions, and generally ends by "squealing." Some prisoners under this ordeal are not so easily brought to confession. A few hours sojourn in a cell, however, pondering over the inspector's parting words frequently brings them to terms, and ready to impart such information as the authorities desire at the next interview.

The interview ended, John Jones goes back before the "Deacon," and if he has not yet been searched, that operation is in order. The man who "goes through him" has become expert by long experience. His search is not an ordinary one of pockets merely. It is thorough. It includes from hat to boots, seams, tailors' "pocket tricks," hat band, hat lining, boot heels, watch case, underwear, even the prisoner's person,—all are ruthlessly examined, and each article found in his possession is placed upon the broad shelf in front of the "Deacon," by whom it is subjected to a close scrutiny. Such articles as relate to the charge against the prisoner, and any instruments with which he might inflict injury upon himself, are laid aside. Generally he has returned to him possessions of no value, small sums of money and so on. If

PRIVATE ROOMS, CENTRAL OFFICE.

the prisoner's photograph is not in the possession of the police, or has been secured by them at such a remote day as to be valueless in recognizing him, he is walked off by the detective, in the same apparently friendly way as that with which he came to headquarters, to one of three Bowery photographers. The conversation during the walk is almost invariably the same. The prisoner ranks his captor as among the dearest of his friends, and addresses him by his Christian name, asking him confidentially concerning the nature of the charge against him, the evidence in possession of the police and his "chances." The detective does not, of course, answer all the questions put to him, but generally outlines what he has against him, and seldom omits to interject a few grains of

CHAS. WILLIAMS. (No. 843.)
(From a Photograph taken under Duress.)

comfort. At the photographer's the prisoner is treated as an ordinary customer. He poses, as a rule, to the best advantage, vanity impels him to look his best, the negative is examined, pronounced satisfactory or otherwise, and when a good likeness is assured, the detective and his man chat on their way back to the Central Office.

First-class "professionals" undergo the process of having their faces handed down to infamy with bad grace. Not infrequently they resist the taking of their photograph in a most vigorous manner. Under the old method, such a prisoner was difficult to photograph. Even when force was used it was found impossible to obtain other than distorted features for the gallery. Now-a-days, however, by means of the instantaneous process, and by catching the reluctant sitter at an unguarded moment, portraits sufficiently correct for the required purpose are always obtained.

When once more back at the Central Office, John Jones is treated kindly, and his personal wants are inquired into. If he is hungry, a generous meal is soon provided, either from the kitchen of Mrs. Mary Webb, the matron, or from a neighboring restaurant, if the prisoner has money. His defence is not neglected, either, if he can defray the cost of employing a messenger. The majority of thieves have their pet lawyers, and a message speedily brings the latter to their clients. Such visits, except in cases where it would be possible for an unscrupulous lawyer to thwart the ends of justice by making away with evidence or property necessary to convict the criminal, are regarded as sacredly confidential.

The prisoner is now handed over to Turnkey Birney, who conducts him down the corkscrew staircase and places him in whatever cell may be empty at the time. All the cells are alike. The furniture consists of but one article—a slanting board, with a raised ledge at the higher end in lieu of a pillow. If, on the next morning, he desires to employ a barber, he can do so, provided that in the process of shaving no hair is cut from the head or from the whiskers or mustache. It has now and then happened that, in order to avoid identification, prisoners have gone so far as to burn their beard and mustache off. Others have been known to hack their whiskers with a pocket-knife. But the most remarkable instance of all was where a man, with whiskers on his chin, actually pulled out the hairs one by one rather than run the risk of being identified the next morning in court. The agony he endured must have been excruciating, but he had his reward—the witnesses were unable to swear to his identity.

The police force of New York City is without doubt the finest organization of its kind in the world. The men composing it are finer looking, better paid, more vigilant than the protectors of any other large city. No organization is more effective either; and even if our police do not exercise that perpetual espionage over individual citizens that the Parisian gendarmes exercise, they are better trained, more athletic, more resolute and hardy. The *esprit de corps* which prevails is unequalled in any other city. Then, too, the men are given to understand that their actions, when governed by a desire for the public good, will be protected and upheld by the courts. In this respect the New York police have unusual liberty of action—more by far than the London police, who dare not lay a finger on a man unless he is engaged in the very act of violating the law. Here, however, it is often a case of "giving a dog a bad name and then hanging him,"—men being arrested merely because they are known to have been law-breakers or persons of bad character. But in London, and in other large cities of the Old World, thieves, burglars and criminals of all classes march past the guardians of peace and law, feeling confident that they are safe from arrest so long as they are not caught in the act of law-breaking. A band of pickpockets may rush through a crowd at Hyde Park, or hustle the throngs that gather upon Epsom Downs on the "Derby Day," but the police are powerless. A howling mob of ten or twenty thousand rascals may gather in Trafalgar Square with the declared intention of sacking Buckingham Palace, but the police can only stand round, waiting for the commission of some illegal act—the throwing of a stone, the tearing down of a fence—before taking any active part in stopping the performance.

With "the finest," as the New York police are sometimes called, criminals do not experience such forbearance. A New York police officer knows he has been sworn in to "keep the peace," and he keeps it. There's no "shilly-shallying" with him; he doesn't consider himself half patrolman and half supreme court judge. He can and does arrest on suspicion. In times of turbulence, or threatened rioting, he keeps people moving. If men or women who are notorious enter places of amusement, a policeman is very

POLICE PARADE, BROADWAY.

likely to eject them. If they don't go quietly and without many words, the station-house becomes their abiding-place for the night.

The London police do not arrest for gross intoxication and disturbance in the street, or for street-walking, as our police do. In New York, prostitutes are not allowed to pursue their calling in a bold and shameless manner. When I was in London I remember standing by the "Old Bailey" and seeing a drunken sailor between two drunken women, chaffing the policemen as they went along and shouting and swearing at the wayfarers. This would not be allowed here one minute.

I stood by Charing Cross one day with Police Commissioner Matthews. Two of his friends stopped him, and while they were talking, a woman who was very noisy and drunken came staggering along. She accosted them with some ribaldry and they moved away to avoid her. She then came and harangued me. I said:

"Get out! Move on! I'll have you arrested if you don't go away."

She turned around and denounced and defied me with a profane and obscene expression. Policemen were close by, but they paid no attention to her. In London and Liverpool are seen multitudes of lewd women in the streets, and the police never molest them.

When I was captain of detectives I assumed a liberty which had never been taken by any of my predecessors. That was, on every public holiday, or in the event of large parades, to issue this order to the detective force: "Arrest all known pickpockets on the streets, and take them in." Of course my action caused considerable consternation in the ranks of the "crooked" fraternity. Some remonstrated, and not a few were furious at my "restraining the liberty of the subject." A considerable number clubbed together and hired a lawyer to argue the matter before the courts. It was no use; my order was sustained and remains to this day. When the Prince of Wales visited this country he expressed his astonishment at the ease with which the police of New York controlled the large crowds in the streets. The Duke of Newcastle noticed the same thing. As a contrast, the fact may be mentioned that afterwards, when the Prince and Princess of Wales gave a reception in London, the mob there overpowered the police, seven persons were killed and hundreds were wounded, to say nothing of the robberies effected in the consequent confusion. When the "Great Eastern" was on exhibition in England, the pickpockets reaped a rich harvest, many thousands of pounds being reported stolen. When the mammoth steamship was exhibited here, however, not a dime was known to have been taken, although she was visited by more than a hundred thousand persons and only six policemen were on duty.

CHAPTER XV.

KIDNAPPING OF CHARLEY ROSS.—MYSTERIOUS LETTERS.—ON THE TRACK OF THE CRIMINALS.—SEARCHING LAND AND WATER.—A TREACHEROUS AID.—THE BURGLARY AT VAN BRUNT'S HOUSE.—DEATH OF THE ABDUCTORS.

OF all my experiences while connected with the police I recall no case which gave me greater solicitude than the abduction of Charley Ross. This occurred on the evening of Wednesday, July 1, 1874, at Germantown, a suburb of Philadelphia. I became superintendent of police on July 23, and in consequence I took an active part in the search for the child and the discovery of the kidnappers.

The crime was one which called for vigorous and continued action. For some years after the futility of the search became evident the abduction was repeatedly brought to my memory. In this case my sympathies were particularly enlisted.

The first intimation the public had of the abduction was gained from the following advertisement which appeared on July 3 in the Philadelphia *Public Ledger:*

"Lost, on the first instant, a small boy about four years of age; light complexion, and light curly hair. A suitable reward will be paid on his return to E. L. Joyce, Central Station, corner of Fifth and Chestnut streets."

The name "Ross" was not mentioned in this notice, as Mr. Christian K. Ross, the father, did not wish to alarm his wife, who was spending a few weeks at Atlantic City. When Mr. Ross came home on July 1 he discovered that his two youngest children, Walter and Charley, were missing. He began search, and before night learned that two strange men, with a horse and wagon, had passed his house and had induced the boys to take a ride. After driving about eight miles toward the city the men deserted Walter. He was found and returned to his father's house. But Charley has never since been seen by his parents.

The community became alarmed, and with the entire police

force of Philadelphia a vigorous search was begun. On the evening of July 4 Mr. Ross received the first unsigned letter from the abductors. It was in a disguised handwriting, and contained much purposely-incorrect spelling, as the following extract will show:

"July 3. Mr. Ros: be not uneasy you son Charley bruster be all writ we is got him and no powers on earth can deliver out of our hand. you wil hav two pay us befor you git him from us, and pay us a big cent to. . . . if any aproch is maid to his hidin place that is the signil for his instant anihilation."

CHARLEY ROSS.
(From a Photograph.)

July 7, posters, giving an account of the abduction of Charley Ross, and offering a reward, were sent to the New York police. All this time the Philadelphia police, as well as that of the cities and towns in Pennsylvania, Delaware and New Jersey, continued their search for the abductors. In a short time the people of the entire country became interested in the matter, and all did what they could to discover the criminals and restore the missing child. Much sympathy was also expressed in Europe, and wherever newspapers were read the fate of Charley Ross was discussed and deplored.

A long correspondence followed with the unknown abductors, through the post and press. They frankly admitted that Charley had been stolen with the hope of getting a large ransom. They declared that he would not be returned until the money was paid.

Acting upon the advice of the authorities and friends, Mr. Ross decided not to pay the sum asked, but to offer large rewards for the recovery of the child, and the capture and conviction of the kidnappers. The Mayor of Philadelphia, at the request of many citizens, offered a reward of $20,000 for the arrest and conviction of the abductors and the restoration of the child to its parents. The publication of this reward drew a letter from the abductors, dated " Philadelphia, July 24," in which they said :—

" We have him so that we feel at ease against all the detective force in the country ever feritin him out. the authorities have offered $20,000 for the recovery of the child an detection of us if they had yu interest at hart this would be the worst thing they could do. this is only oferin a reward for the sacrifice of yu child."

The abductors continued the correspondence for a long time, and made many attempts to induce Mr. Ross to pay them $20,000 for Charley's return. Finally the correspondence closed, and the search proved fruitless.

The first information received in Philadelphia that there was any clew known in New York was through a telegram received on the evening of August 2, as follows :

" *Chief of Police of Philadelphia :*—Send detective here with original letters of kidnappers of Ross child ; think I have information.
"GEO. W. WALLING,
" *Superintendent of New York Police.*"

The next day Captain Heins, of Philadelphia, and Mr. Joseph Ross, brother of Charley Ross's father, came to New York with the original letters of the abductors. They met me at police headquarters.

" We hope that you at least have some trustworthy information," said Captain Heins.

" I think I have," I replied. " Through Captain Henry Hedden, of the Thirteenth Police District, I have heard of a man who professes to know who the abductors are. I will send for Captain Hedden." Mr. Ross was impatient to learn the news.

" Have you any idea who the abductors were ? " he asked.

" We suspect two men named William Mosher and Joseph Douglas," I answered.

" If we have their names," he exclaimed, eagerly, " they can be hunted down."

"Undoubtedly. And that is what we hope to do."

I do not think, before the publication of this autobiography, that the exact reasons have been given why William Mosher was first suspected. A policeman named Doyle came to me one day and said:

"Superintendent, I have been talking with 'Gill' Mosher, and from all I have learned I think his brother William had a hand in carrying off Charley Ross."

"Bring 'Gill' Mosher to see me, as soon as you can," I ordered.

After a great deal of searching and trouble, "Gill" Mosher was found. After asking him many questions I finally said:—

"What are your reasons for suspecting that your brother William took part in the kidnapping of Charley Ross?"

"Well," he replied, "I was approached by Bill, who asked me if I would join him in carrying off some child who had rich parents. The plan was to steal one of Commodore Vanderbilt's grandchildren."—(Some child of the late William H. Vanderbilt.)

"Which one of the children was to be taken?" I asked.

"The youngest one we could get."

"What would you do with it?"

"Hold it for a ransom."

"Where did he propose to conceal the child?"

"In a boat," said "Gill" Mosher. "And," he added, "I was to negotiate for the ransom."

"Well, what then?"

"I refused to have anything to do with the business."

"Why?"

"Because I thought there would be too much risk in trying to get money from the Vanderbilts. They are too rich, have too much power and are not the kind of people to be frightened. There would be no trouble in stealing the child, the difficulty would be in negotiating for its ransom."

"So you gave up the plan?"

"Yes; I would not run the risk of being detected. I did not think it was a safe enterprise."

"Gill" Mosher's statement made a strong impression on me. I was convinced he did not come to me from any honest motives. He hoped he might secure a share of the reward. He was a notorious character, and had been in State Prison for horse-stealing.

It was principally from the clew given by "Gill" Mosher that we followed his brother William, and Douglas. When Captain Hedden arrived at police headquarters he told Captain Heins, of Philadelphia, the story as narrated by "Gill" Mosher. He added:

"If my suspicions are correct, this William Mosher is the leader of the conspiracy. He arranged the plot and is the writer of the letters sent to Mr. Ross. I am familiar with Mosher's writing, and can tell if I see the letters whether he is the author of them."

"Before we show you the letters," said Captain Heins, "describe to us the peculiarities of Mosher's handwriting."

"He writes very rapidly," was the reply, "and is careless. He seldom finishes a page without blotting it. He often writes either above or below the lines. When he folds a letter it is in a peculiar and awkward way."

The letters were produced.

"They are his, without the shadow of a doubt!" exclaimed Hedden. "Here is the handwriting, blots and all, just as I told you. And you see for yourselves, gentlemen, that the letters are folded in a peculiar and awkward manner."

This identification of the letters seemed conclusive. It produced a profound impression upon Captain Heins and Mr. Ross.

"At last!" exclaimed Charley's uncle.

Arrangements were made with the New York detectives that the Philadelphia police should be kept informed of all that transpired, and whatever assistance could be given in Philadelphia should be forthcoming.

Captain Hedden afterwards learned that Mosher and Douglas manufactured a moth preventive, which they called "Mothee." They travelled about the country with a horse and wagon, selling this with other small articles. He also discovered that Mosher had a brother-in-law, William Westervelt, a discharged police officer, of New York, who was probably implicated in the abduction.

I wrote the following letter to Captain Heins, of Philadelphia, on August 11, 1874:

"*Dear Sir :*—The bearer, Officer Doyle, and another man, go to your city, and intend going on to Baltimore, where the family of Johnson (Mosher) lived a few weeks since. Johnson, we think, is the prime mover in the Ross abduction. Mr. Doyle and the man who is with him both know Johnson and his family well. This Johnson has a wife and four children. Sometime since he escaped from jail at Freehold, N. J., while awaiting trial for burglary. His correct name is William Mosher. It may be that we are on the wrong scent; but I think not. If they can locate Johnson's family, we can certainly find his whereabouts.

"Yours respectfully,
"GEO. W. WALLING,
"*Superintendent.*"

The search for Mosher in Baltimore and Philadelphia was disappointing, and the two men returned to New York. On the 13th I wrote again to Captain Heins, as follows:

"*Dear Sir:*—If we are right in our suspicions, and the parties that Detective Doyle and his companion are searching for in Baltimore are guilty of abducting the Ross child, in all probability the child is kept on board of a small boat, and may be in your vicinity.

"Yours, in haste,
"G. W. WALLING."

I knew that "Bill" Mosher lived on the water, and as he had been implicated in cases with river pirates this made it tolerably clear that a boat would be used by him and Douglas to evade pursuit. Pinkerton's men were engaged for awhile on the case, yet with all their endeavors they failed to discover anything relating to the mystery.

On August 24, 1874, I wrote to Captain Heins the following:

"Yours of 22d received. I am more confident than ever that the parties, Clark and Mosher, *alias* Johnson, are the parties we want. I knew before receiving your letter that they were somewhere in this vicinity. Some one has let them know that they are being looked after, and that is the reason for their change of tone. They are frightened, and would, I believe, make terms very moderate, provided they could be assured of safety. There is no danger of their going to Europe; they have no money, and Mosher's wife and children would keep him here. Of this you can assure Mr. Ross, providing I am right as to the parties, and I have no doubt of it. I think it would be well for Mr. Ross to keep in communication (if possible) with them.

"Yours, in haste,
"GEO. W. WALLING,
"*Superintendent of Police.*"

I sent for Westervelt, the brother-in-law of Mosher, on August 18, and asked him to assist me in finding the men and recovering the child. After considering the matter a few days he agreed to help the police. I freely confess that Westervelt's entrance into the Charley Ross case was unfortunate. I well knew his relationship to Mosher. "Set a thief to catch a thief" may be a good method, but I am forced to say it failed utterly in this case. I thought, as did many with whom I consulted, that Westervelt could be induced, by a share in the reward, to inform where the child was. I do not think Westervelt knew where Charley Ross was, but that he took some part in the abduction I feel positive to this day.

The following letter was sent by me to Captain Heins on September 11:

"*Dear Sir:*—Since writing you this A.M. I have seen Westervelt; he says he knows nothing of the whereabouts of Mosher. He says Mosher lived in your city, about four months ago, on Monroe, near Third Street, and that he had a stable between Third and Fourth streets, in some street, name not known, but the third or fourth street from Monroe, towards Washington Avenue. The stable was an old wooden building with very large doors, and was near Third Street. A wagon answering to the description you gave me was in said stable at that time, and may be there yet, but probably not; they kept in said stable a dark bay horse. He is confident the horse has been sold, but does not know to whom. I showed him the drawing of the wagon you gave me, and he says he could not make a better one had he the wagon before him, except that he thinks this would not be quite so much rounded at the top.

"Yours, etc.,
"GEO. W. WALLING,
"*Superintendent.*"

It was ascertained that a family named Henderson had lived at No. 235 Monroe Street, Philadelphia. This proved to be the name Mosher assumed when he went to Philadelphia. It was also learned that Joseph Douglas had lived with the family, and that Mosher's wife and children removed to New York on August 18. It was also discovered that there had been an old stable on Marriott's Lane, which had been since torn down. A part of this Mosher rented, and there he kept his horse and wagon.

An effort was made to find some of Mosher's writing. Westervelt was asked to procure a letter or any paper that he knew Mosher had written; but he would not or could not get any.

It is certain that when Westervelt was aware that we were on the track of his brother-in-law he put Mosher and Douglas on their guard. By means of newspaper advertisements he kept the kidnappers thoroughly informed as to the methods to be employed by the police in tracking them. He never would admit that he had seen the men, but always professed that he was looking for them. I finally learned that he had seen them, and told him so. Then he admitted that he had met them twice, but asserted that he could not have informed me of the meeting in time to have been of any service.

It was one of the most delicate and difficult of cases. I sometimes dreaded that if probed too closely one of the ruffians would murder the child, so as to efface all traces of the crime of abduction. The tracking of Mosher and Douglas was continuous, and a weary chase it was, I having followed what I thought were traces of them for days and nights. I was often close to them. The vigilance of the kidnappers was that of those who were hunted. The innumerable bays and water-courses about New York gave them the fullest opportunity for concealment. I had the evidence that the men rarely stopped in one place more than one night in their boat. Often we were so near to their hiding-place that we passed close by it in the dusk. But the search for the men continued; they were hunted as relentlessly as by blood-hounds. So hard were they pressed by the police of New York that they were forced to remain almost wholly on the water, visiting the city at rare intervals, and then in the night. Soon they were brought to want, because of this, and resorted to burglary.

At two A.M. on December 14, the night pitch-dark, cold and wet, Mosher and Douglas attempted to rob the summer residence of Judge Van Brunt, at Bay Ridge, overlooking the Narrows. When they entered the Judge's house, which was unoccupied, a burglar-alarm telegraph rang a bell in the house of Mr. J. H. Van Brunt, the judge's son, who lived across the way. He roused his son and two men-servants, and arming them, the party stood guard at the front and back doors of the judge's residence.

"Now, boys," said Mr. Van Brunt, "we have work to do and must understand each other. We must capture the thieves if we can without killing them, but if they resist we will have to defend ourselves. Albert, you and Scott stand before the front door; Frank and I will take the rear, and whatever happens afterwards let us remain in the positions we first take up, because if we move around we will be certain in the dark to shoot one another instead of the thieves. Whichever way they come out, let the two who meet them take care of them as best they can. If they come out and scatter both ways then we will all have a chance to work."

The men took their places and watched for an hour, while the thieves went all over the house. At length they came down to the basement. Through the window of the pantry Mr. Van Brunt could see the faces of the two burglars. He could have shot them as they stood, with perfect safety to himself, but he did not wish to take life unless forced to do so. He was getting numb from the effects of the cold.

"Frank," he said to his hired man, "we may as well push things. Take the key and open the back door quickly."

The burglars heard the rattle of the key in the key-hole. Instantly they put out their light and began to ascend the basement or cellar stairs. Mr. Van Brunt heard their footsteps.

"To the trap-door of the cellar, Frank!" whispered Mr. Van Brunt.

The lock of the door had been broken. The door was soon opened, and the form of a man started up, followed by the head of another.

"Halt!" shouted Mr. Van Brunt.

Two pistol-shots flashed almost in his face. They did no injury. He fired at the first man, and a cry of agony followed.

The other man fired and ran towards the front of the house. There he met young Mr. Albert Van Brunt, at whom he fired two shots, missing him. Before he could fire again Albert shattered his arm with a blow from his shot-gun.

With an oath the thief retreated, when the elder Mr. Van Brunt shot him in the back. He staggered for an instant and fell dead.

None of the Van Brunt party were injured, while the burglars were riddled with shot and bullets. One was dead, with his empty revolver under his head. The other lived about two hours. The neighbors came rushing to the place. Water was given the dying man.

"Who are you, and where did you come from?" several asked.

"Men, I won't lie to you," said the dying man. "My name is Joseph Douglas, and that man over there is William Mosher. Mosher lives in New York City. I have no home. I am a single man and have no relatives, except a brother and sister, whom I have not seen for twelve or fifteen years. Mosher is a married man and has five children."

Believing himself to be mortally wounded, he said:

"I have $40 in my pocket. I wish to be buried with it. I made it honestly. *It's no use lying now. Mosher and I stole Charley Ross from Germantown.*"

DEATH OF THE ABDUCTORS.

"Why did you steal him?"

"To make money."

"Who has the child now?"

"Mosher knows all about the child; ask him."

"Mosher is dead."

The men then lifted Douglas up so that he could see his dead partner.

"God help his poor wife and family!" he exclaimed.

"Can you tell us where the child is?" he was again asked.

"God knows I tell you the truth," he replied. "I don't know where he is. Mosher knew."

The same question was repeated. "Superintendent Walling knows all about us and was after us, and now he shall have us. Send him word. The child will be returned home, safe and sound, in a few days."

"How did you get here?" he was asked.

"We came over in a sloop which is down in the cove," he answered. "Please do not ask me any more questions. It hurts me to talk or move."

Writhing in agony, lying on the ground, drenched with rain, surrounded by darkness, the life of the miserable man who had caused so much sorrow and outraged the feelings of every parent in the country, went out. He died like a dog, as was fit.

On the morning of December 14, Justice Church, of Bay Ridge, sent me a telegram, saying that Mosher and Douglas had been killed. I at once dispatched Detective Silleck to Bay Ridge, who, as soon as he saw the dead bodies, said:

"That is Joe Douglas, and that is 'Bill' Mosher. Take the glove off his left hand and you will find a withered finger."

The glove was removed, and the finger found, as indicated. The first finger of the left hand was withered away to a point, the result of a felon.

Little Walter Ross was brought on from Philadelphia, and fully identified the two bodies as they lay in the Brooklyn morgue. But this was all; Charley Ross was never found. I think he is dead. I can conceive of no possible reason why, after the two kidnappers had been killed and Westervelt was in prison, Charley Ross should not have been returned had he been alive. The promised immunity from punishment and the reward offered by the Mayor of Philadelphia are good reasons for supposing that the child, if alive, would have been returned to its parents.

CHAPTER XVI.

BURGLARS.—HOW THEY WORK.—PRETTY SERVANT GIRLS.—A LITTLE PIECE OF SCARLET RIBBON.—THIEVES ON THE ROOF.—A LEAP IN THE DARK.—"STUTTERING JOHN" ASHORE IN JERSEY.—HOW PICKPOCKETS OPERATE.—A MAN WHO KNEW IT ALL.—ARRESTED AT SIGHT.—HOW I WAS FINED.—THIEVES WHO TALKED FROM THEIR CELL DOORS.

THERE can be no doubt that burglary is a fine art, when considered in all its various phases. The night is usually the time when the burglar plies his vocation, and his operations are upon the property of all classes in the community. Any one who possesses anything worth stealing is liable to be paid an unexpected and unwelcome visit by the house-breaker. In a city like New York the number of criminals of this class is very large. Drinking or sleeping is their usual avocation during the daytime, while at night they are engaged in plundering their unfortunate neighbors. The complete prevention of their depredations has always seemed to me to be impossible, and the only safeguard against their operations is incessant vigilance on the part of store-keepers and householders.

To the uninitiated it may seem to be almost an impossibility in some cases for burglars to gain impressions of the keys of a large store, for instance. But there is nothing easier or simpler. Having selected the store to be robbed, the rascals will first attempt to fit a key to the door from their own stock-in-trade. If they succeed, there will be no further trouble. If not, they will watch for the opening of the store in the morning by the clerk or porter, and follow him in as if in a great hurry to buy some small article. It happens ten times out of twelve that the clerk lays his bunch of keys down on the counter while he goes for the article required. A lump of wax, kept handy for the purpose, disposes of that little matter in a trice, and the key is made at leisure. But suppose the clerk should place the key on a desk inside the office? Even that is a difficulty easily surmounted. The thief very politely asks leave of the clerk to address a few letters which he is desirous of mailing immediately.

"Certainly, sir," says the unsuspicious clerk, bowing his customer into the office. With the wax in his hand the thief accomplishes his work in a second.

It is queer, though, that people will nearly always furnish their front doors and windows with the most formidable bolts, bars and locks, while they will leave the back entrances to their buildings almost entirely unguarded. This is just what the burglar wants. He doesn't care to " work " on the front street. The rear of the building is more secluded, and the thief is less liable to interruption. Should the door prove too formidable an obstacle, the window is frequently pried open with an ingeniously constructed " jimmy." Still another way is for the burglar to gain admission to a house or store in the daytime, and conceal himself in some unoccupied room until dark. Then he emerges from his hiding-place and ransacks the place at his own sweet will.

Servant girls are often in league with thieves, and make things easy for their confederates by admitting them into houses after the family has retired to rest. One such instance I well remember, and as it was nearly the first case in which Inspector Byrnes, now chief of the detective force, was engaged, it deserves to be told. A burglary, committed in a very skilful manner, had occurred on Madison Avenue. It was very evident the perpetrators were expert hands at the business. The house had been entered, a safe unlocked, the money and jewels extracted, and yet there was nothing to show how it was all done. Despite all this, however, Inspector Byrnes (he was a patrolman then) found a piece of scarlet ribbon which had been caught between the sides of the safe and the inner drawer. It was not large, only a few shreds, but it suggested an idea to the detective. He put it carefully away in his pocket-book and closely scrutinized the apparel of the dozen or more female servants employed in the house. Only one of them, he noticed, was partial to wearing scarlet ribbon. She was a pretty girl, and was seen by the officer on several occasions to wear a ribbon the color of which was the same as that found in the safe. He waited and watched. One day, some time after the robbery, she announced to her employer that she had obtained another situation which suited her better. She left in the middle of the night. Byrnes "shadowed" her, and rode on the front platform of the Madison Avenue car which she boarded. Going down town she left the car at Canal Street, and hurrying along towards the East River, entered a small tenement house on one of the side streets. Byrnes was still at her heels, and with the aid of two policemen the pretty servant girl, together with two well-known rascals, were captured. Completely cornered, they admitted that the girl had only taken the situation in order that they might more easily rob the house.

INSPECTOR HENRY V. STEERS.
(From a Photograph.)

It should be remembered that burglars always have in mind a way to escape if they are discovered or interrupted. As a rule, they will sooner run than fight. But get one of them in a corner and he will fight to the end in order to escape arrest. Searching for a thief in a house on a dark night is what tries the nerve of a police officer. He often gets in a tight place, taking fearful risks.

I remember one experience which fell to the lot of Inspector Steers. An alarm had been given and Steers found his man on the second story of a high building, picking out an assortment of valuable articles to carry away with him. Upon seeing Steers the thief leaped up the stairs towards the roof, almost like a flash of lightning, while the officer followed as best he could. All this was in the dark. Out through the scuttle upon the roof the thief and his pursuer went. Steers did not hesitate even when the fellow jumped off the side of the house. Where he was going to land he didn't know; it seemed an age before he struck, and when he did it was with a force that nearly drove his legs up into his body. But he caught his man and took him to the station-house. The next day Steers went round and took a look at the scene of his adventure of the night previous, and found that he had jumped from one roof to another, a distance of about twenty feet. He has never fully recovered from the shock, and never will.

It would be impossible for me, without going over ground that has long ago been covered, to give an account of all the big burglaries committed during my service on the force; but one or two incidents occurred in connection with such crimes which are not generally known. For instance, during what I might call a period of "off-duty," I was standing on the dock at Keyport, N. J., looking at the craft in the bay. The month of February on the coast is rather a stormy one, and on this particular day a fierce gale was blowing, accompanied by snow squalls. Through the rather obscured atmosphere I made out a small boat struggling with the waves. She was close hauled, and it was with great difficulty she could be kept on her course. True to my instincts and training (for my first years of service on the police force had developed a certain amount of watchfulness), I watched the boat with considerable interest. She was too small for a fisherman's or oysterman's craft, and did not look like a "clammer"; it was not the season for pleasure boats; and as she came nearer the shore I determined to watch her. After some time she was almost upon the sand. The individual in charge seemed unused to the place, and finally the wind drove her on the beach near by. Concealing myself behind a convenient bulkhead, I watched the crew of three as they walked up the beach. They presented a pitiable condition—drenched to the skin and stiff with the cold.

"Perhaps," I said to myself, "they are a lot of fellows on a spree who have been blown up the bay."

But it wasn't natural for men to start upon a pleasure cruise in February. Scanning the party closely, I noticed that one of the men had a familiar look about him. It was more in the way he

ASHORE IN JERSEY.

carried himself than in his face, for at this time it was too dark for me to distinguish his features. The storm showed no signs of abating, but blew harder every minute. The men, therefore, I knew, would be obliged to seek shelter somewhere or other, and as the whole thing looked suspicious I thought it would do no harm to keep an eye on them.

When they had taken to the main street I carelessly examined the boat. Had they run off with her? Were there any stolen goods in her? Should I try to gain admittance? They might have left a man on board. I therefore thought it wiser to leave the boat alone for the present and follow the men. The villagers— for Keyport in those days was a smaller place than it is now—were also curious. A man named Poling, noticing the strange arrival, wanted to find out the character of the craft. He strolled on board, and looking through the windows of the little cabin—the door was locked—saw what he thought were bolts of silk. He and I were acquainted, and on making the discovery he came directly to me with the information. I was then absolutely certain that things were "crooked." The crew of the boat had gone to one of the hotels in the place, and there I went. Entering cautiously, who should I see, warming himself by the stove, but John Monahan, commonly called "Stuttering John"—a well known river thief. John and I had come in contact some years previously. Though he did not speak, my recognition of him was immediate. Perhaps he was not quite thawed out, for he did not notice my opening the door. Having put my head in, I immediately withdrew it. With "Stuttering John" there were three other men. One I knew by his face as a river pirate. The others I did not recognize.

I was well acquainted with Keyport oystermen, a brave and honest set of men, and I enrolled several of them to help me. At once I returned to the hotel, and, facing "Stuttering John," told him he was a thief, and that I should arrest him and his party. John gave in at once, and offered no resistance, and his companions followed the action of their leader. We held them prisoners at the hotel, sitting up with them all night.

On the next morning we escorted them to the steam-boat and took them to New York. Captain Arrowsmith was in command of the steamer, and at my request he ran the boat near the dock, so that I could jump off first. When I had done that the boat was backed off into the stream. I ran as hard as I could to Mr. Matsell's office, and reported my haul. I was so much out of breath that I had some trouble in making my matter plain. Strange to say, my sudden entrance into the office had interrupted Mr. Cunard, of the Cunard line of steamers, who was explaining to Mr. Matsell the particulars of the robbery of a bonded warehouse in Jersey City, two nights before. When I had concluded, Mr. Cunard said: "The goods stolen were silks."

"I have got them," I cried—"the thieves and the property." It was one of those lucky accidents. At once Mr. Matsell touched his bell, and several officers were called, who accompanied me to the North River. I signalled the captain of the steamer. The boat made a landing and the thieves were taken to the chief's office.

Now that I knew the offence had been committed in New Jersey, the prisoners had to be conveyed there. Of course we had secured the silks in the boat. "Stuttering John" obtained the services of a lawyer, who served a habeas corpus, declared that we had no legal right to convey Monahan from New York to New Jersey, and insisted that a warrant from the governor, or extradition papers, were necessary. I had to show that the shortest way from Keyport to Jersey City was via New York, by steamer, as there were no railways in those days. I had the party lodged in the Hudson County jail. Justice, even Jersey justice, is not always swift or sure. Some of the thieves escaped. Monahan's punishment was not in proportion to his crime. The silks were worth $2500, and with the exception of one piece all were recovered.

How Monahan and his party had found themselves at Keyport was afterwards explained. The robbery of the bonded warehouse took place at Jersey City. The goods had to be carried across by the thieves to New York for concealment and subsequent disposal. In crossing the North River and trying to round the Battery, the gale took them and they were carried down the bay. The weather was so thick that they did not know where they were going, and at last they were blown clean twenty-six miles from New York, glad enough to make a landing anywhere. They had been probably all night on the water, and without fire or food, and had suffered a great deal. A man subsequently claimed the boat, which had been stolen.

There is an amusing sequence to this story, not so amusing to me at the time, as it will be to the reader. I had to pay for the supper and breakfast of the prisoners, the escort of oystermen for their time and the fare of the whole crowd on the boat—amounting in all to $40, a good deal of money for a policeman to pay out of his pocket in those days. The owner of the silks would not reimburse me; the bonded warehouse people respectfully declined; the great Cunard Company was unwilling to pay, all preferring to let the man who had restored the property suffer by their gain; so this little bit of detective work was carried out at my own private expense. This, however, I did not so much mind. The sense of justice done compensated me. I suppose that my subsequent promotion was due to several fairly clever pieces of work of somewhat the same character.

On the occasion of the public reception offered to the Japanese ambassadors upon their arrival in New York in 1860, a tremendous crowd assembled in the streets. On Broadway, especially in the neighborhood of the Metropolitan Hotel, the sidewalks were thronged. As captain of the detective force, it was my duty to be constantly in the streets, and to do my best to prevent those depredations on the public which are always committed on such occasions; for a large crowd in the streets or elsewhere is the pickpockets' carnival.

It happened that on the very evening the Japanese arrived I had about my person a large amount of money. I was not in uniform, and in order to mix better with the crowd and be unobserved, I donned a rough suit of clothes; and, taking my roll of bank bills, stuffed it down my boot-leg, tucking my trousers inside my boots. I mingled freely with the people, and saw that my men were properly distributed and on the alert.

When on the edge of the crowd, near the Metropolitan Hotel, I noticed a very well-dressed and pompous-looking man, who was elbowing his way through the throng. He wore a handsome gold chain, to which a big watch was attached; for I could see the outline of it in his waistcoat pocket. His coat was wide open; in fact, he was making a display of his jewellery. He was a walking invitation for a pickpocket.

As he pushed up near me, I said, very quietly, to him, "My friend, if you go into this crowd in that manner you will be very likely to lose your watch."

The gentleman turned on me in an aggrieved manner, as if resenting my officiousness, and said, "Who are you?"

"No matter who I am," was my reply; "I only warn you that you will pretty certainly lose your watch if you go in there. That's all."

"Sir," was his angry retort, "I want to know who you are, and why you presume to give me advice?"

"Well, if you desire to know, I am an officer, and belong to the detective department," was my answer.

"All right!" he retorted spitefully, "if I do lose my watch I shall never ask you to recover it."

"Very well," I replied, in perfect good humor; and a moment afterwards I had left him and was working my way into the crowd.

On the very next day, I was sitting at my desk in the basement of the detective office examining some reports, when who should I see approaching me but this very gentleman, who had, notwithstanding my advice, insisted on decorating his manly breast with a conspicuous gold watch and chain. At once, from his expression, which was not quite so pompous and self-assured as on the evening before, I made out that something was wrong. The gentleman asked quite meekly:

"Can I see the captain? I have a complaint to make."

"I presume so, sir," was my reply. "You lost your watch and chain before the Metropolitan Hotel last evening, at about seven o'clock."

"I did," was his astonished answer; "but how do you know that?"

"I am the identical person," I replied, "who took every measure to caution you yesterday evening, and you said to me that if you lost your watch I would be the last person you would come to in order that you might recover it; but it looks as if you have come to me after all."

The gentleman seemed to be quite taken aback. His loss annoyed him exceedingly, and there was certainly reason for it, because it had been entirely his own fault.

"Do you think you could get the watch and chain back?" he inquired.

"I do not know, but you may be assured I will try and do my very best," I answered.

It was of course my duty to make every exertion to recover any stolen property, but my pride in this particular matter made me work very hard to get that watch. It was months before I had to give it up, and I regret to say the gentleman never saw his watch and chain again.

Persons who have never been robbed by a pickpocket believe that they enjoy a certain immunity from such depredations, and flatter themselves that it is owing to their own superior cleverness and watchfulness that they have hitherto escaped. But experience tells me that even those most on their guard suffer at times from the operations of pickpockets. It is never safe to get into a crowd in New York; that is, if you have anything valuable in your pockets, for a crowd, as I have said before, is the pickpocket's opportunity. Thieves in this particular calling work in parties of from three to five. One of the rascals will tip a man's hat as if by accident, while another jostles him. The man, who is afraid his hat will fall off, raises his hands to secure it. A third person pushes him, and the fourth pickpocket, called "the wire," takes the watch or the pocket-book. Prior to all this, the man to be robbed has been carefully looked over, and the way his watch is secured or the location of his wallet has been determined. If the wallet is in a deep pocket in his trousers two hands may be used by the pickpocket, one to lift or press the wallet upwards, and two fingers of the other hand to extract the treasure. A wallet put in a pistol pocket is readily lifted in a crowd. When a watch is to be taken, the thief, with his thumb and forefinger, forces the ring of the watch open, which disconnects the chain, and as this springs readily the time-piece is easily removed. The old-fashioned way of keeping the watch and chain in the fob pocket is the safest, for then nothing is exposed. The best place to keep money is in a pocket inside of the waistcoat, which should be secured by a button. Then when the waistcoat is fastened up it is very difficult for a pickpocket to get at the money. Nevertheless, I have known wallets to have been taken when placed inside waistcoat pockets. There is but one rule for those who venture into a crowd in New York, and this is to leave watch, money and all valuables at home, and never to carry more than some small change.

In the street-cars losses are frequent. A crowded car is just arranged for a pickpocket's work. The man to be robbed is hanging on to a strap, and before and behind him is a thief, the one who is to be the "wire" being generally provided with an overcoat or duster, which he carries on his arm. In the swaying of the car the opportunity is found. Nothing is easier than for a pickpocket to filch a diamond breastpin under such circumstances. If the diamond be of some value the wearer of it will have been followed many times, and at all hours. The pickpockets wait patiently for the favorable opportunity. A half dozen futile efforts may have been made before the thieves are finally successful.

I have never had my pocket picked, though in the course of my duty I have been in all parts of New York, and of course a great deal in crowds, and in such dress as did not show that I had any connection with the police force. Once when in a crowded car in the Bowery I saw the car invaded by a rush of men who I knew were pickpockets. I at once addressed them in a short speech, which was neither very chaste or polite. They recognized me at the very first word and a stampede was instantaneous.

While I was captain of the detectives, the losses inflicted on the public by pickpockets, when crowds were assembled, were so serious at one time, occasioning so many complaints, that I adopted a rule that has been kept up ever since, which was to arrest all well-known pickpockets when seen in a crowd, or in the vicinity of large assemblies, and to keep them in durance until the crowd had dispersed. When this method was at first sanctioned, a well-known criminal lawyer came to police headquarters and protested against my arresting suspicious characters, insisting that I had no right to do so, as they had committed no crime, and, as he argued, "they were not amenable to justice." It was, he stated, a base usurpation of the rights of free men, etc., etc. This gentleman's peroration was peculiarly dramatic. "I have advised my clients," he said, "to shoot the officers down the very next time they arrest them, when the latter have not been engaged in committing any crime."

I do not think what this advocate said impressed me very much, for my reply was, "Pshaw! Two can play at that game."

"You know you have no legal right to make such arrests unless you have some charges against them, and they can bring suit against you for false imprisonment," he continued.

"Yes, sir," I answered, "I know that, and I will pay all the judgments your clients may get." So the matter ended.

The excellence of this method became immediately evident, for the practice of the trade of a pickpocket in a crowd became more difficult. As he might be arrested on sight, he found it wisest to be absent.

The female pickpocket abounds in New York, but she preys only on her own sex. The habit women have of keeping their porte-monnaie in their hands is a constant source of temptation. As it cannot always be kept in the hand, the female pickpocket watches patiently until the woman puts it in the pocket of her dress, which, though not visible to men, is at once located by a woman who is a thief, and a porte-monnaie is much more readily abstracted from a woman's pocket than from a man's. As women rarely go into streets where crowds assemble, it is in cars and principally in the stores where these female pickpockets carry on their business. The work is generally done by two women, and shop-lifting often enters into the line of business of these female depredators. When an old, or even a young lady, carries too ostentatiously in the street a bag containing her purse, it is occasionally snatched from her by some young thief, who trusts to his legs to escape capture. In such cases it has generally turned out that the amount of money the lady is in the habit of carrying has been the object of study beforehand.

I was fined ten days' pay once for violating the law, and that, too, when I was at the head of the machinery established to enforce it. How it happened the reader will learn from the following story:

Detective "Dick" King reported at headquarters one day that he had found a lot of bonds, payment of which had been stopped because they had been stolen. We found that some time before, on January 17, 1875, the Adams Express Company had been robbed. The company had kept quiet about it, and instead of confiding the matter to us, had put it in the hands of private detectives. Some persons prefer that way. But when the bonds were found by Detective King I put him on the case. He tracked the missing papers and laid his hand on the thieves. Chief of these was Daniel Haurey, the man who drove the Adams Express wagon containing the safe on the night of the robbery. This man carted express packages across the North River to the Jersey City depot. With miscellaneous packages of all sizes and shapes, there was a little iron safe containing money, bonds and jewellery. Investigations at the Adams Express Company's office revealed the facts that this safe was securely locked; that it was put in Haurey's wagon; that Haurey drove off; that the safe was apparently never

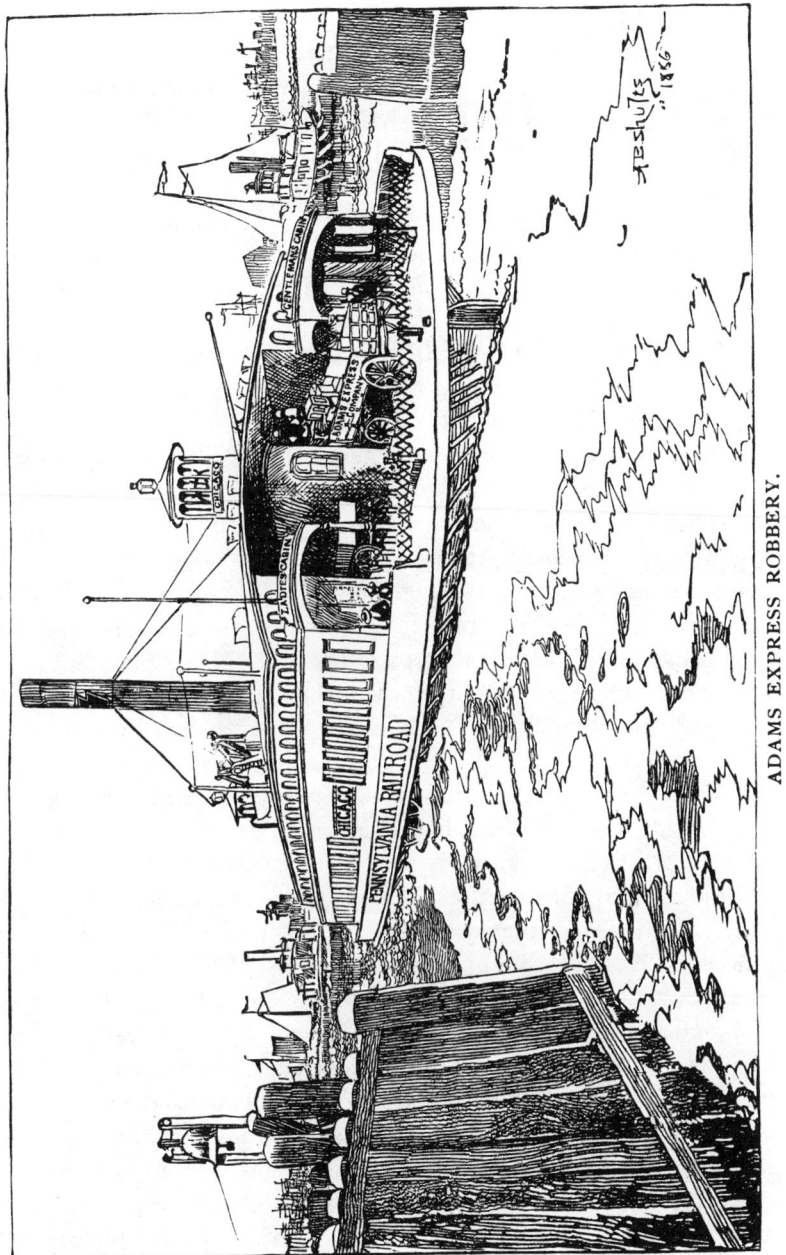

ADAMS EXPRESS ROBBERY.

received in Jersey City; and that Haurey came back without it and swore he delivered it. The loss was over $50,000.

When a portion of the missing goods was found, we arrested Haurey and a crony of his named John Sweeney, and confined them in adjoining cells, cautiously letting them know that they were neighbors. It was not long before they began to talk, each from his cell door. Our detectives overheard them, of course, and the robbers, as usual, "gave themselves away." It was disclosed that the bonds and most of the money were concealed under the flag stones in the cellar of a plumber's shop somewhere in Nassau Street.

We confronted Sweeney with his crime, and told him so much that he concluded his "pal" had "peached;" and then he was eager to tell all he knew. He said that some of the "stuff" had been sold to a receiver by the name of Moses Ehrich. Moses was arrested, gave bail, and fled to Canada.

From Sweeney's disclosures, it was ascertained that when Haurey got over to the Jersey City depot he shoved the little safe up nearer the wagon seat, flung a horse blanket over it, and failed to deliver it. He then drove to a secluded place, where the robbers broke open the safe with tools and obtained the contents, and on the return the safe was thrown in the river. Sweeney took and secreted the plunder in the Nassau Street cellar, then Haurey drove directly back to the New York office, to escape suspicion.

Sweeney went on the stand; and Haurey was convicted within a month of the time of the robbery, and was sent to prison for five years. Most of the valuables were recovered.

Now as to my fine. After Haurey's conviction, his counsel, A. Oakey Hall, asked that sentence be deferred. The request was granted. He then sent up a charge against me, enclosing a written communication to the police commissioners, alleging that I had violated the law by keeping Haurey over Sunday after arresting him, before taking him to a police court. The law requires that a man under arrest shall be taken before a police magistrate at the next sitting of the court. I did not send Haurey up for examination till Monday morning, because I had reason to believe that greater promptness would defeat the ends of justice. I was morally, and Hall was technically, right. He asked me before the commissioners if I did not know I was violating a clause of the police law.

"Yes," I said; "I knew it was a technical violation."

"How came you to violate the law?" he asked, with some harshness.

"I did it purposely and deliberately," I replied, "in order that I might insure not only the conviction of the prisoner, but the recovery of the property. I had reason to fear that if I brought the prisoner to court on Sunday the property would escape from its hiding-place."

The charge made against me was sustained by the police commissioners. They knew I was right, but found that the law did not allow them any option, for it imperatively prescribed a positive penalty—either dismissal or a fine. They fined me ten days' pay—about $160. The law ought to give commissioners some option in cases like this. John Hoey, of the express company, offered to refund the money to me; but I declined to receive it without the consent of the police board. Of course their own action prevented their giving their sanction to my being reimbursed; so that was the last of it.

After Haurey's liberation he sought fresh fields. He finally attained the position of a police-marshal in New Orleans, his native city, and about Christmas time, 1884, he got into a quarrel and was killed.

CHAPTER XVII.

THE COMPLETE STORY OF THE ROBBERY OF A. T. STEWART'S GRAVE.—WORK OF THE GHOULS.—CONCEALMENT OF THE BODY.—DEMAND FOR A RANSOM.—MRS. STEWART'S DISTRESS.—JUDGE HILTON'S REFUSAL TO PAY THE ROBBERS.—FINAL NEGOTIATIONS.—THE BONES OF THE MILLIONAIRE EXCHANGED FOR MONEY UPON A HILL IN WESTCHESTER COUNTY.—RESTORED AND BORNE TO THE CATHEDRAL VAULT.—THE GOBLIN BELLS.

"My God!"

This exclamation sprang from the lips of a man unused to so vigorous an utterance, and he turned pale and clutched the tall iron fence near him. The speaker was Frank Parker, the assistant-sexton of old St. Mark's Church, whose grounds are bounded by Second Avenue, Stuyvesant, Tenth and Eleventh streets—a church once fashionable, and still rich and powerful.

It was an hour after dawn one wet and gloomy Wednesday in November, 1878. Parker had just entered the ancient churchyard, and he stood as if paralyzed as his eyes were fixed on new earth that had been upturned at the mouth of the vault where the remains of A. T. STEWART, the merchant-millionaire, had been deposited thirty months before.

"My God!" he repeated, with a tremor of fear and grief in his voice. "They've done it at last!"

He understood that the Stewart tomb had been probably robbed; that he was one of the only two or three men who knew its exact location; that the horrible crime would convulse the city; and that he would be suspected of participating in it by those who did not know him. He stood a minute gazing nervelessly, and then gathering up his thoughts, he walked across the grass to the tell-tale heap of fresh clay. Thence he ran and told his superior officer, Sexton Hamill, who was still in his home near by on Tenth Street.

Hamill hurried to the spot, and descended into the vault.

There he found his fears confirmed—it had been rifled of the remains of the dead millionaire. Then he ran over to the great store, a block up Fourth Avenue, rushing breathless into the glass office, only to find that Judge Hilton had not yet arrived. The sexton did not wait. He at once called a cab and drove to the judge's house, next door to Stewart's marble palace on Thirty-fourth Street. He gave the butler a message that his business

was of extreme urgency, and the master of the house soon made his appearance. The sexton exclaimed:

"The vault has been robbed, sir; Mr. Stewart's body has been taken away!—I am sorry."

The lawyer made no reply. He thought a moment, took a chair, and then without asking his visitor to be seated, looked long and earnestly at him. The sexton was ill at ease. He stood with furtive eyes and fidgeted with his cap. "All gone; no traces left as I can see," he added, to relieve his embarrassment. Hilton still regarded him fixedly.

"You say you are 'sorry' such a thing should happen?" he suddenly asked, cross-examining.

"Why, yes, sir; very sorry, of course."

"'Sorry,' eh?" repeated the judge, with sarcastic emphasis. "That's singular."

"Singular!" said the sexton, quickly looking up. Then he saw what was in the judge's mind, and he regretfully added: "Will you come over and look for yourself, sir?"

"No; I'll go down to police headquarters," replied the judge, reaching for his coat.

Hamill hurried down town and went to the vault again. "Sexton right here for twenty years," he said, bitterly, "and a member of the church and living an upright life, to be suspected now of this horrid thing!"

I was not at headquarters when Judge Hilton got there. When I did arrive of course I was amazed. It was the first time I had ever seriously considered a crime of that sort. I went over and examined the premises. The vault was in the centre of the yard, east of the church, and seemed, prior to the digging, to have been unmarked and concealed from sight. It would be impossible to imagine a more exposed or difficult location for a grave-robbery. An iron fence, ten feet high, runs around the yard. The members of many old New York families were buried here, the Stewart vault being flanked by those of Thomas Bibby and Benjamin Winthrop.

The rifled vault was of brick, 10 x 15 feet and 12 feet deep; the top was covered with three feet of earth. It was entered by a square hole in the roof, from which descended twelve stone steps to the bottom. This entrance was covered with three marble slabs, and these in turn with three or four inches of sod on a level with the surrounding turf, entirely hiding any suggestion of an entrance. It did really look as if one of the sextons must have been implicated in the robbery, and on this Judge Hilton firmly insisted, as he explained:

"You don't know, I suppose, that an attempt was made to steal the body last month? Yes. On October 9th, just four weeks ago, the sexton discovered that the Stewart slab had been lifted from its bed and put back again. It had been done clumsily, and one end of the marble had been dropped on the grass; perhaps

ST. MARK'S CHURCH.—STEALING STEWART'S REMAINS.

the intruders had descended to the vault, but neither the casket nor the brick pedestal on which it rested had been tampered with. I discovered clay on the lock of the Eleventh-Street gate, like that over the vault, and I had new patent locks put on the gate, and the name-slab, which was before exposed, taken up and removed to a vacant spot some ten feet south-west and sunk in the grass to mislead other ghouls. The old place was carefully sodded over. I then hired Michael Burton, night-watchman of the livery stable across the street, to visit the churchyard every hour and warn trespassers from the enclosure, without saying anything to him about Stewart's vault. There was no disturbance, and Burton's services were dispensed with three days ago."

That is what Judge Hilton said.

We sent for Sexton Hamill next, and he came and told all he knew about it, adding to the information already in hand this:

" I can't imagine how anybody knew where that stone was. Its approximate location was known to three of us only, and even I, who knew it best, couldn't have gone straight to it the first time, on a dark night, as these villains seem to have done. They must have obtained perfect measurements of the place. Perhaps they were watching from a convenient nook when we took up the name-stone and hid it."

The night before the robbery had been a rainy one. At midnight snow fell. The police saw nobody near the yard. The persons in the adjacent houses saw no one. The Rev. Dr. Rylance had married a couple in the vestry as late as 9.30 P.M. He left at ten o'clock, walking out past the Stewart vault and noticing nothing unusual.

The robbers did their fiendish work in the blackness of the night and left hardly any clews. I put inspectors Murray and Dilks on the case. The following alarm was sent out that afternoon:

"CENTRAL OFFICE, *Nov.* 7, 1878.

" *To All:*—The remains of A. T. Stewart were last night stolen from the family vault, St. Mark's Churchyard. The casket was found broken and the body removed. The decomposition of the remains is so offensive that they cannot be concealed. This is apparent from standing at the opening of the vault this morning; consequently the body cannot be taken across the ferries or placed anywhere above ground without discovery. Cause diligent search to be made in your precinct, as the remains were evidently stolen in hope of reward.

"INSPECTOR DILKS."

The robbers seemed to have gone directly to the spot, without experimenting in surrounding sod. The decoy name-slab had not been touched. Only just enough dirt had been removed to uncover the mouth of the vault, closed by a slab three feet and a half by two feet.

Two of the coffins within the vault were of Mr. Stewart's infant children, and two of adult relatives of Mrs. Stewart. The burglars unscrewed the cover of the newest cedar-wood box, cut through the second receptacle of lead, and then forced the enclosed coffin of Mr. Stewart by breaking the locks and hinges. They tore off the costly silver inscription-plate, and carried it with them; also a piece of the velvet lining which they cut out in the shape of an irregular triangle. They left behind a new coal-shovel and a tin bull's-eye lantern.

It was thought that the body of Mr. Stewart weighed about 100 pounds; and as it was not embalmed, it was said by physicians that the flesh would liquefy soon after being exposed to the air.

Mrs. Stewart was in her seventy-eighth year, and quite ill and feeble.

On the morning after the robbery the following reward was offered:

"$25,000 REWARD!—Whereas, in the early morning of Nov. 7, 1878, the vault of the late Alexander T. Stewart, in St. Mark's Churchyard, in this city, was broken into, and his remains removed from there, the above reward is offered by direction of Mrs. A. T. Stewart, and will be paid for the return of the body and information which will convict the parties who were engaged in the outrage. Or a liberal reward will be paid for information which will lead to either of these results.

"HENRY HILTON."

The whole country was convulsed. Newspapers published page after page of comment, rumor and theory. A double guard was set over the tomb of Commodore Vanderbilt at New Dorp, Staten Island. We found out where the shovel and lantern were sold, and there the clew ended. We shadowed suspicious-looking persons; investigated newly-made graves; tracked old malefactors and made them account for their whereabouts on that eventful night.

The emotions excited by the robbery of Stewart's grave were various, even contradictory. Some, who were neither thoughtless nor heartless, were glad. A semi-anarchist newspaper said, virtually : " There is a sort of grim justice in it, and the very irony of greed, that this cruel, avaricious, hard-hearted man, who oppressed his employees, ruined his creditors and drove his poorer competitors to bankruptcy should now have his flesh drop off and his bones rattled in a thieves' bag, while the millions he earned are enjoyed by others."

Mr. Stewart began business in the very humblest way, and was his own salesman, book-keeper, porter and errand-boy. He lived over his store, in a room which served as parlor, bedroom and kitchen. He worked eighteen hours a day. He possessed an indomitable will, great industry, energy, shrewdness, and the foresight to see this week what would be needed in trade the next. He did business for cash only, told the blunt truth about his goods and sold at the cheapest possible price. He bought for cash, controlled high-priced laces, silks, ribbons, furs and gloves, and levied on the world of fashion. He defied competition, and of course ruined a good many of his rivals. Half of his clerks were broken-down merchants. He did some harm incidentally, but he offset it by much good, for he sold goods cheaper than they were ever sold in this market before; set a much-needed example of honesty, and laid the foundation of systematic and comprehensive methods which underlie the great dry-goods bazaars of which New York City boasts. He died worth $30,000,000.

He had no children that lived more than a week. He had few if any friends. His mien was forbidding. He was undersized and slim, with reddish hair, sharp, avaricious features, furrowed with care, a clear, cold, gray eye and an unfriendly, suspicious voice.

James Kealy was captain of detectives at that time, and he followed several promising clews to the end, but in vain. A lawyer named General Patrick H. Jones, who was at one time postmaster of this city, came to me one day, and in an excited tone, said : " A man who formerly served under me in the army claims to know something about the Stewart body. I believe that with proper encouragement I can get information that will lead to its recovery."

By "proper encouragement" he meant some assurance that Hilton would negotiate for it. I declined to commit myself, but I told him to go ahead, and I would call on the judge, and lay the matter before him from that point of view. I did so; the judge

NOT "PROPER ENCOURAGEMENT." 231

declared that he would never pay one cent for Mr. Stewart's bones, unless they came accompanied by the thieves in irons.

I felt and expressed my serious doubts about the correctness of the information, but Jones was persistent and wanted to work up the case and make arrangements for buying the body. He brought a letter or two, which he asserted had come from the thieves. To complete the demonstration he walked into my office a few days later with a package sent to him by express from Boston, in which was the original coffin-plate stolen with the remains. The engraver was sent for; he came and looked the plate over, and at once exclaimed: "That's the very one."

I sent to Boston and interviewed the officers of the express office; but I got no information, except that the package had been left by a lady muffled up to her eyes.

Hilton was still obdurate. He would have nothing to do with a purchase, he said, unless it included the villains themselves. As they were the party of the first part in the negotiations, they were not at all likely to be included. To complete their identification, the robbers sent a piece of paper that fitted exactly the hole in the velvet cover of the coffin. This piece of paper is now in the hands of Sexton Hamill; the coffin-plate is at police headquarters.

Hilton's suspicions in regard to the sextons were not only not confirmed, but were substantially disproved. The two men were of high personal character, and the Rev. Dr. Rylance, pastor of St. Mark's, took up their cause very warmly, giving Judge Hilton a piece of his mind, and condemning his accusation.

The authentic story of the recovery of Stewart's body has not yet been publicly told, but a gentleman who is in a position to know the exact facts recently rehearsed the narrative, and for the first time it is given here.

Two years had passed since the body was stolen, and its recovery was apparently as far off as ever. Judge Hilton had repelled the offers of the criminals to negotiate, and had resolutely opposed Mrs. Stewart's desire to meet their advances.

"We must never compound a felony," he said. "It isn't, of course, the money, but the principle. If we were to pay these infamous scoundrels, what rich man's or woman's dead body would hereafter be safe? We will never pay a cent except for the conviction of the criminals."

The position taken was morally correct, but a mourning widow could hardly be expected to regard the affair so coolly. Her affections were trampled under foot. This difference between the two seems to have been known and appreciated by the robbers, who, therefore, incessantly strove to re-open negotiations with Mrs. Stewart directly. Her nights were almost sleepless. She was well nigh driven insane.

It was towards the spring of 1881 when correspondence with the robbers was resumed.

No trace of the body or thieves was found until January of the following year, when General Patrick H. Jones, of No. 150 Nassau Street, called upon me at police headquarters. He brought with him a parcel and showed me the contents. They were the silver knobs and several of the handles belonging to the coffin in which the body had been buried. He also showed me some letters which he had received. They purported to have been written in Canada, and were signed by "Henry G. Romaine." With tne first letter a hundred-dollar bill was enclosed as a retainer for him to act as attorney for the return of the body, upon the payment of $250,000. The letter then went on to say:

> "The remains were taken before twelve o'clock on the night of the 6th and not at three o'clock on the morning of the 7th of November. They were not taken away in a carriage, but in a grocer's wagon. They were not taken to any house near the grave-yard but to one near One Hundred and Sixtieth Street. They were then enclosed in a zinc-lined trunk and left on an early morning train. They went to Plattsburg and from there to the Dominion. There they were buried. Except that the eyes have disappeared, the flesh is as firm and the features as natural as the day of the interment, and can therefore be instantly identified. The enclosed piece of paper is exactly the size of the piece of velvet taken from the coffin, while the small strip sent you will prove to be of the same piece as that on the coffin. If any additional proofs are required the plate will be sent you upon inserting the following 'personal' in the New York *Herald*:
>
> "'Canada—Send P.—Counsel.'
>
> "If you decline to act, a friend will call for the retainer sent you. When you are satisfied that the relatives of Mrs. Stewart will talk business, insert the following 'personal' in the New York *Herald*:
>
> "'Canada—Will do business—Counsel.'
>
> "Then you will hear from me again.
> "HENRY G. ROMAINE."

The package with the articles mentioned arrived a few hours before the letter. It, with the letter, was at once brought to me. Three days later the personal calling for the coffin-plate was published as directed. The following reply came:

"BOSTON, MASS., *Jan.* 31, 1879."
"P. H. JONES, *Counsel, New York City:*

"Immediately on arrival of *Herald* containing 'personal,' I decided to express the plate from this city, and thus avoid the discovery and publicity which would certainly follow the examination of the package by the Customs officials of the Dominion. Having satisfied the representatives of Mrs. Stewart of its genuineness, you will await further instructions, which will be forwarded after the insertion of the second personal:

"'Canada—Will do business—Counsel.'
"HENRY G. ROMAINE."

The coffin-plate was received from Boston, and brought at once to me at police headquarters. On the 5th of February, at the request of Judge Hilton, Mr. Jones put the second "personal" in the *Herald*, and a couple of days later Mr. Jones wrote to Romaine, agreeing to act as counsel, and saying that Judge Hilton was anxious to recover the remains. The reply which came from Boston on the 11th of February set forth the terms upon which the body would be restored. They were as follows:

"1. The amount to be paid shall be $200,000.
"2. The body will be delivered to yourself and Judge Hilton within twenty-five miles of the city of Montreal, and no other person shall be present.
"3. The money to be placed in your hands or under your control until Judge Hilton is fully satisfied, when you will deliver it to my representative.
"4. Both parties to maintain forever an unbroken silence in regard to the transaction.
"These are the first, last, and only terms which will ever receive attention.
"Having communicated the contents of this letter to Judge Hilton you will await his decision. You will inform me of that by a 'personal' in the *Herald*—
"'Canada—terms accepted.'
"Until this appears you will not hear from me again."

Judge Hilton refused to agree to the terms proposed, and, further, declined to negotiate through the medium of "personals."

"Romaine" was then written to, General Jones informing him of the condition of things. His reply was soon received, ordering Mr. Jones to break off all communication with Judge Hilton and open negotiations with Mrs. Stewart. No notice was taken of this request, but in March Judge Hilt : made an offer of $25,000 for the body. General Jones made the fact known to "Romaine," who "respectfully but firmly declined."

This closed the correspondence.

But the distracted widow and her relatives, without the consent of Judge Hilton, opened negotiations on her own account. The lawyer was still the medium of communication with the ghouls. Foiled in their first attempt to secure money, they had become partly discouraged, and now, instead of expecting $200,000, were willing to dispose of their dreadful booty for half that sum.

Mrs. Stewart, after a wakeful night, gave orders to have the offer accepted; but her representatives obtained a reduction of the price to $20,000, which sum they agreed to pay.

The conditions of the delivery were made quite as severe as those which accompanied the negotiations for the return of

THE MEETING.

Charley Ross. The criminals declined to take any chances. They did not demand that the money be flung from a flying train in a leathern bag without any guarantee, but the man with the money had to surrender himself absolutely into the hands of the robbers, trusting to their "honor."

He was to leave New York City at ten o'clock at night alone, in a one-horse wagon, and drive into Westchester County along a lonely road which the robbers indicated on a map which they sent marked. "Sometime before morning," if the man was acting in good faith, and was not accompanied or followed by detectives, he would be met and given further directions.

A young relative of Mrs. Stewart undertook the hazardous errand, and drove out into the country. Two or three times during the night he became certain that he was closely watched, but it was three o'clock when a masked horseman rode up, gave the signal agreed on, and turned the buggy up a lonely lane. The strange visitor here left him, directing him to drive on. At the end of another mile he became aware that another wagon was blocking the way. He paused. A masked man promptly appeared, and brought forward a bag to his buggy, saying, "Here 'tis; where's the money?"

"Where is the proof of identity?" asked the messenger, as the bag containing the mortal remains of A. T. Stewart was lifted into the buggy.

"Here!" said the other, holding up an irregular bit of velvet, and opening a bull's-eye lantern upon it with a click. The piece was compared with a bit of paper of the same shape which the New Yorker had brought with him to this lonely spot.

"Come, hurry up!" was the command.

The messenger obeyed by producing the money, and the robbers retired a few feet and counted it by the light of their lantern.

Then they moved off with their vehicle, and the messenger of Mrs. Stewart drove back the way he had come, glad to escape from such company.

The next night a freight car went out to Garden City containing nothing except a trunk, and on it sat the man who had spent the previous night in the loneliest part of Westchester County. An empty coffin had already been deposited in the Cathedral, and at the dead of night two men transferred the bones to it from the trunk. They then placed the coffin in an inaccessible vault beneath the dome. And now, they say, if any fiend should ever again touch, unbidden, the vault which holds the bones of the merchant-millionaire, the touch would release a hidden spring which would shake the chime of clustered bells in the tower, and send an instant alarm throughout the sleeping village.

CHAPTER XVIII.

BANK BURGLARIES.—KINGS AMONG THIEVES.—"FOUR-FINGERED JACK."—THE SATCHEL IN THE HALL.—MAKING THE CASHIER UNLOCK A BANK VAULT.—"RED" LEARY'S BRAVADO.—"IF THE FUNDS HAVE GOT TO GO, I WILL GO WITH THEM."—A HEROIC CASHIER.—A TERRIBLE DISCOVERY.—UNJUST SUSPICIONS.—THE HOLE UNDER THE PRESIDENT'S CHAIR.—THE SCHEME THAT WAS HATCHED IN A BROADWAY BILLIARD PARLOR.—SMOULDERING BAGS OF GOLD.—THE LITTLE BLACK TRUNK ON ELIZABETH STREET.—BARON SHINDELL.—BUGGINS, THE BANK MESSENGER.

THE successful bank robber is a king among thieves, and so far as the skill and cunning which he exercises are concerned, he undoubtedly earns his reputation. As a rule, it is the most intelligent members of the criminal class who drift into this branch of wickedness. Experience has demonstrated that the expert bank burglar is possessed of more than ordinary mechanical skill, and an amount of energy and patience that is phenomenal. Thousands of dollars are expended in purchasing tools, and in experimenting with new mechanical contrivances. They are enthusiastic in learning every detail of their occupation. Thus it is that every succeeding year adds to the knowledge of the criminal, and makes absolute protection against detection seem more possible.

But the most notorious bank burglars, like famous men of action, are known by their achievements rather than by their reputation among their fellows. To the burglar the sacking of a bank is as the sacking of a town to a great warrior; if he accomplishes his object without suffering a maximum of loss he is for the time peerless and much sought after by the people—or their representative, the district attorney.

There was some very curious incidents in connection with the robbery of the Hatters' Bank of Bethel, Conn. Some time before the robbery, two excellent officers on the detective force—John McCord and W. G. Elder—reported to me one day that they had seen young Jack Wright, commonly known as "Four-fingered Jack," because he had lost a thumb. Wright was a noted bank robber, and McCord and Elder, who worked together, followed him to see what he was about to do. They informed me that the rascal had entered a number of safe-stores, and had carefully examined the various styles and makes. Afterward he had gone into a tenement house on Charles Street.

"We believe, Captain," said Elder, "that Jack is up to some kind of a job. We are afraid, too, that we are known to him, and if he should see us watching we should lose him. However, he doesn't know you; you might arrest him."

"That will hardly do," I replied. "I know the fellow well by reputation. We had better shadow him further. If he has any job put up, we surely ought to be able to find it out. To arrest him now, with no proof against him, would be useless. You take me with you, and we'll watch him."

We secreted ourselves in a coal office at Charles and Hudson streets, and watched Jack's house. In a short time he came out, and I had a good view of him. "Four-fingered Jack" was a fine-looking man, tall and well built, and tastefully dressed. Leaving Elder and McCord to watch the house, I set out to follow the burglar. He was evidently bent upon a thorough and practical study of safes, for he went into nearly every establishment where they were sold. That he did not want to buy a safe was evident enough to me.

After an extended tour around the city, "Four-fingered Jack" got aboard a Fourth Avenue car. I did also, but he did not seem to recognize me. He rode as far as the terminus of the line, then at Twenty-seventh Street, where the New Haven depot stood, on the site of the building now known as the Madison Square Garden. Here he loitered for a short time and was finally joined by a light-complexioned man. The two exchanged a few words, and then, as they went aboard the New Haven train, I left them. If they had a job in hand it would be at some point east of New York, I thought.

I returned immediately to McCord and Elder, who had been watching Wright's house on Charles Street. This they continued to do for some time. Eventually, they found that their man had returned and was about to remove to some other part of the city. The difficulty now was to track him to his new lodgings. After some trouble the new quarters were discovered in the suburbs of the city, and Jack and his partner kept coming and going, always leaving town *via* the New Haven Railroad. On his last excursion he was absent three days—somewhat longer than usual. This looked suspicious. I might have sent men to follow him on the railroad, but had this been attempted, "Four-fingered Jack" would have "tumbled" at once to the fact that he was being shadowed. He was a clever rascal, and doubtless had his own spies about. Then, again, if the job were in a country town, the presence of any strangers in the place would have at once been sufficient to put Jack on the alert. On the fourth day of his absence from New York the news came to me of the robbery of $100,000 from the Hatters' Bank, of Bethel, Conn. The moment I heard of it I suspected "Four-fingered Jack."

His house in the suburbs was still under surveillance, and when he returned we immediately arrested him, together with another well-known bank burglar called "Peppermint Joe." The house was carefully searched, but, to my discomfiture, none of the stolen money was found. I telegraphed to the officers of the bank at Bethel to come on to New York, and they did.

When our prisoners were brought before the bank officers, "Four-fingered Jack" and "Peppermint Joe" were strangers to them. We sent to Bethel and brought some of the townspeople to look at the men, but they did not recognize them. In fact, no suspicious characters had been seen in Bethel. As usual under such circumstances, the robbery had been committed on Saturday night, and on Sunday the safe had been broken into. There had been some clever burrowing, the heavy floor-stones broken, the bolt of the lock blocked with wood and it was Monday afternoon before the bank officers could open the vault, and then the robbery was discovered. Of the $100,000 stolen, $80,000 were in the Hatters' Bank notes, and the rest in general currency. The bills of the Hatters' Bank were of the denomination of $50 and $100.

Bethel being a small manufacturing town, large bank-bills were not much in use. The Hatters' Bank sent to all the other moneyed institutions in the country an account of the robbery, with a description of the notes. It was impossible to hold the men. I was positive that "Four-fingered Jack" was one of the robbers, but there was no evidence against him, and the magistrate was forced to release him and his "mate."

As Jack was leaving the court-room a free man I said to him, "You have got clear now, but those bills of the Bethel Bank will be of no avail to you. They will lead to your detection."

I regret to say that my prophecy did not come true, as far as the detection of these robbers went, but something quite extraordinary in its way did happen.

I was living then with a friend, named O'Donnel. About a week after the dismissal of "Four-fingered Jack," on returning to my house one evening, Mr. O'Donnel said to me:

"Captain Walling, I suppose some of your people are coming home from the country."

"Not at all," I replied.

"O, yes, they are," was his answer, "for some of them have sent you a travelling-satchel."

"How is that?" I inquired.

"Just before you came in the door-bell rang. The servant girl answered it, and a man put a travelling-bag in her hand, saying, 'This is for Captain Walling.'"

"That's very strange," I said.

O'Donnel went for the article, which was a common-looking black bag. He put it on a chair in the hallway, and lit a candle so that I might better examine it.

"I never saw it before," I said, looking it over. Just then there had been a scare about infernal machines and Mr. O'Donnel said, "Watch out, Captain, maybe you and I will be blown sky-high."

"Nonsense," I said. "Nobody is going to blow me up." Then I felt of the bag, and it seemed to have a parcel in it. Having no key, I opened it with a knife. There was a bundle about eight inches wide and two feet long wrapped up in coarse straw paper. What could it be? I had the wrapper off in a trice, and when I saw the contents I was excited perhaps more than I have been at any other time in my life, for there were the bills of the Hatters' Bank, of Bethel! I sent off in post-haste for McCord and Elder. They could hardly believe their eyes when they saw what was in the satchel. They sat down and we counted the bills. We made the bundle out to contain exactly $60,025. I lost no time in telegraphing the Bank of Bethel, and made a special deposit of the money in the Nassau Bank. The president of the bank came at once to the city, claimed the property and carried

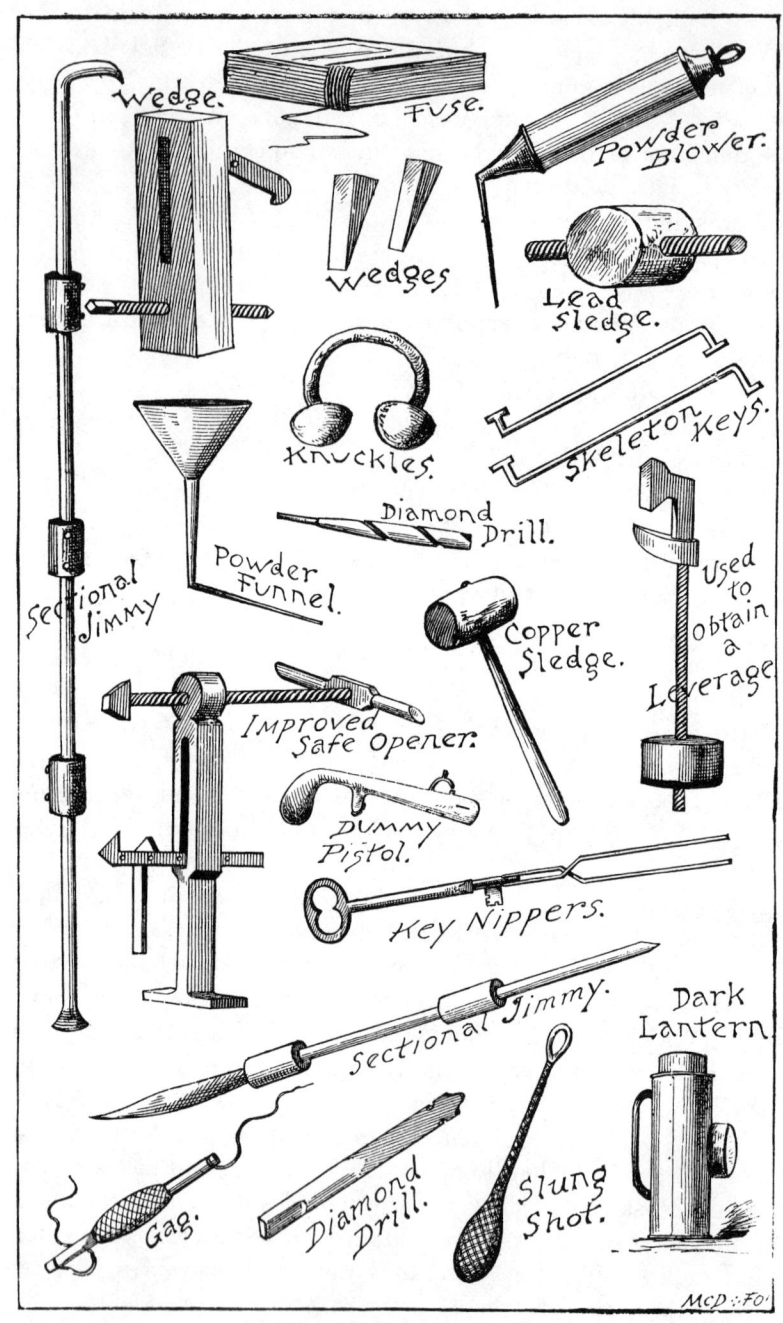

BANK BURGLARS' OUTFIT.

it back to Bethel. Still there was about $40,000 of the amount stolen which was unaccounted for. Some years afterward, the city marshal of Buffalo, Mr. Tyler, got hold of $20,000 more of the bills, but of the remaining $20,000 nothing was ever heard. The robbers were never arrested. Then, as now, I was perfectly convinced that "Four-fingered Jack" was the burglar. I do not regard the restitution of the $60,025 as entitling Four-fingered Jack to the least credit. There is no magnanimity about thieves. Probably his continued possession of these notes might have been a temptation to the rest of the gang, and the circulation of the notes might finally have led to his re-arrest and punishment.

After this exploit, "Four-fingered Jack" disappeared from sight forever. I don't know what became of him. The public often hears of an individual who figures during a very long career of crime. This I am inclined to think a rather exceptional condition of things, because the life of a thief, robber or burglar is not usually a long one. Take a hundred of the criminal class, and the larger proportion of them are dissipated. Drink kills them. Theirs is a calling that carries with it constant and tremendous risks. It is sometimes difficult to follow a thief by his *soubriquet.* A criminal may call himself, as in this instance, "Four-fingered Jack," and at once he has imitators. There will probably spring up in various parts of the country a large crop of Four-fingered Jacks. There have been Jack Shepards in and out of prison walls ever since the time of Jonathan Wild. I do not think that criminals are over fond of these catch names. There are of course many aliases, but those oftenest adopted or applied are familiar through history or fiction. I have more than once startled a criminal who sported a long list of aliases by saluting him with the name given him by his father and mother. An officer of the police, in constant intercourse with the criminal class, may have his sympathies blunted, but I have sometimes felt sorry for even a hardened rascal when his own true name was thrown back at him. It was as if all his disguises had been mysteriously stripped off, and he was suddenly brought face to face with the recollections of his innocent boyhood.

The subject of the Northampton Bank robbery, on January 27, 1876, was on everybody's tongue for several years after it occurred. It was an interesting robbery by reason of the large amount stolen, the notorious thieves who were believed to be implicated, the boldness of their operations and their escapes after capture.

The thieves were seven: "Shang" Draper, "Red" Leary, "Billy" Connor, James Burns, George Howard (or George Leonidas Leslie), Thomas Dunlap and William Scott. There is some doubt, however, whether Howard was actually concerned in the work of the burglary or not. The criminals used considerable strategy in their operations. They wanted to rob a bank, but were not particular as to which one. It was necessary first to find out where there was a bank whose safes and vaults were easily opened. So they made the acquaintance of William D. Edson, an expert in locks and safes, who was a travelling agent for Herring & Co. Edson was not a man with very stern moral convictions. He smiled on his new acquaintances and soon became confidential. The burglars' plot was finally laid before him, and he was promised a generous share in the proceeds if the scheme was successful. They wanted him to point out a weak bank, from a burglar's point of view, and this he did, directing their attention to that at Northampton. With this much learned, the rest of the task was not difficult to thieves of such broad experiences. Northampton was a small town, and boldness, the burglars thought, would most successfully accomplish their designs. Certainly it did.

On the night of January 27, 1876, having reached the town and assembled at their rendezvous, they put on masks and proceeded at once to the residence of the cashier, Mr. Whittlesy. They aroused him from slumber, and after binding his wife, children and servants, made him march under the cover of their pistols to the bank. There they compelled him, by threats of instant death, to unlock the vaults and surrender the contents. Under such circumstances the boldest cashier is apt to lose courage, and Mr. Whittlesy was no exception. He meekly followed his masked captors and surrendered all they asked for. They succeeded in getting $1,500,000 in money and negotiable securities. But even when the booty was in their possession there was no feverish haste to get away. They coolly walked back with the cashier to his house, gagged him and made secure the bonds of his family, and then departed.

So large a sum had been stolen from the bank in the form of securities, upon which the burglars could not readily realize, that

ARRESTED AND SENTENCED. 243

the bank officers tried to recover their lost property before attempting to secure the conviction of the thieves. This plan was followed by negotiations which lasted a year and then brought no satisfactory result. Detectives advised that as many of the thieves as could be caught should be arrested, and acting upon this advice, the bank officers soon had the satisfaction of knowing that Edson, the travelling agent who had conspired with the thieves, was under arrest.

Edson was piqued at not getting as much money from the robbery as he had been promised, and it did not require much urging to get him to turn State's evidence. The names of the burglars were disclosed, and soon afterward Scott and Dunlap were arrested in Philadelphia, just as they were about to take a train southward, where they intended to commit another bank burglary. They were taken to Northampton, and tried, not on the charge of robbing the bank, but on that of entering the cashier's house and threatening the lives of the inmates. Conviction on the former charge would give the culprits only twenty years' sentence, while on the latter charge a life-sentence was possible. The trial on this charge proved a failure, and the second was taken up. Scott and Dunlap were found guilty and were sentenced to twenty years' imprisonment in the Massachusetts State prison, at Charlestown. Scott died in captivity.

Meanwhile, the New York detectives were continuing their search for the remainder of the gang. "Shang" Draper was taken in 1877, and soon afterwards "Billy" Connors fell into the clutches of the law. He was confined in Ludlow Street Jail, but while his extradition papers were preparing he secured an impression of the key of the jail, and one day, at meal time, he unlocked the iron door and walked out. It was on February 4, 1881, that he was re-captured in Philadelphia as he was leaving a dram shop. He was taken to Northampton for trial.

Leary had been arrested about the same time that Connors was first arrested, and was also lodged in Ludlow Street Jail. The desperate character of these thieves is again illustrated when it is told that Leary also broke jail in 1879. Friends of his had rented a brick house adjoining the jail, and dug through the walls to a closet, making an excavation large enough for Leary to crawl through. He was re-arrested in Brooklyn on the same night that Connors was re-taken in Philadelphia. Of the other burglars, one was already serving a term in Sing Sing before it was known that he was engaged in the Northampton bank robbery; Howard, if he was really implicated, was killed, after a remarkable career, in Yonkers, and Edson, of course, got free by turning State's evidence. The bank recovered all its property save $100,000 in securities, $40,000 in Government bonds and $12,000 in cash.

The anniversary of Washington's birthday in 1878 was a raw, cold day in Dexter, Maine. Since it was a holiday, most of the villagers were enjoying themselves in various ways suited to their tastes. On the second floor of what was known as the Masonic Building, however, was one citizen who was not spending the day in idleness. His name was J. W. Barron. He was the cashier of the Dexter Savings Bank, which had offices there. He had left his wife in the morning, and told her that he would return about 3 o'clock—he wanted to go to the bank "to do a little figuring."

There he sat in the offices of the bank on that chill afternoon, and turned the pages of his books or added up a column of figures. The fire in the grate became low, and the cashier shivered now and then as he went on with his work. Finally the room became too cold for him to endure the temperature any longer, so he arose from his desk and walked down to the coal room to bring up some more fuel. Little did James Barron suspect that several pairs of eyes were watching every step he took. Unconscious of coming doom he stooped over and filled the iron scuttle. The rattling of the coal drowned all other noises. He arose to lift his burden, and then fell, struck by a sudden and unlooked-for blow. Three men were upon him in an instant, three men whom that old cashier recognized at once as desperate criminals. He saw determination and brutality written in their faces. He knew at once their intentions.

But Cashier Barron was no coward. A short time before he had read of the Northampton Bank robbery, how the burglars had bound and gagged the cashier and made him divulge the combination of the safes, and Mr. Barron then had said to his wife: "If the bank funds have got to go that way, I prefer to go with them." And down in that dimly-lighted and dusty coal room, with three of the most desperate bank burglars in the country upon him, the gray-haired cashier did not flinch. Again the words he had used to his wife came back to him, and he murmured to himself: "If the funds have got to go, I will go with them."

So he struggled, and there was a desperate fight in the coal room, in which the brave old man's head was cut and his face bruised. His eye-glasses were afterwards found amid the coal, broken, and a set of false teeth glistened brightly against the black diamonds.

But three men can easily overpower one. Mr. Barron struggled until his strength was exhausted, and then the ruffians tied his wrists behind him and fastened them with hand-cuffs. After gagging him so that he could not scream for help they lead him to the bank vault and tried to force out of him the secret of the combination. But although the old man's strength was gone his spirit was not bowed. That firm determination with which he said, " If the funds have got to go I prefer to go with them," stood by him still. He absolutely refused to divulge the combination. How this enraged the burglars! They became perfect fiends. They beat the cashier, slashed him with knives, assaulted him with all sorts of indignities, and in short tried to murder him by slow torture. But all was in vain; their victim was a martyr. The thieves, fearing discovery, for it was broad daylight, abandoned their task and fled. They secured only about $100.

In the mean while there was growing anxiety in the home of Cashier Barron. When 3 o'clock came around and her husband had not returned, Mrs. Barron became fearful lest something had happened to him. She smothered her fears, however, and went on with her household duties. Then the shades of that February day began to fall. The sun shone out clear for a moment just above the western horizon, and then fell behind the hill. The air grew chillier with the approach of dusk. Mrs. Barron left her comfortable seat by the grate fire, and walked to the window to ascertain if she could see her absent husband. There was no sign of him. She walked into the kitchen, and there saw a hired man, named Bement, to whom she expressed her fear that Mr. Barron had met with an accident. Bement offered to go down to the bank and find out if his employer had been detained there.

As the hired man approached the Masonic Building and looked up into the second story, where the bank offices were, he saw no light in the window. He started to go up the steps, when he met Cashier Curtis, of the Dexter National Bank, which was in the same building, and asked him if he had seen anything of Mr. Barron. Mr. Curtis replied that he had not, and together with Bement walked to the door of the building. They listened and heard a faint groan. This was enough. They tried to burst open the door, but it withstood their efforts. There was another entrance, and through this they climbed and made their way to the bank offices. The door by which entrance was had was open a mere crack. They pushed against it, but could not open it sufficiently to get through. The groans became more audible and horrible. Something had to be done. They found a slender lad, who climbed up over the door and into the room. It was dark, but by feeling around he discovered that it was a man's body which blocked the door. By much tugging and straining he managed to pull the body along so as to allow the door to open more widely. Then a Captain Weed, who had been attracted by the noise as he was passing, squeezed through the aperture. Bement, the hired man, handed him his lantern. The captain turned the rays full on the creature behind the door, and a cry of anguish broke from his lips. It was a sickening sight that met his searching look. By the lantern's light he saw Mr. Barron wedged in between the vault and the door—his face livid, his eyes set, his jaws stretched apart by a blood-soaked gag, a rope around his neck, his hands fastened behind him with hand-cuffs, and the man himself dying.

Mr. Barron was at once removed to another part of the building, and his wife was summoned. At midnight he died.

Further examination of the premises revealed the false teeth, the broken eye-glasses, a lead pencil and the coal-hod, half tipped over. There were, however, no clews to the burglars. The little town was of course very much excited. Stories of strange men who had been seen in the village multiplied. Several sleighloads of suspicious-looking men had been seen driving across the country, but whether they included the murderers of the old cashier was never ascertained. Detectives from Boston and Portland were employed to work up the case. It was a huge task. A rumor got abroad that Barron had not been murdered, but had committed suicide after having misappropriated the funds of the bank. His accounts were examined, and for a time his widow lived confronting the unjust suspicions. But the expert accountants soon discovered that Barron, instead of being a thief, was a hero. Finally suspicion centred on a well-known gang of bank burglars, among whom were "Worcester Sam," "Johnny" Dobbs, "Jimmy" Hope, "Abe" Coakley and George Leonidas Leslie, alias George Howard. The Boston detectives called on the police of New

York for assistance, and Richard King and George Dilks of the Central Office were put upon the case. They watched Coakley's house attentively, and after some further investigation were so convinced that the above-named rascals were implicated in the murder that they felt ready to make arrests. The matter was finally allowed to drop because of insufficient evidence, and the murderers of Cashier Barron were never brought to justice.

The peculiar circumstances surrounding the robbery of the Ocean National Bank, at Fulton and Greenwich streets, New York, on June 27, 1869, gives the burglary another interest aside from that which springs from the cleverness of the thieves' work. There was stolen altogether in money and securities $768,879.74, but there was left in the bank vaults, or scattered outside on the floor, $1,806,958.

The burglary occurred between Saturday night and Monday morning. The news came to headquarters on Monday, and detectives Elder, Kelso and Farley were dispatched at once to the building. They arrived at the bank shortly after nine o'clock, and found a very confused state of things. Outside the bank the streets were crowded with persons who had learned the fact of the robbery, and it required the efforts of several policemen to keep the throng from pushing through the doors. Within, the confusion was of a different sort, and greater. Of the persons connected with the bank there had already arrived the colored janitor, Peter Grant; W. H. Dunn, a messenger; Joseph D. Martin, the porter; Edward Dunn, another messenger; Mr. Lyon, the receiving teller; Mr. Clark, the paying teller; C. S. Stevenson, the cashier; Mr. Morgan, a director, and Theodore M. Davis, an attorney of the bank. Sergeant Phillips, of the Twenty-seventh Precinct, had been notified and was in command.

The bank offices included the large business room, the president's private room, and the vault. Around the latter was assembled a very excited and nervous group. The outer door of the vault was open, and smoke issued from the aperture. The floor was covered with papers, books and old clothing left by the burglars, all thoroughly soaked with water. Bags holding nickel coin were smouldering. The detectives examined the outer vault door. It showed no sign of having been violently tampered with. The lock worked as usual.

The vault was in three compartments, with a door to each.

The outside wall was built of large blocks of granite, which were lined on either side by heavy plates of boiler iron. The first door, which so surprised the detectives, was of iron, very strongly put together, and held tight by bolts and a combination lock. The second was also of iron, and was secured by a Yale lock. The

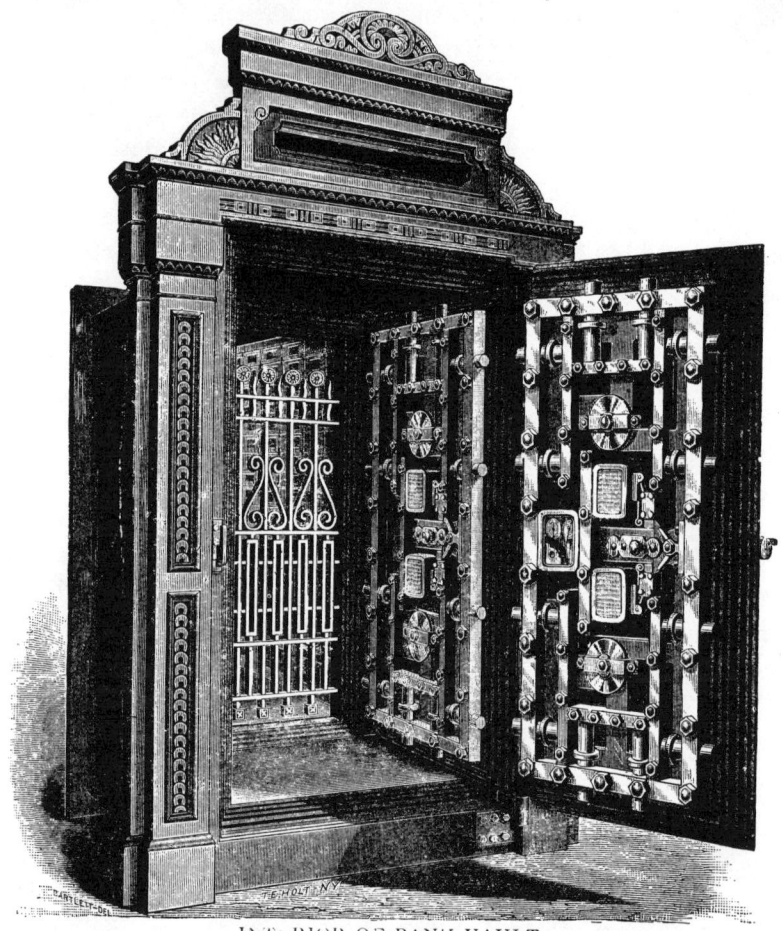

INTERIOR OF BANK VAULT.

keys to this hung on the door, so that having forced the main door it had only been necessary for the burglars to use the keys which they found. The third door, or that leading to the inner vault, was of inch-and-a-quarter iron, and had a different lock from either of the others, a combination Butterworth, No. 3. In this inner vault were two safes, supposed to be burglar proof, and holding the cash and securities of the bank.

Through all this iron and stone the burglars had worked their way. The evidences of their toil and its results were everywhere visible. In some mysterious way they had unlocked the outside door and found the keys which took them through the second; but through the third there was no such easy passage. Here they had to use their jimmies and wedges, and when they got to the safes they brought into service all sorts of ingenious tools. There was a strong smell of powder in this inner vault when the detectives entered. The floor was covered with powder cans, fuses, drills, blow-pipes, bits, wedges, jack-screws, and steel and copper sledges. More wonderful, though, than all the burglars' tools was the wealth which lay scattered over the floor, left by the thieves. Here were bags of gold and nickel coins, bundles of checks, bonds, notes, books, papers and fractional currency, all mixed up in a hopeless confusion, and all soaked with water. Inside the safes were bags of gold untouched; in one box was $160,000 in gold and gold certificates, yet the burglars didn't seem to care for it.

More signs of the burglars' depredations were noticeable outside the vault. The floor of the business room, behind the counter, was littered with depositors' boxes and their contents. The thieves had gone through them, but had taken very little. At the windows the small diamond-shaped apertures above the iron shutters were covered with black muslin and silk. In the floor of the president's room had been bored a hole, two feet long and twenty inches wide. It was directly in front of his desk, and had apparently been worked at several days previous to the robbery. In the basement, below the bank offices, were found a bundle of United States bonds, a lot of silverware, hundreds of dollars in notes and mutilated fractional currency, half-eaten sandwiches, a dark-lantern, tools and old clothing. The basement windows were fastened and the doors locked.

Our detectives looked at all this, and, it cannot be denied, they were mystified. The work had been done very systematically and intelligently, and yet it seemed as if the robbers had cherished just a little contempt for "filthy lucre," so much had they left scattered on the floor. It could not have been that they were frightened away, for they had stopped to close doors and windows after them. Indeed, there seemed no way of accounting for the state of things which we found. When the officers of the bank had made an investigation into their losses they found that $768,879.74 had been carried away, and that $1,806,958 was left.

As soon as they had recovered their senses they requested Theodore M. Davis, who had been the bank's attorney at one time or another, and who happened in the bank on the morning that the robbery was discovered, to undertake an investigation into the burglary. He accordingly established headquarters at once in the president's room, and called in the detectives.

Subsequent search on the part of the detectives only added to the mystery. Strange as had been the conduct of the thieves on the night of the burglary, stranger was it afterward. Early on Tuesday morning, only twenty-four hours after the robbery, Patrolman Donahue, of the Sixth Precinct, brought to the station-house a small trunk bound around with a cord, and having attached to it a piece of paper on which was written, "For Capt. Jourdan, of Sixth Ward." The patrolman reported that while on his beat, two men, John Hilton, of No. 8 Franklin Street, and John Gowan, of No. 202 Catharine Street, had pointed out to him the trunk, which was then in front of No. 2 Elizabeth Street. As they called his attention to it, they remarked:

"Perhaps there's a dead baby in it."

There was no baby in it, however. It contained nothing less than a portion of the property which had been stolen from the Ocean Bank. There were a few hundred dollars in cash, and the remainder, amounting to more than $275,000, was in securities. Among the checks was one of the cashier of the Exchange Bank, payable to the order of D. R. Martin, the president of the Ocean Bank, for $75,000. Another was drawn by President Martin for $20,000, payable to himself, and still another was drawn by the cashier, C. S. Stevenson, for $4000, payable to himself. The two latter had been paid on the Saturday before the robbery.

The policy of the bank, as expressed and carried out by Mr. Davis, was to get possession, not of the thieves, but of the stolen property. For this reason the police thereafter worked against great odds. They did the best they could, however, and what they found is herewith given. The entire mystery of the case was not solved and probably never will be.

Until February 8, of the year of the robbery, the Globe Insurance Company had occupied the basement of the building in which the Ocean Bank was situated. The general manager was

Edgar E. Holly, an intimate friend of President Martin. One morning in May, 1868, Mr. Holly discovered some wax, such as is used by burglars, around the keyhole of the front basement door. A few weeks later he found the lock badly out of order, and on several occasions saw suspicious persons in the neighborhood of the building. Each time his suspicions were aroused, and he told President Martin that he feared a burglary of the bank was threatened. The president laughed, and boasted the strength of the vaults. Later on, the porter of the bank reported that on one or two occasions he had seen strangers inside the railing near the vault. Once also he had seen a suspicious-looking man in the president's room, who had jumped out of the window into Fulton Street as soon as he was discovered. Other warnings came. Sergeant Phillips reported the presence of suspicious characters in the neighborhood of the bank, and two months before the robbery Detective Keneally told the bank officers that an attempt on the Ocean Bank was probable. In spite of all these warnings the president did not heed. He had implicit trust in the strength of the vaults, and declined to have the bank watched. On the morning of the robbery, when Mr. Holly entered the bank, he said to the president, significantly:

"Well, they've done it, haven't they?" Whereupon Mr. Martin, who was greatly agitated, whispered to Holly:

"For God's sake and mine, never speak of any conversation that has passed between me and you in relation to the robbery of this bank."

It was in William J. Sharkey's handsomely fitted billiard parlors in Broadway that the robbery of the Ocean Bank was schemed. Sharkey was a notorious character. The son of a prominent church member, he became early in life a pickpocket. From this occupation he drifted into other criminal pursuits, until, in 1869, he was one of the biggest rascals in New York, and at the same time had such a political influence that he was the companion of judges, legislators and office-holders. Into the crime which he had now in mind he enticed William McKay, called sometimes "Canada Mac," a great sporting man, but known to the police as a burglar. The first plan agreed upon by these conspirators was to employ a sneak thief to do the burglary. For this purpose, Charles King, an expert English thief, was brought over to this country. He it was whom, in 1868, the janitor of the Ocean Bank Building saw leap out of a window in the president's room.

For a whole year Sharkey and McKay were planning the robbery, but their efforts met with no success. Then they changed their tactics. There was a man whom McKay knew, called William O'Kell. This individual was a broker, and did business under the Stuyvesant Bank, on Broadway, above Grand Street. He had previously assisted thieves in disposing of their stolen property. Sharkey and McKay arranged with O'Kell that he should lease the basement under the Ocean Bank Building, recently vacated by the Globe Insurance Company, and sublet the rear part of it to McKay, who was to be known by the name of Lewis K. Cole. This was done early in June, 1869, and unbeknown to everybody save themselves the work of getting at the Ocean Bank's vaults went on. About this time also they enlisted in their plans two well-known thieves, Max Shinburn and George Miles White. To the basement they brought their tools and lanterns. In some way they got information regarding what was in the bank, what the combination for unfastening the outside door of the vault was, and where they were to find the keys to the second door. To such a degree was their task lightened. To effect an entrance to the president's room they bored the hole which was found afterwards in the floor under his desk.

At last everything was completed. Sunday night was chosen for the burglary, because the janitor was in the habit of being away at that time. One by one the thieves crawled up through the hole, and then they began their operations. Sharkey pointed out what securities they should take and what they should leave. They obeyed his commands, mysterious as the latter were, and stole the amount which has already been mentioned. They carried the plunder to a wholesale liquor house near by and divided it. Within twenty-four hours, however, after the robbery was discovered negotiations had been opened between the burglars and the bank officers, which resulted in the former returning the securities found in the little trunk on Elizabeth Street, and making off with the remainder.

Some time during the month of March, 1874, a man named J. J. Gilmore became the lessee of what was known as the Gilmore Building, corner of Eighth Avenue and Fourteenth Street, at a rental of $7000 a year. This Gilmore Building adjoined the premises occupied by the New York Savings Bank, the entrance to which was on Eighth Avenue, near the corner. Previous to Gilmore's tenancy, the Gilmore Building had been occupied by John Arthur as a billiard hall, saloon and restaurant. Under Arthur's management even, the place was never kept in decent shape, but when Gilmore came into possession it was allowed to go to "rack and ruin," and it was a subject for wonder among those who resided in the locality as to how he made a living. Rumors were circulated among a certain class that Gilmore was none other than J. J. Clare, a noted bank burglar, but these suspicions never came to the ears of the officers of the bank, and they therefore took no particular notice of their neighbors. And so matters went along until shortly before midnight of Friday, June 27, when Patrolman Keller, of the Sixteenth Precinct, passed the building. A peculiar "click, click, click" was borne to his ears, seemingly emanating from the bank premises. What could it mean? Then the noise ceased, only to be resumed in a minute or so. "Click, click, click!" There it was again. From whence did it come? Suddenly there flashed to his brain the thought that there was something wrong going on in the bank. "Click, click, click," once more. This time there could be no doubt about it. He at once ran to the corner, and despatched Officer Sinclair, whom he found there, to the Twentieth Street Police Station for assistance. This soon arrived in the person of Captain Cherry, accompanied by three or four patrolmen. They listened, and could plainly hear the same noise which had attracted Keller's attention in the first instance. He also was convinced that all was not right in the bank. By his directions, the officers under him attempted to force an entrance into the Gilmore Building at the Eighth Avenue entrance. The door was a stout one and resisted their utmost efforts. Dashing up the front steps, Captain Cherry gave the bell-handle a vigorous pull, and a resounding peal followed. In response, a window on the second floor was opened and a head appeared.

"What do you want? Who are you?" it asked.

Captain Cherry shouted that they were police officers and wished to be admitted immediately.

"All right," replied the head, which at once disappeared, and the window was closed.

A minute or more elapsed, during which the sound of hurrying footsteps was heard in the basement. Impatient at the delay, the captain was about to ring the bell again, when three men were seen to jump out of a rear window and run in the direction of Ninth Avenue. The officers followed, and after a short, sharp run, managed to capture them. Two of the prisoners, Wm. Morgan and John Simpson, were well known as "crooks," but the other, who gave his name as Charles Sanborn, was a perfect stranger.

Meanwhile, Captain Cherry had not been idle, but had succeeded in entering the Gilmore Building by prying open a window. Once inside, further research was not difficult. A trap-door in the restaurant floor led to the basement, where he found ample evidence that Officer Keller had heard the "click, click, click" just in time. In the southerly wall of the building a hole about four feet square had been made. Four courses of brick had been removed, exposing to view the granite slabs of which the outer casing of the vault of the New York Savings Bank was constructed. No attempt had been made to blast the slabs, but in one of them the captain noticed a clearly-drilled, polished hole, one inch in diameter and two deep. He at once saw that no hand-drill had been used. Groping around in the dungeon-like basement he soon came across a diminutive upright boiler, attached to which was a portion of the machinery necessary to the working of a drill. The whole floor of the basement was covered with the bricks taken from the breach, but the only tool found was a heavy iron mallet, tipped with lead so as to deaden the sound.

Nothing else was discovered, but it was evident that much time and labor had been expended in the "enterprise," which was brought to such an untimely conclusion.

Gilmore, the lessee of the building, managed to escape, and what became of him or his companions I have never ascertained.

Dan Noble, *alias* Daniel Dyson, was originally a pickpocket, but after some years' practice in that direction graduated as a bank sneak of the highest grade. His most brilliant exploit was his "snatching" of $100,000 from the Royal Insurance Company's office on Broadway in broad daylight. He is also said to have been concerned in the famous Lord bond robbery, when $1,000,000 were stolen. Being sentenced to five years' imprisonment at Auburn for burglary at Elmira, New York, he there made the acquaintance of Jimmy Hope and James Brady, and escaped with them. Subsequently he went to England, where he associated, largely with "sporting swells." He visited France on one occasion, but the surroundings were uncongenial and he returned to England, where he was sentenced to twenty years' imprisonment for forgery. His health broke down, and in 1878 he died in prison, after serving about half his term.

Max, or Mark Shinburn, who was one of the confederates in the Ocean Bank burglary, was an aristocratic criminal. It was his habit to remark with great earnestness to his companions that

DAN. NOBLE.
(From a Photograph.)

as soon as he got wealthy he was going back to the Fatherland and become a nobleman. He was the one economical criminal I ever encountered. Instead of dissipating his booty among male and female companions, he bought letters of credit and made them payable to friends in Prussia. He was never the inmate of a prison for any length of time, and only had to do with the "safest" kind of robbery. On the 8th or 9th of February, 1869, while I was inspector, John F. Young, at that time captain of the detective force, received information from General Frank Spinola to the effect that certain men had offered to sell him some stolen bonds. A plan was accordingly set on foot to entrap the parties. General Spinola hired a room at No. 60 Broadway, and fitted it up with the necessary furniture, desks, chairs, safe, etc. A formidable and imposing-looking package of counterfeit bills was obtained from United States Marshal Robert Murray, and given to General Spinola so as to enable him to show the holders of the stolen bonds, who had been notified by him meanwhile that he was ready to negotiate, that he was going to pay cash. On February 10 they put in an appearance. The general received them in the most polite and agreeable manner, giving them to understand that he was willing to buy the bonds if a price could be agreed upon. Opening the safe he took out the package of counterfeit money, and remarked : "You see I'm ready to trade, and will pay cash down for the bonds." After some further conversation an arrangement was made by which they were to call the next day with the bonds. Captain Young was notified by General Spinola to this effect, and at the time agreed, the captain, together with detectives James Irving and Edsell, concealed themselves near the office and were to put in an appearance upon a certain signal. The two men came, bringing the bonds, and the signal was given. The officers rushed into the room and arrested them. Upon being questioned they gave their names as James Weaver and James McCabe, but the former was recognized as no less an individual than Max Shinburn, while the latter was known as "Canada Mac." They were taken to police headquarters, where $99,500 in bonds, stolen from the First National Bank of Maryland, was found on them. Within the past month, in looking over some of the minutes of this capture, I have had occasion to examine the returns of arrests made by the Detective Bureau at that time, but after a careful search I failed to find any record of the occurrence at headquarters. The fact of the arrest was kept a secret at the time, as the two prisoners, it was said, agreed to return to Maryland without waiting for the formality of extradition papers. The two were thereupon delivered into the custody of a private detective agency, having its office in Baltimore. The officers of this agency conveyed Shinburn and Canada Mac to Jersey City, *en route* for Baltimore. Upon arriving in Jersey City, so I have been informed—and I have every reason for placing implicit confidence in my informant—the prisoners delivered to the private detectives about $20,000, the balance of the amount stolen from the bank,

STATE OF NEW YORK.

Executive Department

JOHN T. HOFFMAN,
Governor of the State of New-York.

To the Sheriff of the County of _New York_
And the Sheriffs, Constables and other Peace Officers of the several Counties in the said State:

Whereas, it has been represented to me by the Governor of the State of _Vermont_ that _Max Shinburn_ stands charged with the crime of _Burglary_ committed in the County of _Bennington_ in said State and that _he_ has fled from Justice in that State, and has taken refuge in the State of New York; and the said Governor of _Vermont_ having in pursuance of the Constitution and Laws of the United States, demanded of me that I shall cause the said _Max Shinburn_ to be arrested and delivered to _Leander Powers_ who is duly authorized to receive _him_ into his custody, and convey _him_ back to the said State of _Vermont_

And Whereas, the said representation and demand is accompanied by _Affidavits and Complaints_ whereby the said _Max Shinburn_ _is_ charged with the said crime and with having fled from said State, and taken refuge in the State of New York, which _are_ certified by the said Governor of _Vermont_ to be duly authenticated.

You are, therefore, required to arrest and secure the said _Max Shinburn_ wherever _he_ may be found within the State and to deliver _him_ into the custody of the said _Leander Powers_ to be taken back to the said State from which _he_ fled pursuant to the said requisition.

Given under my hand, and the PRIVY SEAL of the State, at the City of Albany, this _Thirtieth_ day of _March_ in the year of our Lord one thousand eight hundred and sixty-_nine_

By the Governor:
Edgar K. Apgar
Acting Private Secretary

John T. Hoffman

A few hours afterwards Shinburn and his companion were seen walking up Broadway. Early in 1870, while John Jourdan was superintendent, a warrant of Governor Hoffman's was placed in my hands on a requisition from the Governor of Vermont, directing the arrest of Max Shinburn. In the words of the requisition he was "to be delivered to Leander Powers, duly authorized in the State of Vermont to receive and carry the prisoner to the said State." The date of the warrant was March 30, 1869. When I asked the authorities from Vermont why the warrant had been held over so long, the answer was that, judging from former transactions with the New York police, they feared a miscarriage of justice and that the warrant would not be executed. They added that a Mr. Stone, a dry goods merchant of New York, had recommended the placing of the warrant in my hands, and then they would be assured the warrant would be executed. Somewhere about the time of my receiving the warrant, Shinburn had been seen in a restaurant on Broadway, near Thirty-fourth Street. I told Superintendent Jourdan of this, and also of the fact that I had a warrant for Shinburn's arrest, asking him whether I should serve it or hand it over to some one else. His reply was:

"Keep it, and serve it—if you can."

A week elapsed, and the next information I received of Shinburn's whereabouts was that he was in Canada.

Comments on the whole transaction are needless. So far as the police department of the City of New York was concerned it was disgraceful. A door was actually opened for the escape of two notorious criminals, while the absence of any record of the matter at headquarters convinces me that there must have been a terrible amount of rottenness permeating many grades of the police force.

Max Shinburn, I have since learned, finally became as wealthy as he desired, and bidding farewell to his associates he sailed for his long-wished-for Fatherland. There he bought an estate, employed servants, dazzled the natives, and finally, after announcing to the country about his estate that he had been a bank president in America, bought the title of Baron of the principality of Monaco and became a nobleman. His acquaintance with affairs and interiors of banks bore out his claims of being a retired bank president and as "Baron Shindell" he shines.

But perhaps the most audacious and withal amusing robbery

which was intimately connected with a bank was the experience of a messenger of the Greenwich Savings Bank, in 1868. This messenger was a man of unimpeachable honesty and of great strength. He had frequently carried large sums of money from the savings institution to the bank of deposit and had never met the smallest or most uninteresting adventure. This man is still alive, and as publicity will not benefit him I shall call him by the euphonious name of Buggins. His great pride always was that he was seldom known as Buggins, the bank-messenger, but "Buggins, the gentleman connected with the Greenwich Savings Bank." His air of respectability was so penetrating and infectious that one was always inclined to accost him, not with the breezy and flippant inquiry concerning the weather, but about last Sunday's sermon or the latest quotation in "Governments."

Now on certain days of the week Buggins was accustomed to go through the following procedure: he would first go to a closet where hung a respectable hat; removing this hat from its peg he would place it upon his head; then drawing on a pair of respectable gloves he would take a cane, after which a large black bag; all this slowly and methodically. Thus armed he would proceed to the bank of deposit, where he would obtain a sufficient number of bank-bills of small denominations to fill the black bag. He would then return with these bills to the Greenwich Savings Bank, where they were used to pay depositors who desired bank-notes of a small denomination.

A thief with a vivid imagination had long watched these proceedings with the most profound interest, and his mouth had watered at the sight of his bag. "So near and yet so far"; and "he said to himself said he," "I will have that there bag and I will get it without putting my precious carcass in the slightest danger." So one day he boldly walked up to an officer in uniform who was standing on a street corner, and said:

"I am a detective from headquarters, and Superintendent Kennedy [who was at that time Chief of Police] has instructed me to arrest a notorious counterfeiter whom we have long been watching, and who will probably soon pass this way with a black bag full of counterfeit bills. I shall require your assistance."

The policeman, seeing in his mind's eye his name in the morning papers, coupled with such expressions as "Gallant conduct of an officer.—Arrest of a dangerous criminal by Policeman X," with perhaps a sergeant's baton in the background, joyfully acquiesced, and when in due course of time Buggins, with his bag of money, drew near, the officer bore down on him and seized him with such an iron grip that he was for the moment completely paralyzed. The thief, who had, simultaneously with the officer, grabbed poor Buggins and the bag, but especially the bag, said to the patrolman in an authoritative tone:

"Take him to the station-house while I go with the bag to Superintendent Kennedy. We will join you at the station." And then he at once made off with the bag, in spite of the imploring and confused imprecations of the horrified bank-messenger. By this time a large crowd had collected, and one gentleman asked the policeman what the prisoner had done.

"Done!" replied the patrolman, stopping and holding Buggins off at arm's length for a moment while he gloated over his triumph. "Done everything—counterfeiting, bigamy and arson."

"I am a bank officer," howled Buggins, "and you shall suffer for this."

"Oh! yes," howled the crowd, "you are a nice bank officer, you are. He a banker! Look at the villain!" Did the officer require assistance in taking the hardened vagabond to the station? Hundreds of willing hands were stretched out to aid him. And the unhappy Buggins was marched to the Twenty-Seventh Precinct station followed by a delighted crowd, sarcastically jubilant at his claims to be a banker. When he reached the station the officer in command of course promptly informed Supt. Kennedy and the bank. Then came the furious Chief of Police, next the president of the bank with every hair erect with anger and dismay, afterwards the cashier, with a pale face. With this re-enforcement to his reputation, Buggins was discharged.

A general alarm was sent out for the arrest of the thief with the bag, but too late; the thief had disappeared, and neither he nor the money were ever afterwards heard of. The credulous patrolman was tried and dismissed from the force.

CHAPTER XIX.

ROBBING THE MANHATTAN BANK.—A SYNDICATE OF BURGLARS.—A NARROW ESCAPE.—THE DUMMY MISLEADING.—QUICK WORK.—LOADED WITH WEALTH.—A LOQUACIOUS POLICEMAN.—NABBED.—A GENIUS AS A BANK BURGLAR.—THE DECOMPOSING BODY.—A MISTAKE AT NORRISTOWN.—A YOUTHFUL BRIDE.—THE SOUTH KENSINGTON BANK.—A WIFE'S DISCOVERY.—THE LAST TIME ALIVE.—PROBABLY THE MURDERER.

THE bells of old Trinity and St. Paul's had barely finished striking the hour of ten on the morning of Sunday, October 27, 1878, when a man, almost breathless, and quivering with excitement, rushed into the little barber shop in Bleecker Street under the Manhattan Institute for Savings. For a moment he was unable to utter a word in explanation of his unceremonious entrance. At length he gasped out:

"The bank's been robbed!"

Louis Werckle, the janitor of the Manhattan Bank Building, was the person who imparted this startling information. When sufficiently recovered to converse coherently, he said that shortly after six o'clock that morning, while he was dressing, seven or eight men burst in the door of his bedroom. They all wore masks, and securely binding him, his wife and his mother-in-law, left one of their number to guard the terrified trio. Shortly before ten o'clock he and his family were released, and going into the bank he found to his dismay that the vault had been broken into.

The police were at once informed, and an investigation began which finally resulted in the arrest and conviction of at least two of those engaged in the robbery. It was found that the total sum stolen amounted to $2,747,700, of which $2,506,700 was in registered bonds, $241,000 in coupon bonds and $12,764 in cash.

Three years previously, a syndicate of some of the foremost burglars in America had planned this daring robbery. The chief partaking in that conspiracy were George Leonidas Leslie, *alias*

Howard; "Jimmy" Hope, "Jim" Brady, "Abe" Coakley, John, *alias* "Red," Leary, "Shang" Draper, "Johnny" Dobbs, "Sam" Perris ("Worcester Sam"), Pete Emerson ("Banjo Pete"), Mother Mandelbaum and John D. Grady, known as the "Banker of the Burglars." The preliminary expenses of working up the burglary were largely borne by Grady. Mrs. Mandelbaum also furnished considerable money. The remainder came from the pockets of the clique. It was an "inside" job from the start, and

PETE EMERSON, *alias* BANJO PETE.
(From a Photograph in the Rogues' Gallery.)

was managed chiefly by "Shang" Draper and Leslie. In thieves' slang it was a "pudding"; the bank was wealthy, and always kept a large amount of cash and negotiable security on hand; the vault, although apparently impregnable, was easy to enter, and enough police protection from subordinates in the department was assured to render surprise in the commission of the burglary difficult. The bank premises were as accurately surveyed by Leslie as they would have been had a professional architect been employed. Every nook and corner was perfectly well known to the members of the gang.

During the three years preceding the robbery several "mobs" were got up for the purpose of consummating the scheme. It was at first proposed to become possessed of the wealth of the bank by a brutal, coarse and vulgar burglary, which should be accompanied by the forcible overcoming of those who guarded the bank at night. Then more cunning schemes were devised. The nature of the fastenings of the bank vault were ascertained, and the conclusion was reached that it was better to enter by gentler means than by wedges, mallets and jimmies. The use of powder or dynamite was not to be thought of. In the first place, the bank had large plate-glass windows, which would not permit of an explosion within, without disastrous results, and in the second place, there were persons living in the adjacent buildings who would most certainly be aroused by such a shock.

The thieves thought that the combination of the lock of the vault could be easily discovered. The task of finding how this could best be accomplished was assigned to the arch-mechanic and business man of the rascally clique—George Leonidas Leslie, whose history was most adventurous and whose fate was tragic. Leslie was then living with his wife, Mary Henrietta, *née* Coath, at No. 861 Greene Avenue, Brooklyn. Knowing the style of the combination lock to the vault, he procured one of the same make from Messrs. Valentine and Butler, and, with Draper, experimented on it at his home. He found that the combination could be thrown out of gear, and the notches of the tumblers, of which there were four, brought into line by boring a hole under the indicator, and working the tumblers around with a fine piece of steel inserted in the hole. When this much was decided upon the clique planned to introduce a confederate into the service of the bank. After months of scheming they succeeded. A few weeks later Leslie was admitted to the bank at night by the confederate, and attempted with the real lock what he had done with his "dummy" at home. He was delighted when he found he could throw two of the tumblers into line. This work was done under circumstances which would make most men nervous.

The time had not arrived when the policeman on duty in the street outside should become one of the clique. The man then on patrol was a faithful officer, and his virtues were known to no one so well as to Leslie; so that, working at the lock, under a black screen which shaded the light he was using from passers-by in the street, he did not succeed in moving all the tumblers. He believed he had ample time to perfect his plan on a subsequent occasion. Accordingly, he puttied up the hole he had made under the indicator dial and left the bank. He had experimented with the tumblers so much, and was so nervous, that he neglected to place them as they were when he began his operations. The consequence was that when the bank authorities tried to open the safe the next day there was found to be something wrong. The maker of the safe was sent for, and when the lock plate was taken off the hole made by Leslie was discovered. Strangely enough, the officers of the bank took little notice of this extraordinary circumstance.

Later on, another similar attempt was made by the gang (the composition of which had been greatly changed, owing to various reasons), but it was again thwarted, simply from the fact that the construction of the dummy lock was slightly different from the real one, and it would have been necessary, in order to insure success, to have bored the hole one-eighth of an inch lower than they did. The attempt to open the vault by mild means, therefore, was abandoned. The gang managed, however, to introduce into the bank a second confederate as watchman—Patrick Shevlin—and it was now arranged to commit an extraordinary burglary in an ordinary, every-day manner.

Thus it came about, that at six o'clock on Sunday morning, October 27, 1878, the gang entered the bank and bound the janitor and his family, as before described. It is now almost certain that the men actually engaged in the robbery were "Jimmy" Hope (who did the hardest work), William Kelly, "Abe" Coakley, and "Pete" Emerson, who were aided outside by John Nugent, a policeman of the Eighteenth Precinct who was on the sick-list, and afterwards arrested in Hoboken for an atrocious and daring highway robbery on a bank officer. Louis Werckle's story that the burglars were seven or eight in number is generally conceded to be incorrect, as information obtained from men who were allowed their liberty in consideration of the confessions they made, places the number at four.

After securing Werckle and his family, the burglars proceeded to the bank and began operations on the safe. They had brought

MANHATTAN BANK.

with them the finest kit of tools ever used in a bank burglary. Every article composing it was of the best workmanship and material, and the cost of getting up such a collection could not have been less than $2500 or $3000. Forcing the main door of the safe, they broke open the various compartments, making so much noise that it was distinctly heard by Werckle in his room. No one in the street, or in the St. Charles Hotel, next door, heard the noise. It was not even heard in the barber's shop underneath; but this is explained by the fact that the foundations of the vault were of enormous thickness and imbedded in cement. The interior compartments were constructed of the hardest steel, and offered great resistance. To get at their contents, the burglars had to wreck them utterly; but they failed to open several which contained large amounts of cash. The whole "job" was completed in the most expeditious manner, only two and a half or three hours being consumed in the operation. Having obtained possession of all they could get hold of the thieves placed it in satchels, and left the bank unobserved. One of the "carriers" on the occasion, so it is said, was Policeman Nugent.

How near the thieves came to being discovered may be judged from the fact that while they were at work Policeman Van Orden, of the Fifteenth Precinct, who is still a member of the force and has an excellent record, passed the bank and mechanically looked in. He saw a man inside, whose face was not familiar to him, dusting the desks. The man was in his shirt-sleeves and hatless, and nodded familiarly to the policeman. Van Orden thought so little of this circumstance, because the man appeared to be so slightly interested in the policeman's looking into the place, that he went on about his business, and could not afterwards fully remember the features of the man he had seen.

Within an hour after the discovery of the crime all the resources of the police department were called into requisition by me. The detectives assigned to the case all agreed that never before was such a safe-wreck seen. No such "ripping out" had occurred in any bank burglary that had come under their notice. For awhile the case was a complete mystery, and the public came to the conclusion, when some time passed and no arrests were made, that we had given up a perhaps hopeless search. But we had not. Captain Byrnes, of the Fifteenth Precinct, now inspector, had, by winning the confidence of men with whom the actual burglars were allied, obtained a vast amount of valuable information. The most important knowledge thus gained came through Policeman Nugent's loquacity. He had "snickered" about the burglary, had spoken of the "boodle," and had declared that he carried it on the morning of the burglary.

It was not until late in May, 1879, that we were in a position to make any arrests. Action then was brought about by the confes-

1475.
JOHN HOPE.
(From a Photograph in the Rogues' Gallery.)

sion of Shevlin. In substance, Shevlin said that the gang had gradually won his confidence, and at last showed him how he could make a fortune. He was poorly paid, he said, and the temptation was too great for him. Finally, he consented to enter partnership with the thieves. This partnership was negotiated by outside members of the gang—"Little Tracy" and "Big Kid." They introduced him to "Jim" Brady, and the result was the two attempts to "work" the combination. Then came the decision to break open the safe by violent measures. The "mob" which actually committed the burglary was made up in New York City on Friday night, October 25. It was decided to rob the bank, with Shevlin's connivance, the very next time he should be on duty as watchman. This occasion presented itself two days afterwards. Shevlin acted most injudiciously after the burglary. He abandoned his former frugal habits, spent plenty of money and associated with men suspected of being the burglars. When cornered by the police he made damaging admissions, and, finally, a full confession. The result was that on February 11, 1879, Johnny Hope, son of the redoubtable "Jimmy," was arrested by Detective Dolan as he was coming out of the Theatre Comique. He was fully identified as having been seen in front of the bank on the morning of the robbery. On June 2, of the same year, Captain Byrnes had in custody Shevlin, Hope, Kelly, and a man named Patrick Ryan, a bartender in a grog-shop at Avenue C and Seventh Street, who escaped conviction, but who is even now suspected of having received part of the proceeds of the burglary. The arrest of Coakley and "Pete" Emerson followed. At the trial of Kelly and John Hope (whose father is now in San Francisco "doing time" for a bank robbery there) Policeman Nugent was an interested spectator. The police had been informed that a man answering his description was implicated in the robbery. He was accordingly arrested in the court-room and charged with being one of the gang.

Hope and Kelly were convicted, but Nugent, it is said, escaped conviction at the time by bribing one of the jurors, and afterwards was convicted in Hoboken of highway robbery.

The loss to the bank was comparatively small, all the registered securities being replaced. Some of the coupon bonds were recovered. The principal loss was in the ready money. What was stolen from depositors' boxes has never been ascertained, but was probably not far from $100,000.

New York's Thirty-fifth Precinct is a straggling annex of the great city, and in some parts it is as sparsely settled as the Adirondacks. In no part of it were there fewer houses than in the neighborhood of what is known as "Tramps' Rock." This landmark is close to the dividing line between Westchester County and the County of New York, which runs from Clara Morris's country villa to Williams Bridge over the Bronx River. No more favorable neighborhood for the commission of crime, or for the concealing of its results, could be selected.

On the 4th of June, 1884, Mounted Patrolman E. Johnstone, while riding over his district, was not very much surprised when he found, near the base of the rock, the partly decomposed body of a man who, he supposed, had committed suicide. There was nothing startling in the appearance of the body or its surroundings, so far as casual observation went. It was carried to an undertaker's morgue in Yonkers, where it remained for some days. The man appeared to have shot himself with a white-handled revolver. The weapon was found near the body.

Under ordinary circumstances the body would have been buried at the expense of the county, and there would have been an end of the matter. But local reporters for the New York press investigated the finding of the body, and published an accurate description of the corpse and the clothing on it. Equally singular was the lack of common prudence displayed by Madame Mandelbaum, the notorious "fence." A "client" of hers—George Leonidas Leslie, *alias* Western George, George Howard, J. G. Allison, George K. Leslie, C. G. Greene, etc., *ad infinitum*—had been missing for several days. In a certain sense, Leslie was the chief of her clique of silk-stealing and bank-breaking friends, a man who had brought to her coffers many thousands of dollars. Mrs. Mandelbaum dared not appear at Yonkers, but instead sent her chosen associate, Herman Steid, to ascertain if the body was that of Leslie. Steid's usual self-possession deserted him when confronted with the dead. His emotion was so manifest that the local coroner felt assured that the visitor could tell something of the supposed suicide. He questioned him, adroitly obtaining a sufficient clew on which to base further inquiries, and allowed him to return to New York. Pursuing his investigations, the coroner visited New York and made his errand public. The press became interested, and by degrees the particulars of one of the foulest and best-planned murders of the age was obtained.

George Leonidas Leslie was by descent an Englishman, his father, in 1840, emigrating to this country with his wife—a Miss Rodh—and settling in the western part of the State of New York. He had three children, of whom George was born in this country. Leaving New York State, Leslie's father went to Cincinnati and established a brewery. There young George was educated, first in the local schools and then in the university, whence he was graduated with high honors. His mother died in the interim and his father married again. The second wife ill-treated her stepchildren. George left home, came East and fell into bad company. He had been brought up in luxury, was a spendthrift, and the tastes he had acquired for ease and good living led him to spend money rapidly. Possessing great mechanical genius, and prompted by the acquaintances he had made among the criminal classes, he speedily drifted into their ranks. His forte was architecture and the use of house-breaking tools. From his father he inherited the business tact, which never deserted him. He was above committing depredations himself. In the course of a criminal career extending over a period of twenty years, he was never known to be connected with what is termed a "clothes-line affair." He started in at the top of the ladder; and supposing he had been interested in a thousand burglaries, those in which he was indirectly concerned would number more than three-fourths of them. During the latter years of his life he was sought for by active criminals, first as a "putter-up," or planner of robberies, and, second, as a disposer of the plunder. He was such an expert mechanic and so able a negotiator, that his fame spread wherever first-class criminals associated. Supposing him, for instance, to be in Cincinnati. A telegram might summon him to Boston, Philadelphia, New York, or any other large city, simply to "look over" the scheme for a burglary which might be carried out by others. Or, it might be he was wanted to dispose of what had been obtained by a previous robbery.

His early training left an impression on him. When his association with criminals is spoken of, it does not mean that he was constantly with the men who were enriched by his ability to plan raids upon property, or that they were his only companions. He was always well-dressed, had a taste for the fine arts, was somewhat of a bibliomaniac, loved the stage not simply for the amusement it afforded him, but to gratify his critical disposition; and many men, prominent in respectable society, knew him more or less intimately as a man about town, seen at theatres, opening of Academy exhibitions, poring over stands in book-stores, and as a frequenter of all libraries to which access could be had. His exterior and bearing were those of a *dilettante* and business man. He was somewhat short of stature, but robust, with a clean-cut, handsome face. Patronizing only the best and most fashionable tailors and haberdashers he always appeared to advantage. Certainly in this city he lived a double life. Many men yet live who remember him as an enigma. They had met him under circumstances which precluded any doubt of his respectability. Of course, in his rôle as a first-class criminal, he did not neglect to associate and ingratiate himself with such of the detective fraternity as might injure or help him.

There is only one instance on record of his having fallen into serious trouble with the police. This was in 1870, at Norristown, a village near Philadelphia. A plot had been laid to rob a jewellery store. It was one of those occasions when Leslie found it necessary to take an active part in the crime. His companion was Gilbert Yost, also known as Charles Howard, *alias* Heard, *alias* Wilbert. By the veriest mischance, probably due to Yost, they were discovered just as they were about to enter the store, and both were captured. Leslie was bailed by a woman who came post-haste from Chicago. It is hardly necessary to say that the bail was estreated. Yost was convicted and served a term of two years in Montgomery Prison.

It happened that shortly before this, Leslie found it convenient to make the City of Philadelphia his headquarters. He moved there in a certain class of society, just as he had done in New York. Of course, the first-class detective talent in that city knew just as well who he was as they did the superintendent of police. But this hidden knowledge was profitable and his identity was kept a profound secret in expectation of prospective lucrative favors. Thus he became an inmate of No. 508 Locust Street, a boarding-house kept by Mrs. Mary E. Coath, the grass-widow of an hotel-keeper whose domestic affairs were so involved that he found it expedient to make a bee-line for the Western mining regions. In this boarding-house Leslie became acquainted with his landlady's daughter, Mary Henrietta Coath, a very fascinating, blue-eyed girl of fourteen years, who had been tenderly brought up and well educated. She fell in love with the strange, handsome, well-dressed, courteous boarder. His courtship was sincere, and she married him when she was fifteen years old, believing him at that time to be an Internal Revenue detective. Even while paying attentions to the girl, however, he kept up his criminal connections, and aided and advised in several large burglaries. The honeymoon was hardly over when the scheme of a gang of first-class burglars to rob the South Kensington National Bank was carried out. The burglars began operations by sending one of their number to the bank in question and informing the cashier that a plot had been set on foot to rob the bank that very night, and it would be best for them to allow none but officers in uniform to enter the premises after banking hours. This messenger professed to have been sent from police headquarters. The watchmen were put on the *qui-vive*, and so when, late on the evening of February 2, 1871, men in the police uniform knocked at the door of the bank and imparted the information that they had been sent as an additional protection, they were immediately admitted. As soon as the door was closed one of the men drew from his pocket a bottle of whiskey, and offered the watchmen a drink. The latter were—well, they were watchmen. One of them found tumblers, and the other drew a little ice-water from the cooler. Before these pleasing preliminaries were completed, however, one of the pretended policemen invited watchman No. 1 outside for the purpose of identifying some suspicious persons who were near by. The other watchman, "Old Murphy," remained inside, and was considerably startled by an unlooked-for occurrence. Before he had an opportunity of realizing what was going on, he was bound and gagged by the very man who had been sent to the assistance of the bank. The other watchman with the alleged policeman knocked, was admitted and likewise bound and gagged. They were completely powerless. In a few moments sufficient safe-breaking tools were brought into the bank by the seeming policemen to open its vault. Short work was made of all obstacles between the burglars and the round $100,000 in cash which the safe contained.

It is to be doubted if Leslie did more than survey the building, locate the safe, estimate the force necessary to get at the plunder, and stand watch for the actual perpetrators of the robbery, who were James McCoy, "Tom" McCormick, "Jim" Casey, "Johnny" Dobbs, "Jim" Brady, Harry Glenn, "Ike" Marsh and "Jimmie" Hope, the last named, Leslie's sole peer, now languishing in jail at San Francisco.

It is said that Joshua Taggart, who at this time controlled the "optional intelligence" of the Philadelphia detective force, was a friend of Leslie's. No arrests were made. When it became necessary to make public the facts of the robbery, it was jokingly said that the car horses even in Philadelphia had been talking about it twenty-four hours after its commission.

Leslie did not stop at the Kensington Bank robbery. He took a part in April, 1872, in the robbery of the Lycoming Insurance Company, at Muncy, Pennsylvania. The "gang" got away from there with only $30,000, but they improved upon that when, five months afterwards, they made a raid on the Third National Bank of Baltimore and secured $140,000. Two months later they levied on the Saratoga County Bank, of Waterford, N. Y., to the extent of $300,000. These depredations were followed by the robbery of John Brennan's jewellery store, No. 13 South Eighth Street, Philadelphia, $30,000; the Wellsbro' Bank, Pennsylvania, $90,000; and the Milford (New Hampshire) Bank of $100,000. There is not the slightest doubt that Leslie participated either in the commission or the division of the plunder of each of these crimes.

It was not until late in 1874 that Leslie's wife knew the real character of the man to whom she was married. When the revelation came, her infatuation for him was such that she was willing to share his fortunes as a confessed villain. 'Tis said that the discovery was made mainly through a dispute with the Philadelphia detective talent. Taggart thought that his share of Leslie's good fortune was not equal to his appetite for hush money. A scheme was accordingly arranged to entrap Leslie. He was arrested; he promised to be more generous; a spoke was put in the wheels of justice and he was given his liberty, to find that his wife was acquainted with his past and prospective career. After the discovery husband and wife went to Brooklyn, N. Y., and resided there in several localities: at the Clinton House in Fulton Street, No. 478 Fulton Street, and No. 861 Greene Avenue, where the Manhattan Bank robbery was planned. Then they went to Harrison Street, Stapleton, Staten Island.

Up to this time, despite the wife's knowledge of her husband's business, her relations with him had been happy. Leslie had ample means at all times, gratified his wife's every wish, was as careful as ever of living before the world as an honest man, and as prudent in conducting his criminal schemes. While at Stapleton, however, Mrs. Leslie noticed that her husband had changed; he often appeared pre-occupied, was harsh to her, not liberal as heretofore, and often absented himself from home for periods varying from a few days to several weeks. It is now known that at first his attentions were devoted to "Babe" Irving, sister of the Johnny Irving who was killed by "John, the Mick," in "Shang" Draper's saloon on Sixth Avenue. In one instance he spent several weeks with "Babe" and a convivial party in the Catskills, neglecting his wife. Leslie was also enamoured of the wife, or mistress, of "Shang" Draper, and it is probable that the money he received from the syndicate was not all spent at home. These liaisons completely changed his mode of life. His proverbial sagacity and prudence deserted him.

When, in February, 1878, it was planned to rob the Dexter Savings Bank, at Dexter, Maine, Leslie did what is known as the "outside" work. In committing the robbery, which netted a very small amount of money, the cashier, James W. Barron, had to be gagged. The scheme was consummated on the 22d of February, 1878. The burglars, sneaking in through the open door, surprised Barron, who was poring over his accounts late at night. The old cashier made such a determined resistance in defending the property of the bank and his own person, that in silencing him the burglars dealt with him so roughly that he was found dead when the robbery was discovered.

Leslie was completely unnerved by this murder, and hurried to his wife, who was then in Baltimore. He told her he was tired of the life he was leading, and determined to end it. He said he had means and proposed to go somewhere and do a legitimate business; open a cigar store in some great city, and silence those who knew of his past career. He left his wife with the understanding that he was going to Albany, N. Y. This was in April, 1878. He returned three weeks later, utterly prostrated and apparently in terror. He said he had made a mistake, and spoke of assassination, but very vaguely. All Mrs. Leslie inferred was, that in some way or other he had got into ill-repute with his associates in crime. When the facts of the Dexter Bank robbery came out she said she had no doubt that Leslie, unnerved by the murder, had dropped a hint, of which some detective in his confidence had made capital.

She saw him alive for the last time on the 10th of May. He then gave her a small sum of money, and told her he had secreted another sum in the house, which might prove very useful to her. There is no doubt that when Leslie left his wife—they were then in Philadelphia—he went directly to Brooklyn, to the house No. 101 Lynch Street, where lived "Shang" Draper, Jemmy Mooney and Gilbert Yost. Hard by, at No. 152 Patchen Avenue, lived "Billy" Porter and "Johnny" Irving. There is little less doubt that two weeks afterwards Leslie was murdered there by his associates, and his body carried to Tramps' Rock, Yonkers, where it was found as already related.

The police having no special interest in shielding those who

BILLY PORTER.
(From a Photograph.)

were implicated in the crime, named "Shang" Draper, "Billy" Porter, "Johnny" Dobbs, "Johnny" Irving and "Sam" Perris, alias "Worcester Sam," as being concerned in it. The police fortified their theory by saying there had been a quarrel over the division of spoils, that Draper was jealous of Leslie, that Irving was opposed to him on account of his intimacy with "Babe," and that Leslie had become "leaky" in regard to professional secrets—notably so in the case of the Dexter Bank robbery. This theory of the police was, in a certain sense, substantiated. In the first place, when the body was found at Tramps' Rock there was straw near it, and also along the road leading to the rock. It was remembered by a countryman that a wagon (of which an accurate description was obtained), drawn by a sorrel horse, was seen in the neighborhood about Decoration Day, at which time the body must have been placed where it was found. One peculiarity about this wagon was that wisps of straw were sticking out from it, and

396.
EDWARD GEARING, *alias* EDDIE GOODIE, BUTCHER-CART THIEF.
(From a Photograph in the Rogues' Gallery.)

there was something covered with straw on the floor of the vehicle. This description traced the wagon to the Astoria Ferry, over it, and thence towards Williamsburg, where all trace of it was lost.

"Ed" Goodie, a burglar associated with the Mandelbaum-Leslie clique, possessed such a horse, and a wagon similar to the one described had been used by him, both in New York and Brooklyn, in removing stolen goods and the furniture of members of the gang. Moreover, when, shortly afterwards, a burglary in Brooklyn was traced to the inmates of the Patchen Avenue house, and thence to Lynch Street, old "Marm" Mandelbaum went to the latter place and carefully superintended the taking away of a vast amount of property, which included a valise! I was particularly anxious to procure this, and while public excitement was at its height I sent out the following "general alarm":

> "Make inquiries of all persons having furnished rooms or apartments to let, for a square sole-leather trunk, marked 'G. L. H., Phila.' If found, notify me at once.
>
> "G. W. WALLING."

JOHN IRVING.
(From a Photograph.)

This trunk, or valise, was traced to Chicago, and there the trail was lost. I supposed, and had good grounds for my belief, that it contained securities in which Leslie had invested his ill-gotten gains. His wife estimated him to be worth anywhere from $40,000 to $70,000. She never received one penny of it.

Corroborative testimony as to the complicity of the men named in the murder was obtained by Detective Wiggin, of Boston, while hunting up clews to the killing of Cashier Barron, at Dexter. His researches led him to Yonkers, where he obtained information that at the time the body must have been placed at Tramps' Rock

"Johnny" Dobbs and "Sam" Perris were seen in the neighborhood of Yonkers. The day after Leslie's body was found, Porter and Irving disappeared.

Mrs. Leslie was advised of the death of her husband by "Marm" Mandelbaum. She came to New York to the funeral (the expenses of which were borne by the noted receiver), was entertained by that lady, given a small sum of money and sent back to Philadelphia. Just before going she heard that Irving and Porter had been arrested on "general principles" by certain detectives. She went to the Tombs and saw them, but they treated her coldly, as though afraid of her. She paid another visit to New York some time afterwards, in order to recover property taken possession of by the coroner at Yonkers, which had been found on her husband's body. Again she made Mrs. Mandelbaum's house her headquarters, and there met Porter, who had been released. He treated her as before, and sneered at her, evading questions in regard to the possibility of George's associates having killed him. Porter's wife—a shop-girl in a Grand Street store—treated her as though pitying, yet dreading her. On this occasion, Mrs. Mandelbaum was "economically" generous to Mrs. Leslie.

Interest in the Leslie murder has waxed and waned since its commission. At times it has appeared as if the secret would out; at others to be as far from solution as ever. It is said that the actual murderer has been often named. He now occupies a liquor saloon on Sixth Avenue under cover of a dummy proprietor, and his place is the resort of thieves and detectives.

The operations of the Leslie gang—composed of men bound by the strongest of ties to "Marm" Mandelbaum—in nine years, in this city alone, amounted to a round half million of dollars. Throughout the United States their plunderings cannot have been less than $7,000,000, comprising 80 per cent. of all the bank robberies perpetrated from 1860 to the date of Leslie's death.

CHAPTER XX.

MOTHER MANDELBAUM, THE QUEEN OF FENCES.—THE OLD WOMAN'S WORD NEVER DOUBTED.—THE HOUSE IN CLINTON STREET.—A PATRON OF CRIMINALS.—THE FIRST MISTAKE.—A DETERMINED DISTRICT ATTORNEY.—DETECTED.—OF FFOR CANADA.—A MOTHER AND HER DEAD DAUGHTER.

RECEIVERS of stolen goods, or, in thieves' slang, "fences," are numerous in New York. That they are known to the police is not of much avail. The great trouble in convicting them is in the matter of identifying the goods they receive. Many robberies are instigated by receivers, and the means for prosecuting them provided by them. Nor is it simply the cost of the jimmy or other special tools. The criminal must live. Having spent the proceeds of a first robbery, the thief may, and often does, become the pensioner of the receiver until a new job is planned and executed. It takes money for a first-class thief to go through a store properly; and to frustrate watchfulness the criminal must spend money freely. A building must be watched for days prior to a robbery, and its ins and outs located. If fellowship is to be cultivated with the watchman of the building, sometimes months elapse before the thief and the guardian are on intimate terms. Invitations to drink are continuous. I have even known women in the employ of burglars becoming acquainted with the wives of the watchmen of large stores, and in time the men were introduced. Not infrequently a horse and wagon must be provided. If there is money in the job, money is required to launch it, and in all this it is the receiver who is the financial backer of the robber. Affiliations between the receivers and the criminal classes are constant. If there were no markets for stolen goods, there would be no robberies. The police may be morally certain a person is a receiver, and for years be known to associate with criminals. In the courts, when men have been arrested for robberies, such receivers have furnished the money necessary to defray the expenses of the defence. Goods, doubtless stolen, have been traced to the "fence," and yet no conviction has followed. The almost insurmountable difficulty in obtaining the conviction of a receiver lies in the fact that the major portion of the goods in which he deals cannot be identified. One piece of silk, velvet, cloth, or calico, looks like another when it has been stripped of its private mark, or such printing as may have been on it originally. A merchant has been robbed and his goods taken. The articles found in the "fence's" possession are brought into court, but the merchant has sold many of the same kind. Both the thief and the receiver know their business perfectly. Say a store has been robbed and the goods have been carried off to a secure place. Every bit of silk, velvet, or cloth, is immediately unwound, a most careful search is made for private marks, and all tickets, tags, or printed labels are destroyed. The thief's careful efforts to efface the identity of the goods does not suffice a clever and cautious receiver. If he agrees to buy the goods he is not satisfied until he, too, has them examined once more, and then only does he pay for the goods. But before the business has come to this stage, a great deal of caution has been exercised. It may be dangerous for the thief to sell the goods to the receivers too soon after the robbery; and accordingly some months may elapse before the transfer to the "fence" takes place. During the interval, however, the receiver may deal out some money to the thieves, as an advance. Sometimes it happens that the receiver has one or several agents in his employ, who act as go-betweens, or brokers, in "shady" goods. It can be understood readily how goods, coming from a robbery in New York, may be sold in Philadelphia or Boston, or may be shipped to a southern or western city for disposal at auction.

MOTHER MANDELBAUM.
(From a Photograph.)

But what of the "Queen of Fences"?

A quarter of a century ago, William Mandelbaum kept a haberdashery shop in this city. He was a bustling Israelite, but his wife, Frances, or Fredericka, was his superior in business capacity. They started as dealers in the proceeds of robberies in a very small way. The woman took the lead in these nefarious transactions, speedily acquiring a knowledge of the machinery by which criminals are brought to justice. She formed an acquaintance with those who apprehended rogues of all degrees; knew where the wheel of justice could be clogged, and learned the value of a little money when criminals were "in trouble." She was a thorough business woman; her husband was a nonentity. He passed away many years ago, leaving her an adept in discovering where tact, correct knowledge and a little or more money would do the most good.

"Marm" Mandelbaum was a wonderful person; she changed character like a chameleon, and was as adept in her business as the best stock-broker in Wall Street in his. The best of her days were passed less than fifteen years ago. Her acquaintance with policemen and the machinery of the law became more and more accurate. She knew the routine by which the suspected persons reached the grand jury as well as the district attorney himself. Her knowledge of criminals was fully equal to that of the venality of certain lesser members of the police department. In a few words, she established a "Bureau for the Prevention of Conviction" of certain first-class criminals.

Some enjoyed her highest favor, others were simply used to make money. As time went on, her dealings in stolen property are believed to have been enormous. She was known not only throughout the United States, but in Canada, Mexico and Europe. I am morally convinced that she had transactions in stolen property chiefly "collateral," which consists of gold, silver plate, precious stones, etc., in all parts of Europe. She attained a reputation as a business woman whose honesty in criminal matters was absolute, by her adherence to criminal ethics so far as they regarded men who had been graduates in the school of housebreaking and shop-lifting, and the promptness with which she settled her accounts with them. And not only this, she never left a criminal her creditor. When he was in need—caught *flagrante delicto*, red-handed, under circumstances which she could not control—she became his banker, and he could draw on her for sums which, in her estimation of the capabilities of a first-class criminal, he could not hope to repay within many years.

Her establishment in the matter of receiving stolen goods was perfect. It is said she paid a retainer of $5000 a year to the well-known criminal lawyers, Messrs. Howe & Hummel.

The ramifications of her business net were so widespread, her ingenuity as an assistant to criminals so nearly approached genius, that if a silk robbery occurred in St. Louis, and the criminals were known as "belonging to Marm Baum," she always had the first choice of the "swag."

At the police court, the arrest of one of her "gang" was the signal for the instant appearance of one or more of the tribe of lawyers allied with her, and paid liberally for their assistance. Suspicions are not wanting that some of the clerks who drew up

659.
"BIG" FRANK McCOY.
(From a Photograph in the Rogues' Gallery.)

the "informations" knew too well the value of English grammar to neglect slurring it in her interests.

There were many unimportant and less direct channels by which cases reached the grand jury and the district attorney's office, but the Hon. Wm. M. Tweed's advice in this regard—"look after the little things"—was not disregarded. Cases might be mentioned where petty matters were so well taken care of on their way from the police-court to the district attorney's office and the grand-jury room, that the prisoners escaped indictment with an ease that they marvelled at until the "old woman" claimed the credit for the miscarriage of justice. And no man of that class of which she was the head ever doubted her word.

Her methods were extraordinarily simple. She kept what appeared to be a thriving dry goods and haberdashery shop, at No. 79 Clinton Street. The house was rated as "fourth class" by the insurance company, being possibly one-sixth brick and five-sixths wood. It was a straggling, ill-built, yet curious looking building, more pretentious at its angle with Rivington Street than at any other. This angle was the business concern which concealed the real occupation of its owner. Sprawling away from this angle down Clinton Street was the actual business part of the establishment. This was a two-story, clapboarded wing, some twenty-five feet long. On the first floor was one of the best furnished apartments in this city, a room the like of which was not to be found anywhere in the region known as *Kleine Deutschland*, or Little Germany. Whether " Marm " Mandelbaum intended to astonish her clients by a display of her wealth, or to show that she lived in a style befitting her position, cannot here be discussed. There were chairs which would have attracted the cupidity of an antiquarian; a massive mahogany sideboard, and on it a magnificent display of silverware, such as would have been rated as "A 1 swag" had a "client" of the old woman called on her to dispose of it.

On the shelves of the store where the ostensible business of the concern was conducted were displayed the usual assortment of dry goods suitable to the needs of the neighborhood. The attendants were usually Mrs. Mandelbaum (the presiding deity), one of her two daughters, a hired shop-woman, and the successor to the Hon. William Mandelbaum (her late and lamented spouse), Hermann Steid, a stalwart looking man, with curling blonde hair. Mrs. Mandelbaum, thanks to her business capacity, could have easily earned an excellent living simply by keeping a dry goods establishment. She preferred " minting " money by dealing with thieves.

Right here a glance at the proprietress of the store will not be out of place. She was a woman above the middle height, sufficiently corpulent to be easily caricatured, who never, possibly, had enough of coquetry to indulge in corsets, with a large mouth and thick lips. But she was shrewd, careful, methodical in char-

MANDELBAUM STORE AND HOUSE.

acter, and to the point in speech. Wary in the extreme, she never admitted any one unknown to her and unvouched for beyond the precincts of the little dry goods store. Once the entrée given by a hint, note or personal recommendation from any one she depended on, and the little wing of her establishment was wide open to him or her.

Passing from the store to the real office of the concern was a dumb-waiter let into the wall.

"Marm" Mandelbaum's methods grew bolder as her reputation

MICHAEL KURTZ, *alias* "SHEENEY MIKE."
(From a Photograph when under Duress.)

increased. The majority of her transactions were conducted by correspondence, or through messengers. It is almost certain that within the last ten years of her life in New York she rarely received stolen property in bulk at her Clinton Street shop. Suppose, for instance, there had been a robbery of silk in the city. The "swag" would be first "planted" (stored). A messenger would call on her, and she would send a trusted agent to examine the goods thoroughly and report to her.

She would estimate their value to her, make an offer, haggle enough to satisfy her race instinct, pay cash for the "stuff," take the risk of shipping it or secreting it elsewhere, and afterwards make arrangements for its disposal at a profit.

In the case of what is known as "collateral," she usually transacted business at home, first having obtained from the thief a good description and inventory of the plunder. She then made an appointment elsewhere for appraisement and settlement of the matter.

Her interest in professional criminals of a certain class has been spoken of elsewhere. It was far reaching. She has sent money to defend a man "in hock" to the uttermost parts of the United States, and, in several instances, to Canada and Europe. Not only has she sent money for the defence of criminals, but, aware of the objects of their trips abroad, on receipt of information that their operations were delayed by want of funds, she has promptly sent out generous letters of credit. Among those who were especially favored by her were: First, last, and all the time, the champion burglar of America, Michael Kurtz, *alias* "Sheeney Mike"; "Billy" O'Brien, *alias* "Billy" Porter; "Jim" Brady, "Shang" Draper, "Red" Leary, "Big Frank" McCoy, "Jimmy" Wilmot, "Jimmy" Hope, "Ed" Goodie, "Jim" Casey, "Joe" Dollard, "Johnny" Dobbs, "Sam" Perris, "Jimmy" Dunlap, Oscar Decker, "Tom" McCormick, "Piano Charley," "Pete" Emerson, "Billy" McKay, "Pete" Curley, "Bill" Connors, "Jack" Rand, "Ike" Marsh, and a host of smaller fry.

But "Marm" Mandelbaum had to come to grief sometimes. Twelve years ago there was an awkward inquiry about the robbery of $12,000 worth of silk (her specialty). The losers by the theft—prominent merchants—were not to be placated by any sophistries. They would have spent the whole capital of the firm in convicting either the thieves or the receiver. But despite all efforts in the interests of justice, Mrs. Mandelbaum came safely out of the ordeal, although arrested as nearly red-handed as it was possible for a receiver of stolen goods to be. She was not convicted.

And here I must say that the higher officials of the police force were most active in the attempt to convict her. She was watched on all sides, and it was only her great cunning and shrewdness that enabled her to continue her nefarious business for such a length of time.

She had not been without anxiety. Nothing disturbed her so

much as the "fuss," as she termed it, which was made about the murder of George Leonidas Leslie. She got out of the scrape at a cost of (it is believed) not less than $12,000.

Her next great trouble came to her through the well-meaning and active, but, owing to circumstances, almost impotent district attorney, Peter B. Olney. Mr. Olney undoubtedly took the utmost aggressive interest in "Mother" Mandelbaum's affairs. If his private utterances are to be believed, and there has never been, among respectable persons, a doubt in this regard, he thought that the existence of a woman who by various means had been enabled to control the most dangerous and wealthy criminal interests of America, was a burning shame. He employed the Pinkerton agency, in order to discover a plan by which either the woman might be brought to justice or her business broken up. Special officers, detailed to watch her, visited her place in the guise of petty thieves. Gradually they obtained her confidence. Others were detailed to purchase goods from her by representing that they wanted to drive a hard bargain in stolen goods, knowing that she was the right person to whom to apply. Accordingly, on the one hand they obtained absolute proof that "Mother" Mandelbaum bought "stuff" from persons who represented that they had obtained it by criminal means, and on the other hand they were assured that she sold goods at less than cost price, which she said had been obtained feloniously. In the latter instance the detectives were able to corner her.

Among the goods sold were pieces of silk which had been stolen, and on them were certain marks by which they could be recognized. These goods, purchased by one of Pinkerton's "operatives," were identified by Jas. A. Hearn & Son, of West Fourteenth Street, and Messrs. Simpson, Crawford & Simpson. And so it came about that on the 22d of July, 1884, Mr. Olney had so far perfected his case against Mrs. Mandelbaum that he ordered her arrest. She was arraigned in the Harlem Police Court. As was to be expected, the prosecution encountered a tremendous array of the best criminal talent of the New York bar, and a big fight was made through the many agencies she controlled in her behalf. Her son Julius and Hermann Steid were arrested with her.

"Marm" Mandelbaum got the worst of the fight. She appreciated this fact on December 4, 1884, when, seeing that a conviction was made inevitable, she made the best of her way to Canada.

GEO. MASON, *alias* OSCAR DECKER, BURGLAR, No. 1027.
(From a Photograph taken under Duress.)

Her bondsman, George Speckhardt, of No. 161 Rivington Street, who had become surety for her appearance before the grand jury in the sum of $3000, was a loser of that amount.

Mrs. Mandelbaum selected Toronto as her residence, and four days after her arrival there, was arrested by the Canadian authorities, but was as promptly released.

Since her flight from New York Mrs. Mandelbaum has lived quietly in Canada. Her exile has been cheered by frequent visits from emissaries of her council, and saddened by the intelligence of the death of her younger daughter. It is asserted, and the fact has never been contradicted, that when the unfortunate and beautiful girl died, the motherly instincts of Mrs. Mandelbaum were so excited, that, braving arrest, she left Canada in disguise and travelled by a circuitous route—from Montreal to Rouse's Point, then by the Rome, Watertown and Ogdensburg Railroad to Utica, thence by private conveyance to the Erie Road—to New York. She dared not follow the body to the grave, but saw the funeral on its way and immediately went back to her forced home in Canada.

It is estimated that despite her misfortunes, lawyers' fees, loss of "business," and a sojourn in a country where every fugitive, once spotted, is considered fair material for "bleeding," "Marm" Mandelbaum can command at least $125,000. She has told persons who have seen her in the "land of the bank cashier" that she would gladly forfeit every penny of her wealth in order to once more breathe freely the atmosphere of the Thirteenth Ward.

As a woman and a mother she is spoken of with respect. Her family consisted of two sons and two daughters. Of the boys, one clung to her as her *alter ego*. The other is a respectable citizen. Of the daughters, one, as beautiful a girl as any of her race in this city, died just as she came to know what her mother really was. The other, strangely enough, is married to a private detective. This daughter was so deeply interested in the shadowy part of her mother's "business" transactions, that when times became threatening she took apartments within a block of the store, with the intention of receiving such "informers" as her parent could not conveniently see, and to watch prowlers who might be investigating the "business" of the little store at Clinton and Rivington streets.

As a receiver of stolen goods, "Marm" Mandelbaum had no peer in the United States. In New York, the shop of the great

BARON MÜNCHAUSEN'S DINNER-PARTY.

Grady was simply an annex of the Clinton Street establishment. He dealt mainly in collateral of which Mrs. Mandelbaum found it inconvenient to dispose, and considered dangerous to have in her possession.

Madame Mandelbaum's favorite article of plunder was silk. Next of importance, in her estimation, came gold and silverware. Then ranked the miscellaneous booty resulting from a burglarious or shop-lifting excursion in a dry goods store, such as laces, gloves, etc. Her first care was to look for trade-marks, and in this branch of her calling she was very expert. Labels and tags, of course, were immediately removed. Private marks were also searched for. Now and then she dealt in stolen bonds, having a safe outlet for such things among a certain class of brokers, who for a large percentage would deal in securities whose ownership was doubtful.

Mrs. Mandelbaum depleted her income in good living. She had a cellar of choice wines and liquors and was a liberal patron of the local synagogue, of which she was considered a consistent member. In the winter she frequently gave entertainments to thieves of both sexes and outside friends, and the receptions were conducted with as much attention to the proprieties of society as though Mrs. Mandelbaum's establishment was in Fifth Avenue instead of in a suspicious corner of the East Side.

CHAPTER XXI.

ESCAPES FROM PRISON.—THE STRANGE WOMAN IN BLACK WHO WALKED OUT OF THE TOMBS.—THE BANK BURGLAR'S SWEETHEART.—" YOUR TICKET, PLEASE."—THE MAN WHO SOAPED HIS BODY AND WRIGGLED THROUGH A HOLE.—DESPERATE FIGHT IN A BOWERY BEER SALOON.—A BOLD LEAP FOR LIBERTY.—THE STRANGE MAN ON DE KALB AVENUE WITH TWO COATS.—THE WAX IMPRESSION FOUND IN LONG MARY'S ROOM. — " RED LEARY'S ESCAPED ! "

A YOUNG and pretty girl was standing on the sidewalk in front of the iron gate which admits visitors to the Tombs prison, on the morning of November 19, 1873, waiting for the keeper to unfasten the lock and allow friends of the prisoners to enter. When ten o'clock came the heavy gate swung open, and the throng outside passed in. One, at least, this same young and pretty girl, was well known to the keepers. Her beautiful face appealed to their sensibilities, and perhaps as she stood before them they did not perform their duty of searching her as thoroughly as they might have. At any rate, she received her ticket and passed by the keepers until she had reached cell No. 40. Here she stopped, and peered between the iron gratings. He whom she had come to see stepped forward quickly, and the meeting of the prisoner and his visitor was cordial. The cell was richly fitted up and the occupant evidently was not leading a very restricted life.

The man in the cell was William J. Sharkey; the woman outside was Maggie Jourdan. Sharkey had been a pickpocket, a gambler, a notorious bank burglar, a politician of no mean influence, and the murderer of Robert S. Dunn. For this last crime he had been tried and found guilty. While awaiting his sentence a stay of proceedings was granted, but the arguments on the case had not been heard when Maggie Jourdan, the criminal's sweetheart, walked into the Tombs on that November morning.

If the keeper who was at the door when Maggie Jourdan entered and was given her ticket of exit had searched this bright young woman more thoroughly, he might have discovered that she carried on her person, not one set of raiment, but two. But the keeper did not notice this, so Sharkey's sweetheart brought up to his cell a woman's complete outfit, which, as soon as she could get from her person, he put on his. To make him look more feminine he shaved off his mustache. At last the disguise was complete. He took the key which Maggie held closely in her hands and

WM. J. SHARKEY.
(From a Photograph.)

found that the lock worked perfectly. At one o'clock Maggie left him and walked out of the prison.

It was scarcely a half hour after Maggie Jourdan had passed out that another woman came from the prison corridors, and giving up the usual visitor's ticket was allowed by Keeper Phillips to walk out without molestation or undue scrutiny. This second woman was dressed in a dark woollen dress, black cloak, and an Alpine hat. She wore a thick green veil, which she kept close to her face. She was large and rather masculine in appearance. An hour later, Mrs. "Wes" Allen, a sister-in-law of "The" Allen whose husband was in the Tombs, attempted to pass Keeper Kennedy who was then at the door.

"Your ticket, please," Kennedy remarked, as he looked at the woman.

The latter stopped, put her hand in her dress pocket, and after fumbling about her clothing for a moment, exclaimed.

"Why, I must have lost it. I'm sure I put it in my pocket!"

But Keeper Kennedy was not to be moved by such an excuse as that, and Mrs. Allen did not make her exit from the prison that morning as soon as she expected, for she was at once put in care of the officer, while an alarm was given and the cells were searched. When the investigating officers had reached cell No. 40, they discovered that its occupant was not there. The door was unlocked, and Sharkey's clothing lay on the floor. On a little shelf were found some locks of hair which were supposed to be the remains of the murderer's mustache. The whole thing was clear enough now. The masculine-appearing creature who had walked past the keeper with her green veil drawn tightly over her face was none other than William J. Sharkey, the pickpocket, politician, burglar and murderer, the one man of all who were then in the Tombs that should have been constantly watched.

To say that there was excitement in that gloomy old building is expressing it mildly. Of course the police were at once notified and began work on the case. Mrs. "Wes" Allen was arrested for complicity in the escape, but was afterwards discharged, as no actual proof could be secured against her. The same was true of Keeper Phillips. On Maggie Jourdan something stronger than suspicion rested. It was discovered that previous to the day of Sharkey's escape she had taken an impression in wax of the lock on her lover's cell, and, assisted by Sharkey's confederates outside the prison, had managed to have a key made. The first key tried would not move the lock, but the second worked successfully. Maggie was arrested and tried on the charge of helping Sharkey to escape, but although everybody believed her guilty the jury failed to agree upon a verdict, and the girl was set at liberty. Her boldness in assisting Sharkey was universally wondered at. The fact was that she was deeply infatuated with the man. He had a pleasing appearance, and was undoubtedly fascinating to certain persons. Her devotion to him was constant. She visited him every day in prison, and after his escape, while she herself

ESCAPE OF SHARKEY.

was in custody and knew her lover's whereabouts, she did nor said nothing by which the police could guess where he was.

In fact it is not known to this day where Sharkey went directly after his escape. It is pretty certain that he remained in New York for three or four weeks, but he managed very shrewdly to elude the detectives who were after him. When at last he did leave New York, it was on a small schooner bound for Baracoa, Cuba. From Baracoa he went to Havana, where two years later he was joined by Maggie Jourdan, whose affection had not dwindled in spite of time and separation. The girl's devotion, however, was but poorly rewarded. With base ingratitude he soon began to ill-use her. To his harsh treatment she at first submitted, but when it continued day after day her infatuation ceased, and indignant at Sharkey's insults she left the man for whom she had perilled so much, and returned to New York.

There is something daring in an escape from prison that appeals to popular interest. Here are gigantic walls, massive iron bars, complex locks, all built and put together with the greatest ingenuity and skill, and with the express purpose of preventing escapes; and yet here is a shrewd prisoner who has been successful in defying them all. It is not strange that people want to know how he did it. As a general thing they are far more interested in a clever escape than they are in a dexterous burglary, or even in a murder. With the great caution which is exercised in our prisons it must be a bold mind which would even think of trying to escape. But to succeed in breaking through bars and eluding the watchful eyes of keepers displays cunning and ability of no mean order. To the credit of the men who have had charge of the Tombs prison be it said there have been in the last thirty-five years only twenty-eight escapes from that place of confinement.

The first of these of which we have any record is that of Henry A. Clark, who managed in some way to break out on December 21, 1851. We have no details as to his manner of escaping. There were two escapes during the following year: James Hampton leaped through a window in the court-room, and Robert Green, who was imprisoned on a charge of grand larceny, got out of his cell on the second tier, and surrendering a forged ticket at the keeper's gate walked quietly out into the air and freedom.

At four o'clock on the afternoon of April 11, 1859, six boys, named Bartholomew Upton, Edward Upton, Peter McCann, Frederick Lowe, Thomas Flynn and John Mahoney crawled through a window on the Franklin Street side of the prison. There were some laboring men near by who watched the escape, but gave no alarm. The boys got safely away and were never re-captured. A shrewd trick was played by Henry Hawk, a noted burglar, who made his escape in July, 1860. When the names of prisoners who were to be discharged were called, he walked boldly up and out.

An escape which ranks with that of Sharkey was made on September 19, 1863. The prisoner was Conrad Smith, alias Schrader. With two other prisoners he was confined in a cell on the second tier. Assisted by them he removed the iron lintel under the window, leaving an aperture twenty-nine inches long and six and a quarter inches broad. When this had been done he soaped himself from head to foot, and then managed to wriggle through the small space. He dropped to the ground below, and from there climbed to the roof of the cook-house, which was in the rear of the prison. The top of the outer wall was thirty feet from where he stood, but in some way he got upon it and then jumped to the street—a free man. He went immediately among his "pals," who kept him secreted for a month. At the end of that time, however, the police found him in a Bowery lager beer saloon, and attempted to arrest him. But Smith resisted. He did not care to go back to prison and was willing to fight for his liberty. It was only after a desperate encounter that he was re-captured.

In 1879 there was a very bold escape of a man who had been imprisoned on a slight charge of disorderly conduct. Dennis Sullivan, while waiting in the prisoners' pen at the Tombs police-court for his turn to be arraigned, suddenly vaulted over the railing, sprang to the open window near by, and leaped through to the street beneath. The thing was all done with such dexterity of movement that none of the numerous policemen in the court-room could interfere. Indeed there was one policeman within four feet of the window, and although he jumped to catch the escaping prisoner, he had the pleasure only of seeing the latter's coat-tails disappear through his fingers. The crowd of persons who frequent the court-room were greatly excited. In spite of the efforts of the judge to preserve the dignity of the court, there was a rush of spectators to the doors and great consternation among the officers on duty. At least twenty policemen started in pursuit of the fugitive. He ran from Centre Street through Mulberry, and from there to Bayard Street. Here he was lost sight of and has never been seen since.

It was early in the morning, but broad daylight, on June 1, 1879, when "Billy" Porter and John Irving turned their backs upon Raymond Street Jail, Brooklyn, where they had been deprived of their liberty for the last ten months. They had the "run" of one of the corridors, and were in the habit, between six and seven o'clock in the morning, to pass down to the kitchen and get their cups filled with coffee. Porter and Irving rose a little earlier than their fellow-prisoners on that eventful morning. The two cooks who were in the kitchen were not at all surprised when the notorious criminals entered with cups in hand. But when they put down their cups on the table, and walked boldly across the kitchen and up the stairway leading to the jail-yard, then the cooks were struck dumb with amazement and raised neither hand nor voice to prevent the escape.

Having reached the jail-yard, Irving and Porter walked boldly across and entered the stable-yards. There were some men at work here, but just as the two convicts entered the yard the attention of the laborers was diverted by heavy knocking outside the wall. So believing themselves unseen by the men, Irving and Porter stepped stealthily across the stable-yard to some excavations which were making in the wall. Through these they crawled and were soon outside the jail limits, and in the adjoining grounds of the city hospital.

But some one after all did observe the transit of the convicts across the stable-yard. This person was John Cassin, one of the men who were employed in the yard. He ran at once to Keeper Joseph Evans and exclaimed:

"They've got out!"

"Who?" asked the keeper, all excitement.

"Irving and Porter," gasped the man, whose breath had been exhausted by his hasty run.

This intelligence was enough to send a dozen fears through Evans's mind. He rapidly asked a few questions and then hastened out to Raymond Street and looked up and down to see if he could see some sign of the runaways. But he saw nothing. He ran back into the jail and told Warden Bryan what had happened. The warden became excited too. He telegraphed Sheriff Riley at the latter's house, and sent out a general alarm to the police headquarters of Brooklyn, New York and adjoining cities. From there in turn went out instructions to all the precincts to watch for men of Irving's and Porter's description. Inside Raymond Street Jail a search was instituted, and the manner of the escape was soon ascertained. Subsequent investigations revealed the fact that after the convicts had got outside the jail walls they went immediately to De Kalb Avenue, where they were seen to receive two coats from a strange man. From here all trace of them was lost, and when at last they were re-captured, it was not for breaking jail, but for worse offences.

Porter and Irving belonged to what was known as the Patchen Avenue gang, one of the fiercest which at that time infested Brooklyn. They were all notorious burglars, but none were better known than Irving and Porter. The two were close friends and often "buckled" together to avenge wrongs or insults which one had received. They were arrested on August 11, 1878, for burglary, and had been in jail ten months when they made their escape. Porter had been tried and found guilty, and was awaiting sentence. He had been meditating escape for some time, and there is reason to think that his delay in attempting it was only from a hope that he might not be found guilty. When the jury's verdict upset this hope he was ready to carry his plot into execution. There is no doubt that he and Irving were helped by confederates outside the prison, and the knocking which the laborers in the stable-yard heard outside the walls on the morning of the escape was doubtless the work of the convicts' friends, who hoped thereby to divert attention from the runaways. Sheriff Riley offered a reward of $2500 for the return of the prisoners, but so far as I am aware no one ever secured the money. The two men were conspicuous figures in subsequent crimes which startled the country. Irving met his death a few years later in "Shang" Draper's saloon on Sixth avenue, at the hands of John Walsh. Porter was supposed to have avenged his colleague's death by killing Walsh, but he escaped conviction and promised to lead a different sort of life in the future. How little his reformation amounted to may be seen when I add that during the present summer he was arrested for robbing a jewellery store in Troy, and having given bail to the amount of $20,000, returned to his old haunts in this city.

At dusk one night in the autumn of 1873, a man named Henry Smith and a woman named Lilly Miller set out from Tarrytown in a small boat and pulled for Sing Sing. Having reached their destination they got stealthily out of the boat, and took with them a large bag in which was concealed something of considerable weight. This they carried over to the prison yard and concealed in a lumber pile. In some inexplicable way the contents of this bag—which were nothing more or less than a powerful jackscrew and some smaller tools—reached gallery No. 19 in the prison, where "Jim" Brady, who, previous to his lodgment in Sing Sing, had been publicly flogged and sentenced to twenty years' imprisonment at Newcastle, Delaware, for burglary, and W. A. Miller, a notorious rascal, were confined. One day this illustrious pair of striped convicts walked out of their cells, out of gallery No. 19, and with their jackscrews and other tools having forced the iron bars at the window overlooking the prison yard, squeezed through the aperture and dropped to the ground beneath. Having reached the yard, escape was comparatively easy.

There was no little consternation when Miller and Brady were missed from their cells. Keepers of course appeared as much astonished as any one, and everybody wondered, first, how the convicts could have secured possession of their tools; and second, how they could have obtained the keys which unfastened the doors leading into the gallery. The mystery deepened when days and weeks went by without any light having been shown on the manner of the escape, and when subsequent sudden departures of convicts from Sing Sing seemed as easily accomplished as that of Miller and Brady. Among the desperate characters who made their way out of the prison about this time was "Jimmy" Hope, the notorious burglar, who had suffered with Brady in Newcastle, Delaware, and for the same offence. Others were Sophie Levy, W. C. Harrison, Joe Howard, and John O'Keefe. Ned Lyons and his wife were both imprisoned. "Ned" got out, but instead of leaving the vicinity of Sing Sing, he loitered near the prison, and one day drove into the grounds in a carriage, picked up his wife, who was in the female prison, and drove off without interference.

Such things as these made people think that there was something "rotten" in Sing Sing. New Yorkers began to grow excited over the number of escapes. The newspapers called loudly for reform in the management, and the department of police came to the conclusion that it was time for it to take a hand in ferreting out the mystery. Accordingly, there were put on the case Captain

Irving and detectives Thomas Sampson and Philip Farley, of the Central Office. These gentlemen worked for some time without any success. Finally, by mere accident, they stumbled upon a clew. Mary Moon, called "Long Mary," was arrested on February 18, 1874, for shop-lifting. Her room, which was on Third Avenue near Fifty-second Street, was searched by the same officers who were engaged in the Sing Sing mystery. They found numerous articles which they thought would help in proving the charge of shop-lifting against the woman. Suddenly one of the detectives came upon a suspicious-looking tin box which was hidden in a bureau drawer. The box was taken out and opened. Inside, carefully wrapped in soft paper, was the wax impression of a large key. It is needless to say that these officers were familiar with the key which unlocked the doors in gallery No. 19 at Sing Sing, and at once they recognized in the wax impression a familiar shape.

Of course they lost no time in confirming the suspicion which at once entered their minds, that "Long Mary" was an accomplice of the jail-birds' confederates. They had a key made according to the impression, and then went to Sing Sing. They saw Warden Hubbell, who, although not told of their errand, received them kindly and conducted them through the prison. When the detectives reached gallery No. 19 they tried the key, and found it to be a perfect fit to the lock. Now they had a definite clew to work upon. Without telling the warden their suspicions they came back to New York and proceeded to look up Long Mary's friends in the city. They found one, Henry Smith, whom they arrested on suspicion. By clever work they secured from him a confession which implicated John Steurer, a German locksmith, whose establishment was at No. 106 Hester Street.

The next move on the part of the detectives was to find out all they could from Steurer. So pretending to be burglars they went to Steurer's shop one afternoon, and found him at dinner. He left his meal to see what his visitors wanted, but they assured him that they wished to have a few words with him in private and would wait until he finished his dinner. The old German "tumbled" at once, and chuckling to himself over securing more valuable customers went back to his sauerkraut. He soon returned to the basement where his shop was and asked the men what he could do for them. The detectives tried a "bluff" game on him.

They began to upbraid him for selling them such poor tools recently.

"Why, that jackscrew was good for nothing," said Detective Farley.

The old fellow had no doubt now, if he had been suspicious at all, that his visitors were men whom he had previously worked for through third persons, and he began to beg their pardon and explain that the second jackscrew was all right. By careful work they trapped Steurer several times, he growing more confidential all the time, and finally they induced him to accompany them to the house of a friend of theirs, where they wished him to see a certain tool of which they were to order one similar. The unsuspecting manufacturer of burglars' outfits willingly followed their guidance, nor did he turn back when they had led him into police headquarters. It even took him some time to believe that he was under arrest, and that his three customers were not burglars after all, but Central Office detectives.

With the information which Steurer had already divulged, and what was subsequently got from him, it was learned that Henry Smith and Lilly Miller were the outside confederates of Miller and Brady, the escaped Sing Sing prisoners. They, it seems, had gone to Steurer's shop and ordered the tools which were afterward taken to Tarrytown, and thence by boat to Sing Sing and placed in the lumber pile. Smith had already been arrested, and now Lilly Miller was taken to police headquarters. But the detectives had still to prove who had assisted the escaped prisoners inside the prison. By this time, however, the warden had become alarmed, and was making an investigation on his own account. Through Keeper Gale, he forced a confession from Keeper John Outhouse. This confession implicated David Manny, another keeper, who was said to have taken the wax impression of the key to No. 19. Manny was afterward acquitted, however, of any complicity in the escapes. Outhouse admitted that he had taken the tools to Miller and Brady, and that he had received $1000 for his assistance.

After these revelations escapes from Sing Sing were not such frequent occurrences.

A few minutes before eleven o'clock on the night of May 7, 1879, Roundsman Hirney ran breathlessly into the Eldridge Street police station, and cried out: "'Red' Leary's escaped from

Ludlow Street Jail!" The policemen who were around the room looked up in amazement, and the sergeant in command began at once to order out a number of men for the search. No sooner had he given the order than another man ran excitedly into the station-house and gave the alarm. This person was Bernard Fitzsimmons, who was acting-warden of the jail at the time. The men whom the sergeant had ordered out accompanied Fitzsimmons to the jail, and he posted them at different points about the block,

"RED" LEARY.
(From a Photograph.)

so that the jail-breaker might not escape from the immediate vicinity. When some time had passed and no sign of "Red" Leary had been seen, the policemen searched through all the buildings in the square, but with no better result.

In the mean while, however, the excited condition of the employees in the jail had given way to coolness, and a close examination revealed the manner of the notorious burglar's escape. Leary's cell was on the first tier. On the third tier there was a corridor, at the end of which was a water-closet. Leary was allowed the run of the corridor until 10.30 P.M. The floor of the corridor corresponded to the second story of the jail. It was Keeper Wendell's duty to see that Leary was in his cell at the proper time, and at 10.30 o'clock he made his nightly round. When he reached the door of the prisoner's apartment he found it partly opened. He looked inside and called out, "Hullo, there, Leary!" No answer came. Thinking the prisoner might be asleep he walked into the narrow room, but found no one there. He looked under the iron bedstead and still saw no one. "He must be up in the corridor," thought the keeper, and proceeded up stairs. But there was no Leary in the corridor, nor in the closet. Wendell now was thoroughly aroused. He rushed down stairs and told Acting-Warden Fitzsimmons, who at once started for the police station. While he was absent, and the men from the Eldridge Street station were searching the block, a vigorous investigation was made about the jail. One of the keepers went into the closet again at the end of the corridor on the third tier of cells, and there the mystery was solved. A huge hole was found in one corner of the room. Assistance was summoned, and surrounded by a crowd of excited employees of the prison, one of the keepers entered the hole to explore it. He did not know where it would take him, or what obstacles he would meet at the end of it. Perhaps Red Leary himself was there with a club in his hands to dash out the brains of the first man who stuck his head through. But whatever fears the keeper had he did not show them, and worked his way on through the aperture. He crawled at least five feet and then found himself in a room on the fifth floor of the tenement house which adjoined the jail. Then the manner of the burglar's escape was solved. A search of the tenement house was made at once, but no "Red" Leary was found.

The investigation, however, showed that some weeks previously a woman named Mrs. Myers, whose husband was a 'longshoreman, had taken three rooms in No. 76 Ludlow Street, the large tenement house next the jail. About the same time two men took rooms in the third story on the side near the jail, and then almost immediately moved to the fifth story. The second floor of the jail was three feet below the fifth floor of the tenement. From these rooms the men burrowed with mathematical precision down through the five feet of wall into the water-closet of the jail. Leary was kept posted as to their progress by his wife, who visited him frequently. She was there on the day of the escape at 12 o'clock, and again from five until eight o'clock in the evening. During this last visit it is likely that the final arrangements were made for the arch-rascal's gaining his liberty. When the room into which the hole from the jail entered was searched, nearly a wagon load of bricks were found in the fireplace. As they had been taken out they had been carefully piled and concealed. A broken hydraulic jimmy was found near the scene of labor, and scraps of food and cooking utensils lay scattered around the room.

Leary was in jail awaiting extradition papers by which he was to be taken to Northampton and tried for the famous burglary which was committed in the National Bank of that place. After his escape he went to Europe, but returned again to this country, and was re-captured in Brooklyn on February 4, 1881.

CHAPTER XXII.

PERSECUTING THE RECTOR OF TRINITY CHURCH.—ONSLAUGHT OF THE CHILDREN OF ISRAEL.—NOT AN EPILEPTIC FIT.—UNWELCOME LIQUOR BILLS.—A "HERALD" PERSONAL.—AN INDIGNANT HUSBAND.—TRACING THE HANDWRITING.—FOUND IN BALTIMORE.—"GENTLEMAN JOE'S" DEATH.

ONE of the most extraordinary mysteries that ever puzzled the police, the press and the people was the daring persecution of the Rev. Dr. Morgan Dix, the rector of Trinity Church, by "Gentleman Joe," in the winter of 1880. To this day those concerned in the capture of the rascal who kept the aged clergyman, the police department and the leading members of several professions and trades in a ferment for a month, and those who knew him before and afterward, are unable to decide whether "Gentleman Joe" was merely the feather-brained crank he seemed, or whether some sinister design, involving a deep, ulterior motive, inspired his remarkable conduct.

It seems almost incredible that a man of the soundness of mind in ordinary matters that he manifested should have cut up the pranks he played for mere amusement, and yet the circumstance that the only threats of blackmail he made were incidental to his scheme of persecution, indicates that money was not the object he was striving to attain. On the other hand, he had no incentive for the malice he displayed toward the victim of his attentions, since Dr. Dix had been but one of several in the only matter that can possibly suggest itself, if vengeance were the motive of "Gentleman Joe's" persecutions. Another mystery in the affair was the rascal's source of income. No one knew how he obtained the large amounts of money he spent, not only in carrying on his campaign against Dr. Dix, but for other purposes during his previous career. He possessed no property and had no bank account; the only swindles or thefts he was ever known to perpetrate were on a scale so small that their sum total would not have supported him for a week; and yet he lived in good style, and bore all the outward evidences of prosperity in his career in several American and European capitals.

The malicious ingenuity that "Gentleman Joe" displayed in his tricks upon the venerable clergyman saved him from the clutches of the police for so long a time that they had almost given up hope of ever laying hands upon him. During the entire period that he kept the community stirred not a single clew was found to the perpetrator of the outrages. His final discovery and arrest were due rather to a fortunate accident than to his own carelessness in leaving any of his tracks uncovered.

The attention of the police was first called to this remarkable case in February, 1880, though for some time previously Dr. Dix had been annoyed by his unknown persecutor. About this time nearly every large manufacturing concern in the West received postal cards purporting to come from Dr. Dix, speaking of their goods in a favorable way, saying that the writer wished to make large purchases for the supply of several charitable institutions under his control, and requesting the fullest information regarding prices and cash discounts. At the same time all the leading seminaries, boarding-schools and institutions for female education in the country received letters, signed with the name of Trinity's rector, asking for information and terms, with a view to placing two or three little girls in one of these academies.

The result was that for a week Dr. Dix received every day an immense mass of circulars, hundreds of letters and innumerable samples of dry goods, while from seminaries and boarding-schools came long and enthusiastic communications, offering special terms to the wards of so distinguished a clergyman, while many of the institutions sent members of their faculties to call on the doctor in person. Morning, afternoon and evening the door-bell was rung, commercial agents and educators called at the pastoral residence, who kept Dr. Dix explaining and insisting that he had sent no communications to the dry goods houses, and that he had no children under his care whom he desired to place in educational institutions. Many Western houses had sent agents to New York to secure Dr. Dix's order, and a number of college instructors had travelled long distances to explain the superiority of their methods of education. In spite of the annoyance, and the fact that he was in no way to blame for the hoax of which he was jointly a victim with them, the clergyman felt it to be his duty to make a personal explanation of the matter to each one of his unwelcome callers.

The newspapers and the police made strenuous efforts to ascertain the identity of this wholesale joker. Many of the postal-cards and letters to which Dr. Dix's name was signed, and which had brought about the trouble, were procured and were found to be all in the same handwriting. The rascal had even gone to the expense of obtaining engraved letter-paper with the title, " Trinity Parsonage, No. 27 West Twenty-fifth Street," across the top, to more completely establish his hoax in the minds of the persons who received his letters. An effort was made to get some clew to his identity through the engraver of this letter-paper, but he had received the order through a messenger-boy, and another boy had called for the package and paid the bill. A search of the district messenger offices failed to find the boys who had done this errand, and the trail was lost there. The letters were all good examples of literary composition, and the writing of the hundred or more that the man sent out must have occupied several days. Whoever the writer was, the police thought he was playing a great deal of a jest upon himself as well as his victims, but the apparent lack of motive in the affair was the most puzzling feature of it.

Dr. Dix's commercial mail was only beginning to fall off a trifle, when the most distinguished clergymen and bishops of the Episcopal church, particularly throughout the East, received curt letters, on the Trinity Parsonage paper, signed with the pastor's name, demanding to know why they had ignored his letters. As a result the unfortunate Dr. Dix began to receive numerous grave and stately documents from these clerical gentlemen, assuring him that they had not received previous letters from him, and expressing regret at the unchristian tone of his address to them in reference to the matter. Of course this necessitated an immense amount of explanatory correspondence on the doctor's part, and the good old rector began to realize that life was a burden. But he had not concluded his explanations when the various Bible societies and religious book concerns began to pour in circulars, letters and agents in response to postal cards requesting that terms for supplying Trinity Sunday-school be sent to the rectory.

Dr. Dix and the police gave the fullest information in all these cases to the newspapers, in order that publicity might warn any persons receiving communications purporting to come from the clergyman. But, strangely enough, the warning seemed to have no effect. The most amusing feature of the entire series of hoaxes—if there is an amusing side to such a mean persecution—came the next in order.

On February 21, Dr. Dix received a postal card, mailed at the general post-office the day before, informing him that he would receive calls on the following Monday from the "old clothes ladies," of Baxter and Chatham streets, who would be prepared to enter into negotiations with him for the disposal of his wife's wardrobe. In fear and trembling Dr. Dix waited for Monday to arrive. It came, and the feminine part of the old clothes trade came with it.

The pastor of Trinity had hardly finished his breakfast, when a rickety little wagon, drawn by a mournful little horse, rattled up the fashionable thoroughfare and stopped before his door. On the seat sat a very fat woman of Semitic profile, in stately grandeur. A small boy, whose countenance was a miniature reproduction of her's, held the reins in one hand, while with the other arm he supported an infant of perhaps four years, that to all appearance had not been washed since its birth. The fat woman descended ponderously from the wagon, almost bearing the mournful little horse to the ground as she steadied herself by placing a hand upon his haunches, and then climbed laboriously up the front steps. Dr. Dix opened the door.

"Madam," he said, courteously, "I am afraid you have been made the victim of a hoax. I haven't——"

"Ah, ha!" interrupted the matron, suspiciously. "You sell dose glothes already, heh?"

"No, no," said the doctor, "I haven't any to sell."

"Vot's der matter?" said the lady, in an injured tone. "I gif you der best brice in der market. Come, you trade mit me vonce, an' you nefer trade mit anybody else again. I vas shoost so much of a fool dat I sheat mineself always when I trade mit a shentleman."

"But you've made a mistake," began the unfortunate clergyman. "You——"

"Shoost show me dose glothes, an' vhen I tell you vhat I gif you, you sell 'em right avay," pursued the fat woman, overlooking his protest.

DR. DIX'S VISITORS.

"I tell you," said Dr. Dix, firmly, "that I have no clothes to sell, and I must request you to leave the house."

"I gif you der money down," insisted the visitor, "I gif efferything——"

A scream from the sidewalk interrupted her, and the horrified Doctor of Divinity beheld another Jewish female ascending his steps, shaking her finger and exclaiming:

"Don't you trade mit dot woman, she sheat you haluf vot dose glothes is vort. I buy dose glothes at your own brice, mit der cash on der spot."

"I bought dose glothes already," remarked the first comer, with dignity. "Shakey," she called to her younger son, "come right avay an' bring dose glothes into der vagon. Mosish can hold der horse."

In despair Dr. Dix closed his door, but not until he had caught a glimpse of three other women hurrying toward the house, one drawing a clattering hand-cart behind her on the sidewalk. The two women on the steps held a short conference, pulled the bell a couple of times for luck, endeavored to peer through the stained-glass side-lights and then descended to the pavement and sat placidly down upon the bottom step. The other women rang the basement bell, and Dr. Dix, being aware that it was no fault of theirs that brought them there, opened the door and began to explain the circumstance to them, when the other two women left the steps and ran excitedly in to hear the conversation, jabbering the high prices they were willing to pay. The clergyman again shut the door in self-defence, and when he got up stairs and peered through the parlor curtains, there were three additional women and two very dirty boys in his door-yard. A moment later another wagon, bearing the name of Isaacstein, of Baxter Street, on the side, drove up and two more females were added to the assembly. At this interesting juncture a street gamin contributed to the complication by shouting to a group of companions:

"Hi, fellers! Git onto de Sheenys! Here's de Essex Street women's rights a holdin' a conwention!" And in another moment a group of street boys were leaning on the iron fence, making solicitous inquiries relative to the market rates of wearing apparel, and openly comparing the relative sizes of the Hebrew noses.

Dr. Dix observed that his neighbors were becoming highly interested in the goings on in his premises, but none of the women manifested any intention to leave, while, on the contrary, new arrivals were continually appearing. At noon there were twenty-eight women and twelve children in the yard and on the steps. Each one obviously thought that a sale was to take place, and that the one who waited the longest would be able to make a good bargain, and hence each was determined to out-stay the others. But Dr. Dix, observing that there was no disposition among them to leave of their own accord, finally telephoned to police headquarters, and a squad of officers was sent to disperse them. This was not accomplished without a great deal of difficulty. Each one of these women had received a note requesting her to call at Trinity parsonage to purchase the wardrobe of the rector's wife.

The last one of these women had scarcely been driven away, and the police had hardly departed, when a carriage whirled rapidly around the corner from Fifth Avenue, stopped before the parsonage, and one of the leading physicians of the city sprang hastily out and ran up the steps. He had scarcely pulled the bell, when two more carriages came swiftly down the street and also stopped in front of the house, and two more eminent physicians hurriedly entered the house. Each one told Dr. Dix that he had been summoned by a messenger to come directly to the parsonage, as the pastor had gone into an epileptic fit and was feared to be dying. The same summons had been sent to twenty or thirty physicians, and their visits continued until late in the evening.

The following day Dr. Dix received a note from his unknown tormentor, in which he said that he had witnessed the arrival and the exodus of the children of Israel from his window, and suggesting to the clergyman that they would have been more agreeable associates if he had had sufficient foresight to call out a fire-engine to play upon them with a stream of cologne. The hint that the man lived in the neighborhood was eagerly taken up by the detectives, and every house that commanded a view of Dr. Dix's residence was at once enquired at, and a complete census of all the residents taken without any success. That afternoon a troop of shoemakers, each one of whom had received a postal card requesting him to call and measure some children for shoes, put in an appearance; and at least fifty men and women who had advertised for employment, and received notes requesting them to call upon Dr. Dix, visited him during the afternoon and evening. The latter callers were very persistent, and many of them called several times to make sure that their letters were in reality hoaxes. The man who had victimized them wrote to Dr. Dix the next day that he had himself been one of the callers among those seeking employment, and complimented him upon the courtesy he had shown in dismissing him.

A day or two later this nuisance took on a new form, scarcely less annoying. Messrs. Arnold, Constable & Co., A. T. Stewart & Co., Stern Bros., Lord & Taylor, and other well known dry goods houses received letters, telling them that their impertinent letters had been received and turned over to counsel, who would proceed against them. These firms made haste to respond that no such letters had been sent by them, only to find that, on the other hand, no such letters had been written to them. About the same time many well known clergymen received invitations to dine with Dr. Dix, to meet the bishops of York and Exeter, only to find upon arriving at the parsonage that the rector and themselves were the victims of another hoax.

After this freak the rascally author of the various forgeries turned his attention for a day to other victims. He mailed a number of postal cards to eminently respectable citizens, signing the communications with the names of various liquor dealers, and informing each recipient of a card that he would get himself into trouble unless he called at once, or sent to the undersigned the amount of his bill for liquors and cigars. Only the names of respectable liquor dealers were signed to these cards, while the victims themselves were citizens of wealth and respectability, most of them being members of churches. They were naturally very much incensed, and many of them placed the matter in the hands of their lawyers before the true state of affairs was discovered.

Then came the first letter that hinted at anything like blackmail to Dr. Dix. The clergyman was informed that all the annoyances to which he had been subjected would cease on payment of one thousand dollars to the writer. He was instructed in case he accepted this proposition to insert a personal in the *Herald*, addressed to "Gentleman Joe," saying: "All right." Dr. Dix at once communicated with the detectives who were at work on the case, and they advised inserting the personal. The next day there were three personals in the *Herald* addressed to "Gentleman Joe," each one making the same communication, "All right," but Dr. Dix's persecutor, who had probably inserted two of these advertisements himself, did not pay the slightest attention to the other one. Whether he really intended black-mail and was frightened out of his scheme, or whether he only desired to put the doctor to the annoyance of advertising, has never been ascertained. However that was, the scoundrel now discontinued his annoyances for a couple of weeks, after having kept lawyers, detectives and reporters on the *qui vive* for nearly a month.

Dr. Dix was just beginning to congratulate himself that his tormentor had ceased his attentions for good, when, on St. Patrick's Day, he received another letter in the too familiar handwriting, in which "Gentleman Joe" informed his "Dear friend, Dr. Dix," that his house would be again besieged on the following Friday, unless he paid the writer $1500. He inclosed a name and address to which the money was to be sent. No notice was taken of this communication except that the clergyman put the detectives in charge of his house, while he, to avoid the threatened annoyance, spent the day at his office in the church. As "Gentleman Joe" had promised, Dr. Dix's house was besieged by all classes of men on all kinds of errands. In spite of the publicity that had been given to the case by the newspapers, not one of the callers had any idea, until he arrived at the house, that this, too, was a hoax. "Gentleman Joe" had adroitly begun all his letters on this occasion with an allusion to the mischievous tricks of which the supposed writer had been the victim, in such a manner as to throw them all off their guards.

Early in the morning came a member of a well known firm of lawyers, who had received a letter purporting to come from Mrs. Dix, who desired to consult them relative to proceeding against her husband for divorce. Then other lawyers called on the same errand during the day, and another firm sent word that a representative would visit her the following afternoon. Another caller was the agent of a steamship line, who had received notice to bring two tickets for Havana. Other callers were persons who had advertised in the newspapers of the previous two or three days, offering rewards for lost or stolen property, they having been directed to call at Dr. Dix's number and bring the reward with them.

One man, who had advertised one hundred dollars reward for

the return of two stolen one-thousand-dollar bonds, had been notified to call with the promised amount, and get his bonds that morning. He was not aware that No. 27 West Twenty-fifth Street was Dr. Dix's number, and, therefore, he brought a private detective with him. The gentleman entered the house and the detective stationed himself opposite, it having been previously agreed that if the money was paid and the bonds received, the gentleman on coming out of the house was to scratch his right leg with his left foot, when the detective was to rush in and arrest the negotiator of stolen goods. It is hardly necessary to say that the gentleman came out scratching his head instead of his leg, and feeling very foolish over the fact that he, too, had been victimized by the man whose pranks had been so thoroughly advertised.

Dr. Dix returned home at night to be informed of his numerous visitors and the various purposes for which they had called, and the next day he received a letter from "Gentleman Joe," in which that audacious trickster gleefully related the details of his visit to the house on the previous day, pretending that he had been sent for in response to an advertisement. He informed the doctor that he was always in sight of the house and hugely enjoyed the rare sights it furnished. That afternoon he meanly insulted Mrs. Dix by sending her a pair of exceedingly dirty stockings, together with a note, in which he said that he had another pair which he would place at her disposal when the first were sufficiently worn.

The adventure that came the nearest to resulting disastrously to the good old clergyman was "Gentleman Joe's" most audacious trick. About ten o'clock, a few mornings after the occurrence just related, Dr. Dix's bell rang violently, and a servant hurried to the door. A very determined looking man, who carried a light and supple cane, stepped quickly into the hall as soon as the door was opened and inquired sharply:

"Is Dr. Dix at home?"

"Yes, sir. What do you want to see him about?" inquired the girl, who surmised that he was probably the victim of a hoax.

"It's none of your d—d business what I want to see him about," returned the visitor, savagely, "send him down to me."

The affrighted servant fled, and informed her master that a very cross man was waiting for him in the hall, who declined to state his business. Believing that this was probably another detail of his tormentor's scheme, the clergyman descended to the front hall, where his visitor was leaning against the wall with his hat on and his hands behind him.

"What can I do for you?" Dr. Dix asked, mildly.

The stranger did not reply at once. He glanced the minister over scornfully from his worsted-work slippers to his gray head, and then sneered:

"You leacherous old hypocrite! You're a fine plum for a minister of the gospel, you are—you sniffling, sanctimonious old sinner."

"Sir," began Dr. Dix, haughtily, "what do——"

"Shut up," thundered the visitor, taking a step toward the clergyman. "Don't you dare to open that old Bible trap of yours until I get through talking to you."

"I'll call a policeman," cried the doctor; "I'll see if——"

"D—n you, I tell you to shut up," shouted the stranger, with a scowl so black that the clergyman's knees knocked together. "If you call anything you'll call an ambulance, and I'll have you ready to go to a hospital in it, you bow-legged old pelican."

"Wh—what have I ever d—done to—to you?" faltered the clergyman.

"What have you ever done to me?" repeated the stranger, violently. "D'ye mean to say you don't *know* what you've done to me —or rather what you've tried to do to me? Do you want to make the matter worse by lying about it? By G—d, it makes me sick to think of you standing up in your old doxology works every Sunday, and ladling out religion with that sanctimonious mug of yours, and all the time sizing up the women in the pews. O, I'm right onto *you* with all four feet. Now I'll tell you what I am going to do. I ought to take you out in the street and cane you publicly; but this time I'm going to be easy, and I'll thrash you in the privacy of your own hall. But if you dare to yell or call for help, I'll finish you up out on the steps."

"But what for?" gasped the agonized Dr. Dix, as the stranger took a firmer grip upon his lithe and slender cane. "What have I done?"

The stranger paused, and gazed upon the clergyman with unfeigned astonishment. Then he broke out:

"Well, for clean cheek if you don't get the medal! What for? —D—n your old slippers! For writing that letter to my wife you **hoary-headed old scoundrel!**"

The stranger produced a letter, and waved it excitedly above his head. "I'll teach you to make an appointment with a respectable woman, you old ruffian," he said. "I'll not only give you such an everlasting thrashing that you'll wish you'd died before you were born, but I'll placard you in the street. Call my wife, whom you never spoke to, your 'darling Annie,' will you? Well, I'll wager you won't again."

"I never wrote such a letter," cried the minister.

"You unblushing liar," cried the visitor, "there's your name to it."

"It's a forgery," cried Dr. Dix.

"Is it, though," snarled the stranger, contemptuously. "Well, I'll tell you what I'll do. I'll give you one chance for a whole skin. Get me some of your handwriting and let me compare it with this letter."

"I'll do it," cried the doctor, "I can convince you in a moment. I was just writing a sermon, and I'll get you my last page of manuscript," and he started to run up stairs.

"Here!" said the visitor, sternly, "come back here! You can't come that dodge on me. You'd run up stairs and get a revolver or climb out on the roof, wouldn't you? I'll just go along with you, my reverend old boy. You don't get out of my sight until you've either cleared yourself or had a thrashing."

Accordingly, Dr. Dix and his unwelcome visitor mounted to the minister's study, where the clergyman readily proved that his handwriting was very different from that of the offensive letter. But the stranger muttered a few remarks about writing in a disguised hand, and finally said that he guessed he'd go and see a lawyer about the matter and get some money out of it.

Dr. Dix was in a state of terror after this incident until the following day, when he received a note from "Gentleman Joe," declaring that the writer had enjoyed his call the day before exceedingly, and that he hoped the doctor had recovered from his fright. The savage stranger was none other than "Gentleman Joe" himself, but Dr. Dix's description of him gave the police no clew.

Strange as it may seem, notwithstanding all the annoyance he had caused, "Gentleman Joe" had thus far committed no legal offence, save when he had written a letter threatening to publish in the daily papers charges of adultery against the clergyman. But all the other annoyances he had caused did not then come within any of our criminal statutes, since no such offence ever having been committed before, there had been no law made to punish it. But the threat to make charges of adultery came under the blackmail law, and the aid of the Post-Office department was now invoked to discover the identity of the rascal. In order to make sure of his detection, detectives were actually set to watch every letter-box and branch office in the city. The officers were provided with keys, and with samples of "Gentleman Joe's" handwriting. They stood at short distances from the boxes, and whenever any one mailed a letter, the box was at once opened and the handwriting on the envelope examined. If "Gentleman Joe's" neat chirography had been discovered in any of these instances, whoever had deposited the letter would have been summarily arrested. Though this surveillance was continued for a week, Dr. Dix's tormentor did not use the mails during that time.

At length, every method of detecting the rascal that could be devised having failed, it was resolved to make random inquiries, with the hope of securing some clew by a piece of luck. For this purpose detectives consulted personally every clergyman in the city to ascertain if perchance some hint might be obtained upon which action could be taken. None of these gentlemen could offer the slightest help or make any suggestion, much as they sympathized with the rector of Trinity. One clergyman, however, of another denomination, happened to mention to a detective that he had seen in the city only a few days before a man who called himself Eugene Fairfax Williamson. He had left New York several years previously, upon being found guilty of extremely bestial conduct by the trustees of Trinity church, in whose Sabbath-school he had been a teacher.

The detective thought that even so remote a circumstance as the fact that Dr. Dix was at the head of a church that had detected this man and forced him to leave the city because of another case, might possibly account for a motive in lack of any other. Acting on the hint, Superintendent Gaylor of the Post-Office Department at once made an examination of his books, to see if Williamson's handwriting was in their possession. His name was found in the book in which are registered the names and addresses of persons requesting their mail to be forwarded from one address to another. The Post-Office files all orders of this nature, and upon turning to this file the postal-card Williamson had written, asking that letters addressed to him be sent to the Windsor Hotel, was found. The writing on this card was identical with that of "Gentleman Joe."

The detective at once visited the Windsor Hotel and found that Williamson had registered there on February 17, just before the persecution of Dr. Dix began, and had left the hotel only that day for Baltimore. He had left directions at the Windsor to have his letters sent to Barnum's Hotel, in Baltimore, and Superintendent Gaylor traced him through his letters to a private boarding-house in that city.

Williamson was arrested in this boarding-house and charged with being the author of the annoyances to which the pastor of Trinity had been subjected. He at once admitted that he had written all the offensive cards and letters, and caused Dr. Dix's sudden popularity with the trades and professions, but he said that he had no motive except the fun of watching the besieged house, of reading about the matter in the newspapers, and of puzzling the detectives. He said that neither Dr. Dix nor any of the persons to whom he had written had ever annoyed or injured him, and that he only selected the rector of Trinity because he considered that his distinguished name, his standing as a minister and his popularity in the community, made him an eminently available person to have fun with.

The career of Williamson, or that much of it as was afterward learned, shows him to have led an extraordinary life. He had apparently given himself up to the commission of small crimes and petty offences, not with the object of making anything out of them, but only to amuse himself. He had an abnormal fondness for notoriety, delighted in causing a sensation of any kind, and was very fond of writing letters.

But only the last twelve years of his life could be traced, and who or what he was previously is not known. In 1868 he travelled extensively in Europe as an English gentleman, calling himself Eugene Edward Fairfax Williamson. Early in 1870 he came to this city, where he spent that year and the one following. His only exploit here at that time was to steal a lot of fine stationery, gold pens and similar articles from a shop opposite the Gilsey House, in Broadway. He became well acquainted with the proprietor of this shop, and made use of the confidence reposed in him to steal small articles upon every possible occasion. Williamson was in the habit of boasting of his experiences in Turkey, and of his participation in vices peculiar to the East. He became, however, a teacher in Trinity Sunday-school.

After the exposure of his early misdeeds he left for Europe, announcing his engagement to a certain Countess de Maralles. He was not married, however, but went to London, where he played a series of tricks upon a well-known Hebrew gentleman similar to those with which he afterward persecuted Dr. Dix. He sent out the same kind of invitations and business proposals in this gentleman's name, and hired a room opposite his house from which to witness the fun. He was detected by the London police, tried, convicted and sentenced to Newgate for one year.

After serving this sentence, he returned to America in 1875, and took up his residence in Pittsburg. He moved in the best society there and always had plenty of money. The source of his income still continues a mystery, since, as has been said, he kept no bank account, and had apparently no resources except swindling, though, as the only swindles that were ever discovered dealt with very small amounts, these could not have furnished him with the amount of money he expended. It is possible that he perpetrated larger frauds, which were never discovered, but if he did he was the most adroit and skilful thief that ever operated in America. During his residence in Pittsburg, he swindled several New York and Philadelphia jewellery firms out of small amounts. Another strange feature of his extraordinary career is the circumstance that he wrote a great deal of poetry, and even had a play produced, his literary efforts meeting favorable recognition by the newspapers in New York and other cities. These works were afterward discovered to be the productions of a nun in a New Orleans convent, but under what circumstances he had procured them is not known, nor has the identity of the real author ever been disclosed.

"Gentleman Joe" came to New York from Pittsburg, and at once began his peculiar system of tormenting Dr. Dix, as has been related. He was convicted of an attempt at blackmail and sentenced to a term in Sing Sing prison, where he died. The secret of his life and conduct, if indeed there is any mystery aside from the circumstance that his mind was disordered, died with him.

CHAPTER XXIII.

A LAW-BREAKER AS KNOWN BY HIS FAMILY.—SOME MISCONCEPTIONS.—NOT AN AGENT OF THE ASSOCIATED PRESS.—PHILIP SCHUYLER OR JOHN SPICER?—A FIFTY-YEAR-OLD SON WHO DIDN'T KNOW HIS FATHER.—A SOMEWHAT COMPLICATED WILL CASE.—ISAAC M. SINGER AND HIS MANY WIVES.—FIRST A STROLLING PLAYER AND THEN A MILLIONAIRE.—CHARACTERISTICS OF CRIMINALS.—WHAT MAKES A LAW-BREAKER.—THE FIRST STEP IN EVIL-DOING.—THE HARRIS FAMILY.

It is a preconceived and not always well-founded notion of the vast majority of persons that men who war upon society must of necessity bear the brand of their evil doings on their brows. This is not so. As chief of police of one of the greatest cities of the world, I have been brought into personal contact with the most consummate criminals. With few exceptions, the men who have been accredited with the most daring violations of the law have been persons who could not have been marked by the most learned physiognomist as of accommodating morals. As a rule, a man to be a successful criminal must be an individual of rare cunning, great determination, and capable of masking his real character under the guise of a respectable and respected member of society. I speak, be it remembered, only of the more dreaded enemies of good order. Thieves, pickpockets, highway robbers and men capable of brutal crime are marked even to the most unsophisticated citizen. Criminals who live by their wits, generally termed swindlers, are almost without exception persons of winning address and fascinating manners. In fact, without this power to engage the attention and secure the confidence of their victim, their careers would not be very profitable. Law-breakers are compelled by the exigencies of civilization to lead double lives. They are children of the serpent—smooth, glistening, charming, only to spring upon the unsuspecting and enjoy the results of their trickery. A friend relates the following :

" I once knew a retired gambler. He had kept a 'hell' on Barclay Street for many years, and had lost the end of his nose—bitten off in a fight. One of his fingers was also missing, from the same cause. I was a boy when I first met the man, and was much more afraid of him then than I was of any boat, horse, or gun, as my subsequent experience on tne police force had not yet taught me that most villains are only villanous at certain times, and in the regular course of their evil deeds. He was, however, of a mild and placid demeanor and engaging conversation. I gradually got accustomed to him, and finally became fond of him. One day he was sitting beside me, smoking a cigar, when suddenly we heard the shriek of a child. The retired gambler evidently recognized the voice, for he immediately dashed round a corner in the direction of the cry, and quickly reappeared, tenderly carrying his daughter's child in his arms. A dog had jumped against it and knocked it down in the road. He hugged and kissed the little one with all the fervor of a woman, brushing its hair, wiping its eyes and loading it with caresses. But he was a rogue and a swindler for all that.

Comparatively little is known of the lives of many persons in New York. Acquaintances are formed which ripen into intimacy among men and women who know nothing of one another's past history, and there are many who pass for being thoroughly respectable whose lives would not bear much scrutiny.

Not very many years ago a family resided on Lexington Avenue, the members of which were popular and well liked among their neighbors. The wife was a pretty and hospitable little woman, and the two daughters—bright, engaging and well-bred girls—were just coming of age. In fact, it was as happy a little family as could be found anywhere, and everything about the house was well ordered. The husband was tall and gaunt, and was somewhat irregular in his hours and habits. This fact, however, was accounted for by the fact that he was supposed to be connected with the Associated Press. For more than four years the relations of a friend with the family were of the most intimate nature, and he never had the slightest suspicion that there was anything "crooked" about them, until one night when he happened to be in a gambling-house up town, where there was a very brisk game of baccarat in progress. About forty gentlemen, all more or less well known about town and of good position, were seated around the green table, and two young men who had bought the bank were winning money very rapidly. Everybody else was losing. The faces of most of the men looked solemn and ill-natured; a few were flushed, while others were as calm and imperturbable as though carved out of marble. The run of luck in favor of the bank was evidently something out of the common. A smooth-faced young fellow who sat inside a big iron cage and sold chips to the players, had climbed upon his desk so as to get a good view of the table; and even the waiters, usually so obedient and prompt of service, forgot to fill orders. At one end of the table the cards were dealt to a young man who had been losing heavily, and whose hand shook so much with excitement that he turned over one of his cards. The banker saw it. The flushed player called for another card. It was turned up suddenly; there was a "false play," and an instantaneous howl of rage (I can call it by no other name) from the players. All the men were heavy loosers, and matters looked very squally.

The players all jumped to their feet, everybody shouted at once, and the waiters closed the doors. A row was evidently imminent. Suddenly, the attendant in his iron cage rang a bell; the door of the adjoining room opened quickly, and was then closed again with a bang which could be heard above the babel of voices. The heads of all were turned towards the doorway—my friend's along with the rest—and there stood that very respectable head of the very respectable family who resided on Lexington Avenue, and with whom my friend had been so intimate for four years or more. He was precisely as he always seemed; his frock coat hung in loose folds upon his gaunt figure; there was a cigar in his mouth; his cold, blue eyes were as devoid of animation as ever.

Immediately upon his entrance he was appealed to by a dozen different individuals. He asked whether a decision by him would be accepted as final. And the answer of the majority was in the affirmative. Then he entered into a lengthy analysis of the rules of the game on the point in dispute. He spoke with labored politeness, and looked around from face to face with a forced smile as each word was spoken. He finally wound up by saying:

"There can't be a question or doubt, gentlemen, about this decision. I have known the point to come up fifty times in Paris, and so universally is the ruling understood that it no longer raises even a word. It is accepted at once as final."

That settled it, and within ten minutes the game was in full blast again, and half a case of champagne had been disposed of. That is the sort of Associated Press agent the gaunt gentleman with the highly respectable family was. His wife may have known all about his business, but it is doubtful if his daughters did.

It is astonishing how thoroughly things can be concealed in New York. Men lead double lives for years without any one being the wiser. Persons have even been known to support two establishments within a very short distance of each other—two wives, two families—and yet the fact has only come to light after death.

Philip Schuyler, the railroad millionaire of twenty years ago, was one of these two-faced individuals. He was known by his family, who lived up town, as John Spicer. He did business on the Stock Exchange, and maintained an office at No. 10 Broad Street, under the name of Philip Schuyler. And the way in which the whole thing was discovered was this:

A young fellow and companion, as they walked Broadway, passed a handsome gentleman to whom they both bowed. One said:

"Why, Bob Spicer, how came you to know that man? I didn't know you knew him."

"Well, yes, I know him slightly," said young Spicer sarcastically. "Why shouldn't I, seeing he's my father?"

"Your father!" exclaimed the other with a laugh; "not much! That's Philip Schuyler."

"'Tain't either," exclaimed Bob Spicer, excitedly. "Don't I know my own father? What are you talking about? Haven't I seen him every day since I could remember?"

"But have you seen him evenings, Bob?"

"No, he works down town evenings."

"Works! I tell you he's a Fifth Avenue swell, Schuyler is; and he goes to all the Patriarch Club's parties and balls; and he is a bachelor, and he is sweet on my Aunt Emma; and he plays billiards at our house every few evenings. They say he's awful rich."

"See here," said Bob to his companion; "if you go on talking that way we can't be friends any more. Talk's cheap. Come home with me at five o'clock, and see what mother says about it. Father will be there too."

Thus it came about that the matter was investigated, and Bob found that his loving and indulgent father, John Spicer, was known on the Stock Exchange and at No. 10 Broad Street as the railroad magnate and bachelor millionaire, Philip Schuyler.

Not more than two or three years ago there was a contest before the New York Surrogate over the will of William Austin. He was an importer of Scotch linens, and died in 1875, leaving personal property to his wife valued at $800,000, together with a house on West Twenty-third Street, in which they had lived for many years and reared a large family. Down town, on Cedar Street, where he had his office, he was known as William Hutchinson, and none of his business acquaintances ever suspected him of being married or having a family. In church he was known as Austin and on the Stock Board as Hutchinson. A most remarkable fact in connection with this case is that Mr. Austin-Hutchinson lived this double life undiscovered for more than fifty years.

When he died his oldest son was fifty-one years old, and the next, forty-six. But these two old boys do not seem ever to have suspected that they were anything else than unadulterated Austins; or that they had an enterprising and acquisitive relation named "Hutchinson," doing a good deal of business in Cedar Street, with his gilt sign out over the sidewalk—"Hutchinson"—for fifty years, working six hours every day, doing millions of dollars worth of business. They never discovered that he was else than the respectable and domestic Austin of Twenty-third Street! Austin for fifty years, for eighteen hours of the day and night, and never once inopportunely revealed as Hutchinson of the Stock Board, and the note-shaver of Cedar Street! It seems to me that that fifty-year-old boy could not have been very wide awake.

I remember a very strange revelation about a will, contested more than thirty years ago in our Surrogate Court. In the old times there was a very stylish house of prostitution in Chambers Street, known as "The Palace of Mirrors"—the name being descriptive of the place. It was kept by a famous courtesan named, or at any rate called, Kate Ridgeway. She was brilliant, refined looking, and with modest manners, and she sometimes got into a box at the opera without attracting undue attention, except from the men about town to whom her face was known. Years and years passed. She was prudent. She became wealthy. Suddenly the house was closed, Kate disappeared from view, and nobody knew whither she had gone.

Some years afterward a lady of distinguished appearance,

of about middle age, took up her residence on Fifth Avenue with her wealthy husband, and, to a certain extent, was admitted into the select society of that thoroughfare. They thrived. A circle of friends assembled about them. They were prominent members of a fashionable church. Their name was foremost in conspicuous charities. Her husband, a retired hardware merchant of Warren Street, died a couple of years later, leaving her a comfortable fortune. She left here for a residence in a moderate-sized Western city, where she was regarded as a very wealthy woman.

After awhile she returned here and died, and her will was presented for probate in the Surrogate Court. Objections were filed by a very beautiful and accomplished young lady, who claimed to be her only daughter. The will bequeathed the bulk of the property to her niece, a Philadelphia woman. The evidence brought to light the origin of the parties and their relations.

The testatrix proved to be no other than the famous Kate Ridgeway. She was the sister of Matilda Heron, the powerful but eccentric tragic actress, who was the first representative Camille in the English language. The contestant produced some forty or fifty letters from the decedent, in which the writer addressed her as "My Dear Daughter," and lawyers and court were confounded by the marked manifestations of affection by the decedent, and were nonplussed by the fact that the object of these terms of endearment was disinherited under the will. The claimant was strikingly handsome and refined, about twenty-two years old, intelligent and lady-like, and she impressed everybody most favorably. Pending the litigation, the attorney for the will bethought himself to inquire of the records to see if a guardian had ever been appointed for this mysterious girl. The search was rewarded.

It was found that her real name was Louise West, and that she was the child of the keeper of an assignation house in the rear of the Palace of Mirrors, who, on dying, left her property to Kate Ridgeway for the benefit and education of her child, enjoining upon her that it should be used for her maintenance and training, and that Louise should never know the secret of her birth. The guardianship had been respected and the trust carried out. When the infant arrived at sufficient age she was taken from the Palace of Mirrors and placed in the Convent of the Sacred Heart above the city, where she remained during several years' absence of her guardian in Europe. On the return from Europe, the name Bishop was substituted for West, and the now educated young woman was taken into the Fifth Avenue family to reside. She shortly married without her guardian's consent, and left the city with her young husband, remaining away till she heard of her "mother's" death. The whole queer business being cleared up, the will was admitted to probate.

On the 23d of July, 1875, at No. 83½ Boulevard Malesherbes, Paris, Isaac M. Singer died, aged sixty-three years. In 1836, when eighteen years old, he met in Baltimore Mary Ann Spousle, a native of Carlisle, Pennsylvania, and fell in love with her. Her father was an oyster-packer. Singer was a strolling player and extremely poor. Travelling about the country, he acted in temperance plays in churches. He told Mary Ann that he was already married to one Catherine Maria Haley, whom he had left for cause, and from whom he proposed to get a divorce. He induced Mary Ann to go to New York with him, as his wife, promising to marry her after procuring the divorce. The latter he neglected to do, and the marriage ceremony was never performed. About a year after this arrangement he deserted Mary Ann, and she returned to her father's home, where she remained until 1839. Singer and Mary met again and the two travelled over the country for many years. Mary also became an actor, although she was ignorant and could not read. She lived with Singer for twenty-five years, and bore him ten children. For thirteen years they went up and down the country, residing at different times in Pittsburgh, Pa., Fredericksburg, Ohio; and Chicago. They were still very poor.

In 1838 Mr. Singer invented a machine for drilling rocks by horse-power. He received some income from this. He also invented a machine for carving wood types, and went into that business in Ohio. As an actor he played under the title of Isaac Merritt. In 1850 he perfected his first sewing-machine, and came to New York to live, on Fifth Street, near the Bowery. He afterwards lived on Fourth Avenue, near Twenty-seventh Street, and subsequently at No. 14 Fifth Avenue, then in Yonkers, and Paris.

The Singer Manufacturing Co. was started with a factory on Elizabeth Street, and a grand office on Broadway, at the corner of Browne. Money flowed in and the Singers became wealthy. At No. 14 Fifth Avenue they kept six carriages and ten horses, and a troupe of servants. Mr. Singer always introduced Mary as his wife, gave her money to pay all bills, etc.

Everything went well until August 7, 1860, when Mrs. Singer took a ride up Fifth Avenue in her coupé. She met Mr. Singer coming down the avenue in an open carriage with one Mary McGonigal. Mrs. Singer was astounded at Singer's apparent perfidy, and screamed. She then drove home, and found Mr. Singer there waiting for her. He gave her a severe beating, and she had him arrested for ill treatment. She also began a suit for divorce. In her complaint she said:

" During the whole of her married life she had received the most cruel and inhuman treatment. He frequently beat and choked her to insensibility. On August 7, 1860, he assaulted her at No. 14 Fifth Avenue. He beat his daughter Violetta, until she became insensible, and he was alarmed for her recovery. He was finally obliged to send for Dr. Wm. H. Maxwell. Mother and daughter were both confined to their beds several days. On September 19, 1860, Singer went to Europe with a woman of easy virtue, Kate McGonigal, aged nineteen years. They sailed from Boston under assumed names. He formerly visited her at No. 40 Christopher Street. From 1855 to 1860 he kept as his mistress Mary McGonigal, sister of Kate. Other women with whom it is known he had illicit relations were Mary Matthews, a Mrs. Judson, an operative in the establishment; Mary Waters, Ellen Brazer and Ellen Livingstone. These women bore children by him. Another woman, known as Lucy, he seduced in England, and she followed him to this country. He lived with her at No. 110 West Thirty-seventh Street. He is in the habit of seducing his female operatives, and employs them both in England and New York for that purpose."

The divorce was never procured, since the lawyers agreed to a compromise, and Judge Barnard ordered the papers sealed up and returned to the attorneys. Singer agreed to purchase a house for Mary, and support her family. He bought the house, No. 189 West Twenty-eighth Street, for $16,500 and furnished it. He paid $40 a week for the care of the children. A few weeks after this settlement Mrs. Singer went to Boston, where she was married to John Edward Foster, a young man, twenty-five years old, a railway clerk.

When the Singer will was probated at White Plains, N. Y., in September, 1875, Mrs. Foster appeared in person to contest the will, claiming to be the widow of Mr. Singer. At the close of the proceedings, the surrogate, Judge Coffin, adjudged that Mary Ann Foster was never the wife, and therefore was not the widow, of Isaac M. Singer, and was not entitled to intervene.

The estate left by Singer amounted in round numbers to fifteen millions of dollars. It has largely increased, since each " part " spoken of in the will represented $250,000.

In his will Mr. Singer made provision for the following persons:

"I give to my wife, Isabelle Eugenia Singer, all the plate, furniture, carriages, etc., in my possession; also the house and lands belonging thereto which I occupied as a home, for life, and afterwards to her children.

To my children, born of her who was Maria Haley: to William A. Singer, $500; to Lillian A. Singer, $10,000.

The rest of the estate shall be divided into sixty equal parts:

To Isabelle Eugenie, four parts;
To Adam Mortimer, six parts;
To Winnaretta Eugenie, five parts;
To Washington Merritt Grant, six parts;
To Paris Eugene, six parts;
To Isabelle Blanche, five parts;
To Franklin Morse, six parts.

I give to each of the following named persons whom in this, my will, I call by the surname of Singer, they being my children, born of Mary McGonigal, of San Francisco, and who is commonly called by the surname of Matthews:

To Ruth Merrit, two parts;
To Clara, two parts;
To Florence Adelaide, two parts;
To Margaret Alexandria, two parts;
To Charles Alexander, two parts;
To Alice, born of Mary E. Walter, of New York, commonly called Merritt, two parts.

To each of the following persons whom I call Singer, my children, born of her who is now known as Mary Ann Foster, of New York:

To Isaac Augustus, two parts;
To Violetta Theresa, nothing;
To John Albert, two parts;
To Fanny Elizabeth, one part;
To Joseph Camet, one part;
To Mary Olive, one part;
To Julia Ann, one part, and
To Caroline Virginia, two parts.

But to return to "respectable" criminals. Look at the "confidence" man, or "bunco steerer," for instance. The greater part of his stock-in-trade consists of his wardrobe and his personal attractions Without good clothing and good looks he would be unfit for his "business." In making up his general appearance his fashionable attire, of course, goes a great way. He must be careful, too, not to offend the susceptibility of his intended victims by any "loudness" in his dress, or anything that makes him singular or cònspicuous. The "confidence" man, therefore, carefully avoids anything remarkable in his address, seeking, rather, the general appearance of easy respectability. A sprinkling of gray hairs is a great help to him in his operations. A bald head and a clerical figure is positively a fortune. His hands must be white and delicate, and his voice softly modulated. With such an "outfit," together with an immaculate shirt and collar, he has the "open sesame" to the wallets of his "dear friends" from the country. When on the look-out for a "pigeon" no one could be more diffident and retiring. He is politeness itself, and no amount of pushing, crushing or crowding can put him out of temper.

The bank thief dresses well, lives well, and is, in fact, upon the highest plane of criminal life. He must, like the "confidence" operator, be a person of good address; and, above all, must have some pretensions to good looks. Good pickpockets (if there are any), those who "work" the largest kind of game, are generally well and stylishly dressed, easy in their manners and correct in speech. The hotel thief is usually a man of suave and polished manners. Ask him a question as he strolls about the corridors of the hotel which he has selected as his field of operations. His answer is always ready, and you can touch upon no subject with which he does not appear to be perfectly familiar. Well dressed, of good appearance, the more you see and converse with him the better you like him. He can suit his ways, too, to the company in which he may happen to be—laughing with those who laugh, and sympathetic or dignified with those who are sorrowful and sedate. You may meet him at one hotel by the name of Brown, and a week later at another by that of Robinson. But this little apparent inconsistency doesn't trouble him in the least. Remind him of it, and he is ready with some pleasant little fiction which it is ten to one will pull the wool over your eyes in the most complete manner.

Shop-lifters are dangerous, too, as far as detecting them by their attire is concerned. It has frequently happened that a man and a couple of women of this class have gone about the city during the holiday season, when stores are crowded, in a carriage with servants in livery and other surroundings equal to their pretentions, riding from place to place, robbing as they went. They go into our best and largest jewellers', silk-merchants', and lace shops rustling in silk or robed in velvet and satin; and yet all the time, and none the less, they are thieves.

Even the burglar, that nightmare of the householder, is very rarely brave; and it is only when driven into a corner, and at bay, that he becomes bold and desperate. The burglar would much rather run than fight. Frighten him, and if there is a chance to escape he will avail himself of it.

I have known thieves, brutal and murderous enough, if disturbed when engaged in any depredation, who in their homes were kind husbands and affectionate fathers. For years they have concealed the nature of their "work" from their families; their wives living lives of respectability and comfortable confidence.

The question has been very often asked me: "How are thieves made—what makes them commit their first crime?" It is a difficult one to answer. It is not always the naturally vicious men who join the ranks of our great army of criminals. Over and over again instances have come to my notice where young men, and women, too, who have been well bred, and whose natural traits are far from vicious, have drifted (and I can find no better word in the English language) into crime purely and simply through want. Their first offence escaped detection, and they have thus been induced to follow it as a business or profession. There is a certain young man now serving out a sentence of seven and a half years at Sing Sing for various burglaries, whose experiences will illustrate what I mean.

When he first came to New York, the young man in question was as modest, quiet and respectable as could well be imagined. His references were excellent, and he had no trouble in obtaining a situation in a down-town wholesale house, where he soon gained the confidence of his employers. Consequent upon the general depression in business which occurred in 1884, he was discharged, along with numbers of others. Day after day, week after week, he tramped the streets, going from store to store seeking work. The little money he had saved was soon gone, and then an unpaid board bill stared him in the face.

With no friends to aid him, it is no wonder he became desperate. An idea entered his head, and one evening he left his boarding-house, taking with him all the keys he could find. He had determined to raise money in some way, and, as honest labor offered him no opportunity, he determined to try house-breaking. One of the keys in the bunch which he had enabled him to open a house in a certain side street, and entering one of the rooms, he stole a quantity of jewellery and made his escape without being detected. The pawn-shop was resorted to, and he thus obtained funds with which to get along for a time.

Now the success attending him in his first robbery deceived him. If he had been caught then and there the chances are ten to one that his whole future would have been changed. But success in his first venture ruined him. He went on and on in the downward path until, when he was arrested, he confessed to as many as forty burglaries. His career is but a sample of several which have come under my observation. Want and starvation drive many more into crime than most persons imagine. Education in crime by professional thieves is not the cause of making half as many criminals as is the fact that young men of much more than average ability are fairly driven to thievery by want, and also the fact that they can see no way of making an honest living in the immediate future.

On the other hand, however, it is wrong to say that there is no such thing as hereditary viciousness. There is, and I'm sorry to say I've seen plenty of it. Take the case of the Harris family. Five of the brothers are now in prison! Just think of it. A drunken mother with seven sons, only the two youngest of whom are not within the clutch of the law. What a picture! Four strapping young men, who might, if they had started aright, be earning a good living to-day! Save the wages of stripes and hard labor for a convict contractor, they have earned little from their arduous profession of thieving. Few tenements in the city were more bare of comforts than those which they and their female companions inhabited. There were no carpets on the floor and nothing which could be termed "furniture," even by the greatest stretch of the imagination. But what hard work they endured to obtain all this; what nights of peril and discomfort while watching and waiting for a chance to "crack a crib"; what weeks of hiding in garrets and cellars from the police; what hard bargains driven with unscrupulous "fences"; what constant calls for drink-money by the mother who had done more than her share in helping them into the harness of crime; and, on top of this, fifty years between them of an existence seen through an iron grating.

Again, only recently, I noticed the case of a man who was eighty years of age, tottering on the edge of the grave, who actually begged the judge of a circuit court in Indiana to sentence him to such a term of imprisonment as would enable him to spend his few remaining days in jail. Forty years he had passed behind brick walls and iron gratings; no sooner had he been released on one sentence, than he had committed another crime in order to prolong his life behind the bars. His last offence was burglary, and in response to the questions of the court told a story of crime which indicated as near an approach to total depravity as can well be imagined.

Said he: "I have no relatives, no friends and no money. I would rather be in prison than in the poor-house. I will not beg, and I want to pass the remainder of my life in the penitentiary. Yes, Judge, send me up for just such time as you like. I don't know how long I will live. I cannot say that five years will be enough."

And the old man's face wore a contented, happy expression when he heard his sentence of five years' imprisonment—a punishment which to some men would be as the crack of doom, but which to him was as an invitation to partake of a good meal.

Such instances as these are almost sufficient to arouse a suspicion in the minds of most persons that there must be something radically wrong in our social system, or else the mode of punishment for crimes committed cannot be sufficiently severe.

The intention of the law is not so much the punishment of any one thief who may be captured, as to deter others from committing similar crimes. On not a few criminals the best efforts of the philanthropist are completely lost. Their efforts are as futile as carrying water in a sieve. The most irksome manual labor and most rigid discipline should be the portion of such men.

Upon the other hand, those convicted of a first offence should be dealt with leniently. My conviction for a number of years has been that criminals should be made to understand distinctly, upon their conviction, that their punishment will be carried out in the most rigid and inflexible manner—that they have nothing to hope for in the way of a pardon. Of course, I believe it to be perfectly right to offer premiums for good conduct in the shape of a reduction of their sentence; but so-called " philanthropists " do far more harm than good by their promiscuous and ill-directed struggles for the relief of the imprisoned. Men who are desirous of reforming and leading a correct life in the future should be afforded every facility to do so, and encouraged in their endeavors.

The problem is a gigantic one, and its solution this side of the millennium is a matter of doubt.

CHAPTER XXIV.

FORGERS AND FORGING.—THE ARISTOCRATIC AND WEALTHY MEXICAN DOCTOR.—"A MOST CONSUMMATE VILLAIN."—THE SUNDAY-SCHOOL TEACHER WHO FORGED CHECKS FOR $250,000.—THREE MEN WHO CAME FROM A HOUSE IN ALLEN STREET ON A DARK WINTER'S NIGHT.—HOW JAMES A. GARFIELD WAS NEARLY DEFEATED.—THE FORGER WITH BLACK EYES AND RAVEN HAIR.—LORD ASHBURTON AND HIS ROMANTIC CAREER.—ROCKY MOUNTAIN BLACK-MAILERS.—THE UNION BANK OF LONDON FORGERIES.

In 1874 there lived at No. 50 East Fifty-third Street, New York City, a man whose name was as complex as his character. Dr. Gabor Nephegyi, for such was this person's name, was a gentleman whom many prominent New Yorkers felt proud to say they knew. He was to them a man of enormous wealth. He lived in a fashionable part of the city and lived gorgeously. His house was elaborately furnished. The works of art, the books, the tapestries and Persian rugs with which the building seemed crowded, demonstrated that there was no vulgarity about this man's riches. He was unmistakably a man of taste, education and refinement. His conversational powers were extraordinary. He had travelled extensively, and seemed well posted on a great variety of subjects. He was said to be a member of the New York Historical Society, as also of the Geographical Society, and he frequently entertained his fellow members at his house. These receptions were always the envy of those who could not attend them, and those who came once seldom remained away when the next one occurred.

Why this attractive man was called Doctor was never clearly ascertained. He was known to be a Mexican, and that covered a multitude of curious questions. All sorts of explanations were made by those who admired the grandeur of his turn-out as he rolled in his carriages over the avenues or through the Park. No livery was quite so faultless as his, no coachmen understood quite so well their business. His horses were magnificent specimens of brutes, and none in the city stepped along more proudly. The doctor's servants were legion, and they were managed like clockwork.

Yet this apparently faultless man, who had been dined and wined and fêted by the "nabobs" of fashionable and cultured society, was as great a rascal as lived in New York. He continued his almost princely life for some time, and then fell—fell like Lucifer, never to rise again.

The Doctor had had some alterations and repairs made to his house, and in payment had given forged checks on the Gallatin National Bank. Among those who thus suffered was E. M. Knox, who lost $3000. Mr. Knox had the wealthy Mexican arrested, and the prisoner was held to await the action of the grand jury. This was a blow from which Nephegyi had not quite audacity enough to recover. He was bailed, as he had been many times before, though the New York club men with whom he associated had never suspected it, by a man named H. P. Norton, who was believed to be his confederate in nefarious schemes. At the trial the forger made a vigorous defence. His counsel submitted an inventory of his client's possessions, showing that there could have been no fraudulent motive on the part of the prisoner. The prosecution, on the other hand, hurled a bombshell into New York society by unfolding Dr. Gabor Nephegyi's past record. It proved him to have been a professional confidence man. In 1866, under another name, he had been arrested for making counterfeit money on Staten Island. A year or so later he had swindled a Boston business house out of $10,000. In 1869 Asa Packer and others, of Bethlehem, Pennsylvania, lost thousands of dollars by this arch-rascal. "He is one of the most consummate villains, rogues and swindlers that ever disgraced this part of the country," wrote John G. Miller from Asa Packer's home. He had been confined for some time in the jail at Eaton, where he had shown his cleverness and carelessness by writing over the cell door: "Private entrance to the hotel of free lodging. No exit except on bail. Regulations: *First*. Guests are not permitted to leave without the express permission of the landlord. *Second*. For the better security of guests, iron and locks are constantly in the windows and doors."

The last and most astounding incident in this man's career, as spread before the public by the district attorney, was his swindling the City of Mexico out of $600,000 by fraudulent gas contracts.

It was on the proceeds of these deeds of villany that the cultured, aristocratic, wealthy and fashionable resident of Fifty-third Street supported his gorgeous turn-outs, gave his magnificent dinners, and aroused the admiration and envy of his less talented and poorer acquaintances. Yet in the end his money did not save him, and the law showed the cultured Mexican no more leniency than it did a Bowery prize-fighter.

The case of Dr. Nephegyi illustrates well the character of the men with whom, as forgers and swindlers, the police of New York are constantly coming in contact. At the bottom, these men are as unscrupulous and as vicious as the roughest looking criminal that is arraigned in our police courts. Yet frequently their associates are persons of eminent respectability and refinement. Forging is often refined bank robbery, and forgers are cultured bank robbers. It is necessary for the successful accomplishment of their fraudulent schemes that they should dress well and act well. The most adroit, or those whose aim is to get large sums of money, must live like persons who are accustomed to handle plenty of money. Their work of fraud lies among the rich and educated part of the population, and to avoid arousing suspicion they must be careful not to show any signs of vulgarity or of crookedness. The successful forger is always a very smart man, and this very fact frequently aids him, as it aided Dr. Nephegyi, in getting the entrée to the best and cleverest society. It has been my experience as a police officer that one of the hardest criminals to detect and convict is the forger, and I attribute this in no small degree to his habit of ingratiating himself, by his suave manners and gentlemanly appearance, into the affections of those who ought to be his accusers. It is the most difficult thing in the world sometimes to convince reputable people that the stranger who has gained their confidence is the man who has defrauded them. So unwilling is human nature to admit that it has been imposed upon.

Another of these accomplished forgers, whose case has also its pathetic side, was William C. Gilman, a broker of good reputation, who lived at No. 31 West Thirty-sixth Street. One day in October Gilman sent to the office of Henry Talmadge & Co., bankers, of No. 39 Pine Street, as collateral security for money borrowed, two certificates of scrip of the Atlantic Mutual Insurance Company for $10,000 each. The firm sent the certificates to the insurance company for identification and there it was learned that they were not genuine. It was found that certificates for $100 each had been issued to Gilman in 1876, and there was every evidence that these presented by Henry Talmadge & Co. were the same ones, but the amount had been raised in each from $100 to $10,000.

The fact of the forgery was soon made known, and the greatest surprise and consternation followed. Business men had looked on William C. Gilman as a model of honesty and fair dealing. He belonged to the firm William C. Gilman & Co., which had been respected on the street for forty years. He had entered the house when a boy, and had finally succeeded his father in control. The latter had died thirteen years before and left his son $100,000. Gilman's manner of living was such that his friends thought he must be doing a good business. He was a member of the Union League Club, and very popular with his associates. His social position was excellent. Above all, he was a devoted church member and a teacher in a Sabbath-school.

Yet the revelation on that second day in October pronounced him a swindler of the blackest type. His crime was not only the forging of two certificates of $10,000 each, but the swindling of other firms and corporations out of ten times as much. As soon as the attempted fraud on Henry Talmadge & Co. was discovered and made known, there was great excitement at all the banks where Gilman was accustomed to do business. His securities which they held were at once overhauled and critically examined. The further the investigation went the more astounding revelations were made. The Third National Bank discovered that it held $20,000 of forged paper; the American Exchange Bank, $87,320; a trust company, $74,000; and other corporations, $30,000. Gilman was believed to have fraudulently secured altogether about $250,000. The forgeries had all been committed by raising certificates from comparatively small amounts to large ones.

The excitement among business men and Gilman's acquaintances was intense, and when almost simultaneously with the discovery of the forgeries it was made known that Gilman himself had fled, those who had for an instant cherished any doubts of the forger's guilt were ready to believe it now. No plausible theory, however, was suggested for the man's conduct.

Two weeks later Gilman turned up, and surrendered himself to the police. I confess I have seldom felt more touched by the arrest of any prisoner. His fall was so complete, and the broken-down man realized it so entirely. He issued a confession to the public, in which he blamed no one but himself, and said that he had been tempted to wrong-doing by business troubles and his extravagant habits. It was a very humiliating recital. In court soon afterward he pleaded guilty to forgery in the second degree, and was sent to State's prison for five years.

On a dark cloudy night early in the year 1877 three detectives, with their overcoats buttoned closely around their throats to keep off the biting air of winter, paced slowly up and down in front of a house in Allen Street, New York. Now and then they cast anxious glances toward the house, and stopped and stared curiously when there was any sign of life about the dwelling. They noted the entrance of one or two men into the house, and then were gratified to see an expressman drive up before the suspected house, and, leaving his horse and wagon, rapidly mount the steps and ring the bell. There were a few words exchanged at the door with the person who responded to the call, and then the expressman returned to his wagon. A moment later three men emerged from the doorway, carrying a large bundle which they placed carefully in the wagon. At that instant three revolvers were pointed at their heads, and the three detectives demanded the men's surrender.

So quick was the action of the detectives and so surprised were their prisoners that the latter offered no resistance. The driver started to run, but was told to stand still. Then the six men, followed by the terrified expressman, filed silently toward a police station, and thence to headquarters. There I saw the three prisoners, and recognized in one of them, to my great surprise, " Little Joe " Elliot, an aristocratic criminal, a man who has committed crime in nearly every State of the Union, and in half the countries of the Old World, and who is familiar with at least a score of prisons. The other two prisoners were Charles Becker and " Old Man " Hearing, as he was familiarly called, two well-known forgers.

The crime for which these men were arrested on this dark night was that of forging a check for $64,000, purporting to be drawn by the New York Life Insurance Company upon the Union Trust Company. The forgery was wrought in this manner: On January 3, " Little Joe " called on George L. Maxwell, a

Wall Street broker, introduced himself as an agent of the New York Life Insurance Company, and asked the broker if he would purchase for the company $50,000 in gold, tendering him at the same time a certified check for $64,000. There was nothing in Elliot's manner or appearance to arouse suspicions. He was dressed fashionably, had pleasant manners, was good looking and had an agreeable way of talking. The broker felt flattered at being asked to do commission business for the New York Life Insurance Company, and readily agreed to do the work which Elliot requested. Two days later the gold had been bought and put in "Little Joe's" hands, and the certified check was deposited in the Mechanics' Bank and duly honored.

The fraud was not discovered until January 16, when the account of the insurance company with the Union Trust Company was audited. At first sight it was hard to believe even then that a forgery had occurred. The president was astounded that his signature could have been copied so exactly. But that fraud had occurred was beyond dispute, and the matter was put in the hands of our detective force. The officers of the company were suspicious of the broker, Mr. Maxwell, and at their instigation he was arrested, but when the matter had been thoroughly exploited, was discharged.

The first effort of the detectives was to find the note from which the signatures on the forged check had been made. This, strange to say, was found among the papers of the company, and subsequent investigation proved conclusively that it had been taken from the company's papers and put back among them again by Charles W. Pontez, a clerk. To the detectives, Pontez had been known before as an associate of Joseph W. Chapman, a well-known forger. Pontez was watched constantly. These curious creatures of the day and night whom we call "shadows," followed him when he left the office at night, saw him go to his home, went to the theatre behind him, and kept their eyes on him until he was safely housed for the night. One night he was seen at the theatre with "Little Joe" Elliot, but after that they were not observed together. Again, on a night when the cold winds were sweeping across the North River and causing the passengers who were hastening to the Cortlandt Street ferries to shiver, one of these omnipresent shadows saw Joseph Elliot greet warmly by a hand-shake the notorious forger, Charles Becker.

After this the trio were seen to go frequently to the house in Allen Street, and it was determined that this was their headquarters. Accordingly it was watched, and with the result mentioned. After the arrest of the three forgers the house was searched, and metallic dies, checks, lithographic stones, prints of bank-notes, etc., were found, as well as proof sheets of the forged check of the New York Life Insurance Company. Pontez was arrested on the next morning. The exposure of the affair showed that he had stolen the check and handed it over to Elliot. Becker engraved the check and "Old Man" Hearing printed it.

The trial of the forgers came on, and created a great deal of interest. But "Little Joe" had his mind on something else than the trial. He was thinking of escape, and one day while the officer who took him to and from court had his eyes turned away, Elliot took to his heels and fled. He was afterward re-captured, and with two of his associates in crime paid the penalty for his misdeeds. Pontez died before his sentence was pronounced.

"Little Joe" began stealing when a boy. As a youth he was quite a dashing young fellow, had lots of money, and kept company with many of the most aristocratic young "bloods" about town. He married Kate Castleton, the actress, having met her when she was playing with the San Francisco Minstrels in this city. Their wedding was in the Little Church Around the Corner after a courtship of three days. She retired from the stage at his request, but afterward, when their domestic happiness was clouded by discord, returned to her old profession. When her husband was serving his term in prison for forgery, no one was more constant in devotion than his wife, and she tried in vain to secure a pardon for him from the governor. She afterward secured a divorce from him and married Harry Phillips, the manager of the "Crazy Patch" company. Elliot is suspected of having been implicated in the murder of Mary Chapman, in London, many years ago. She was the wife of Joseph B. Chapman, the notorious American forger, whom Elliot met in Constantinople, and in whose company he committed several crimes.

Charles I. Brockway, one of whose operations is referred to in another chapter, was a forger whose name will always be a familiar one in the traditions of the police department of New York. He was the leader of a bold gang which included such men as William Ogle, Andrew Gilligan, James Williams, popularly known

WM. E. BROCKWAY.
(From a Photograph in the Rogues' Gallery.)

as "Big Kentuck," George Lockwood, alias "Cully," and "Tommy" Moore. The amount of his forgeries in this city alone amounted to $300,000, and there is scarcely an important city in the Union that has not seen some of his handiwork. Some of his victims in New York were the Bank of the Republic, the Chemical Bank, the Bank of the State of New York, the Phœnix Bank, the Second National Bank and the firm of Fiske & Hatch. Brockway himself frequently escaped detection and conviction, because he was clever enough to put most of the work into the hands of a man of pronounced bad character, and because he seldom had communications with the members of his gang, save through this accomplice. After successfully forging a check on the Bank of the Republic, the gang got into a dispute over the spoils, during which "Tommy" Moore objected to Brockway's creed, and fired a pistol at him. Ogle sprang to his chief's defence and fired back at Moore, wounding him. Afterwards Ogle, Gilligan and Williams were arrested for committing a forgery on the Phœnix Bank. Williams gave the conspiracy away, and the arrest of the other members of the gang followed. Brockway was sentenced to prison for ten years, but was afterward pardoned by President Johnson. In 1874 Detective King, of the Central Office, arrested him again and he was taken to Massachusetts, where he served three years. He turned up later in Chicago, and again was found plying his trade in New York. Captain Kealy, the chief of detectives, got evidence that he was implicated in other forgeries, and arrested him in a Bleecker Street saloon.

Brockway was a handsome man, with black hair and eyes, tall and well formed. He is now not more than forty-five years old. He was born in New York and has lived here always, save for such absences as his business would necessitate. Soon after the war he ran a faro game in this city, and dealt largely in counterfeit money.

No forgery ever occurred more famous than the Morey letter, which was published in fac-simile in *Truth* during the presidential campaign of 1880. No other forgery probably had such far reaching consequences. Others have wrecked commercial companies and wiped out the fortunes of private individuals, but this Morey forgery nearly changed the result of a presidential election.

Everybody is familiar with the story. The letter purported to have been written by James A. Garfield, the Republican candidate, to a Mr. Morey, a manufacturer in Massachusetts, and dealt with the Chinese question in such a way as would undoubtedly lose the Pacific States to the Republican party had the genuineness of the letter not been doubted. Mr. Garfield himself wrote a prompt denial, but the denial scarcely reached as many persons as the letter itself, for a fac-simile of the letter in electrotype was published in every Democratic newspaper in the land.

The Republican national committee were determined that they would trace this infamous imposition to its source, and put the matter into the hands of Colonel George Bliss and John I. Davenport. These gentlemen employed almost the whole Detective Bureau to discover the author of the forgery. It was not long before he was supposed to be found in the person of Kenward Philp, a brilliant but erratic journalist, who was one of the writers for *Truth*. He was arrested, charged with forgery and libel in writing and publishing the letter. The trial lasted for some time; but Philp was finally acquitted, not, however, until several witnesses had been indicted for perjury. During the trial a friend of Philp's happened into the court-room and asked him what the charge was. His reply was: "For being the author of 'Beautiful Snow.'" The inference is, therefore, that had Philp been convicted, this long-vexed question would have been decided. Poor Philp! He died in Brooklyn the first part of this year.

A romantic, varied life, capped by a most successful tour of forging through this country, is the picture I have now to present to the readers of this autobiography. The life of William Griffis, *alias* the "Earl of Ashburton," "Lord Ashburton," George M. Saville, William J. Hadley and Henry C. Walters, is told best by tracing his career from childhood. The rounded work of crime is much more impressive and full of moral than any incidents of this career of infamy.

Griffis was born at Totnes, a small village near the mouth of the River Exe, in Devonshire, England. His father was a wealthy, enterprising and respected timber merchant. He determined that his son should have education, fortune and the choice of the army or navy, or one of the liberal professions. The boy first went to the Butchers' School, in London, a very famous institution for preparing lads for a collegiate career. From there he went to Eton, and was in the class of '61-2. Here his conduct did not please his father, and although the boy was destined for Cambridge University, it was decided that it would be best to start him in the banking business at once. So it came about that influence obtained for him a desk in the Bank of England—"The Old Lady of Threadneedle Street." This was in the fall of 1862. He was a born financier. In 1865 he had learned all that could be learned in Threadneedle Street, and took a trip with an officer of the bank to China. He visited Hong Kong and Shanghai, returning to England in 1867.

At this time his bad characteristics were developed. He always possessed an innate cussedness, which cropped out just at the wrong time. He suddenly left the bank, abandoned home and friends, and came to New York. Unfortunately for him, as it subsequently proved, he had learnt engraving and lithographing. When he landed here he had ample means, and remittances from home were assured. His choice led him into "tavern" society. Naturally bright and conspicuously intelligent, he attracted the attention of certain individuals who frequented the places he chose for his headquarters. He continued to perfect himself in engraving and lithographing, and so fell across men who were agents for the most powerful gang of forgers that ever infested this country.

Griffis's financial knowledge was a mine of wealth to those who gradually drew him into the vortex of crime News of his doings had reached his father, who remonstrated with him for his gambling, his association with females of doubtful character, and his intemperance. Finally, the father virtually discarded him, but Griffis did not trouble himself about this He could earn his living as an engraver and lithographer, and his criminal associates warped his honest instincts by degrees. When he was financially embarrassed they lent him sums of money At first these sums were small; then the amounts would be hundreds of dollars. Finally he was head over heels in debt, and the only way to get out of it was by doing the bidding of the men who had him in their power. To "handle" him became easy in 1878, because of a little adventure with a girl whom he had betrayed. From 1869 till 1875 he had done all sorts of little "jobs" for the clique of forgers. He had given them valuable information in regard to financial business in Europe, had done some engraving on bonds, commercial paper and bank-notes, and had shared in the profits. There is no doubt that between the years named the clique made at least $300,000 out of his intimate knowledge of the banking business, and his skill with the graver.

But the grand *coup* had not yet been proposed to him.

In 1876 he was at Syracuse, N. Y., with a few hundred dollars in his pocket, when he made the acquaintance of a German girl who called herself Lola Walters. She was fairly respectable, and averred that Griffis betrayed her under a promise of marriage. In February of the following year they lived at No. 126 West Twenty-ninth Street, and were very hard up for money. In the same house was an actress—Lizzie Kelsey—who was fond of ostentatiously displaying her wardrobe and jewellery. The girl Lola is believed to have prompted Walters, as he now called himself, to the commission of a burglary; and in it were associated an ex-policeman and a professional criminal. The burglary was not as successful as the perpetrators wished. It netted property worth less than a thousand dollars, which, sifted through the hands of a receiver, realized but a couple of hundred dollars—hardly enough, as the thieves afterwards confessed, to "pay expenses." All of those who participated were arrested. One was not tried, another pleaded guilty to petty larceny and went to the penitentiary for a short term. Lola and Griffis, who were each under an *alias*, invoked "influence" at the district attorney's office which secured a delay, resulting in the disappearance of witnesses. Finally they were discharged. Griffis came out of prison as poor as the proverbial church mouse, and fell an easy prey to the men who knew his worth as an engraver and financier.

It had long been plotted to flood the country with circular notes and letters of credit of the Union Bank of London (England). The scheme had so far progressed that even the paper on which the notes and letters of credit were to be printed had been ordered and manufactured in Europe, together with the bulk of the engravings. Griffis was given general charge of the whole business, and directed what should be done in England to bring the matter to a head, and to secure the circulation of the paper without a hitch. When the whole scheme was completed and everything was ready, the forgers had prepared the following "paper," all directed against the Union Bank of London: Circular letters of £54,000 ($270,000) with the privilege of unlimited credit on drafts, and with circular notes running from £10 ($50) to £500 ($2500); circular note for £43,000 ($215,000), circular letters for £20,000

($100,000) and £6000 ($30,000), and two of £1000 each ($10,000), the last four having circular notes of £10 ($50) each. The aggregate was $625,000!

No one not thoroughly conversant with the intricacies of banking, letters of credit, circular notes, engraving, printing and general business matters, can have the slightest idea of the pains and nicety required to mature such a scheme of plunder. When Griffis started to cash these spurious drafts there was not a flaw in the whole arrangement. He was not alone in the business of reaping the harvest of his and his associates' infamy. His share was to be the letter of credit for $270,000; his field of operations, Denver, Ogden, Salt Lake City, Virginia City and San Francisco.

In October, 1878, he arrived in Boston, Massachusetts, literally loaded down with money. There he met his fate, in the person of Georgetta Saville, a corrupt but beautiful auburn-haired woman, who had been launched on a career of infamy by a New York stock-broker. This gentleman's means had begun to fail when Griffis met Georgetta, and she was glad to find a new protector with plenty of the needful. Taking her name, Griffis came to New York and began to victimize our tradesmen, one of whom was Mr. Thomas Kirkpatrick, the Broadway jeweller. From him, for thirty-two of the forged £10 notes, he obtained $1600 worth of jewellery. Griffis fared equally well with a dozen other tradesmen, and then cut a swathe through Chicago, Toledo, Cleveland and Kansas City. The woman accompanied him, and became as expert in disposing of the forged paper as the man.

Unfortunately for them, an indiscretion on the part of one of the forgers—Walker F. Floswell, *alias* Esmond—at the office of Jesup, Paton & Co., the William Street bankers, got the gang into trouble. The blunder led to the discovery of the forgeries, and in forty-eight hours hundreds of telegrams of warning and inquiry had put every banking institution in the United States and Canada on their guard. Wall Street was appalled at the responses which came in from east, west, north and south. It was at first imagined that the scheme had netted $2,000,000, but when the accounts were balanced it was ascertained that the epidemic was not one-eighth as bad as was supposed.

One of these telegrams of inquiry and warning reached a corrupt and black-mailing clique in the Rocky Mountains. It was called the Rocky Mountain Detective Agency. Now, it so happened that

Griffis and Georgetta were "papering" Denver at the time. The agency swooped down on them, kept them under surveillance, and sent me the following telegram:

"We have got those Union Bank forgers—man and woman. What reward is there out for them?"

I replied:

"Will give $100 reward. If any more you can have it."

Whereupon the boss rascal of the agency, D. J. Cook, sent me this reply:

"Sum named will not do at all. Would not pay railroad fare."

That closed the negotiations with me; but the "agency" proceeded to reward themselves for any little trouble they might have had in following Griffis and his auburn-haired companion. They fleeced them out of $11,000, but were kind enough to pay the forgers' railroad fare to the place they desired to go to. The woman quitted her companion to go East. Griffis chose to go to Cheyenne, and as he got on the train the Rocky Mountain Agency kindly handed him $300,000 of the forged Union Bank of London paper, hoping, no doubt, that he would be successful enough to be able to repay future attention.

The Rocky Mountain men, however, were too greedy. They stuck to Griffis like his undershirt, and spoiled his "business" at Cheyenne and Ogden, until he was compelled to give them a hint "not to come so darned close to him." They saw the point, allowed him a little more latitude, and despite the warnings flashed from New York, he was able to do quite a respectable little business in the line of forged circular notes. But the Rocky Mountain boys knew whenever and wherever he made a "haul," and at the very first opportunity "shook him up" and divided the profits. In this way, from the adventure at Denver to the time he arrived in San Francisco, they fleeced him out of $21,000.

At San Francisco he stood at bay and defied the detectives. The 'Frisco police had got wind of the affair, and interposed just when Griffis had planned to lay a little money aside for himself. He had disposed of $125,000 more of the notes in the purchase of mining stocks. But he fell between the upper and the nether millstone—the Rocky Mountain agency and Chief Lees of the San Francisco detectives—and was prosecuted by the Bank of Nevada. It was an easy matter to convict him. His sentence was eight years' imprisonment. He was then in failing health, and in some remarkable and mysterious manner excited so much sympathy that two other indictments, which would have consigned him to prison for the rest of his natural life, were not pushed. Griffis continued in prison until November, 1882, when influence secured his release, on the representation that he was dying. He had relatives in San Francisco, one of them a young lady of undoubted respectability. She constantly visited him, and upon his release from prison they were married. The ceremony was performed while he lay on a bed of sickness, from which he never expected to move unless to be placed in his coffin. He was carried, however, by short and easy stages, to Southern California, and remained in bed for nine weeks. Then he came East, intending to go home to Devonshire to die. His lungs were affected, and he suffered from hæmorrhages several times a day. He arrived at New York, *incognito*, but news of his movements had been telegraphed to Mr. Kirkpatrick, who resolved to ascertain if the reported illness of the forger was true. He communicated with me, and through the officers of the Twenty-ninth Precinct I tracked him to East Fiftieth Street, where he was arrested. When in custody he made a full and unreserved confession.

CHAPTER XXV.

SWINDLERS AND BLACK-MAILERS.—"HE CAN'T BEAT ME PLAYIN' POKER."—A SWINDLER SWINDLED.—DIVORCES PROCURED BY WHOLESALE.—SWINDLING A GREAT DRY GOODS HOUSE.—A BANK BILL.—HOW TO PUNISH A BLACK-MAILER.—"I CAME IN HERE TO KILL YOU."

ON one night in August, 1883, the brilliant electric light which hangs outside the entrance to the Madison Square Theatre shone down on the faces of a well-dressed, hurrying crowd of men and women who were anxious to reach their seats inside the building before the curtain should rise. Standing just inside the main entrance, with rather a dubious look on his face, was a stout, healthy-looking man, with rough clothes and bronzed face, whom a veteran New Yorker would at once pronounce a countryman. Now and then this stranger to the city walked over to the box-office and in hearty tones cried out, "Any seats yet?" The play which was on then was a popular one, and on this particular evening all the seats had been taken. The stranger had waited until coming to the play-house before securing a chair, and as a consequence found himself unable to get one. Now he was waiting in hope that some of the stalls which had been taken would be returned.

The ticket agent looked up with a smile at the stout man's question, which was then asked for nearly the dozenth time, and responded blandly, "No, there are none in yet."

Just then from one side of the lobby where he had been examining the pictures of actresses in a glass case, a young man, dressed in a stylish suit, walked over to where the stranger stood, and in polite and modest tones asked:

"Pardon me, but were you trying to get a seat?"

"Wall, I should say I war," the stranger replied.

"Then won't you take one of mine? I bought two expecting to meet a friend here, but he hasn't turned up and I don't believe he will come."

The man with the bronzed face was overcome with gratitude and gladly consented to sit beside the handsomely dressed young man. They went into the theatre, took their seats and enjoyed the play. The young man was exceedingly agreeable, and his elder companion talked with him frankly and without restraint. He told him that he was a ranchman from Abilene, Kansas, and that he was in New York for the second time in his entire life. This led to conversation about the sights of the great metropolis, and inasmuch as his polite young friend professed to be thoroughly familiar with the ins and outs, it was only natural that the Westerner should comply with the young man's suggestion that they should go together and visit some of the notorious places.

"I'm stayin' at the Fifth Avenue Hotel," said the ranchman, as they parted for the night. "Come round an' take dinner with me to-morrow night." The young man accepted the invitation.

On the next night, after the two men had more than satisfied their stomachs' demands, and had imbibed liberally of claret and champagne, they walked out of the dining-room into the corridor and stopped at the desk, while the Westerner took a well-padded pocket-book out of his trousers, and counting out five hundred dollars in bills of large denomination deposited them with the clerk. The young man appeared to take no interest in this proceeding, yet all the time his eyes were on the well-filled wallet and the green bank-notes.

The ranchman and his young companion left the hotel. Late that night the older man returned.

After breakfast the next morning, Benjamin Ashley, for such was the name which the man from the West had written on the hotel register, was lounging in the corridors, when he was addressed by the clerk, who, after apologizing for his boldness, asked the hotel guest if he was aware of the character of the young man who was with him on the previous night. Mr. Ashley replied that he had met him since he had come to New York and was very much pleased with him.

"Let me give you a pointer," said the clerk. "That young man is 'Hungry Joe,' the biggest swindler in this town!"

Benjamin Ashley was startled. He said nothing for a moment, then became thoughtful, and finally replied: "That's the kind o' huckleberry he is, is it? Wall, all right. Let him blaze away. He can't beat me playin' poker."

"HUNGRY JOE'S POKER GAME.

The clerk smiled sarcastically, but considering that he had done his duty dropped the subject at once, and without further remark handed over from the safe the $1000 which Mr. Ashley asked for.

After this, "Hungry Joe" and his innocent friend were often together. They drove through the Park and up the Boulevard; they went to the theatre and they played—poker. Mr. Ashley grew more confidential, and told his companion that he owned a valuable ranch in Kansas, and that he was about to sail for England to have his eyes treated. More poker games were played, and more bank bills were drawn from those on deposit in the hotel safe. A week after the clerk had warned him of Hungry Joe, Mr. Ashley had lost nearly $4000. Yet he was unwilling to give up.

One afternoon he was in his room with "Hungry Joe," and two friends which the latter had introduced. They had played poker and the Westerner had met with his usual poor luck. He grew despondent.

"I'll tell you what I'll do, boys," he said at length, "I didn't think you could beat me at poker, but, by golly, you've done it, an' done it bad too. Now I've got to get to Europe somehow or tother, an' I don't see how I'm to do it on what I've got left of my pile. So, as I said, I'll tell you what I'll do. I'll give you a mortgage on my ranch for $4000."

The whilom friends expressed their sympathy for Mr. Ashley and offered to think about it. They soon left the hotel and went into a saloon. Here they concocted a scheme. They would telegraph to Abilene, to the postmaster, to find out if Ashley's representations were correct, and if they were they would buy the ranch outright at a reduced figure. The telegram read something like this:

"Postmaster, Abilene, Kansas: Telegraph full particulars about Benjamin Ashley at my expense.
"R. Dickson."

The answer came and was entirely satisfactory. Hungry Joe and his companions managed to scrape together $14,000, and with this sum in their pockets the two repaired again to the hotel, and offered Mr. Ashley $14,000 for his ranch. The offer was promptly accepted, the papers were drawn up, and $14,000 went into the Fifth Avenue Hotel safe to wait until Mr. Ashley wished to draw it out.

Two days later a Guion line steamship left its dock amid the waving of handkerchiefs. Among the little knot of persons who stood on the edge of the pier to get the last glimpse of their friends were Hungry Joe and the two companions who were with him in Benjamin Ashley's room when the latter sold the deed to his Western property for $14,000. The bronze-faced ranchman waved his slouch hat at the trio as the huge black hull of the steamer swung loose from its moorings. The trio politely tipped their stylish derbies in acknowledgment of the farewell greeting. A few moments and the vessel was out of sight. The trio turned, chuckled to themselves, and hurried away with the remark, " Well, he's safely out of the way ! A neat little pile we'll make out of that ranch too, eh ? " What the ranchman said we may only surmise when this story's sequel is told.

Two weeks from the time this steamer sailed there was registered again at the same hotel " Benjamin Ashley, Abilene, Kansas." Hungry Joe heard of the arrival and hastened to the hotel to pay his respects. He sent up his card and was soon ushered into the presence of a total stranger.

" You are not Mr. Ashley ? " he inquired. " There must be some mistake. I was looking for Mr. Benjamin Ashley, of Abilene, Kansas."

" I am the man, sir," responded the gentleman.

" Why, that is strange. Is it possible there are two men of the same name in your town ? It was only a few days ago that I bought a ranch of a Mr. Benjamin Ashley, of Abilene."

" You did, eh ? Well, then, I guess you were swindled, my friend," answered the traveller, dryly. " There is but one Benjamin Ashley in Abilene and that is myself, and I haven't any recollection of selling my ranch to you or to any one else. I just got in yesterday from Europe."

Hungry Joe turned pale. The vision flashed across him that he, the arch-swindler of New York, had been himself swindled. The thought was humiliating. For a moment he said nothing.

" But, by the way," continued this new Mr. Ashley, " what kind of a looking man was this double of mine ? "

Hungry Joe described him. A flash of recognition crossed the stranger's face. He laughed as he said:

"I see it all now. That man must have been Harry Barnes, one of my cowboys!"

The mystery was easily solved now. The genuine Benjamin Ashley had gone abroad some time before for the purpose of having his eyes treated. The cowboy had followed, determined to have a good time by using his employer's name, and perhaps money. After becoming acquainted with Hungry Joe he lost nearly all he had, and to his great chagrin a "city chap" had beaten him at poker. He would get even with him in some way, and so devised the scheme of selling his employer's property. It worked successfully, and at the same time that the real Mr. Ashley was leaving London for New York, the false Mr. Ashley was leaving New York for London, with $14,000 in his pocket.

Hungry Joe went thoughtfully from the hotel. One who was close enough to him might have heard the murmur, "Beaten by a cowboy! What a d–n fool I am!"

For some time previous to February, 1884, there appeared in several of the New York papers a number of advertisements which read, " Divorces procured without publicity." It was just such an advertisement that would strike the eye of the hundreds in this metropolis whose domestic lives were not that fulness of uninterrupted bliss of which poets sing and young people dream. How many wives remain joined to husbands whom they would leave in an instant save for the publicity caused by suit for divorce! It is not strange then that such an advertisement would be clutched at as if it were a last straw to the dying by those who suffer the pangs of married infelicity.

To the police, however, this notice in the public prints was a thing to arouse suspicion. An investigation was made, and a most appalling state of things was discovered. It was found that fraudulent divorces were obtained almost by wholesale in Brooklyn. It seems that a clique of lawyers in this city, notably one Monro Adams, was in collusion with a clerk of the King's County Supreme Court, who issued the decrees by forging the name of the judge and county clerk, and stamping the documents with the county seal.

This fraudulent business had been carried on for a long while and on an enormous scale, and it is estimated that there are thousands of these bogus divorce certificates throughout the country. When Adams's papers were examined it was found that this system of securing divorces had patrons in nearly every State in the Union.

In 1884 men and women of the upper circles in New York were startled by the announcement that Henry C. Pedder, the proprietor of the *Manhattan Magazine*, had swindled Arnold, Constable & Co. out of thousands of dollars. Fifteen years before he had entered the firm's business as entry clerk at a salary of $600 a year. He worked his way up until he became manager of the firm's real estate. Although his chances for making money honestly were not great, he owned at the time his false character was discovered a house at Llewellyn Park, Orange, New Jersey, valued at $200,000. He lived in great style, but in spite of his rather cultivated tastes he was a thorough rascal. He sunk money in real estate in speculation, in the Gorringe Ship-building Company, and in his magazine, which died soon after Pedder's dishonesty was made public.

The discovery of Pedder's illegal transactions was made by investigation into other cases of swindling which had occurred in the house of Arnold, Constable & Co. The cases had been put into the hands of Inspector Byrnes, and his men had ferreted the swindlers out. It was found that several persons, including Mrs. B. F. Burke, of No. 345 East Fifteenth Street, her son Joseph, William Devlin, a porter in the employ of the house, and a man named Cornelius O'Leary, who had at one time been receiving clerk, had entered into a conspiracy to systematically rob the firm. Their method was to impose fraudulent checks on the house payable to the order of Mrs. Burke, from whom it was asserted that bills of goods had been purchased. Checks from $100 up to $1000 were thus paid, and altogether the firm had lost about $50,000. O'Leary pleaded guilty and was sent up for five years, and the others were treated accordingly.

Years ago a florid-faced Englishman entered Tiffany's old downtown store on Broadway. He was dressed in the height of fashion, wore a profusion of jewellery, and carried himself with an air of importance. He asked to be shown some diamonds, of which the firm had a remarkable display, their value being not less than a million dollars. The customer was rather particular in his tastes; but finally selected a varied assortment of fine stones. Ostentatiously he handed out in payment a bank bill of large denomination, and at the same time presented his card, which bore the name of Muchler. The bill was sent to the desk.

Suddenly the cashier appeared with the bill in his hand, and declared it a counterfeit!

The Englishman asserted his respectability, and his high " position," and became so noisy and indignant as to attract the attention of all those in the store. Neither was the cashier backward, and the altercation became warm. The clerks gathered round. The cashier, waving the bill in the air, cried out:

" You're a swindler ! "

In an instant the bill was snatched from his hand, and Muchler made for the door. Now thoroughly aroused, the clerks grabbed him and took him into a private office by main force.

Word was sent to me at police headquarters that there was trouble at Tiffany's and I immediately sent two detectives. Upon their arrival, they searched Muchler thoroughly; but to the astonishment of every one the counterfeit bill could not be found upon his person; and he had had no possible opportunity for destroying or throwing it away. Here was a mystery. We had the man safely enough, but without the counterfeit bill it would be impossible to convict him of any offence. The detectives finally brought him to my office at headquarters, together with the clerk and cashier. When Muchler was conducted into my presence the facts were told me, and I ordered him to be searched again, thinking that the bill might have been overlooked. That it was secreted somewhere about the Englishman's person there seemed no doubt, so we searched every square inch of each article he wore, both inside and out, as well as every portion of his body where a human being could possibly conceal a bank bill.

But our efforts were futile ; no bill could be found! My officers were in a dilemma ; it seemed as if we should be obliged to let the man go. Suddenly, one of the detectives whispered to me.

"You are right; just the very thing," I responded to the whisper. Calling a messenger, I gave him some secret instructions and sent him out of the office.

All the persons in the room, including the prisoner, looked surprised and puzzled at my action. In a few minutes the messenger returned. By my directions, Muchler was laid upon his back on a table. The two detectives held his head firmly while I opened his mouth, and taking from the messenger a small packet emptied the contents down his throat and forced him to swallow. He struggled violently; but it was too late. Before the man knew my intentions, the object was accomplished. Presently his face twitched, his throat contracted, there came a spasm, and at our feet fell—a bank bill! He had swallowed the counterfeit, and I had given him an emetic.

The finding of the bill, I may say, led to Muchler's conviction. The method employed for its recovery, I know, was not very enjoyable, but it was harmless; and the end certainly justified the means. While I would never permit anything approaching brutality to prisoners, there are times when, in order to obtain the necessary proofs, one has to employ heroic methods. This was a case in point.

The bill in question, I believe, is now on exhibition at police headquarters.

In 1859 a young man came to me and told me that a rascal was trying to black-mail him, on account of a woman to whom he was paying attentions. The fellow had followed the pair, and the next day called upon the lady and demanded money from her as the price of keeping her secret.

"Well," said my visitor, "she hadn't any money to spare; but he scared her with his threat of exposure and she hurried to tell me. I have come to you for advice. What shall I do?"

"I can arrest him for attempted black-mail; but even if he is punished, that may not be the end of it," I replied.

"Yes, I was thinking of that," said the young man. "That is what bothers me."

I asked him if he could thrash the fellow.

"Don't know," he answered; "I haven't sized him up. I can if he isn't a real good man, Cap. Anyhow, I'll be glad to try it if you say so."

I asked if he didn't sometimes stay behind and lock up the store where he worked.

"Oh, yes," he answered, "occasionally; I can do it any time."

"Then let the lady send him to you for money. When you've locked up the store, you can give him a dressing down."

In a week the young man made his appearance again, in a glow of grateful appreciation.

"Thanks, Cap!" he exclaimed, "it worked like a charm. He came. I told him I'd settle with him after the rest had gone, and when we were alone I gave him the worst licking a man ever had in his life. He begged me not to kill him, for he thought it was his last hour, and he swore on his knees never to say a word about me or about any of my affairs. I'm awfully afraid I have crippled him for life, though I didn't mean to; but when he went over the first time he fell across the stove and broke his arm."

He had scared the fellow so badly that the rascal told just who he was and where he lived and all about himself. It was the last of the trouble. I saw the injured would-be informer walking about nearly a month later with his arm in a sling.

At about midnight on November 7, 1881, half a dozen congenial spirits were gathered around a table in Dick Darling's saloon at No. 1217 Broadway. Half drained glasses were in front of them, and jokes and jesting were the order of the occasion. It was a jolly good-natured crowd, although in their number were some desperate criminals. The six men were Bill Bowie, George Law, Jr., Harry Rice, Charles Crawford, Billy Temple and Charles R. Miller, the "king of the bunco men." For an hour the men sat chatting and drinking. Once a man whom the drinkers recognized as Billy Tracy, a bad fellow, but a coward, opened the door of the bar-room and peeked in only to quickly withdraw. A few minutes later the same man opened the door again, walked up to the bar, and ordered a whiskey sour. Suddenly he turned around, and addressing the king of the bunco men, exclaimed:

"I came in here to kill you!"

No sooner had the words left his mouth than a revolver was pointed at Miller's head, the trigger was pulled, and a No. 32 cartridge sank into the bunco man's stomach. Miller doubled up, reached for his revolver, and then fainted. In a few moments an ambulance appeared and the wounded man was taken to the New York Hospital, where he soon died. Tracy was caught and arrested.

In the sensational death of Charles P. Miller was ended the life of a notorious swindler, a man whose talents were so marvellous that he earned for himself among the fraternity of sharpers that name by which I have called him—"the king of bunco men."

In person he was slim, fair, polished, agreeable and one of the best conversationalists that ever frequented the first-class resorts of the Twenty-ninth Precinct. He was invariably well-dressed, clean-shaven and good-looking, liberal to a fault, slow in making confidential friends, equally slow in making enemies. He was the son of a county officer in Texas. Parental indulgence spoiled him. He learned to drink to excess when he was fifteen years of age, fell into bad company of both sexes, was outlawed by his father and took to railroading in Louisiana, where he completed his knowledge of the art of gambling.

He began his career as a gambler by "capping" for one of the New Orleans establishments, and finally started a cheating concern of his own. While conducting this he became proficient as a "confidence" and "bunco man." When he had amassed about $35,000 he came to New York and "doubled up" with a gambling clique. He soon got ahead of his tutors, secured another partner who knew a little more than his first, and battled in a contest of wits with the "chiefs" of the New York swindling fraternity, including such men as Hungry Joe and McDermott. His ability was such that they were soon willing and pleased to acknowledge him as the "chief operator" in the United States. Miller had so ingratiated himself by his intelligence, suavity and liberality with persons who have a great deal to do with the surveillance, arrest and conviction of this very slippery class, always difficult to convict, that he could "pull the strings" of the law whenever he chose, and the first person whom a "confidence" man thought of when he got into trouble was Miller. It is hardly necessary to say that in his new position Miller did very little "work." His principal occupation was keeping an eye on the operations of the various cliques—the Ferry, Astor House, Fifth Avenue Hotel and other gangs. He was rarely seen down town. His headquarters were within a few feet of the lamp-post which stands on the south-west corner of Broadway and Twenty-eighth Street. It is within reason to say that he had a shake-hands acquaintance with a thousand men who never dreamed that he was a rascal. He knew every police officer by sight, at least, every politician, every man and nearly every woman about town. He lived like one of the "gilded youths" of Uppertendom, disdaining whiskey, strong drinks and cheap cigars, and taking his meals in none other than first-class restaurants.

He passed his time "in the season," which may be said to last from November to May, in the principal bar-rooms and hotels. If he operated at all it was in the summer months, and then he only aimed at high game. He was as well known at Long Branch, Saratoga, Newport, Nantasket Beach, Richfield Springs and other resorts as the millionaire habitués. He never visited one of these places without having an eye to business; that is to say, he was always accompanied by a clique of operators, whose movements he directed. His personal expenses could hardly have been less than $20 a day, and his liberality did not permit him to amass a fortune. Had he been prudent he would have died worth several hundred thousand dollars. One of the circumstances that militated against his prosperity was his love for horse-racing. He was known to have lost $20,000 in one day's racing. He eschewed faro after losing $18,000 at one sitting at Saratoga.

One of the few enemies he made was Billy Tracy, his murderer. The latter was an Irish-American, born in the Eleventh Ward, who was graduated as a petty thief at the age of sixteen, and went through the various grades until he was considered an expert bank forger. But this was simply because of his associates. He was always a coward, but with such companions as Red Leary, Jimmy Dolan, Whitey Bob, "Old Jake" Tierney, Dan Noble and Jimmy Griffin he had no difficulty in attaining reasonable success in his vocation. He had been arrested often for various crimes by Central Office detectives, and as frequently escaped conviction.

The feud between Miller and Tracy began in the spring of 1881, and came pretty nearly to an end one night when they drew pistols on each other in Tracy's own saloon, No. 33 West Twenty-ninth Street. As Miller strolled into the place, Tracy began to bully him. When Miller appeared likely to retaliate. Tracy backed down. Miller kept his eye on him, expecting a cowardly attack, and when the latter, in a burst of courage, said: " I'll fix you," the threatened man drew a revolver and quickly fired three shots, one of which hit Tracy. The bullet only wounded him slightly. He fell on the floor and called for the police. Miller and his friends crowded around him, laughing at him until they were tired, and then left the place. There were no arrests. Miller's hilarity, however, rankled in the breast of Tracy who resolved to get even, and did it in the way that has been mentioned.

Perjured testimony saved the murderer from the gallows. He went scot-free, and is still keeping the little saloon where the first encounter between him and Miller took place.

CHAPTER XXVI.

A PLOT OF NIHILISTS.—THREATENING LETTERS.—LITTLE ROSA STRASBURGER.—A CAUTIOUS RABBI.—DETECTIVE CAMPBELL'S WATCH.—"I'LL BLOW YOUR BRAINS OUT."—A BLACK-MAILER'S DEATH.—LETTERS TO JAY GOULD.—INTERESTED IN "SALVATION."—WATCHING THE MAILING-BOXES.—THE MYSTERY SOLVED.

A PLOT only second in interest to the Charley Ross case, and equal to it in its tragic conclusion, was brought to an end in the early part of 1881. It was concocted by men who were proved to be Russian Nihilists. Mr. Louis Strasburger, a wealthy diamond merchant, of No. 15 Maiden Lane, whose name is known wherever there is a market for these gems, lived at No. 128 East Sixty-first Street with his family, which consisted of his wife and their charming little daughter Rosa. The first scheme set on foot was to extort money by frightening the object of the attentions of the clique; and so, on the day before Christmas, 1880, they addressed the following letter to Mrs. Strasburger and her sister, Mrs. Adler, who had married Mr. Strasburger's partner:

> "You doubtless know that your husband has been sentenced to pay $60,000. We appeal for the last time to you, and if you don't wish to have a funeral in the house at an early day you had better pay it. If you desire to prevent bloodshed take a car precisely at 1.30 to the corner of Broadway and Barclay Street. Have the money ready. Between half-past three and four go alone from the corner of Broadway and Barclay Street to West Broadway, three times, with an envelope in your hand.
> "EXECUTIVE COMMITTEE."

Mr. Strasburger ridiculed the communication. His wife and her sister were nervous, however, and upon second thought Mr. Strasburger quietly informed Pinkerton's Detective Agency of what had happened. Subsequently, he called upon Captain John Gunner, of the Twenty-eighth Precinct, who took the matter in hand, and strove, with Detective Campbell, to discover who had written the letter. Upon their advice, Mrs. Strasburger followed the instructions laid down in the anonymous communication. She provided herself with a dummy package encased in a large envelope, and, as directed, ostentatiously displayed it. Detectives were watching her all the time, but no one accosted her. Nothing more was heard of the "Executive Committee" until the end of March.

Rosa was in the habit on Sunday of attending school at Dr. Heubsch's synagogue, Lexington Avenue and Sixty-fifth Street. She went there as usual upon the occasion indicated, and in the course of the afternoon Dr. Heubsch was called from his duties by one of the scholars, who gave him the following letter:

"*Dear Sir:*—I request you to permit my daughter to leave school, as a member of the family has been suddenly taken sick."

Dr. Heubsch was very bright and keen. The handwriting of the note did not satisfy him, although it was that of a lady's, and on paper which such a person would use. It flashed through his mind that Rosa was an only and cherished daughter, her father was extraordinarily particular in regard to her, and if any illness had occurred in the family he would not wish to have her startled by the breaking of the intelligence to her by a stranger. Dr. Heubsch, therefore, made inquiry as to the delivery of the letter, and the child who handed it to him pointed out a man who was lounging against the railing near by. At Dr. Heubsch's bidding the child went to the man and asked him to come to the doctor. His appearance was unprepossessing; he could not look the doctor in the face, was shabbily clad, and was certainly not a person whom Mr. Strasburger would choose to escort his child home. To the doctor's inquiring: "Who entrusted you with this note?" the man made some muttered reply in German. Dr. Heubsch "caught him up" in that language, and interrogated him sharply. He said that the missive had been put in his hands by a man with a long goatee, and gave a further description which tallied with that of Mr. Strasburger. He added that after giving him the note the gentleman had darted down Fifty-first Street. This last statement impelled Dr. Heubsch to extreme caution. He told the man that he could go—that it would be all right. When the man had gone Dr. Heubsch sent Miss Strasburger home, when it was discovered that no such letter had been written by any member of the Strasburger family. Mrs. Strasburger at the time was in delicate health, and this evident plot to abduct her child, in addition to the letter of the "Executive Committee," brought about a nervous crisis, so that Mr. Strasburger urged on the police to spare neither pains or expense in relieving him and his family of the intense anxiety from which they were suffering. Then came the following letter to Messrs. L. Strasburger & Co., dated March 27, 9.30 P.M.:

"We attempted to-day to abduct your daughter, but as we desired to show you what steps we can take when needed, you no doubt have an idea what we shall do. We warn you again to comply strictly with our wishes, and if we are not assured on Monday at 4 o'clock that you have what is desired safely in your pocket, we shall satisfy you that there will arrive a moment for us which shall be a momentous one in the history of your family. Should you not comply, you will compel us to work our several plans and to doubly strengthen them. We are not afraid of any kind of crime.
"EXECUTIVE COMMITTEE, 3 A 1 S."

This was followed in twenty-four hours by another letter, which ran:

"*March* 28, 1881.
"MESSRS. L. STRASBURGER & CO.,
    "NO. 15 MAIDEN LANE,
        "CITY.

"*Mr. Strasburger:*—Confirming our letter of yesterday, we call your attention to the necessity of your carrying the desired envelope in your hand wherever you go, and in such a manner that every one can see it. We hope to see this affair settled in the prescribed way. Otherwise, unless you do not give us immediate cause, we cease further correspondence. Should you not comply with our wishes we advise you not to permit your family to breathe too much sea air during the coming summer. We have time for vengeance.
"THE EXECUTIVE COMMITTEE, 3A1Sex."

Nothing was done by Mr. Strasburger except to place these terrible letters in the hands of Captain Gunner. He laid them before me, and acting on my advice, suggested to Mr. Strasburger that he should take care of himself and permit no member of his family to go out of the house without proper and sufficient escort. Upon the 5th of April, 1881, Captain Gunner showed me the following letters:

"LOUIS STRASBURGER, ESQ.,
    "NO. 128 EAST 61ST STREET,
        "CITY.

"*Dear Mrs. Strasburger:*—Without having the slightest interest, I can write to warn you once more, although I am afraid that it will be useless. In your own interests, so as not to be left a widow in this heartless world, try with Mrs. Adler to persuade your husband, or another, to settle this business yourself. I offer you my aid; more I cannot do. If I find in the *Staats Zeitung* of Sunday the following advertisement: 'LUDWIG KLABEKSKY, THIRD AVENUE,—Recommend all sorts of tobacco,' then I am certain you desire my help. I subscribe myself,

"SECRETARY,
"*Executive Committee.*"

The second letter was dated April 4, and ran as follows:

"MRS. L. STRASBURGER:

"*Most Respected Ladies:*—Excuse me for addressing you. I am a Polander and was drawn among the Nihilists by the hatred my race bears towards the Czar of Russia. I entered into the enterprise with a great zeal, as my generation is tyrannized over by Russia and we are breeding vengeance. I receive a very high salary as secretary of the Nihilists, which makes my life very comfortable, and I have only in return to translate from other languages. The negotiations with your husband cover a period of six months. The correspondence proved a failure, and it was intended a week ago that your daughter should be abducted, but I prevented it, as I advised threatening letters should be first used. The attempt to carry away your daughter from school was only a stupid affair. The real plan was to carry Rosa away from the street, to force or coax her into a coach. I prevented it. Then came threatening letters without any result. Last Thursday night we tried to avenge ourselves on Mr. Strasburger by a bomb, but I prevented that. When Mr. Strasburger went home with the boy, one of us saw a package in his pocket and cried out 'The envelope,' and at once the orders were countermanded. All this was my doing. You ask me why I have so much sympathy for you. I am the only Jew among the Section of Sixteen; all the others are Catholics. Therefore I concluded to warn you. But, ladies, I now only warn you that it may be too late. On Tuesday a resolution will be adopted. I will advise you what will be done. I am afraid this will be adopted on Tuesday night. The Fourth Section (the section of vengeance) consists of six men. It will be authorized to use the tools of their goddess. Then it will be too late for me to warn you, as every one will act independently. For the present, do not let Rosa leave the house alone, or with Miss Spelden. Do not walk any distance yourselves, particularly at night. I do not know what your husband can do for your safety, as the people charged with the execution of this resolve prize their success more than their lives. This very hour, friend, should you be able to comply with the wishes of the Nihilists, though to a reduced amount, you will find more rest and safety than at present. Were I in your situation I couldn't sleep a wink. If you comply you might be able to open other negotiations. Assuring you that I have acted without any interest in the Nihilist cause, I remain,

"SECRETARY,
"*A. E. 3d Avenue.*

"P. S —I can be found by advertisement over a well known name in the *Staats Zeitung* of Tuesday and the *German News* of Monday night, in which you might shortly announce what your conclusions are. Be brief, short and quick."

I suggested that Mrs. Strasburger should comply with the suggestion in these devilish communications, and in the papers named the following advertisement was inserted :

"I am not afraid. Cannot give much. State lowest price and place."

Also this one:

"I have $4600. May raise $5000."

Then came in an envelope the following suggestion from the Nihilists.

"Hurry them up."

It was followed by a scrap clipped from a German newspaper which read:

"REWARD OFFERED.—Mayor Howell was empowered by the Board of Aldermen to offer a reward for the discovery of the criminals who on March 12 laid a grenade, filled with dynamite, on the doorstep of James McKesney, No. 175 Clinton Street, Brooklyn."

All of us were now very much exercised over the turn affairs had taken. It is hardly necessary to say that both Captain Gunner and Detective Campbell were working zealously. A day or two later they were chagrined from the fact that either the principal or an accomplice of the black-mailers had been seen at Mr. Strasburger's house. When one of the letters was received, the door-bell was rung, and the governess, Miss Spelton, answered the summons. A frowzy-looking fellow handed a note to Miss Spelton, who looked at the address and said that Mrs. Strasburger was not in. Upon this the fellow snatched the missive from her hand, ran away, and it was afterwards received through the mail. Detective Campbell was worn out by his activity in the case. One day he would appear as an Italian rag picker; another he masqueraded as a coachman; then as a ragged laborer, and again as a tramp. Finally, it was resolved to post him in the neighborhood, so that he could be constantly on the watch. Upon the 7th of April a lad, who was evidently ignorant of what he was doing, went to Mr. Strasburger's house and left the following letter on the stoop :

"What is the meaning of all this? If, on receipt of this, before any one leaves the house, Miss Speldon will, with an envelope in her hand, go through Sixty-first Street to Central Park, and enter the same, I will regret I have written to you. These are my thanks. If it is done as before indicated, Miss Speldon will have to drop an envelope as soon as she hears a pistol shot, and not look round. This will probably be done on Sixty-first Street."

It so happened that Detective Campbell was in the house at the time. He told Miss Spelton to do precisely as the letter requested, and then he got out of the house by strategy, knowing perfectly well that the house was watched. Scaling a fence, he reached the basement of a house on Sixtieth Street. Here he was delayed somewhat by the suspiciousness of a servant, but he succeeded in gaining her confidence by exhibiting his badge, and then darted towards Fourth Avenue. He eventually gained the corner of Madison Avenue and Sixtieth Street, where there was a vacant space, which gave him a clear view up and down and toward the Park. Concealing himself near a low fence, he scanned the neighborhood and saw a youngish looking man, evidently a foreigner, lounging at the corner of Madison Avenue and Sixty-first Street. Campbell immediately came to the conclusion that this was one of Mr. Strasburger's persecutors. In a short while he saw the man signalling to some one, and a few moments afterwards another fellow came along Sixty-first Street, from the east, making signals for the first man to retire. The second man passed on without speaking, crossed Madison Avenue, and continued westward until he halted between Madison and Fifth avenues. Then he signalled to the first man to go up the avenue. Campbell now knew that Miss Spelton was coming, and accordingly creeped up towards the first man. Miss Spelton finally appeared, and Campbell braced himself for the coming struggle. As the lady turned the corner of Sixty-first Street, the second man discharged a pistol and Miss Spelton dropped the envelope. In an instant the first man darted forward towards the supposed fortune. Campbell glided towards where the envelope lay, keeping pace with the man, who, in his anxiety to reach what he thought was the treasure, did not notice his Nemesis. A few more steps, and then, looking up, he caught sight of Campbell. Putting his hand in his pistol-pocket he exclaimed in broken English:

"You son of a ———, I'll blow your brains out!"

Campbell, undeterred, seized him by the collar and put the muzzle of his revolver close to the man's face. The prisoner immediately seized the weapon and in so doing struck Campbell's hand.

The detective's finger was on the trigger and the pistol was discharged, the bullet entering the Nihilist's left eye and killing him instantly. His body was carried to the East Fifty-ninth Street station, where an examination of his clothing revealed his identity. He proved to be Edward Herman Johannes Sagart. He was born in Berlin, was only twenty-three years old, and had at one time been a butler.

The plotted abduction of Miss Strasburger was not, after all, such a "stupid affair" as some people supposed. Documents in the dead man's pockets led to the discovery that before Sagart visited Dr. Heubsch he had hired a room in a secluded neighborhood, and had actually provided garments and food for the little girl. His association with Nihilistic organizations was also amply proved.

There is no doubt that his companion—Felix Vogel—who was arrested the same day, was as deeply in the plot as Sagart; but it is to be doubted if any one beside these two knew anything of the details of the affair. There were, however, several individuals to whom Sagart had spoken, in a general way, of making money by frightening a rich man into the payment of many thousand dollars for peace, and of taking the rich man's daughter away to hold for a ransom. Had those individuals been honest they could have saved Mr. Strasburger and his family much anxiety, and the life of Sagart would have been spared.

Although Jay Gould is perhaps the wealthiest man on this continent to-day, the criminal classes regard him as a person who has resources of such a peculiar character that it is well to let him alone. Once, however, his name appears as complainant on the records. In October, 1881, Colonel J. Howard Welles, a relation of Gideon Welles (once Secretary of the Navy), whose father was Richard J. Welles, a New York lawyer, conceived the plan of extorting money from the arch-financier. Colonel Welles believed that Mr. Gould could be frightened into paying a large sum of money to secure peace of mind. And so, on October 17, at the Windsor Hotel, he wrote the following letter and sent it to Mr. Gould:

"*Dear Sir:*—It is my painful duty to inform you that within six days of the date of this letter your body will have returned to the dust from whence it came. I, therefore, entreat you to make your peace with God, and prepare for the fate which awaits you. It is no wish of mine to take your life, but I am inspired and requested by the all-living God to do so as a public necessity, and for the benefit of the community at large. You must undoubtedly be aware that you have been a rogue of the first water all your life. Through your artful cunning you have ruined thousands of people of their birthright; you have had no mercy; you have robbed the rich and the poor, the father and the fatherless, the widow and the orphan, indiscriminately, of their last dollar; and through your villany have wrought ruin and destruction on thousands of families. All this you have done under a cloak, by circulating false reports, bribing newspapers, making false statements, committing perjury, and by artful cunning. In fact, you have robbed both great and small, and now the law says that you must pay for all with your death, as a public necessity, in order to save thousands of others from pain and destruction.

"Your death will be an easy one, for I propose shooting you through the heart, if possible, and if my first shot is not instant death, I will give you the *coup de grace* with the second shot, so that your death shall be quick and easy. Don't hold out the hope that this is a threatening letter, sent for stock-jobbing purposes, for I don't own a single share of stock of any kind, neither am I interested in any. This is simply the will of God, and He has chosen me to carry it out. He has appeared to me in a dream, and requested me to consult you as the party interested, and in doing so God has assured me that it is by Divine Providence I am chosen to do this act, and that by so doing I will become a public benefactor; and I have sworn and taken a solemn oath before the all-living God that I will put you to death. I intended to have shot you last Friday (yesterday), when I saw you with Barrow and Sage. I had my pistol, ready cocked, but a voice from the Lord sounded in my ear, saying: 'Hold on; give him time to repent, lest he be sent into everlasting punishment.'

"Now make your peace with God and prepare for the fate which awaits you, and may the Lord have mercy on your soul. I am only an agent of the Lord. The Lord appeared to me again last night and said: 'Jay Gould must surely die;' and when I reasoned with the Lord in my dream I told Him my life would also be required, and that I should be hung. The Lord answered me that no harm should come to me; the rope was not made, neither was the hemp grown to make the rope to hang me with, and that He would deliver me out of the hands of mine enemies. It is by the express will and command of God that I am chosen to put you to death, and I have sworn before the all-living God, the great Jehovah and the Redeemer of the world, and having taken a solemn oath I will carry it out within six days if the proper opportunity occurs. Therefore, be prepared to meet your fate at any moment, and may God have mercy on your soul.

"I remain, sir,
"An Old Victim."

This letter was read by a confidential employee who was not at first disposed to trouble Mr. Gould about it. But there was something in its tenor which indicated that the writer meant at least part of what he wrote, and that it would be just as well to become acquainted with him. Mr. Gould was not in the imminent peril his correspondent indicated. For many years Mr. Gould rarely moved in this city when engaged on business without a confidential agent having him under surveillance. Mr. Washington E. Conner was immediately placed in charge of the case. He naturally went to police headquarters, and, as naturally, Inspector Byrnes was directed to do whatever might seem necessary in the premises. His first act was to put "shadows" on Mr. Gould, in order to watch any man who might be lying in wait for him, or dogging his footsteps.

Meantime, the "Old Victim" continued his correspondence and began to insert advertisements in newspapers. He also sent Mr. Gould, in order to carry on the advertising correspondence, a cypher key, in which familiar words were to represent certain stocks. Gradually, the plan of the "Old Victim" was developed. He said in one of his written communications that he had gambled in Wall Street and lost hundreds of thousands of dollars. He desired to recoup himself. In other words, he wanted "points" on the stock market direct from the bosom of Mr. Jay Gould. The matter ran on for three weeks, when "Old Victim," having received many "points" which did not appear to have been taken advantage of, addressed Mr. Gould the following letter:

"NEW YORK, *Nov.* 11, 1881.

"*My Dear Sir:*—I thank you for the two personals in to-day's *Herald*, though I expected none from you this morning, as I had no intention, when writing to you yesterday, of giving you the trouble of replying to my letter. I gave you the information asked for in your personal of yesterday, namely, the cost of the two stocks I had purchased through your advice; and if I asked too much in too short a time, as you say, it was owing to my anxiety on account of the decline of 'Salvation,' early yesterday afternoon. I had no intention, I can assure you, of advancing the price of 'Salvation' simply on my account, only I did hope, for the reason I gave, that you would not let it go below its cost to me. The 'Salvation' my relative purchased for me on Wednesday was on the usual margin, but his brokers yesterday, as I mentioned, refused to carry any more for him under a 20 per cent. margin. This forced him to purchase for me five hundred shares of 'Salvation' yesterday from another house, who bought it for him on the usual margin. I think commission houses are disinclined to purchase 'Salvation' except for *good parties* with good bank accounts."

Now, it is necessary to explain that the cypher key previously mentioned makes "Salvation" the indicator for Manhattan Elevated Railroad stock, while the personals referred to were:

"TEXAS CORRESPONDENT.—Up-town Salvation. Then let me know at once how you stand. Who is using the same heading? Are you trifling?"

"Up-town Salvation" meant "bull Manhattan Elevated," and the question about the two persons using the same heading arose from some one who was curious trying to solve the mystery by inserting misleading notices. The second personal was:

"NEGOTIATE SALVATION.—Yes. Keep Windsor. Let go Concord. Give me the cost of Salvation."

This was in regard to a query by letter from the "Old Victim." It meant "Keep Western Union. Sell Pacific Mail." Then came the personal alluded to in the "Old Victim's" letter, which said he asked too much in too short a time. It added:

"Be more reasonable."

After that came:

"NEGOTIATE.—Can't understand how it costs so much. Give me particulars. Do not be alarmed."

This had reference to the complaint that exorbitant demands of the brokers forced "Old Victim" to take a twenty per cent. margin.

And so it went on—letters and personals and the police playing at cross purposes, until it was discovered that the bulk of the letters addressed to Mr. Jay Gould by "Old Victim" came from Post-office Station E. Still, this afforded a small chance of reaching the writer, as some letters were posted in other districts. However, a watch was kept on the letter-boxes, and letters received at Station E for Mr. Gould were, by an arrangement with the postal officials, allowed to be scrutinized by Central Office detectives. This plan failed, because it was found necessary, in order to catch the correspondent, to have a watch kept on each letter-box, and arrest any man who put a letter in for Mr. Gould in the handwriting of "Old Victim" on the spot.

A plan was first devised to have employees of the Post-office work in concert with the detectives, but this did not appear feasible, as it would first have necessitated the giving away of the secret to men who might be "leaky," and they might not be sufficiently alert, or sufficiently expert in handwriting to be of service. Finally it was agreed that each box of the district should be watched by an employee of the Post-office and one or more detectives. If a letter was dropped into a box the Post-office employee would keep an eye on the depositor and also scan the letter. If it were addressed to Jay Gould he would be particularly careful to note whether there was any resemblance between the handwriting of the address and that of "Old Victim."

The day chosen was Sunday, November 13, 1881. The letter-boxes were under surveillance from an early hour, and the plan worked well until about noon, when a patrolman of the Twenty-ninth Precinct, who was not in the secret and who had been watching the actions of two Central Office detectives who had charge of a box in company with a Post-office official, became suspicious. He was not satisfied with the explanation of one of the officers that they were detectives acting under orders from Inspector Byrnes, and was about to take one of them into custody when another detective passed who was acquainted with the patrolman, and the matter was explained. Fortunately the "Old Victim" did not choose that box as his depository. But at three o'clock a sprucely-dressed man with a military bearing went to the box at the corner of Thirty-fourth Street and Seventh Avenue, carelessly dropped in a letter, and walked off. John Healy, a postman, quickly opened the box and found a letter addressed to Jay Gould. Detectives Phil Riley and Wood were instantly informed of the fact, and a glance at the handwriting of the address satisfied them that the man who had dropped it in the box was worth detaining. He was halted, questioned, the letter was re-examined, and Detective Riley at once decided that he had Mr. Gould's tormentor in his grasp.

The prisoner was taken to police headquarters and proved to be Colonel Welles. When confronted with Mr. Washington E. Conner and other gentlemen in the interest of Mr. Gould he made some very lame excuses and shammed insanity. The same defence was made for him when he was arraigned at the Tombs police court. He was able to exercise the strangest kind of personal influence over Mr. Gould, and after passing a few weeks in prison was released and was never prosecuted.

It was not believed at any time that "Old Victim" had any accomplices. He coined the scheme without aid, and if he had been a sharper man he would have made money out of Mr. Gould, as it was in Mr. Gould's interest to humor him in the matter of giving "points." Many a stock gambler would have given Colonel Welles a check for $100,000 if he had known the plot, and that Colonel Welles had driven in an entering wedge by getting up a newspaper "personal" correspondence in which a cypher key was brought into requisition.

CHAPTER XXVII.

PRIZE-FIGHTING AND FIGHTERS.—THE LAW ON THE SUBJECT.—EARLY HEROES IN THE " RING."—AN ADVENTURE WITH " BILL " HARRINGTON.—JOHN MORRISSEY.—HIS ARRIVAL IN NEW YORK.—JOHN L. SULLIVAN.—HIS LIFE.—FARO.—" EDE " NORRIS AND HIS VISITORS.—LEGAL ASPECT OF GAMBLING.—WHY IT IS NOT SUPPRESSED.—A REMEDY.—PLAYING ON A SYSTEM.—A SUCCESSFUL GAMBLER.—POLICY, KENO AND POKER.—MATTHIAS DANSER'S MONEY.—CUTTING COUPONS BY CANDLE LIGHT.—$8000 UNDER SEWING-MACHINE PLATES.—A GAMBLER'S FORTUNE GIVEN TO THE CHURCH.

THE Penal Code of the State of New York contains not a few sections relating to the "manly art of self-defence." First, prize fighting of every description is expressly forbidden, and the dire penalties consequent upon a breach of this law are fully set forth. There are other sections prohibiting any one from leaving the State with even the intention of engaging in a prize-fight. The punishment for this offence is very severe. And last, another provision is made in this Code for disciplining such publishers of newspapers and others who print or send challenges with a view of engaging in a prize-fight. It can be seen, therefore, that the law is determined to put down prize-fighting and everything connected with it—in theory. But not in fact. The columns of the daily and weekly press contain numberless challenges. That the law is a dead letter in this particular is patent to all; perhaps the majority of people are not aware that such a statute is part and parcel of our laws. Prize-fighting takes place every day under the very noses of the authorities, and yet no steps are taken to prevent it, except in very rare instances. Once, however, some years ago, Mr. Richard K. Fox, the proprietor of the *Police Gazette*, was indicted for publishing some such challenges. What that indictment accomplished has always been a mystery to me and everybody else. Nothing ever came of it to my knowledge, and I was in a position to have heard.

"But," some persons will say, "if you knew prize-fighting was against the law, why didn't you put a stop to it when you were superintendent of police?"

Let me relate what happened once when I made an attempt to enforce it. In 1884 it was announced that John L. Sullivan and Greenfield were to fight at Madison Square Garden. Mr. Edson was mayor at the time, and it was at his instigation that I took steps to prevent the fight taking place. When consulted, the police commissioners concurred, and both Sullivan and Greenfield were arrested on a charge of intending to engage in a prize-fight. The arguments were heard before Judge Barrett, who decided that it would be perfectly legal for the two principals to engage in a sparring contest for "points." If it came to "slugging," then the police were empowered to stop the fight. I accordingly attended the "exhibition," accompanied by Inspector Thorne and Captain Williams. In the first two rounds the fighting was confined to scientific sparring for "points," but after that it became evident to me that Sullivan intended to "knock out" his opponent, who was cut and bleeding profusely. It became a "slugging" match, and I accordingly had them arrested; and they were indicted by the Grand Jury.

At the trial, however, I was the only witness who would swear that it was anything else than a mere scientific contest. Inspector Thorne and Captain Williams said they had often seen harder fighting, as if that was any excuse for breaking the law. Inspector Murray, who saw the fight, agreed with me, but although it had been arranged to have him called as a witness, he failed to put in an appearance, nor was his name mentioned in court.

Thus it will be seen that it was very little use for me to attempt an enforcement of the law in this matter.

In my time I have been acquainted with a great many prize-fighters, particularly during my early connection with the force. I knew "Tom" Hyer, an adventure with whom is told in a previous chapter. He was really the first champion of America, and his fights with "Country McCloskey" and "Yankee" Sullivan proved him to be one of the greatest pugilists who ever stood in a ring. Then there was "Bill" Harrington. He was a fine, well-built young fellow, a regular giant in strength. At the time of my first meeting him—in 1849—he was in his prime. He introduced himself to me. The way it happened was this: I was on duty on

Broadway early one Sunday morning, and met him coming up the street making "Rome howl," with a number of equally noisy companions. The party had evidently been making a night of it and were on their way home. I went up to them and requested that they should refrain from making such a disturbance, as it was Sunday morning.

"Who the —— are you who talk so big?" asked the largest man of the crowd. (It must be remembered that in those days the police wore no uniform.)

"I'm an officer," I replied, exhibiting my star; "and if you don't keep quiet I shall have to run you in."

"Well," he said, " I don't think you can take us all in ;" when another of the party, who afterwards told me he was Harrington, interposed, saying to me : "You've spoken in a gentlemanly manner, and "—then he turned to his companions—"if he can't take you in, he and I will. So keep quiet." There was no further noise.

"Awful" Gardener was another bright and shining ornament of the "mystic circle" in those days. I was well acquainted with him.

I knew John Morrissey, too—knew him when he was a long way from being the John Morrissey of Saratoga, with white flannel suits and huge diamond rings. I knew him when he was John Morrissey the prize-fighter, John Morrissey the drunkard, without money or friends, battered in clothes as well as in person. Before coming to New York he kept a veritable "rum hole" in Troy, then the favorite resort of gamblers, thieves and dissolute persons of the lowest grade. Such a nuisance did his place become, in fact, that it was closed by order of the authorities. At the time he arrived in this city a local election was about to be held in one of the up-town wards, and threats were openly made by a certain element—the Plug Uglies and others—that they would smash the ballot-boxes and keep the respectable voters from the polls. Violence must needs be met with violence. Morrissey was engaged to hire a gang of as big ruffians as himself to protect the polls. He did so, and from that time began his upward course. He opened a small gambling house, dressed decently, and became a teetotaller—almost. He made money rapidly, and in a few years his establishment was the most elegantly furnished of the kind in the country.

Morrissey now and then broke loose from his self-imposed restraint in regard to the use of liquor, and was very quarrelsome when intoxicated. Early one morning in May, 1853, he and a friend named Patterson attempted to "clean out" the Girard House in Chambers Street. They first threw a large water-pitcher at the bar-tender, and then, when one of the other employees, named Conway, interfered Morrissey fired at him. He missed his aim, and the ball, after shattering a window, passed through the hat of a gentleman who was walking along West Broadway. Conway ran for a policeman, but even when he returned with two they were afraid

JOHN MORRISSEY.
(From a Photograph.)

to arrest Morrissey, who drew an ugly-looking dagger and threatened to rip open any man who approached him. The officers retired, but returned very shortly with assistance. Morrissey and his companion then surrendered, and were locked up.

John Lawrence Sullivan was born on the 15th of October, 1858, in that part of Boston, Mass., now known as the Highlands, but which then formed the town of Roxbury. He received a common-school education at the Dwight School, and was an expert in ball-playing from his very earliest days, having been connected with

JOHN L. SULLIVAN.

such clubs as the old Tremonts and Ætnas, etc., long before any professional nines were put into the field. Shortly after leaving school, young Sullivan commenced studying for the priesthood, but after eleven months application in this direction concluded he was not intended for a priest, and so it came about that he drifted into playing ball for a living. He had always been "handy with his fists," and had gained quite a reputation among the "boys" at the South End by the manner in which he disposed of his antagonists. It was not until October or November, 1878, when he was just twenty years of age, that he made his first public appearance as a pugilist. It was in Boston Music Hall, and the occasion was a benefit to Dan Dwyer. His opponent was "Cockey" Woods, whom he bested easily, and in such a scientific manner as to arouse the enthusiasm of the knowing ones. In the year following he had a lively set-to with Dwyer himself, who was knocked out in short order. Upon April 6, 1880, he sparred with the veteran Joe Goss, and on the 28th of June, of the same year, with George Rooke, and in both of these contests he came off victorious. A trip to Cincinnati in the fall of 1880 resulted in his sparring John Donaldson at the Opera House. Subsequently, the two fought on Christmas Eve, Donaldson being pretty badly used up. His first exploit of any account in New York was his fight, March 31, 1881, at Harry Hill's, with Steve Taylor, whom he defeated in two minutes and a half. Then he fought eight rounds with John Flood, on the 16th of May, on a barge up the Hudson River. Sullivan had not a mark on him to speak of, while Flood was badly punished. His great fight with Ryan took place near Kansas City on the 7th of February, 1882, when nine rounds were fought in eleven minutes. Then on the 14th of July, of the same year, came his famous contest with "Tug" Wilson, resulting in what was called a draw, although Sullivan was undoubtedly the better man and outfought Wilson at every point.

Sullivan's next venture was with an athletic combination, and this led to travel over the greater part of the United States. It was at this time that Sullivan issued his famous challenge, open to all, offering $100 to $10,000 that no man could "stop" him in four rounds. This challenge was accepted by not a few, but in no case was Sullivan defeated—he always won, with plenty to spare. On July 14, 1883, he fought Charley Mitchell, and on August 6 following, Slade, the "Maori," made an exhibition of himself. Both events came off at Madison Square Garden. For the next eight or ten months Sullivan travelled with Al. Smith's company of athletes. Then, on the 10th of November, 1884, a match was made between him and Greenfield. This is the occasion on which, as previously stated, I ordered the arrest of both Sullivan and his opponent. Until lately Sullivan resided in Boston, where he kept a gorgeous saloon on Washington Street, near the corner of Kneeland. Recently, however, he has removed to this city, and is now in partnership, I believe, with Bennett, the proprietor of an hotel on the corner of 59th Street and Seventh Avenue. Sullivan is not a brute and bully, as some newspapers would have the public believe. For my part, I have always found him gentlemanly in demeanor; and when complaints have been made concerning his conduct, they have been found to be more the outcomes of petty spite than anything else. "Our John," as he is termed in Boston, does not like to be imposed upon; he is but human, and has doubtless "given as good as he got."

But to turn to gaming. Of all the many games of chance, not one is played so extensively, or has such an army of followers, as faro. The haunts of the "Tiger" are dotted all over the city.

For me to say that nothing has been done by the proper authorities to stamp out gambling in New York would not be exactly true. Still it would not be so very far from the truth. Spasmodic efforts are made, with the only result of closing up the "hells" for a few nights, to re-open again with redoubled barefacedness. I well remember a somewhat laughable incident which occurred during 1856, when Fernando Wood was mayor, in connection with one of these spasmodic efforts to put down gambling. I was captain of the Eighteenth Ward at the time. "Ede" Norris and his brother ran a snug little place on the Bowery, and were making a large amount of money. They had a clever corps of "ropers in"; business was in a flourishing condition. Early one evening, before the regular night's game had begun, two well clad men strolled into their place, and looked round in a disappointed way, as if they wanted to find something and didn't like to ask for it. "Ede" jumped to the conclusion that they were countrymen and wanted to "buck agin the tiger." He jumped up from the chair in which he had been sitting, removed a cigar from between his lips, and remarked insinuatingly:

"If you like, gentlemen, I'll open the game for you."

The visitors observed that they didn't understand anything about gambling; but might be induced to try their hand if the thing were explained.

"Ede" withdrew a cloth from a table in the room and disclosed to view a faro lay-out. Then he explained how the game was played, in the usual manner. A game was opened, and several of those present joined in it. Presently, one of the men who "didn't understand" the game stepped up to "Ede" and said:

"Well, Mr. Norris, since you've been so kind as to open the game, I'll close it. Here's a warrant for your arrest."

The two visitors were myself and an officer named Knapp.

"Ede" was too dumfounded to say a word at first, but was much incensed, and threatened vengeance. As usual, nothing came of his threats. His brother laughed at the way in which he had been caught.

That same night raids were made upon numerous other gambling resorts in the city, this movement on the part of the police having been prompted by certain suggestions from Mayor Wood, who took this method, among many others, of improving his reputation among certain classes in the community. Whatever may have been its effect in that particular direction, it certainly did not put a stop to gambling. For a day or two the "tiger" lay quiescent in his lair, but was soon as rapacious and savage as ever in entrapping and destroying his victims.

Practically speaking, the superintendent of police has no power whatever to suppress gambling. Be he ever so honest or determined in his personal efforts, the whole matter rests solely with the captains of the various precincts. The entire suppression of gambling in all its forms, both public and private, is of course entirely out of the question, for obvious reasons. But make the captains directly responsible to the superintendent, and give them to understand distinctly that they will be dismissed the force unless public gambling-houses are closed in their several districts, and the nuisance will be soon abated. It is within the power of each captain—and I know it from my own experience when in that position—to so harass the proprietors of gambling-houses that it will not pay to keep such places open. And when the investment doesn't pay, you may be sure the business will be dropped quickly.

Granted that it is a difficult thing to obtain a conviction in such cases, that even when persons who have been swindled at "skin" games are ready to come forward and make a complaint, the parties most interested get hold of the man and "fix" things, so that the case never comes to trial. They pay him back his money and send him out of the city; and further still, should the Grand Jury indict the offending party, the indictment will soon be covered with dust in the district attorney's office, unless some unusual pressure from the outside is brought to bear upon that department of our legal machinery. Granted all that, and much more besides.

JIMMY ELLIOTT.
(From a Photograph.)

One swallow does not make a summer, neither would any number of convictions for gambling show a clean bill of health unless the captains exercised their full powers in the desired direction.

I remember on one occasion, shortly after my appointment as superintendent, taking vigorous steps to shut up all the known gambling-houses in the city. Evidence—conclusive evidence—was secured against many individuals who stood high in the community, and warrants were about to be issued for their arrest. But there was a stumbling-block in the way, and one which I could not surmount. The police commissioners stepped forward and passed a resolution prohibiting me from taking any proceedings against gamblers without first consulting and laying the whole evidence before them. That resolution remained on the books some time, and, as a natural consequence, the proper enforcement of the statute was rendered almost next to impossible.

At one time, in 1873, however, when Mr. Matsell was superintendent, the commissioners co-operated with him most cordially for a short period in the suppression of gambling-houses, showing that such a thing is possible. One member of the board had a quarrel with the famous John Morrissey, and it was for the purpose of "getting even" with and injuring him, more than anything else, that the gambling-houses were closed for the time being.

If you gain admittance to some of the more fashionable gaming establishments in this city, many of those whom you see there would not care to have the fact generally known. Gentlemen well known on the Stock Exchange and in public life, merchants of high standing, and whose names adorn the reports of our benevolent and charitable organizations, are seen in these places. To one not accustomed to such a sight it is rather startling to see men occupying prominent positions in church and state seemingly quite at home at their seats around the green cloth-covered table. The greatest gamblers of all are those who in the day time are accustomed to the excitement of Wall Street. Most of them play deeply and lose heavily of course. Merchants, bank cashiers and clerks often play until they lose all, then pledge their watches and jewellery, their salaries even, to meet their "debts of honor," as they are termed. Embezzlement, forgery, theft follow as an inevitable consequence. Very rarely is it that a gambler saves any money. Generally he spends it in the same reckless way as that in which it was obtained. Of course, there are some men who make gambling their regular business, and pursue it with the same amount of energy, carefulness and system as a dry goods merchant. I know of one such who resided up town in fine style, and was reputed to be worth half a million dollars. For more than thirty years he has gambled steadily and persistently. In every other way he is a model man, attends church regularly three times every Sunday, does not use liquor or tobacco in any form. He has made set rules for his guidance—loses a certain sum and then quits playing for that night, but continuing as long as he wins or breaks the bank. He has been successful, but thousands of others who have tried the same plan have been hurried to nothing but irretrievable ruin.

Policy was a generally played game some years ago, but owing to the "dead-set" made against it by authorities it has now gone out of fashion. There are at present very few places, in fact, where policy is played openly. Those who formerly ran a "shop"—generally in the guise of a broker's office, cigar store, coal and wood agency, etc.—are now compelled to walk round to their customers, "backing their own books," as it is called. The colored population is not by any means, as is generally supposed, the chief patrons of this fascinating game of chance. Their Caucasian brethren are far more eager in their quest after the shadow of the "almighty dollar" in this way. Keno, too, is going out of date and is rarely heard of now. Poker is a favorite game, and large sums are lost and won at this alluring recreation in our fashionable hotels, clubs and private residences.

One of the most successful gamblers I have met was Matthias Danser, and about him there is a somewhat interesting story. Danser was one of the shrewdest men in his mode of living. He was after the "main chance" all the time. Some persons have said that he never "ran a square game," and that in the early days of the war he thus laid the foundations of a vast fortune. He had establishments in various parts of the city, at one time running both up and down-town "hells." His last venture was at No. 8 Barclay Street. Shortly after the close of the war he began to prepare to retire from business, and in 1872 he ceased to be a director of the Board of Green Cloth. He was then worth anywhere from $700,000 to $1,000,000. In justice to him, however, it should be said that despite the way in which he made his money he kept his family aloof from his transactions. No one could be more devout than his wife and daughter. "Matt" tried hard to "get religion," but, to all outward appearances, signally failed. That fact, however, did not interfere with the piety of his family. He was the most extraordinary man I ever saw in respect to facial development. A slight stroke of paralysis had affected one side of his face, so as to draw his mouth sideways into a pucker; and when he talked and swore it was hard to keep one's countenance when looking him in the eye. "Matt" was not only not a miser, but he was careless in looking after the securities into which he had turned his money. In a trunk with a lock which could have been forced open with a tooth-pick, and in a room which was never secured, in his house at No. 50 West Eleventh Street, he kept securities and bonds worth certainly $400,000, and possibly a great deal more. He was reckless, too, in the choice of the domestic servants of his establishment.

In April, 1875, there entered his service a sly, repulsive-looking woman—Mary Logan. I was afterwards told that Danser's establishment had been "surveyed" by persons intent upon getting a share of "Matt's" fortune, and that Mary was "planted" in the house to enable them to attain their ends. At any rate, Mary soon found out where the bonds were kept, and made no mistake when she saved Mr. Danser the trouble of cutting off the coupons. She did this by the light of a candle in the coal cellar. When she had cut off coupons representing $21,640, she hid about $6000 of them under the coal, together with bonds worth $200,000. The other coupons she put in her trunk. On or about May 26, 1875, she was suddenly taken ill, went to St. Luke's Hospital, and died three days afterwards. Her relatives—Michael and Ann O'Farrell—came in suspicious haste to Mr. Danser's to claim her trunk, which they carried away. Mr. Danser did not miss his bonds until nearly a month later. He took the affair as nonchalently as he did the "nipping" of a thousand-dollar bill from his fob pocket by a boot-black in Union Square shortly before. But he called upon Sergeant (now Superintendent) William Murray, who, with Detective (now Detective-Sergeant) Slevin, became very much interested in the search for the missing securities.

A clew to the robbery was found by Mr. Danser's cook, who in overhauling the cellar unearthed the bonds and coupons. Then Mary Logan's antecedents and associations were looked into, and suspicion fell on the O'Farrells. They were not discovered for a long time, but finally Sergeant Murray located them up town on the west side. They were running a large and lucrative clothing establishment, employing many hands and a dozen sewing-machines. When the police made a descent on the place, husband and wife quibbled about their connection with Mary Logan and the contents of her trunk. The place was searched, but no trace of the bonds was found at first. Sergeant Murray was just coming to believe O'Farrell's story—that he found in Mary's trunk a lot of little pieces of paper with printing on them, and that not knowing that they were of value he had burned them—when he decided to make a further search, and under the plates of the sewing-machines he discovered seven or eight thousand dollars worth of the coupons.

Then Mr. O'Farrell volunteered the statement that he had sent about $3200 worth to Patrick O'Farrell, his brother, at Lower Cragie County, Edinburgh, Scotland. Sergeant Murray took upon himself to write to Patrick in Michael's name, requesting the immediate return of the coupons. They came in a letter addressed to " Michael Reynolds, care of D. A. Demey, No. 749 Ninth Avenue." This letter was impounded at the Post-Office through the connivance of the authorities. The O'Farrells, husband and wife, were tried for receiving stolen goods. The husband alone was convicted (the wife pleaded coverture), and he was sent to State's prison for five years.

Before this, however, the Danser establishment had another startling experience. On the 12th of July, 1875, Mr. Danser had business down town, and his daughter went out to church, leaving Mrs. Ann Louise Danser at home. This was in the morning. Shortly after Mr. Danser left the house, three spruce young men halted in front of the house. One of them took out a note-book, scrutinized the house carefully, and appeared to be taking voluminous memoranda. Then they rang the bell at the basement door. Mrs. Danser responded, and, as she afterwards said, understood them to say that they wanted to see something about the water. She took them to be employees of the Department of Public Works, sanitary officers or plumbers sent by her husband, or " something of that sort." They entered the house, and two seconds after the door was closed Mrs. Danser was in their grasp. They conducted her to a rear room on the third floor, and the first question asked her was :

"Where's them bonds?" showing a prior knowledge of Mr. Danser's investments. Mrs. Danser protested, the rascals bullied and cajoled her, demanded her keys, and, leaving her under guard, went down stairs and admitted confederates to the number, it is thought, of three.

Then they ransacked the house, using, among other tools, a hatchet. They were evidently nervous and on the lookout for the return of Mr. or Miss Danser, or calls from chance visitors, as they did their work bunglingly, overlooking much property of value. At length they found a bundle of $40,000 worth of Virginia City bonds, worth in the market $17,000, and a halt was called. A consultation was held, and Mrs. Danser was left, bound, in the third-story room, awful and profane threats being made against her if she attempted to regain her freedom before an hour had elapsed. It was barely twenty minutes after they left the house that her husband returned and found her in the predicament in which she had been left. He rushed to the Mercer Street police station, and his endeavors to make himself intelligible are spoken of as earnest but ludicrous in the extreme, by reason of his infirmity. The police did much to try and bring the perpetrators of the robbery to justice. I believe that the job was arranged by "Jim" Brady. But although this may be so, no one was convicted of the crime and only one arrest was made—that of a man named Frank Moss, who was very soon released.

These adventures so affected the Dansers that Matthias died in August, 1876. His wife followed him in November, and Miss Danser, who was engaged to be married to one of the telegraph operators at police headquarters, died in February, 1877, leaving her affianced husband $30,000. The bulk of Matthias Danser's fortune went into the coffers of various religious organizations, so that what had been gained through the instrumentality of the devil went, in the end, to the service of God.

CHAPTER XXVIII.

A GLIMPSE OF PRISONS.—A NIGHT IN A STATION-HOUSE CELL.—SOBBING BOYS AND CURSING WOMEN.—SHRIEKS OF TERROR THROUGH THE CORRIDORS.—LUXURIOUS LIVING IN LUDLOW STREET JAIL.—WARD'S DINNER-PARTIES.—BECKY JONES'S GOAT-RACE WITH JAMES D. FISH.—LIFE IN THE TOMBS.

If there is one place among those which are used for the purpose of confining criminals (or alleged criminals) that is known to a greater number of persons than another, it is the station-house. This, so to speak, is the reception-room before reaching the inner office of punishment, and no small proportion of those admitted here get no farther. Many persons are continually being arrested on suspicion, and are perhaps locked up over night. When brought before a police justice in the morning they are discharged. Drunk and disorderly persons, as well as those who are more vicious, find their first halting-place on the road to punishment in the station-house cell. Perhaps this place of confinement sees, on the average, a greater number of prominent prisoners than the Tombs or Ludlow Street Jail or Sing Sing. For under our laws a policeman can arrest a man or woman on suspicion, and this fact accounts for many an innocent and respectable person spending a night behind prison bars. To the residents of any precinct the station-house occupies the same place as the "coop," "cooler," "jug," etc., do to the inhabitants of a country town. In the down-town precincts especially, every new arrest is witnessed by a crowd of youngsters, and frequently by children of a larger growth. To persons of delicate sensibilities or of previously reputable character, whose lot it is to be brought a prisoner to the station, such a reception is most humiliating.

When a person has been arrested, either on suspicion or by a warrant, he is taken at once to the station house in the precinct where the arrest is made. A sergeant sits behind a railing and a high counter-like desk, and as the policeman enters the building and walks up to the desk the sergeant enters the name of the prisoner, together with the charge which is made against him. Sometimes it happens that the prisoner is a man of wealth, and then frequently he gives bonds for his appearance at the proper time to answer to the charge.

In most cases, however, the prisoner has no such easy fate. He must take his lot as it comes, and usually it comes very hard. To spend a night in a station-house cell is not one of the pleasantest experiences a man can have. Of course the class of persons the officers have to deal with is a low and vicious one. They are often brought to the cells in a state of beastly intoxication. They shout and scream and curse worse than any furies which ever existed. All this perhaps goes through the mind of the accused as he stands before the sergeant.

The man behind the desk orders the policeman who has brought the prisoner to search him thoroughly, and, feeling more and more like a criminal, the accused submits to have his valuables taken from his pockets. Then the sergeant taps a bell, and at the summons a doorman appears.

"Show this man to No.—" is the next remark of the sergeant, and the prisoner is led away to make his bed on a hard board and in a loathsome cell. His night, it is safe to predict, is not a restful one. In the first place, the thought of the cell itself is repulsive, and its suggestions of filth are nauseating. The room is cramped and the air foul. The occupant cannot get a comfortable position, and his limbs become lame and paralyzed. He tries to sleep; the trial is a failure. Perhaps in an adjoining cell a howling Jezebel has been placed for the night. She is mad with liquor, and raves and swears in a horrible manner. Then one of the keepers comes to quiet her. His admonitions are of no avail, and he enters the cell to carry out his orders with force. The woman strikes him, and there follows a tussle in which the screams and oaths become tenfold more terrible. For a while, perhaps, the creature is quieted, and then spasmodically during the night her paroxysms of madness break forth again.

In another cell near by there may have been a woman of a different stamp—a tender, refined, intelligent woman, whose weakness has caused her to commit the sin with which she is charged. She appreciates the enormity of her offence; at least whatever its magnitude is it seems great to her. This is the first time she ever was in a prison cell. The disgrace is terrible. She moans and groans in her grief, and sobs as if her heart was breaking. Now and then can be heard her tearful words of prayer.

"O, why did I do it?" she cries out in tones of anguish, and there is no one to answer the question or to comfort the grief-stricken one.

In another cell is an old man. He, too, is half maniacal through the constant habit of drinking. He has been brought in stupidly drunk, but after awhile his stupidity gives way to howls and ravings which are fearful to hear—they must be awful to behold. He has delirium tremens, and the strange creatures of his vision which haunt his cell frighten him and make him shriek in supposed agony and in real terror.

Near by, again, is a sobbing boy. This is his first night in a station-house cell, too, and thoughts of the disgrace and anxiety he has brought on his mother are enough almost to distract him. But the boy's nature causes him to weary of his grief after awhile, and he sobs off to sleep to dream about his sorrows, not to taste them in their reality.

Such sounds as these come to the man whom we have consigned to a cell. The tales they tell or suggest of human woe and misery are heart-rending. How gladly would he drop off to sleep and forget these dismal reminders of evil. But, no; that is impossible. The night grows into weeks, apparently. Now and then the iron gates clank, and a fresh victim has been brought to satisfy that grim, stern avenger whom we call Justice. Worn out, pale and haggard, the prisoner thanks God when he sees the first glimmer of daylight which reaches the interior of his cell, and when, some hours later, he is brought forth and taken before a police justice, the outside air, and even the police court, seem the most like paradise of anything he has ever seen.

It is said that William M. Tweed was the contractor of Ludlow Street Jail, in which he died. If so, he showed again the trait of character for which, with all his faults, he was famous. It does not look much like a jail, and in this respect was fortunately planned. It is situated on Ludlow Street, just north of Grand. Essex Market is beyond. The building is of red brick, and the main entrance is on Ludlow Street. The structure has about 100 feet frontage. It has the appearance of a library from the outside. The windows especially give it that look. In the northeast corner of the building is a large prison-yard, well guarded by lofty brick walls. The jail had previously been used as a place for the temporary confinement of United States' prisoners and for debtors. The prison was built about thirty years ago, and it is estimated that no less than 40,000 prisoners have been confined there since its erection. About half this number were residents of New York previous to their incarceration. The jail has held many prominent rascals. It was here that Tweed was kept, and in recent times James D. Fish and Ferdinand Ward. Red Leary made his famous escape from Ludlow Street Jail, and around its walks cluster many of the traditions connected with prison scenes and prominent prisoners.

In order that the reader may understand just what confinement in Ludlow Street Jail means, let us suppose the case of a man who has been arrested for attempting to defraud, or something similar, and after having been brought before the court is remanded without bail to the jail. As he enters the iron gate at the main entrance the deputy sheriff who has brought him hands him over to the warden's care, who makes a record of his coming, and speedily finds out whether the prisoner wants to become a "boarder," or to remain a common felon. For there are two distinct castes in Ludlow Street Jail, of which the public generally hears of but one—and that the higher one. These two castes may be named the "paying" boarders, and the "non-paying boarders." The former class are the aristocrats of the jail. They pay the warden fifteen dollars a week for the privilege of sitting at his table and eating the luxuries of the market. This sum includes also a respectable room, not cell, and fair attendance. Except for the restraint of confinement the paying boarder's life in Ludlow Street Jail is not such an unhappy one as most persons think. There are sometimes prisoners who are even more aristocratic than the paying boarder, but these are rare—they do not appear in the jail very often. When they do, they get a nicely furnished room with all the luxuries, have their meals served in their rooms and live in royal style. For this privilege, however, they have to pay from $50 to $100 a week. Of course the warden is glad to see such prisoners, and you may be sure he tries to keep them as long as possible.

Tweed belonged to the paying class of boarders, as did also Becky Jones, and Ward, and Fish. It used to be said of Ward and Fish that they frequently met in the jail corridors, but "never spoke as they passed by." Becky Jones was continually protesting that the only reason for her continued incarceration was the warden's wish to make as much money out of her as possible. And in spite of the $15 a week which Becky paid, she did not get a very good room. It was small and cramped, but she kept it neat and in first-class order. She had a way of collecting pictures, advertising cards and other cheap articles of decoration, and one side of her room was literally covered with them. I always thought Becky was considerably "off" in the upper story, and I remember well peculiar stories she used to tell; for she was a voluminous talker. Once she told a visitor that she had spent the morning in having a goat-race in the court-yard with James D. Fish. The gray-haired ex-president of the Marine Bank had mounted one goat, she said, and she had mounted another, and the two had a mad race around the court. She came out ahead, I believe.

When Tweed was a paying boarder in the jail many stories used to be told of the luxurious way in which he lived, and I have no doubt they were true. The same was true of Ward. He used to have cases of champagne and wine in his room, and cigars almost by the wholesale. Occasionally he would give dinner-parties, at which several of the old friends of his better days would be present. On such occasions as these Ward would lay himself out. He would order the choicest courses of food and the best china, and an extra supply of wines. At each of the ladies' plates he would have placed an expensive boutonnaire. Ward was an omnivorous reader, and most of his time in jail was taken up in smoking or reading the newspapers. Perhaps those who are at a loss to account for some of the missing funds of the Marine Bank might trace them to the merchants who furnished Ward with his luxurious supplies.

But to go back to our prisoner whom we left before the warden waiting to say whether he wished to be a pay-boarder or not. The prisoner did not hesitate half as long as it has taken me to write this parenthesis, for circumstances prevented him from being able to live luxuriously, and he had to be satisfied with the lot of the common prisoner. He was sent up to a cell near the roof. Vermin were plainly visible on the floor, and his quarters were scant and uncomfortable. He wished he had money enough to be a pay-boarder, but there is no chance of his getting it. He lies down and tries to rest, but it takes weeks sometimes to learn to rest in these places. His daily life is a constant aggravation, because in the court-yard and jail corridors he is brought into contact with the "high-toned" prisoners, and feels the sting of the difference in his position continually.

He is locked up in his cell from 7.30 o'clock at night until 6.30 in the morning. At this hour he arises and puts on his clothes. Then, according to the prison rules, he takes up his slop-pail and carries it down to the sink, where he cleanses it. His own ablutions are performed here too, and then he goes back to the cell, makes up his bed, cleans his room, and then waits for breakfast. Breakfast is a novel meal in Ludlow Street Jail. It comes to the prisoners; they do not go to it. They stand, the non-paying boarders of course, each at their cell doors, and await the carriers of food. These are two prisoners who, in consideration of their work about the jail, are allowed to remain up until 10.30 o'clock at night. The first carries a large basket of bread cut into good-sized hunks. As he passes each cell the man at the door reaches for the biggest piece he can find, and the carrier goes on to the next cell. After the bread-man comes one with a tin boiler filled with coffee and tin cups. He gives one cupful to each prisoner, and this completes the breakfast. After breakfast the prisoner can go down into the court-yard or walk through the corridors. Dinner is served at 12 o'clock, and consists of bread and a soup in which scraps of meat and vegetables are mixed more according to quantity than to the taste of the compound. On Thursdays, Fridays and Sundays the dinner ménu is changed. Fish and a potato are given on Fridays; and on the other two days corned beef and a boiled potato are each man's allowance.

Supper comes at six o'clock, and again the prisoners stand in front of the cell doors and receive their portion. This time it consists of a tin cup of tea and a piece of bread. No knives or forks are furnished, and no spoons, save for dinner, when soup is furnished.

To a non-paying boarder life in Ludlow Street Jail, as in fact in any of our prisons, is a constant tax on the strength and health. The food which is provided is not nourishing particularly, and this, taken in connection with the dampness of the walls, the impure air, and the fact of his imprisonment constantly preying upon one's mind, it is not strange that men come out of jail shattered completely in constitution. This is all the more lamentable in the case of prisoners in Ludlow Street Jail, for frequently they have been confined for years for nothing more than the non-payment of a debt. It is a glorious thing for our State that the poor-debtor law has been recently passed. This has been veritably a loosening of the shackles to many an unfortunate.

To the average person I know of no place of imprisonment, out-

THE TOMBS—EXTERIOR.

side of State institutions, which holds greater horrors than the city prison, ordinarily called the Tombs. It may not be known to everybody that the building in its general architectural design was planned after an Egyptian tomb, but such nevertheless is the fact. Certainly the structure is well-named. I never go past it but I am struck with its gloom and its prison-like aspect. Unfortunate it is that the Tombs prison was built where it is. This region was all a pond and marsh once, and when it was proposed to build a structure like this there, it was found necessary to sink many piles and heavy stones upon which to erect so heavy an edifice. From time since the prison was built there have been evidences of a sinking in the foundations. Large cracks have appeared in the walls, and it would not surprise me very much if some time these massive walls should crush beneath them the hundreds of inmates confined by iron bars. Aside from this danger, however, is that of sickness and disease. Many complaints have been made from time to time regarding the sanitary condition of the prison, and despite the efforts of the keepers to keep things cleanly, the natural situation of the place will always work against them. It will require almost a superhuman effort to destroy the germs of disease which I feel sure must all the time be breeding in this malarial atmosphere.

THE TOMBS—COURTYARD.

The Tombs prison was completed and ready for use in the year 1838. There are 200 cells in the building; but even this number has not always proved sufficient, and it has been necessary to put two and even three prisoners in a cell. The female portion of the prison is separated from the male, and contains about 150 cells arranged in tiers. The officers of the Tombs are appointed by the Commissioner of Charities and Corrections, and consist of a

THE TOMBS—INTERIOR.

warden, two deputies, a physician, record clerk, steward, eleven keepers, matron and two deputy matrons.

As in the case of the other places for the confinement of violators of the law which I have mentioned, the reader will be able to see more vividly the inside life of the Tombs by the suppositious confinement of a criminal than by the mere description of what goes on. Suppose, then, that we take the case of one of the disorderly or vagrant class that daily appears in the Tombs police court.

BLACKWELL'S ISLAND.

He steps before the bar and the police justice hears the charge preferred against him, hears his statement of the facts, and then, as if this mortal was only one out of 10,000, in a cold and business-like manner consigns him to spend a term in the Tombs. An officer in the court-room gruffly says: "Come along," and without remonstrance, and pondering over his sentence, the new candidate for prison discipline meekly follows his blue-coated attendant. They pass through that awful smelling court-room amid the dull and brutish stare of the assembled scum of the lower city wards, through one or two corridors and into the prison. Here they pass a keeper, who, seeing the officer in charge of the prisoner and his commitment papers, allows them to pass. They go through two or three more iron doors into the open area in the centre of the building, across this into another section of the prison. Another keeper unlocks the door for them, and with scarcely a word they approach the desk of the clerk. As the prisoner stands here, waiting for the clerk to get his books ready, he has a chance to look about and get a bird's-eye view of where he is to live for some time. It is not an encouraging view. The floor on which he is standing is merely a narrow hallway, perhaps six feet wide. On either side rise high walls, with glimmerings of light streaming down from the windows at the two extremities of the corridor.

Narrow balconies at intervals are built out from these walls, and denote the different tiers of cells. There is one tier on the same floor that the prisoner is standing on, and by peeping through the narrow grating he gets a glimpse of the kind of room in which he is to be confined.

Finally the clerk at the desk is ready.

"Name?" he asks, without looking up.

THE "BLACK MARIA."

"John Blank," is the response. Then follow in rapid order inquiries as to age, marriage, residence, occupation and so forth. A turnkey now steps forward and leads away the prisoner to his cell. He unlocks the two iron doors and puts the occupant in. Then he slams the doors, locks them, and the prisoner is left to get acquainted with his new quarters.

The cell is narrow and small, but is rather better, on the whole, than one would think from looking at the entrance. The floor is of cement, and gets damp and cold. There is a hard, uncomfortable iron bed, one or two necessary articles of furniture; and these are all. Here, as in Ludlow Street Jail, if one wants luxuries he has to pay for them, and the messengers are said to make a very good thing of it. They offer to get cigars, tobacco, fruit, etc., for them and charge them double prices. The prisoners cannot rebel, and their persecutors have absolute power.

Bread and tea formed the diet which our prisoners got at supper time. The tea was served in large tin basins, and a quart cupful was allowed to the prisoner. Besides this he was given a hunk of bread. These he took into his cell and consumed them at his leisure. At breakfast time there are bread and hot rye coffee passed around, and at dinner time a bowl of vegetable-and-meat soup. During the day the prisoner was allowed to get out in the corridor for exercise.

This dull monotony of existence continues until the prisoner's term expires. Occasionally he sees visitors, who are allowed to talk to him at the cell door. Perhaps he is confined in the Tombs only temporarily before being conveyed to Blackwell's Island. When his time comes to start he is hustled out with a dozen or more other prisoners, all of whom are packed into the " Black Maria" and driven rapidly over the pavements toward Blackwell's Island.

In the Tombs, of course, different rows of cells are assigned to different grades of prisoners. The tier on the ground floor is used for lunatics, *delirium tremens* cases, and for sentenced prisoners. Muderers' Row is on the second tier, and burglars, highway robbers and other desperate criminals are confined here. The third tier is occupied by prisoners arrested for grand larceny, and the fourth for minor misdemeanors.

CHAPTER XXIX.

MURDERS AND MURDERERS.—THE BLOODY AFFRAY IN "SHANG" DRAPER'S SALOON.—RUNNING INTO THE ARMS OF A DETECTIVE.—PROSTRATE ON THE FLOOR IN A POOL OF BLOOD.—THE SNOW ON TWELFTH STREET DEFILED WITH GORE.—THE SKELETON IN THE CELLAR.—KNOCKED DOWN AND KILLED AT EARLY DAWN.—THE MURDERER OF MRS. HULL CAUGHT BY A REPORTER.

THE moon shone bright on the night of October 16, 1883. The clock lacked fifteen minutes of two. The outside door of "Shang" Draper's saloon on Sixth Avenue between Twenty-ninth and Thirtieth streets was locked and the curtains were closely drawn. Inside, the lights had not been all turned down, for there were customers still in the room. Four men stood before the bar. One was John Walsh, a bank burglar, called by his friends "Johnnie the Mick." Another was William Vosburgh, a notorious sneak thief. Pat Leary and Michael Fay, associates of criminals, were the other two. Behind the bar, mixing drinks, was Harry Hope, a son of Jimmy Hope, a bank burglar of no small reputation. The four men had raised their glasses to their lips.

Suddenly the side door creaked on its hinge. The men with the glasses in their hands glanced carelessly towards the aperture. A man's face and part of his figure were there. It was the face of John Irving, himself a famous bank burglar, and the leader of a gang hostile to that in which "Johnnie the Mick" was chief. At the sight of him the men at the bar put down their glasses, and one of them reached almost unconsciously for his revolver in his hip-pocket. It was too late. Irving had cocked and aimed his weapon. The trigger snapped and the ball flew through the lappel of Walsh's coat.

Behind the bar-room was a billiard-room, and into this Irving ran as soon as he had fired. Walsh dashed after him, discharging three cartridges from his revolver as he ran. One of the bullets pierced Irving's heart and he fell dead. Then appeared on the scene his life-long friend and avenger, Billy Porter. Like a Nemesis he swooped down upon his friend's murderer and sent a hot piece of lead whistling through his head. Then he broke for the door of the saloon, reached the street, and started to flee, only to fall into the hands of Detective Sergeant Hickey, who had been attracted by the firing.

In a few seconds the saloon was surrounded by Captain Williams and policemen McCool, Price, Gallagher and Fay. Near them

JOHN WALSH.
(From a Photograph.)

stood "Shang" Draper and "Red" Leary, the heroes of many deeds of infamy, who had been eating oysters in the adjoining saloon. The men waited a moment to see that no one broke away from the saloon, and then entered. A sorry spectacle it was that met their gaze. Irving lay stone dead, with his feet toward the centre of the room. A 38-calibre revolver with five chambers, two of which were empty, lay beside him. Ten feet away, doubled up in a corner, was "Johnnie the Mick," who was just alive. Vosburgh, Pat Leary and Michael Fay were vainly trying to restore him to life.

A solemn procession it was that fifteen minutes later wended its way toward the Thirtieth Street Station-house. A wagon carried the bodies of Irving and Walsh, and on the sidewalk, in a mournful, silent group, walked Captain Williams, the policemen, and as many of that band of criminals and ex-convicts as were left alive. Porter had preceded them to the station-house. The moon shone down as brightly as ever and threw the shadow of the passing men on the flag-stones.

CAPTAIN ALEX. S. WILLIAMS, TWENTY-NINTH PRECINCT.
(From a Photograph.)

For a long time there had been bad blood between Walsh and Irving. They had been engaged in the same burglaries and had quarrelled over the division of the spoils. Both were supposed to have been mixed up in the murder of George Leonidas Leslie, and Irving thought that Walsh knew too much about the affair. Porter had assisted Irving to escape from Raymond Street Jail in Brooklyn, and they were warm friends.

Although Porter was arrested he managed in some way to escape conviction. He is still alive and at large. Only as this is written he is reported in the newspapers as having arrived in New York again, after having been let out of prison in Troy, where he was held for the jewellery robbery at the store of Marks & Son, by procuring a bail-bond for $20,000.

On a Sunday morning in August, 1875, a woman who lived on Greenwich Street heard groans coming from an unfinished house at No. 275. At first she paid no attention to the sounds. But as they increased in volume and number she became startled and instituted a search. On the first floor of the new building lay a man, weltering in his own blood. There was a terrible gash in his head, out of which flowed blood and brain. Spasmodic gasps showed that the man was still alive. Those that found him recognized him as James H. Noe, an elderly gentleman of fortune, and the owner of the building in which he was discovered. It had been his custom to walk over to where the work was going on every Sunday morning, to see what progress had been made during the week.

The old man rallied for a few minutes while he told the story of the assault which had been made upon him. "I went up on the roof," he said, between his struggles for breath, "and found a man there tearing up the lead. I never had seen the man before. I caught hold of him and marched him down stairs. Right here where I lie he picked up a bar of iron and hit me. The next I remember he had tied a handkerchief over my mouth and was searching my pockets. I attempted to resist, but he told me if I made any noise he would come back and finish me."

With this much said Mr. Noe became unconscious again. He was removed to Chambers Street Hospital, where he died within a week, never having regained his consciousness.

The case went into my hands. I put upon it Detective Dorcey, who, after making a thorough examination of the premises, found several clews which he thought might lead to finding the murderer. One of these was the handkerchief which he had tied around Mr. Noe's face. It had a blue border and was saturated with blood. Mr. Noe's gold watch and chain, which had been purchased a few days previously, had been taken away by his assailant. Strangely, too, the murderer had broken his victim's cane in two and carried away the top piece, attached to which was a metal handle in the shape of a monkey. A description of the watch was obtained

SURPRISED AT WORK.

from the maker, a man named Welch, and Dorcey searched a great many pawnshops, but without finding what he wanted. One day, however, the proprietor of a small loan office on Chatham Street brought me a watch which he thought answered the description of the one taken from Mr. Noe. Sure enough it did, in every respect but the number. Mr. Welch, the maker, called with the information that he had inadvertently given me the wrong number. Placing the watch which I had received before him, he declared it was the one he had made for Mr. Noe.

A few days subsequent to this it was found that a cane with a monkey's head in metal for a handle had been seen in the possession of James Dolan, a well-known "tough," by Hendricks, who kept a coffee-and-cake saloon on Chatham Street. The blue-bordered handkerchief, too, was identified as belonging to Dolan by two girls of the town with whom he was on intimate terms. Dolan was arrested, and on his trial was fully identified as having pawned the watch. He was convicted of the crime and suffered the extreme penalty of the law in the Tombs. He never made any formal confession of his guilt, but when a son of the murdered man published what purported to be the conversation between his father and the murderer, Dolan exclaimed:

"That's a lie! I never said anything of the kind," thus practically admitting that he was the man.

The last day of the year 1868 was ushered in by a heavy snow-storm. The pure soft flakes fell noiselessly on the pavement until its nakedness was hidden beneath a mantle of white. On East Twelfth Street, as early as seven o'clock, an elderly gentleman, named Charles M. Rogers, was in front of his residence, at No. 42, sweeping the fallen substance into the street. As he swung his broom, keeping time with a tune which he was humming, a rough-looking man crossed the street and approached him. As he got near he made a dart at old Mr. Rogers's watch and pocket-book, and transferred them to the side pocket of his blue flannel sack coat. But when the highway robber tried to make off with his booty he found he was restrained. The old man had him tightly held. Then began a terrible struggle. The thief fought like a demon to get free, but Mr. Rogers's grip was firm. Finally the assailant reached a hand for the knife which he had concealed about him, and drawing it, plunged it into the bowels of his antagonist. Then with an extra effort he broke away, and the old man fell over, clutching a portion of his assailant's coat which ha · parted in the struggle.

All this happened in broad daylight, and not a few persons were in the street. Yet so far as is known no human eye witnessed the murder, for such it was. A few minutes later Rogers was discovered dying on his own doorstep. He muttered a few words which outlined the story as above told, and then died.

Firmly grasped in the murdered man's right hand was the part of the coat which he had torn from the assassin. The snow was gory with blood. Near by was the garroter's hat and knife sheath. In the pocket of the torn part of the coat was the watch and wallet of Mr. Rogers, and an envelope with the inscription: " James Logan, New York City. This will be handed you by Tom."

This the police considered a good clew, and at once commenced a vigorous search for James Logan. A man with this name was found to be living in the upper part of the city, and he was arrested. It was ascertained that he was a plasterer by trade, and, strangely enough, a small quantity of plaster was found in the pocket of the coat torn from the murderer. Then, too, he was proved to have been in the vicinity of Twelfth Street shortly before the murder. These were suspicious circumstances, but he explained his presence on Twelfth Street by stating that, in company with a friend, he had spent the night in a house near by. This was ascertained to be true, and being otherwise of a good character he was discharged from custody.

The true " James Logan," however, has never been discovered, and who it was that murdered Mr. Rogers is likely to remain forever a mystery. Many individuals bearing the name of Logan were looked up and " shadowed," but no definite results followed.

What is known as the Carleton House mystery created a great sensation at the time it was discovered. The affair is still as much of a mystery as ever, but the people have forgotten it.

The Carleton House is situated at the corner of William and Frankford streets, and is a tall building, occupied by many different kinds of people. It has in times past had rather a bad reputation. The traditions which cluster around its mouldering walls tell tales of crime which gain horror with age. It was just the building for a mystery, and the newspapers, with their keen instinct for what is interesting, made the most of it.

One day in December, 1884, some workmen were engaged in cleaning out a sub-cellar which projected under the William Street sidewalk. The sub-cellar had long been closed, and was half filled with ashes and other refuse which had been dumped through a trap-door from the regular basement of the building. The subterranean apartment was many feet deep, and dark and damp, and suggestive of crime. It was not a pleasant place to work. Two of the workmen were engaged in filling a basket of the debris, which two more would carry to a small aperture on the Frankfort Street side, whence it was hoisted by ropes and pulleys to the sidewalk. Candles were placed here and there in the dark passages to give the workmen light. Such were the odors which came from the sub-cellar that the men inside were obliged to come out at short intervals for fresh air.

On this December day that I have alluded to, the flickering rays of a candle were casting shadows over the ash-heaps, when one of the workmen in his digging came upon a woman's hand sticking out of the rubbish. It was a ghastly sight in such a place. Cold perspiration ran down the workman's face, and he darted for the place of exit and told his discovery to his companions. The first spasm of fright was soon over. The men went back to their work after having summoned a policeman. Further digging brought forth a most horrible sight. It was the skeleton of a woman clothed in a maroon-colored dress, a dark sacque with bead fringe, and striped stockings. A heavy stone lay across her face, and a calico cloth was tied tightly around her throat.

The body was dug out and carried to the Morgue. It looked as if it had been dead five years. The police came to the conclusion that they had before them to unravel the greatest mystery they had touched in years.

Many theories were broached to account for the discovery of the body. There had plainly been a murder. There was the heavy stone across the face, the rag around the throat, and the suggestive trap-door above. But who could have done it? and who was the foul murderer's victim? These were the questions which bothered the police for some time, until finally a theory was accepted as most plausible, but nevertheless not quite satisfactory.

It seems that about the time the murder was supposed to have been committed, the room above the sub-cellar was occupied by Benjamin Gray, a printer. There were witnesses who said that Gray often had visits from two women, one of whom, after awhile, ceased to come, and was never seen again. The police supposed that Gray had killed the missing woman and thrust her through the trap-door. The sub-cellar was never entered, ashes were thrown through the opening in the floor above, and thus the murder was never discovered.

The next thing was to find Gray. After some search he was discovered in the Trenton Penitentiary, where he was serving a ten-years' sentence, for attempting to murder a woman whom he called his wife, and who lived in Dover, New Jersey, where he had struck her on the head and left her on the road-side for dead. He was surly and glum when spoken to concerning the body which was found in the Carleton House sub-cellar, and would neither deny nor affirm the charge of murder against him. His real name was Samuel S. Gray, and he was by birth an Englishman, and about twenty-six years old. His term expires on June 20, 1893, and it remains to be seen whether he will then be re-arrested on this graver charge. His wife in Dover refused to say anything which would in any way implicate her husband. So there is still a mystery hanging about the Carleton House.

Early dawn was just sending its gray shadows against the buildings in Seventh Avenue on the morning of May 24, 1882, when Josephine Hawkes, a woman with a notorious history, was strolling toward the corner of Fifty-seventh Street, arm-in-arm with Louis W. Gutermuth. They had spent the night in carousing, and were out " walking it off." The woman told her companion that she thought they were being followed, and to see if her suspicions were correct they turned into Fifty-seventh Street. As they did so, the man behind them approached rapidly, and coming up behind Mrs. Hawkes made an insulting remark to her. Gutermuth turned around to retaliate on the fellow, when the latter turned on him, and with a blow felled his antagonist to the ground. In his fall Gutermuth struck his head heavily on the curb-stone, and while down he received another blow on the nose from a club. He attempted to rise, but received a third blow on the side of the head with a sand-bag, which stretched him again on the ground. Mrs. Hawkes assisted him to get up; he was very feeble, and she looked round for assistance. After some time she found an officer, who went with her to Mr. Gutermuth's assistance. He was sitting on the curbing, so injured as to be unable to give his exact address, and he was accordingly taken to the Roosevelt Hospital. A member of the firm by which he was employed found him in that institution on the 25th of May and took him to his residence—at Mrs. Jardine's, No. 144 West Forty-seventh Street. There he received such careful attention that on the 3d of June he was able to go to his office. He was still very weak, however, and was told to go home until fully recovered. He went back to Mrs. Jardine's, became worse, aggravating his condition by paying visits to friends, and three days later was a dead man.

The Central Office detectives were tardily notified of his death and the facts connected therewith. On the 13th of June they had in custody Mrs. Hawkes, Robert C. Clapp and John K. Imley, a disreputable private detective. These arrests were made on what appeared to be excellent information in regard to a scandal which had existed for some time, and which grew out of troubles at the Rossmore Hotel between the sons of Hawley D. Clapp (the proprietor), Robert C. (one of the prisoners) and Mortimer R., who were made executors of Mr. Hawley Clapp's will. The father died in 1880, and the sons immediately went to fighting at law. Robert, who was a dissipated fellow, was accused of various offences, criminal and otherwise, and his mother sided with Mortimer R. They had Robert C. arrested on the ground that he was a confirmed drunkard. The charge did not stand in court, upon which Robert turned round and had Mortimer arrested upon a charge of grand larceny. This charge was also dismissed, and the litigation increased the bad feeling between the brothers, Robert on one occasion attempting to stab Mortimer with a knife. They had a sister, named Nellie, who became the associate of Mrs. Hawkes, and was her equal in depravity. Imley, the private detective, was the "familiar" of Robert, while Mortimer and Gutermuth were friends. A singular circumstance was that the latter two resembled each other so closely, that in the gray light of a spring morning they might each easily have been mistaken for the other. The theory of the detectives in arresting Mrs. Hawkes, Robert Clapp and Imley was that the two last-named had plotted to attack Mortimer, and that they followed Gutermuth believing him to be Mortimer. There was a good deal of "volunteer" testimony placed in the possession of the Central Office detectives;

but when the inquest was held it was manifest that the mistaken-identity theory was faulty; and after a protracted examination, it served only to throw additional mystery around the affair. It established that the events which led to the assault were simply a street altercation, a sudden brewing of hot blood and the striking of one or more deadly blows. Mrs. Hawkes, Clapp and Imley were acquitted by the coroner's jury. For nine months afterwards the police worked unremittingly on the case. Several promising clews were obtained, but they ended like a track in the Far West, beginning at a broad wagon-road and ending in a squirrel's "run" up a tree.

Taken as a whole, the homicide in question was one of the most peculiar on record. Gutermuth himself was a mystery, to a certain extent, both before and after his death. It is believed that he was born in Germany, and that his father was a furniture manufacturer and wealthy. Louis received an excellent education and spoke English, German and Spanish fluently. He began life for himself as a book-keeper. Subsequently he went to Cuba as agent for Emil Myer, an exporter; and later on occupied a similar position with the firm of Coombs, Crosby & Eddy, who were in the same trade. In this situation Gutermuth went to the City of Mexico as general correspondent of the firm, and now and then came to the United States. He last visited New York on New Year's Day, 1882. As a business man he was eulogized as sober, industrious and capable. Socially he was exceedingly popular; he had the *entrée* of the best society in Mexico, and was engaged to a young Mexican lady. In New York he belonged to several social organizations and had many firm friends.

Mr. Gutermuth, it should be stated, had a *penchant* for "night-hawking." He was not a depraved or vicious man, but he loved good-fellowship, and his friends said that he often stayed out later than his own tastes would have permitted him because he was unwilling to break up a convivial party. It thus happened that he had formed the acquaintance of Mrs. Hawkes. This woman was born of well-known and respectable parents in the Ninth Ward. Many of her relatives were employed in the city departments, and several of them were policemen. Her maiden name was Josephine Webb. In 1859 she married a shiftless and dishonest fellow named Monyea, who, before the honeymoon was barely ended, was arrested for the theft of a diamond ring. Mrs. Monyea invoked "influence" which enabled him to escape with a light sentence, and she then "took up" with "Con" Stagg, an Internal Revenue officer, and a frequenter of the gambling den called "The Place," on Hudson Street, where Sharkey killed Dunn, the gambler. She has often said that Stagg was the only man for whom she had any real affection. He went with her to San Francisco, where Stagg, wearying of her, speculated on her charms. He opened a gambling house, and his mistress was employed in luring wealthy Californians into the meshes of his net. The place was run as a hotel, with the attraction of a "club" in which faro and other games could be indulged in. While here Josephine met with a great misfortune. She had a luxuriant head of dark hair, which she lost by a fever, and then replaced it by a blonde wig, said to have cost $3000. The young bloods who patronized her "husband's" establishment were not slow in carrying the news all over San Francisco, and visitors to that city may see in sundry nooks and corners the picture of the handsome Josephine without her wig, facetiously labelled "Baldy Josephine," or "Blondy." Lithographs were also published of her with her wig on, but those who possess them hold them at an exorbitant price.

Somehow or other the popularity of Stagg waned, despite the attractions, real and false, of his partner. He drank deeply, gambled recklessly, and lost all the woman's esteem by publicly consorting with the most notorious characters of the Golden Gate. Josephine was not loath, therefore, to accept the offer made her by B. Shafton Hawkes to go East with him. She settled accounts in San Francisco by thrashing her latest successor in Stagg's affections in the public street, while Mr. Hawkes squared matters with Mr. Stagg by *lending* him $10,000. All this occurred in April, 1877, and three weeks later Josephine and Mr. Hawkes arrived in New York. Her story was that she had obtained a divorce from Stagg and had married Hawkes.

Mr. Hawkes was simply "tolerated" by Josephine. He had to submit to her capers and extravagances, and three years after he had made her acquaintance in California he did little more than support her. He travelled extensively in Europe and Canada, now and then going to where "Mrs. Hawkes" lived and appearing in public with her. It is said he fitted up a flat at No. 19 Seventh Avenue and lived with her a few weeks. This was in

June, 1881, and in the fall of that same year Mr. Hawkes dropped out of sight, gave instructions to tradesmen to collect bills from the "lady," and Mrs. Hawkes was thrown on her own resources. Mrs. Hawkes, despite years of dissipation, was yet a remarkably handsome woman. Mr. Gutermuth became, to a certain extent, infatuated with her, and on the night of the assault had been with her, in company with Nellie Clapp and a gentleman whose connection with the murder was so slight that I do not give his name.

Emma H. Conkling, in 1873, when she was nineteen years old, married, at San Francisco, J. Clement Uhler, a stock broker. They lived happily several years, and then came to New York, where Uhler went into partnership with Mr. W. H. Haverstick, the title of the firm being "J. Clement Uhler & Co." At that time Mrs. Uhler had become the mother of several children, but notwithstanding this fact she became infatuated with Mr. Haverstick, who succeeded in seducing her. The injured husband was averse to violent methods of expressing his disapprobation of the liaison, and when Mrs. Uhler left his bed and board he did little besides protest against an act which would bring disgrace on both families. Haverstick's infatuation was such that after the dissolution of his business connection with the man he had dishonored, he cohabited with Mrs. Uhler—the two passing as brother and sister—and in the summer of 1882 they went to live in the Paris Flats, No. 341 West Twenty-third Street, where Haverstick was subsequently slain.

A member of Mrs. Uhler's family—her brother, George W. Conkling, Jr.—had known of his sister's disgrace for some time. He wrote to her in regard to it, being unable to visit New York, on account of his position as an officer of the U. S. Field Service in Nevada. At last, however, in February, 1883, Conkling arrived in New York, with but one end in view—of breaking the liaison, and taking his sister back with him to Reno, Nevada. His first act was to seek out Mrs. Uhler, talk to her earnestly of her situation, and implore her to leave her betrayer. He told her he thought he could pave the way, after a short time, to a reconciliation with her husband, and that all might be well again. But Mrs. Uhler rebelled against any idea of a reconciliation. She said she did not care for her husband, and that in the future, whenever they happened to be on bad terms, he would be sure to "cast up" her association with Haverstick.

Conkling, therefore, gave up his idea of re-uniting husband and wife, but he set himself at work to separate his sister and her paramour. She finally appeared to acquiesce in her brother's wishes, and it was arranged that on a certain evening she should go to the Leland Hotel (where her brother was a guest), place herself under his protection and abandon Haverstick forever. Conkling had so much faith in his sister's decision that he made preparations for their journey westward.

Mrs. Uhler, however, did not keep the appointment at the Leland House, and her brother went to the Paris Flats, resolved to do something desperate if he could not tear his sister from the arms of the man who had betrayed her. Conkling had little to fear personally, although he was much the inferior in physique of Haverstick, who was a swart, brawny individual, taller and broader than the man who sought to remedy the disgrace into which he had brought Mrs. Uhler. But Conkling had the advantage of having passed several years as a frontiersman, and also of being a strictly temperate person. When he entered the little bijou of an apartment on the third floor, which had been fitted up handsomely by the guilty pair, he was confronted by Haverstick, who demanded his purpose, well knowing, through a confession by Mrs. Uhler, for what he came. Conkling said boldly that he had come to take his sister away at all hazards, and that when he left the house she should accompany him. Haverstick bullied and Conkling made a pathetic appeal to his sister, which was offset by an equally urgent appeal from Haverstick. The woman hesitated, and the men grew more and more angry until at last, after Conkling had denounced the seducer's villany in galling terms, Haverstick seized a Dresden vase from the mantle-piece and hurled it at his victim's brother.

Conkling was accustomed on the frontier to the use of fire-arms and knew the necessity of quick action in an emergency. Before the vase, which missed him, was dashed against the wall of the room, his hand grasped his pistol. Just as Haverstick was about to throw the companion vase Conkling levelled his weapon, a shot rang out, and the bullet pierced Haverstick in the centre of his body. Conkling threw aside his pistol, cast a glance at Haverstick, who had fallen and was leaning on his arm gazing appealingly at the sister's avenger, walked out of the apartment, brushed aside his half-frantic relative, and going to the Grand Opera

House surrendered himself to Officer J. W. Mantell, of the Sixteenth Precinct.

Meanwhile physicians were summoned to the Paris Flats, where they found that Haverstick was mortally wounded. Although fully cognizant that his end was near, he was loath at first to name his assailant, probably from feelings of remorse; but at last he endeavored to raise himself from his bed, on which he had been lying, and in a burst of passion exclaimed:

"George Conkling shot me—shot me down like a dog. But I forgive him. I don't think he meant to kill me."

Then he sank back on his pillow and murmured as in a dream:

"God bless my mother!"

A few moments later he was dead. The homicide did not excite any feeling of animosity towards Conkling. By the general public it was considered the avenging of Mr. Uhler and the honor of the Conkling family. Young Conkling readily procured bail. Mrs. Uhler was deeply affected by the tragedy, and was in constant hysterics for several days. At the inquest, however, after acknowledging her disgrace without reserve, she told the story of her brother's endeavor to separate her from the man with whom she had become infatuated. She gave testimony which was very favorable to the defendant. The outcome of the inquest was that Conkling was held for trial on the following extraordinary verdict:

"We find that Wilbur H. Haverstick came to his death by a pistol-shot wound in the abdomen, fired by George W. Conkling, Jr., on the evening of March 19, 1883, at 341 West Twenty-third Street, and that the shot was fired under great provocation."

After Mr. Conkling obtained bail he went West, came back to be tried for the crime, was acquitted and went West again to die.

Mrs. Uhler did not reform. She contracted the opium habit, and died a wretched death in this city.

When Nancy Francis, the cook at Mrs. Jane Lawrence De Forrest Hull's boarding house at No. 140 West Forty-second Street, went to her mistress's room at seven o'clock on the morning of June 11, 1879, to awaken her, she shrieked with terror. The sight which met her gaze was terrible to behold. Mrs. Hull lay flat on her back; there was a bandage tied tightly around her eyes, her throat was bound and bed-clothes were stuffed into her mouth, her hands and legs were each fastened to the sides of the bed with strips of linen torn from the sheets. Her face was purple and cold as death. When the bandage was removed from her eyes they were found to be burned, and the lashes and brows singed. The odor of cologne permeated the atmosphere. The woman was dead.

It is needless to say there was an uproar in that house. Mrs. Hull was the wife of Dr. Alonzo G. Hull, and about fifty-eight years old. She weighed about two hundred pounds. There were about a dozen boarders in the house, who rushed from their rooms in alarm when they heard the cook's shrieks. When they discovered that their landlady had been murdered they were highly excited. The police were immediately called, and Captain Williams was soon in possession of the house. He thought that the enormity of the crime was sufficient to warrant my presence, and at a special summons from him I went to the house.

I found that the room in which the murder had occurred—for that such it was there could be no doubt—was a small one, 12 x 6 feet, at the end of the hallway. There was every evidence that a robbery had been committed. A ring had been torn from Mrs. Hull's finger, and a gold watch, chain, an enamelled ring, a diamond ring and a topaz necklace were missing. Much silverware and jewellery, however, were undisturbed. A colored servant, Nellie West, had found the front door of the house open at five A. M. The thief and murderer had evidently been familiar with the house.

A post-mortem examination was held, and revealed the fact that Mrs. Hull had died of suffocation. Her lungs and brain were congested. I concluded, after I had learned these facts, that the murder had probably been unintentional. Whether there was really a thief in the case I confess I was in doubt. Dr. Hull's actions were very peculiar. He seemed to exhibit no special concern, and I had a suspicion that he was the murderer. I beg his pardon for the suspicion, but I could not help it. Mrs. Hull had speculated largely in stocks, and when this was known it added to the complexity of the case.

I went to work at the case with a vim. I found in a few days after the sad occurrence that some of Mrs. Hull's stolen jewellery had been offered for sale in Boston. The watch had been pawned. When the Boston police ascertained this they telegraphed us a description of the man who had offered the valuables for sale. We identified it as that of Chastine Cox, alias John Cox, alias William

Francis, at one time a waiter in Mrs. Hull's house, and sent back word to the police of Boston to find the man if they could.

About a week after this came the news of Cox's arrest, and the particulars somewhat surprised us. Mr. W. R. Balch, a reporter on the Boston *Herald*, obtained a description of Cox from the police in the course of his regular duties, and mentally photographed him. As he was walking along Waltham Street on Monday, June 23, he noticed a negro in front of him who seemed to answer the description given of Cox. He accordingly followed him and saw him enter a small church frequented wholly by colored people on Harrison Avenue. Mr. Balch at once made known his discovery to Detective Wood, who, with another officer, went to the church in question. The sexton was requested to call Cox outside, which he accordingly did, and upon the suspected murderer stepping into the vestibule, he was arrested. When searched at the police station, Cox had on his person, besides other things, a revolver and a gold watch. The latter was at once identified as being one of the articles stolen from Mrs. Hull's room on the night the burglary was committed and she was so brutally murdered. The following day he was brought on to New York, and shortly after his arrival Cox made what he called a "confession." In it he said he entered the house through one of the front parlor windows which he found unfastened; and that when Mrs. Hull awoke and made an outcry, he tied her hands and feet, put his hands over her face and stuffed up her mouth with a portion of the bed-clothes. He then went on to say that while looking round the room for money he suddenly noticed that Mrs. Hull had ceased to breathe and, seizing a bottle of cologne, he dashed the liquid on her face. It was too late, however; Mrs. Hull was dead. Upon his trial he was found guilty, and while confined in the Tombs under sentence of death, he made what was undoubtedly a true statement of the facts, which utterly contradicted his former story. In this second confession Cox admitted having been Mrs. Hull's lover for some considerable length of time, and that he had been in the habit of constantly visiting at night. In fact she had provided him with keys to the house and her apartment. On the night of the murder he went to her room as usual. For some days previously he had been playing policy, and having lost heavily was in need of money. He demanded the needed amount from Mrs. Hull, who replied that she had no

AT THE PRAYER-MEETING.

money. Going to the dressing table, Cox snatched up some jewellery and observed that he would raise money on it and bring her the pawn-tickets. The unfortunate woman attempted to snatch the jewellery from his hand; there was a struggle between the two which only ended in death, as before described.

This statement, together with affidavits to the effect that Cox had had free access to the house and was intimate with Mrs. Hull, were laid before the governor. That official, however, refused to interfere with the due execution of the sentence already imposed. Although the killing of Mrs. Hull, he said, might have been unpremeditated and unintentional, the crime, nevertheless, was murder in the first degree, as it was undoubtedly committed during the attempted burglary of a house in the night time.

Cox was therefore hung at the Tombs, and met his fate with becoming resignation, so I have been informed by those who witnessed the execution.

CHAPTER XXX.

THE CHINESE QUARTER.—HAUNTS OF CHINESE VICE.—A SUNDAY'S VISIT.—IN AN OPIUM JOINT.—THE GAME OF POLICY.—AT THE FONG TONG TABLE.—THE SOCIAL EVIL.—DEGRADATION OF WHITE WOMEN.—THE EVIL OF THE LAUNDRIES.—CHINESE AND AMERICAN MARRIAGES.—BEFORE THE GREAT JOSS.

OF all foreign colonies in New York the Chinese is the most picturesque. Emigrants from European countries merge themselves in the American population, acquire the English tongue, study the spirit of our institutions, and are content to live and die within the bounds of the great republic. But the Chinaman is a unique and isolated figure. Suspicious as a man who finds himself in a den of thieves, he is ever on the watch while he works for some new manifestation of that American temperament which his own mind, dense with the superstitions of many thousand years, can never quite understand. He scents in the average citizen an alert foe to his nationality, creed and habits. Consideration and kindness never disarm him. He is even distrustful of that tongue which the Americans use with such nervous energy, and year after year passes over his head without an attempt to learn more of the language than suffices for his business relations with the people whom he fears and dislikes. And so it follows that he wears the flowing blouse, the loose trowsers, and the paper shoes of his countrymen at home; lets his queue hang down his back, and eats the peculiar dishes whose secret he brought with him from the remote East. His amusements, too, are essentially Chinese. He clings to the opium habit, and cannot see the good of casting it loathingly behind him. He has his own clumsy methods of gambling, which require the least effort of his enervated mind. When he plays his favorite game of policy he employs a system of counting which is grotesque to the American eye. When he drinks it is a decoction made from the extract of a nut which is indescribably offensive to delicate palates. When he wants music he thrums on a Celestial mandolin an air of unbroken monotony.

His pleasure is grave and subdued, as if he lived under the spell of his impish and wooden-featured gods. It is his taciturn humor, his creeping isolation, his clannish fashions, his uncanny likes and dislikes, and his jealousy of push and progress, that make the Chinaman stand out a conspicuous oddity in our restless population. He is like the figure of one of his own curiously carved and hideous idols. There is probably no American who does not regard the Chinese as beings dissimilar to and dissonant with himself; as a caste shut out by its fantastic personality from his sympathies and associations.

Unless it be San Francisco, there is no city in the United States where the Chinese can be studied to such advantage as in New York. There are between six and seven thousand settled in our midst, forming a compact and well-regulated colony. Their main settlement is in the lower part of Mott Street, with branches running into Pell and Park streets. Here in old, dark and dirty tenement houses they swarm, like coolies on a Pacific steamer. Around and on all sides of them live the crowded Italians, Irish, Jews and Germans; hucksters, rag-pickers, laborers, loafers, thieves and vagrants; but none in darker and narrower quarters than the Chinese. Scattered in other parts of the city, even to the outskirts, are hundreds of laundries. Their occupants have more space to move and breathe in than the Mott Street Chinaman, but every Sunday sees them wending their way to mingle with their friends in the big settlement, with its stores, restaurants and joss house. It was natural that in a colony welded into one whole the fashions and practices peculiar to remote China should prevail and take root. Some of those practices are no doubt bad and vicious, but they have been transplanted and they flourish here. Among them none is more pernicious than the opium habit. And it is to indulge in his beloved drug by smoking it in long, cumbrous pipes that the Chinamen rendezvous in Mott Street Sunday after Sunday.

The "joints" are usually situated at the end of a passage in a weather-beaten brick house, no doubt the scene in other years of brawls and orgies among the debased tenants. The Chinamen glide into these houses as stealthily as shadows, for they know that the opium den is under the ban of the law and that it may be raided by the police at any hour of the day or night. The authorities are disposed to let the Chinamen congregate as friends to enjoy a sociable pipe of opium, but set their faces hard against the practice as it prevails in the notorious joint. With the connivance of some politician, a Chinaman is sometimes able to fit up an opium den with pipes and lounges, where he makes a profitable business of drugging his almond-eyed friends with the narcotic. But the politician, in permitting the joint to exist for a weekly tax, draws the line at the admittance of Americans. Occasionally a degraded white, who has become wedded to opium for the pleasure it affords him, is tolerated among the Chinese smokers. But his introduction is attended with peril to the interests of the keeper of the joint, for no sooner is it known to the Chinaman's accomplice on the police force than the den is raided and indiscriminate arrests of whites and Mongols are made. If an American, however, has had a long acquaintance with an intelligent Chinaman he may get admitted to the joint solely to look on at the opium smoking but not to indulge in it.

This is the picture he sees. A low apartment divided into stalls, between which runs a passage to the kitchen in the rear, where the opium is prepared. In each compartment is a low lounge of matting furnished with pillows for the smoker's head. The walls are covered with a cheap paper and with crude Chinese designs; an oil lamp swings from the ceiling. The effect of the division of the place into stalls is to remind one of the steerage of an ocean steamer, and the indescribable odor that floats in the air strengthens the illusion. Each lounge is equipped with a tray holding the smoking apparatus, which consists of a pipe, needle, opium jar and sweet-oil lamp. It is a rare thing for the compartments not to be well patronized after dark. Reclining on the lounges with their heads propped up by pillows two Chinamen on each lounge may be seen smoking or dreaming away the hours. The process of using the opium is simple. From the little opium jar the smoker takes on the point of a needle a lump of matter which is thick and dark like molasses. He winds it around the needle until it adheres without dropping, and then holds the substance over the flame of the lamp. The opium sizzles and turns to a rich amber color, the Chinaman watching it with a drowsy face, in which there is not the least vestige of intelligence. The cooking, as it is called, lasts perhaps two minutes. Then the smoker takes his long cane pipe in one hand to stuff into it the ball of opium. The stem is about two feet in length and an inch and a half in diameter, and is made of reed or Chinese mahogany. The bowl is a piece of wood of the color of burnt clay, with a hole in the centre about as large as the thick part of a big darning-needle, and it is set into the stem six or eight inches from the end. The mouth-piece of this clumsy pipe does not taper off into a smooth piece of amber, but is of the same size as the stem itself. Into the aperture of the bowl the Chinaman packs the opium with the point of a huge needle. Now his preparations are complete. He turns himself on his side and holds the bowl close to the flame so that the opium can burn slowly. His eyes half close, a look of languor steals over his features, and he sucks in from the big mouth-piece a cloud of smoke which he takes into his lungs and breathes out through his nostrils. In a minute and a half the opium is exhausted, only a charred remnant remaining in the bowl. Reveries, dreams and stupefaction do not come with one pipe. Again and again the smoker cooks his lump of opium, packs it into the bowl, and lazily watches the smoke curl up around the hanging lamp. After awhile the pipe drops from his nerveless hand, there is a glaze on his eyes, which are half-shut, like a dead man's, his lips part, his head falls upon his breast, and he is in that opium trance which is either paradise or hell, according to the degree of his indulgence in the narcotic. It may be that his fellow on the lounge has thrown aside the pipe before its effects have overcome him, and is holding a half-consumed cigarette between his lips. His expression is listless and blank. His companion is wrapped in the opium sleep, limp, pale and motionless, but he does not look at him lying as one dead on the other side of the little lamp of sweet oil which burns with a bluish flame, like an imp of fire in a bottle. The air is dense with an oppressive odor that has a leaden and drowsy effect even on the chance visitor.

In possession of other lounges lie Chinamen in all kinds of postures and in all stages of the opium languor. Now there is a stillness as of death, and now a jerky guttural comes from the throat of a dreamer tumbled into a heap on a lounge in a dark corner. Sometimes a door opens and a new comer breaks the silence with a confused jargon. But there is not much conversation in the opium joint; the genius of the place holds his worshippers in a speechless and inert thrall. The hanging-lamps burn with a yellow flicker through the long night hours, and a cloud of opium smoke is often drawn over them like a veil. The place is rude and often unclean, but the minds of the sleepers are building for them palaces of rare beauty, sunsets of eternal glory, and gardens of musical fountains and blossoming flowers. No one can be so transcendently happy as these wretched creatures in the depth of their degradation. De Quincey has depicted in imperishable language the pageants and forms of beauty he saw in his trances, but fortunately for his fellow-men he has also drawn pictures of the exquisite torture he suffered in the moments when his nerves were drawn out like fine wire through infinite space. As the night wears on a sleeper here and there rouses himself to his feet and with dulled eyes and mechanical movement passes out through the door into the night and the yellow-lighted street. Perhaps his senses mark the staggering gait and hear the shout of a belated roisterer. Wine may be a bad taskmaster but opium is a grinning tyrant who releases his victims only when their nerves are shattered to fragments and death yawns horribly before them. Better to be the wine-inflamed debauchee than the stupefied smoker of opium.

But the stagnant dissipation of the smoker's life in the joint goes on all night. No breath of pure air strays in to cool the dreamer's brow; doors are sealed tight, lamps steadily flame, and the white smoke hangs in layers in the light and is banked up in dark corners. In the rear of the rows of bunks is the opium kitchen, where a boilerful of a black fluid is bubbling audibly. Near it sits the keeper of the joint, a pipe of tobacco in his mouth. He cannot afford to drug and daze himself. He must attend to the wants of his patrons, refill the opium jars, prepare the pipes of nerveless smokers, trim the yellow lamps, and collect his dues. The fluid in the boiler is opium forming into the glutinous mass with which the jars are replenished. A dense cloud of steam rolls up from the iron pot; if you put your head into it you will find the odor suggestive of a grave vault, and loving fresh air you will draw back with repugnance. Daylight can steal in even through the blind windows of an opium den, and when it comes the dreamers know that they must go out to that toil which earns them the price of their indulgence. And so, one by one, they get up with stiffened limbs and issue forth to their laundries and tea stores.

Another Chinese habit that is almost as pernicious in its effects as opium smoking is the habit of gambling. The Celestial is a shameless and inveterate gambler. It is a rare thing to find a Chinaman who is not infatuated with games of chance. His gambling takes two forms, policy and "fong tong." The houses in which these games flourish are designated by white characters painted on the porch or door. If you pass through Mott or Pell streets you will see these places every few steps. It may be that the den is in a basement below the sidewalk, and often it is reached by three or four crooked flights of stairs. The policy shop is the most interesting to Americans, because our own negroes and shiftless whites throughout the United States play the game to a great extent. The Chinese game is not so complex as the American, in which the term "gig," "whip" and "saddle" confuse the uninitiated. The Chinese policy-shop is usually a square room boarded up to the ceiling with pine planks. It is divided into two parts by wooden bars, which run up to the plastering. Behind this partition stands the owner of the game and his assistants. In the space outside tables are set against the walls for the accommodation of the players, and hung above is a sheaf of tickets. In Mott Street two drawings take place every day, at four o'clock in the afternoon and at ten o'clock in the evening. When the Chinaman wants to play policy he tears a ticket from the sheaf on the wall, and pores over it for a few minutes before selecting his numbers, of which there are eighty printed on the slip of paper. These numbers are Chinese characters, incomprehensible to an American. Perhaps the player has had a dream the night before that a certain combination of figures will bring him fortune, or perhaps, like the American gambler, he employs a "system." When his mind is made up he seizes a little stick from the table, dips it in red paint, and daubs the numbers that he fancies. He does this in a very clumsy fashion, and when he has finished the ticket looks as if a dozen strawberries had been crushed into it. He may play five or more numbers, according to the money he risks. He hands his combination to a Chinaman behind the bars, who puts it on file. Hour after hour the Celestials pour in to try their luck. Some of them never miss a drawing, even if they have only a few cents to lose. The dream of their lives is to make a lucky strike. They don't talk very much, except when excited with winning, and then their jerky speech jars the ear like the sound of a rusty wagon wheel. Behind the bars the proprietor is kept busy receiving money and giving change. His expression is always fixed and stolid. For impassiveness the American gambler cannot be compared with him. But if an inquisitive stranger puts his face into the shop and peers at the strange scene, at once a look of ugly distrust comes into the face of the gambler behind the wooden fence. He now has the appearance of a venomous animal in a cage. A hostile light glitters in his eyes, and if the strange white man has been piloted in by a Chinaman it is with no friendly glance that the latter is regarded. Next to an unknown American the Chinaman hates one of his own kind who shows the American the sights and oddities of Chinatown. Uppermost in his mind is the fear that the strangely assorted couple have designs on his business. He thinks he may be black-mailed by threats of police interference. If an American wishes to see an evil expression on a human creature's face he should penetrate a Chinese gambling den and loiter about until the keeper of the place and his satellites have worked themselves into an agony of nervousness. If glances could kill he would be mutilated after a hundred fashions.

When the hours have arrived at which the Celestial policy-player is to learn whether he has lost his wretched stake or is to see it multiplied many times the chief interest begins. About fifteen minutes before the drawing eighty numbers are scrawled on slips of paper, all of the same size. These are rolled up into balls and placed in equal numbers in three white bowls. Then a Chinaman mixes them up by changing handfuls of the balls from bowl to bowl. Finally the numbers are thrown into one large basin, and thirteen of them are picked out at random. They are passed down the table to a Chinaman who keeps the record. Then it is that the waiting gamblers beyond the railing give their strictest attention to the procedure. Their eyes twinkle and expand, they change their attitudes from one foot to the other or plunge their hands under their blouses. But after all, they resemble American gamblers in a studied unconcern and a rigid repression of feeling. The recording Chinaman slowly unrolls the balls. He is the arbiter of fate, and he takes his time. As his eye catches sight of the number he clangs it out in a monotone. Not a word is heard among the gamblers. Some of them stand near the railing with their eyes fixed on the clerk of numbers. Others are sitting down at tables daubing red marks on fresh tickets to designate how the drawing is running. As it proceeds they know how many of their guesses were correct. The harsh monotone rises thirteen times and then ceases. When it has died away most of the Chinamen straggle out with hands in their pockets. They speak not a word, and look neither vexed nor surprised. There is not one of them who shouts an imprecation. Policy is a part of their daily routine. They expect to lose, and lose with the stolidity of wooden images. Those who are winners remain behind to congratulate each other on their good luck, to which they are very sensitive. If five numbers were guessed the player receives the amount of his stake, and it is doubled, trebled or further multiplied according as his guesses have approached the complete number of thirteen. Payments are not made immediately after the drawing, but the next morning. In almost every tea and grocery store in Chinatown you will find a record of the drawings for a month back. This record the Chinese gambler studies as the American sporting man studies the racing guide. He makes all sorts of calculations on the probability of a repetition or change of combinations. If the lucky numbers are all huddled together in the card of to-day he will scatter his guesses all over the ticket of to-morrow, or he will paint them in the form of a cross or circle, as the fancy seizes him. He is full of whims and oddities, and is as much a slave to systems of play as the American roulette or faro gambler. The Chinaman will talk freely with you about his luck. He will tell you that he has not hit the right numbers for a month, or that he made fifty dollars a fortnight ago, and he will show you the numbers he was successful with. The dream of his life is to paint on his ticket the very figures that the Chinaman behind the desk announces in his harsh monotone. Then if his stake was large he will be rich and may return to China and be mandarin. He is full of reminiscence of his lucky days, when he won perhaps three hundred dollars at one clean sweep. But he will admit with a bland smile and a show of teeth that he has lost every cent of it since at policy. As high as three thousand dollars in greenbacks has fallen at times to the lucky Mott Street policy-player. That means nothing less than shaking the dust of New York from the feet and travelling overland to San Francisco on the way home.

But the Chinamen who enrich themselves out of the game of policy are the proprietors of the shops. Profits fall into their laps very fast, and if they can keep their dens open without interference they are reasonably sure of fortune. The every-day gambler finds himself growing poorer and poorer. His blouses get to look shabby, he neglects his person, and his business goes to ruin. If he is wise he moves his laundry to the upper part of the city where it is a long cry to the Mott Street dens.

The favorite game of chance other than policy with the Chinese is fong tong. This is played on a table of matting about three feet high and eight feet in length for four in width. In the middle of it is a square drawn in thin black lines of paint; each side of the square is eighteen inches long, and is numbered one, two, three or four. The player puts down his money, say at the No. 1 side. Then the dealer or *croupier*, as he may be termed, pours a bowlful of Chinese copper coins on the table. With a black stick he separates from the pile four coins at a time, a number the same as the sides of the square. He may have removed twenty series of four when one coin remains, which signifies that a stake on the No. 1 side of the square has won. If two coins remain, the No. 2 side of the square has won. If the player places his chip or counter on a corner of the square he means that he desires two chances for his stake, for he is covering two sides of the square. He can win of course by this play less than if he were backing one chance out of four. All manners of combinations can be made on this simple square.

A popular gambling-house is crowded in the late hours of the evening. The Chinamen swarm in and surround the fong tong table. The place is fitted up as rudely as an opium den, but there is more space for breathing, more light, more talk and laughter. When the gamblers stand and sit in rows about the table of matting it is possible for them to place their stakes only on one side of the square, but they can designate a play on any side by using a little red pointer which they put beneath the counters. They are probably the most absorbed gamblers in the world. They hang on each play as if the fate of the human race hung on the issue, and they watch the *croupier* who parts the coins with the most jealous viglance. If he were to attempt to make the partition with his fingers there would be an outcry at once. He must use the black stick, which he manages as skilfully as he would the chop-sticks with a dish of rice.

The proprietors of the game not only have the benefit of the bad play of their patrons, but exact a percentage of their winnings. Americans are not admitted under any pretence. It has been said that they have sat at Chinese gambling tables in Celestial garments, but no one of sense will believe this, for the Chinaman is as keen-eyed as a lynx. And it might go hard with an American who penetrated into a gambling haunt in the dress of a Chinaman. Red is considered the lucky color by Chinamen. In all the decorations of their gambling dens, whether they are illuminated texts, rude pictures, or knots of silk, you will never see anything red. Walls and doors may be painted blue or green, but not red, for that color would surely mean ruin to the proprietor.

The Chinese, when engaged in playing games of chance day after day, are just as superstitious as the most ignorant negro who pins his faith to the "whip," "gig," or "saddle" of policy. If on his way to try his fortune at fong tong he meets a stranger who greets him pleasantly, he will have good luck. If he visits of an evening and refreshments are set before him, he can go to a gambling-house with impunity after leaving his host. If he dreams of the color red, or sees a conflagration or gorgeous sunset in his sleep, he will have luck at the fong tong table. But if his eye falls on a dead body during the day he will shun games of chance until the effect has passed off. If he has had a quarrel he does not dare to stake his money. On his way to play he will never lend a cent of his capital, for that too would be an evil omen. Gold he may dream about and win, but not so of silver. To dream of blue is also unfortunate. And then he has the same queer notions while at the fong tong square as his American brother at faro. If he is losing and an acquaintance leans on his shoulder or puts a foot on his chair he strenuously objects, believing that the circumstance brings him bad luck. Two thousand dollars is said to be as much as a Chinaman ever won at fong tong at one sitting in New York. From one to eight hundred dollars is not an unusual winning. When a house has gained the reputation of bringing big profits to the proprietor straightway his rent is raised, and no Chinaman thinks it an extortion. The Celestial who can renounce the gambling table after a turn of good fortune usually puts his gains into a laundry and is content to work from daybreak to late at night if he can spend Sunday in Mott Street.

The social evil prevails among the Chinese in New York to an extraordinary degree, despite the fact that the half dozen native women are wives of Chinese merchants and are not prostitutes. In Pell Street and vicinity there are three houses of prostitution whose sole patrons are Chinamen. The inmates are Irish, American, German and Italian females who have fallen from one stage of degradation to another until they are more brute than human. Most of them, sad to say, are very young women. Their appearance is coarse, and their habits are anything but clean. One prominent man among the Chinese residents keeps a disorderly house, in which there are sixteen women. A cousin of his has been overheard to say that death would be the lot of any Chinaman who attempted to break up his nefarious traffic.

But the existence of these houses of prostitution is by no means the blackest feature of the loose life of Mott Street. Young girls of from fifteen to eighteen years of age are in the habit of visiting the laundries of their own free will for immoral purposes. Some of them not only support themselves by this practice but supply the means of dissipation to some chosen male friend. It is a shocking thing to write down the fact that there are wretches low enough to accept money from girls who administer to the lusts of Chinamen, but such is the fact, well known to persons who live in the vicinity of Mott Street. If contempt goes out to these brutalized females what odium is black enough for their white accomplices. It is from this latter class that the worst element in the city is recruited; boys and men who haven't one vestige of manhood, who are ready to steal, stab and shoot without provocation, and who are too drenched in moral iniquity to be held in check except by the discipline of the penitentiary.

The moon-faced, gentle Chinaman who plies his iron all day and slips through the streets fearful of contact with the rude American is an easy victim to the wiles of the immoral white woman. An intelligent Chinaman, who dresses like a European and talks English fluently, once pointed out to a friend of mine a pert young woman in an elevated train.

"That girl," said the Chinaman, " who is less than twenty years of age, wheedled an acquaintance of mine out of eight hundred dollars which he had got together after years of painful toil in his laundry. It all went in three months, and then the girl went her way and the poor Chinaman had to begin the world over again. Such cases are not uncommon."

In New York City there are fifteen Chinamen who are married to American women. They belong to the progressive class of Chinamen who have learned English and have abandoned all idea of returning to the Flowery Kingdom. The women in most cases have made excellent wives, and show as much affection for their offspring as if the blood in their veins ran pure. The children are usually bright and active. They are taught to speak English and attend the public schools. The ignorant Chinese element who raise the barrier of their tongue and creed between themselves and the hated Americans are bitterly opposed to this intermarriage. Not only in their minds does it mean treachery to their country and the faith of their fathers, but it implies that the husbands are preferred by the white women to themselves. Jealousy, by the way, is the ruling passion in the Chinese breast. The Chinese consul in New York is of course a foe to intermarriage, on the ground that the domicile of the husband in America must be the result.

Perhaps the most interesting feature of Chinese life in New York is the social intercourse of these people as seen in the great joss house, their restaurants and lounging places. The joss house used to be a dingy tenement on Mott Street, but a year ago the tea and grocery merchants, having waxed rich and generous, resolved to give their god an elaborate and reverential temple. The distrust of Americans was so deep-seated that none of our skilled workmen were thought worthy of being entrusted with the plainest piece of upholstery or decorative work. An order for the image of the joss, his shrine, and all the embellishments that were to surround him was sent to China. The cost of the god and temple was to be eight hundred dollars. In due time he arrived and was received with imposing ceremony. The Chinese merchants leased the second floor of a building on Chatham Street near Mott, and the joss was at once put in possession. The room in which he looks out from a screen, night and day, is about thirty feet square. It is gaudily fitted up, and is kept as neat as pious hands can keep it. The joss himself sits in a gorgeous shrine of carved wood, mounted with gold. The setting is most fantastic and bewildering. Birds, dragons, antediluvian animals, serpents, crabs and fishes burst out all over the front of the shrine. Almost veiled from view, the joss peers out on the worshipper. He is painted on carved wood, and is as hideous a deity as was ever seen in the most frenzied of opium dreams. In front of the shrine stands a table— a handsome one, with all the appliances of worship upon it. Worship takes the form of burning scented sticks and paper, which is done constantly by pious Chinamen and by Chinamen of irregular habits when the good-will of the joss is desired. Something very curious on that table is the wooden augur, as it might be called.

It consists of two pieces of wood, each shaped like the half of a pear. When the devout Celestial wishes to know the humor of the joss towards an enterprise or journey he kneels before the table, takes the pieces of wood in his hands, and invoking the pleasure of the god drops them on the floor. If the pieces both fall with the flat sides uppermost the joss regards the enterprise or journey favorably; but if the rounded sides show uppermost the joss is inflexibly opposed to the purpose of his communicant. Before the god an oil lamp burns day and night. It is tended by the clerk of the temple, who also sweeps and cleans the room. On the walls are painted mythological scenes; among them you may see the Chinese Santa Claus, a bald-headed man of very benevolent aspect. Handsomely illuminated texts from Confucius in rich frames are everywhere, and from their corners hang bows of silk of colors considered to be auspicious by the Chinamen. Of course, red predominates. The costly furnishing of the room, however, is found in the magnificent two-armed ebony chairs, elaborately carved. The carving was done by hand, and occupied the artists several years. There are a dozen or more of these chairs in a row. The great merchants and teachers of the Chinese colony sit in them on feast days and occasions of solemn conclave. Strange to say, the joss house is not only a place of worship, but a meeting-hall for the consideration of questions affecting the material welfare of the god's worshippers. It was not long ago that the expediency of printing laundry tickets in both American and Chinese characters was discussed in the temple. The unprogressive element opposed the reform and killed the measure. Quite a number of Chinamen are susceptible to Christian teachings and are seldom seen in the house of the god. It is said that the respectable class among them are joining the Baptist and other churches. Upwards of two thousand Chinese now attend the Sunday-schools of New York.

There are three Chinese restaurants on Mott Street; the chief and best of them is called the King Flower House. Banners and great bows of colored silk wave from the second story under the name of this place of entertainment. The restaurant is on the second floor, and on your way up you pass a policy shop with its wooden walls and cage of railings. Colors trikes the eye on the first entrance into the dining-room, gaudy words of welcome, verses in strange characters and florid pictures of Chinese women, gardens and mountains. On one side an opium divan and enclosure attracts the attention. It is encircled with painted railings that run up to the ceiling, and contains easy pillows and the bright little sweet-oil lamps. Very high black tables and chairs are set about the room and the bill of fare in Chinese is pasted on the wall. The kitchen, with its pots, pans and ware, is in plain view through two doors in the rear. In the outer room half a dozen chickens are hanging to hooks, and beneath them, on a large table, dishes full of liver, scraps of pork, Chinese maccaroni and fish are to be seen. The cooks and waiters who whisk about their duties are conspicuous for their loose attire and their indifference to cleanliness. But you will be safe in ordering a bowl of tea, which you will find to have an exquisite flavor. The Chinese sweets and cakes, however, are sickening to the American palate. The tea is not brought in a pot, but in a bowl covered over with a saucer, and a cup is brought with it. After it is filled the saucer is replaced on the bowl. No sugar or milk are used. A Chinaman would be horrified at the bare thought. His favorite dish is boiled chicken or roast pork cut into fragments and thrown into a heap of a peculiar maccaroni which the cook makes himself. With a pair of chop-sticks the diner transfers the food to his mouth with a quick moment and great relish. He is content with the toughest kind of chicken. When he has finished his repast he may try a pipe of opium on the divan. While he eats, it is likely that his attendant will lie down in the railed inclosure and smoke three or four pipes, the while keeping up a running talk with the man at the table. In the King Flower restaurant you may see an elfish little Chinese-American girl, who talks English very fast and is as pert as you please. She is a great favorite with the Chinamen, who always play with her when they come in. On very great occasions—as, for instance, a banquet to the Chinese consul—the tooth of the epicure is tempted with shark's fin, bird-nest soup and mushrooms, all imported from China.

The great feast season is at New Year's, which falls in our February. Then for ten days the Chinamen give themselves up to unrestrained revelry, which to our notions is noisy but very orderly. Then the Celestials gather from all the adjoining cities and feast on roast ducks and unpronounceable Chinese sweets, washed down with their home whiskey, which no American can taste without nausea. Drums, gongs and cymbals wake the echoes of Mott

Street every afternoon and evening, and fireworks sizzle and flash in the sky. Hideous kites of glaring colors float above the garrets of the tenement houses, and Chinamen and street urchins cheer them as they ascend. The prominent merchants close up their shops for three days, and fling themselves, like boys, into the general celebration. Our Christmas is also observed, but more as a season of social calls than as a single day of good cheer. The Chinese then pay visits, and leave cards nearly a foot long in immense red envelopes. Sunday is the conventional day for social gatherings. A Chinaman would think he had passed it ill if he did not journey to Mott Street, smoke his cigar in the store of his friend, the tea merchant, chat about old times, and dine at one of the restaurants. On Sunday, too, he makes his purchases for the following week. His critics say that he really appears in Mott Street only to play policy and fong tong and to smoke opium, and there is a shade of truth in the assertion.

The Chinese, on the whole, if allowed to practise their vices unmolested are orderly members of the community. That the majority of them are incurable gamblers and beings of a low moral tone is unfortunately true, but they mind their own business as they understand it and are never guilty of ruffianism. Even among themselves the bully and swashbuckler is a rare exception. They never appear in the police courts except as complainants against ruffians who have damaged their property or brutally assaulted them. While they are absurdly suspicious of the most amiable American they are very sensitive to kindness, and display the utmost good temper in return. They are keenly afraid of ridicule, and always suspect it in gestures or expressions that they do not understand. To laugh or jibe at a Chinaman is to earn his undying enmity. He would never consent to let an artist draw his picture from the dread that it would find its way into a comic journal.

In their intercourse with one another they exhibit one serious imperfection of character. They are as jealous as women, and nearly all their wrangles may be laid to this fact. If a Chinaman is unusually successful in business, love or pleasure on Mott Street, he is never in haste to announce it to his almond-eyed friends. It is the shiftless Chinaman who creeps along the even tenor of his way who does not raise enemies on every side.

There are, as has been said, between six and seven thousand Chinese in this city. The work of religious and humane societies among them has worked great changes in the last few years. To-day the respectable Chinaman goes to Sunday-school and puts on American clothing without fear of persecution, and he has become ashamed of gambling. There is an earnest wish and effort among them to stamp this evil out, and by living moral lives to prove themselves worthy of the good-will of Americans and the privilege of citizenship.

CHAPTER XXXI.

ABORTIONISTS.—MADAM RESTELL'S PALACE OF WICKEDNESS.—A RAID BY ANTHONY COMSTOCK.—SUICIDE IN A BATH TUB.—THE NAKED CORPSE FOUND IN A TRUNK.—A SHRIEK WHICH STARTLED THE COURT.—" FOR GOD'S SAKE, SPARE MY POOR FRANK."

IN a luxurious residence, built in the most fashionable part of the city, and equalled in magnificence by few structures which wealth and taste have erected, was ended in April 9, 1878, the career of the most infamous female criminal ever known in New York. She was found lying in her bath-tub, which was partly filled with warm water dyed crimson by the blood which flowed from the woman's neck. She had severed her jugular vein, and her weapon, a huge carving-knife, lay blood-stained on the bathroom floor.

The woman who thus ended her life was Madam Restell, known to the police as the most famous abortionist this country has ever seen. Forty years of infamy were behind her; how small and insignificant the crime of suicide must have appeared! Forty years nourishing the most inhuman of vices! Alas! how many murders must that female fiend account for on that dreadful day of reckoning! How many mothers shall rise up in that day and call her—*damned!* She was the very personification of infamy. Under the mask of wealth and refinement she encouraged young women to offer themselves up on the altar of lust, and she made vice easy for those who wished to follow it. Her patrons from the wealth and fashion of the metropolis flocked to her, and they laid their money at her feet. Her services she knew were invaluable; she could charge what she wished and it was paid. A young woman comes to her to prevent the disgrace which would fall after the exposure of indiscretions. A wife of fashion and society comes because she is too cowardly and too selfish to perform her duty as a mother. The little one who would have brightened her household never knows what it is to breathe the air of life.

Man, too, comes to this foul creature and implores her attention to the young girl he has ruined. To them all the hardened reprobate appears courteous and sympathetic. Sure of her fee she undertakes the filthy work.

The career of Madam Restell is like a horrible romance. She was born in England, and married at the age of sixteen. Her real name was not Restell; she got that in Paris and brought it back with her. Her first husband was a worthless fellow, and he died a few years after the marriage. The widow came to this country

MADAM RESTELL.
(From a Photograph.)

and began earning her living as a dressmaker in Greenwich Street. She was handsome, bright and well informed. In the course of her experience as a needle-woman she became acquainted with many nice people. One family in particular were so pleased with her that they induced her to go abroad with them as governess for their children. Paris captivated her and she decided to make it her home. She fell in with a quack doctress who professed to have certain secret remedies whose properties were marvellous. Madam Restell thought she would like to come back to America and grow rich out of the weaknesses of the citizens of New York as her Parisian friend had out of the weaknesses of the French metropolis. So back she came, and with her certain recipes for producing abortions. To assist her in her cold-blooded scheme she married Charles R. Lohman, better known as Dr. Mauricna, an abortionist.

This was in 1837. She took up her residence on Greenwich Street, near Cortlandt, and advertised as a "physician." New York was more Puritanic in those days than it is now, and, I am glad to say, such an occupation was much more repulsive then to the average citizen than it is now. Accordingly this new abortionist discovered that she had obstacles to contend with, and in those early days she learned to get influence as well as shekels. She was frequently arrested, but each time the indictments would be suppressed by a liberal use of both money and influence. But in 1847 she was not so fortunate. Joseph C. Cook, a manufacturer, had seduced a young girl employed in his factory, named Maria Bodine. To avoid any unpleasant consequences he had taken the girl to Madam Restell for treatment. The young woman was attended to and went home. Afterward she became ill and confessed everything.

Upon the facts thus gained were based a complaint and warrant against the abortionist. She was arrested, tried and convicted, but not without a struggle. She brought into play every weapon she could use. She invoked influence, she employed eminent counsel and she spent money freely; but it was all in vain. She went to the Island to spend a year. She behaved like no ordinary prisoner, however, in her island home. Money bought her luxuries here as it had elsewhere, and she lived in handsome style for a convict. Her husband was with her frequently.

When her term here had expired she came back to her old quarters on Greenwich Street, and carried on her business more vigorously than ever. She also became more notorious than ever. Archbishop Hughes denounced her from the pulpit of St. Patrick's Cathedral. Later in her life she got even with him. When the site of the new cathedral was bought, and the archbishop designed to build the Episcopal residence at Fifty-second Street and Fifth Avenue, Madam Restell stepped in, and, after running the property up to a price beyond its value, bought it.

SUICIDE OF MADAM RESTELL.

Here was built the magnificent house in which the female abortionist was found dead on the morning of April 9, 1878. It stands there to this day. Handsomely built, luxuriously furnished, it was a model of comfort and ease. Here she not only sold articles and instruments for procuring abortions and preventing conceptions, but she received as patients in her house such women as desired treatment and could afford the expense. Her charges were exorbitant, but as her patrons were from the wealthy classes she was able to accumulate an enormous fortune. At her death it was estimated that she was worth a million dollars.

The immediate cause of her suicide was undoubtedly her arrest by Anthony Comstock, who in searching her house procured evidence enough both in persons and things to secure her conviction. Her lawyers alleged that the knowledge of this and the memory of her many dark crimes so weighed on her mind as to make her insane, but there seems to have been too much method for madness in her suicide. Her property was divided between her grandson and granddaughter, the latter of whom married a young lawyer of this city. A woman was driven up to the door of the Hudson River Railroad on the afternoon of August 26, 1871. She nervously alighted, walked rapidly to the baggage master's room, and asked to have a certain trunk checked to Chicago. She learned that no train left until night, and then she disappeared from the neighborhood of the depot.

The trunk which she had spoken of was taken care of in its turn. The baggage men took hold of it and were carrying it to a pile of trunks destined for the West, when they noticed a horrible stench. Their suspicions of something wrong were at once aroused. A cold chisel was procured and the attempt was made to wrench the top of the trunk off. After much prying the cover was raised. The baggage men drew back as if shot. A sickening sight met their glance and a foul odor filled the room. There in the trunk was disclosed the naked body of a full grown woman. It lay on its right side, with the legs doubled up and the head bent forward so that the face and knees almost met. A lovely mass of golden hair tumbled in confusion over features whose beauty was not entirely concealed by the lines which pain and suffering had drawn thereon. The corpse was slightly decomposed. Here was a mystery—an ugly burden which the baggage masters wished to have removed as soon as possible. They called in the police. I saw, as soon as I heard of it, that this was an exceptional crime, and accordingly I put my best detectives at work to ferret out the perpetrators.

It was necessary first to find the truckman who had brought the trunk to the depot. This would have been no easy task in itself, and unless this link in the chain of evidence had been found, I fear it might have been impossible for us to solve the mystery of

DR. ROSENZWEIG.
(From a Photograph.)

the cramped corpse. Officers were immediately detailed in search of the truckman and all the customary steps were taken to get upon his track. But our labors in this direction were lightened by the voluntary coming forward of the man himself. News of the matter reaching him in some way or other, he came to Captain Brennan and frankly told him all he knew about the mystery. It was soon found that the man himself was innocent of any conspiracy that might be behind the matter, and he readily told us from what house he had brought the body. This, he said, was No. 687 Second Avenue. The house was carefully watched by my detectives, who finally thought they had evidence enough upon which to arrest the proprietor. Their suggestion was carried out, and very soon Dr. Ascher, alias Rosenzweig, a notorious abortionist, found himself behind prison bars.

The body in the trunk was identified as that of Alice Augusta Bowlsby, a charming and beautiful young woman, who had resided

ALICE AUGUSTA BOWLSBY.
(From a Photograph.)

with her parents in Paterson, N. J. Pieces of underclothing marked with the initials "A. A. B." were found on Rosenzweig's premises. When this discovery was made known the excitement in Paterson was very great. A young man named Conkling, with whom the unfortunate girl had kept company, put a bullet through his brain in order that he might die rather than face the ordeal and disgrace of appearing as a witness.

Rosenzweig's trial came on in the following October. Public interest was intense. All through the trial the court-room was crowded with spectators eager to hear the disgusting testimony which came from witnesses. Rosenzweig's lawyers worked hard for their client. The result of the trial was extremely uncertain. Finally, the opposing counsel had offered their argument, the judge had delivered his charge and the jury filed out of the room. Among those who awaited its verdict was Rosenzweig's little daughter, about ten years old, who was very fondly attached to her father and had remained in court during the whole of his trial.

After a reasonable length of time there was a stir near the door, a buzz ran round the room, followed by a silence like death, and the jurors walked in single file to their seats.

"Have you agreed upon a verdict?" asked the clerk.

Rosenzweig held his head down, but his little daughter's was raised in expectation.

"We have," returned the foreman. "We find the prisoner guilty."

As he pronounced the word "guilty" an unearthly shriek pierced the room, startling the court and terrifying the spectators, and Rosenzweig's daughter fell to the floor unconscious.

The prisoner was sentenced to seven years in the State prison. Subsequently a new trial was granted him, which never took place, in consequence of a change in the law.

A messenger came to Inspector Murray on February 10, 1879, and told him that a woman was dying from malpractice at No. 161 East Twenty-seventh Street. The house was a suspicious one, for it was known to be the residence of Mrs. Bertha Burger, an abortionist. Inspector Murray notified Coroner Flanagan, who with his deputy, and with Sergeant Meekim and Roundsman O'Toole, went to the house and made an investigation. A sad and wicked state of affairs was brought to light. Cora Sammis, a girl, young, beautiful and not long since pure and innocent, was the woman who had been said to be dying. She lay in a poorly furnished room and was surrounded by no comforts. Very different was the house of this abortionist from that of Madam Restell. Here were no soft carpets, luxurious beds and chairs, with servants to heed every wish and cooks to tempt the appetite with delicacies. Mrs. Burger's patients were women in lower grades of life than Madam Restell's, and they could not pay such large fees. No wonder then that they did not receive such good care.

Six months before that night when police officers raided this house to save a dying soul, Cora Sammis had been a bright and pretty country girl at Northport, Long Island. Her father was a well-to-do coal and lumber dealer. Cora went to Sunday-school, and not the shadow of a suspicion was ever breathed against her. In the summer time she met many New Yorkers who came there to spend the hot months, and among the number was one Frank Cosgrove, who was employed in an office at No. 2 Burling Slip. Cosgrove was taken with the girl's charms. Acquaintance ripened into friendship and friendship into love. Passion played a part too and this was what caused Cora Sammis's ruin and death. In December Cora came to Brooklyn to visit an aunt, and Cosgrove saw a great deal of her there. To prevent an exposure of her weakness it was arranged that she should go to the abortionist, Mrs. Burger.

She went, and the abominable practice which this ignorant woman brought to bear upon her case made her so ill that she died. Her last words to the officers who had come to her rescue were:

"For God's sake, spare my poor Frank!"

"Poor Frank" was saved from punishment by law, but not from the misery and remorse of his own soul.

Mrs. Burger was arrested, as were also her married daughter, Rachel Davis, who lived in the same house, and Jennie Williams and Minnie Russell, who were supposed to act largely as Mrs. Burger's agents. Much evidence besides that yielded by Cora Sammis's case came to light, and showed for what degrading purposes this house was used. I rejoice to be able to say that this worse than female devil suffered the penalty of her crimes in prison.

CHAPTER XXXII.

FRAUDS ON INSURANCE COMPANIES.—A NOTABLE INSTANCE.—ERNST ULING AND HIS CLEVER SCHEMES.—CONVULSIONS AND SOAP.—A LIVELY CORPSE.—WHAT THE COFFIN CONTAINED.—THE LAST SAD RITES OVER NINETEEN BRICKS.—HID UNDER THE BED.—A FULL CONFESSION.—FINK, THE UNDERTAKER.—STATE'S PRISON FOR BOTH.

FRAUDS on insurance companies have but rarely come under my observation, but one which occurred in 1874 is certainly deserving of mention. The organization sought to be defrauded was the Merchants' Life Insurance Co., of this city, of which Mr. B. F. Beekman was president at the time. The individual charged with the fraud was a Hungarian doctor named Ernst Uling, *alias* De Bagnicki, who had just previously been accused of malpractice on a woman by the name of Louise Germs, with whom he had a mutual policy of $10,000 in the company in question. It was alleged by Uling that the woman, to whom he professed to be devotedly attached, died while under treatment for a uterine complaint; and he attempted to collect the money on the policy. The officers of the company were somewhat suspicious that all was not as it should be, and inquiries were quickly set on foot to sift the matter to the bottom. The coffin in which Louise was said to have been buried was exhumed from the Union Cemetery, and taken to the New York Morgue, where a Dr. Leo was to hold a post-mortem examination. The fastenings of the coffin were set in white lead, and were removed with difficulty; and when the lid was opened nineteen bricks, wrapped in newspapers and secured in place by laths, were found symmetrically and tightly packed in the bottom of the coffin, which was a very handsome one. The usual trimmings were unsoiled, and there was no indication that a body had ever been placed in it. In view of this discovery, the police authorities were communicated with, and Superintendent Matsell immediately ordered that Uling be arrested, together with Chas. Fink, the undertaker. The latter upon being taken into custody, stated that the coffin was ordered by Uling, and that he had seen the body of a woman placed in it, he himself screwing down the lid. The plate on the coffin bore the following inscription:

" Louise Greimet, died March 30, 1874, aged twenty-three years, three months."

Detectives Tilley and Heidelburg were detailed to work up the case, and they at once decided to call at the apartments formerly occupied by Uling, at No. 160 Eldridge St. Knocking at the door produced no response, and the officers were trying to open one of the doors with a key, when a quaint, livid-featured old lady, apparently about sixty-five years of age, together with a long, ungainly lad, made their appearance. The female said her name was Marie de Bagnicki, while the lad was her nephew—Aurel de Szent-Ivanyi. Both were Hungarians, and could speak but very little English. In the apartments were a quantity of clothes, linen, and documents, which were being packed up ready for removal. The woman said these things all belonged to Uling, notwithstanding the fact that the linen was marked " E. B." When questioned concerning the death of Louise Germs, the old lady became very reticent, but finally said that if the officers went to Mrs. Janitzky, No. 228 East Twenty-fifth St., they might learn something about Uling. Tilley and Heidelburg accordingly went to the address given, but were informed by Mrs. Janitzky that she knew nothing about Uling. During a search of the premises, however, the officers entered a small hall bed-room in the rear of the second floor. Upon the bed was a man's hat, and looking underneath the couch Uling was discovered, in his shirt sleeves and crouched up in a most uncomfortable position. He was quickly pulled from his hiding-place. At the station-house he was searched and the officers found on him a number of papers, amongst which was a portrait of the alleged dead woman, Louise Germs. The next day, following up a clew furnished by some memoranda found on Uling, the detectives visited the house of Mrs. Wechsler, No. 133 One Hundred and Ninth St. They were admitted by Mrs. Wechsler, and Detective Tilley, while entering, saw a woman peep out at the area gate. He took a second glance at her and immediately recognized her as the original of the photograph found in Uling's possession. The officers informed Mrs. Wechsler of the nature of their errand, and Louise Germs, *alias* Greimet, was called into the parlor and placed under arrest. At first she took her arrest in a very nonchalant manner, saying she had learned all about the case from the newspapers; but on the way to the station-house she burst into tears and lamented bitterly the result of her conduct, as also the pain it would cause her father, who believed her to be dead. At police headquarters she made a full confession of the whole conspiracy. Her story was that when the insurance policy was taken out by Uling, she, notwithstanding the fact that she was examined by the physicians of the insurance company, believed she was passing for another woman, who was to simulate death, and thus enable Uling to draw the amount of the policy. In December of the previous year (1873), she was very intimate with Uling, and became sick. Her illness was a serious one, and Uling called in a Dr. Kranowitch, who prescribed for her. The following March she had entirely recovered, and Uling offered her $2500 if she would simulate death and enable him to obtain the amount of the policy from the insurance company. He told her exactly what to do, and then called in Dr. Kurtz, who found her apparently in strong convulsions and foaming at the mouth. Dr. Kurtz pronounced her case a desperate one and left. As soon as the door closed on him she jumped out of bed and burst into a hearty laugh. She had placed a piece of soap in her mouth to produce the froth, and had acted so well as to deceive Dr. Kurtz, who was a reputable practitioner. On March 29, Uling made preparations for the funeral, giving Fink the order for the coffin, which was taken to No. 160 Eldridge Street, and placed on trestles by an assistant, who then went away, leaving Fink to place the supposed corpse in its last resting-place. Louise, who was lying on a bed with a sheet over her, then jumped up and frightened Fink considerably. Uling took him on one side and told him he had a pecuniary interest in Louise's death; that he had mistaken syncope for dissolution, and that his affairs were so embarrassed he was obliged to make it appear that she had died. He offered Fink $250 to assist him, and after some haggling he agreed. Mrs. Marie de Bagnicki then brought in the bricks, and when they had been arranged in the coffin, Fink went back to his shop, procured two strong slats, and fastened them with screws, so that the bricks could not be displaced. Then the coffin was sealed up with white lead as before described. Louise Germs changed her name to "Marie Ley" and took service with a family in Orchard Street, where she remained two days. The "funeral" took place on April 1, at Union Cemetery. This was all she knew; she was completely in the dark as to who attended the funeral of the nineteen bricks.

Before being taken to court, Louise was standing in the corridor when Uling and Fink were brought out of their cells. The former made a sign for her to be silent and then sat down in a manner suggestive of indifference to his fate. Fink acknowledged the truth of Louise's story, and appeared much cast down at his position.

In appearance Uling was apparently about forty years of age, stoutly built, florid countenance, and passably good looking. Louise was a rather interesting little woman, about twenty-five years of age, with decided German features. She had small eyes, high cheek bones and forehead, a pale complexion, and a small, pretty mouth.

As far as could be ascertained, Uling belonged to a noble Hungarian family, and once held a commission in the Hungarian army. In 1845 his position was one of affluence, but he appeared to have spent all his money. He was well educated, and must have studied medicine thoroughly. It was presumed that in 1852 his fortune became exhausted, and after visiting England and France, where he practised medicine, he came to this country in 1854. His career in New York was a checkered one. In May, 1861, he was tried in the Court of General Sessions for swindling Elizabeth Altenhein, of No. 85 West Seventeenth Street, out of $417, but was acquitted. The following year he was tried on a charge of forgery, but a *nol. pros.* was entered. This prosecution arose out of a patent held by Uling, for which letters patent were granted in England. The facts of the case are not obtainable, but the charge was instigated by Uling's agent in Paris, where the invention was favorably received by Dr. Ricord and the faculty of the Hospital Beaujon. Uling had also been "in trouble" in regard to debts contracted with various parties, and papers found upon him at the time of his arrest showed that for some years prior to 1874 his practice had been far from reputable. Only $50 was found in his possession, and as no money or valuables were found at his house, it is fair to conclude that he was not in very good circumstances. After these and other papers had been examined, Fink was taken to Bagnicki's cell and identified him as the person who ordered and superintended the funeral of Louise Germs.

Fink stoutly maintained that when the coffin was taken to No. 160 Eldridge Street he saw the dead body of a woman. Bagnicki asked him to help put her in the coffin. Fink caught hold of her legs and noticed that they were very limp. He remarked to the doctor that the body was scarcely cold, and asked how long the woman had been dead. Bagnicki replied: "Twenty-four hours." Fink thereupon closed the lid of the coffin, screwed it down, and receiving $40 on account of a bill of $50, left. He was shown the portrait of Louise Germs, but could not positively identify it as that of the woman he put in the coffin. At the funeral there was a woman closely veiled, but she remained in the carriage the whole time. She resembled the portrait of Louise Germs, but Fink thought that her features were longer and broader. Then Mme. Marie de Bagnicki was questioned, and frankly acknowledged that she was the wife of Bagnicki; but on account of her age she had given him permission to marry again whenever he thought proper. She identified the portrait of Louise Germs as that of a person she had seen, but she pretended not to know her name or to have had any acquaintance with her. She remembered that one of Bagnicki's patients died at 160 Eldridge Street; she knew this to be true, as she went into the room and saw the corpse laid out on a bed. She did not know the deceased woman's name. The reason why Bagnicki adopted the name of Uling was because his real name was so difficult of pronunciation. When told that her husband had been arrested, a twitching of the corners of the mouth and a momentary spasm were the only signs of nervousness that she exhibited during the examination to which she was subjected. When asked what induced her to pack up her husband's clothes and papers, she replied she thought from what had been published in the newspapers that he had left the city and that she would have to seek a new home. She also declared that she could not recollect where she last saw Bagnicki.

The coffin containing the nineteen bricks was placed on view in the day-room of the detectives' office, where it was an object of curiosity to the police commissioners and several hundred private individuals. Louise was brought from her cell and laughed heartily at seeing what was supposed to be her last resting-place, remarking that she had no doubt but that there were many people in New York who wouldn't object to purchasing the bricks as relics at high prices.

The case was tried before Recorder Hackett in July, 1874. Louise was admitted as a witness on behalf of the State, and Uling and Fink were each sentenced to eighteen months' imprisonment in Sing Sing. Louise was discharged upon her own recognizances.

Of the subsequent careers of the parties concerned in this most extraordinary instance of attempted fraud I have no positive knowledge; but doubtless Uling and Louise are now, if they are not dead, still living together.

CHAPTER XXXIII.

BEGGARS.—THE DUDE MENDICANT.—FROM BEGGING TO THIEVING.—TILL TAPPERS.—SNEAK THIEVES ROBBING RUFUS LORD.—SHOPLIFTING.—HOW THE "CONFIDENCE" GAME IS WORKED.—CATCHING A TARTAR.—THE USE OF DRUGS BY THIEVES.—A MISTAKEN IDEA.

There are all kinds of beggars in New York, despite the efforts of the Mendacity Society, the Charity Organization Society and other kindred organizations. By their agents, mendicants are traced to their haunts, their claim to charity investigated, and should it be discovered that they are impostors they are prosecuted. If these persons are caught in the act of begging they are arrested and taken to the nearest police court, from whence they are sent to places of industry under the city's care.

The tramp-beggar is the genus most commonly met. He makes his appearance on the street just about the time the street lamps are lighted and honest, hard-working citizens are going home from their labor. Usually a tramp-beggar has a very hoarse voice and a half-starved countenance. He informs you, in what is intended to be a very pathetic manner—but which isn't—that he is out of work, can't get any and has quick consumption. Pay no attention to his: "May I ask a favor of you?" or "Mister, would you kindly—." He is a fraud. Another favorite excuse is that the applicant only needs a nickle or a dime to make up a sufficient amount to pay for his night's lodging; but the chances are that he has more ready cash in his pocket than the person addressed.

Then there is what may be called the chronic beggar, who is found in the same place week after week and month after month. As a rule he is blind or crippled. Sometimes he carries in his hand a package of lead pencils, which are never sold; a bundle of envelopes or writing paper, which are never disposed of. It may be that he is equipped with a dilapidated music-box, asthmatical hand-organ, or some such instrument of torture. Others, and there are not a few of them, make no such pretence of earning a living, but come out boldly, tin cup or cigar box in hand, and ask the passer by for largess. Some of them are poor in reality and use the proceeds of their solicitations in a proper manner. Most of them, however, are frauds. Ladies do a great deal of harm by the thoughtless manner in which they give away their small change. The uglier and more horribly mutilated the beggar may be, the greater his chance of getting a goodly share of coppers. One

CAPTAIN ANTHONY J. ALLAIRE.
(From a Photograph. See page 101.)

blind fellow who had a "stand" on Second Avenue for a considerable time was followed to a room in a house in Tenth Avenue one evening, where he handed over his day's receipts—something more than $16—to a number of gamblers.

Then there are the letter-writing beggars. They are very genteel, and from a comparatively comfortable home send out the most heart-rending and pathetic letters regarding their piteous condition. The names and addresses of all the benevolently disposed individuals in the city are at these persons' fingers' ends, and a mistake is rarely made in the character of the person addressed. The heart of the philanthropist or merchant is generally touched by the tale of woe, and without waiting to investigate the truth of the letter he encloses a bank-note in an envelope and the beggar laughs in his sleeve at the credulity of the giver. Not a few women are engaged in this manner of soliciting, and they make a very good living out of it.

Of late years a new genius has made its appearance—the dude beggar. A young man who did not look to be more than twenty five years old sauntered down Broadway one night in 1880. His light overcoat covered a shapely form, his head was crowned with a derby hat of recent fashion. A pair of eye-glasses rested on his nose. One hand was hidden in a neat driving-glove and from the other hand dangled its mate. Altogether, his appearance was that of a natty young man just returning from a late call—for it was midnight. All this was noticed by a tired New Yorker, who was overcome with surprise when this exceedingly fine young man stepped up with:

"Would you kindly assist me, sir, with a few pennies, that I may get a lodging for the night?"

"What?" gasped the almost dumb-struck citizen.

"I am entirely without funds. I have met with misfortune," suavely responded the young man.

Without attempting to reply, the person addressed pulled out a ten-cent piece. When the movement towards the pocket was made, the "dude beggar" lightened his voice of the stress of care and feeling that pervaded it at first.

"I only came over from England a month ago," he volunteered, "and am unable to find work. I am a machinist by trade. I have had no food since last night."

This observation was added when the silent transfer of the coin was made, and its small denomination became manifest in the bright rays of an adjacent electric light. The beggar hesitated a moment; then he touched his hat with a "Thank you," and quickened his pace down Broadway.

The loser by the transaction stood hesitating for a moment. Then he started in pursuit. The latter did not even turn around, and as his pursuer drew near wafted forth a contented whistle. He finally came to a brilliantly lighted saloon, into which he dodged with the familiarity of an old rounder. His follower caught him in the act of tossing off a sherry flip, for which he had thrown down a fifty-cent piece in payment.

His cheek did not pale when he saw the almoner before him. Indeed, he nodded his head in a sort of greeting.

"I admire you, now," said the New Yorker. To the bar-keeper, "I will take the same. Come, sit down. I want you to tell me all about it. Yes, that was with you. You pay."

The young man was led to an adjoining table, and after a little persuading, told his method of following the begging business.

"Since you have fairly cornered me, I will tell you about this affair. I was once a hard-working young man, but owing to circumstances I was thrown out of business and compelled to find means of sustenance as best I could. I had a few decent rags left," and he glanced affectionately at the neat top coat, and nudged with his chin the rather flaming necktie that encircled an upright collar.

"I had to get money somehow, and I took the method you have observed. I joined the ranks of the dude beggars. I am not ashamed of the term. A beggar is a beggar. Yes, there are others like me. You have not happened to meet them, that is all. Indeed, a little more and you would not have met me, as I go to Washington to-morrow. Congress is in session, you know, and it is really about the best time to visit the Capital.

"The success of my method—you are not the only one who has been kind to me to-night"—and the speaker proved his assertion without remark by giving his pocketful of coins a slap—"the success of my method is owing to the astonishment which affects those to whom I make my appeals. My appearance does not imply want or starvation, and when I tell my story the listener immediately concludes, as soon as he recovers himself, that I am telling the strict truth and have been caught without means. He goes away after making his donation feeling extremely well satisfied that he has at last hit upon a case deserving of true charity."

So much for the beggar, who, although not exactly a criminal, still preys upon society, and is not by any means a law-abiding citizen.

From professional begging to thieving is a very short step. As a rule, till-tapping is the ground on which young thieves —boys and youths—first practice. To be a successful till-tapper the boy must have both courage and daring. The way in which they work is as follows: Three or four boys enter a store, one after the other, being careful to select an hour when some of the clerks are absent. One or two of the party make a pretence of purchasing some small article, while the third—who it has been arranged previously shall secure the contents of the till—will probably ask to look at the directory. Sometimes one excuse is made and sometimes another, but if it is sufficient to turn the attention of the clerk for a moment or so, the trick is done and the thieves are off. Occasionally a till-tapper will operate alone, creeping in on his hands and knees behind the counter, and then make a bold dash for the street. But this is a dangerous bit of work, and is very rarely attempted.

Then the molasses trick is played. This is very amusing to everybody but the victim. Two of the thieves go to his store, laughing, carrying their hats in their hands. They tell him they have a bet on as to whose hat will hold the most molasses. He is to decide the bet by filling up one of the hats. But it will ruin the hat. Never mind; the winner can pay for a new one. So the obliging grocer pours in the molasses. At this interesting stage of the proceedings, a third conspirator enters the store and asks for the change of a quarter. The grocer goes to his till, and the moment his back is turned the hat containing the molasses is clapped dexterously on his head from behind. This is where the laugh comes in, for while he is groping about, blinded and half smothered by the sticky mass, his till is rifled of its contents and the thieves make good their escape.

Every commander of a precinct will agree with me in saying that the "mosquitoes" of police duty are the sneak thieves. They grade from the urchin who will snatch an apple from the front of a grocery store, to the clever, plausible, well-dressed fellow who will steal into a mansion like a shadow and disappear with the substance, leaving not a "wrack" behind. In such cases I can hardly blame the captain and his precinct detectives for just making an inquiry into the facts, and advising the householder to be more careful in the future. Of course sneak thieves of the better class could not exist unless there were receivers of stolen goods; while on the other hand there would be no arrests of first-class members of this class in the criminal world, without a friendly hint now and then from persons known to the police as receivers of their plunder. So that where a precinct commander wishes to gain occasional glory by the capture of a sneak thief he must, in gamblers' *parlance*, "play both ends against the middle"—that is, his conscience and reputation against "optional intelligence" in regard to persons he knows to be in league with the criminals.

Strangely enough, the most dangerous sneak thieves are those who work alone. Men have been in this "business" for years without being detected. They have no one to betray them except themselves, and they are generally faithful to their trust. Perhaps the most venturesome is the "second-story" man. In all my ex-

SPENCER PETTIS.
(From a Photograph.)

perience I think I can say truly that there have not been more than six of this class who have come under my notice. There may have been a dozen "working" during that time. If so, six have never come to grief. This is simply the result of the manner in which these "princes of larceny" manage their affairs. A "second-story" man is required to be shrewd, have an absolute knowledge of police methods, be an A 1 judge of human nature, know the ways of servants, profound in divining feminine artifices in respect to concealing valuables, expert in judging the value of precious stones, jewelry, and, but rarely, furs and garments—for these gentry make up their last in small packages, and do not care to appear bulky when returning from a marauding expedition. He must have great architectural instinct, and, above all, acrobatic ability. The hour of the "second-story" man is 6 P.M., in winter, and dusk in summer; but here it should be said that mid-summer business is neither safe or profitable. When dusk comes with the dinner hour, then is the "second-story" man's opportunity. His aim is to be above the inmates of the house when they are pleasantly engaged in discussing the evening meal. No one ever saw a "pursy," asthmatic or feeble "second-story" man. Take a circus acrobat, and you have his model. His aim is to reach a second-story window unobserved. That attained he will take care of himself. It is immaterial to him whether the window be open or shut, no catch ever devised can keep him out. His "tools" can be carried in his hat if necessary. They consist of a jimmy, not more than five inches long; nippers, a piece of candle, matches, a thin bladed glazier's knife; and, in some cases, a piece of paper smeared with Venice turpentine, molasses or any substance that will keep sticky and wet for a long time. This is used when it is necessary to break a pane of glass. A monkey in the tether of an Italian organ grinder is not more agile than a second-story man in ascending by means of window blinds, gutters, or anything which will afford finger or toe hold, or the grasp of an arm. A few seconds suffice to enter a window. Then a hasty survey of the field; and everything is comprehended at a glance.

A second-story man rarely opens anything which does not contain valuables. Few locks are proof against his jimmy. He rapidly stores his plunder in capacious pockets, often fitted with safety-flaps so that in descending to the ground, or in flight, nothing can fall out. An average of two minutes to a room is enough for his purpose. During this time he has to keep a sharp look-out for stray members of the household and a dog. If possible, he chooses other means of exit than those of his entry, so that a knowledge of the various fashions of protecting front doors comes in use. Once in the street, he never hurries until out of sight of the house he has plundered, except when pursued. In such an event he is always "clean" when the hand of the law is laid on him, having thrown his plunder away. I recollect three cases of conviction of such marauders. The very king of these specialists, after a wonderful career in respect to evading arrest, met his fate by the toppling over of a coping-stone, which fell on his head and killed him.

Next in rank is the first-class sneak thief who has no acrobatic ability, but who has a thorough knowledge of the science of opening front or basement doors, profiting from the carelessness of inmates, and occasionally venturing a descent through the coal chute or the scuttle on the roof. I remember the unearthing, in September, 1879, of one of the worst gangs of sneak thieves that ever made a police captain's life unhappy. The party was composed of Michael Murphy, George Leonard, Alexander Higgins, George Thompson and Arthur Dempsey. They had an ally in the person of John J. Sheridan, a liquor dealer, of No. 428 East Thirteenth Street. Their depredations startled the community. They were like the Irishman's flea. One day a robbery up town, next down town, then the east, then the west, and then in the centre of the city. At first no police officer could " place " them. Their principal " tracks " consisted of the following robberies: In August, at No. 47 East Ninth Street, at the residence of the Rev. Mancius C. Hutton. This was a " coal chute job." The house was vacant so far as residents were concerned, and the usual occupant, who was in the country, was an antiquarian. His rooms were crowded with objects of art, precious documents, old furniture, tapestries and books—some of them of great value. The thieves completely gutted the place. No band of brigands ever displayed less regard for property which would not pay for carrying away. When the robbery was discovered it was ascertained that the articles secured by the thieves were worth less than a thousand dollars. In getting this much they had done at least $5000 damage. They had turned over the contents of each apartment in order to select what was "negotiable," ripping, cutting, breaking and defiling what they did not want; and piling the rejected articles in the centre of the room. Only a day or two afterwards the members of the gang visited the residence of Mrs. Mary G. Duykinck. This raid netted them about a thousand dollars. Later, General J. Watts De Peyster was the sufferer. His quaint old home at No. 59 East Twenty-first Street was entered by the coal chute, and the property taken was worth " intrinsically " more than $3000. It included medals and other souvenirs, for which the General would have refused $10,000. Next in order was the robbery of No. 24 Lexington Avenue, the residence of Mr. J. Allen, of the firm of Allen & Dam (Astor House). Mr. Allen's loss was $2000. Then came Mr. T. A. Coakley's house, No. 268 West Twenty-fourth Street, loss, $1200. Then, Mrs. J. H. Billings's residence at No. 117 East Nineteenth Street, where trunks were rifled of property worth $700.

By chance, a week after, a policeman of the Twenty-ninth Precinct, arrested Murphy, Leonard and Higgins in the act of plun-

TIP LITTLE.
(From a Photograph.)

dering No. 140 West Thirty-fourth Street, the residence of Mr. F. C. Manning. The job was a coal chute one, and when Detectives King and Lyons heard of it they were active in examining and interrogating the prisoners. From what they learned, they became assured of the men's complicity in the other robberies mentioned. They found that one of them wore a shirt and necktie which had been taken from Mr. Allen's house. This led to the surveillance of men who might be reasonably supposed to associate with the prisoners; and so, ten days later, the officers had the satisfaction of arresting Thompson and Dempsey carrying valises which contained the bulk of the Duykinck property. Sheridan's connection with the thieves had by this time been more than suspected. It was safe now to explore his place. The result was satisfactory to the police. Not only was much of the other property found there, but also "stuff" obtained in other expeditions. Sheridan's private quarters were fitted up as a store-house, and the display of recovered goods, worth from seven to eight thousand dollars, at police headquarters, was about the best ever seen there. The prisoners were all convicted and sentenced to long terms of imprisonment.

One of the most important sneak thieving operations known in this country was that perpetrated on Rufus L. Lord, capitalist and owner of vast real estate in the neighborhood of Exchange Place. Lord was a financial curiosity, and his wealth in his later years could not have been less than $4,000,000. That he was economical there could be no doubt, and some persons called him a miser. There was some reason for this. At No. 38 Exchange Place he had what he called an "office." It was rather a den, presided over by this Crœsus. His ordinary attire consisted of garments which a first-class rag-picker would disdain to take from an ash-barrel, and, invariably, a pair of slippers which appeared to have done considerable service. The "fittings" of the office were as antique as the attire of its occupant. At the back of the room, behind his desk, he had constructed a fire-proof vault, in which were placed the deeds, accounts and books of his property, and also vast sums in bonds and securities. This vault was known to be so fire and burglar-proof that wealthy friends often asked permission to put their securities and money in it. Mr. Lord's end and aim in life was to amass wealth; he talked and dreamed of nothing else, and what work he did was confined to taking his securities and bonds from the safe, gloating over them and cutting off the coupons.

I well remember how, on the 7th of March, 1866, poor Mr. Lord came to grief. At that time he was almost in his dotage. He was blear-eyed, feeble, and absent-minded to the extent of frequently leaving his treasure unguarded and at the mercy of marauders. Upon one occasion he went home, leaving his office and safe open, with nearly $2,000,000 at the command of the first adventurer who came along. At another time, the janitor in cleaning up the place found the key of the vault in the wash-basin, where Mr. Lord had washed some grime from his usually dirty hands. He was deaf, garrulous, and his attention was easily distracted by any chance visitor who happened to call with a plan for making more money. Upon the date mentioned, Mr. Lord was busy as usual in his den. He was, it is believed, at the time concerning which I am about to relate, sorting coupons into bundles. Two plausible gentlemen called. They had visited him before, and were, therefore, not entire strangers to him. They were " Jack " Rand, *alias* " Greedy Jake," bank burglar and sneak, and so thoroughly dishonest that once, in a marauding expedition in Canada, he got the start of some confederates with whom he was to visit a bank, opened the cash receptacle himself, and got away with the plunder, leaving his " pals " in the lurch. Hence the sobriquet, " Greedy." The other worthy was Horace Ennis, commonly known as " Hod." Both hailed from Boston.

At the former visit these gentlemen had taken a good look at the room in which they were received, and had incidentally discovered Mr. Lord's many infirmities. It was easy, therefore, while they engaged his attention on the first visit, for " Ed." Pettengill, *alias* " Perkins," *alias* " Anderson," *alias* " Boston Pet," to glide into the den, take the key from the vault and obtain a wax impression of it. This was a precautionary measure. On the day of the crime there was no need of using the key which had been manufactured from the wax impression. Pettengill again glided in like a shadow, seized two tin boxes, as silently gliding out. He took with him negotiable and un-negotiable securities worth little less than $1,900,000! This is claimed to be the greatest " haul " ever made in this country by a sneak thief, and in my opinion the claim is a just one. The greater part of the securities—half a million of which belonged to a Mr. Barron—were as negotiable as a double gold eagle, being coupon bonds. For instance, there was a little matter of $275,000 in one bundle, of 7.3-10 per cents. Then there were forty $5000 bonds of the same denomination; a few 10-40, piles of 7-30's, a lot of Oregon War Debt, a quarter of a million in registered stock, sheaves of Warren Railroad stock, of New Jersey, Hartford and New Haven, Delaware, Lackawanna and Western; New Orleans Mechanics' and Traders' Bank, Columbia Marine Insurance, Manhattan Fire Insurance, John Scott bonds, Galena and Chicago first mortgage; St. Louis, Alton and Terre Haute second mortgage; and also income and interest bonds of the same railroad. On top of all there was $26,000 in six per cent. United States coupons.

When Mr. Pettengill had "done his end of the job," Messrs. Rand and Ennis bade Mr. Lord a courteous and dignified adieu.

Wall Street was convulsed by the magnitude and audacity of the crime, while Mr. Lord came very near dying from chagrin and mortification. Superintendent John A. Kennedy, Chief Detective John Young and his aides, as well as all the private detective agen-

JIMMY PRICE.
(From a Photograph.)

cies, were immediately interested in the robbery. Strangely enough, but possibly because it was war time, the newspapers of the day devoted but a few lines to the recital of the affair; but in their advertising columns it took a column to enumerate the stolen securities. What the robbers did with the securities became afterwards very clear. The tin boxes were taken to a liquor store kept by an Englishman, at Spring and Worcester streets, where they were "planted." There was a sort of a "whack-up" among the perpetrators of the robbery, to whom should be added a man named Harry Howard. Ennis started on a negotiating tour with about a quarter of a million of the United States securities—which, by the way, amounted in all to $1,200,000—in Massachusetts. A dozen detectives knew he had gone, but only Captain Young knew of Mr. Lord's wishes and intentions. Mr. Lord's avarice prompted him to request, first, the recovery of his property, and then the arrest of the thieves, if the detectives cared to bother with them. For the recovery of the securities a large percentage reward was offered. And so it came about that Mr. Ennis, at Newburyport, fell into the hands of a grasping sheriff, gave up the bonds he had in his possession, and made the sheriff richer by $25,000. A small percentage of the bonds found their way into Canada; but the bulk of the booty was carried to Europe by the English liquor dealer. Negotiations for the return of these bonds and securities were then begun, through the medium of a "highly moral and conscientious" English solicitor. The result was that Mr. Lord and Mr. Barron got back $1,600,000 worth of their property—a shrinkage of $200,000. It is barely possible that the thieves got more than $75,000 for the job. Some of the securities were lost, a good deal of money was paid out in expenses, and the English solicitor put the balance to the credit of his bank account. Nobody was punished for the crime. Howard and Pettengill were arrested in this city in August, 1866, but were not prosecuted. A pawnbroker, too, was apprehended for having in his possession a five thousand dollar bond of Mr. Lord's; and Mr. F. Hellen, then of No. 9 Wall Street, was arrested and discharged on a complaint of having dealt in some of the stolen securities.

Of the thieves, only Pettengill now survives. He is a broken down, miserable tramp. He has run the gamut of high crime—bank sneak and forger—and is now and then "shown up" at police headquarters, possibly as an antiquarian curiosity, for he is now harmless in his former lines of "business." Jack Rand, who "reformed" some years ago—his "reformation" did not go to the extent of refunding a snug little fortune amassed by villany—dropped dead last year at the Beacon Park race course, near Boston, just after he had purchased a gambling ticket.

A very clever scheme of swindlers is known as the "Custom House racket." A man calls at your house, attired in what looks very much like a Custom House officer's uniform, and produces bills for parcels from the other side of the Atlantic, which are now in hand, and must be released immediately. In most instances no one stops to question the authenticity of the bill which is presented, and it is paid without much questioning. Even if one does question this quondam Custom House officer, he always has an answer ready. He is the most plausible kind of a fellow and always behaves like a "perfect gentleman." In one case a fellow of this class called at a house on Eighty-first Street, and collected a little less than ten dollars on one of his bogus bills. The lady of the house had occasion to bring the money from an up-stairs room, and while she was gone he was left alone in the parlor. Finding the piano open he sat down and played " Nearer, my God, to thee," with great taste and feeling. So much pathos, in fact, did he infuse into the whole performance, that when, after some days of waiting and anxious inquiries, no package arrived, his victims refused to believe he was anything but an honest man. Probably they think so now, notwithstanding the fact that their Custom House pianist is wearing a striped suit within the walls of Sing Sing.

A more impudent and barefaced mode of petty thieving is that adopted by the man in a jumper, who pokes his head in at the door the moment an express package has been delivered and says:

"Beg pardon, ma'am; the driver left the wrong parcel. I'll take it and bring back the right one."

And that's the last of your parcel.

Another "cheeky" thief is the one who makes a good "haul" now and then by following coal carts to their destination—to saloons or restaurants he gives the preference—where he assumes an air of authority which is liable to impose upon the sharpest. He bosses the whole business in the most audacious and barefaced manner, until the driver of the team thinks he is connected with the firm by whom the coal is sent. When the swindler thinks this stage has been reached—and he is an accurate judge—he demands the driver's unsigned receipt, collects the cash for the coal and decamps.

It would be impossible for me to enumerate all the tricks which have been resorted to by this class of criminals to dupe their victims. The way in which the "confidence" game is played is familiar to most persons, but for all that, scarcely a day passes but somebody is victimized by it. Country people are not the only dupes. Not by any means. Look at Oscar Wilde, Charles Francis

Adams and others quite as educated and in just such prominent positions in society.

Shoplifting is almost exclusively confined to women. Generally the shoplifter carries a bag, fastened with straps around the waist, into which she can easily drop anything she may steal. Some women arrange their skirts so that the whole front from waist to bottom forms a bag, which can be stuffed full of feathers, laces, etc., without any outward sign. A very handy receptacle for the storing away of fine goods is a muff. Quite a natural and innocent looking thing in itself, but very dangerous when utilized by a shoplifter. The woman puts her muff on a pile of handkerchiefs, and while she examines something with one hand, quietly pulls handkerchiefs, or anything else within reach, into her muff with the other.

I have been frequently called upon to express an opinion regarding the frequency, or otherwise, of the use of chloroform by the criminal classes to assist in robbery. I may at once say that during the whole of my experience there was never a case of this character where chloroform was alleged to have been used, brought before me, without my regarding the whole business with a considerable amount of suspicion. It is very difficult for me to remember any case in which I was convinced that chloroform was employed by thieves whose intent was to commit a robbery. The very character of this anæsthetic precludes its employment for general criminal purposes. When carelessly applied it has something of a corrosive action, and its contact with the mucous membrane would leave a trace. Being, too, a volatile fluid, with a peculiar odor, its presence would be immediately revealed. It is a solvent and acts quickly on colors, and if it is absorbed by materials which are dyed the colors would be effaced. What is more to the point, however, is this : To administer chloroform, the person taking it must be willing to accept it. If he or she be unwilling, then force or violence must be employed ; and if violence is to be used at all a much easier thing is to knock the victim on the head with a bludgeon. A handkerchief saturated with chloroform is perfectly ineffective, unless it be closely and persistently applied to the mouth and nostrils. It is impossible to make such applications of chloroform to healthy sleeping persons without awakening them. Entirely ignorant of the nature or effects of chloroform, a great many persons suppose that a sponge saturated with it and left in a room will throw a sleeping person into a state of coma. This, of course, is nonsense; and I believe all physicians will agree with me that chloroform as an agent to aid the criminal in robbing his victim is worthless. I do not mean to say that, in case a person is ill, or very old, or feeble, robbery may not be committed by means of chloroform; but the chance of discovery is even greater than if a weapon of some kind had been used to attain the same end. I have found, very frequently, that persons

THEO. BISHOP.
(From a Photograph.)

who have lost money entrusted to them, and who have alleged they were chloroformed, have been themselves the real culprits.

Sensational romance is full of stories of crimes effected by means of chloroform; but all this must be credited to the vivid imagination of the writer. As to the use of drugs, I am inclined to believe that they are very rarely employed. It is quite possible to "hocus" beer by its mixture with a few grains of opium, but authentic cases of drugged liquor are exceptional. Such reports are generally mythical. Why should a man who wants to rob another administer an opiate? If he can induce his intended victim to partake of one glass of spirits it is much easier to induce him to have another than it is to tamper with the liquor. It is far easier and safer to get a man drunk than it is to poison him; and the risk is greatly diminished. If a man's head will resist alcoholic influences longer than a woman's, why, when the latter is the subject, need an opiate be used at all, even from the assailant's own point of view? The use of snuff mixed with liquors is sometimes written about. A little consideration of the subject, or, at any rate, experimenting with it, will show that the administration of a dose of this kind would make the fraud immediately apparent to the person who drank of it. A pinch of snuff would make a glass of beer, or any thing else, positively nauseating.

An almost endless quantity of nonsense has been written about the skill of criminals in the "fixing" of drugged fluids and the administration of them. Criminals are clever enough, in their way too clever, but they possess no secret drugs with which to lull their unsuspecting victims to sleep, sensational novels to the contrary notwithstanding.

I remember one case that came under my notice. A prominent jeweller claimed that he had been robbed. His store was situated under a hotel, and his story to me was that during the night, while he was in bed, chloroform had been administered to him and his money stolen. Always suspicious about chloroform, I put a number of searching questions to him. He described his symptoms to me in a very minute manner—he was half-conscious, but could not move. To make his story more plausible, he informed me that the traces of the chloroform could still be found on his pillow. This decided the matter in my own mind. The man was a fraud, and was trying to humbug me. Sure enough, when the pillow was examined an oily substance was found staining it; but it bore no resemblance, either in color or odor, to chloroform, and a chemical analysis proved that it was simply linseed oil. There had been no robbery, and I believe it afterwards turned out that the man was financially embarrassed and had invented the chloroform story as an excuse for not paying his debts.

It is very certain that if chloroform could be made useful by thieves they would almost always employ it. The fact that they do not do so shows conclusively that if they have tried it they abandoned it long ago, finding it to be of no avail. All "chloroform" stories, therefore, should be examined into most thoroughly. Let me recall another case:

A man in active business, whose credit was good and who possessed some means, was heavily indebted to one of the most prominent grocery firms in New York City. This indebtedness was in the form of notes due at certain dates. The man had always paid his obligations, and his financial condition was regarded as perfectly solvent. He was something of a speculator in real estate, and the opportunity came when he thought he could purchase a piece of property at a bargain. A note to his groceryman was due. He went to the holder of the note and said:

"I have just met with a terrible misfortune—a great loss. I went down on Wall Street to sell some bonds, so that I could meet your note. In a hallway, where I happened to be, a stranger came up and spoke to me, and that is the last I remember about it. When I came to consciousness I found myself on Staten Island in the neighborhood of a friend's house. My bonds were gone! I must have been chloroformed, and that is all I know about it."

That was the extraordinary story he told the members of the firm to whom he was indebted. I was very much inclined to disbelieve his story, and I assured the groceryman that it was all utter nonsense. Then they were convinced, though at first they were inclined to think he had been chloroformed and robbed. The man was sent for, I had a private interview with him, and he repeated his story, varying in no respect from his first narration. When he had finished, I said:

"What stuff! You don't mean to say that you found yourself on Staten Island, and that no one knew of your transfer! A man can't be carried on a ferry boat without being seen by somebody. How were you carried? It's preposterous for you to try and make me believe that you took a lot of bonds somewhere, that you told no one of your intention, and yet that somebody knew it and met you in a hallway on Wall Street and chloroformed you. Don't you see how absurd and unlikely it all is? Why your story is so flimsy that it won't hang together for an instant. Your trick wouldn't deceive a child, even."

My outburst staggered him; and in a few minutes he confessed the whole thing. He had bought some land with the bonds, and so did not have money enough to meet the note which he had given his groceryman.

CHAPTER XXXIV.

A POT POURRI OF CRIMES.—A BLOODY ASSASSINATION IN FRONT OF SUTHERLAND'S RESTAURANT.—THE MUFFLED GROAN OF "MURDER!"—HIGHWAY ROBBERS IN A THIRD AVENUE CAR.—GARROTED IN THE FOURTH AVENUE TUNNEL.—A THIEF TRIPPED UP BY A SERVANT GIRL.—THE RICH MAN'S SON WHO SHOT A LAWYER.—GRADY, THE MASCULINE RIVAL OF MADAME MANDELBAUM.—A RASCALLY THEOLOGIAN.

I DO not remember a bloodier assassination than that of Nicholas W. Duryea by John E. Simmons, outside Sutherland's restaurant on Liberty Street, on the 16th of December, 1872. Duryea represented a Brooklyn clique of policy players. Simmons was one of the Simmons Brothers—"Eph," John E. and William C.—who conducted a Kentucky lottery at No. 17 Liberty Street. There had been bad blood between Duryea and Simmons for some time. On the evening in question they were to have a business talk, and settle some important matters.

What really occurred at this interview will never fully be known. It was certainly not satisfactory to Simmons, for when the two men left the office they came to blows. In the struggle both men fell, Simmons being the "under dog." They rolled on the sidewalk for half a minute, when Duryea cried out:

"G—d d—— you, fight fair! Let me up!"

Simmons's only response was to draw a huge, glittering bowie-knife, sharp as a razor on both edges. With a pumping motion, he thrust the shining weapon into Duryea's body as often as the nervous motion of the assassin's arm would permit.

"Golly! it was red hot!" said a little boot-black afterward, who was asked to describe the fight to the coroner's jury.

After the first lunge of the knife Duryea said little. When his opponent continued to stab, there was a muffled groan of "murder!" and Duryea offered no further resistance. Simmons tried to rise, but the stabbing had been so fierce and so promiscuous that nearly all the life-blood in Duryea's body had been let out, and the sidewalk was covered with the slippery crimson fluid. In rising, Simmons slipped in his foe's blood and fell and fractured one of his ankles. This did not prevent him from shrieking exultingly over his bleeding victim:

"Now I've got the best of you!"

He was led to a chair in Sutherland's restaurant, sat down and calmly awaited arrest. The horrible tragedy and his own personal peril did not appear to affect him nearly as much as the condition of his ankle. He repeatedly asked when the surgeon would come, and when an officer walked into the restaurant and made him a prisoner, he asked whiningly when he could be attended to. He had to be carried to the Second Precinct stationhouse, where Captain Caffrey was in command. Duryea's body had been taken there, and was a hideous sight. Before the combat he had been splendidly attired in the finest linen, with diamonds in his shirt front, a $100 overcoat with a fur collar on his back and patent leather boots on his feet. Now he was one mass of gore. Blood flowed from sixteen wounds.

Dr. F. Le Roy Satterlee attended Simmons's foot, and sent him to the Park Hospital under guard. The knife with which the deed was committed was not found until lanterns were procured; and it was then discovered that Simmons's energy had been so great that the keen point of the weapon had been broken off in Duryea's body.

Simmons had many daring friends, and a plot was arranged to take him by force from the Park Hospital. This plan was frustrated by his being removed to Bellevue under a strong guard. By no means discouraged, his friends influenced Coroner Patsy Keenan to hold a mock inquest at the hospital. Simmons, however, was not smart enough to get out of town, possibly because the bones of his ankle were not entirely knitted. So District Attorney Samuel B. Garvin was able to override the coroner and get the murderer re-arrested. He was tried, convicted and served an inadequate term in the State prison. He is now a gambler in this city.

Among the special instances I remember of unusual boldness and cleverness on the part of thieves was a robbery which occurred down in Nassau Street early in the year 1878.

The circumstances were these: The clerk of James H. Young, a broker whose place of business was in this street, was busy late one afternoon cutting coupons from bonds. There was no one else in the office at the time, until two well dressed and gentlemanly looking men entered and informed the clerk that there was a lame gentleman at the door, who, owing to his infirmity, could not get up the steps from the carriage in which he was, and wished to see the clerk outside. Knowing that one of the firm's customers was lame and supposing the young men to be his friends, the clerk went down to the door without locking desk or safe. When he returned the young men were missing, and so were $8000 in cash and $80,000 in bonds.

Another instance which fell under my official observation was the robbery of a Third Avenue street-car on the morning of August 22, 1880. Car No. 14 was passing through the Bowery at about daybreak. When it had reached Prince Street six determined looking men boarded it. One of them covered the driver with the muzzle of a cocked revolver, while another paid the same attention to the conductor, at the same time varying his occupation by relieving his terrified victim of all the money he had on his person. The other four men went inside the car, and with revolvers cocked and pointed robbed the twenty-six passengers of what money and valuables they had about them. One passenger was brave enough to make resistance, but in the struggle which followed he was seriously injured. A policeman was aroused by the unusual scene in the car and came up on a run to where it was standing. The highway robbers, however, had about made their rounds, and without stopping to greet the policeman, they grabbed their booty tighter and darted at full speed down one of the streets which enter into the Bowery. They escaped.

There was wild excitement on East Thirty-eighth Street at about the noon hour on January 15, 1883. The occasion of it was what is known in police tradition as the tunnel robbery. It was a bold and outrageous attempt to steal money, and for some time afterward produced a feeling of nervousness among the female residents of Murray Hill.

Miss Christina Isherwood, of No. 111 East Thirty-sixth Street, a daughter of the chief engineer in the United States Navy, and her cousin, Miss Carpenter, of Auburn, N. Y., started out just after twelve o'clock for Fifty-seventh Street. They proposed to take a Fourth Avenue car, and Miss Carpenter ran ahead to stop it, while her companion came on more leisurely behind. When the latter had reached the first landing in descending the stone steps leading to the Fourth Avenue tunnel, a man sprang up the stairway and grabbed at the bag which Miss Isherwood held in her right hand, and which contained a pair of opal earrings set with diamonds, and $30 in coin. The young lady clutched the bag more tightly, and the thief tried the harder to wrench it from her grasp. She screamed and struggled; whereupon he seized her by the throat and forced her down upon the steps. At this her hold on the bag was relaxed and the robber rushed off with it.

Both of the young women started in pursuit. A man joined them and all three rushed down Thirty-eighth Street towards Third Avenue. Passers by stopped to see what this unusual sight was going on and then joined the pursuers. A servant girl who was sweeping the sidewalk in front of one of the residences farther down the street, saw the thief coming and slyly putting out her broom tripped him up. He fell on his knees, but recovered himself at once and rushed on. At Lexington Avenue he was lost sight of.

The robbery was reported at the police station in Thirty-fifth Street, and Captain Ryan and his detectives came to me for aid. I sent several of the detectives from police headquarters to the spot where the robbery took place. They soon learned that a man answering to the thief's description had been seen loitering about the tunnel for a day or two. It was also learned that the thief while being pursued ran into a barber shop at Third Avenue and Thirty-sixth Street. He walked rapidly through the shop, passed out of a rear door, crossed a small yard, and entered the back door of a liquor store in Third Avenue. From there all trace of him was lost for some time.

The people living in the apartment house at Thirty-second Street and Broadway were startled on the night of Saturday, March 8, 1884, when they were informed of a dastardly attempt at robbery which had been undertaken in the building.

A Miss Harvey and her little niece were living in the rooms rented by Mr. George H. Sloane. In the absence of Mr. and Mrs. Sloane on the evening in question, Miss Harvey and her niece went early to bed. They had no sooner retired than through the dim light a negro emerged from a closet in the room and stealthily stole toward the bed. He seized the woman by the throat and gagged her, then dragged her from the bed, threw her on the floor, and bound her wrists together behind her back. The black thief then proceeded to ransack the apartment for plunder. Nervously he picked up whatever valuables he could find and thrust them into a bag which he was carrying. Then he disappeared.

At 11.30 o'clock Mr. and Mrs. Sloane returned to find the room turned topsy-turvy, Miss Harvey stretched on the floor unconscious, and the silver missing. A physician was summoned and the stricken lady was soon restored. Then it became time to look for the thief. Detective Price was summoned and as soon as he had arrived he heard Miss Harvey's story. The dining-room window opened out on a fire-escape. When Mr. and Mrs. Sloane had arrived they had found that one of the doors to this window was open. Through this Detective Price walked, and found at his feet a pillow-case with $600 worth of silver in it. He climbed up the fire-escape to the room of a servant girl, where he found, crouched under the bed, a negro, Jesse Williams, twenty-one years old. He was handcuffed and taken to the station-house. The servant, Gertrude L. Ash, was also looked up. She had had the negro in her room for several days, and had been noticed pouring hot water on the fire-escape in the morning, apparently for the purpose of melting the ice which had frozen on the iron work.

A shooting affray occurred in June, 1884, which while not possessing remarkable interest in itself, afterward gained some importance from the course the affair took in court. I refer to the shooting of John Drake by William C. Rhinelander on June 17. Rhinelander was a wayward son. He belonged to the wealthy and aristocratic old Rhinelander family but scarcely upheld the dignity of the name. He married a servant girl, named Maggie McGinnis, whereupon his father disinherited him, and allowed him $100 a week. Rhinelander fancied that Drake, who was a lawyer, stood between him and his wife, and with this idea he threatened vengeance.

On the day in question Rhinelander and Drake were seated talking in the latter's office, at No. 79 Cedar Street, when suddenly the former raised a pistol and shot the lawyer in the shoulder. Drake grappled with this lowly son of an aristocratic family, and held him until assistance came. He pinned Rhinelander against the wall, and held his hands above his head. The lawyer finally wrenched the pistol from Rhinelander's grasp. By this time George Douglas had arrived on the scene. Drake exclaimed, "I'm shot!"

"I'll send for a policeman," said Douglas.

"No," said Drake, "hold him, and let the boy run for a doctor."

By this time Drake was exhausted. Dr. Peck found him in a state of collapse from the shock, but the patient soon rallied. The ball had shattered the bone in the shoulder joint of the right arm. Mr. Drake refused to have Rhinelander arrested, and he was taken away by his uncle, H. Cruger Oakley. Finally, however, he was arrested and taken to the Tombs prison to await the result of Drake's injuries. Drake recovered ostensibly, but died about a year afterward from another cause. Rhinelander's relatives tried to make him out a lunatic, and several commissions were appointed to determine his mental soundness. The accused man was finally discharged, and with his wife sailed almost immediately for Europe.

From 1865 to 1880 no face was more familiar at police headquarters, at the district attorney's office, at the courts, in private houses, in the streets, and in short everywhere, than that of the eccentric and cunning dealer in "collateral," and the felons' banker—John D. Grady. He was always shabby, always carried a satchel, and never, in late years, had less than $10,000 worth of property in it and his pockets. It would have been a safe bet in a bar-room, when Grady was present, to wager that at least one of the crowd could show a genuine one thousand dollar note. Grady would have been worth to the community at least a hundred thousand dollars as a detective; that is to say, such an amount would have been only ten per cent. of the saving to citizens and institutions, from burglaries, sneak thieving and the higher grades of dishonesty.

Beginning in a small way as a pedler of "pinchbeck," Grady took up "collateral" as a business, and found that it paid better to deal with criminals and make from 150 to 200 per cent. than to go down to Maiden Lane, take the risks and chances of depression in stock, and make from ten to twenty per cent. Besides he thus became interested in other lines of business. He had mastered the jewelry trade. No one could judge the precious stones and metals better than he. He could make a watch, and not infrequently was called upon to give expert opinion to honest tradesmen, who knew perfectly well that it was among the not very remote possibilities that some day he might be walking around with part of their stock in his satchel. The new lines of business consisted in "banking" for forgers, bank "cracksmen" and plunderers generally.

He became a sort of masculine rival to Madame Mandelbaum. There was a species of armed neutrality between them; they were civil when they met, and occasionally transacted "business" with one another. But they were rivals so far as influence over the *creme de la creme* of felons was concerned. Grady now and then took care of the proceeds of bank burglaries. In one case he held half a million dollars' worth of securities until negotiations with the losers had terminated, when he delivered up the booty and received a heavy percentage. He occasionally tried his hand at disposing of stolen bonds. In 1874, while conducting negotiations in the Ninth Ward with the notorious Jimmy Brady, he was surprised by detectives Dilkes and Tully. Grady surrendered. Brady ran, firing at Dilkes, who returned the fire and captured him after wounding him in the thigh as he jumped through a store window. Both were tried, but Grady went scot-free, while Brady was sent to Sing Sing. He was helped out of this little difficulty by means of tools furnished by Grady, which enabled him to escape from confinement.

It is estimated that in Grady's career as a pedler, receiver, negotiator and banker, he handled in one way and another $4,000,000 in property, securities and cash.

Brady turned out an ingrate. After his escape from Sing Sing he owed Grady about $12,000. Grady, of course, wished to recoup himself; but Brady was very lazy, found another banker and wouldn't go to "work." His new banker got tired of him. He returned to Grady and got $2000 more from him by threatening, cajoling and promising. Then when Grady showed a disposition to close the account, Brady raised a pistol to his head and made him hand over $2000 in cash. This little adventure was the indirect cause of Brady's downfall. He went to work at his criminal pursuits with a vengeance, and Grady kept himself thoroughly posted as to his friend's movements.

In 1878 Brady and his confederates had been so fortunate that a dividend was decided upon. A private room was hired at the

JIM BRADY'S JUMP.

Hotel Brunswick, and each of the men present pocketed $40,000. Brady celebrated the occasion by getting hilariously drunk. When he left the hotel he decided that nothing but silk underwear was good enough for him. He staggered into a furnishing store at Twenty third Street and Broadway, selected several hundred dollars' worth of goods, and all would have gone well but for his habit of taking that which did not belong to him. He secreted in his pockets some articles of trifling value. The storekeeper detected him and remonstrated. Brady, as was said before, was drunk, and misapprehended the situation. He afterwards said he thought he was "in a bank row." He therefore fled like a deer. The storekeeper pursued and policemen joined in the chase. Brady remembered that he had a pistol in his pocket and began to fire away. After about a dozen shots had been fired by him and the police, he was captured. Then Grady had him. He instigated and aided the prosecution. So it came about that Brady went back to Sing Sing prison under a heavy sentence for a miserable little theft of which a "clothes liner" would have been ashamed.

During his career, Grady consorted with the following criminals: "Sheeney Mike," Billy O'Brien, Johnny Irving, "Johnny, the Mick," "Shang" Draper, Bob Scott, "Red" Leary, Billy Conners, James Dunlap, Johnny Dobbs, "Sheeney" Rose, Sam Perris, Abe Coakley, George Leonidas Leslie, Pete Curley, "Big Frank" McCoy, George Miles, Ike Marsh, Ed. Goodie, Joe Dollard, Geo. Mason, and a hundred others.

In later years—the last two of his life—Grady was in trouble. Men who had protected him had died, or had become impotent; criminals whom he had dealt with, or banked for, had been imprisoned or become no longer useful. He was sued by persons who had good reason to believe that property taken from them had found its way into his hands; and persons who knew his secrets had extorted blood-money from him, until all his fortune, which was once estimated at $1,500,000, had dwindled down to less than $100,000. He died of pneumonia at his office, No. 403 Sixth Avenue, in October, 1880. He was then in partnership with a man who had been in a similar line of business; but for months the firm had pretended to do what they termed a "legitimate business." When the public administrator settled the estate, the amount of it was below $45,000. Taking Grady's own words as a basis, this was a shrinkage since 1875 of about $200,000. He always said he never had had any luck since he quarrelled with "Jim" Brady.

In 1880, much scandal was caused at Tournai, Belgium, by the antagonism between two ecclesiastics—Monsieur Dumont and Monsieur Du Rousseaux—because the latter had succeeded the former as bishop, through Pope Leo, who was compelled to suspend Monsieur Dumont. One cause of Dumont's suspension was his great age; he was in his dotage, and peevish and quarrelsome in the extreme. There was an unseemly wrangle between the two ecclesiastics for many months, mainly owing to a refusal of Monsieur Rousseaux to give up certain property which Dumont demanded. In order to have the property in question, which consisted of valuable church plate and two millions or more of francs, amply protected, Monsieur Rousseaux prevailed on the authorities at Rome to appoint the canon, Leon J. Bernard, as treasurer of the diocese. He immediately took the treasure to his own house, and kept it in safes procured for the purpose.

In March, 1881, the canon concluded to lay up for himself treasures on earth, and ran off with the money just as Monsieur Dumont had made an application to have the property and money inventoried, so as to furnish a ground for action against Monsieur Rousseaux. The flight of the canon caused such apprehension and scandal that Monsieur Rousseaux and the clergy of the diocese decided for a time to keep the matter a secret, hoping to find out the whereabouts of the erring brother and bring him to terms.

For this purpose another canon was sent to follow Bernard, who had been traced to New York. All clue to him in this city was lost, until a lawyer opened negotiations with the ecclesiastical authorities from Quebec, and tried to arrange with Dumont on a basis of 60 per cent. of the stolen money for the Monsieur and 40 per cent. for the lawyer and embezzler. This offer was refused. The lawyer was arrested and was held as a sort of hostage for Bernard. This arrest of the lawyer led to the discovery of some of the stolen money. Two hundred thousand francs of it were found at the Crédit Lyonnais in Paris, and one hundred thousand francs in a London bank. These amounts were seized; but Bernard, meanwhile, had again disappeared. The Belgian authorities communicated with the Belgian minister at Washington, and Mr. Mali, the Belgian consul-general here, was given charge of the case. He engaged the firm of Condert Brothers, who came to police headquarters and conferred with me. The case was turned over to Inspector Byrnes. His choice was excellent when he selected Detective Joseph Dorcy to hunt up the rascally monk.

All that the detective had to start with was a good description of the man. He hunted around the hotels in this city until he found that in June, 1881, Bernard had stopped at the Fifth Avenue Hotel. From this point he traced him to Boston, Montreal, and Quebec. Here the trail ended for a time. It was picked up at Chicago, where Bernard was on the 25th of March, 1882. Dorcy wasted much time in the West, in endeavoring to track Bernard from Chicago. He finally found a clue in Montgomery, Alabama, and went thence to Mobile and New Orleans. Here the scent was pretty fresh. Bernard, under the name of Leopold Bal, had lived at No. 193 Canal Street, and had the imprudence to get photographed. A copy of this photograph fell into the hands of the detective, and was useful to him, because the canon had somewhat changed in appearance. "Bal" had left New Orleans just eighteen days before Dorcy's arrival. The detective found that the man he was pursuing had taken tickets for Houston, Texas. This led him to Galveston, Houston, San Antonio, Little Rock, Hot Springs, Memphis, Selma, Texarkana and Waco.

At the last named place, the train on which Dorcy was riding was stopped by a freshet having washed away a bridge and part of the track. It was a wild, desolate region, with no hotels and few inhabitants. The weather was of the worst. The only shelter Dorcy could find was a miserable hut, and there he subsisted for three days on the staple food of the district—hoe cake and salted horse. Tired of losing time in this manner, Dorcy decided to go back to Texarkana, and was compelled to walk the greater part of the way, knee deep in mud, and obliged to ford two streams. From Texarkana, Dorcy hurried back to New Orleans. He had been in the city but a few hours when he picked up a capital clew at the office of the Morgan Steamship Company. It told him that Bernard had dodged him in Texas, had come back to New Orleans and had taken tickets for Vera Cruz, Mexico. Dorcy made the best of his way to the City of Mexico. He learned from a passenger who saw Bernard on the ship which he took from Mexico, and who remembered well, that on shore the rascal was exceedingly anxious to get to the City of Mexico.

There Dorcy found the hotel in which Bernard had lodged as

"L. Brown." He left it on May 10, 1882, giving instructions for his letters to be sent to San Luis de Potosi up to the 25th of June; and up to July 10, to the City of Leon. This, however, was simply a ruse on the part of Bernard to throw possible pursuers off the scent. It resulted in Dorcy losing all track of him, although he searched thoroughly in Pueblo de los Angeles, Orizaba and Cordova. He was almost in despair when, on the 19th of June, he arrived at Vera Cruz. Here he discovered that Bernard had taken passage for Havana on June 2, as "J. Lyon." Dorcy consulted a steam-boat guide, and knowing that Bernard had a passport for St. Thomas, readily understood that as the steamer left Havana on the 21st of June for that place, he had but little time to spare. The telegraph was called into requisition, and a despatch sent to the Governor of Havana resulted in Bernard's capture just as he was leaving his hotel to go on board the steamer. He had in his possession $20,000, and keys for thirteen safe depositories in the United States and Canada, where he had secreted the stolen money. In his travels he had become well versed in methods of arrest and extradition, and had copies of the various extradition laws, as well as blank forms of writs of *habeas corpus*, ready for any emergency.

Dorcy took the next steamer for Havana, sympathized with Bernard, and returned to New York. Bernard was sent to Madrid first, and thence to Belgium, where he was tried and convicted. All the money stolen by him, with the exception of a few thousand dollars, was recovered.

CHAPTER XXXV.

THE DIVES OF NEW YORK.—FROM THE HAYMARKET TO THE MORGUE,—IN THE CREMORNE.—TOM GOULD'S DIVE.—HARRY HILL'S THEATRE.—AT THE AMERICAN MABILLE.—VICE IN THE BLACK-AND-TAN.—THE CAN-CAN IN ITS GLORY.—BILLY MCGLORY'S SYSTEM.—THE WRECK OF A WOMAN.—THE SAILORS' DIVES.—A FRENCH BALL.

THE dives of New York are the hot-beds of its crime. Under the brilliant glare of gas-jets and the seductive strains of music vice germinates, grows, buds and yields its bitter fruit. Every stage of crime is reflected in a true picture of these holes of viciousness. The "dance of death" begins with the Haymarket, grows feeble in "Billy McGlory's," or the "Black-and-Tan," and ends in the river or the potter's field. A pure girl who visits the Haymarket, if such a one ever does visit it, attracted by the gay scenes and the fascination of the waltz, may feel sure of her own power to keep from going lower in the scale of sensuality; but as surely as a displaced stone goes tumbling down a hillside, she rushes onward to the black fate which awaits her, and virtue, youth, beauty, health and soul are lost in the downward course to ruin. A terrible fate it is, yet many are they who reach it yearly.

New York is well provided with what is commonly known as dives, although fortunately, under the awakening moral sense of the community, some of the more notorious dens of iniquity are being closed. There are enough left, however, to amuse and corrupt the crowds which nightly flock to them. For the uninitiated let it be said that by dives is meant, in general, the dance-halls in various parts of the town, where abandoned women congregate to try their charms on easily tempted men. These dance-halls are all more or less alike. They vary only in the classes of people patronizing them. I will not say they vary in the degree of vice carried on, for I believe there is as much wickednes in the Cremorne and Haymarket and Tom Gould's, as in the low resorts down town. They all have music and dancing and female attachés and gaudily decorated halls, and liquors. One of these attractions would be worthless without the others. All taken together make a combination which many men find it hard to resist.

The men who own and run such places are *sui generis*—of their own kind. From the enormous amount of their ill-gotten gains they are able to own expensive houses and live in extravagant style. Beneath their smiling features there is the consciousness, no, perhaps not the consciousness, but at least the remembrance of almost every sort of crime. Conscience is a foreign word to men of this foul business. Honest and generous are they sometimes called? Well, yes, when it pays. ··They are tyrants of the worst sort. The women who frequent their resorts are not their accomplices in iniquity, but their tools. They use them as travelling showmen do a trained bear—prod them when they refuse to dance or when they become useless, treat them as we do faded flowers —throw them into the gutter to die.

In order that the full significance of the evil influence which surrounds these places may be appreciated, I have thought it best to describe in detail each of the better known dives. Some may seem almost too well known to need description, but it strikes me they cannot be made too familiar.

First, there is the Haymarket, situated on Sixth Avenue, just below Thirtieth Street. On the outside it is not a particularly ornate building; in fact, by daylight the structure is rather repulsive, but then the Haymarket is only an ordinary building in the daytime. At night it shines with the brilliancy of a Broadway theatre and becomes animate with the licentious life of the avenue. The easily swinging doors which open from the sidewalk creak half the night with the entrance or exit of depraved women and their masculine escorts. Let the reader who has never visited this illuminated den go with me in imagination, and see the wicked character of the place, pictured as well as I am able to paint it. At the entrance one reads by the pale electric light the only indication of the purposes to which the building is put—"Haymarket, Grand Soiree Dansante." We push the swinging doors and pay our entrance fee of twenty-five cents for males, nothing for females, to a man behind a narrow window. We push another swinging door and then pause to become accustomed to the gay glare and the whirl of human figures. We are in a long and broad room, whose centre is a polished dancing floor. At the extreme end is a sort of a stage with a brilliantly painted curtain, and the chairs of the musicians. The latter are playing their instruments at full blast, and to the entrancing strains of a waltz a dozen or more young men and women are moving in slow measure over the floor. Along on either side of the wall is a row of seats, and here we sit for a few moments and look about us. We hear the clink of glasses and look up to discover that the dancing-hall is not all of the Haymarket. There is a gallery above us and it seems to be the popular part of the place. It is crowded with men and women, drinking and smoking and filling the room with ribald laughter and blasphemous words. The galleries extend around three sides of the room; and so well filled are they with the Haymarket's patrons and patronesses that it is with difficulty that the waiters, who carry everything, from lemonade to whiskey, are able to work their way through the throngs, without smashing glasses and tipping over tables.

The galleries are arranged with tables and chairs, and on the northern side, connected by passage-ways with the gallery, is the bar. There are tables in the bar-room also, and they are well filled with glasses, and surrounded by abandoned women and the men whom they have "roped" in. It does not take us long to discover that the attraction of the Haymarket is not so much in its dance floor as in its gallery. It is here that the habitués of the place congregate, and mingle vile jokes with beer and whiskey and tobacco smoke. There are all sorts of women here. Some are extremely young and pretty; others are fat and homely and awkward. Some are demure, others coarse and loud-mouthed. Some have painted their faces to hide the ravages which vice has been making in their features. Some are dressed with taste; others are arrayed in brilliant colors and cheap tawdry fabrics. Some even are bashful and modest appearing, hesitating to approach the men who patronize the place. Others are brazen in their conduct. They address without compunction those with whom they wish to talk—even fling their arms around them and breathe lascivious thoughts into their ears.

The females who visit the Haymarket range in age from seventeen to thirty-five years, and most of them are not more than twenty-five. They are most of them inmates of disreputable houses, and congregate in this dance-hall like harpies, to seize upon and devour the weak. The owners of the Haymarket allow them free admission to and from the building, and pile up their riches by squeezing the prey of these prostitutes. The amount of liquor that is sold here is enormous. Of course fancy prices are put on every drink, and the girls who frequent the place are supposed to call for the most expensive liquors, and drink as much as they are able.

As I hinted in the previous part of this chapter, I consider the Haymarket as bad in its influence as some of the down-town resorts. The language and conversation which one hears here are something terrible in their way. I remember once when I was obliged to be in the place in an official capacity, I noticed a young girl there whose face was peculiarly sweet and winning. She had an air of refinement about her that at once distinguished her from her companions. She looked bright and seemed to talk with vivacity. I was struck by the girl's face, and made up my mind that she must have been persuaded to visit the resort by companions who were older in years and depravity. My curiosity to confirm my good opinion of her was great, I admit, and I had not long to wait before my curiosity was satisfied in a most shocking manner. The girl saw me standing alone and came where I was. She introduced the conversation with some flippant remark, and after a word or two in reply from me, she launched into such a tirade of oaths and foul speech as fairly took my breath away. I was almost struck dumb. The shock to my impressions was impossible to overcome. I have seen many hardened human beings in the course of my life, but the depravity of none of them ever surprised me as did the foul words which came from what I supposed were pure lips.

So the demoralizing effect of the Haymarket is not in the actual crime committed there, as is the case in the Bleecker Street dives for instance, but in the temptations which are held out so seductively to young men by the devils in female forms who make their homes there.

Not far from the Haymarket is another dive where debauched women congregate. It is known as the "Cremorne," and is situated just west of Sixth Avenue on Thirty-second Street. Out over the sidewalk in large, glittering letters shines the name of the concert hall. It must not be confounded with that other institution which Jerry McAuley founded next door, and which goes by the same name. That good man was bold enough to pitch his tent beside Satan's and fight with the devil for the possession of souls. It may have been a foolish thing to establish a mission next door to a hell, but that was what Jerry McAuley did, and all honor to his memory for his bravery.

The "Cremorne" dive occupies the basement or ground floor of the building in which it is situated. The entrance from the street leads directly to the bar, and through noiselessly swinging doors at the other end of the hallway comes the gleam of the electric light, and now and then the strains of music. At the end of the bar sits behind a desk a pompous, well-built man who, with a face stern and defiant, acts as cashier and general manager. An ugly-looking club hangs behind him on the wall, and occasionally his duties as money changer are interrupted by those of the "bouncer." For the men who come to his establishment sometimes get unruly, and then it is that the cashier unbends his dignity and restores the "respectability" of the hall by dexterously clubbing the drunken offender.

The "Cremorne" is not a dance-hall. There are women and music here, and all kinds of liquors. The women and music are attractions brought by the proprietors to aid the sale of liquor. The concert hall is a large room gaudily decorated with mirrors and bright colors. Here and there stands a statue, more notable for its nudity than its artistic merit. A balcony rich in velvet, and statues of historic personages separates the musicians from the main floor of the hall, which is covered with tables. At each of these tables sits one woman or more, who remain helpless and awkward until they are joined by men who are willing to pay high prices for liquors in order to drink them with these harlots. The female attachés of the "Cremorne" are usually well dressed, and many are handsome and attractive. They get a commission on the number of drinks that are sold under their influences, and consequently they employ all their powers of fascination on their male companions. "Ladies' drinks" are all twenty cents in this resort, and no gentleman would think of sitting down and drinking without the companionship of one or more of the females present, according to the etiquette of the avenue.

Here again the women are largely "runners in" for the houses of disrepute in the neighborhood. They have more pecuniary resources than the commission which they get from the "Cremorne's" proprietors. Some of these I can only hint at. I have no doubt that in the wine rooms which are connected with the concert hall of the Cremorne, many a man loses what money and valuables he may have had in his pockets. He drinks and jokes with his female companions until reason and wit begin to dull. He enjoys in a low, sensual way their pawing over his face and whiskers, and notices naught amiss when these light feminine fingers slip into his pockets and abstract his valuables. He does see something wrong, however, the next morning, but he is unable to account for it.

Tom Gould's is another of the up-town resorts, where vice is none the less abundant because it is better concealed. It is in Thirty-first Street, between Broadway and Sixth Avenue, on the south side of the street. It is nothing more or less than a house of assignation. The hallway by which it is entered leads into a long room, at the end of which is a platform used as a stage. The room is decorated with flowers and potted plants. There is a bar from which all kinds of liquor are sold. Tables are scattered about, and, like those of other dives, are attended by women of by no means doubtful characters. They are not as well dressed as the frequenters of the Haymarket.

On the stage, negroes and white men sing popular songs and musicians play the latest operatic airs. The proprietor, Tom Gould, is rather a good-looking man. He is about five feet, seven inches in height, has regular features and a long mustache. At present I believe he is running his establishment without a license, and the authorities should take measures to close it up. The great obstacle I experienced when superintendent, in this as in other cases, was the laxity on the part of excise boards about granting licenses. It is well known that the former Board of Excise granted licenses to many improper places.

Harry Hill's is one of the least harmful dives in the lower part of the town. In saying this, however, I do not mean to imply that debauchery and crime are not greatly fostered here. The gleaming diamond on Manager Harry Hill's shirt-front has probably reflected rays of light on many an evil deed and on many a vicious act around him. The genial proprietor's rotund form and smooth shaven face have made him almost a demi-god among the classes which frequent his resort.

His notorious place, situated on Houston Street, one block east of Broadway, is much frequented by strangers in the city, and by the residents near the Bowery. The building is well known; a structure facing the corner, with a large brazen eagle surmounting the entrance. The visitor enters the bar-room from the street, and after buying his ticket of admittance to the concert hall climbs up the dark stairs. To Harry Hill's sense of personal advantage may be attributed the few disorderly scenes which are enacted in this house. The concert and dance-room of the dive is small and cramped. There is no such wide expanse of floor for waltzing as there is in the Haymarket. There is plainer music, too. A small stage furnishes the most amusement. A regular program is presented on it each night. It consists of boxing-matches, ballads, ballets and comedies. Perhaps a homely woman, dressed in radiant colors, sings a pathetic song in a squeaky voice, or a young and pretty girl in short dresses and long hair puts life and bathos into a touching ballad. The comedy presented is of the lowest type, and the jokes of the comedians are coarse and flat. Yet the open-mouthed spectators stamp their feet in applause, and many a rustic heart is touched with emotion by the forced and creaky notes of a gaudily dressed ballad singer.

There is no formality at Harry Hill's. Everybody is supposed to feel at home. Therefore, when one of the favorite "artists" has finished her part on the program, she slips, in all her made-up finery, gayly to the gallery over the stage and does her best to make the visiting males buy her employer's liquor. They gather around the tables, and at the expense of their male acquaintances order drinks. Now and then they succeed in getting their victims "half seas over," and then complete mastery is easy. They become affectionate in their disposition, and caress them with the deceitful hand of the prostitute.

Far different from the dives which I have described is the "Black-and-Tan," at No. 153 Bleecker Street. No enormous globe holding an electric light attracts people to its entrance. Vice is not resplendent here. No attempt is made to conceal it, or to make it appear less like vice. It is carried on openly, flagrantly and defiantly. The wicked nature of the place is betokened as one enters. Imagine the house—an old-fashioned, well-built brick building, once the home of some proud and wealthy family, now abandoned to the very rot of society. No one would ever dream, as he passed the front door, of the scenes that go on nightly within. Yet he descends three steps and finds himself at the basement door.

This and the windows are heavily curtained, and only here and there where the curtain had not been securely fastened gleamed forth rays of light. We enter a door at the right and find ourselves in a narrow hallway, black as the waters of the East River on a foggy night. We feel our way along the damp walls and follow the sounds and the faint glimmer which come from the remote end

A BOWERY DIVE.

of the hall. Here stands Frank Stephenson, the alleged proprietor of the Black-and-Tan. He has no such genial appearance as Harry Hill. He is not particularly muscular—is slim built and has a bloodless, brutal expression. His sneaky, vicious appearance is a good index of the character of the resort. The men who frequent the Black-and-Tan are the "crooks," the thieves, the criminals of the town.

It would not be difficult to say where the Black-and-Tan got its name. It is the resort of black men as well as white, but the girls are all white! This mixture of races is all the more revolting; and the scenes which go on here in this underground dive are as bad as imagination can picture them. The main room is only about thirty feet square and is low ceiled. There are tables around the sides of the room, and the space in the centre is reserved for dancing. At one end is the bar, kept by four bar-tenders, behind each of whom hangs a murderous-looking club to which the patrons of the dive are not strangers. One will see fifteen or twenty women in the room, and as many burly, brutal negroes. There are only traces of beauty in the women's faces. Whatever sign of womanhood that might have been there once is gone now. Persons who have become too depraved for the up town dives find their way here. There are no bounds to license. It takes a good deal to satisfy the best of these dull-sensed negroes. They dance until the perspiration rolls in streams down their faces, and then they drink until they are stupid. The other male visitors besides negroes—sailors, young clerks, countrymen—indulge in sensuality almost as vigorously. The air becomes close and hot, and as impure as the moral atmosphere of the place. Later in the evening, the women amuse their male friends by the can-can dance. There is a contest among them to see which can kick the highest, and they take their skirts in their hands, and amid the applause of the spectators kick a cigar from the lips of one of the men.

Women parade the Bowery at night and bring their victims, who too frequently are countrymen, into the dimly lighted dance-room. The bar-tenders, women and proprietor are all in one great conspiracy to make money by means fair or foul. A visitor orders a bottle of wine and he gets perhaps the wrong change back. He appeals from the bar-tender to the proprietor, but the latter smiles grimly, assures him that he must be mistaken and pockets the ill-gotten gains. Let the wronged man make a disturbance, and out he goes into the dark hallway, probably bruised and battered by the murderous clubs wielded by the bar-tenders.

I am told that, until recently, there was an old woman with a pathetic history who used to frequent the Black-and-Tan. Her name was Crazy Lou, and she would come in promptly at midnight and go away at two o'clock. Her face was wrinkled with years of vice. She wore an old worn shawl, and shivered in the warm room as if she were cold. No one spoke to this woman more than to say: "Hello, Crazy Lou!" and her only answer was a smile. She had began her career in the Haymarket, a beautiful, attractive girl of seventeen. She had sat at the tables in the Cremorne and at Tom Gould's. She had danced at Harry Hill's and Billy McGlory's, and finally at the Black-and-Tan. One night while the winds were blowing chill she gathered her shawl about her and went out from the dance-hall into the street. Slowly she picked her way along, and then those who were watching her lost sight of her. The next morning a corpse was found floating in East River. Crazy Lou came to the Black-and-Tan no more.

The worst feature of the American Mabille, as the brightly illuminated building is called which stands in Bleecker Street, near Broadway, is the temptation which it offers to young girls. Young women who have worked all day in shops and factories have a natural longing for relaxation of some sort when evening comes. So they go out into the brilliantly lighted street, and thence easily find their way to such places as the Mabille. Once there, and fascinated by the gay whirl of the waltz and the soft speeches of masculine flatterers, it is a great temptation to come again. And they return night after night, the slow poison of vice gradually working to the very centre if their moral consciousness, absorbing every good trait in their bodies. Finally they give up their positions in the shops and factories, and earn their living in the dance-hall. Self-respect and virtue are speedily lost, and they sink to the lowest depths of infamy.

For such downfalls as these Mr. " The." or Theodore Allen, the proprietor of the American Mabille, and one of a family of criminals, is largely responsible. Yet what cares he for young girls' souls? His path to wealth is strewn with them, and he has grown accustomed to the sight ere this.

The Mabille differs in no important particular from the other low resorts that have been mentioned. There are two parts of it; the main room, entered from the street, where there are tables and a bar, a few worn-out musicians, and bar-tenders with ominous clubs. Women frequenters who are not directly employed by Allen sit at the table and persuade men to pay large prices for poor wine and worse beer.

There is a stage also in the concert room, upon which a poor **variety** performance is given. Dissolute women in gaudy tights dance and sing ribald songs, and rough-looking men shout—I could hardly say sing—the latest vulgar burlesque.

In the basement is the dance-hall, and it is here that the young girls of the neighborhood get their first taste for vice. There is a bar down here too, and there are musicians who make worse music than their fellows up stairs.

Billy McGlory is, in the neighborhood of Hester Street, what Tom Lee, a discharged deputy-sheriff and an Americanized Chinaman, is in Chinatown—an uncrowned king. He is a man out of whom forty devils might be cast were it possible to get at him. He was born in crime, and has grown up in it. The Five Points, thirty-five years ago, was the seat of the worst dens of infamy in America. Surrounded by everything evil, McGlory was born. He got his education in the dives, and there he is finishing it. As a boy he was one of the worst " toughs " of Chatham Square and the Bowery, but was shrewd enough to keep out of the clutches of the police. He is now about thirty-five years old, a slim man, with dark sunken eyes and thin lips. A huge diamond sparkles on his shirt-front.

The realm of this king is only in the immediate vicinity of the dive over which he presides. But his name is world-wide, and his infamy is as well known as his name. " Armory Hall," or " Billy McGlory's," is at No. 158 Hester Street. It is very much like the American Mabille, only " more so." It is better known and perhaps more brilliantly conducted. This makes it all the more fascinating to the youth and pleasure-seeking classes of the Bowery and vicinity. The "attractions" begin at about eleven o'clock. They consist of much the same performances as we have seen at the other dives. Perhaps here the women throw their legs a little higher, and display a larger extent of nether garments. This makes the spectators laugh and cheer the more loudly, and attracts greater numbers of the vicious classes. There are "crooks" and criminals of the worst sort in attendance here. It makes a sort of diversion for them, and gives them exceptional opportunities for plying their foul trade.

Billy McGlory's supplies largely with inmates the houses of ill-fame in this and other cities. Shop girls go to Armory Hall to dance, and just as surely as they become habitués of the place their horrible fate as prostitutes is settled. The can-can dance is the favorite one here, and the debauchery and licentiousness exhibited is terrible. The wonder is that young girls are not warned by the shocking immoralities displayed by their elders: but they seem to be only fascinated.

There was a sunny-haired maiden there once, who looked and was, I believe, as pure as the freshly fallen snow. I saw her again only two years later, and her plump cheeks were hollow; the lustre of her eyes was gone, and a pallor as of death was on her coun-

OWNEY GEOGEGHAN.
(From a Photograph.)

tenance. The grim terror, consumption, was standing over her and waiting to grasp its victim. A woman with delicate physique cannot lie half drunk in the damp streets many nights without endangering her life.

A haggard woman was once brought into police headquarters, raving like a maniac. She was taken to Blackwell's Island, but before she went I had learned that she had been found in a fit of delirium tremens outside of Billy McGlory's. She had danced in

Harry Hill's once, and had been a favorite at the Black-and-Tan and the American Mabille. Later she had appeared at Armory Hall, where she drank until even brain was gone.

A pretty girl who was once thrown out of Billy McGlory's, because she would not go with a man who invited her, was found by police officers in a raid on a Mott Street opium joint, whither she had gone to dream life away in the fumes of the Oriental drug. I am informed that the king of the Hester Street dives has made it a rule that any female habitué of his place who refuses to go out for immoral purposes with the man that asks her, shall be denied the " privileges " of the hall. He gives orders to this effect to his door-keepers, and no king's orders were ever more faithfully obeyed than Billy McGlory's.

But arising from the degradation of vice to the glitter it assumes when surrounded by the splendor of the ball-room, and leavened by such pseudo-respectable persons as wish to watch the immorality of others without indulging in it, perhaps the French ball is the most conspicuous of all questionable assemblies. This ball is known as that of the Cercle Française de l'Harmonie.

Although this event is termed French, it is thoroughly an American institution. Most of the attendants are Americans and Germans. It is one of the most "populous" balls of the city, and perhaps the most disreputable of the reputable ones—hovering just on the border line.

It is given under the auspices of a society of Frenchmen, who clear from $15,000 to $25,000 every year. A ticket of admission is $5, a hat-check $2 more, and supper $2 additional for each guest. So popular has this ball grown to be that it is generally held in three of the largest halls in the city : the great Academy of Music, opening one way through a short vestibule into Neilson Hall, and the other way over a temporary bridge above the street into Irving Hall. So important are the alimentary features of the entertainment deemed, that the two smaller halls are allotted wholly to the gratification of the palate, Irving Hall being used for a supper-room and Neilson Hall as a wine-room. The orchestra chairs of the Academy are covered by a flooring to be used as a dancing floor, and at the back of the stage is an enormous circle of gas jets, forming the luminous legends of the society. Two bands, numbering 175 instruments, play alternately dancing and promenade music from the galleries. The Stars and Stripes, trimmed with the tri-color along the foot-lights, and shields and crests crossed with spears hang on the columns. The boxes are handsomely trimmed with patriotic devices, and deep festoons of blue and crimson velvet, interspersed with banners, decorate the galleries, the chandeliers, and the lobbies, as well as the bridge spanning Irving Place to the second floor of Irving Hall. This bridge is lighted by electricity.

The ball begins late. At ten o'clock there are not fifty persons on the floor, and but few in the seats; but almost all are masked, and the ladies' dressing-room is already a crush.

"It'll be lively by midnight, though," somebody said, and somebody was exactly right about it.

If it was lively at twelve, what adjective will describe it at two?

The French ball is an assemblage of the higher class demi-monde and the club men of New York City, a congress of the more particular of disreputable women and of business and professional men. It is taken for granted that most of the *jeunesse dorée* will go—sometimes, if not always—and that respectable women will not go. Yet respectable women do attend the ball. There are usually more than a hundred on the floor and in the dress circle, deeply and thoroughly masked beyond recognition, except to those who know their forms and methods of walking. Husbands and wives often go—generally with somebody's else wives and husbands.

At one of these balls held recently the centre of attraction seemed to be a Miss Western, a woman of much notoriety, formerly an intimate friend of the notorious Josephine Mansfield, and one of "Jim" Fiske's "Twelve Temptations." She occupied the best proscenium box in the Academy—the box owned by the Astor family. She was unmasked, and evidently proud of her position as the acknowledged queen of the ball. Scores of club-men stood grouped together on the floor below the box all night, staring up into her face, and indulging in free comments on her appearance. She was very tall, but well proportioned; her complexion, a rich, deep olive; black eyes and dark hair lending considerable beauty to a round, full face. She was costumed in a Worth dress of black satin, square corsage, with black gloves reaching far above the elbow. There was no color in her ornamentation; her jewellery was of gold and diamonds. In her ears flashed two superb solitaires; about her arms wound two great

FRENCH BALL.

snakes of woven gold, almost from her shoulders to her wrists, where four eyes of the largest diamonds gleamed from wicked-looking heads.

Some hundred or two of the "solid men" of the future New York called on her in the box during the evening, and made her acquaintance. Indeed, she held a regular court, and was the cynosure of all eyes. It seemed very odd that the gleaming and glittering creature should be sitting there, enthroned and complacent, in the chair which Mrs. Astor usually occupies, so demurely listening to the opera. Bouquet after bouquet was brought to her, and she threw a fleeting glance of coquettish recognition upon each giver, and piled them upon the balcony and chairs around her till she was fairly embowered. She was said to have on $10,000 worth of jewels. She reminded one of the "Dame with the Camellias."

The other boxes in the vicinity were similarly occupied by the most disreputable women in the city—a stout and sober-looking matron occupying the front of each box, with a bevy of gaudily or fancifully dressed girls grouped behind her.

At ten o'clock there are 7000 persons present—500 couple madly struggling for a chance to waltz at once. Perhaps one-third of the people are in fancy dress, at least 1000 being in character; and perhaps half of the ladies and a quarter of the gentlemen wear masks. There is a terrible crowd. The heat is like the fiery furnace. Actors and actresses come in from the theatres. A good many well-known politicians were on hand. A distinguished Western journalist had a box, but he was soon enticed to the floor.

The dancing floor is now a picturesque jam. A Neapolitan fisherman dances with the "Mascotte;" a Prince of the Caucasus whirls "Little Red Riding Hood;" one of the half dozen Oscar Wildes present dances the can-can; and turning about the floor are a gaudy butterfly; a nymph in pale green silk, embroidered with pearls, is arm-in-arm with a water lily; a Moorish chief charges upon a dozen Æsthetes, and then comes an assorted lot of Napoleons, Cleopatras, Joan of Arcs, gypsies, nuns, brigands, vivandieres, sultanas, Magyars, Bedouins, "Olivettes," Indians, fairies and demons; women in black tights, women in red tights, women in blue tights; men and women in every picturesque garb imaginable. There is by this time a good deal of reckless behavior.

Wine is having its effect. A Charles II. cavalier comes rushing down from the lobby, and seizing a handsome woman kisses her frantically. Her escort interferes, and there is a fight. Somebody strikes somebody else who cannot be seen, for the policemen step upon the scene and vanish with their victim.

Policemen have been noticed quietly stealing in,—coming one by one—so softly that their entrance was not noticed by the dancers generally, and taking position around the outside of the auditorium, at the entrances to the vestibule. Every species of amusement that belongs to masked balls is in full swing. Some of the club men are riotous. Others are languid and look bored; but these are the dissolute and *blasé*, who have drank all sorts of beakers to the dregs and always look bored. Men yawn and pay little attention to the creatures, padded and painted and powdered, with hard-finish faces and harsh, rasping voices, that go flitting past.

We walk down the *foyer*, just on the borders of the dance floor, when a woman approaches us, attired in a brocaded pink silk dress, shirred down the front with pink satin, ornaments, laces and diamonds, and tries to kick our hats off. We quit the terrible person, and retreat to the stairs, where a gentleman, well known in New York parlors, is tugging away at something. It is a woman, apparently; a very heavy weight. He has clasped her wrists over his shoulders, and is trying to carry her up stairs on his back.

"O, Harry! Drop that mountain of loveliness!" shouted an acquaintance to him, and the "mountain" rolls off in a rage, and rushes for the speaker, who flees.

We walk down to the floor again. Pandemonium has broken loose. In the clatter of voices, quiet conversation is no longer possible. A friend speaks in our ears.

"Do you want to see hell?"

"Yes! Where?" we cry eagerly. "Where is it?"

He takes us by the arms and leads us fifty steps to the entrance to Neilson Hall. We stand at the top of the four steps between the halls and look down upon the scene. This, it will be remembered, is the wine-room. Sure enough, it is an inferno. It is so full of smoke that you can scarcely see a form, except those near, though there are fully one thousand persons there. As for the noise, it seems not so much like a Babel of voices, as like an incessant roll. The sound is pitched high and the tone slightly rises and falls, but the screech is unbroken; it sounds like the cry of agony of a hundred persons being burned alive in a wrecked railroad train. Here and there a loud laugh pierces the din.

Now I see that most of the drinkers are sitting at tables. Every chair in the great hall is occupied, and persons stand behind in relays, waiting for a chance. One third of them are women. Some are sitting on the tables. Some lying on the window-sills. Each one of them seems to be screaming to the other. There is found that wild abandon—that freedom of speech, gesture, and attitude—belonging exclusively to the French Masquerade ball. Every body speaks to everybody without reserve, and the person spoken to puts his hand to his ear and scoops in the utterance like a sailor in a hurricane.

When we first entered the building the halls were all of them gloomy, cold, quiet, almost unoccupied; now there is found a bacchanalian orgie—a hot and crazy revel, and whirl of passion.

At three o'clock some of the tireless foot flingers are still on the floor, but the fire of revelry is burning low.

NOTE.—I wrote the preceding chapter in the summer of 1886. Since that time Abram S. Hewitt has been elected and is now (1887) mayor of New York. Thanks to his untiring efforts and inflexible determination every so-called "dive" described by me has been closed and the city is to-day freed of those cradles of crime and debauchery. There is no reason why they should ever be re-opened. —G. W. W.

CHAPTER XXXVI.

BUTCHER-CART THIEVES.—STARVING CHILDREN IN "THE SHEPHERD'S FOLD."—GARFIELD'S MURDERER AT POLICE HEADQUARTERS.—THE WOMAN WHO THOUGHT SHE WAS SHADOWED. —THE NOTORIOUS FLORENTINE FORGERS.—A VISIT TO EUROPE.—HOW THE EXCISE LAWS ARE EVADED.

A CERTAIN class of thieves who flourished back in the fifties had a bold and novel way of pursuing their vocations. Numbers of young men, who either owned or hired horses and wagons, would ride up suddenly to butcher shops in the upper part of the city, and seizing a carcass would throw it into the wagon, and make off at full speed. Such marauding expeditions led the thieves into trouble, of course, unless the carcass-snatchers possessed well-built vehicles, with faultless running gear, and trusty horses of more than average speed. These robberies opened up to thieves a new field for men of nerve, so that, a few years later, watches and other valuables were snatched from citizens by men who escaped in wagons, and in the order of evolution persons were waylaid in the streets by these bold depredators, and deprived of packages of money and bonds. It came to be so, after awhile, that "hog" and "butcher-cart" thieves, as they were called, were all considered A. 1. in the "profession."

The first important robbery of this kind which I remember occurred on the morning of January 19, 1866. Samuel Terry, sixteen years old, a messenger of the Farmers' and Citizens' National Bank, of Williamsburg, was despatched to the Park National Bank, of New York, with a satchel in which were $7,000 in money and $7,000 in checks. He crossed the Roosevelt Street ferry, and was in Beekman Street, near Park Row, when two men, who wore soldiers' blue smocks, sprang from a butcher's cart and approached him. One struck the boy a blow which made him dizzy, and the other seized the satchel. Both then jumped into the cart again, whipped up the horses and escaped easily.

Upon May 12th, of the same year, J. H. Higgins, cashier for E. S. Higgins and Company, carpet-makers, at No. 358 Broadway, went to the bank to draw the wages for the hands, as it was Saturday. He put $16,400 in a bag, and started for the factory, which was situated at the foot of West Forty-third Street. He left an Eighth Avenue car at Forty-Third Street, and was half way down the block when he passed a man who scanned him closely. An instant later the man crept up behind him and dealt him a stunning blow on the back of the head, while a confederate, springing from a butcher's cart near by, gave the cashier another blow, seized the bag, and threw it to a third man in the cart. The two assailants then leaped into the wagon and escaped. They were chased as far as Third Avenue and Forty-Second Street, but here trace of them was lost.

On December 13, 1867, Lewis J. Kinsley, seventeen years old, junior clerk of the Bank of the City of New York, had just left the Clearing House and was at the corner of Wall and William Streets, carrying a satchel which contained $500 in money and $3,600,000 in checks, when he noticed a Portland sleigh, in the shafts of which was a bob-tailed horse, standing near the curb. As he passed it he was felled to the ground, and in the twinkling of an eye the satchel was thrown into the sleigh and caught by a man sitting in it. Another man jumped in, and the horse was urged on. Meanwhile young Kinsley had partially recovered from the shock of the blow, and had caught on to the hind part of the sleigh. He hung on bravely for about a block, lustily yelling "Thieves!" but a film came over his eyes, his hands relaxed their hold, and he was picked up in an unconscious condition. The money was never recovered by the bank, but the checks, it was reported, were "negotiated" back for a small sum.

So far there had been no arrests of any consequence for such offences as these, but on February 1, 1869, Edward Francis, alias "Steve" Boyle, alias "Gus" Shaw, was arrested in front of S. P. Squires' jewellery store at No. 182 Bowery. He had a butcher-cart near by, and when captured was no doubt meditating an attack on Squires. The evidence against him, however, was insufficient to warrant an indictment, so he was turned over to the Michigan authorities for the murder of Sheriff Orcutt of that state.

There was a lull in the butcher-cart business up to June 10, 1878. On that day Joseph W. Laffetra, conductor's receiver of the Third Avenue Railroad, started from the Harlem depot for the main office with about $150 on his person. Usually he carried a much larger amount. He boarded a Third Avenue car at nine o'clock. In it were a number of persons who had been at a picnic, and some soldiers of the Eleventh Regiment. The car was followed, at a respectable distance at first, by a wagon in which were five men. At Ninety-Fourth Street these men drove the wagon close up to the car, and jumping out attacked Laffetra, got the bag which contained the money after a severe fight, and escaped. The soldiers in the car rendered Laffetra no assistance. For this offence J R. Titterington, John Hogan and Peter Culkin, well known desperadoes, and identified with former crimes of the same nature, were arrested. There was not sufficient evidence against them, and they were discharged.

The last butcher cart robbery of note occurred on December 31, 1883. Mr. Alfred Church, the aged superintendent of John Dwight and Company's soda-water factory in East 112th Street, went to the Chatham National Bank for the purpose of drawing money to pay wages. He had done this often, and his movements had been closely watched by the notorious "Ed." Goodie, alias Gearing. Mr. Church had to get off the Second Avenue Elevated road at 111th Street. Goodie, who for years had furnished the horse flesh for such expeditions, had his best horse hitched to a butcher's cart near the station. At that time there was only one way to reach the street from the platform, and as Church began to go down the stairs he saw a villanous looking man, attired in a blue jumper, sweeping the steps. The sweeper allowed Mr. Church to pass. Near the bottom of the stairs Mr. Church encountered a fair-complexioned, clean shaven man, who was also sweeping. As he was about to pass him, the fellow threw aside his broom and snatched the package of money, amounting to $2250, from under Mr. Church's arm; while the first sweeper put the old man *hors du combat* by a blow from a piece of lead pipe, prepared for the occasion. The two thieves then rushed for the butcher's cart, into which they climbed and escaped, despite the fact that they were chased as far south as Seventy-Second Street. An excellent description of the thieves was given at Police Headquarters, so that in less than two months afterwards Goodie was sentenced to twenty years' imprisonment, Farrell to fifteen years, and Titterington to ten years.

One of the best executed "jobs" of this class was what is known as the "Messerschmidt affair." It occurred on the 15th July, 1881. Mr. Charles Messerschmidt was a trusted employee of Jacob Ruppert, the brewer, and had been for years employed to take the vast collections of his employer to the Germania Bank. On the day in question, accompanied by Gustave Aengele, a boy, he started from the brewery at Ninety-First Street and Third Avenue in a buggy, with $9600 in bills, made up in a package, on which he sat; $5000 in checks, and $1000 in silver. He drove down town by way of Lexington Avenue, and remarked nothing until between Forty-Seventh and Forty Eighth streets, when what appeared to be a licensed vender's wagon was driven violently against the buggy horse, so as to force it on to the curb. At the same instant a man sprung out of the wagon into the buggy and throttled Mr. Messerschmidt with one hand while with the other he held a revolver to his head. A second man then jumped out of the wagon, ran round to the side of the buggy and took the package of bills from under Mr. Messerschmidt. Still a third man cut the harness of the buggy horse, so as to render pursuit impossible. There was a signal given—"All right,"—the three men got into the wagon, in which there were two others, and they then started down town at a 3.20 gait. Some citizens, a policeman and a fireman took up the chase at intervals, and the thieves showed of what metal they were made by firing several shots at their pursuers, one of the bullets passing through the window of a store. Several arrests were made, but no one was even brought to trial.

Horrifying disclosures regarding the treatment of the children in the "Shepherd's Fold" created much public indignation during the year 1880. This institution was situated at No. 157 East Sixtieth Street in this city, and was managed by the Rev. Edward Cowley, whose name will be handed down to posterity as one of the most cold-blooded, canting hypocrites with which this world has ever been afflicted. Under his charge at the "Fold" there were between thirty and forty children, ranging in age from four to sixteen years. Cowley's wife was associated with him in the management of the institution. This confederate in iniquity, on one day in the latter part of December, 1879, appeared at St. Luke's Hospital with a child called Louis Victor, who was five years old, and who, she said, had been an inmate of the Fold, and needed better care and treatment than she could give him there.

Truly the little waif did need better care. According to Dr. Riolon, the physician in charge of the hospital, the child was in a state of emaciation almost beyond relief; he was simply skin and bones, and had nothing on his body which looked like fat or muscular development. He was very stupid. In the presence of Mrs. Cowley he made no cry or complaint; but after he was taken to the ward, he cried continually for food, especially meat. His pinched face had a dark, bloodless color. Beyond all question his condition was due, simply and wholly, to improper and insufficient food—in plain English, he was suffering from starvation!

The condition of the little starveling was critical, and on the sixth of January, 1880, the officers of St. Luke's Hospital notified the Society for the Prevention of Cruelty to Children. The president of the society, Mr. Elbridge T. Gerry, at once called at the hospital, and a photograph of poor little Louis was taken, showing his physical condition. The facts of the case were laid before the Supreme Court by the society, and a warrant was issued by Justice Donohue for the production of all the inmates of the Shepherd's Fold. The result of this was that the following children were brought before him: Fannie McCurdy, 16 years, Bessie Lawrence, 15, Minnie St. James, 15, Lillie Hawes, 14, Emma Bowman, 15, Lizzie Hunter, 13, Mary Shaw, 8, Rockwell Macan, 9, Philip Macan, 5, Lilian Anderson, 8, Edith Anderson, 4, George Predeau, 5, Mary Metzler, 11, Gussie Sweeney, 12, Charles Sweeney, 9, Frederick Sweeney, 7, Maggie Sweeney, 3, Lawrence Martin, 7, Robert Wood, 3, Alfredo Lauzi, 9, Estelle Staudenback, 13, John Staudenback, 10, Thomas Banks, 10, and John Banks, 7 years,—Louis Victor, 5 years, being in St. Luke's Hospital, was not produced. James Fox, 14, and John Campbell, 16 years, were surrendered later.

The grand jury found no less than twenty five indictments against the Rev. Edward Cowley, and on one of them, in which he was charged with cruelly ill-using and neglecting little Victor, he was tried during the month of February, 1880.

The evidence adduced at the trial showed that the Shepherd's Fold was incorporated under the laws of the State of New York for the purpose of "receiving and adopting children and youths of both sexes, between the age of twelve months and fifteen years, who are orphans, half-orphans, or otherwise friendless; these to keep, support, and educate, apprentice and place out to service, trades and schools." It was under these promises that Louis Victor was received into the "Fold" on the 23d of January, 1878. He was then in a perfect state of health—plump, lively, healthy and stout. The testimony went to show that almost the only food served to the children was oatmeal mush, milk and water, which was served to them on soap boxes in a damp, dingy basement. A physician was called in to see Louis Victor once, and fresh air and exercise, together with nourishing food, were prescribed. But all the exercise and fresh air he and his fellow inmates got were obtained in a little back yard, into which the sun never entered. Meat, the children never saw, and the squalor, discomfort and misery of the place must have chilled and darkened the entire block in which the "Fold" was situated. "Nourishing food" meant three raw tomatoes a day!

Poor little Louis gradually wasted away before the eyes of the Cowleys, until he was on the very verge of the grave, and then they took him to the hospital.

Shepherd Cowley made a strong fight in the courts, but it was of no avail. The evidence of his neglect and cruelty was overwhelming, and he was found guilty, as might have been expected. Recorder Smythe, before whom the case was tried, sentenced him to one year's imprisonment in the Penitentiary, and to pay a fine of $250, or to stand committed until the fine was paid. Cowley appealed, but the conviction was sustained, and he served out his sentence. But prison fare such as he got would have seemed sweet to the orphans whom he maltreated.

Every one is conversant with the tragic circumstances which attended the assassination of President Garfield by Guiteau—how, when the President, walking in the Baltimore and Potomac railway station at Washington, arm-in-arm with James G. Blaine, was shot down in cold blood by a political crank. When the appalling news of the assassination was made known in New York, I was immediately struck with the similarity of the name of the assassin— Guiteau—with that of a man who had once been brought before me. A few days before the trial of Guiteau I happened to be in Washington, and saw him in his cell. Any doubts I may have had as to his being the fellow I had arrested in New York were at once dis-

THE SHEPHERD'S FLOCK.

pelled by his appearance, and by his exclaiming, as if he recognized me, "How do you do, sir?"

The way in which he came under my notice was as follows: He had conceived a passionate admiration for a young lady, and began showing it by following her about when she went shopping and when she went to church. Then he wrote her love-letters, in a high-flown style, expressing his ardent affection and devotion. These were followed by small presents from time to time. Such attentions became exceedingly distasteful to the young lady, and she made the facts known to her friends, who reported the matter to me. The letters were numerous; all had passed through the Post-office and were written on Fifth Avenue Hotel note paper. The writer was apparently a man of some education, as the penmanship was fairly good, and the language, though lofty and grandiloquent, appropriate and grammatical. As an inducement to the young lady to accept him as her husband, he mentioned that he was about to receive from the Government an appointment abroad as diplomatic representative of the United States. He drew a flattering picture, showing the grace and dignity with which the young lady, as his wife, could assist him in filling the position. The lawyer who came to me in behalf of the young lady pointed out that the would-be suitor was evidently under the impression that the subject of his admiration was an heiress; but that in this he was mistaken. The gifts, too, I learned, were of a cheap and trashy character. The letters were all signed "Charles Guiteau."

I sent a very careful officer—John McNamara—to enquire into the matter. He watched the lady's residence, and also the church she was in the habit of attending. In a day or two Guiteau appeared on the scene, and was immediately recognized by the officer from the description furnished him. The suitor was loitering about outside the church, waiting for his lady love. He did not see her, however, for McNamara arrested him, and he was brought before me. It did not strike me then that there was anything remarkable about his appearance, and he made no particular impression on me. He was a small man, with dark complexion, black eyes, and was respectably dressed. His demeanor, when in my presence, did not differ in the least from those under arrest for similar offences.

"So you've been writing letters to a lady?" I said.

He admitted as much, informing me, also, that he had sent her presents.

I gave Guiteau a severe lecture, upon the conclusion of which he promised never to annoy the young lady again. As he was leaving the office, I said:

"If this same complaint is made against you a second time, I shall certainly send you to the Penitentiary."

Instances of this kind were not uncommon in my experience; and it had almost passed out of my mind, when one day Officer McNamara reported that he had again found Guiteau in the vicinity of the church, evidently lying in wait for the young lady. The officer took hold of him and nearly frightened him out of his boots by saying:

"I am going to take you before the superintendent, and you'll have to go to the Penitentiary this time."

Guiteau was very much alarmed, and begged and prayed in a piteous manner to be let off. This was done, and that was the last time he came in contact with the New York police. It would have been difficult to prosecute the man, which is nearly always the case in accusations of this nature. The publication of particulars is unpleasant for the persons who have been annoyed.

The number of persons who are reported to the police as being missing from their homes is something incredible. As for lost, stolen or strayed children, their name is legion. A parent rushes wildly into the station-house, her hair dishevelled, and her eyes almost starting from their sockets, and cries out that her child has been lost. It had been last seen with a strange man or woman, therefore it must have been kidnapped!

As a general rule, however, the missing individual soon turns up with a very simple explanation as to the cause of absence. Right here comes in the greatest difficulty with which the police have to contend. Instant information is given when a person is supposed to be "lost," but very rarely is it that the friends of the lost remember to inform the police of the absent one's return.

A number of precautions are taken by the police for the protection of those who are strangers in the city and who happen to meet with any accident. When persons are found sick on the sidewalk, and are unable to tell their names or addresses, but are identified by an address card found on them, they are at once sent to their homes. Otherwise, if there is no such clue, a description.

of the individual found is telegraphed to an officer at headquarters, who has charge of all such matters. In the case of a child found wandering about the streets, if it can tell its name, we telegraph to its parents, who come to headquarters and recover their darling. If no information can be obtained from the child, it is placed in charge of the matron, Mrs. Webb, until some one claims the child, or it is sent to some public institution.

One of the most famous cases of disappearance which occurred during my term as police superintendent, and one which perhaps is freshest in my memory, was that of Charles Delmonico, the proprietor of the well-known restaurant, on January 5, 1884. On that day he left his home in West Fourteenth Street and disappeared so effectually that for a week, in spite of large rewards, the police and detective force were unable to get track of him. It came to be generally supposed that he had been kidnapped, or, worse yet, murdered; but the police knew that the missing man had shown signs, previous to his mysterious departure, of dementia, the result of a long and severe illness; and they worked on the theory that he had wandered off somewhere and either lost his way or met with an accident.

We finally learned that he had been seen last on a ferry-boat leading to Jersey City, and accordingly our search was confined largely to New Jersey. After days of disagreeable searching, for the weather was wintry and cold, we came upon his body in a little ravine near Orange. Evidently he had fallen, and injured himself so severely that he could not rise nor attract others to his condition. So he gradually starved and froze to death.

Women have very often proved troublesome upon being arrested, especially when intoxicated. Policemen Maxwell and Carney came across two of them one evening, raising a disturbance on the Bowery. Maxwell collared one and his companion the other. Maxwell's prisoner made no particular resistance until they had walked some distance, when she suddenly sat down on the sidewalk and commenced to disrobe. Bonnet, shawl, boots, stockings, and other garments went flying into the middle of the street. As fast as Maxwell replaced one article she divested herself of another. At length, with the assistance of bystanders, the policeman got enough clothes on her to hide her nakedness, and again started for the station-house.

Before reaching there, however, down she went on the sidewalk again, and this time she managed to pull her dress completely off. The policeman was then close to the entrance, and so, gathering up his prisoner's clothing in one hand, took hold of her with the other, and marched her in. To say that the sergeant in charge was astonished at seeing this half-clothed woman is but half expressing his impressions. It took three men to dress her again and put her in a cell. Maxwell has since confessed to me that whenever he saw her on the street afterward he always gave her a wide berth.

On one occasion, while superintendent, I was standing at the corner of Pine and Nassau streets, talking to two gentlemen, when an old woman, pretty well intoxicated and carrying a basket on her arm, came up and addressed me. Although I was attired in citizen's dress, she evidently knew me, because when I told her to go away and not make a noise she commenced to abuse the police in general and me in particular. A crowd quickly collected, and despite all my urging the woman would not go away. Among those in the crowd was a well-known stock broker. With the intention of disconcerting me and having some fun, this gentleman remarked in a loud voice:

"I thought it was the duty of the police to arrest intoxicated and disorderly persons on the streets."

Thus challenged, as it were, although I might easily have called a patrolman, I took hold of the woman and started with her towards the First Precinct station-house on New Street. The crowd followed. Among the various contents of the woman's basket was a bag of flour, with which, having one arm free, she vigorously pelted me. I was covered with the white powder from head to foot. The numerous brokers and others who witnessed the scene were most uproarious, yelling and shouting at the top of their voices, while the smaller boys were no less backward in their demonstrations of delight at my whitewashed appearance. I appeared against the woman the next day at the Tombs, and she was sent to the Island for a term.

The habit of people to fly to the police upon the very slightest provocation is astonishing. All nervous and excitable persons apparently look upon the force as having been organized for their own personal benefit. The complaints made, and the grievances elaborated by these imaginative individuals, are countless. The most natural movements and actions on the part of perfectly innocent persons are distorted, by the aid of vivid imaginations, into plots to commit crime or to destroy the happiness and peace of mind of those making the complaint. Very often, I confess, have I been provoked when investigating these "baseless fabrics of a vision." Yet I could not pass these complaints over without taking some notice of them, as the very next thing in order would have been a charge of negligence against the police.

Of intercourse with "cranks" I really think I have had more than my fair share. It is strange how these unfortunate individuals always go directly to the Superintendent of Police, seemingly having little or no confidence in any of his subordinates. The most common form of aberration of mind which these half-balanced individuals possess is the fear of being waylaid and attacked by enemies who, they think, are pursuing them day and night.

I well remember one nice old lady who came to me in evident fear and distress of mind. That she was well-bred there could be no doubt—her dress and demeanor plainly showed that. She informed me, in a very earnest but somewhat rambling manner, that certain persons, with none of whom she was acquainted, were constantly following her about, to do her some injury. I saw at once that her mind was affected, but nevertheless listened attentively to all she had to say, with apparently the deepest sympathy. She was so evidently a lady in every sense of the word that I hadn't the heart to send her about her business, as I might have done. A fortunate thought entered my head and I hastened to act on it. I rang my bell and instructed the officer who answered the summons to send me two of the smartest detectives on the force. They came, and pointing out the lady to them I said:

"You will see that hereafter this lady is not molested in any way."

The old lady then left the room, thanking me over and over again for my kindness, and evidently was greatly pleased with the result of her interview. A few months afterwards, however, she again made her appearance in my office. She had come, she said, to inform me that she was entirely free from her enemies in New York; but as she was going to spend the summer at Newport she thought it would be best if I gave her a letter to the Chief of Police there. This, I told her, was impossible, but I would, however, see to it that the Newport chief was made acquainted with her case and that the necessary protection would be afforded her. Once more did she almost overwhelm me with her professions of gratitude, and then retired.

Upon returning to New York, however, she again proved troublesome, paying frequent visits to Police Headquarters and annoying me in many ways. One day, therefore, I informed her that she must call on me no more. She became very indignant and exclaimed in a very angry manner:

"Superintendent, you are a cruel man! and God will not be good to you."

Another good example of a crank who paid me a visit was a highly educated Englishman. He, literally as well as figuratively, had electricity on the brain, and believed he was powerfully charged with the volatile fluid. In his imagination a brick wall presented no obstacles, and the never-failing reservoir of supply was, he thought, located somewhere in his head. He was taken before a magistrate, to whom I explained the poor fellow's hallucination, and he was sent to an insane asylum. He was subsequently released and returned to England, whence he wrote me. His letter was a bright and clever composition, very sensible except for the final sentence, which ran thus: "I am still suffering from the electric fluid; and I will never come near you again because you were cruel enough to send me to an asylum."

Once, when I was captain of the Eighteenth Precinct, a German actually came and wanted the aid of the police simply because his horse wouldn't stand still and he couldn't harness him. At another time a woman told me a long story about a mackerel, which another woman had promised to watch for her while it was being cooked. This woman had neglected her trust, the mackerel was burned and the complainant wanted the woman arrested, and made to pay for the cremated fish.

I have even known business men to make the most reckless charges, without considering the legal aspect of the case. I have been asked to order the arrest of drummers travelling in another state, who had sold their samples, the applicant forgetting that such a crime, committed in one state, is not punishable in another. Men frequently want their wives arrested for stealing property from them, and also on the charge of adultery. This is no offence, in law, in New York state, as I found out to my cost on one occasion. I received a despatch from the Montreal chief of police requesting me to arrest a married woman who had eloped from Canada with a man not her husband, and who was on her way to this city. When the two arrived here I had them arrested and taken to Jefferson Market Police Court. The woman employed Messrs. Howe and Hummell as her counsel and was immediately discharged, as there was no statute under which she could be held for adultery. Afterwards, a resolution was introduced in the assembly by Hamilton Fish, Jr., asking that an enquiry be held into my action, but nothing ever came of it. I was, however, more careful in the future.

The methods of that dangerous class of criminals known as forgers, and the passers of spurious money and securities, were never more thoroughly exposed than in a confession made to Col. J. Schuyler Crosby, at Florence, Italy, in the early spring of 1885 It occurred after the arrest of those famous forgers and counterfeiters: Willis, Burnes, Hamilton and Wilkes, in connection with what is known as the Florentine forgeries. "Pete" Burnes, otherwise known as James J. Julian and Henry Wood; and George W. Wilkes, alias Willis, were arrested in Florence, Italy, on Christmas Day, 1880. Almost at the same moment, "Shell" Hamilton, alias Colburt, their confederate, was captured in Milan. They had been engaged in freebooting expeditions against bankers and hotel keepers all over Europe, using forged bonds, counterfeit money and spurious letters of credit.

After a long trial, they were all convicted. Burnes died in prison, leaving a fortune of nearly half a million dollars, for which three women, who pretended to be his "wives," had a long legal squabble. But Wilkes, in some way or other, managed to get released after a short term of imprisonment. It is believed that his release is due to his confession to Consul Crosby, which threw great light on the operations of these and other celebrated forgers in Europe and America.

Wilkes was undoubtedly the equal of any man who ever forged, counterfeited or dealt in "doubtful" securities. Such men as "Andy" Roberts, George Engels, Charley Becker and a host of others, who have been considered "specialists," acknowledged his superiority by seeking his services from time to time. It was he who engineered the infamous $64,000 check forgery on the Union Trust Co.; and he had a share in at least 75 per cent. of all such operations in this country and Europe in which Americans, or villains sailing from America, were connected.

The confession of Wilkes is now among the archives at Police Headquarters. In it he tells the story of his life. He was a native of Orange Co., N. Y., and was born in 1837. After clerking a while for the Erie Railroad Co., he was graduated as a professional gambler, and once kept a "hell" at the corner of Broadway and Fourth Street, with John Tollman and Charley Schaffer. His gambling career lasted a couple of years, and during this period he associated with the better class of criminals. His first venture in forging was with a third-rate man named Sudless. They forged a check of the Board of Education, as well as some small drafts. They were arrested, but discharged. Then Wilkes indulged in a fraud on the Custom House, known as the "Brandy Ring," which netted him $40,000. He was next interested in the forgery of a fifty-dollar greenback on the Tradesman's National Bank of New York. His succeeding venture was with Joseph Chapman (now in prison in Europe) and William Denneran in a "starring" forgery trip. After several failures, at Cheyenne, Chapman passed a draft for $3000. The gang then went to San Francisco, where they had poor luck, only succeeding in cashing a draft for $2300. About this time they went into partnership with N. V. Clinton, a "Hoosier," and organized a scheme of plunder against South American merchants. Clinton, however, broke loose, cheated his partners and came to grief, much to the delight of his former companions, for stealing a letter of credit from a fellow-passenger while on the journey from Panama. Wilkes also left the gang to come to New York, and made arrangements to meet Chapman, who at San Francisco had obtained a small draft on the Bank of British North America. Wilkes "doctored" the draft until it called for $5000, and Chapman negotiated it by means of false letters of introduction.

The two then went to Boston, and when prepared for another starring tour took in George Barlow. They raised funds to meet travelling and hotel expenses by altering a check for a paltry amount to $1600. Their next exploit was the raising of a small draft, obtained in Chicago, to $5000, which was cashed in Louisville, Kentucky. All this, however, was poor business. Besides, several detectives were on the track of the forgers, and Clinton, who was in jail at Panama, had to be supplied with money to bribe his keepers. There was some clever work done in raising checks from small amounts to thousands of dollars, and this kept the gang from starving until the winter of 1876, when they were in possession of funds to the amount of $8,000 or $10,000. At that time the gang was increased by the addition of "Eph" Holland, Patrick Riley and James Hogan. They had money enough to be idle for a time, and at Chicago perfected their knowledge of banking methods. In this they were greatly aided by "Phil" Hargraves, who was nearly as expert as Wilkes.

Early in 1877 they made a descent on Louisiana, raking in from $20,000 to $30,000. They lived recklessly, however; and when they meditated operations between St. Louis and San Francisco, and it was necessary to raise as much money as possible, they were unable to count on much more than $10,000. They, however, rang the changes between the two cities named so cleverly that they netted about $30,000. By this time Wilkes had formed other connections, and had accumulated enough money to enter into bigger business. Forged bonds of the Central Pacific Railroad had been made by Charley Becker, and $10,000 worth of them were disposed of by Wilkes and the others in Chicago. Then, in company with "Josie" Spencer and $34,000 of the bonds, Wilkes started for Europe. Hardly had they landed at Liverpool than a telegram from Chapman announced that "the snap had been given away," and the forged bonds were therefore immediately destroyed. Hunted by the police, Wilkes and Spencer fled to London, and thence back to America, landing at Baltimore. Then they went into the draft-raising business again. At their very first attempt they made $13,500. There was a quarrel among the members of the clique, the result being that Wilkes joined his fortunes with those of Decker and John Phillips, who had just emerged from prison in Pennsylvania. Accompanied by their wives, the trio started for England to dispose of bonds stolen from the Bank of Trenton, New Jersey. In London they met "Andy" Roberts, and had fair luck. Wilkes came back to America, to return almost by the next steamer. This sudden trip was to aid in a plot for placing a "block" of $200,000 worth of Buffalo and Erie Railroad bonds which had been prepared by Roberts. In addition to these bonds there was about $150,000 worth of the bonds of the Chicago Western and Southern Railroad. These securities, however, were not altogether perfected. The finishing touches to the Buffalo and Erie's were put on by "Andy" Roberts, while Walter Sheridan completed the Chicago bonds.

The plot, however, fell through, owing to bad management. The gang dissolved partnership, and Wilkes returned to New York depleted in purse, but far richer in experience. He formed a combination with John Donahue, Charles King, James Greene, and "Phil" Hargraves to buy $50,000 worth of counterfeit greenbacks to dispose of in Europe. The counterfeits were obtained from Charles Ulrich and William E. Gray, at twelve and a half per cent. of their face value. Of this sum $20,000 was lost in Europe by Greene and King, who ventured to Italy and did not know the language sufficiently to place the "queer." Very little was done with the balance.

Then Wilkes went into the speculation of forging letters of credit, etc., spoken of in the history of William Griffis, alias Lord Ashburton. His next plot was to victimize the banking firm of Seligman & Co. of New York. He obtained genuine drafts of £1000 and £10 from the firm in question, upon their London (England) correspondents. In London the gang had the drafts certified and stamped in due form. Then they proceeded to forge other drafts on the firm, and netted $40,000. These forgeries were accomplished by raising smaller drafts on the London correspondents, and stamping them with the spurious certification.

Late in 1879 a gigantic scheme of forging French certificates of three per cents was entered into between Burns, Wilkes, Decker, a Dr. Hamnell and a man named Picon. The certificates were forged by Decker, and the venture proved a gold mine to the gang. They next started on letters of credit of the Société Génerale, of Brussels; but this scheme hung fire, and only about 13,000 francs were made by them. Then they prepared for an Italian raid. Decker and Engels had got ready certificates of Italian stocks to the amount of 600,000 francs, and the gang started to negotiate them. In the hands of such expert "negotiators" as Burns, John Carr, James Poswell, Engels, Wilkes, Charles Baranoff, and Charles Silvio Bixio the certificates went like hot-cakes. The forgers separated into several parties, some going as far as Russia even. The rascals were not content with more than a moderate success, but they were desirous of trying their hand again with the balance of the five per cent. Italian stocks. The plot was to "sack" Naples, Rome, Livorno, Turin, and other places. Luck followed them everywhere, but they came to grief, as before stated, in Turin and Florence.

I don't think I shall be very much out of the way in saying that during Wilkes' career he and his associates dealt in at least $4,000,000 worth of forged and stolen securities, and that they "realized" at least forty per cent. of that amount.

A policeman who had a mistaken idea as to his duties was Patrolman Purvis, of the Sixteenth Precinct, who arrested a well-known saloon-keeper for selling liquor on Sunday. He was informed unofficially by the liquor interest, that in consequence of this arrest he would be transferred to some other precinct. Sure enough he was, for in a very short time he was assigned to duty in the Twenty-ninth, the Police Board passing an order making the transfer. While he was in the Twenty-ninth Precinct he one day received the following anonymous letter:

"Purvis, my old boy, you were told you would be transferred, and you have been. I hope you won't be quite so fresh in arresting people for selling on Sunday."

Let the police do what they may in the matter of making arrests for violations of the excise law, they cannot stop them. Suppose, in the first place, a policeman, in citizen's clothes, enters a saloon on Sunday and sees beer and spirits sold freely. He arrests the bar-tender, who is taken before a magistrate. The law says that if the accused demands a trial by jury it must be granted him, the amount of bail being fixed at $100. Then the case goes to the General Sessions, where it is placed on file, never to come up again probably while he lives. Why? Because I suppose there are not far from twenty thousand such cases on file there now, and the machinery of the court of General Sessions is totally inadequate to deal with them.

I know of one case where a patrolman entered a lager beer saloon on Sunday, saw several sales of liquor, and then arrested the seller. The magistrate before whom the accused was taken asked the officer how he knew that what was sold was lager. He even asked whether the policeman had tasted it or not. The officer replied that he had not, but that he heard persons ask for lager; that they were served with something drawn from a lager beer keg; and that they paid the regular price for lager. The magistrate thereupon discharged the prisoners.

In another case of a like nature, the officer was roundly abused by the magistrate as a spy and a sneak, for having entered the saloon in citizen's attire. Shortly afterwards the same magistrate threatened to prefer charges against that very officer for going into another saloon while wearing his uniform! The police are hampered in every possible way, and it is no wonder some of them give up as useless attempting to enforce this part of the law.

While I was superintendent it was my practice to send a complete record of all the arrests for violations of the excise law to the Excise Commissioners. If they would only do their duty, and revoke the licenses of those who break the law, they would quickly put a stop to all such infractions.

The Roosevelt committee, in their report, credited the inspectors and captains of police with having used all due diligence. My opinion is that the finding of that committee was not justified by the evidence. Its members were influenced in some way or other. I know that a fund was raised through the captains from the men in the force, and turned over to the inspectors, who paid it to some one connected with the committee. The force raised about $13,000, and after the committee got through, the lawyers put in their bills. There was not enough left to pay them, and they had to take up a second collection. Many of the men refused to pay. Anonymous letters came to me from members of the force protesting against it. The method taken to collect the assessments was to have each member of the force "interviewed" while on duty, and on pay-day he was expected to hand his contribution to the person designated to collect. The information relative to the amount paid to some person connected with the committee came to me some months after the occurrence.

In company with Police Commissioner Matthews I went to Europe on June 28, 1882. We sailed from New York on the *Germania*, for Havre. From there we went to Rouen, and called on the Prefect of Police. We told him who we were, but he wasn't visibly impressed. He only touched an electric button on his desk and told the man who answered the call to show us around. There wasn't much to be seen. The next day we got an interpreter, an Englishman who was building a horse railway, and we conversed with the Prefect at second-hand. Americans who have been on the Continent can best understand such enjoyment. Then we went to Paris. I sent in my card to the Prefect there, and he requested me to call the next day; but it turned out that he had mistaken me for the Chief of the Newark, N. J., police, who had a letter of introduction to him, from the American minister. So he sent me to Macé, the Chief of Detectives. The latter showed me his collection of burglars' tools, but they did not amount to much. Finally we were presented to the Prefect, through the introduction of the American Consul, Gen. Walker. We had an audience with him.

I met Miss Kate Field at Mr. J. S. Hooper's, the American vice-consul. We stopped in Paris ten or twelve days. We took breakfast with the Prefect one morning at Mr. Walker's house.

I went into one or two of the police barracks, which are equivalent to our station-houses. One cannot compare the two police systems. The French consists more in doing military duty, nearly all the members of the force having been in the army. The gendarmes didn't seem to attempt to regulate vehicles in the streets at all. I never saw but one disturbance, and that was a very slight one, occasioned by one team running into another.

While in Paris, Mr. and Mrs. Hooper gave a reception, to which we were invited and had a very pleasant time. From the pen of our hostess are the delightful Paris letters to the press signed Lucy H. Hooper. On July 14 we went to see the review of the troops at Versailles—which was a grand sight.

In London we visited Scotland Yard, and I had an interview with Superintendent Williamson. He knew me by reputation, and I had had frequent correspondence with him. The police there have three "watches"—eight hours each—from ten to six o'clock, six to two, and two to ten again. There are three sets of men.

After staying a week or ten days in London, we went to Glasgow by the London and North-western Railroad, and then came home.

CHAPTER XXXVII.

THE DETECTIVE OF ROMANCE.—SOME POPULAR ERRORS CORRECTED.—LOST CHILDREN.—MYSTERIOUS DISAPPEARANCES.—MISSING MR. SMITH.—HOW I FOUND HIM.—STEPPING OVER THE COUNTY LINE.—LIVINGSTONE THE FORGER.—A CHASE AS FAR AS CHICAGO.—AN ACCOMPLISHED PENMAN.—MORTGAGING A DEAD MAN'S PROPERTY.—CLEVER TRICK ON A LAWYER.—THE STORY OF A WATCH.

TAKING a clew from the detectives found in novels, one portion of the public believes that the member of this special branch of the police service possesses almost supernatural powers; while the other portion, more sceptical, has little faith in the abilities of the detective as he is pictured in books. The detective of current romance is a superlative being, endowed with such prescience, fitted out with such a wonderful brain and gifted with so many more senses than the average man that I fear his true character is likely to be misunderstood.

In a large city, there must always exist a body of men entrusted with the preservation of public order. Their duties are distinctly defined. They serve the purposes of dealing with the ordinary offences which are likely to occur. These men, the rank and file of the force, become familiar with those portions of the city entrusted to their charge, and their services are all the more effective on that account. Outside of this force, there must exist another one, of a more mobile character, which ought to be in a certain measure independent of the first, though under the control of the principal officer of the police. The function of such a body of men is obvious. To draw a simile from army organization, the main force of the police is the infantry; the detectives, the cavalry and the scouts. The latter make the reconnoissances. Their duties are multifarious. Ready to move anywhere at any time, their province is to anticipate, if they can, the commission of a crime; or, if a criminal act has been already perpetrated, to track it to its source.

I confess that I have found some difficulty in making clear to my own mind what the peculiar traits are which make a man an efficient detective officer. That he must be endowed with courage and intelligence, have alacrity and adaptability, and, above everything, a good memory is quite evident to all. As to what is called quick-wittedness, I am rather doubtful as to the indispensableness of that, because I have rarely found that the one whose deductions were very rapid was a safe man. The rapid generalizer turns out usually to be one who shapes his facts to his theories. A slow-thinking man, however, without powers of mental combination, never could make a good detective. I have rather liked the hesitating man, the officer who doubted the correctness of his own theories, providing he constructed any. The cock-sure man, I have always found, made a mess of his business. The man with a poetical imagination, who gets greatly excited, and who frames every day a new scheme, and tries them all one after another, always follows his nose up a blind alley.

I know of nothing more like a game of chess than the game of thief catching. Edgar Poe never could have tracked a robber. Clews are good things, but some of them are very thin and impalpable; straws which do not show which way the wind blows. Some men who are detectives have been often lucky; and I may say that I have been lucky a great many times. I have started from a mere nothing, something which I thought at first was insignificant, and which has proved to be the thread which led me straight through the labyrinth.

But such good fortune does not always smile upon the best equipped of detectives. My own experience has shown me hundreds of times how futile were my hopes. All of a sudden, when the scent was hottest, when the tracks were freshest, when I thought that a capture was positive, every trace of the malefactor has disappeared. I might have been right up to a certain point and then gone wrong. Looking back at my work, studying it carefully, step by step, I would sometimes find where I had been in error; but as often as not, where the blunder I had been guilty of was I never could discover. I may as well confess here that I never gave myself any credit for extra keenness, but generally attributed my failures to my own fault.

It is satisfactory, however, to recall the fact that in a majority of the cases when criminal acts were followed up by the police, the capture of the perpetrators has followed. I am inclined to believe that the difficulty of catching offenders rather augments than diminishes as the years go by. The skill of the detective has increased, but the cunning of the criminal has not lessened and means of concealment are more readily attainable.

In a large city like New York, to find a certain man is like hunting for a needle in a hay-stack. As the avenues of travel multiply, the methods of escape become easier. When the perpetrator of a criminal act in New York may, within a week, notwithstanding the use of the telegraph, be walking safely in the streets of San Francisco, the increasing difficulties of detective work are at once apparent. Our system of surveillance differs entirely from that employed in France, especially in Paris, where the goings and comings of their criminal class are closely watched. I have some acquaintance with the methods employed at the Rue Jerusalem, in Paris, acquired by personal examination there, and I am quite certain that the probability of the capture of thieves and the restoration of property is about the same in New York as in Paris. In London, the comparison made by me between the work of the English and the New York detective was rather creditable to the superior skill or, at any rate, success, of our own men.

In describing not so much a perfect detective as the peculiarities of his calling, I should be doing an injustice if I did not state that there is a certain element of romance about his work. The detective must have, at times, histrionic traits, and must be able not only to wear a disguise, but to enact the personage he assumes to be. If the thief ingratiates himself among honest men in order to plunder them, so the honest man associates with thieves in order to frustrate their plans. It requires no small amount of *sang froid* and self-command to shadow a man for days, and to assume an indifferent manner; I can allege from my own experience that it is very trying and exasperating work.

After weeks of apparent idleness and unconcern, all of a sudden, in an instant, the time of action comes. Like everything else, after a while the detective gets accustomed to his peculiar work, and rather likes it. To ride with a man in a horse-car, whose every action it is your business to know; to find out all you can about him; to stamp his features indelibly on your memory; to see him on the steps of his own house; to try to make out what he would look like without his disguise, while you are apparently doing anything else than paying particular attention to him, is an art not acquired in an instant. Remember that the man you are watching is no fool. He is expecting to be watched. He is never entirely off his guard. If you caught his eye, if you made any uncalled-for movement, he would be as the wily fox, who scents the dogs from afar.

If the suspicious man has been for any considerable time engaged in criminal pursuits, you may be quite certain that he is well up in his knowledge of the New York detective, and not alone the New York detective, but those on similar service in many other cities. He has a nose for a detective. Your assumed indifference as a detective may be humored and recognized by him. When he once believes you are after him, he will lead you an interminable chase, which nine times out of ten will terminate in your losing him entirely.

The preliminary study necessary before the regular detective work begins is sometimes very great. A crime is committed, a murder for instance, and in the confused condition of public alarm three or four or more persons are suspected. All the details of the lives of these persons have to be looked up—their past, their present condition, their character, their motives. Often such information is most difficult to obtain, because investigations have to be prosecuted in a noiseless way. It frequently happens that it is the head of the police department who, having unravelled these tangled threads, gives the winding up of them to the detective. The public then blindly credits the detective with the capture, entirely overlooking the person who at his desk has laid the elaborate plan which led directly to the execution of justice.

Sometimes, what might be called the refinement of detective work is carried out. It may be that a counterfeiter is to be captured. He has issued spurious coin. The laws have been, however, so framed that unless the man is discovered in the act of manufacturing the false notes or the false coins, punishment would be difficult. To get into the forger's or counterfeiter's confidence and to catch him in the very act of counterfeiting may be called one of the triumphs of detective skill. The successful accomplishment of an arrest of this character is often more difficult than to trace a murderer.

Murders, it may be said, are not as often the work of clever criminals, as of unaccomplished ones. Putting aside the elements of passion, as hate, or love, or jealousy, Cain kills Abel most frequently for his money. The house-breaker does not wish to kill. Occasional killing may be said to be one of the accidents of his calling. He may turn suddenly when cornered or discovered, and desperately use his knife or pistol. In such a case, when a man has been killed for the sake of plunder in a city, it is wiser to seek for his murderer in the lower stratum of society. But when death seeks a victim from jealousy the clews are more apparent.

How frequently do we read in the papers that John Smith or William Jones left his house at a certain time and has not been heard of since. And as for children, the number of them who are daily reported as having disappeared is remarkable. The parents rush to the station-house, saying their child had been seen with a woman and they concluded it had been kidnapped. The friends and relatives of missing people get unnecessarily alarmed, and conclude that something dreadful has happened to them should they be absent for a few hours beyond their usual time. But then, as a rule, the children all return home, and so do the adults. This is the greatest difficulty the police have to contend with; they are told when people are lost, but no one bothers himself to vouchsafe information as to when they return. We send orders to the captains of precincts to make inquiries as to whether parties had returned home, and to notify us immediately of the fact. Frequently a man would be absent for a day or two, and would explain the matter on his return by saying that he was carried off by the cars, omitting to state, however, why he had not got off at the first station.

We adopt a number of precautions to protect people who are strangers in the city, or who have met with some untoward accident. The orders are very precise on this point. When people are found sick in the streets, and are unable to tell their names, but are identified by papers found on them they are sent to their homes. The order is if a person is found sick on the streets and is unable to tell his name, a description of him must be telegraphed and that description is sent to a man who has special charge of such matters. When inquiry is made about an individual, the record of arrests and accidents is first examined. The police are bound to keep a book for this purpose. Let us suppose, for instance, that a young lady has fallen ill on the street, and is unable to tell her name and address. The police telegraph that a lady was found in such a condition, describe her age, if they can guess at that, size and other points by which she might be identified. Should she be able to tell her name, or her address be found upon her, we immediately send word to the house in question. If no address is to be found, we put her in the hospital. In the height of summer, when people are prostrated by the sun, such cases are of common occurrence. I have known as many as from twenty to thirty children a day brought to us in July and August. A full description is telegraphed to the Central Office, if the child can tell its name; parents come to headquarters and recover their darling. If we can get no information from the youngster on this point, it is placed in the care of the matron, Mrs. Webb, until somebody comes along and claims the child.

During the earlier portion of my career on the police force, I remember several cases of persons missing from their homes; but the one which stands out most prominently is that which I will now relate:

Mr. Thomas Smith, whom I well knew, was a constable residing at Middletown Point, now named Mattawan, Monmouth Co., N. J., in 1856, and in the Fall of that year mysteriously disappeared. The information was brought to me by two gentlemen, Messrs. David Warner and Eusebius Walling, the latter of whom was a relative. Mr. Smith's family, they said, were very much distressed over his disappearance. When he left home, over a week previously, he told his friends he was going to New York on business, and as the garrotting scare was then at its height, they feared foul play. Somewhat curious as to the cause which induced Messrs. Warner and Walling to take such an interest in the matter, I made inquiries, and learned that Smith, in the course of his regular duties, had collected some $2000 of taxes for which he had not accounted, and that the two gentlemen above mentioned were his bondsmen. To find any trace of Smith was a difficult matter, but I found out from Warner that the missing man had once told him that he had some relatives in the western part of New York State. This was not much of a clew, but still there was a chance that Smith might be there. I was not on duty at the time, and had an idea that some experience might be gained by following the matter up. I therefore took the train for a station not far from the terminus of the road. I walked some miles on foot until I reached the place. Before starting, some of Smith's letters had been handed me, and during the journey I had studied the handwriting thoroughly and was perfectly familiar with its peculiarities. Arrived at the only hotel in the place, I at first made no inquiries. Entering a fictitious name on the hotel register, I scanned the pages. There was no "Smith" on the first or second pages, so I turned further back, and finally made out a signature, the handwriting of which closely resembled that of the missing constable.

I questioned the hotel proprietor: "Did he remember one of his guests of some days previously—the gentleman whose name was written there?" pointing it out.

"Yes," he did; and he proceeded to describe Smith, who was a man past fifty years of age—tall, slim, wrinkled face, and carrying a gold-headed cane.

"Where did he go?" I inquired.

"I'm sure I can't tell. I remember he wanted to hire a conveyance of me, but as I don't keep a horse I sent him to the livery stable round the corner. Guess he got a team there."

I immediately called upon the livery-stable keeper.

"Do you remember a slim, oldish-looking man, pretty well wrinkled, with a gold-headed cane, who hired a horse and buggy of you about a week ago?" I asked.

"Certainly I do," was the prompt reply.

"Did he drive himself, or did you send some one with him?" was my next question.

"One of my men took him," said the liveryman.

"Well, then, send round a horse and wagon to the hotel for me," said I, "and, above all, that same driver."

In less than ten minutes, horse, wagon and driver were at the door.

"Now, my man," said I, "I want you to drive me exactly to the place where that old gentleman went with you. Put me down precisely at the same spot."

The driver took me quite a long journey, but finally stopped at a small village and let me out. I walked to the hotel, had some dinner, and then engaged in conversation with the proprietor. In the course of our chat I asked him if he remembered a certain old gentleman coming there a week previously, who had a gold-headed cane with him.

"Yes," he said; "he wanted to know the way to a family of the name of Smith, who lived not far from here. Real nice, pious old man; goes to church; I saw him in the village last Sunday."

That was enough for me. I sought a Justice of the Peace and procured a warrant. The charge I made against Smith was the embezzlement of public money. I needed a constable too, and accordingly secured one. This constable, if he was a country one, was bright enough, for he said to me: "Look here, that warrant is all well enough; but it's only good for this county. Smith's house is on the other side of the road, in another county. I'm afraid you won't be able to get him."

"Much obliged to you," I remarked; "but for all that we must find some way of getting hold of him."

Hiring a team, towards evening the constable and I started for the house at which we supposed Mr. Smith was staying. By-the-bye, I took the precaution of carrying with me a carriage lamp, the utility of which will appear later on.

"There's the place," said the constable, pointing with his whip to a little farm house, set a short distance back from the roadway.

"Now light the lamp," I said; "and haul the wagon up on the side of the road which is in your county."

He did so, hitching the horse to a fence. There was a light in the kitchen, and walking up the path I looked in at the window. There was the missing man, seated very comfortably and engaged in reading a newspaper. I went back to my companion and informed him that our man was inside, sure enough. "You are acquainted with the people," I observed; "so you go ahead. I'll follow."

The constable knocked, the door was opened, and we entered.

"How are you, Mr. Smith?" said the constable; and

"How are you, Mr. Thomas Smith?" was added by me.

Smith had known me ever since I was a boy, and at once rose from his seat.

"Why, how are you, Wash," he said, "what are you doing here?"

Smith was very effusive, and really played his part very well.

"The fact of the matter is, Mr. Smith," I replied, "I've come to see you. Your people were fearful that you had been garroted in New York, and that your body had been thrown into the water. But now I find you alive and well I should like to see you in private for a minute or two. Come outside." Suspecting nothing, Smith came to the door.

"I have a letter I want you to look at," said I; "but it's too dark here," and I led him to the lamp in the wagon. As soon as he put his foot over the county line, the constable clapped his hand on his shoulder and told him he was a prisoner. For my part, I at once taxed him with having run off with $2000, and carefully searched both him and his baggage, but found only a few dollars in his pockets.

Upon asking him what had become of the money, Smith solemnly avowed that he had been robbed of it in New York. This story I did not believe for one instant, but hurried him to New York, and turned him over to Supt. Matsell. Of course I was exceedingly annoyed at my failure to recover the money, and watched my prisoner pretty closely. While I was communicating the facts in the case to my chief, Smith appeared very uneasy and nervous, protesting his innocence in a manner that was really pathetic. Suddenly I noticed a furtive effort on the part of Smith to handle and fumble with his waistcoat. He did this two or three times, and all at once it flashed across my mind that he had at one time been a tailor. That waistcoat concealed something, and I must have it. He took it off, and I scrutinized it all over very carefully. The stitches in the lining were apparently all right; but still I was not satisfied. I took out my pen-knife, ripped open the inside seam near the button-holes, and there was the money or, at least, $1800 of it, nicely quilted in!

That afternoon Smith was taken, under my charge, to Keyport, N. J., and confronted with his bondsmen.

"If you will go to my house," said he, "the rest of the money will be found." We went there, and the remaining money, $200, was found concealed in a bed. It was a singular case. Here was a man ostensibly honest for forty years, who all at once could not resist temptation.

The news of Smith's capture made a decided sensation at Keyport. The whole town was out of doors when Smith was brought there. Perhaps what was hardest for Smith to bear were the mocking taunts of some of the Keyport bad boys. It is probable that some of these urchins had held Smith in awe, and he might in former days have threatened them with punishment for some trifling delinquencies. I remember some of them, notwithstanding my efforts to the contrary, jeering Smith with their cries, such as: "Tried to run away with money that wasn't yourn, did yer? But Wash ketched you."

It is not generally known, but Thomas Worth, the artist, was at one time a teller in the City Bank, and it was only by the merest accident that he did not remain in that position all his life. And the way it came about was in connection with one of the cheekiest forgeries I ever remember. It happened in July, 1867, one day in which month a stout, good-humored fellow, attired in a sort of "cheese-cutter" cap and a short sack jacket, drove up in front of the City Bank in an express wagon, drawn by a pair of magnificent black horses. The man alighted, and walking into the bank in an easy, off-hand manner, laid on Worth's desk a check for $75,000, seemingly signed by Cornelius Vanderbilt in favor of "Henry Keep." Apparently, the signature was genuine, and as it was no uncommon occurrence for the Commodore to withdraw his money in just such an unceremonious manner, the cash was done up in a package and delivered to the man. He carefully examined it to satisfy himself as to the correctness of the amount, engaged in conversation with the cashier for a minute or so, then strolled leisurely out of the bank, mounted the seat in his wagon, and drove off. Nothing more was thought of the matter by the bank officials, until at the expiration of seven weeks, when Mr. Vanderbilt disclaimed any knowledge of having given such a check. In fact, it was a forgery! When asked to describe the personal appearance of the individual who had presented the forged check, Worth was unable to do so verbally, but taking his pen drew a rough sketch of the man as he remembered him.

Detective George Elder (poor fellow, he died only a short time ago) was shown the rough sketch, and immediately exclaimed:

"Why, that's John Livingstone."

Here was a clew certainly, but the daring forger had seven weeks' start of his pursuers. Elder was detailed to work up the case, and he very soon discovered that his man had located himself somewhere not far from Chicago. Knowing that Livingstone had a weakness for horse-flesh, Elder learned, by judicious inquiries in that particular direction, that his man had purchased some fine horses, etc., at various points on the road, saying he was going to set up a stock farm. By this means Elder traced him to a farm which he had purchased, about forty miles from Chicago. Thither, one morning, the detective, in company with some two or three friends, went, and accosted the suspected forger, who met them at the front door, with:

"Good morning, Mr. Livingstone."

Livingstone made no reply, and Elder tried again.

"Did you leave everybody well in New York?"

"Sir," was the reply, "I never was in New York in my life. I don't understand you."

"Well, then, you'll soon have a chance of going there;" saying which, Elder put the handcuffs on him, at the same moment imparting the information that he was under arrest for forgery.

Livingstone was a sensible man and consented to return East with his captor, so Elder quickly hitched up the same pair of horses with which he had driven up to the bank, and made the best possible time for Indiana, pursued at no great distance by Chicago lawyers armed with writs of *habeas corpus.* Elder, however, managed to get his prisoner aboard a train in safety, and soon landed him in New York.

Elder succeeded in recovering about $50,000 of the amount which had been obtained by means of the forged check, but even this did not satisfy the bank authorities, who strongly hinted that more might have been obtained if he had desired. Naturally enough, Elder, who had really worked hard and faithfully on the case, was very indignant at the accusation, and hot words ensued. The bank refused to pay any reward, and it was only with the greatest difficulty that Elder could induce them to refund him the amount he had disbursed in following up the criminal.

Worth's reputation as an artist was brought about and assured through his rough sketch of Livingstone from memory. He soon afterwards left the employ of the bank, and his subsequent career is well known. Elder won renewed laurels by his skilful work in successfully following up the clew afforded by the picture, while Livingstone also reaped a benefit from it in the shape of a long term of imprisonment in Sing Sing.

Some thirty years ago there resided in Chicago an individual named Thomas D. Lawson, a most accomplished penman. His skill was something wonderful, and had his energies been directed in the right path he might have won for himself a respectable position in society. He obtained distinction, however, in quite another way. Contemporaneously with Mr. Lawson, the brewing firm of Gunsenhauser & Co., was also famous in the annals of Chicago. This firm was uniformly prosperous, and Gunsenhauser himself died in 1858, leaving a large fortune. The shrewd brewer had the foresight and judgment to see that there was much wealth to be acquired by the purchase of land in the already fast-growing city, and therefore invested the greater portion of his means in realty. When he died, his extensive estate was naturally a big temptation to sharpers, and a band of them determined to see what they could make out of it. With this end in view, they managed to gain the good graces of Lawson, who under their direction executed a number of deeds and mortgages, transferring portions of the deceased brewer's landed property, all drawn up and engrossed in proper form. All these documents were antedated, as if they had been executed during the lifetime of Gunsenhauser. Each of them, too, was also recorded. To have offered these deeds for sale in Chicago would have led to certain detection, so some of them were disposed of in other places. New York, however, became the principal base of operations, and thus, when in charge of the detective force, the matter came under my notice.

The swindlers were at first very successful. The parties with whom they entered into negotiations for the purchase of the mortgages took the usual precaution of sending to Chicago for information. The examinations were made, and the transactions having been reported apparently correct, large sums of money were paid to the forgers on the completion of the purchases.

Not long after, the buyers discovered that they had been swindled, the brewer's heirs showing very clearly that no such mortgages had ever been made, and that the whole of the transactions were fraudulent.

I set detectives on the track and in a very short time I had a number of the suspected persons under arrest. One of these was Lawson, who secured the services of Mr. Francis B. Cutting, an eminent lawyer, well known in New York, who occupied an elegant house on Fifth Avenue. Lawson succeeded in convincing his counsel of his innocence.

Mr. Cutting, as is usual, insisted upon the entire counsel fee of $1000 being paid. This seemed at first impossible, as Lawson's brothers in crime had turned a cold shoulder to their accomplished penman; however, after some delay, the money was paid. The day of the trial came. Mr. Cutting made a very eloquent appeal to the court, pointing out that Mr. Lawson was not only innocent but a persecuted and much-wronged man. His address created a great impression on the jury, but in spite of this Lawson was convicted. He felt grateful for his counsel's able efforts, and did not regret the payment of so large a retainer.

It transpired afterwards that the cause of the delay in raising this money was that Lawson was negotiating the mortgaging of some New York property. At length all arrangements were completed, and the mortgage was duly executed and recorded. The consideration was $1500, $500 of which Lawson kept for himself, paying the remainder over to his counsel. But imagine Mr. Cutting's astonishment and rage when, upon looking over the records, he found that his own mansion on Fifth Avenue was the identical property upon which the money had been advanced. It was a clever dodge, no doubt. Criminals very seldom play any such tricks on their lawyers, but this one certainly displayed a grim humor that was notable.

One day, some fourteen or fifteen years ago, while I was in command of the detective force, I was sitting in my office, which was then at the corner of Broome and Elm streets, when two of my men—Thomas Sampson and James Bennett—came in, bringing with them a well-known thief and fence named Dreyfus. The officers were walking along the Bowery, and saw him slip into a saloon by the side door, in a manner which suggested the idea that he had particular reasons for not being seen. They followed him in, and finding he had taken refuge in the water-closet concluded to bring him to me. Upon arriving at my office, his clothing was searched, but nothing was found which could criminate him. At length I told him to hold out his hands, which he did, and in one of them was a gold watch.

"Ah! gold watch, eh? Where did you get this?" I asked.

"That watch," replied Dreyfus, "is one I've had for twenty years, and I was just going to have it mended."

"All right," was my only observation, saying which I opened the case of the watch and found that the pin had been removed, so that the works could be taken out at a moment's notice. This was suspicious, to say the least, and I accordingly ordered Dreyfus to be locked up. He could not have been in his cell more than an hour, when in rushed a man,—a stranger to me,—loudly exclaiming: "I've been robbed!"

When he had calmed down a little, I learned that he was a watchmaker and jeweller on the Bower and that very afternoon.

he had been visited by two young men, who looked at quite a number of watches, but did not make a purchase. After they had left he found a valuable gold watch was missing.

I should say that I had written on my blotter the number and description of the watch taken from Dreyfus, while the watch itself was on the desk, covered with a newspaper. I asked the man who had complained to me the number, etc., of his watch, and it corresponded. Calling him behind the railing, I lifted the newspaper and asked:

"Is that your watch?"

"Mine Gott!" he exclaimed, raising his hands in astonishment, "Vere you get dot vatch. It vas mine."

Telling him he would see in a few minutes, I ordered Dreyfus to be brought up from his cell. When confronted with the storekeeper he was at once recognized as being one of the young men who had paid him a visit in the afternoon.

While it was never my custom to bandy jokes with prisoners who were brought before me, I could not refrain on this occasion from remarking to Dreyfus it was very funny he had carried the watch for twenty years, and yet the watch dealer was able to describe it accurately, even mentioning a slight scratch which there was on the inside of the case.

"Yes," was the reply which Dreyfus made, with the gravest imaginable look on his face; "dot was very funny." Despite this assertion, however, he was sent to Sing Sing for a term of years.

CHAPTER XXXVIII.

TRAIN ROBBERS IN HOBOKEN, N. J.—THE CASHIER'S SATCHEL.—A BALKY HORSE.—CLEVERLY CAPTURED.—EX-POLICEMAN NUGENT'S EXPLOIT.—THE CHARLTON STREET GANG OF PIRATES.—SILK STEALING ON A STORMY NIGHT.—BANK BURGLARS FOILED.—HOW MR. ALEXANDER'S PLAN MISCARRIED.—POTS OF "JAM."—THE CONSPIRACY FOILED.—"JOHNNY" ROWE AND HIS CLUBHOUSE.—HOW THE PLUMBER WAS ROPED IN.—HIS REVENGE.

IN Chapter XIX. reference is made to one Nugent, a police officer, who was suspected of complicity in the great Manhattan Bank robbery. Some interesting details have been given me concerning his subsequent fate by that very able and distinguished police official, Chief Charles A. Donovan, of Hoboken, who has been at the head of the Hoboken police force for nearly twenty-one years, and who, I trust, has still many honorable years of service before him.

It is not an uncommon thing to read of the exploits of Western train-robbers. The Jameses, the Youngers, the Colemans and others have cast a sort of infamous halo about this detestable species of crime. But it will hardly be believed that not so very long ago, within sight of the metropolis, a bold attempt was made to introduce the Western methods upon a railroad centring in the very heart of civilization.

In the year 1883, Mr. Thomas J. Smith was (and perhaps is now) cashier of the First National Bank of Orange, N. J. It was his custom, when in need of currency, to procure it himself in New York, and carry it himself to his bank. For purposes of security he had made a strong leather satchel with a stout lock. To this satchel he attached a steel chain, which was so made as to fasten around his wrist.

On the morning of July 28, 1883, Mr. Smith was returning from New York to Orange with ten thousand dollars in his satchel. Afterwards he recollected that on the ferry-boat three men kept unpleasantly near him, and even jostled him once or twice, but at the time he paid no particular attention to their behavior. Arrived on the Hoboken side, Mr. Smith proceeded to the Delaware and Lackawanna railroad station, purchased his ticket for Orange, and immediately took his seat in a car of the waiting train. It wanted about five minutes of starting time.

Scarcely had he settled himself comfortably in his seat than three men entered the car. He immediately recognized them as the men of the ferry-boat, and instantly it flashed across his mind that they were following him for no good purpose. Still, the idea seemed absurd; there were a number of other passengers in the car, and Mr. Smith smiled at his own folly.

But while these thoughts were passing through his mind, one of the men walked rapidly to one end of the car and stood at the door with a drawn pistol. Another of them remained at the door by which they had entered, also displaying a formidable revolver. Then the startled passengers heard the short, sharp command:

"Keep in your seats. The first one to move is a dead man!"

Meanwhile, the third man, armed with a short piece of lead pipe, walked straight to Mr. Smith and attempted to snatch the satchel from his grasp. Quite undaunted, Mr. Smith wasted no breath in words, but settled himself down to a firm hold of the satchel. The robber, realizing that he could not terrify the cashier, began savagely striking Mr. Smith about the head with the lead pipe. So thick and fast came the murderous blows that Mr. Smith involuntarily raised his hands to protect himself. The robber made another snatch at the satchel, but was again baffled by the steel chain, which, as usual, was tightly secured to the cashier's wrist.

Meanwhile, the other passengers had partially recovered from the stupefaction of their first surprise, and, though not daring to rise from their seats, were flinging up the windows and calling loudly for assistance. Answering cries were coming from without, and the confusion was brought to a climax by the ringing of the engine bell for the train's departure. And still the steel chain held, although the cashier's wrist was bruised and bleeding.

Not daring to be carried off on the train, the would-be bandits relinquished their attempts, and, weapons in hand, bolted from the car. It seems incredible that three men could traverse a crowded station uncaptured or unstopped, but an unarmed crowd is naturally the most cowardly of gatherings, and the baffled desperadoes gained the street, with the yelling mob behind them. A light baker's wagon stood outside the depot and into this the three jumped, but the horse, terrified at the unusual noise, became balky and refused to move—the more they lashed him the more obstinate he became, till, in despair, the men jumped to the ground and scattered in different directions.

It so happened that at this moment Chief Donovan was standing on Hudson Street, between Newark and First Streets. A man came running along at a rapid rate, followed by a crowd. The Chief promptly collared him, despite a very vigorous resistance.

"Now, my man, what's the trouble?" asked the chief.

"O, I got into a row with a longshoreman, and hit him on the nose," was the reply.

Swinging the man around, so as to get a view of his face, the Chief recognized him. It was the notorious thief, Peter Emerson.

"Hallo! Is it you?" said the Chief, genially.

"Do you recognize me?" asked "Pete," in a disgusted tone.

"Of course," replied the Chief, "and you are altogether too distinguished a gentleman to be practising on longshoremen's noses. You will honor me with your society to the station-house."

Proceeding stationward, the Chief again recommended Mr. Emerson to confide his trouble to him, but he wasted his politeness on the desert air, for all he could get out of "Pete" was the surly growl: "You'll find out soon enough."

He had no sooner said this than a butcher wagon came dashing along at a tremendous rate, with one man in it. He turned round the corner of Second Street, where he collided with a tree and was thrown out. Quickly regaining his feet, the man jumped on to a grocer's wagon which was passing, and taking the reins from the boy in charge, drove off. An officer close by, who had seen the whole transaction, also jumped on the team and captured the man, who turned out to be no less a personage than Edward Farrell.

The march to the station-house was resumed, but before the Chief reached there he saw another man racing down Court Street towards the Ferry. A roundsman started in pursuit, seeing which the fleeing man threw down a pistol which he still had in his hand. This man was soon captured, and proved to be the John Nugent alluded to at the beginning of this story. He had rapidly been promoted to the aristocracy of crime.

The assault upon the cashier took place at 10.35 A. M., and in less than six minutes all three of the assailants were lodged in the station. Such was the inglorious ending of this attempt to transplant the Western crime of train robbery to a crowded centre of population. To succeed, the robber must have at hand the vast loneliness of the prairie for his asylum.

Nugent and Farrell pleaded guilty, and were each sentenced to ten years' imprisonment, which they are now undergoing. Emerson stood trial and a great sum of money was spent in his defence, but in vain. He was convicted, and received the same punishment as his comrades.

Mr. Smith received no lasting injuries from the blows dealt him, but never again travelled without an escort when carrying money.

It was in 1877-8 that the "Charlton Street" gang of river pirates, under the leadership of the notorious Mike Shannon, was at the very zenith of its prosperity. But it was at this period also that it received its death-blow. For many years the members of this ruffianly horde had preyed upon the shipping in both the North and East rivers, along the Staten Island, Brooklyn, and New Jersey shores, and Hoboken as well. They were not very particular as to the plunder which they picked up, and less so as to the means adopted to secure it. "Dead men tell no tales" was their motto, and many a poor seafaring wanderer has been foully murdered by them, within sight of the home from which he had been so long absent, for daring to defend his property.

Mike Shannon was the leader and director of this gang. He was a resident of the Eighth Ward, and his political influence there was very great, a fact of no small importance whenever any of his associates were " in trouble." One day, however, in the latter part of 1878, I received a visit from Chief of Police Donovan, of Hoboken. During the previous night, which had been a particularly wet, dark and stormy one, a large quantity of valuable silks had been stolen, so he informed me, from the Bremen Dock, Hoboken, the property of the North German Lloyd Steamship Co. Could I help him in discovering the thieves, as he had a suspicion they had come from my side of the river? Captain Schultz was at that time in command of the New York Harbor Police, and so I sent for him. The details of the robbery were again gone over in a brief but comprehensive manner by Chief Donovan.

"A shoe-string against a row of apple-trees that I know who was in that job," instantly exclaimed Captain Schultz.

"Who was it? How do you know?" exclaimed the Chief and myself in the same breath.

"One question at a time, gentlemen, if you please," laughingly remarked the burly captain. "Who was it? Why it was Mike Shannon's gang. How do I know? Well, if you'll just listen a while I'll tell you, and you see if I ain't somewhere near right. I've had my men watching those fellows for a good long time, and know a lot about them, but not enough to make sure of a conviction. Now I think I've got them 'dead to rights.' Last night, you know, was a pretty rough night, as rough a one as I want to be out in. The rain came down in regular sheets and the wind blew a hurricane, while it was so dark you couldn't see half a boat's length in front of you. As I said before, I had been watching Shannon and his gang for some time, and last night, as luck would have it, I had one of my men stationed on Charlton Street. That's where Shannon and his lot hang out. At about ten o'clock, when the storm was about at its worst, a couple of rough fellows, named Scanlon and Cassidy, well known to be hand-in-hand with Shannon, were seen by my men to go down the street towards the water. They were muffled up round their necks, and they had on wide-brimmed tarpaulin hats, well slouched down over their faces, so as to protect them from the pelting rain, which was beating right against them. They walked quickly down to the pier, where they were joined by another, similarly muffled up. My man crept up pretty near them and could just distinguish their forms as they got into a boat and then rowed off in the darkness, headed for the Jersey shore. Now there's no other gang working round here now, and if we can get hold of those fellows I named we shall learn something more, you bet! It's lucky I stationed that man on Charlton Street." Saying which the Captain leaned back in his chair with a look on his face as if he already had the gang under lock and key.

It certainly did look as if we had a clew to the robbers, and so I ordered Captain Schultz to pursue his investigations in the direction indicated, and to give Chief Donovan all the assistance in his power. Within three or four weeks, five of the gang were in custody, namely, Shea, Grady, Scanlon, Cassidy, and Shevlin. Unfortunately, Shannon, the ringleader, came to know we were in search of him, and was lost sight of for some months. But more of him hereafter. There was quite a chase after Grady and Scanlon, who were captured in Buffalo. At first none of the gang would say a word, but when they found themselves deserted by Shannon, and that he did not come to aid them with his political influence, as in times past, they "peached."

From them it was learned that there were nine of the gang implicated in the robbery. They had three boats, too; one starting from the foot of Charlton Street, and the other two from Houston Street pier, with three men in each boat. No lights were carried, save dark lanterns, and these were only "flashed" now and then for a second or so at a time, in order to get the proper bearings. The job had been planned several days previously, and they knew just where the cases of silks were located in the warehouse. Through the inky blackness of the night, and pulling right in the very teeth of the heavy gusts which blew across the river, the three boats slowly made their way to the Bremen Dock, which is situated a little to the northward of the Hoboken Ferry. Watchmen patrolled the wharf and warehouses throughout the night, "pegging" their clocks at stated hours. In the interval, the thieves succeeded in effecting an entrance into the warehouse. Holes were bored in the wooden partition with augers, and then with the aid of a saw an aperture, measuring 3 x 6 feet, was soon cut. Before this was accomplished, however, they were interrupted several times by the approach of the watchman, and then they would suspend operations, crouching in the bottom of their boats, and in the darkness they were not observed. When he retraced his steps, operations on the boarding were resumed until completed. Quickly and noiselessly, two cases of silk were transferred from the warehouse to the boat. A slight noise alarmed the watchmen, who came to the edge of the wharf and peered over. This alarmed them and they pulled away out into the stream, with one boat short of cargo. What they had secured, however, was safely landed at the foot of Houston Street, and concealed under the wharf there, until a favorable opportunity occurred for its removal to a more secure hiding-place. But that opportunity never came. The silk was found there by Chief Donovan and Captain Schultz, and was finally returned to the rightful owners. The five thieves mentioned were tried and convicted, and were sentenced to ten years' imprisonment each in Trenton State prison.

As to Shannon, he was arrested four or five months after the robbery, in Baltimore, when he had just landed from England. He told us he had gone from New York to Canada and from there sailed for Queenstown, Ireland, where he remained some four months. He was brought on here, and put upon his trial, but notwithstanding the fact that two of his accomplices were brought from prison and testified against him, the jury failed to agree and he was shortly afterward discharged from custody. He was never tried again, and is now, so I am informed, leading an honest, hard working life.

Nearly all will recollect the sensation which was produced when the almost successful attempt was made to rob the Jersey City National Bank, some ten or twelve years ago; but there is a sequel to it which has never before been made public, and which was confided to me by my friend, Chief Donovan, of Hoboken. There were four of the most notorious bank burglars that this country has ever produced concerned in the affair—Frank Denning (*alias* "Dago Frank"), "Bill" Proctor, Moses Vogel and "Dave" Cummings. These four hired a room in a building adjoining the bank, and had succeeded in digging their way to within a few feet of the vault, when their strange behavior aroused the suspicions of their landlady, who informed the police that she thought her lodgers were up to some roguery. The house was raided by the police, the result being the capture of Denning, Proctor and Vogel. Cummings, who was attending to the "outside," escaped, and has since made his name infamous in Europe. The three prisoners were soon lodged in the Hudson County Jail to await trial, and for a time public interest was diverted from them.

And now comes the sequel, or, rather, a little bit of by-play.

Late one night, about a week after the arrest of the men in question, a respectably dressed middle-aged man was found by a policeman lying drunk in the gutter on Court Street, Hoboken. To all appearances he was unable to walk, and was accordingly carried to the station-house and locked in a cell. He gave his name as Wm. Alexander. The next morning, in accordance with an invariable custom, Chief Donovan walked along the cell corridor for the purpose of taking a look at those who had been brought in during the night. Alexander was a very respectable looking fellow, and in answer to the Chief's inquiries said he had been on a spree the night previous and had taken more than was good for him. The man's appearance was in his favor; he did not look like an "habitual," and so, when arraigned in court, the Chief spoke a good word for him to the judge, and he was discharged with a caution. But that very same night "Mr. Alexander" was again found lying in almost the identical spot, and, as before, in a drunken condition. This time, however, a pane of glass had been broken in the window of a cigar store close to where he was lying, and his hat was inside. He was again arrested, and was sentenced to thirty days' imprisonment in the county jail. Out of consideration for his apparent respectability, however, he was not sent to the jail, but was kept in Hoboken along with the "ten-day" men. What subsequently transpired will show how fortunate a circumstance this was.

"Alexander" had served about half of his term, when one afternoon a stylish brougham was driven up to the door of police headquarters in Hoboken, and a fashionably attired man alighted. His clothes were of the latest style and cut, while a magnificent diamond pin in his tie almost dazzled Chief Donovan, who happened to be "at the desk," and to whom he addressed himself.

Did the Chief know anything about a man named Alexander, who had been arrested for drunkenness.

The Chief replied that he did, adding that he had been "sent up" for thirty days.

Was there no way of getting him out? asked the gentlemanly stranger. He would be willing to pay a hundred dollars rather than have him remain in prison any longer. The fact of it was his sister was to have been married to "Alexander," and his non-appearance on the day set apart for that interesting ceremony had almost rendered the poor girl frantic. Could not something be done to secure the imprisoned man's liberty? No monetary considerations should stand in the way. And so the stranger urged and pleaded, but with no avail. There was no flaw in the commitment, and nothing could be done. "Alexander," it was decided, must serve his full term.

A day or two after this scene, a young lad, a resident of Hoboken, was arrested and sent to the county jail for picking pockets. Chief Donovan knew him and his aged mother well, and through his influence the old lady was allowed to visit her boy in the jail rather more frequently than the rules permitted. One day she conveyed a message to the Chief that her son wished particularly to see him, as he had some valuable information to communicate.

The Chief accordingly called at the jail, and there obtained from the boy a clew which led to the frustration of one of the most daring attempts at escape which has ever been heard of. The lad told the Chief that some time previously he had been approached by the three "bankies," as he called them, Denning, Proctor and Vogel, who induced him to allow his mother to go to some friends of theirs in New York and get some pots of jam, etc., for them. These "pots of jam," the lad said, were so numerous that he thought there was something wrong. And, indeed, it looked very much that way. The next jam pot, therefore, that the old lady brought, was opened and examined, and found to contain, not jam, but dynamite cartridges, fuse, etc. The cells of the three "bankies" were at once thoroughly examined, and the astounding discovery was made by the jail officials that the men had already dug a tunnel which extended to the outer wall of the jail. The wall, it was intended, should be blown up with the dynamite, but the little pickpocket's forethought brought the conspiracy to light. In conversation with one of the bank burglars, Chief Donovan learned that the man "Alexander," who was twice arrested for drunkenness, was no less than another of the gang, the notorious Scott, who hoped to get committed to the jail, where he could arrange the details of the plot for their release. The gorgeous young man to whose sister he was to have been married was no less a personage than Dunlap, also a well-known bank burglar. Both were subsequently engaged in the Northampton Bank burglary, and are now "doing time" in Massachusetts State Prison.

It was only a short time ago that I noticed in the daily papers an account of a murder and suicide in Washington, D. C., in which "Johnny" Rowe, as he was called, shot his mistress with a revolver, and then put an end to his own miserable existence with a bullet from the same weapon. I knew Rowe well, and was pretty well posted concerning some of the many "jobs" in which he was engaged. In personal appearance he was a perfect gentleman: his clothes were made by a fashionable tailor; his linen of spotless purity, his boots brilliantly polished, and his face always clean shaved. His favorite stand during the day, or when not engaged in the pursuit of "business," was on Broadway, at the corner of Twenty-eighth Street. This was in the days when the Brower House, near by, was generally considered by the "fraternity" as their headquarters. In that then gorgeous temple of chance,

"Johnny" was one of the leading spirits. He was a gambler of the first water, and, like all of that ilk, did not hesitate, when "pigeons" were scarce and legitimate gambling was dull, to descend further in the scale of crime and try his hand at common, every-day swindling. I couldn't begin to enumerate one-half the "hells" with which Johnny was connected from time to time, in one way or another. Two years ago, however, when we made a big raid on all the gambling establishments up town, he "ran the game" at a place on Sixth Avenue, between Thirty-first and Thirty-second streets. He was a clever conversationalist, cool, plausible and calculating, and the possession of these qualities tended in a great degree to his almost invariable success in the various operations in which he engaged. When preparing for a raid upon any one's pocket-book, he was always very careful to make himself thoroughly acquainted with his intended victim's "soft spot" or hobby, and then he would work it for all it was worth. He "spotted" a Brooklyn plumber (of course he was a wealthy man), and ascertained that his hobby consisted in making bets on almost every conceivable matter or occasion. But the plumber was also a politician; he had "travelled with the boys" for a number of years, and could not be plucked by any common, every-day trick. He knew all the ropes, as they say, and Rowe saw it would be no easy job to pull the wool over his eyes. So he hired a couple of nicely furnished rooms, with sliding doors between them, located down town, and then sent a polite note to the Brooklyn plumber, asking him to call upon a certain day and give an estimate on a big job in his line. Always having an eye to business as well as to politics, the plumber gladly accepted the invitation and called upon the day indicated. Rowe ushered him into one of the rooms, the sliding doors being closed, and at once began to explain that he wanted new wash-stands, closets, pipes, etc., put in of a gorgeous and costly nature. The plumber, of course, was deeply interested in the long list of things which would be required; but his meditations upon the vision of future profits were suddenly broken in upon by a familiar sound, faint but distinct, which came from the other side of the sliding doors. It was the rattling of "chips," and voices could be heard making bets. The effect upon the plumber was like that of the scent of powder on an old war-horse. He raised his head, almost involuntarily, and asked:

"What's that?"

"Oh!" replied "Johnny," lifting his forefinger with a mysterious and warning air; "keep quiet. Don't say a word."

"But there's a 'game' going on there," said the plumber, pointing in the direction from whence the sounds came. "Who's in there? What's going on?"

"Hush!" again said Johnny, in a hoarse whisper, and with a well-assumed look of terror on his face. "Don't give it away, will you? The fact is we've just started a little club of our own. You see there's any number of respectable men about this neighborhood who are fond of a game of cards on the quiet, and so we fitted up this place especially for 'em. There's one or two in there now."

The natural curiosity of the plumber was aroused, and he asked Rowe if he had any objections to his taking a look at the game. "Johnny," at first, wouldn't hear of such a thing; the club was a very select one, and those in the next room wouldn't like such an intrusion upon their privacy. It might be the means, too, of getting him into trouble.

"Well, you know I'm all right," replied the plumber. "Just let me have a look, won't you?"

And still Johnny made a show of resistance, but finally he acceded to the plumber's urgent entreaties, and pulling back the sliding doors introduced him to the three or four gentlemen in the room, who, it may be remarked, were "Johnny's" confederates, located there "for this occasion only."

The plumber watched the play for some minutes without saying a word. At length he could not resist the fascination, and began to wager on the turn of the cards.

The inevitable result followed. Before the plumber "let up" he had been absolutely *swindled* out of no less than sixteen hundred dollars. Of course he was far from being pleased at losing such a sum of money; but just imagine his state of mind when, an hour or two later, upon informing a friend of his adventure, he learned that the "club house" proprietor was no less a personage than the notorious "Johnny" Rowe. To say that he was mad is but a faint way of expressing the rage which burned within the plumber's breast. He vowed to get square, and so, the very next day, when a gentlemanly looking young fellow called on him with the information that his "brother" wanted to see him at the club, the plumber was very polite, as if nothing had occurred.

"Very sorry," said he, "but I'm very busy just now. Tell Mr. Rowe to come over here to my place. I want to see him very much."

The young fellow left, and as soon as he had gone the plumber, with a broad anticipatory grin on his countenance, procured a formidable looking butcher knife, and placing the blade in the stove, heated it red-hot.

He was doomed to be disappointed, however. The messenger returned with the information that Mr. Rowe was also very busy, much to his regret. This was too much, and so, seizing the knife, the plumber went for "Johnny's" brother without any preliminaries, pricking him in a dozen or more tender spots before he could make his escape.

"Johnny" saw that the game was up, and prepared to shift his quarters, but before he could get clear away, the plumber, accompanied by some Brooklyn boys, appeared on the scene, and made him disgorge a portion, at least, of the plunder.

"Johnny" was not even true to those of his own fraternity, and never missed a chance of exercising his peculiar talents in the field of roguery. A well-known man about town, named "Wine Harry," once backed Rowe in going into business with McLane, the betting man. Some money was needed, and Rowe was commissioned to raise $5000 on a mortgage of property belonging to "Harry." He did so, but that was the last seen or heard of him for some time. At length it leaked out that he was in Washington, in company with a young woman who had accompanied him from New York. He had set her up in "business," but Rowe took to drink, and at length she left him, and went to live with a fast young fellow of the Capitol. This was the cause which led to the double tragedy alluded to at the commencement of this narrative.

CHAPTER XXXIX.

REMARKABLE CRIMES IN BROOKLYN.—SUPT. CAMPBELL AS A DETECTIVE.—THE HEAD THAT WAS FOUND IN A LUMBER YARD.—A HORRIBLE SMELL.—THE DETECTIVES' DISCOVERY.— WHAT WAS BOILING IN THE POT.—AN INHUMAN DEED.—THE GOODRICH MURDER.—LOOKING FOR KATE STODDARD.—A FEMALE DETECTIVE AND HER PROVIDENTIAL MEETING WITH THE MURDERESS.—ONLY A LOCKET.—CRUMBS OF CONGEALED BLOOD.—SEARCHING EVERY HOUSE IN BROOKLYN.—SUCCESS AT LAST.

THE city of Brooklyn has been the scene of some very remarkable crimes; and the manner in which they were unearthed, and the success which attended the efforts to bring the criminals to justice, have combined to make the name of Superintendent Campbell famous as one of the most skilful detectives in the country. In view of the fact, therefore, that Brooklyn, since the completion of the East River Bridge, has been brought into still closer connection with New York, I cannot do better, perhaps, than give one or two cases as examples of Supt. Campbell's skill as a director of criminal investigation.

Early on the morning of January 27, 1876, some men on their way to work, found the ghastly head of a man lying in a lumber yard at Greenpoint, not far from the ferry. A casual examination showed that it had been severed from the body with some not very sharp instrument, and the edges of the flesh of the neck where it had been cut were irregular and jagged. It was partially wrapped in a half sheet of a German newspaper, and that was the only clew. The police were notified—in fact, the head was taken to Chief Campbell's office, and was there subjected to the closest scrutiny by medical men and others; but for some time the mystery was as far from elucidation as ever. During the afternoon following the discovery, however, the head was viewed by a number of individuals, one or two of whom said it looked very much like that of a man named William W. Simmons, who had been employed for some time in Williamsburgh at one of the sugar refineries. Search was accordingly made for Simmons, detectives being despatched in every direction by Mr. Campbell with instructions to report to him hourly by telegraph. While they were absent, a man who gave his name as Andrew Fuchs called upon

PATRICK CAMPBELL.
(Superintendent of the Brooklyn Police.)

Captain Woglom, of the Fifth Precinct. He had heard it rumored, he said, that the head which was found was that of Simmons, and he should like to see it, as he knew him well. It was shown him, and he positively identified it. Fuchs said he had been a "helper" to Simmons for some years, and told about his partiality for the society of the fair sex, how he would boast of his conquests in that direction, and that he was particularly fond of a certain woman of Greenpoint, who resided not far from the yard where his head was found. Fuchs then left the office after having given his address. Officers were then despatched to hunt up the woman alluded to by Fuchs, but she could not be found. In the course of their investigations, however, they learned that a short time before the finding of Simmons' head a man had been seen in the neighborhood carrying a market basket, the top of which was covered with a sheet of paper. This apparently trivial incident was reported to the Captain, who asked for a description of the man. It was given him, upon which he immediately exclaimed:

"Why that's very much like Fuchs, his helper, who has only just gone out. Follow him and tell him I want him. Here's his address."

The officers departed on their errand, but found that the man they were in search of had gone directly home, and thither they followed him. As they entered the house a peculiar and unusual smell was perceived, but they thought nothing of it at the time, although they subsequently remembered it with startling vividness. Fuchs was seated at the table eating his dinner, knife and fork in hand—the former being an immense and formidable looking article.

"You are wanted down at the station-house," remarked one of the officers.

Fuchs gave a slight start, and came to a full stop with his eating, staring fixedly at the detective, who repeated what he had previously said.

With his eyes still fastened on the speaker, Fuchs deliberately, and in an apparently absent-minded manner, drew the blade of the knife across the ball of his left thumb, and then wiped his bloody hand on his trousers.

When taken before the Captain, that gentleman subjected him to a rigid verbal examination.

"What's that blood on your pants there," asked the Captain, pointing at the crimson stain.

"That?" was Fuchs' reply, "oh, I just happened to cut my hand with my knife, as I was coming away," and he turned towards the officers who had arrested him with an inquiring look as if asking for their confirmation of his statement.

The Captain, however, motioned them to remain silent.

"But that's fresh blood," remarked Capt. Woglom. "I mean this dry spot. What's that?"

Fuchs mumbled out some half inaudible answer, to the effect that he didn't know; but his demeanor was anything but that of an innocent man, and he was fast becoming nervous. He was searched, and the very first article almost which the officer pulled out of his pocket was a watch.

"Is that yours?"

No answer.

The landlady with whom Simmons boarded in Williamsburgh was sent for. On her arrival she was shown the watch and at once identified it as the property of the murdered man.

There could be very little doubt but that Fuchs was his murderer, or, at least, was connected in some way with the tragedy. But further evidence against him was necessary for the ends of justice.

The detectives were again despatched to Fuchs' house, with instructions to make a thorough search of the premises. Upon opening the door their nostrils were once more assailed by the same peculiar and penetrating odor with which they had been saluted on the occasion of their first visit. Every minute it grew more powerful and nauseating. At length one of them raised the lid of an iron pot which was standing on the stove, and the mystery was solved.

Horrible and almost incredible as the statement may seem, there, boiling in the pot, was the trunk of Simmons' body! Hardened and inured to all sorts of sights as the detectives were, this was too much for even their iron nerves. How any man could have sat coolly eating his dinner as Fuchs did, with that ghastly human broth stewing on the stove within reach of his arm, is something which passes comprehension.

His wife and child, who were in another room, were then arrested and taken to headquarters.

When the detectives arrived and communicated their discovery to their horrified listeners, Fuchs, who was present, admitted everything. A night or two previously, he said, Simmons came to his house, and they partook of considerable liquor together.

Finally, Simmons despatched him to a neighboring saloon for a further supply of whiskey. Having procured it, he was about to re-enter the house, when a suspicion as to his wife's fidelity entered his mind. He peered through the window, and, as he declared, saw her and Simmons in a position which left him no alternative but to come to the conclusion that they had been infringing one of the Ten Commandments. Almost frenzied by the sight, he caught up an axe which was lying near the stove and struck Simmons on the back of the neck with it, felling him to the floor. He then got a large carving-knife—the one with which he was eating his dinner when the detectives visited him—and completely severed the head from the body. He next cut the legs off at the knee-joint, then the thighs, and finally the arms. The head he threw into the lumber-yard where it was found; while the other members he hid at various points along the banks of Newtown Creek. The trunk of the body, however, was too bulky to be disposed of in a like manner, so he conceived the idea of boiling it!

Mrs. Fuchs, while admitting that her husband had murdered Simmons, gave a far different version of the circumstances leading up to it. Her story was that she, together with her child, retired to their room some time during the evening, leaving Simmons and her husband sitting in the kitchen drinking. At about ten o'clock she heard her husband leave the house with a bottle in his hand. In a short while he returned, to find Simmons lying upon the sofa half stupefied with liquor. Going up and bending over him, her husband stood gazing for some time and muttering to himself. Suddenly snatching up the axe, he knocked Simmons off on to the floor, and then proceeded deliberately to hack him to pieces. Horrified and astounded at the bloody butchery, both she and her child rushed into the kitchen, but were silenced by the most terrible threats of a like fate if they dared inform any one of what they had witnessed. So they held their tongues.

The various pieces of the body were found where Fuchs had hidden them, and, after a lengthy trial, he was sentenced to imprisonment for life.

During the year 1873, no crime excited such wide-spread interest and attention as the Goodrich murder in Brooklyn, and the circumstances attendant upon it. The victim was Mr. Charles Goodrich, who resided in a handsomely furnished house (his own property) in one of the most fashionable portions of Brooklyn. On the morning of March 21st, of the year before mentioned, a report was made to the police that Mr. Goodrich was lying dead in his kitchen. Officers were despatched to his residence, and, sure enough, Mr. Goodrich was dead, shot through the head. He was lying on his back in the front basement, a pair of boots under his head for a pillow, while on his feet were a pair of slippers. The linen he wore was fresh and clean, and his hair, which was wet, had evidently been combed and brushed only a short time before the body was discovered. In the back basement were hung some two or three towels, damp, as if they had been recently used. From this and other little circumstances which were noticed by the detectives who had been detailed on the case, it was concluded that the murder had been committed by a woman ; and so it afterwards proved. But who was the woman ? So far as was generally known, the murdered man lived by himself, and there was no female inmate of his house. By dint of close inquiry, however, Chief Campbell succeeded in ascertaining that a woman named Lizzie King, *alias* Kate Stoddard, had been living with him up to within a short time of his death. They had had a misunderstanding of some sort and parted; and it therefore became very necessary to find Miss Stoddard. But she had vanished in a most inexplicable manner. Her features and general appearance were unknown, and so the only clew which could be obtained as to her whereabouts was that she had been employed at a straw works on Broadway, New York City. This branch of the trail was thoroughly followed up, and finally it was learned that the missing woman had some time previously become the inmate of a certain home for fallen women in the upper part of New York. For a day or two the name and location of the institution remained unknown, but at length it was found. Alas, it was too late! The bird had flown. She, however, had roomed while in the home with a young woman of good education. Her name was Mary Handley, and Chief Campbell had a lengthy interview with her. The result of that interview was that she became a detective for the nonce, her task being the hunting down of Kate Stoddard. Months passed and still no trace of the missing and mysterious murderess, as she was alleged to be. Mary Handley, however, did not give up the chase, neither did

Chief Campbell, who cheered her on when she appeared despondent at her lack of success. She travelled here and there over the country, watching and waiting for a glimpse of the familiar face and form of her erstwhile room-mate. At last on July 8, 1873, the time came; but in a most unforeseen and providential manner. She had just had an interview with Chief Campbell in his office, and was about leaving, when he remarked to her:

"Oh! by the bye, Mary, have you got any money?"

"No," was her reply; "I wish you would let me have some. I'm going over to New York, and may want it."

He handed her a five-dollar bill, and she left the office, still carrying it in her hand in an absent-minded manner, thinking of what the prospects were for capturing the supposed murderess of Mr. Goodrich. Entering a horse-car for the purpose of riding to the ferry, still absorbed in her reflections, she carelessly rolled the five-dollar bill which the Chief had given her between her fingers. The conductor's abrupt: "Your fare, miss," brought her to her senses, and without thinking, out of the open car window went the little rolled-up greenback. She realized in an instant what she had done, and managed to stammer out, in reply to the conductor's reiterated request for her fare:

"Oh! my fare. Please stop the car. I've just thrown my money out of the window."

The car was stopped, and alighting, Mary Handley retraced her steps, finding the bill on the edge of the curb-stone. She was not a very great distance from the ferry now, and so concluded to walk. Before she had gone many yards, however, she happened to glance on the other side of the street, and there was Kate Stoddard. Thrilled with excitement at this providential meeting, Mary followed the woman for whom she had so long been searching, until she came to a police-officer. Accosting him, she said:

"Arrest that woman; the Chief wants her."

The officer, as was but natural, demurred somewhat.

"I'll go with you," observed Mary, noticing his hesitation; "but if you let her escape you'll never forgive yourself."

The arrest was made, and the much sought-for Kate Stoddard was soon before Chief Campbell in his private office. At first she denied that her name was either King or Stoddard; it must be a case of mistaken identity, she said, and she had never roomed with, or seen Mary Handley before in her life. All these disclaimers were made in a matter-of-fact manner, and with an air calculated to convince even the most sceptical.

But Mary Handley was positive she was not mistaken, and finally Mr. Campbell observed to the suspected woman:

"Madame, we don't want to hold you here if you are not Kate Stoddard. Be kind enough to tell me where you reside, and I will at once despatch an officer and ascertain if you are telling me the truth."

"That I'm sure I wont do," was the somewhat unexpected reply which came from the woman's lips.

"Then," said the Chief, "you will have to remain in custody; but first you must be searched."

Fastened around her neck by a chain was a large gold locket, and as she refused to hand it over to Mr. Campbell herself it was taken from her. The Chief found it a difficult matter to open it, upon which the woman remarked, with more excitement than she had hitherto exhibited:

"Now, be careful," at the same time watching every movement of the Chief's fingers in his endeavors to make the spring work.

At length the locket opened and disclosed a few dark-colored crumbs or lumps, some one or two of which fell upon the floor. Falling quickly on her knees, Kate Stoddard hastily picked them up and placed them in her mouth. Fearing they might be poison, Chief Campbell grasped hold of her hands and asked:

"What's that?"

"That's blood—dried blood," was the startling reply.

"Why what do you mean?" questioned Mr. Campbell, whose curiosity was now fully aroused, as well it might be, by such an announcement.

"Never mind," she said; "I guess I wont talk to you any further on that subject now."

And she didn't. All efforts to induce her to disclose her place of residence were fruitless, and she was finally consigned to a cell for the night.

I should have stated that when first arrested, and when on her way to the station-house, she was seen to take a couple of letters from her pocket and throw them in the road. They were picked up and handed to Chief Campbell, who noticed that they were addressed to parties in New York and New Jersey. From this, and the fact that she was on the east side of the river when arrested, he concluded that she lived in Brooklyn. But whereabouts? Brooklyn, even then, was a pretty extensive city, and the task of locating her residence seemed a hopeless one. Chief Campbell, however, although comparatively a novice in police matters, was determined to find out where the woman lived. He adopted a plan, too, which had never before been tried and it is doubtful whether it ever will again. First consulting with the Police Commissioners and obtaining their consent to the extraordinary plan which he unfolded to them, Mr. Campbell called all the captains before him and ordered the entire force on duty, reserves and all, with instructions to inquire at every single house in the city whether any female had been missing for several days—since the arrest of Kate Stoddard. The result of such a course of procedure can be better imagined than described. Chief Campbell fully appreciated the odium which would attach to him if his plan turned out a failure; but he never faltered. Inquiries were made as ordered and in less than two hours over 300 females were reported as having been absent from the usual place of abode since the previous Tuesday, including those whose whereabouts were known. Towards evening, one of the captains went to the Chief and said :

" I've found it for you."

" Indeed," was the reply ; "where is it ? "

" On High Street."

A latch-key had been taken from Kate's pocket when she was arrested, and taking that with him the Chief tried it in the door of the indicated residence. It fitted.

Upon inquiring of the landlady it was ascertained that Kate Stoddard had a room there, fitted up in a very neat and comfortable manner by herself. Her trunks were there, and when opened were found to contain, besides books and papers, etc., the murdered man's watch, chain, charms, pocket-book, etc. There was now not the slightest doubt but that Kate Stoddard was the murderess.

She was never tried for the offence, her insanity being proved beyond the shadow of a doubt, and she is now an inmate of the State Asylum at Utica.

CHAPTER XL.

CHIEF STEWART OF THE PHILADELPHIA POLICE.—STORY OF A CRANK.—SAVED FROM HIS ENEMIES.—CHIEF KELLY, OF THE PHILADELPHIA DETECTIVES.—POOR KIRBY, AND HOW HE WAS KILLED BY POLITENESS.—CLEVERLY LAID PLANS MISCARRY.—A PLOT TO STEAL $11,000,000.—COPPER INSTEAD OF GOLD.—DISAPPOINTMENT AND DEATH.—" GOPHER BILL," THE CUNNING COUNTERFEITER. — HIS CAREER AND HOW HE WAS CAPTURED. — WALTER SHERIDAN.—A CURIOUS HISTORY.—A CASE OF SHANGHAI.—THE " BUNDLE " GAME.—PRINTED DESCRIPTIONS OF THIEVES.—SOME CURIOUS SPECIMENS.—A BRUTAL MURDER IN PENNSYLVANIA.—ROBBERY OF THE PHILADELPHIA MINT.—A BAR OF SILVER THAT WASN'T MISSED.

IN a previous chapter I have adverted to the tribe of nuisances called cranks, who are constantly coming to police headquarters with various and absurd complaints. General James Stewart, Jr., Chief of the Philadelphia Police,* who is not only the finest looking chief of police in America, but is a royal good fellow as well, relates his experience with one of the above-mentioned fraternity. He was quietly seated in his office when the door opened and one of the most remarkable looking heads that he had ever seen was thrust into the room. Every individual hair was standing perfectly erect, giving the face a combined expression of surprise, anger and terror that was perhaps never before seen on a human being. Now there are three kinds of men who wear their hair after the manner of Shakespeare's indignant porcupine : poets, Russian Nihilists and those who have been confronted with danger so great and sudden that it caused their hair to stand on end. As the head was followed by a well dressed body, the chief decided that he could not be a poet, and when the man asked in broken English if he had the honor of addressing the chief of police, he was found to be a Russian. He stated that he had recently arrived in the city, but ever since his advent had been constantly followed by two men. He said that while one of the men was only

---

* Since writing this General Stewart has resigned from office.

GEN. JAMES STEWART, JR.
(Ex-Chief of the Philadelphia Police.)

eight feet high, the other had attained the unusual altitude of nine feet in his boots. He further said they hardly ever left him. When he arose in the morning there was the nine-footer solemnly peering in at the window, while his side partner, who had come down the chimney during the night, was glaring at him from the hearth rug. Did he draw the curtains closely, and stop the chimney, the sleepless eye of the one glared through the key-hole, while the loud breathing of the other could be heard through the crack underneath the door. He said it was not agreeable to have seventeen feet of humanity constantly with one, sleeping or waking. He declared that the taller man was one of the most agile persons he had ever met, that he thought nothing of turning a handspring over a lamp-post, and on one bright cool morning, when he seemed to be feeling remarkably well, he had taken a flying leap over the top of one of the tallest telegraph poles in the city. His eight-foot friend was not such a jumper, but for getting through key-holes and cracks of doors hardly wide enough to admit the blade of a pen-knife, for balancing himself on the top of a lamp or a chair during the entire night, and sleeping with one eye open, he was without an equal. He had spoken to several men, including some policemen, who were too polite to deny the truth of his statements, but were so discourteous as to laugh at him, and when he pointed out the giants, the officers either through fear or because they were subsidized by the long men, pretended not to see them. Sometimes they were dressed as policemen, and he had frequently seen the nine-footer on Chestnut Street, dressed in the magnificent uniform with which a grateful city clothes its defenders. Of course he knew they were not real policemen, but assumed the garb to more effectually terrify inoffensive foreigners, and he now demanded the protection of the chief of police. General Stewart replied that he heartily sympathized with and would protect him; that such specimens of humanity instead of spending their time in following and annoying strangers, should confine themselves to dime museums, where they would draw trade, and help swell the resources of the municipality of Philadelphia. Asking the Russian to be seated he sent for two officers, and after relating the story told them to go out and look for the two men described, and when found to arrest them and bring them to headquarters. The officers gravely assented and departed. In about a half an hour they returned, and told the chief, in the presence of the Russian, who had in the meantime been anxiously waiting in the office, that they had found the giants on Chestnut Street and arrested them, and they were now locked up in the strong cells beneath. A radiant expression overspread the face of the Russian, and he heartily thanked the chief for having relieved him of his persecutors. In about a week the Russian again came into the office, and showing the chief a ticket to Europe said that he intended to go home, and had bought his ticket; but on going to the wharf where the steamship lay he found his two old enemies stationed at the foot of the gangplank, and that they absolutely refused to let him go on board. Would the chief once more aid him and remove them from the wharf.

The chief said that he would do so, but if he sent his officers, the men, whose astuteness equalled their length, would suspect danger and would at once board the ship; but could they be induced to leave the wharf and remain until the vessel sailed, the Russian would be rid of them forever. The chief proposed to put some of his men into women's clothes, and as all giants are notoriously susceptible to female charms, they would undoubtedly follow them from the dock, when the Russian could depart in safety. The crank cordially thanked the chief and departed in a very happy frame of mind, went on board the ship and sailed away with illimitable faith in, and immeasurable admiration of General James Stewart, Jr., Chief of the Police of Philadelphia.

Among the many detective chiefs of the United States, I know of none other more worthy of mention in this volume of my reminiscences than Francis R. Kelly, Chief of the Detective Bureau of Philadelphia. He is comparatively a young man yet, but has seen more real service than almost any other man in the country occupying a similar position. In view of this fact, therefore, it will not be out of place if I make brief mention of a few of the notable cases in which he has been engaged.

I never knew or heard of a better example of the power of politeness than the following one. It happened that in February, 1885, Chief Kelly made up his mind that it wouldn't be a bad thing to let the dangerous classes of society know that Philadelphia was not going to be a pleasant abiding place during his term of office, and that they would not be allowed to ply their usual vocations with impunity. Many a thief, pickpocket, burglar, or what not had been "sent up" through his instrumentality, and there were not many rogues in town. But still there were a few rogues left, and although they were keeping pretty quiet, Chief Kelly determined to get rid of them as quickly as he could. And the manner in which he did it in one instance is worth mentioning, not only by reason of its amusing originality, but for its effectiveness as well. One day a complaint was made to him that an overcoat had been stolen from the house of a prominent resident, and "from information received" the Chief made up his mind that the theft had been committed by a well-known "professional" named Kirby. There was no proof against the man from a legal point of view, and it would be no use to arrest him on mere suspicion. Mr. Kirby was well aware of this fact, and was therefore considerably astonished at receiving a very polite intimation that his presence was urgently desired by Chief Kelly at his office. He accompanied the messenger to headquarters, where his mind was somewhat relieved by the assurance that he was not "wanted" on any specific criminal charge. But Kirby's disgust may be better imagined than described when he found that the Chief had also invited the whole of his detective force to attend the reception. Poor Kirby was introduced in turn to each one present by Mr. Kelly, who was very particular to observe every little law laid down in society's etiquette. At length the introductions were concluded, and then Chief Kelly outlined to him the sort of life which he would have to live if he decided to reside in Philadelphia. Other men might step an inch or two over the line with impunity; but as for Mr. Kirby, he must see to it that his deportment was as correct as that of the most straight-laced Puritan. The slightest infraction of the law on his part would be followed by the most condign punishment; and it therefore behooved him to be careful in the extreme. This was too much for Kirby. He looked at the Chief in a bewildered manner, as if he could hardly believe his own ears, and then bolted from the room most unceremoniously. The next day he packed up his "duds" and left Philadelphia for the West, remarking that there was "no good in this confounded town, anyway."

In 1880, Mr. Alexander Tutton, in addition to holding the office of Collector of the port of Philadelphia, was also custodian of the U. S. Sub-Treasury, then located in the Custom-House Building, and one day in the early part of the year mentioned he was called upon by an individual in clerical attire, who represented himself as the Rev. Dr. Haddock, pastor of the Spruce Street Church. The "reverend" gentleman had called, so he announced to Mr. Tutton, for the purpose of soliciting the position of watchman in the Sub-Treasury for one of his parishioners—a very worthy, honest, sober and capable man. Now, Mr. Tutton was a very religiously inclined gentleman, and expressed himself as being not only willing but anxious to oblige such an upright and distinguished divine as Dr. Haddock, whose personal acquaintance he had not previously made. A vacancy occurred very shortly afterwards in the force of watchmen, and Dr. Haddock's protégé was appointed to the position. This was some time in March, and the newly appointed watchman performed his duties in a manner satisfactory to his superiors. At three o'clock, Saturday afternoon, April 26, the vaults, which contained about $15,000,000 in gold, silver and bills, were properly secured, the usual guard of watchmen set, and the outer doors of the building locked, not to be opened, in the ordinary course of affairs, until the following Monday morning. But something extraordinary occurred in the interval, and that the doors were opened subsequent discoveries plainly showed. Adjoining the Custom-House Building was a bonded warehouse, and when the laborers employed there entered on Monday morning they found that a hole had been dug through the wall, on a level with and in the direction of the Sub-Treasury vaults. The consternation, when this startling piece of information was imparted to the Sub-Treasury officials, was something almost ludicrous at first, but it disappeared when it was learned that the diggers of the hole had failed in their endeavors to reach the gold and bill compartments, and had only succeeded in possessing themselves of a bag containing about $20 in copper coin. As a set-off they left behind them a well-finished kit of burglar's tools, the making of which must have cost the expenditure of considerable time and money.

The fact of such an audacious attempt having been made was kept a profound secret from the outside public for some time, as it was feared the disclosure of it would tend to defeat the ends of justice. Chief Kelly, who was at that time an officer of the U. S. Secret Service, was put in charge of the case, and followed up the slight clews with which he was furnished. After several months of investigation in various directions, travelling hither and thither over nearly the whole country, Kelly succeeded in sifting the matter to the very bottom. He argued to himself that one or more of the force of watchmen on guard in the treasury had been in collusion with the burglars, and had admitted them into the warehouse adjoining the Custom House. The antecedents of each of them was looked into closely, and all gave a satisfactory account of themselves, with the exception of the individual who had been appointed through the influence of the Rev. Dr. Haddock. His story of his previous life was rather vague, and the clergyman himself was applied to.

"Did Mr. Haddock know anything about his parishioner?" asked Kelly.

The divine was puzzled; he knew nothing about any parishioner of his who was a watchman in the Custom House, neither had he recommended any one for such a position; didn't know Collector Tutton, and had never called upon him. Further inquiries developed the fact that the "parishioner" was no other than "Shang" Miller, an old-time thief and crook, and the individual who called upon Collector Tutton in the guise of Dr. Haddock, was another of the gang. "Shang," it had been arranged, was to furnish his confederates with a plan of the vaults, and it was only through his carelessness that the most important part of the plot was a failure. By some miscalculation "Shang" failed to locate the different vaults properly. After he had things all "O. K.," as he supposed, he let in "Big Jack" Eberman (who was the originator of the "job"), Bill Cutler and a couple of others, stowing them away until after dark in a little loft under the roof. They worked Saturday night, all day Sunday, until Monday morning, when they found themselves in the copper vault, having missed the gold compartment by a few inches. Their disgust can be more easily imagined than described. In fact, their failure to get the $15,000,000 in gold actually broke "Big Jack's" heart, and he died six weeks afterwards. He kept a saloon on Vine Street, below Sixth, Philadelphia, at the time of the robbery, but was well known among police officials and others all over the country.

Another noted criminal with the capture of whom Chief Kelly had considerable to do when he was a Secret Service Agent, was William H. Robinson, better known as "Gopher Bill," the well-known counterfeiter and "shover of the queer." It was in the summer of 1880. For some considerable period prior to the month of June in the year mentioned, the city of Philadelphia had been flooded with $5, $10 and $50 bank-notes, and although every effort had been made to discover the source from which they emanated, there had been no tangible results. Kelly, with another secret agent of the Government, was placed on the case,

FRANCIS R. KELLY.
Chief of Detectives.

and the two soon made important discoveries. They learned, by means which it would not be policy to divulge even at this late day, that the members of a certain gang in Philadelphia were operating in conjunction with another, the headquarters of which were in Baltimore. Kelly and his "side partner," therefore, watched the trains and boats arriving from the latter city pretty closely for several weeks. At length their patience was rewarded one day by the sight of Frederick Umneck and James Lock, the character of neither of whom would bear investigation, walking down the gangplank of a steamer. Both the men mentioned walked slowly along Delaware Avenue, followed by the detectives, and were met a few blocks below the landing-place, by the "Gopher," who, after a few minutes' conversation, handed them a small package. Knowing Mr. Robinson's tricky nature, the officers allowed him to go his own way unmolested for a time, but followed up Umneck and Lock. And a weary following up it was, too,—first into one saloon for a drink or cigar; then into another; next, a small purchase was made in a store, the officers all the time close at their heels. Finally they landed in the Broad Street station, and boarded a train for Baltimore. But as they sat in the smoking car, each puffing away at a good cigar, they were utterly unconscious of evil from the two innocent-looking men who sat behind them, seemingly intent upon watching the country through which they passed, but who, in reality, were closely watching every action and listening to every word. Baltimore was reached, and the two men, after having wished each other a cordial "good night," were about to separate, when heavy hands were laid on their shoulders, and a pair of voices simultaneously declared that they were both under arrest. The game was up! When searched in the station-house to which they were at once taken, it was discovered that the package which they had received from "Gopher Bill" in Philadelphia contained sixty-two ten-dollar bills, purporting to be issued by the Muncy (Pa.) National Bank; five fifty-dollar notes of the Central National Bank of New York, and spurious silver coin to the amount of $200. The next day, Umneck and Lock were both committed to prison in default of $10,000 bail, to await trial. Kelly and his comrade then went post-haste to Philadelphia and devoted their best energies to keeping a watchful eye upon "Gopher Bill," with a view of ascertaining whether he had any partners in his "business." They soon noticed that the "Gopher" was often accompanied by a respectable, quiet and inoffensive looking man, whose identity was at first unknown to the detectives. It was soon ascertained, however, that his name was Alfred L. Hubbard, and that he lived, with his wife, in a two-story brick house at No. 632 McKean Street. Watching their opportunity, the officers made a descent on Hubbard's residence one evening, and in a closet in a rear room were found twenty-five packages of counterfeit Bland and trade dollars, as well as eight rolls of half dollars—amounting altogether to somewhere about $900 of spurious coin. Mr. and Mrs. Hubbard were accordingly arrested, and the very next day "Gopher Bill" himself was in custody. Mrs. Hubbard was not held for trial, but was discharged. Her husband and "Gopher," however, were both tried and sentenced to eight years' imprisonment in the Eastern Penitentiary. Before sentencing "Gopher," Judge Butler asked him what he had to say. His reply was that so many of his years had been spent in crooked ways that it was a matter of impossibility for him to become "straight." That fact, he thought, should be taken into consideration. Judge Butler, however, said his chronic crookedness was all the greater reason that society should be protected, and he should accordingly send him where he would no longer be a menace to the public.

Few men, indeed, have attained more notoriety in the counterfeiting business than "Gopher Bill." He commenced his career away back beyond the memory of the oldest detectives now in the service. His specialty seems to have been to receive bogus money from the manufacturers, and to make all the necessary arrangements for disposing of it among the "circulators." His slyness and cunning was such as to very often baffle the skill of the shrewdest detectives, the great difficulty being to find the spurious money in his possession and to locate the parties with whom he dealt. As compared with the number of counterfeiting enterprises in which "Gopher" engaged, the number of times he has been arrested is very small. He was a great organizer, and was consulted by those high in the "profession" whenever any scheme of unusual magnitude was proposed. In 1877 he was arrested by Agent Drummond, but as only one counterfeit coin was found on him when he was searched, it was found impossible to convict him. It is believed, though there is no positive proof, that it was he who supplied "Big Frank" McCoy with the tools which enabled that notorious and enterprising criminal to make his escape from the Newcastle (Del.) Jail. "Gopher," however, came to grief in the summer of 1878, when he was " caught dead to rights," and sentenced to eighteen months' imprisonment. He served out his time, and shortly after his release, in October, 1879, was again in custody on suspicion of being concerned in the robbery of the Bailey Brothers, at Kennett Square. He gave certain information to the police, however, and he was released. His companions, Charley Miller and Charles Jones, alias "Blake," were sentenced to long terms of imprisonment in the Penitentiary. Miller's friends, of course, were furious at the treacherous conduct of the "Gopher," and vowed to be revenged. Some time afterwards, "Gopher" was attacked by James Cassidy, one of Miller's "pals," and left lying for dead on the pavement at the corner of Eighth and Vine streets. He was laid up for some time, but finally recovered, and carried on his "business" again, until captured by Chief Kelly as previously narrated.

Chief Kelly, too, was well acquainted with Walter Sheridan, the famous forger and diamond thief. Very seldom, indeed, is it that these two branches of crime are "worked" by one man; but Sheridan, so Chief Kelly informed me, always was a peculiar fellow, but probably united the two "businesses" so that he might always have something to fall back upon. Sheridan was a native of New Orleans, where he first saw the light in 1832. His parents were moderately well off, and he received a fair education. When but a mere lad he drifted, as it were, into crime, and at a very early age made his appearance in Western Missouri in the *rôle* of a horse thief. Subsequently, he became an accomplished general thief and confidence man, but he more especially distinguished himself as a bank sneak. In company with Joseph Moran he was arrested in 1858 for being concerned in a bank robbery in Chicago, and was sentenced to five years' imprisonment in the Alton Penitentiary. The next operation of any magnitude in which he engaged was the theft of $35,000 from the vaults of the National Bank of Springfield, Ill. He had with him as partners on that occasion Charles Hicks and Phil. Pearson, two noted experts in their line. Sheridan, who was a plausible and entertaining conversationalist, engaged the attention of the teller of the bank, while his companions crept in behind the counter and stole the money. Months afterwards, Sheridan was arrested at Toledo, Ohio, by Wm. Pinkerton with $22,000 of the stolen money in his possession. He was placed on trial, but as the prosecution could not prove that he did any more than engage the teller in conversation while the theft was being perpetrated, he was acquitted. Then he came East, and in Baltimore robbed the American Fire Insurance Co. of $50,000, but again escaped conviction. He was equally fortunate in June, 1870, when arrested for stealing $37,800 from the Mechanics' Bank of Scranton, Pa. Probably the neatest "job" ever performed by Sheridan was, when, some six or seven years ago, he accosted Mr. Blatchford (father of U. S. Judge Blatchford) at the corner of Nassau and Liberty streets. The gentleman named held in his hand a package of bonds of the value of $75,000 and stopped at a street stall to purchase an apple. Sheridan spoke to him, and so interested Mr. Blatchford in the conversation that he unthinkingly laid the bonds upon the stall. In a moment it was snatched up by one of Sheridan's confederates, and Mr. Blatchford was "out" $75,000. Nothing, of course, could be legally proved against Sheridan, and he was not even arrested. A portion of the bonds, however, were subsequently recovered, but in what way, I was never able to ascertain.

I have already given an account, in a previous chapter, of the attempt made by George Wilkes and others, in 1873, to swindle Wall Street brokers by the wholesale issue of fraudulent stock. Sheridan was one of the "gang" and was also concerned in the plot to forge letters of credit on the Bank of England. He became disgusted with the way in which the affair was being conducted by certain confederates on the other side of the Atlantic, and declined to have any further hand in the "job." In the same year, too, one of Sheridan's "enterprises" raised quite a commotion in financial circles. After months of planning and negotiating, he succeeded in obtaining a loan of $84,000 from the New York Guaranty & Indemnity Co., depositing as security Buffalo and Erie Railroad bonds, of the face value of $100,000. Close scrutiny showed these bonds to be expert and clever forgeries. Previous to this *coup* Sheridan had, by some means or other, become a member of the Produce Exchange, under the assumed and somewhat romantic name of Charles Ralston. Immediately upon the discovery of the swindle, detectives were put upon Sheridan's track, but he managed to get away from New York with the money. In less than a week he was heard of in Washington, D. C., where he was arrested and brought back to this city. The evidence brought against him on his trial was overwhelming. He was convicted and sent to Sing Sing for five years. Upon the expiration of his term of imprisonment, Sheridan formed a co-partnership with Joe McClosky, one of the shrewdest thieves in the country, and the pair "worked" together for some time. They stole a tray of diamonds from a jewellery store in Philadelphia, and afterwards robbed a travelling salesman's sample trunk of a considerable quantity of jewellery in the same city. The Jewellers' Association of New York took the matter in hand, and Sheridan's photograph, which was in the Rogues' Gallery, was shown the individuals from whom the goods were stolen. They identified him immediately, and soon afterwards he was arrested by the Philadelphia police. It cost him three years in the Eastern Penitentiary. Drifting out West, upon his release, Sheridan, in the fall of 1883, was arrested in Topeka, Kansas, for passing three counterfeit $500 bills, and was sent into retirement for two years. Sheridan is now in the House of Correction at Oporto, Portugal, having been detected in attempting to pass three bogus £500 Bank of England notes upon the cashier of the London and Brazilian Bank.

The only case of "Shanghai," as it is called, which has occurred in recent years in Philadelphia, was one which came under the notice of Chief Kelly in the month of October, 1884, although the event actually occurred some considerable time previous to that. One day, in the first week of the month above mentioned, Chief Kelly received a letter from the Chief Constable of Rochdale, England, giving certain details concerning what was alleged to have been the kidnapping of a young man in Philadelphia during the previous August. Chief Kelly was informed in the letter that in June, Frank Tansey, a resident of Rochdale, sailed from Liverpool for Philadelphia, on board the steamer *Lord Gough*. Shortly after arriving in the city he secured employment in Messrs. Morris & Tasker's Iron Works, and went to lodge at X. Kaufman's saloon, No. 22 Morris Street. He worked at the foundry for several weeks, and was then discharged on account of the slackness of trade. One day, as young Tansey was walking along the wharves, "near where the steamers came in from Boston," he entered into conversation with a strange man, who finally asked him if he was in search of work. Tansey replied that he was, and his chance companion at once volunteered to get him work " down the river." Both then got aboard a small steamer, and after a long run down the Delaware, Tansey was placed upon the Swedish barque *Selina*. Once on board of her, although he knew nothing about seamanship and protested against his treatment in a vigorous manner, he was compelled to work " before the mast." The vessel arrived at Hamburg, her destination, in thirty-five days, and here Tansey was most unceremoniously discharged with just £1 in English money as his pay. He informed the British consul of his condition, and that official immediately forwarded him to his home in Rochdale.

Inquiries were set on foot by Chief Kelly upon receipt of the above mentioned letter, and he found ample evidence that Tansey's statements were correct. His trunk was found at Kaufman's saloon, but £13 which it contained when he was spirited away was missing. From all appearances, Chief Kelly was convinced the affair was a case of "Shanghai," a term which originated many years ago, when the crime of forcing seamen and others on board vessels just as they were about to leave port was a common almost every-day occurrence.

It was in the same month and the same year that Chief Kelly, assisted by two of his men, made a clever capture, one morning, of two notorious burglars, and also recovered considerable valuable property which had been stolen the night before. When Mr. Kelly reached his office that morning he found two complaints of robberies, one of which is known as the "bundle game." A messenger boy was taking a package of goods from the store of Messrs. Murray & Wilson, Thirteenth Street, when at the corner of Tenth and Chestnut streets, he was accosted by a man who asked him to take a note a short distance for a pecuniary consideration. The lad assented, and started off with the note, leaving the bundle, which contained $50 worth of dry-goods, in the hands of the man, who said he would await his return. Needless to say, the man did not wait, and the boy returned to his employers in a disconsolate mood. The second robbery was perpetrated at the cutlery store, Nos. 1927 and 1929 Market Street, not far from $400 worth of razors, forks, knives and spoons being secured by the burglars. For some time previous to this Chief Kelly had suspected that some of the inmates of a cheap lodging-house, situated on North Eighth Street, were not as honest as they might be. The messenger boy, too, gave a description of the man who relieved him of his bundle which tallied with that of an individual who had been seen at the house in question. Without any delay, therefore, Chief Kelly visited the premises, and hurrying up stairs to the third-story back room, took the thieves completely by surprise.

So unprepared were they for the Chief's visit that they had made no effort to conceal the stolen property, which was lying on the floor. The men proved to be "Boston" Crandell and Frank Wilson, both of whom had served terms of imprisonment in not a few prisons of various States.

I don't believe that over ten rogues in a hundred are ever caught by the printed descriptions of them, which may be sent broadcast all over the country without any result. The embezzler, the forger, the murderer, all know how to guard against recognition from such a description as a general rule. But when the authorities are furnished with a photograph of the suspected criminal, the case is different. A man cannot change the expression in his eyes, which is, after all, the main point. The English police officials are very profuse and minute in their descriptions of criminals of whom they are in search. Take, for instance, the following, of a man named Harry Hammond Swindells, suspected of having fled to this country after committing a murder at Oldham, Lancashire: "He is 49 years of age, five feet three and a half inches high, sallow complexion, dark brown hair and beard American fashion, whiskers shaved off, dark blue eyes, Roman nose with blue mark on the bridge, high cheek bones, large mouth, has only one or two teeth in upper jaw, scar on right side of neck, little finger of right hand crooked, walks with a swinging gait, dressed in a black-ribbed, double-breasted slap-back jacket (the right shoulder and arm of which may bear traces of lime-wash), trowsers and vest of same material, new black soft billy-cock hat with a large brim, and new spring-side boots, with square toes."

Another, selected at random, was from Bromberg (Germany), dated October 23, 1883, and headed "Warrant of Caption." Translated into English it read as follows:

"It is notified that the imprisonment for inquiry has been decreed by judgment against the below-described banker, Nathan Szkolny, of Inowrazlaw, Prussia, on account of fraudulent bankruptcy and counterfeiting of documents referring to section 209, No. 1, of the bankruptcy law, and sections 267, 268, No. 1, 74 of the penal code. It is requested to arrest him where he is met, to seize the money and effects found with him, and to give me notice. Szkolny has falsified bills of exchange to the amount of about 200,000 marks, and has escaped with the money he has got thereby.

His creditors guarantee to any one who seizes him a reward of fifteen per cent. of the amount being in his possession.

"For the Royal Attorney of State,
"SCHULZE-VELLINGHAUSEN."

The description which follows is unique in its way, and includes the following "special marks," as they are termed:

"Szkolny wears blue spectacles, has a glass eye, stutters and has two false teeth in the under jaw. He walks slowly and the *legs are 'O' formed.*"

Quite a prepossessing sort of a fellow, but not quite as handsome, was an individual once "wanted" in Chicago, where he had succeeded in winning the heart and person of a trusting maiden, and then cruelly refused to fulfil his promise of wedding her. His name was Erastus Judson Stillwind, and the description furnished is quite unique in its way:

"He claims to be forty-five years of age, but looks twenty years older; is smooth shaven and wears a dark brown wig, reaching over the forehead. He squints a great deal, and is constantly chewing tobacco; complexion sallow, with hollow cheeks, receding chin, prominent nose, on the left side of which are two warts; about five feet six inches tall, stoops considerably and has a halting gait, caused by a club foot and knock-knees. Weight, about 130 to 140 lbs., but made up to look much heavier."

What an Apollo! None of my men ever came across such a one, and I have often wondered whether his inamorata was as good-looking and well-favored as he.

As a general rule we always had enough to do with looking after our own criminals; and unless a man was very distinctly marked, and the crime freshly committed, it was very seldom he was captured unless by accident. It has often happened that an individual has been arrested on suspicion, or for some petty offence, and has turned out to be a fugitive from some other city or State. Then the printed description, for want of a photograph, comes in very handy.

Circulars in relation to eloping couples are very numerous, and I have noticed that in nearly every instance where rewards are offered the advertiser is the husband and of German birth. The women, too, are usually well advanced in years. For instance, some years ago, Mr. B. Hettisheimer, a resident of Cincinnati, was anxious for the return of his wife, forty-three years old, who had run away with a young man not half her age. Then there was a dangerous young flirt of fifty, who had eloped from her lawful lord and master, a Mr. Tremble, of Pittsburg, with a Frenchman named Shew. Twenty-five dollars appears to be the average amount which husbands are willing to pay for the return of their erring helpmeets, but a woman never offers to pay anything for a missing husband. Strange, isn't it?

In October, 1884, I received information from the Philadelphia police authorities that an Italian had been brutally murdered in the woods near Linwood, Deleware Co., Pennsylvania, and that the suspected murderer, also an Italian, would doubtless attempt to sail from New York on his way to his native land. The body of the murdered man, who was employed on the Baltimore and Philadelphia R.R., and was known as "No. 25" by the contractor, was discovered in a deep ravine near Upper Chichester, by an Italian lad named "Pete". The head of the poor victim had been beaten into an almost shapeless mass, and a formidable hickory club about five feet long, covered with blood and hair, was found near by. His pants pockets were turned inside out, and the belt in which he carried his money, and wore around his waist, had been cut open. The identity of the murderer was shrouded in mystery, and various theories were broached by the police and detectives. A lot of apples were on the ground near the body, which, it should be mentioned, was lying in an orchard on the farm of two German brothers, and this, together with the fact that the blood-stained club had evidently been taken from a wood-pile in the vicinity of the farm-house, led to the belief that the killing had been done by one of the inmates who had caught him trespassing and stealing the apples. For a long time no clew was obtained as to the murdered man's name. The contractor in whose employ he worked as a stone-mason only reconized him as "No. 25." At length it was discovered that the dead man, together with a friend whose name, also, was not ascertainable at first, but was subsequently discovered to be Giuseppi Davino, had lived in a shanty kept by a fellow countryman, and known as "Frank's Hut." In this shanty the detectives found an old trunk belonging to the deceased, containing some clothing and other effects; and a passport in the pocket of a coat, gave his name as Nevaciante Ciampi. His friend Davino had also disappeared just previous to the finding of the body. By diligent inquiries it was also found that on October 21st, Ciampi and Davino had visited a place called Belleview, a mile or two from the shanty, and had remained there nearly the whole of the day. They were seen to leave Belleview in company the same evening, walking in the direction of their camp, where, however, they did not put in an appearance. Three days afterwards Ciampi's corpse was found as above stated, three miles from " Frank's Hut." He had always been an industrious, sober and hard-working man; while his companion, Davino, was described by those who knew him as a worthless, lazy fellow, never working when he could possibly avoid it and sponging on his fellow countrymen. He was always longing to return to Italy, and had begged his friends there time and time again to remit him money enough to pay his expenses. They always refused, and his sudden disappearance, therefore, caused much comment. He was traced to this city, where towards the end of December my detectives, who had been furnished with Davino's description, found that he had sailed for Italy on the 3d of the month named. Upon learning this, Chief Kelly communicated with the Italian authorities, and at length had the satisfaction of receiving a letter from the Pretor of Frigento (Italy) that Davino had been arrested there—his native town. A watch had been found upon him which was identified as having been the property of Ciampi; and his own daughter testified to having heard him confess to her mother one night that he had killed Ciampi. Davino was never returned to this country, but was, I believe, tried and convicted in Italy, the laws there permitting such a course.

With all the numerous safeguards which exist against dishonesty in the Mint at Philadelphia, I remember one instance, at least, in which they proved to be insufficient; and although every effort was made by Chief Kelly and his detectives to fix the responsibility, they were unable to ferret out the thief. One afternoon, in the early part of February, 1885, Mr. B. F. Cohen, a jeweller, of No. 6 Maiden Lane, in this city, called at the office of Mr. Charles S. Platt, assayer and refiner, No. 4 Liberty Place, with a bar of silver, weighing seventy pounds, stating that it had been sent him by some parties in Philadelphia to dispose of. Mr. Platt was well acquainted with Mr. Cohen, and would undoubtedly have purchased the precious metal immediately, had he not noticed the name of the Omaha & Grant Smelting and Refining

Co. stamped upon it. This was rather suspicious to Mr. Platt, as he knew that the silver of the company mentioned was generally sold in large quantities—50,000 ozs., or more at a time. The company, too, were in the habit of numbering all the bars sold by them, and the number of the one presented by Mr. Cohen was "16,929." It weighed 1023 70-100 ozs., and was 999 fine. After noticing all these things, Mr. Platt said he could not purchase the bar unless Clark, Dodge & Co., the agents for the Omaha Smelting Co., said it was all right. A message was accordingly sent to the firm, and on investigation it was found that the bar in question had been sold some time previously to the well-known bankers, J. & W. Seligman & Co., who declared that, with a number of others, it had been purchased by the Government and delivered at the Philadelphia Mint. The Messrs. Seligman said they had been paid, and had also received an official notification that all was correct. That notification was dated January 24th and yet up to February 13th the bar of silver in the possession of Mr. Cohen had not been missed from the Philadelphia Mint. The matter was reported to me and a telegram to the authorities at the Mint made them acquainted with the theft for the first time. How a bar of solid silver, weighing over eighty-five pounds, could be carried out of the Mint without detection, is beyond my comprehension; but the fact remains that it was stolen, and that the thief was never discovered. A saloon-keeper named Hugh Daly, who kept a place on South Street, was arrested by Chief Kelly on suspicion of being concerned in the affair; but nothing could be proved against him, and he was discharged.

I might fill a volume, if I chose to give a detailed account of the many excellent services rendered, not only the city of Philadelphia, but the country at large, by Chief Kelly. It will be remembered that in 1882 there was considerable excitement in England over what was known as "the dynamite scare." A number of so-called "infernal machines," had been shipped to England, where they were seized. It was discovered that they had been manufactured in this country, and the English Government communicated with Minister West upon the subject, authorizing him to take what steps might be necessary for unearthing the makers. It should be stated that previous to this, Sir Stafford Northcote (later Lord Iddesleigh) had offered a reward of $10,000 for reliable information upon the subject; and it is now known that the sum mentioned was actually paid, but to whom has never been made public. In accordance with his instructions, Minister West secured the services of Chief Kelly, then a secret agent of the U. S. Government, and also those of Detective Gilkinson. They received from England the very barrel in which the machines were packed, and also one of the machines themselves. The work of investigation was long and tiresome, occupying over nine months' time and leading the two officers along the whole line of coast, from the Gulf to Maine. They found that the barrel had been made in Philadelphia, and that the infernal machines were the productions of a man named Holgate, who then resided at No. 1502 South Juniper Street. This machine was nothing more than an ordinary zinc canister, about four inches square at the ends and twelve inches high. The "works" were simply common clock works, and, it was ascertained, had been furnished by an individual doing business on Eighth Street. As to the explosives with which the machines were said to be filled, their contents, on close examination, turned out to be harmless gypsum powder, which had been obtained from the ruins of an old factory at Gray's Ferry Road and the Schuylkill river. It also transpired that the English Government had paid the reward of $10,000 to the very parties who had shipped these harmless infernal machines to London. Chief Kelly reported what he had learned to Minister West, and shortly afterwards further investigation was ordered to cease, the authorities evidently having come to the conclusion that they had been nicely fooled by the parties who had shipped the machines.

CHAPTER XLI.

JUSTICE'S JUSTICE IN NEW YORK.—HOW THE WHEELS ARE "COGGED." —AN INADEQUATE JUDICIARY.—EVASION OF PUNISHMENT. — SEVERAL INSTANCES.—"BUNCO" MEN AND SWINDLERS.—WHY THEY ARE NOT BROUGHT TO TRIAL.—ROUGH ON THE COMPLAINANT.—SEVENTEEN WEEKS IN THE HOUSE OF DETENTION.— "FINE WORK."—SOMETHING ABOUT GAMBLERS.—NOT A SINGLE HONEST ONE.—WALL STREET'S INSATIABLE MAW.—SOLITARY MR. SMITH, OF RHODE ISLAND.—WHERE ALL THE MONEY GOES.— POLICE CAPTAINS SHOULD BE MADE RESPONSIBLE FOR THE EXISTENCE OF "HELLS."—BLACKMAIL LEVIED ON GAMBLING HOUSES. —REMEDIES SUGGESTED.

THE reader will naturally ask why justice in New York is very often so long delayed in the case of the wealthy defendant, and as often denied the poor complainant. That the wheels of the blindfolded goddess's car are often "cogged," is a fact beyond dispute. How is it that such a state of things exists; and to what is all the more than suspicious laxity in the enforcement of the laws and the proper administration of justice to be attributed? Any one at all conversant with the workings of the *lex mechanico* in our city, will at once perceive the difficulty of answering such a question in an off-hand manner.

Take, for instance, violations of the excise law; they are numerous enough; arrests are made every day, and yet one very rarely hears of a liquor dealer being sent to prison. Why, I suppose I should not be far wrong in saying that there are anywhere from eighteen to twenty thousand complaints against parties for violations of the terms of their licenses now on file in the District Attorney's office. They have been accumulating there in the pigeon-holes for years and years; most of them are covered with dust and many of them are actually mouldy with age. A violator of the excise law is arrested; he gives bail and elects to be tried by a jury in the General Sessions. This he has a perfect right to do. The consequence is that the facilities for trying such cases be come peculiarly inadequate; and the District Attorney, in the very nature of things, cannot prevent the vast accumulation of papers to which I have previously referred. He is obliged to try what are known as "prison cases," such as murder, manslaughter, burglary and other crimes against person or property. If these cases were not dealt with, and the time of the court were occupied with liquor, gambling and lottery cases, a man, charged with a serious offence, who has been in jail a certain length of time without being brought up for trial, would have a right to demand his discharge. Unless, therefore, our judicial machinery—the number of courts as well as the number of judges—is increased, this evil in our system of justice will never be regulated or decreased. Even supposing an offender is brought to trial, and a conviction ensues — and this has happened now and then — political and other influences are invoked, and the culprit is pardoned. Let me give an instance or two. The case of Thomas Doyle, of No. 87 Third Avenue, charged with a violation of the excise law, came up in the Court of General Sessions on Oct. 4, 1878, before Recorder Hackett, who imposed a sentence of thirty days' imprisonment in the Penitentiary. Doyle's counsel at once procured a writ of *habeas corpus*, the arguments on which, however, were adjourned from time to time over a space of two weeks. Doyle was a prominent and powerful politician, and among his friends were Major J. W. Saner and Councillor F. Rand, who proceeded to Albany while these arguments were pending before the courts, had an interview with Governor Robinson and procured a pardon for Doyle! Comment is needless.

Then there was the case of Jacob Berry, proprietor of the infamous Columbia Opera House, which stood on the corner of Twelfth and Greenwich streets, which was raided some time in March, 1878. After many delays, Berry was sentenced to eight months' imprisonment in the Penitentiary. The case was taken on an appeal to the Supreme Court, but the decision of the lower court was affirmed by Judges Davis and Ingalls, Judge Brady dissenting. The Court of Appeals at Albany was then applied to, but with a like result, and the papers were returned to District Attorney Phelps. Berry, however, remained at liberty; the reason he was not brought up for sentence, so I was informed, being that a recommendation for his pardon had been presented to Governor Robinson. And sure enough, on the 9th of June, a pardon was granted, political influence having evidently been brought to bear in certain quarters. Then, again, Phillip·Cantlan, No. 39 Washington Street, indicted in 1878 for violation of the excise law, has appeared ten or fifteen times in court, but on each occasion the case has been adjourned, and nothing has yet come of the complaint.

The common run of juries, too, if they think a severe sentence is going to follow a verdict of guilty, are unwilling to convict in cases where the offence charged is a violation of the excise law. In July, 1879, a man named Julius Kohler was convicted of such an offence, and was thereupon sentenced by Judge Cowing to thirty days' imprisonment in the City Prison. A regular howl went up from those in the court-room when they heard the sentence, and the foreman of the jury informed Judge Cowing that had he and his fellow jurymen known so severe a sentence would have been imposed, they would not have returned a verdict of guilty; and yet this Kohler's place was one of the worst possible character, and the evidence against him overwhelming.

The reasons why "bunco" men and swindlers of a somewhat similar nature are not convicted as a general rule, although complaints against such characters are numerous, are somewhat different. The victim, in nearly every instance, is a resident of some other city or State. The magistrate before whom the parties are taken holds both complainant and defendant for examination, fixing bail at the amount required by law. The procuring of a bondsman is an easy matter with the sharper; but with the poor victim it is different. Failing to furnish the requisite security for his appearance, he is bundled off to the House of Detention.

As an instance of the injustice committed in this way let me give just one sample, the records of which are before me. It is the first that came to hand, although I could mention dozens of a similar nature. A young man named N. T. Fox (never mind what his business, or where he came from; but the name is genuine) visited that notorious gambling house, No. 15 Ann Street, some time in February, 1880. In one evening he lost as much as $1000, and the next morning came to me with his story, saying that all he cared about was to get his money back. At my request he made an affidavit as to the facts, and that same night the place was raided. Peter DeLacy was the proprietor of this "hell," and was arrested. Upon being taken before a police magistrate, he gave bail and was allowed to go at liberty, while Fox, the complainant, was sent to the House of Detention, and held as a witness. Time and time again were efforts made, at my direction, to have the case tried, but in every instance DeLacy's counsel, by some means or other, which I have never been enabled to fathom, managed to have it adjourned. Finally, in October, after no less than seventeen weeks' imprisonment in the House of Detention, Fox was set at liberty, the only explanation given him being that the case would come up some time or other, and that he would be notified. In April, 1881, District Attorney Phelps was asked to place the case against DeLacy on the calendar. This he refused to do, giving as his reason that DeLacy had " gone out of business." And yet No. 15 Ann Street has long been known to be one of the worst places in the city. True, DeLacy may not be the proprietor in the eye of the law, but he hung round the place most of his time.

It is when the complainant is about to be sent to the House of Detention that the friends of the swindlers get in their " fine work," as it is termed; that is, they make overtures to the complainant; they point out the inconvenience it is, to say nothing of the unpleasantness, to remain incarcerated, when by merely promising to go to his home and not appear against the accused on the day of trial, a bondsman will be procured, the money of which he was despoiled will be returned, and there will be no further bother about it. Of course the complainant is only too glad of the chance. He gives the required promise, a bondsman is supplied, he leaves the city or State, and there's an end of the matter.

It is not very likely that the aggrieved party, having received back his own, is going to remain in the city at considerable expense, to say nothing of the inconvenience, in a business point of view. He therefore goes home, and there is no legal power which can compel the attendance of a person in another State as a witness here.

And now, although I have alluded to the subject of gambling in a previous chapter, I have something more to say in that connection. It has always been a popular delusion that somewhere or other, and at some time or other, there has existed an *honest* professional gambler. I don't believe it. During my whole experience I never met with such an one. They don't all of them steal, however, because they find it pays them better to live by gambling. But all the gambling that goes on in the City of New York is not confined to the playing of cards and the betting on horse races, etc. Wall Street itself is nothing more nor less than an immense gambling concern, and among the many defaulters for large amounts, who have from time to time been brought before me, nine-tenths of them have admitted that their social and moral ruin had been brought about by speculating in Wall Street. How many retire from it with a fortune? Very few. Only a short time since, in the course of conversation with the head of one of the largest firms of brokers in this country, the question was asked how many men, of all the thousands who were constantly investing money in stocks, etc., through his agency, retired from the "street" possessed of more than they had put into it.

"A few," said he.

"Can you give me an instance?"

He hesitated, thought awhile, and finally admitted that he could not recall any just then. His chief clerk, who was standing near, listening to our conversation, remarked:

"Yes; I remember there was Smith, of Rhode Island, who made $30,000 through us, and then retired from the city to his farm."

"Do you remember any one else?" was the next inquiry.

He did not—could not recall a single other instance.

So I asked further concerning this wonderful Mr. Smith:

"How long ago was it that Smith left the 'street' with his $30,000?"

"About a year and a half," was the reply of the head clerk. "And I'm perfectly confident," added the head of the firm, "that Mr. Smith will return to Wall Street and lose it all."

Seeking further enlightenment on the matter, I inquired of another leading broker as to how many of his customers made money in the long run by their speculations. He told me that not one did; and to back up his assertion he stated that only a short time previously he had gone over the books with his accountant. The result of his investigations, covering a number of years, showed millions to the debit of the customers, balanced almost entirely by commissions paid to the broker. Think of it. Of all the thousands and thousands who had marched into the offices of these two large firms, there was only this solitary Smith who had retired with more money than when he went in! Who gets these untold millions that are being constantly poured into Wall Street's insatiable maw? It finds its way, partly into the pockets of those who, when they die, leave fortunes of hundreds of millions; and partly to brokers, whose legitimate commissions sometimes amount to as much as a million dollars a year. If this is not gambling, I should like to know what is.

Apart from Wall Street, however, it will, of course, be of no use for me to attempt to deny, even if I had the desire, that during my term of office as superintendent, this great and crying evil was in a flourishing condition. Under the present system, too, it can and will never be otherwise. The suppression of gambling of every description, under the present form of police government, does not, by any means, lie with the superintendent. It is wholly and solely within the power of the captains of the various precincts. I do not mean to say that they can put a stop to poker parties, etc., in private residences; but having occupied the position of captain myself for a number of years, it may be justly supposed I know something about the matter. This I do know: that when first appointed captain, I was called upon by a professional gambler, who asked for permission to open a gambling house in my precinct. I refused him in language more forcible than polite, and he was wise enough to think I meant what I said, and therefore did not invest any money in such a venture as proposed. There were no public gaming houses in my precinct, and it is within the power of every captain to order the same state of things. It is an utter impossibility for a public gambling house to exist in any precinct for a length of time, without the connivance, direct or indirect, of the captain. While I have no positive personal knowledge on the subject, still I am morally convinced in my own mind, that the great majority of gambling establishments in this city have in the past, and do even now, pay for the privilege of being allowed to conduct their business without being molested. The only possible way in which such a state of things as this can be remedied, is by making every captain directly responsible for the condition of his precinct in this regard; instant dismissal to follow the existence of a public gambling house.

But, after all, the only way in which to obtain a fair, just and thorough enforcement of the law by the police, is to separate the force entirely from politics. Have but one commissioner with unlimited power, independent of any or every political clique. Four police commissioners are just about as much use as if we had four mayors. The superintendent, for his part, should have power commensurate with his responsibility.

Just think of it! Prior to the year 1882, the police commissioners had the power to remove me from the office of superintendent by a simple vote at one of their meetings. Why, my position was more unstable in that respect than that of any other member of the force—from inspectors down to door-men, who had the right of demanding written charges, and of being heard in their own defence. Time and time again have I attempted, one way or another, to have fuller power placed in my hands, but for the last four years during which I was superintendent, my position was that of a mere figure-head. What I claim is, that a man who is held responsible for the actions of certain subordinates in any public department, should have absolute control over those under him as to assignment and transfer.

CHAPTER XLII.

THE "SOCIAL EVIL" AGAIN.—HOW TO CLEAR A RESPECTABLE NEIGHBORHOOD.—A NOVEL PLAN.—CAPTAINS NOT UNAWARE OF ILLEGAL RESORTS IN THEIR PRECINCTS.—"FIXED UP" REPORTS. — MISREPRESENTATIONS WHICH HAVE OCCURRED. — BLACKMAILING BY DETECTIVES. — HOW I CAUGHT THE OFFENDERS. — A STORY WITH AN INTERESTING SEQUEL. — "PLIN" WHITE'S WONDERFUL CAREER.—HOW HE WENT HOME TO DIE.

IN connection with the problem of how to deal with the "social evil," one incident recurs to mind, which happened when I was captain of the Eighteenth Ward. Complaints were made to me by certain residents in a decidedly respectable neighborhood to the effect that a house of assignation had been started in their very midst by a notorious woman. How could they be ridded of her company? Some sort of a self-appointed committee, I was informed, had waited upon the female in question, and had offered to pay her quite a considerable sum of money — something over $1000—if she would remove from the locality. The "strange woman," however, was obdurate. $2000, or nothing, she said, was what she wanted. This, in the opinion of the deputation was not only more than they cared to give, but was more than their cash in hand amounted to. Could I aid them in any way, so as to rid the locality of the disgrace of having a house of such a character right in its very midst? None of them were willing to go so far as to make the scandal worse by making a complaint against the objectionable female in the courts, and the question was an open one as to how I should get her to move. After considerable cogitation I at length hit upon a plan which I thought would be successful in attaining the desired end. By my orders an officer in plain clothes was stationed in front of the house in question all the time, both day and night. Anyone—whether male or female —who was about to enter the premises, was accosted with the remark (accompanied at night by a flash from the officer's dark lantern):—

"Beg your pardon, but the captain is going to 'pull' this house, and if you take my advice you will not go inside."

In almost every single instance the intended visit was indefinitely postponed, and as a natural consequence the woman very quickly found it would be to her advantage to seek fresh fields and pastures new.

This method may not have been a strictly legal one, but it at least possessed the merit of being sure in its result, which is more than can be said of a resort to a court of law. As a general rule, juries have something almost amounting to an aversion to convict in such cases, and especially is this so when the jury is made up largely of elderly men; they seem to sympathize, strangely enough, with the elegantly accoutred and apparently repentant Delilah, who sometimes sheds "crocodile" tears, or else looks as prim and demure as a Puritan maiden fresh from the "Mayflower."

And while writing upon this matter, it may be as well to let the public become acquainted with the fact that in each precinct station-house a private list is kept of all the houses of assignation, gambling resorts, policy-shops, etc., a copy of which is also to be found at police headquarters. These lists are constantly being revised from time to time, as reports are made by patrolmen and detectives, and it is all nonsense for a captain to declare that he is unaware of the existence of an illegal or immoral resort in his precinct until it has been brought to his notice by private citizens, who have known of it for a longer or a shorter period. It has happened—and more than once, too—that curious and inexcusable blunders have been made by captains in writing out their lists. An energetic mayor or spasmodically moral police commissioner will call for a list in a hurry, and one is "cooked" for the occasion, in the almost certain conviction that no investigation will be made as to its correctness, or otherwise. Now and then, however, as I happen to know, such a captain reckons without his host. In one list which came to my knowledge, submitted by a certain captain who shall be nameless, a couple of residences were set down as gambling houses. Officers were sent to investigate privately. One of the so-called gambling houses turned out to be occupied by the widow of one of our most distinguished generals during the Rebellion—a lady of undoubted culture, refinement and uprightness of character! The other house was vacant.

In another chapter I have alluded to the difficulty experienced by a chief of police in convicting his officers of blackmail on offenders against the law. I remember an incident, however, which occurred while I was an inspector under Superintendent Kennedy, and which is worthy of being related in this connection. A man walked into the office one day, and without any preliminaries said to Mr. Kennedy: " Chief, I'm a pickpocket, and have been systematically blackmailed by two of your detectives (giving their names), and now they threaten to arrest me if I don't comply with their demands."

Mr. Kennedy, as was but natural, in view of the fact that the detectives in question had been many years on the force and bore excellent characters, expressed his disbelief in the man's assertion.

" Well," said the self-confessed pickpocket, " I don't want you to believe my simple statement. I didn't expect you would; but if you have some honest man in whom you have implicit confidence, and will send him with me to-morrow, when I'm to meet them again, I'll prove to your satisfaction that what I say is true."

Mr. Kennedy accordingly sent for me, and I had a long talk with the thief. I myself doubted his story, but he stated the facts so circumstantially that I concluded to investigate the matter thoroughly. He told me that he had met the officers the night previous and that they had demanded a certain sum of money from him. He told them he had not that much in his pocket, but gave them all he had, promising to furnish the remainder on the following day. After listening attentively to the man's story, I furnished him with a worthless bill on a broken bank, writing on the back of it " George W. Walling, Inspector of Police." We also arranged a neat little plot, having in view the capture of the detectives red-handed, as it were, the details of which will appear hereafter. The next day I followed the man to Thirteenth Street, where he said he was to meet the officers. He ensconced himself in a doorway, while I seated myself on the shafts of a convenient cart, which stood on the opposite side of the street, with an old slouch hat drawn down over my face somewhat. Very shortly afterwards the detectives appeared on the scene, shook hands with the pickpocket, and after some little conversation the money was handed over to one of them, who placed it in his overcoat pocket. Both then walked away in the direction of Fourteenth Street, where, followed by me, they entered a saloon. Keeping close at their heels, I also went into the place. They were standing at the bar, and were just ordering something to drink.

"What'll you take?" said one to the other.

He was the fellow who had taken the money from the pickpocket, so I stepped up to him and put my hand on his shoulder.

Said I, "I'll take the money that thief has just given you."

The effect on him was wonderful. He jumped away from me, and his face grew pale, as he replied:

"What do you mean, Walling? No thief has given me any money."

"He has, though," I persisted. "I want it, too, and am going to have it. If you don't produce it immediately I'll throw you on the floor and take it from you by main force," saying which I stepped quickly to the other side of him, put my hand in his pocket, and pulled out the worthless bill which the pickpocket had given him. I showed him my signature on the back, and observed:

"See what an egregious ass you have been."

"For God's sake, Walling, don't give me away," he said, imploringly.

But I had my duty to perform, and telling them I should report the circumstances to Supt. Kennedy, walked down town in the direction of headquarters. They followed me as far as the Cooper Institute, begging me to let up on them. However, I related my story to Mr. Kennedy. The detectives could offer no excuse for their conduct; they could only beg not to be publicly exposed. No doubt they deserved to have been indicted by the Grand Jury, but in consideration of their many years of service and previous good behavior, Mr. Kennedy finally gave them permission to hand in their resignations. This they did at once, and that was the last heard of the matter.

Another similar case with which I was connected, was the outcome of a complaint made to Supt. Kennedy by Mr. Robert Murray, United States Marshal, to the effect that some of the detective force were in the habit of blackmailing certain criminals.

In his impulsive, off-hand manner, Capt. Kennedy at once exclaimed:

"I don't believe a word of it."

"If you will do as I say, Mr. Kennedy, I'll prove it to you," was Mr. Murray's rejoinder.

"If you can I'll be very glad to have you do so," replied the superintendent, and Marshal Murray at once unfolded his plan.

In accordance with that plan Mr. Kennedy sent for Capt. Bowen G. Lord, of the sanitary squad, and myself, and gave us our instructions.

We were told that a well-known thief, named Hyer, had informed the "super" that certain detectives were in the habit of "sponging" on him for money, and that he had agreed to meet one of them that evening in a little yard in the rear of the Metropolitan Hotel, near the corner of Prince and Crosby streets, for the purpose of paying him something. Lord and myself accordingly stationed ourselves in a stable on the opposite corner, and watched through the window for anything which might transpire. Very shortly, the man Hyer came along and seated himself very comfortably upon a hydrant, whistling softly to himself in an unconcerned and haven't-got-a-care-in-the-world manner.

I should have previously stated, however, that earlier in the day Superintendent Kennedy had sent for Capt. John Young, who was then in charge of the detective force, and informed him that if any of his men were engaged in the affair they would most assuredly be caught. One would have thought that with such a warning as this none of the detectives would have been foolhardy enough to keep the appointment with the man Hyer. But it proved otherwise.

Hyer had been seated on the hydrant, as before related, about a quarter of an hour, when a well-known detective approached him, and, standing as he did, right under the lamp-post, everything that passed was seen by Capt. Lord and myself. The conversation which passed between the two was inaudible, but we distinctly saw Hyer pass something to the detective, who immediately placed it in his waistcoat pocket, and then walked rapidly away in the direction of Broadway. Lord and I followed, and just as the detective was in front of Niblo's Garden I accosted him with :

" Good evening, ———, I'm very sorry you did that."

" Did what ? " he asked with an air of astonishment which I'm certain was not assumed, as he did not dream of his little transaction with Hyer having been overlooked.

" Why, take the money from that thief Hyer," I replied. " Give it to me. You put it in your right-hand vest pocket."

Without a word, he handed me the money then and there. Mr. Kennedy was waiting rather impatiently in his office to hear the result of our inquiries, hoping to hear that the charge against the detective was unfounded. I told him the facts and laid the money on the desk. The detective was present, and turning to him he simply said:

"Just write out your resignation."

The detective retired to the waiting-room, wrote it, and returning in a few minutes, handed it to the superintendent.

And now for the sequel, which is more interesting and instructive in a certain way than the story itself.

Hyer, who was said to have reformed, became the proprietor of a liquor saloon in the Eighth Ward, and appeared to be doing a good business. One day, some months after the events previously narrated, Captain John Jourdan, who subsequently succeeded Mr. Kennedy as superintendent, walked into Hyer's saloon, accompanied by one or two others.

"Hold out your hands," was Jourdan's command.

Hyer did so. Click! and the handcuffs were on his wrists. "Having counterfeit money in his possession" was the charge. It was sustained, too, by the prosecution, the witnesses, if I remember aright, testifying to finding base money in his till; and Hyer was sentenced to a long term of imprisonment in Sing Sing. Whether Hyer was guilty or not I have no means of judging. I have simply given the facts and leave the reader to draw his own conclusions. But there is something I had almost forgotten, which is that the detective to whom Hyer was seen to pay the money was an especial friend of Captain Jourdan, and served under him as a patrolman in the Sixth Precinct.

Away back in the "thirties," there resided in the little town of Wethersfield, Vt., a family by the name of White, consisting of Mr. and Mrs. White and two sons, one of whom was named "Plymouth." Young Plymouth attended the village school, and stored his mind with such crumbs of learning as were distributed in those days. There was nothing remarkable about the lad; his pursuits and amusements were about the same as those of others of his age and station in life; there was no indication of the extraordinary career which it would seem was his by destiny. Leaving school, Plymouth White, still a mere boy, went to work in a small printing-house in Montpelier, the State capital. For some years he busied himself with mastering the intricacies of the "art preservative of all arts," and then emigrated to Boston. There he succeeded in obtaining work as a compositor on the *Atlas*, and by his energy and natural aptitude for the newspaper business soon managed to elevate himself to the position of editor. In this capacity he met with no small degree of success, his writings attracting considerable attention in literary circles. He was well known among newspaper men generally, with whom he was always "hail fellow, well met." About this time, too, he became somewhat convivial in his habits, and was a pretty frequent visitor at one or two first-class saloons in the neighborhood of the theatres and newspaper offices. He lived in an expensive manner, always dressed well, and had quite a standing in society, being on friendly and familiar terms with many of Boston's leading men. His salary was comparatively small for a man of his luxurious inclinations, and the inevitable result followed. Finding himself short of money he resorted to tricky methods of "raising the wind," and was compelled to leave the "Hub" in rather a hurried manner.

And this was the beginning of the criminal life of "Plin" White, as he had now come to be called, the most notorious and successful "confidence" man that ever lived, the whole of the complaints against whom it would be impossible to enumerate. He was, undoubtedly, the "king pin" of the great army of those who gain their living by the exercise of their wits, and those who knew him might truly have said: "We ne'er shall look upon his like again." In personal appearance he was not unlike that other great diplomatist, Prince Bismark. Massive, regular and striking features; deep-set, resolute eyes; high projecting forehead; mouth covered with white mustache, and his head bald, with the exception of a snowy fringe of hair—such was "Plin" White according to his latest photograph, taken under the auspices of the Boston police when he was sixty years of age. Earlier "counterfeit presentments" of him, however, depict him as quite a slim young fellow, rather good-looking, with black hair and mustache. Still, even in his youthful days he had more the appearance of a young divinity student than anything else, coupled with an air of frankness and integrity which imposed upon even those most deeply versed in the ways of the world. As a conversationalist he was both plausible and convincing, while in his manners he was a perfect gentleman. With such an outfit of both mental and physical qualifications, then, "Plin" commenced his career as a confidence man. Leaving Boston, he journeyed "down East," and located himself in Bangor, Me., where he found quite a lucrative field for the exercise of his peculiar abilities as a swindler. He wheedled himself into the confidences and good graces of many of the most wealthy business men in the town, and succeeded in making more money in a month by his swindling operations than he could in a whole year by editing a newspaper. It paid immensely; but his quarters in Bangor soon became too warm for him, and he therefore returned to Boston, where he "operated" on a rather more pretentious and extensive scale. Finding his abilities appreciated, as it were, "Plin" came to the conclusion that his greatest talents lay in the cheating of his fellow-men, and thought that the city of New York would not be a bad place in which to exercise his wits. So he came here in 1850, and established what he announced as a "general brokerage business," the name of the firm with which he was connected being "Winn, Hawkins & White." This combination lasted but a very brief period; and "Plin" became the defendant in any number of civil suits. But this didn't trouble him in the least; he was far above being annoyed by such small matters as that, and in a few weeks he was on his feet again. At this time the city was fairly overrun with returning Californians, who brought with them large quantities of gold-dust and nuggets, which they were anxious to dispose of. White considered them fair game, and accordingly became a speculator in the precious metal. Success attended every venture in which he engaged, and he soon amassed quite a decent fortune. He purchased a costly residence on Fifth Avenue and lived in the most extravagant and luxurious manner. One of his victims was Major Hall, proprietor of Lovejoy's Hotel, whom he somehow or other induced to sign notes to the amount of $50,000. White told the major that he only wanted to use the notes as collateral security in some of his gold speculations, and entered into an agreement not to dispose of them. "Plin" no sooner had the notes in his possession than he sold them, and Hall realized that he was a ruined man. He remonstrated with White and threatened him with a criminal prosecution, but he only laughed in the major's face and defied him.

"You can't have me locked up," he said.

And so it proved, but Major Hall brought a civil suit, out of which White came with flying colors. Thirty years afterwards, so consummate was White's impudence, that he actually called upon the major at his residence, and begged forgiveness. But this was not the sole object of his call. Would Major Hall oblige him with the loan of $1200 for a few days, and accept as security a blue envelope, which he produced, saying it contained $6000 worth of bonds. The major hesitated, and was lost. He drew the money from the bank and handed it to White, receiving the blue envelope as security, and signing an agreement not to open it until the expiration of two months. Mrs. Hall, when she heard of the transaction was not quite as confiding as her husband. She accordingly called upon me one Sunday afternoon at my private residence, No. 311 East 19th Street, and showed me the contents of the envelope—nothing but bogus and worthless bonds. Mrs. Hall informed me that "Plin" was to call upon her husband that evening, and I immediately telegraphed to police headquarters, instructing a couple of detectives to arrest White when he called upon Major Hall. They did so, and White eventually served a three years' sentence in Sing Sing. Immediately after his first dealings with Major Hall, White retired, for a time, to Vermont, where he completely dazzled the natives by the stories which he told them concerning his enormous wealth and resources. He succeeded in gaining the confidence of many wealthy men, and purchased large tracts of real estate, paying for them with notes which were worth a little less than the paper on which they were written. Then he raised money by mortgaging the property so purchased, and finally fled to Europe to escape arrest. Here he spent several years, swindling everybody with whom he came in contact and who was worth the "plucking." Returning from Europe, he favored the good people of Louisiana with his good offices, and helped to elect a governor. He was rewarded for his services by being appointed State printer, and while holding that office purchased an island off the coast of Texas. Here he went into the business of raising chickens, but his efforts in this innocent direction were interfered with by a tremendous storm, which swept away the whole of his stock and nearly drowned White himself. Portland, Me., was his next abiding place, where he made the acquaintance of a Mrs. P. O. Williams and her brother, whom he induced to go into partnership with him and open an immense dry goods establishments in Denver, Col. The firm failed, and White was richer by $75,000. The number of his dupes is amazing, and among them I may mention Ex-judge James R. Whiting (his lawyer), Charles Whiting; C. G. Sanford, of Williamsburgh; H. C. and J. H. Stevens, bankers, of Broadway and Chambers Street; Clinton Lovell, of Boston; Alderman Libby, of New York; Albert H. Dolliver, Sixth Avenue; J. M. Shelly & Co., of Kansas City, and hosts of others. Altogether, I shall not be very far wrong if I estimate the total amount obtained by "Plin" from his too-confiding friends during the last twenty years of his career, at $1,500,000!

He is said to have married three women, two of whom were living at the same time; but he was always very close regarding his domestic arrangements, and I never heard anything on the subject which I considered reliable.

But after all, he died without a penny almost. Hunted by the police, suffering from a disease which he knew would terminate his existence in a few weeks (a carbuncle at the base of his brain), the once dashing confidence man arrived at Reading, Vt., in the early part of 1886, a mere shadow of his early self. Bowed down with the weight of sixty years of as adventurous a life as falls to the lot of but few men, he passes along the old familiar streets, unrecognized and unknown. Slowly and sadly he walks to the home of his brother Edward, and there asks for shelter. His life, he tells his relatives, has not been what it should have been. He knows that well enough. Prison fare had been his portion, at times, but full well did he deserve the punishment. Drink had been his downfall! It was the old tale told over again. But all was over now; he had not many days to live, and in the name of the mother who bore them both he begged that he might be allowed to die beneath his brother's roof.

And so he did!

CHAPTER XLIII.

INFORMATION TO REPORTERS.—ABUSES WHICH CREEP IN.—A CASE IN POINT.—BLISSFUL IGNORANCE OF THE PUBLIC.—PUNISHMENT NOT THE SOLE PURPOSE OF A COURT OF JUSTICE.—ITS REAL END AND AIM.—FULL PUBLICATION DESIRABLE UNDER CERTAIN RESTRICTIONS.—A PARALLEL CASE WITH THAT OF MR. COMMISSIONER SQUIRE.—HOW MR. DISBECKER BECAME A POLICE COMMISSIONER.—WHY HE DID NOT RESIGN.—PERSONAL APPEARANCE OF THE "FINEST."—HOW IT CAN BE IMPROVED.—A PROPOSED "SCHOOL OF DEPORTMENT."—THE ART OF WEARING CLOTHES.—MR. E. BERRY WALL AS AN INSTRUCTOR.—A POLICEMAN WITH A PERFECT MENTAL EQUILIBRIUM.—WHAT A VICTORY!—EFFECT OF POLITENESS ON THE LOWER CLASSES.—A POWERFUL OBJECT LESSON.

As nearly everyone is aware, it has been the almost invariable practice for those in authority at police headquarters to furnish representatives of the press with only such information as they may consider advisable concerning complaints made of crimes committed. That the law gives them the authority to hold back from the public any information which in their opinion would tend to defeat the ends of justice, there can be no doubt; and in certain cases it is only right that they should have this discretionary power placed in their hands. But, on the other hand, this very power, when exercised in an indiscriminate and intemperate manner, certainly opens a gateway through which many abuses can creep.

When a case is successfully "worked up," the fact is invariably given out to the reporters and blazoned far and wide over the country with a grand flourish of trumpets. If the story furnished the reporters were strictly in accordance with the facts, I should be the last person on earth to make a complaint. The trouble has been and is that greater stress is laid upon the efforts of the detective than is most times deserved. It has frequently come to my knowledge—while I was connected with the force, and since—

that credit has been given certain detectives for "working up" a case successfully, when, in reality, the capture of the criminal has been effected by that much sought for individual giving himself up, or else it has been the result of a "squeal" by one of his companions. One glaring instance of this sort of detective "work" recurs to my mind at the present writing. A forgery had been committed on a leading banking establishment, but the matter was not reported to the police. The bank kept quiet until a second check was presented by the same man, when they detained him on some excuse, sent for an officer and gave him into custody. In a few days a spread-eagle account of the capture of the forger was published in the papers, certain detectives being credited with having been "shadowing" the unfortunate criminal for weeks, whereas the very fact that a forgery had been committed was unknown to them. This instance is by no means a solitary one; it occurs frequently, and arises as much from the desire of the reporter to "keep in" with the detective corps, as it does with that of the detective's wish to pose as a successful thief-catcher. But otherwise—should no such happy event occur—no information is ever furnished the representatives of the press, and the public remain in blissful ignorance of the real state of affairs; they have, in fact, no means of judging of the real effectiveness of the detective department, self-constituted, as it were, into something very nearly approaching a "Star Chamber." It is, of course, a truism that the machinery of justice, as represented by the police department and the courts, is not set in motion by society for the sole purpose of punishing crime, or enabling individuals who have been made the victims of criminals to obtain restitution or revenge. The first and primal object of police and court organizations is to *prevent* crime. Punishments are awarded, not to inflict suffering on the criminal, but to warn others from the wrong path. This is the modern and sound idea, to which all humane and enlightened people are compelled to subscribe.

Now, I take it that if every person perpetrating a crime, or contemplating the perpetration of a crime, should know of an absolute certainty that if detected it would be utterly impossible for him to suppress facts, utterly impossible for him to keep his name out of the public press, and thus become a warning and an example—that this alone would exercise a deterrent influence. Of course this would seem a great hardship in very many cases. The feelings of families and innocent people would often be sadly wounded, but the result arrived at would be the benefit of society at large; and in contemplating such a result, true humanity does not permit us to consider the feelings of individuals.

As for the effect on the police force itself of a full publication of police news, it could not fail to be beneficial, as the public would learn of failures as well as successes, and the spur to greater effort would be immediately felt. I am aware that I am writing on a delicate subject, and my own experience teaches me that there are many cases in which suppression of news is, to a certain extent, absolutely necessary for the detection of the criminal, as the mere fact of publication might warn him to take to flight. In such cases I should advocate large discretionary powers in the hands of the superintendent of police—not for the suppression of news, but for a reasonable delay in giving such news out. Let that delay, as now, be left entirely to the judgment of the superintendent.

I throw out these suggestions with diffidence, because I am so thoroughly aware of the many complications surrounding this question; and I do not put them forward in any spirit of criticism of present method, but merely as the result of my own reflections upon the subject, which may lead some wiser heads than mine to give it mature consideration.

The publicity given not so very long ago as to the methods which prevailed in connection with the appointment of Mr. Squire as Commissioner of Public Works, recalls to my mind an instance almost identically similar in character, which took place in 1873. When Mr. William F. Havemeyer became mayor of this city he was asked to appoint Abraham Disbecker as one of the police commissioners. Mr. Disbecker's most urgent and persistent endorser was Mr. A. D. Barber, of Albany, who had helped Mr. Havemeyer to get legislation through the assembly affecting the relations of the mayor to the police commissioners. Disbecker had been a clerk of one of the committees that had the bill in charge, and was a great friend of Mr. Barber. There was, of course, considerable "dickering" and "negotiating," but the result was that Mr. Havemeyer agreed to appoint Disbecker as a police commissioner, provided the latter would give him a written promise to resign, which it was understood should be used when the mayor saw fit. In accordance with this arrangement, therefore, on the day previous to that on which the appointment was to be made, Disbecker handed Mayor Havemeyer a letter which read substantially as follows:

"I hereby agree to resign my position as commissioner of police whenever requested by Wm. F. Havemeyer, mayor."

In due course of time it came about that Mayor Havemeyer arrived at the conclusion that it would be as well if Mr. Disbecker exercised his peculiar talents at some other place than the sunny quarters of the police board on Mulberry Street. In short, Mr. Havemeyer called upon Commissioner Disbecker to resign. Mr. Disbecker said he couldn't think of such a thing; he was very comfortable in his berth, and saw no good reason why he should willingly cast himself adrift upon a cold and unsympathetic world. Mr. Havemeyer insisted, and reminded Mr. Disbecker of the existence of a certain document by which he promised to relinquish his office whenever so requested. This didn't trouble Mr. Disbecker in the least; the document in question, the authenticity of which he did not for one moment call in question, was not worth the paper upon which it was written. He pointed out to the mayor that the date on the letter was that of the day previous to his appointment as a commissioner. It was not, therefore, a legal resignation in any sense of the term; it was merely a private communication, such as one citizen might write to another, and had no official force whatever.

The position taken by the astute and far-seeing Mr. Disbecker was indisputable, and Mr. Havemeyer, to his great discomfiture, was obliged to retire from the field, leaving his appointee in possession of his commissionership. In fact, Disbecker continued in office until Mr. Wickham became mayor, when he was removed on charges preferred.

Since I have left active police life I have often thought of the wonderful change that has taken place in the character of the force during the time I was connected with it. Thirty-five years ago but little attention was paid to the *personnel* of applicants for appointment as patrolmen. Now a very close investigation is made of the strength, constitution and general physical well-being of the policemen, and it is unquestionable that great improvement has been the result of the application of the methods of examination now in vogue. But I venture to suggest that there is still very wide room for broadening the field of police education. It is undoubtedly an excellent thing to secure stalwart, hearty and vigorous men; but there are other qualifications which civil service examination does not provide for, but which would most certainly go a long way towards making up the acquirements of an ideal officer. I have sometimes fancied that it might not be wholly impossible to attempt to endow policemen with those elegancies and courtesies of life which make refined social intercourse so pleasant and improving.

Let us imagine an institution in which the guardian of the peace can learn to make a pleasant bow, to walk with grace, to shake hands with dignity, to lift his hat in a courtly way, or to extend his protecting arm to a lady with Chesterfieldian decorum. Such arts are teachable, and could be eloquently lectured upon and illustrated by some great actor, famous for his grace of manner, say Mr. Frank Mayo, for example. Another art which goes far toward making a man popular and effective is the capacity to speak readily and to the point upon matters which come within his ken. In my imaginary School of Deportment I can see Mr. Chauncey M. Depew filling such a "chair," and imparting to his scholars some of the secrets of the fascinating elements which make him so happy a speechmaker; and with what unctuous humor and fine rhetoric could our distinguished senator, Wm. M. Evarts, unfold the mystery of how to crack a pleasant joke.

Another of the amenities of life, which is taught nowhere, is the art of how to wear one's clothes. How often have I seen the effect of a fine new uniform, donned by a well-built policeman, spoiled because the man inside did not know how to wear it; and how much must this detract from the impression sought to be produced by clothing the officer in a uniform? Could he not be taught how to wear it? I maintain that he could, and have but to mention the name of Mr. E. Berry Wall, for every citizen of New York to instantly recognize the proper gentleman to act as instructor of this branch of polite accomplishment.

At first sight, these propositions may seem somewhat fanciful, but if the reader will think a little he will perceive that I am really advocating a most serious matter. Certainly, the practice of the arts which make men agreeable to their fellows is as much to be desired as the practice of the rules which make them formidable. Indeed, more than that. A strong man who is also a polite and affable person is the possessor of enlarged powers for good. I think, if such a curriculum were instituted for policemen, that the beneficial effects which would be obtained would make themselves notable; and that the idea would spread as it ought to, and that before long we should see similar professorships ordained in our public schools. And no one can dispute for a moment that much good would be done if the coming generation were not only taught how to read, write and cipher, but also how to be graceful, courteous, and sociable ladies and gentlemen. In fact, it would accomplish a revolution in the social life of our country; for the most ardent lovers of American institutions, of whom I count myself one, cannot deny that our social life is somewhat lacking in the refinement of what are commonly called small things, but which really are very important things, and which go far toward making existence pleasant and enjoyable. I have no doubt that the eminent gentlemen I have named would heartily co-operate in a movement looking to the ends I have indicated; and certainly a School of Deportment under such distinguished patronage would speedily become a national institution that would find imitators throughout the length and breadth of the Republic.

Imagine a policeman so trained! Why, the transaction of business with him by the average citizen would be both a pleasure and an instruction. A request for the locality of a certain street would be cheerfully answered with a pleasant bow, that would send the citizen on his way refreshed and light of heart. A lady compelled to cross Broadway amid a throng of jostling vehicles, would find herself escorted with a courteous consideration that would land her on the opposite side-walk positively pleased with her perilous trip; and the unfortunate gentleman who should have worshipped too long and too often at the rosy shrine of Bacchus would find himself guided to his home, or when too far "gone," to the nearest police-station, with a dignified and shocked formality that would not only make him feel perfectly safe, but would positively shame him into a better line of conduct, because, for the moment at least, he would be the churl and the officer the gentleman. I do not know whether, in surprising a burglar at his nefarious occupation, a police-officer so schooled could stop to consider how the burglar should be accosted; but I can imagine a policeman brought to such a fine pitch of mental equilibrium that even then he would carefully weigh his words and actions, with a view not only to effect the capture of the burglar, but to preach to him in his person and bearing an effective moral lesson. This, of course, would be an extreme case, but if it could be accomplished, who knows but that the burglar's mind would be so startled and so powerfully affected by the living sermon before him, that it might prove the starting point that would turn his feet into ways of righteousness. What a victory would that be!

There are certain districts in New York, as in all great cities, where life is seen in its crudest and most revolting forms. If the police squads that patrol such districts were living specimens of all that is lovely and courteous in mankind, they would breathe out an atmosphere about them that could not fail to impregnate the minds of the dullest of the denizens of these purlieus; and in due course of time it might come to pass that Mulberry and Baxter streets would begin to rival Rotten Row and the *Bois de Boulogne* in the exchange of courtesies and the practice of politeness; and every philosopher who has ever written bears testimony to the fact that good manners breed good morals. So, not only might the poor creatures named be improved in their style, but ultimately elevated in all their relations with their fellow-men. The development of the Kindergarten system demonstrates that no lessons are so powerful as object lessons; and what more striking and delightful daily instruction can be imagined than the perpetual appearance and reappearance of a corps of policemen so admirably trained as to be positively fascinating.

I will particularize no further, but will leave this fruitful theme to the consideration of the public, with the firm conviction that some great reformer will at some future day arise, who will crown his name with glory by inaugurating the "Era of National Politeness."

CHAPTER XLIV.

TWO MAIN CAUSES OF CRIME.—MUNICIPAL GOVERNMENT IN NEW YORK.—" POLITICS " SYNONYMOUS WITH POWER AND PLUNDER.—THE PREDOMINANT IDEA IN A POLITICAL CAMPAIGN. —ALL THE SNEAKS ARE REPUBLICANS AND ALL THE ROUGHS ARE DEMOCRATS.—NEW YORK RULED BY THE WORST ELEMENTS IN THE COMMUNITY.—WHY THE BETTER CLASSES DO NOT ATTEND THE PRIMARIES.—RESULTS OF OUR FORM OF GOVERNMENT. — EXCESSIVE TAXATION. — SHAMEFUL STREETS. — DISGRACEFUL DOCKS.—INSUFFICIENT SCHOOL ACCOMMODATION.— THE JUDICIARY.—NOT AN EDIFYING SIGHT.—HOW JUSTICE IS PERVERTED.—WHY JAY GOULD COULD DEFY THE LAW.—PERSECUTING A PROSECUTOR.—OUR LIBERTIES CURTAILED.—ONE LAW FOR THE RICH AND ANOTHER FOR THE POOR.—THE EXCISE LAWS.—SOME SUGGESTIONS.—THE SOCIAL EVIL AND HOW TO DEAL WITH IT.—THE COMMISSIONER OF JURORS.—UNIVERSAL SUFFRAGE A FAILURE.—DIFFICULTIES IN THE PATH OF REFORM.—THE ROOT OF THE EVIL.—REMEDIES.—THE LAST PAGE.

I HAVE finished my record. Looking over the many pages that precede this, many telling of what is worst in human nature, it fairly appals me to think that such a record lies within the recollection and experience of a single human life. But I pursue the reflection, and realize that my own knowledge of crime is but as a drop of water to the infinite ocean of vice. What causes crime? There seem to me to be two main originating forces. First: crime that springs from the instincts of nature, and that ever has been, is and will be committed by human beings, whether savage or civilized. Second: crime that springs peculiarly from society; or, to put it more plainly, crime bred by the social environment of the criminal. With the first species I do not propose to deal; it is properly the field of the philosopher and the clergyman. But the second species, I think, may fairly lie within my province; and I may venture to claim that a chief of police has unusual opportunities for observing and noting the many phases of corruption which are possible and existent under our present system of government. I shall, of course, confine my remarks entirely to municipal affairs.

Municipal government in the United States is not conducted as it is in the rest of the civilized world. It is based upon universal suffrage, and its campaigns are carried on, not on the basis of what the city needs, but the needs of the politicians of the two great political parties. As every one knows, there are two political factions, so called, in New York—Republican and Democratic—but politics implies principles, and I do not believe that one man in five hundred can explain understandingly the foundation principles of either of the parties mentioned. To call them "political" parties is clearly a misnomer, for the very simple reason that the only basis underlying their existence, here in New York, at least, is power and plunder. No intelligent man, in fact, believes that these two parties are kept alive for any other purpose than that of catching votes by the use of the old watchwords—"Republican" and "Democrat." If any proof be needed of this, it can be found in the oft-repeated fusions of the rings of the two parties, for the purpose of getting an office, and the spoils belonging thereto, within their grasp. In a "political" campaign of the present day, one idea is predominant and overwhelms every other—that of nominating the man who can command the greatest numbers of votes. Why, I verily believe if Judas Iscariot were alive, and it were supposed he had the "pull" in any single ward in the city, he would stand a good chance of being nominated for an office. I have noticed one remarkable fact in connection with the intimate relations between politics and crime, which is this: All the sneaks, hypocrites and higher grade of criminals, when questioned upon the subject, almost invariably lay claim to be adherents of the Republican party; while, on the other hand, criminals of the lower order—those who rob by violence and brute force—lay claim in no uncertain tones to being practical and energetic exponents of true Democratic principles. Of course, it is far from my intention to say that every Republican is a sanctimonious sneak, hypocrite or forger; or that every Democrat is a burglar, foot-pad, pimp or rough. Nevertheless, what I have alluded to is the fact. I will not pretend to account for these remarkable phenomena, but leave them rather to future philosophers and scientists, who will, doubtless, enlighten humanity. It is beyond my power to do so.

The city of New York is actually ruled by some twenty thousand office-holders, most of whom are taken from and controlled by the very worst elements in the community.

The "gentleman" is practically debarred from any active participation in politics. One does not see the merchant princes, nor the great editors in the aldermanic chamber. But we do see the face of the ward "heeler" and the "tough." Observe the countenances of some of our "City Fathers," court *attachés* and city employés. You will find the square jaw and large back head of the man who rules by brute force rather than by intellect; but the face of the student and of the refined gentleman is rarely seen. In fact, the ruling class in New York has its counterpart almost in the land of the Hindoo, where the "Thugs" dominate certain portions of the country by the exercise of brute force and criminal violence, although we are supposed to have a government by the people, of the people and for the people; instead of that we have a government by the politician, of the politician, and for the politician. To me the question very naturally arises, why the better classes of society do not attend the "primaries." I know the "gentleman" considers it useless for him to do so; and it certainly requires some courage to enter the low saloons and rum-shops in which the primaries are almost invariably held; attended, too, as they are in most instances, by gangs of roughs in the employ of the "boss" of the district. It is claimed by the respectable element that even if they did attend, there is not much chance of their being heard; and even if they are not thrown down stairs or pitched out of window before the voting commences, the ballot boxes are stuffed with impunity, for the simple reason that the law regarding the proceedings at these gatherings has fallen into a state of "innocuous desuetude." Granted that such is the state of affairs, and I am fully aware of its truth, I shall have something further to say upon the subject.

Let me ask, What are some of the results of such a form of government? Why, the rate of taxation is so high that the owner of a house has to disburse more per annum in that direction than he would have to pay for the rent of a similar residence in almost any city of the Old World. And what do we get in return for this enormous outlay? Streets, many paved with cobble stones and full of holes, which would be a disgrace to any country village, and only the chief of which are watered in order to lay the dust, a county court-house without a roof; docks which are a disgrace to any civilized community; a system of public schools so inadequate in the matter of accommodation that thousands of children are obliged to attend private educational institutions; while the cost of justice is so great, the loss of time so considerable, and the annoyances of such a nature that many men submit to the depredations of the petty thief and the loss of small debts, rather than risk ten times the amount in uncertain and ruinous litigation. Our judiciary and prosecuting officers are elected and controlled in a great measure by the very elements they are called upon to punish and keep in check. A Russian official, in the very nature of things, dares not cross the purposes of the Czar, nor does the office-holder in New York dare anything which might prejudice him in the opinion of those to whom he must appeal for re-election. Not infrequently our police justices have been men with no knowledge of law, and sometimes so illiterate as to be unable to spell even the simplest words correctly. It is not an edifying or unusual sight to see a low politician demanding that some disorderly person be discharged from the prison to which he has been relegated on account of his inability to produce a bondsman for his good behavior. Indeed, a politician often peremptorily demands the discharge of a culprit after he has been proved guilty beyond the shadow of a doubt, and not infrequently a prisoner is allowed to walk out of the court-room, a free man, even after he has been committed to the Island for a term of months.

Although, of course, all things are possible, yet I would not count among probable contingencies, under the present system of government in New York, the hanging of any one of its millionaires, no matter how unprovoked or premeditated the murder. Those individuals who have been executed during the last generation have all been without money, and, usually, with no friends. Many murders have been committed by rich men, but they either did not come to trial, or they were found to be insane by an "intelligent" jury. I believe that Mr. Jay Gould could to-day commit any crime in the decalogue with impunity. I do not mean to say that Mr. Gould is a dishonest man, nor would I have the reader infer that he would wrong any one, but I believe that Mr.

Gould, backed by his fifty million dollars, could defy justice in the city of New York.

I have already alluded to the disinclination of persons to "go to law," and the fact that many a business man who has been robbed, prefers to put up with his loss rather than submit to the waste of time, the vexation, annoyance and interruption of business which attendance at court would entail. The consequence is that the accused is discharged from custody; a fact which, I have no doubt, encourages others in the commission of crime by the expectation of similar leniency. In my opinion a man should be compelled to prosecute in such cases. A magistrate should not allow any compromise in his court, but should enforce the attendance of witnesses on behalf of the people. In not doing so he is simply permitting what, under other circumstances, would be a criminal offence—the compounding of a felony. That is what it is morally, if not legally; and it is constantly winked at by our judges. With our present judicial machinery, however, it is very evident that we cannot expect the laws to be properly enforced. I have known numberless cases where the "lines" of a prosecutor have not, by any means, "been cast in pleasant places." Political friends and adherents make life unpleasant for him; on the streets he is hounded by prize-fighters and bullies; his business threatened with ruin; bully-ragged in court by low, shyster lawyers, as criminal as those by whom they are employed, until he comes to the conclusion that his life is in danger—which is not probable—and considers it policy on his part to withdraw from the prosecution.

While I admit that, as a nation, we have the best form of government there is in the world, under our municipal system here in New York there is less liberty and protection to person and property than in almost any city in Europe, Russian cities not excepted. To such an extent is the public demoralized that they no longer consider the policeman in his true light, that of a preserver of the peace; but actually, and with some degree of justice, deem him a public enemy. This, of course, inevitably reacts on the police force itself, until a policeman very naturally comes to consider himself not unlike an armed soldier in the midst of a hostile camp. Further, the police are by no means supported by the authorities in the enforcement of the law, and as a natural consequence, are sometimes dilatory in bringing culprits to justice, or, as has happened time and time again, mete out punishment themselves.

Two incidents which come to my mind just now will illustrate what I allude to exactly. Upon the day the Crystal Palace was opened in London, certain streets were ordered to be closed against the passage of any but pedestrians, and police-officers were detailed to enforce this order. A captain in the Coldstream Guards, mounted, attempted to ride through one of the thoroughfares in question, and was stopped by the policeman on duty. He persisted, and finally struck the officer several severe blows across the face with his whip. He was promptly arrested, and despite the fact that his friends were willing to spend any amount of money to procure his acquittal, he was convicted and sentenced to a term of imprisonment. An appeal was even made to the Queen herself in his behalf, for he was of high lineage, but with no avail. Now, mark the contrast. At about the same time there was a procession passing through the streets of New York, and a detachment of officers was at the head of it to clear the way. A well-known gambler and politician, seated in his carriage, was met and was requested to turn into a side street. He refused, became very abusive and beat the officer who remonstrated with him in such a severe manner about the head and face as to draw blood. And then he drove on. Nothing was ever done about it, except that the police-officer, if I remember rightly was soon afterwards transferred to a precinct where he would not make himself obnoxious by interfering with the guileless pleasures of the gambler. Is it any wonder, under such circumstances, that members of the force sometimes forget that they are sworn to preserve the peace, and hit back, just as an ordinary citizen would, when abused, threatened and assaulted, instead of invoking the aid of justice—heaven save the mark!

Another crying evil is the system of excise laws. Standing as it does at present, it is neither more nor less than a farce. Under the present laws the excise commissioners are empowered to revoke the license of an individual who has been convicted; but that individual, in the boldest possible manner, simply puts a "dummy" in his place and procures another license. What is needed is an act of the Legislature giving the commissioners power to suspend the license to the place itself, as well as the individual. Owners of property in the shape of saloons, dance halls, etc., would then pretty quickly find it to be to their interest to secure decent, respectable tenants. I would also advocate the granting of licenses for the sale of liquor between such hours as the customs or needs of the locality in which the saloon is located demanded. Such, for instance, as in the vicinity of the Washington, Fulton and other markets. Why not allow them to be open between 3 A.M. and 9 P.M. every day, for that is the period during which those who do business there need refreshments?

And now a word or two upon a subject, distasteful to all, but at the same time one which must be considered in connection with the proper government of a large city like New York. I refer to the "social evil," so called. I am well aware, both from personal observation abroad and what I have read, that in this respect our city will bear favorable comparison with any other. Not that the number of prostitutes is smaller, but the existence of the evil is less apparent to a stranger, who does not find himself accosted on the street in broad daylight, as would be the case were he walking on certain streets in London. But for all that, some stringent regulations are required in order to deal properly with this important problem. While I am not prepared to advocate the adoption of the French system in its entirety, still I would place the "strange woman" under the surveillance of the police. They should be restricted to a certain section of the city, and be subject to arrest at sight if found anywhere outside the prescribed limits. Under no consideration whatever should a woman be allowed to approach or solicit men on the street. Such a system would undoubtedly prevent the wholesale blackmailing to which I have every reason to believe the poor degraded women who sell their bodies for gain are forced to submit at the hands of unprincipled police officials. I say "have every reason to believe," because, while it is a moral certainty this blackmailing exists, it is almost impossible to obtain the evidence of a third party as to the payment of money in such instances. When one of these women makes a charge of this nature, it is simply a question of veracity between her and the police-officer. Those in authority have always demanded that the complainant's story shall be substantiated by the evidence of citizens of reputation and standing before they were willing to arrive at the conclusion that the charge was proven. It reminds me of the story of the man who went to his neighbor and requested the loan of his jackass. "It's not at home," was the reply. At that moment the animal's braying was heard in the adjoining stable. "Why, you said it wasn't at home!" remarked the would-be borrower. Upon which the owner retorted: "Whose word do you take—mine or that jackass's?" Neither do the police commissioners care to believe the word of the erring and sinful, but much-to-be-pitied, woman against that of the police officer.

Another radical evil has been revealed by the recent disclosures in connection with the preparation of the lists of talesmen for the trial of "boodle" Alderman McQuade. It has been shown most conclusively that there is no small amount of corruption in the office of the Commissioner of Jurors, and some sweeping reforms and changes are needed in that department. I would suggest, also, that the judge of a criminal court should have the power, when he deems fit, to try criminal cases with "struck" juries, as certain civil cases are now.

Think of all these things, and then talk about this being the land of liberty. Look at the manner in which the elevated railroads occupy a street to the utter disregard of the rights of the public. Certainly they are a public convenience, but as certainly should the people, who are the chief parties interested, be consulted in the first instance, which they are not.

Our liberties are interfered with and curtailed in so many ways, that it is useless to attempt an enumeration. We are robbed and swindled right and left—by the wealthy corporation, which seizes upon our property with impunity and without remuneration, down, through all the various grades, to the thief with political influence who "snatches" your watch; while human life, as I have previously observed, can be taken with safety by the great millionaire or party leader.

What are the remedies for the existing state of things? First, I believe that universal suffrage, when applied to the municipal government of large cities, is a failure. I think the same opinion is held by the editor of every newspaper in this city, but none dare give public expression to that opinion, as such a course would woefully damage the subscription lists. A man should have some qualification other than simply that of being a resident. If it were possible to draw a plain, unmistakable line, I should say make honesty, intelligence and integrity the prerequisite for the exercise of the ballot; but such a demarcation, as yet, is beyond our powers. By no means would I advocate a property qualification. Suppose, for instance, a law were passed requiring the possession of property to the value of

$50 as a pre-requisite. A man owns a mule worth that much, and as long as that mule lives his owner can exercise the franchise. It dies, and the man loses his vote! Ergo, by a species of inductive logic, the mule votes, not the man!

Admitting, therefore, the present impossibility of attacking universal suffrage, the efforts of all reputable citizens should be to see that the suffrage is cast in the most honest manner possible and for the most honest purposes. To secure this, what can be done? The expression of the public will at the polls must, in the nature of things, be moved by the machinery of a party or parties. Let the gentlemen of New York cease to vote in municipal affairs as so-called Republicans or Democrats, and let them band themselves together in defence of their persons and lives against lawless violence; in defence of their property against excessive and illegal taxation, which, if allowed to run unchecked, will one day end in confiscation; and in defence of their natural and inalienable right to rule themselves, which right, through carelessness and lack of interest, they have practically delegated to the professional politician, the ward bummer, the heeler and the tough.

The very root of the whole trouble is that the respectable business men, those having an interest in the good government of the city, not only for their own sakes, but for the sake of those who will come after them, do not take that interest which is clearly their duty in the preliminary skirmishes of a political campaign—the primaries. It is all very well to say that such gatherings are controlled by a rough element. Whose fault is that? It is within the power of the better classes of the community to overcome this pernicious element, by taking their proper part in the conduct of primaries. They do it in cases of riot or disturbance; ruffians, may, for a short period, have the upper hand, but the moment they meet the law-abiding citizens they are crushed. Why should not the "gentlemen" exercise their power, enroll themselves in district organizations, organize primaries, and see to it that those who are nominated for office are in every way qualified? The only real reason they do not do so at present is that they do not care to spare the time from their mad race after wealth, coupled with a dislike to come in contact with a lower element in society. At present here in New York we have taxation without representation. Our forefathers revolted from the British yoke because they were taxed without their own consent. We walk up to the tax-collector's office and hand in our money without our opinion having been paid the empty compliment of being asked for.

But the taxed have none to blame except themselves. The only hope and salvation for the future of the city is that the better element will awaken to a full and complete appreciation of its danger and rights, and, knowing them, will dare maintain them in the face of all the politicians, ruffians, thieves and rascals with which every branch of our city government is infested. We have had enough of the rule of the " tough "; now let us try the rule of the " gentleman."

An organized effort of the better classes to purify municipal politics will inevitably entail a bitter struggle, because things have gone so far to the bad. It will be necessary to meet and repel at every step the most shameless tricks, and the most audacious and unscrupulous efforts that will be made to deter the " gentleman " from claiming his own. The ballot and the ballot-box itself will not be respected; and in this connection I would most strongly urge the adoption of the Australian system of voting, which has lately been adopted in England, and which, in brief, is this: Previous to election the names of all the candidates for each office are recorded. On the day of election ballots are furnished for the offices to be filled, containing the names of all the candidates for each office. One of these is given to each voter, by a qualified officer, as he comes up to vote; the ballot is stamped with an official mark; the voter on receiving it goes into a small retiring room by himself, and there places opposite the name of the candidate for whom he wishes to vote, a cross; he then folds the ballot in such a way as to conceal the names, but to disclose the official stamp, and then deposits it in the ballot-box, which is locked. This plan, it will be seen, secures perfect secrecy, independence and certainty.

I would also most strongly advise that the Bureau of Elections be taken away from the control of the police commissioners. The connection of the police with an election should be absolutely limited to preserving the peace and affording the safe and easy access of every voter to the poles. To allow them to count the ballots and certify the result is to clothe them with a ministerial function, whereas the police force should be simply executive. A separate and entirely independent bureau should be in existence at times of voting, for the sole purpose of counting the votes and declaring the result; and so completely would I wean it from municipal control, that I would advise its being placed in the hands of some perfectly independent officer, to be appointed by the governor.

But let us suppose that such a party as I have alluded to has been organized, and has elected a certain number of officials. A new and deadly danger can at once be foreseen. The professional politicians, rendered desperate by such a defeat, would inevitably contest everything connected with the election in the courts, and whom should we find on the bench? Judges elected by the so-called political organizations, and hoping for re-election at their hands. This brings me to the discussion of a very grave matter. I am forced to the opinion that it is wrong to elect judges. It is next to impossible that a mass of voters, however organized, can select candidates for the judiciary on account of their fitness for the bench. Now, it goes without question that the political opinions of a man have nothing whatever to do with his legal abilities; but so long as judges are elected to their offices, just so long will they be elected because of their ability to control votes, and not because of their mental and moral requirements. It would seem to me a better way to have judges appointed by the governor, with the consent of the senate. Even under this method I am quite aware that a certain amount of political bias could not be escaped, but I think a much more able and pure judiciary would be secured in this way, than by leaving the bench as a plaything for municipal associations, and part of the spoils to be trafficked in.

Any citizen of New York can recall the terrible depths to which the judiciary sank during the days of the Tweed regime, when certain judges were simply the creatures of a bold and infamous ring, absolutely subject to the command of political bosses. It is true that an indignant public sentiment was aroused, which swept from the bench those who had disgraced the ermine; and it is true that to-day New York enjoys a pure and able bench; but under our elective system we have good judges in spite, and not by reason, of it. Let public sentiment again become dulled, and let some other ring, by slow and insidious methods, gain possession of municipal politics, and once again, to an absolute certainty, we should see the creatures of that ring mocking justice in our courts. And what is true of New York city is equally applicable to all our other great centers of population.

I do not wish my preceding remarks to be taken as implying dissatisfaction with our Republican institutions. I believe heartily in the theory of the American system of government; but I am forced to the conclusion that in the practical carrying on of that government, at least in so far as it deals with municipal affairs, the rules of safety are departed from. Republican government means, of necesssity, self-government; and, as I have said before, the citizens of our great cities have tacitly surrendered the exercise of their prerogative. The evil can be checked if taken in time; but if allowed to grow until the franchise shall become a mere empty form, by which the professional politician operates his machine, the decadence of Republican institutions will not be far off; and this great republic, to-day the hope and glory of the world, will follow the fate of the republics of old.

I do not believe in a monarchy; but if we are to be ruled by individuals practically vested with monarchical powers, let us have one king who is a gentleman, rather than twenty thousand kings who are "toughs."

* * * * * * * *

On the ninth day of June, 1885, my duties and cares as superintendent of the New York police force ended. I left the office, in which I had spent so many pleasant hours, and met so many varied experiences, with something of regret. Regret, because my life had been one of almost continuous activity of a nature that falls only to the lot of those in my position. The constant concentration of ideas upon a certain series of subjects is inclined to leave a man exhausted when confronted with new duties, or the needlessness of any at all. And so with me. For some time the routine of my past life remained with me with such potency that it was only after effort that I could avoid going to police headquarters and assuming my former duties. The training of my life as an officer was demanding recognition. Little by little habit grew less imperative in its demands. I began to form new ties, new associations, new duties. My time now is mostly passed in travelling, fishing and hunting, and I can congratulate myself upon having become a private citizen of the greatest commonwealth in the world.

With this last page of the record of my life upon the desk before me, I can say, with the confidence of a man under no obligations, that I have done my duty to the extent of my understanding; and that my service as a police officer has been untrammelled by either political or personal influences. I have endeavored to discharge my duties to the citizens of New York, and in this I think I have succeeded.

HON. WOLFE LONDONER, MAYOR.

Historic Supplement

OF THE

DENVER POLICE

A Review From Earliest Days to the Present Time

BY A. KAUFMANN

ILLUSTRATED

Specially Published for the Benefit of the Denver Police Mutual Aid Fund

DENVER COLORADO
1890

PREFACE.

In presenting to the citizens of Denver this historic review of the Police Department the object intended to be conserved is twofold : First and foremost, the interest of the Mutual Aid Association of the members of the Department, and, Secondly, to bring the citizens and the Department into closer relations. A knowledge of the men, and system, will help to a better appreciation and a greater realization of the hazardous duties of our police officers. The editor desires to thank Chief Farley and his staff for their uniform kindness and courtesy for the valuable aid they have extended to him while gathering data and information. Thanks are also due to the respective Photographers, Messrs. Bellsmith, Post, Rinehart and Wells, who kindly furnished the photographs from which the different portraits, that embellish this supplement, are made.

THE EDITOR.

CONTENTS.

CHAPTER I.

EARLY DAYS.—ORGANIZATION OF A PROVISIONAL CITY GOVERNMENT.—BIOGRAPHIES OF FORMER MAYORS.—THE HON. WOLFE LONDONER, MAYOR, PP. 615–619.

CHAPTER II.

A CHANGE FROM A MUNICIPAL TO A METROPOLITAN POLICE FORCE NECESSARY.—BIOGRAPHIES OF FORMER CITY MARSHALS AND CHIEFS OF POLICE FROM W. E. SISTY TO DAVID J. COOK, PP. 620–626.

CHAPTER III.

BIOGRAPHIES OF FORMER CITY MARSHALS AND CHIEFS OF POLICE FROM DAVID J. COOK TO JOHN F. FARLEY, PP. 627–637.

CHAPTRR IV.

CHIEF FARLEY.—A THRILLING INCIDENT IN INDIAN WARFARE.—THE INDIAN DEPREDATIONS.—FARLEY SEVERELY WOUNDED.—A DESPERATE SITUATION.—FOUR AMERICAN SOLDIERS HOLD OFF A FIERCE BAND OF APACHES FOR SEVERAL HOURS.—FARLEY ESTABLISHES THE THIEL DETECTIVE AGENCIES IN SEVERAL CITIES.—APPOINTMENT AS CHIEF OF POLICE, PP. 638—644.

CHAPTER V.

INSPECTOR HAWLEY.—THE HAYWARD MURDER CASE.—TRACKING OF THE MURDERERS SEMINOLE AND WOODRUFF.—INCIDENTAL CAPTURE OF THE NOTORIOUS MAIL ROBBER "BILL" JOHNSON.—

HAWLEY CAPTURES SEMINOLE IN DAKOTA.—ON THE TRAIL OF WOODRUFF.—HAWLEY ARRESTS WOODRUFF IN IOWA.—WOODRUFF BROUGHT TO DENVER.—SEMINOLE AND WOODRUFF LYNCHED.— PP. 645–650.

CHAPTER VI.

LIEUTENANT PHILLIPS.—THE SLAYING OF JIM MOON.—THE ARREST OF CLAY WILSON.—THE BELLE WARDEN CASE.—LIEUTENANT NEWMEYER. — SERGEANTS NORKETT — BOHANNA — M'NEIL — TEETER — CLAY—GREEN—MACDONALD, PP. 651–657

CHAPTER VII.

THE DETECTIVE DEPARTMENT.—DAN SINKS' NOTORIOUS CAREER.— EXPERIENCE OF CHIEF FARLEY WITH SINKS.—SINKS LEAVES TOWN.—THE SAFES CRACKED OF THE UNION PACIFIC TICKET OFFICE AND OF PRYOR & NOAH.—SINKS ARRESTED.—SINKS AND THE DETECTIVES.—RECENT ARREST OF SINKS IN PUEBLO.—RESIGNATION OF CHIEF LOAR.—CHIEF FARLEY TAKES CHARGE OF THE DETECTIVE DEPARTMENT.—ASSISTANT CHIEF OF DETECTIVES SAM HOWE.—HOWE'S LONG AND USEFUL SERVICE, PP. 658–662.

CHAPTER VIII.

THE ROUTINE OF OUR POLICE DEPARTMENT.—CHIEF FARLEY'S SYSTEMATIC AND ADMIRABLE IMPROVEMENTS.—DENVER A WINTER RESORT FOR TRAMPS AND "VAGS."—GREAT NEED OF A WORKHOUSE.—FREE THE POLICE DEPARTMENT FROM POLITICS AND POLITICIANS.—LET THE LEGISLATURE MAKE THE DEPARTMENT METROPOLITAN, PP. 663–667.

CHAPTER IX.

DENVER BREWING COMPANY'S SAFE CRACKED.—THE TRAP.—THE HAUL.—MOST IMPORTANT ARREST OF BURGLARS IN THE UNITED

CONTENTS.

STATES FOR A NUMBER OF YEARS.—CLEVER WORK OF THE DENVER POLICE.—THE MAGNIFICENT KIT OF TOOLS.—OFFICIAL CORRESPONDENCE IDENTIFYING THE BURGLARS, PP. 668–673.

CHAPTER X.

THE DENVER POLICE MUTUAL AID ASSOCIATION.—OUR POLICE FORCE MUCH TOO SMALL.—INCREASE THE FORCE, PP. 674–675.

APPENDIX.

THE ROSTER OF THE DENVER POLICE FORCE.

ILLUSTRATIONS.

The Hon. Wolfe Londoner—Mayor.
John F. Farley—Chief of Police.
Chas. A. Hawley—Inspector of Police.
John E. Phillips—First Lieutenant.
Henry Newmeyer—Second Lieutenant.
Clay, Green, MacDonald, Bohanna—Sergeants.
Norkett, Teeter, McNeil—Sergeants.
Sam Howe—Assistant Chief of Detectives.
The Famous Kit of Tools Recently Captured.

HISTORIC SUPPLEMENT

OF THE

DENVER POLICE.

CHAPTER I.

FROM PROVISIONAL MAYOR, JOHN C. MOORE, TO MAYOR WOLFE LONDONER.—1859–1890.

It would be a difficult task to attempt a historic resume of the Police Department of the City of Denver, without, at once, making it a history of the City as well, since the two, though separate and distinct, are co-relative

Both are young institutions, of co-eval birth; but they rival in vicissitudes, cities and their departments which began their growth in the early years of American history; neither of the two is fully matured; still each is ripe and rich in experience.

Thirty-two years ago, on the 24th day of October, 1858, Anselm H. Barker erected the first log cabin somewhere within the limits where now is the great Rocky Mountain metropolis, Denver, with its population of some one hundred and fifty thousand souls. There were no railroads then; not even a good wagon road, and the hardy pioneer, the gold hunter and the adventurer sought each, at the risk of his life, the gold fields of Colorado.

The blood-thirsty savage and the beast of prey barred the line of progress and had to be overcome as step by step the white man forced onward and upward toward the crest of the continent. To-day an empire stands redeemed and created as the achievement of daring, hardihood and steadfastness of purpose.

Many are the pioneers that have passed away, but still many remain to marvel at the results of their own efforts and endeavors. Among these belong the first mayor, now a resident of Pueblo, and the present mayor of the City of Denver.

When it is considered what this little more than a quarter of a century has brought forth; when the mind dwells upon the fact that already is it possible to chronicle historical data which read partly not unlike "ancient history," the startling pace of development during the latter half of the Nineteenth Century strikes one with amazement.

In the summer of 1859 a mass-meeting of the early settlers of Denver, then known as Auraria, a little camp on the west shore of Cherry Creek, was called to assemble. The object of this meeting was to organize a provisional territorial government of what was then known as Jefferson Territory. Resolutions memorializing the people of this territory were adopted and Messrs. William N. Byers, J. C. Moore and Richard Sopris were appointed a committee. This committee prepared a short memorial, providing for an election in the scattered settlements and mining camps, to test the sense of the people on the subject of a provisional government, and also for delegates to a constitutional convention. Within a few weeks the convention met and in ten days had completed its work. Shortly after an election was held for territorial officers and members of the legislature. W. P. McClure and J. C. Moore were elected members. The legislature, among other things, consolidated the rival and warring towns of Denver and West Denver into one municipality, and under the name of Denver granted it a charter and designated a time for the election of city officers. A result of this election was the selection of Mr. Moore for Mayor and the late Mr. W. E. Sisty as City Marshal, the first and pioneer police officer of Denver.

What the social conditions of the town were prior and partially during Mr. Sisty's tenure of office, may best be imagined and understood when contemplating this terse summing-up of a chronicler: "During the year they managed to get a bridge across the Platte river, (Cherry creek?) and established and maintained pretty good order in the town—that is to say, put a stop to mob violence and hung people, when they needed hanging, legally and decently."

Mr. Moore, since his occupancy as first Mayor of Denver, has led a very eventful life. He left Denver in 1861, during that greatest of all civil strifes, and cast his fortunes with the Southern Confederacy. He joined General Sterling Price's army in Missouri as a private. At Corinth, Miss., he was elected captain of the re-organized St. Louis Battery. After the fight at Farmington, and the battle of Iuka, he resigned and went west of the Mississippi. He was made Adjutant of General Shelby's regiment of Infantry, and early in 1863 was transferred to the cavalry as Assistant Adjutant of General Marmaduke's division. After Marmaduke's capture he was assigned as judge advocate general on General J. B. Morgan's staff, and early in 1864 he was sent north of the Arkansas river as an officer of General Shelby's cavalry division, Shelby himself expecting to follow in a few weeks.

After the close of the war he went to Mexico and served six months in the French Contre-Guerrillas, a command especially organized to fight Guerrillas. On leaving the service he was offered a commission in the regular French army, but declined.

In 1866 he returned to Missouri from Mexico and in 1868 established the Kansas City *Times*, which he edited for nearly three years. Afterward he established the *Mail* in Kansas City, and again became editor of the *Times* in 1878, during the rancorous compaign between Crisp and Sawyer for Congress. Still later he held an editorial position on the St. Louis *Times*. He returned to Colorado in 1881.

Mr. Moore is now editor of the Pueblo *Press*, and is one of the most vigorous writers of the west.

The second mayor of Denver—the first one elected at the polls—was the Hon. Charles A. Cook, who was elected in November 1861 to 1863 and was succeeded by the Hon. Amos Steck, who in turn was succeeded in 1865, by his predecessor, Mr. Cook. The Hon. Hiram J. Brendlinger, third mayor of Denver was elected in 1864 and he was followed by the late Hon. George T. Clarke in 1865. In 1866 the Hon. Milton M. DeLano was chosen for mayor by the people of Denver and was re-elected to the same office in from April 1867 to 1868. Under Mr. DeLano's administration the Denver Fire Department was first organized. Hon. W. M. Clayton succeeded Mr. DeLano in 1868 and he in turn was followed in 1869 by the Hon. B. B. Stiles who was re-elected in 1870. In 1871 the Hon. John Harper was elected mayor of Denver, and was succeeded by Hon. Joseph E. Bates in 1872. The successor of Mr. Bates was the Hon. Francis M. Case, 1873, and in 1874 the Hon W. J. Barker was elected to this office, which he occupied for two terms. He was followed by R. G. Buckingham M. D., who also served the city two terms. This brings us down to 1878 when the Hon. R. Sopris was elected mayor and re-elected in 1879 and again in 1880, serving three consecutive terms in the capacity of mayor of Denver. In 1881 the Hon. Robert Morris was elected mayor and re-elected in 1882. Hon. John L. Routt succeeded Mr. Morris in 1883 and succeeded himself the following year 1884.

Mr. Routt's services as mayor form but an incident in his distinguished career. After three years service to his country in the late war he retired to private life from which he emerged in 1869, accepting the position of Chief Clerk in the bureau of the Assistant Postmaster General. In the Spring of 1870 President Grant made him United States Marshal of the Southern District of Illinois and in 1871 the President offered him the position of Second Assistant Postmaster General, which he accepted. As such he served until February 1875, when his old friend President Grant appointed him Territorial Governor of Colorado. When in 1876 Colorado became a state, John L. Routt received the nomination for the Governorship and upon being elected the last Governor of the Territory became the first Chief Magistrate of the Centennial State. At the recent state elections the Republican party again testified to the confidence and respect in which it held Mr. Routt by once more electing him Governor of the State of Colorado.

In 1885 the newly amended charter of the City of Denver passed the Legislature. One of the changes consisted in the extension of the mayor's term of office from one year to two years, and the first incumbent under the new order was Mr.

Jos. E. Bates, for the second time honored by election to the city's chief magistracy. Mr. Bates was succeeded by the Hon. Wm. Scott Lee in 1887, and Mr. Lee was succeeded in 1889 by our present mayor, the Hon. Wolfe Londoner, whose term expires in March, 1891.

Wolfe Londoner was born in New York City in the year 1841, and came to Colorado in May, of 1860, in the fall of which year he drifted to California Gulch where he was engaged in the mercantile business for a period of five years. Four of these years he was clerk and recorder for the district, and part of the time County Treasurer and Commissioner. In 1865 he returned to Denver where he has since been one of the leading merchants and in every sense a prominent citizen, having been both a member of the city council and County Commissioner. Mayor Londoner has ever applied, in his official capacities, the strict methods of the business man and his administration is marked by good judgment, economy and a general conservation of the best interests of the community.

One of the distinctive features of Mr. Londoner's administration consists in the selection of Mr. John F. Farley as the head of the Denver Police Department. In making this choice Mr. Londoner ignored all precedents of former mayors of the city, who were always, more or less, prompted by political motives in the selection of their marshals and chiefs. Mr Farley had never been identified with politics further than to cast his vote as an American citizen and a good Republican. He was known as an efficient officer of one of the greatest detective systems in the land, and a man of sterling character, courage and intrepidity.

CHAPTER II.

CITY MARSHALS AND CHIEFS OF POLICE.—FROM W. E. SISTY TO DAVID J. COOK.—1859–1866.

There is perhaps no modern city on the globe which has passed through the same stirring events during so brief an existence as the City of Denver. If the first child born here were to turn historian and record the events during his own life, in his own birthplace, he could fill a mighty volume and still have matter left.

From a frontier post, remote from civilization, in the very heart of the desert, Denver has grown, within a third of a century, into the greatest and most important city between the Missouri river and Pacific Coast. The vicissitudes during the various stages of development, from hamlet to town, from town to city, of this wonderful community, would fill volumes. The limited space of this supplement does not permit delving into detailed accounts and the writer can only in a general way recount the origin and growth of the department of Public Safety up to the present time. He would however call attention to a very important fact relative to our police system. With the unprecedented growth of Denver it is but natural that the city should have outgrown many of its early institutions, one of which is the Police Department—the most essential department of a community. Our force is by no means adequate to the exigencies and demands of the times.

Denver's fame has attracted the attention of the civilized world, and with the great influx of men and money it is scarcely remarkable that the criminal classes of all lands should be liberally represented here. In the face of this deplorable fact an economy which retards and baffles the usefulness of the Police Department by limiting its numbers and stinting it in the sinews of war, thus exposing it to every grumbler and fault-finder, is to say the least, to be deprecated;

and as long as these conditions shall last, our fair city will remain the Mecca and abiding place of the predatory class; and so long will the rough and tough continue to lord it in this community.

Times and circumstances demand a change—a thorough reorganization of our police system. It is now ripe for conversion into a metropolitan force and must be freed from the influences of local politics, which hamper and impair its usefulness to an alarming degree. Our present police officials are thoroughly competent and experienced men and the force, as far as its personnel is concerned, compares favorably in capacity, taking into consideration its limited numbers, with any in the United States. It however, does not reach far enough; neither in numbers, opportunities nor means. There is actually not sufficient appropriation for the workings of the detective branch of the department and yet the community expects and exacts the same efficiency which, for example, exists in New York or Chicago, where similar departments are absolutely and entirely free to move and act as arising exigencies may demand.

It has become necessary and the time is ripe for the city council to give this matter their most serious attention and to see to it that a bill shall be prepared and submitted to the General Assembly which shall give to the metropolis of the Inter-West a metropolitan police department. This once effected, causes for criticism and complaint, as they now arise, will rapidly disappear.

In reviewing the personnel of the present executive staff of the department it must be apparent to the careful observer that in point of character its individual members stand on a high plane of excellence. They are each and every one trained and experienced men in their profession, and all have been selected, or advanced, for their proficiency and because of the general confidence reposed in them. At the same time, going back in review of the different heads of the Denver Police Department, from its inception, we find a list of names comprising honorable and efficient men and some extraordinary ones. The first one of these was

WILSON E. SISTY.

The organization which resulted in the municipal government of Denver-Auraria-Highland, and which elected the Hon. John C. Moore provisional mayor, forwarded the following document to Mr. Sisty:

DENVER, AURARIA AND HIGHLAND, }
DECEMBER 21, 1859. }

MR. W. E. SISTY,—*Sir:*

You are hereby notified that you are duly elected marshal for the City of Denver, Auraria and Highland at an election held for the election of municipal officers on the 19th day of December, 1859.

[Signed] JOHN J. SAVILLE,
President of Board of Canvassers.

W E. Sisty was born in Pennsylvania in the year 1826, and after a few years in school, he entered, when but ten years old, the office of the Wilkesbarre *Advocate* as "printers' devil;" but, being restive, he remained there only two years, when he struck out for "green fields and pastures new," and after visiting different places and following various occupations, he enlisted as private in a company raised by Captain E. L. Dana at Wilkesbarre, Pa., in the year 1846, at the outbreak of the Mexican War. This company was mustered into service as one of the first regiment of Pennsylvania volunteers, at Pittsburgh. He accompanied his regiment to Mexico and participated with it in all the engagements before Vera Cruz and in the battle of Cerro Gordo, and passing through the entire war, he was among those who entered the City of Mexico under General Winfield Scott. At the close of the Mexican War, Mr. Sisty returned to his home in Pennsylvania where he became superintendent of a coal mine. At the breaking out of the Pike's Peak gold excitement, in the year 1859, Mr. Sisty was seized with the fever and started on his way West. Arriving at Council Bluffs, Iowa, he fitted out an ox team and after a journey of several months he arrived in Denver early in May. The wonderful discoveries reported at that time from Central, which attracted the attention of thousands, drew Mr. Sisty with the tide and reaching Black Hawk he located at this point and devoted himself to mining for a few years. Subsequently following the trail to Russell Gulch and down Virginia Canon, he went to Russell Gulch and with a party established the mining district of Downeyville. In the summer of 1859 he came back to Denver, where he was appointed deputy sheriff by John H. Kehler, the first sheriff of Arapahoe, then a portion of Jefferson Territory. In May, 1860, he returned to Idaho Springs, where he engaged in mining until 1862, when he again returned to Denver. Mr. Sisty was a most intimate friend of the famous writer of wild and vivid Western fiction, "Ned Buntline" (E. C. Judson.) In 1856 the latter wrote and dedicated to his friend Sisty a poem entitled "A Song of Friendship," the original manuscript of which was among Mr. Sisty's effects at the time of his death, which sad event occurred on the 14th day of October, 1889. Mr. Sisty was a man of excellent traits of character and enjoyed great popularity throughout the entire State, where he had a multitude of personal friends. In 1876 he was made the first fish commissioner the state ever had, by Governor Routt, in which position he was re-confirmed by Governors Pitkin and Grant. Aside from having been the first chief officer of the Denver Police Department, Mr. Sisty may be regarded as the father of fish culture in Colorado.

W. M. KEITH.

In 1861, after the provisional government of the city ceased and the regular municipal government came into existence, the Hon. Charles A. Cook, Denver's first regularly elected mayor, selected Mr. W. M. Keith to fill the position of marshal. Mr. Keith was a Scotchman by birth. Early in life he came west and went into the hotel business at Omaha, where he was for some years proprietor of the Douglass House. In 1859 he came to Denver and opened the old Cherokee House, on Blake Street between Fourteenth and Fifteenth streets. He was also, at one time, connected with the old Platte Valley House. He was city marshal from April 1861 to April 1862. He, later on, removed to Pueblo, where he died of paralysis. Those who knew him speak highly of him as a good officer and estimable citizen.

GEORGE E. THORNTON.

The first man who bore the title of "Chief of Police" of the city of Denver was Mr. George E. Thornton, who is another of the early pioneers, having come to Denver in 1859. Mr. Thornton was born in the state of New York November 2, 1829. While still a young man he became a member of the New York Police Force, in 1855-56, where he enjoyed the esteem of his superior officers as a man of integrity and an efficient officer. Mr. Thornton was among the first to build his cabin in Auraria, of which little home early settlers still speak. At the time of his appointment as Chief of Police desperadoes from all parts of the world infested the town, which was a refuge for the very worst criminals the country produced. Every man went armed to the teeth, and such "terrors" as Coal Wood, George Strute and Jim Gordon were representatives among the "bad men" of that time. It was the delight of the hard characters of that period to designate themselves as "bad men from Bitter Creek," until the phrase became a byword the country over. This was the element which Mr. Thornton had to face, and the acceptance of the call was sufficient in itself to stamp the man as one possessed of extraordinary nerve and courage. Mr. Thornton commenced his administration of the Denver Police Department with making a series of very important arrests, attended by some hair-breadth escapes on his part. But his intrepidity and heroism soon made him a terror to the rogues and cut-throats who infested the town and vicinity, and he soon won a reputation as an officer of fearlessness and merit. Mr. Thornton's experience as Chief of Police would supply matter for a large volume of intensely interesting reading in criminal literature. Accounts of his arrests, escapes and adventures would shame the imagination of the most vivid romancer of western fiction. In 1870 Mr. Thornton was appointed acting warden of the Colorado penitentiary, which position he held until 1882, when Capt. Burger, his successor, was killed and five prisoners succeeded in making their escape. Then Mr. Thornton was appointed warden. Always successful in the handling of criminals, possessed of an unusual amount of executive ability, and never flinching in his duty, no matter what the dangers of the occasion might be, Mr. Thornton's name became a terror to the desperate characters of that time and to him the community of those days was indebted for such law and order and immunity from crime as it soon learned to enjoy. Mr. Thornton is still living among us and enjoys the esteem of all who know him.

ANDREW J. SNYDER.

In April of the year 1862, Mayor Chas. A. Cook appointed Mr. "Andy" J. Snyder as City Marshal of Denver. Mr. Snyder was born in Pennsylvania and was among the first to follow the golden allurements which the Pike's Peak excitement promised for the venturesome. He located in Auraria, now West Denver, and served one term as the head of the local police force. Sometime afterward he again turned his face eastward, located in Kansas City, Mo., where he embarked in business as a pork packer, and is now one of the most prosperous packers in the West. Mr. Snyder is a several-times millionaire and while no event of particular or great importance during his term of office, as Marshal of Denver, occurred, his marvelous success in business would stamp him as a man of uncommon qualifications.

JOSEPH L. BAILEY.

Another who was attracted to this region of sunshine and precious metals, in ante-bellum days, is Mr. Joseph L. Bailey. Of an old Maryland family which was among the first settlers of that state, Mr. Bailey himself is by birth a Pennsylvanian, his native city being Philadelphia, where he was born in 1835. A grand-father of Mr. Bailey was a soldier of the Revolution of 1776. After receiving a good public school education, Mr. Bailey learned the trade of carpenter and builder, like his father, who was a practical builder and contractor. When twenty-two years of age the young man went west to Leavenworth, Kansas, where he devoted himself to his trade, and was there through that terrible struggle, known as the "Border Ruffian War," which was one of the causes of the War of the Rebellion. Mr. Bailey himself belonged to the free-state party.

In 1859 Mr. Bailey started for "Pike's Peak," and in June of that year he pitched his tent on the banks of the now historic Cherry Creek. Later on we find him in Gilpin county, where he and his partners worked a claim on Casto hill, in which they exhausted their funds. Returning to Denver, Mr.

Bailey embarked in the butcher business, in which venture he was exceedingly successful, not to say fortunate, since he is credited with clearing up the neat profit of thirty thousand dollars within eighteen months. This he possessed in the shape of gold dust, which in lieu of a safer place of deposit, he buried in the ground under his store. When the Civil War broke out Mr. Bailey suffered the double loss of his bookkeeper and his funds, both at the same time. After this misfortune he was appointed, successively, Street Commissioner, City Marshal and Provost Marshal, under Mr. Wanless, and Deputy United States Marshal under Hon. A. C. Hunt. He served as City Marshal during the administrations of Hon. Amos Steck, Hon. H. J. Brendlinger and Hon. Geo. T. Clark, and made a splendid record as an officer and a gentleman. Mr. Bailey has also served, at different times, as Deputy Sheriff, and was twice elected to the office of Councilman. Prominent in business and ever public-spirited, Mr. Bailey is one of the best and most favorably known of Denver's citizens. He is one of the organizers of the Colorado Cattle Growers' Association, of which he was president for two years.

CHAPTER III.

FROM GENERAL DAVID J. COOK TO JOHN F. FARLEY.—1886-1889.

DAVID J. COOK.

He is indeed a "tenderfoot" who does not know, or has not heard of General David J. Cook, Denver's City Marshal of 1866-67-68, Chief of Police in 1880 and the head of the Rocky Mountain Detective Agency since 1863.

David J. Cook was born August 12, 1840, in Laporte County, Indiana, where his father was a farmer and land speculator. After receiving a moderate, but what was then considered a liberal education, he worked on farms in the states of Indiana, Iowa and Kansas until the year 1859. The same tales of the "golden fleece," which allured thousands who now comprise the "solid" citizens of Colorado, attracted Mr. Cook and he struck out for "Pike's Peak." Locating in GilpinCounty he dug for gold some two years or more, but not "striking it lucky" returned to Kansas whence he removed to Rolla, Mo., in 1861, and there engaged in the running of supply trains. Subsequently he joined the ordinance department of the army of the frontier and in 1863 he again drifted to Colorado, since which time he has been connected with the famous Rocky Mountain Detective Association. He enlisted in the Colorado Cavalry and in 1864 was detailed by the quartermaster of the Denver Post as government detective, which position he held until 1866, when the post was abandoned.

In April of the year 1866 Mayor De Lano appointed Mr. Cook City Marshal, in which capacity he served during Mr. De Lano's two terms and also during the administration of Hon. William M. Clayton.

In 1869 Mr. Cook was elected to the office of Sheriff of Arapahoe County; at the end of his term he was re-elected and served for two more years. In 1873 he was appointed Deputy United States Marshal, which position he occupied until 1875, when he was again elected Sheriff of Arapahoe county and re-elected at the end of his term, his last term ending in January, 1880. In 1873 the Hon. Samuel J. Elbert, then Territorial Governor, appointed Mr. Cook major-general of the Colorado Militia in the continuation of which post he was honored by both Governors Routt and Pitkin. In 1880 he was ordered to Leadville by Governor Pitkin to quell the railroad riots which then occurred and which caused the Governor to proclaim martial law in Lake County. General Cook most promptly and effectually put an end to the disturbances. On the 30th day of October (Sunday) 1880, the memorable Chinese riots broke out in Denver and for a while the wildest state of anarchy and lawlessness prevailed. Mayor Sopris called on General Cook to subdue the rioters and restore order. Taking charge of the police force, and swearing in fifty special policemen, General Cook very quickly became master of the situation. He arrested the ring-leaders and placed them behind the bars. But for the prompt action on the part of the municipal government and the efficiency of General Cook and his forces, the outrages on the inoffensive Chinamen, and the sacking and pillaging of their quarters, might soon have spread and become general, for the blood of the mob was up to fever heat, and the direst calamity in the city's history might have been recorded.

General Cook's services to Denver and the State of Colorado are not easily estimated. He has, in his many years of service, both in his capacity as public official and private detective, been a terror to murderers, horse-thieves, foot-pads and general all-around hold-ups. His is a career which teems with adventure and episode but rarely experienced by an individual. His name is known as a warning to thieves from the Atlantic to the Pacific; from the British line to the Mexican. He has perhaps brought more criminals to justice than any half-dozen men in the Rocky Mountains. In his reminiscences, which General Cook published some years ago, under the title of "Hands Up," he recounts many experiences which might well be taken *cum grano salis*, but for the fact that there are too many living witnesses of the occurrences therein detailed. The most exaggerated Western sensationalism of blood-and-thunder authors is overmatched and out-done by the extraordinary and blood-curdling experiences of the head of the Rocky Mountain Detective Association, and his picked lieutenants during the days of Colorado pioneerdom. It was during General Cook's term of office that the notorious Musgrove gang was hunted down and dispersed. Musgrove himself was lynched in broad day light by the populace of Denver, and while the rope, which was suspended from the Larimer Street bridge, crossing Cherry Creek, was being placed about his neck the desperado stood coolly puffing away at his cigarette. He veritably "died game." Many were the stock thieves which were brought to book through the agency of General Cook and to him is due the breaking-up of these particular bands of desperadoes in Arapahoe and adjoining counties; and in fact in distant counties of Colorado.

General Cook is still an active man and at the head of the detective agency whose name and fame are identical with his own.

G. M. HOPKINS.

Among the city marshals of Denver there is not one who is more kindly remembered than the efficient and exceedingly popular Mr. G. M. Hopkins. Born in the State of Illinois, November 15, 1835, where he passed the earlier years of his life on a farm, receiving the customary education of a prosperous farmer's child of that day, Mr. Hopkins at the age of twenty-five, was induced, by premonitory symptoms of lung trouble, to seek, like thousands of others in quest of life and health, the restorative climate of Colorado. That Mr. Hopkins found his panacea is demonstrated by his physical appearance. He arrived in Denver on the 10th day of January, 1860, and like the majority of new arrivals immediately sought the gold fields and their fascinations. After a brief activity at Chicago Bar, near Idaho Springs, he enlisted in the First Colorado Volunteers and with that regiment participated in the battles of "Apache Canon," "Pigeon Ranche" and "Paroalta." After three years service he was mustered out with an honorable discharge and the reputation of a gallant soldier. After the war he again turned his attention to mining and in

1866 he entered the police department of which he was a faithful member for two years. Early in his career as an officer he arrested James Allen on a charge of murder committed on the Maxwell Grant in the territory of New Mexico, and delivered up Allen to the territorial authorities. He was also mainly instrumental in working up the "Cheap John" murder case, which occurred in West Denver in the winter of 1886-1887, and in company with Mr. Richard Sopris, then sheriff of Arapahoe County, arrested the murderer, George Gorman of Central City. Though Gorman was acquitted at his second trial his guilt was never doubted by a majority of the people.

Mr. Hopkins was elected City Marshal in 1869 under the mayoralty of Hon. B. B. Stiles and was re-elected in '70, '71 and '72. Though called upon to run again for the office in 1873 he declined to do so.

One of the most thrilling events recorded in the criminal annals of Colorado is that of the surprise and plundering of the United States mail coach on its way from Cheyenne to Denver in January of 1870. Suspicion pointed to five men who had terrorized the country about the old town of Burlington in Boulder county at the crossing of the St. Vrain. On the 6th day of February 1870, warrants were issued by Orson Brooks, United States Commissioner, to Mark A. Schafflinberg, then United States Marshal, for their arrest. Schafflinberg requested Mr. Hopkins to raise a strong posse of determined men for the purpose of going to Boulder county and to make the arrests. His reply was that he required but one brave and determined man to go with him for that purpose.

He was made a Deputy United States Marshal and a suitable comrade having been found he started on his daring and dangerous enterprise. His companion was Jesse Burton, now of Ouray. They left Denver in the night in a two-horse conveyance and within 48 hours they returned with W. C. Duboise, Perry Walker, George Morris and Theodore Smith. The fifth of this gang of desperadoes, W. E. Tucker, was not found. The men were tried but discharged. Duboise returned to his home in Left Hand, and on meeting a young man named McKinney, whom he suspected of "giving him away," shot him down. The people, in their outraged feelings, turned out and surrounded his house. He kept them at bay until day-break, when, mounting a swift-footed horse, he dashed through their lines, amid a shower of bullets, and made good his escape. After a close pursuit he was surrounded, later in the day, and, finding escape impossible, he turned and emptied two six-shooters at his pursuers, and then fell from his horse a corpse, riddled with bullets and buck-shot. This was the last attempt at robbing the United States mail in Colorado.

Mr. Hopkins also worked up the famous Wall murder case. Wall was a sheep-herder, who lived on Dry Creek, about fifteen miles south of Denver. His mysterious disappearance was reported to Mr. Hopkins, who immediately suspected a man named George Witherell, who had suddenly become the possessor of a large flock of sheep. This man was also suspected of having stolen a large number of sheep from J. K. Doolittle. Mr. Hopkins had Witherell arrested for the larceny of these sheep, but his real design was to get Witherell in custody for the murder of Wall. If the body of Wall were discovered other evidence in his possession would convict Witherell of the murder. The case was compromised by Witherell turning over six hundred head of sheep to Doolittle. The body of the murdered man was afterwards found, Witherell was tried for the murder and is now serving a life sentence at Canon City.

These are but a few instances among the many extraordinary and marvelous episodes in the apprehension of desperate criminals in the official career of this excellent police officer. Mr. Hopkins is now jailor of the Arapahoe County jail, is hearty and well-preserved and esteemed as an efficient and meritorious official.

WILLIAM A. SMITH.

One of the ablest and most determined Chiefs of Police Denver has known was Mr. William A. Smith, a gentleman still among us in the enjoyment of health, prosperity and popularity.

Mr. Smith was born in Lancashire, England, November 5th, 1840. When ten years of age he came to America with his parents, who located in Brooklyn, New York.

In 1851 he accompanied his father to Chicago, and in 1857 he moved to Kansas City, Missouri. In 1860 he came to Colorado and settled in Black Hawk, Gilpin County. Here he erected several stamp-mills and engaged in the construction of others in Empire, Clear Creek County. In conjunction with his father he put up a quartz mill of his own. When the war broke out he sold his interests and enlisted in company C, First Colorado Regiment of Infantry, under Captain Richard Sopris, who afterwards became Mayor of. Denver. In 1862 the regiment received orders to proceed to New Mexico, but in the fall of the year returned to Camp Weld and went into winter quarters. In the spring of 1863 the regiment was ordered to campaign against the Sioux Indians. In 1865 Mr. Smith obtained a veteran's furlough, proceeded to St. Louis, where he married, and soon after left the army. Upon obtaining a large contract from the government to supply posts in Arizona with corn, he proceeded to that territory. In the year 1866 Mr. Smith sailed from San Francisco to New York, by way of the Horn, and in 1867 he returned to Colorado, and located on Wisconsin ranch near Denver; but owing to Indian depredations he was compelled to leave and then removed to Denver in 1868. He became a member of the police force and was elected Constable. In 1871 he was appointed Deputy Sheriff, in which capacity he served until 1873, when he was appointed City Marshal by Mayor Francis M. Case. In 1875 he again returned to his ranch. In 1876 he was appointed Deputy Sheriff by General D. J. Cook, then Sheriff of Arapahoe County, in which capacity he acted for a number of years.

When the Hon. John L. Routt was elected Mayor, in 1884, Mr. Smith was again appointed as the head of the Police Department, this time as Chief, which office he held during Mr. Routt's entire term.

Mr. Smith's name is connected with some of the most important criminal cases and arrests in the history of Colorado.

JOHN C. MCCALLIN.

In 1874, when Hon. W. J. Barker was Mayor, John C. McCallin was appointed Chief of Police.

Mr. McCallin was born in Ireland in 1839. When he was three years old, his family came to America. His father was a farmer and young McCallin received his education at a township school. His family emigrated West when he was still a young lad. In 1874 Mr. McCallin joined the police force of Denver and his efficiency as an officer attracted the attention of Mr. Barker, who regarded him as an able man to be placed at the head of the department. His term extended through the two administrations of Mayor Barker. Mr. McCallin died at the age of thirty-seven, a young man with a splendid record, respected by all who knew him, and regretted as a good citizen and an excellent officer.

DANIEL W. MAYS.

A prominent, enterprising and useful citizen, a man of highest standing among his fellow-men, is Mr. Daniel W. Mays, and his selection to the head of the Police Department, in 1871 by Mayor Buckingham, could not but meet with the approval of the peace and order-loving people of Denver. Mr. Mays was born in the year 1840 in the State of Missouri. He was educated in the La Grange University in that state. At the age of twenty, at the breaking out of the war he joined the Confederate Army as a private in Colonel Martin E. Green's regiment. The regiment was one attached to the command of General Sterling Price and took part in the battle of Pea Ridge and numerous skirmishes. That Mr. Mays was a good and brave soldier is attested by the fact that he joined the ranks as private and graduated therefrom with an honorable discharge and a pair of shoulder straps.

In 1868 Mr. Mays brought the first drove of sheep to Denver; the first ever driven across the plains. The journey took five months. He disposed of them to advantage and with the proceeds established himself in the flour and feed business. This was the first store of the kind established in Denver. In this business he remained until his appointment as Chief of Police. He served a full term and part of a second, the legislature having changed the election of city officers from April to October. After his term of office Mr. Mays went into the real estate business, in which he has been and is still eminently successful. Mr. Mays is one of the substantial citizens of Denver and no one is more generally respected than he.

CHARLES B. STONE.

Mr. Stone was appointed Chief of the Denver Police by the Hon. B. B. Stiles, when the latter was elected to the mayoralty in 1877.

Mr. Stone was born in Franklin County, Vermont, in the year 1843. He was the son of a farmer and made himself useful upon a farm until he was eighteen years of age, receiving the education farmers were wont to give their sons in that part of the country at that time. At the breaking out of the Civil War, Mr. Stone entered in the First Vermont Cavalry regiment of volunteers as lieutenant of company B., and afterwards served in the third division of the cavalry corps, then under command of General Custer. After serving his country three years and six months, participating in all the battles in which his corps took part, he returned home with an honorable record. He was engaged in the lumber business in his native state, until 1872 when he came to Colorado. Then he followed mercantile pursuits with varied results, succumbing in the panic of 1873, which proved so disastrous to many of the business men throughout the country. Mr. Stone made a faithful and efficient Chief of Police. After his term of office he again turned his attention to business in which he has been very successful, having acquired large interests in this city and elsewhere.

WILLIAM R. HICKEY.

William R. Hickey was born in Ireland in 1844, and was brought to this country when but a child, by his parents. His family located in Ohio and afterward removed to Illinois, where they lived when the war broke out. Young Hickey enlisted in one of the first regiments raised in Illinois, in which he advanced from a private to the rank of first lieutenant, and as such was mustered out. In the year 1866 he removed to Nebraska, where he raised a company of volunteers against the Indians, who were troublesome at the time in that state, and did some good service. After these disturbances he became City Marshal of Nebraska City, occupying the office for two terms. He was afterwards tax collector of the same city. In 1873 he came to Denver and was chosen Chief of Police by Mayor Richard Sopris in 1879. He served one term in full but during his second term of office, in consequence of political complications in municipal affairs, he resigned. Immediately after his resignation he lost his health, and never recovered sufficiently to take part in either politics or business. His reason finally gave way and he was adjudged insane. He died August 25, 1882, in the house of his mother. He was buried with public honors.

JAMES M. LOMERY.

Mr. Lomery was appointed to the office of Chief of Police by the Hon. Robert Morris, in 1881. James M. Lomery was born in St. Augustine, Florida, January 10th, 1842, of English parents. His father was a successful merchant and young Lomery was educated at various institutes in New York, Mobile and New Orleans. In April, 1860, he joined the Second Louisiana Infantry, Confederates, and as ensign served in this regiment until the close of the war. He took part in all the battles of Virginia and Maryland, was in Jackson's corps at Gettysburg, then under command of General "Jeb." Stuart, and an eyewitness of Lee's surrender at Appomatox. After the close of the war Mr. Lomery returned to Mobile, where he was appointed clerk of the Circuit Court, and register and master in chancery. For six years he held these positions and was then elected a councilman. In 1872 he received the nomination for the mayoralty of Mobile, but in the tidal wave of the Greeley campaign, which then swept the South, he was defeated. Mr. Lomery then removed to Colorado and settled in Denver. He engaged in the practice of law, entering the office of Teller, Reed and Dixon. Mr. Lomery is now co-publisher, with Mr. Halsey Rhodes, of the Rocky Mountain *Herald*.

AUSTIN W. HOGLE.

In 1885, when the Hon. Joseph E. Bates was again elected Mayor of Denver, he selected as his Chief of Police Mr. Austin W. Hogle.

Mr. Hogle was born at Henrysville, western Canada, in 1844, whence his parents, while he was still an infant, removed to the United States. They located in Iroquois County, Illinois, where young Hogle received his education at the public school. At an early age he went into apprenticeship, as a printer on the Middleford *Press*. A few years later he went into the drug business.

In 1862 Mr. Hogle enlisted in the Seventy-sixth Illinois regiment of volunteers as a private. A few months later he was made first sergeant of his company, and in 1864 he was commissioned second lieutenant. His regiment was with Grant in his first Mississippi campaign; he took part in all the battles before Vicksburg, Jackson Crossing, Benton, Mississippi and Jackson, Louisiana; was at the siege of Jackson, Mississippi; with Gen. Steele in his Alabama and Florida campaigns; took part in the siege and assault on Blakeley, Alabama, and participated, all in all, in over fifty battles and minor skirmishes of the war. In 1869, after returning to his old home in Illinois, Mr. Hogle was elected treasurer of Iroquois County, which office he held for two years. In 1872 he came to Colorado, settled in Denver and went into the commission business.

Mr. Hogle made an excellent Chief of Police. It was he who introduced the military discipline and drill into the force, without which a police department is but an imperfect organization. A policeman should be in no wise, physically, the inferior of the soldier; mentally, to be a good officer of the peace and order, he ought to be his superior. The soldier moves and acts only upon command; the policeman acts largely on his own judgment, and this ought to be of a high order.

HENRY BRADY.

The predecessor of the present incumbent at the head of the Police Department was Mr. Henry Brady, who was appointed by the Hon. Wm. Scott Lee, in 1887.

Mr. Brady was born at Independence, Missouri, March 23d, 1854, where he lived and attended school, until he reached the age of eighteen. In search of adventure and fortune he started West, reaching Denver in 1872, where he entered the employ of a transfer company, which position he left at the end of two months and went to work on the Colorado Central railway, then in course of construction to Black Hawk.

From a tool boss, Mr. Brady was soon promoted to the foremanship of a gang. He remained in this position until the road was completed, when he went to Georgetown, Colorado, and engaged in mining for nearly five years. In 1878 Mr. Brady went to Leadville. After several months, the climate not agreeing with him, he returned to Denver and again entered the employ of the transfer company for which he had formerly worked. Later on he was in the employ of other similar companies, until he entered the police force in November 1881.

For one year Mr. Brady did duty as patrolman, when he was appointed City Jailer, in December, 1882. In this position he remained until his promotion to a second lieutenancy on the force, by Mayor Bates, in 1886, which position he held until his elevation to the position of Chief of Police. Mr. Brady is a man of courage, and his experience qualified him well for the duties of the responsible position he was called upon to fill. But Mr. Brady is too much of a politician and in the opinion of the writer, this is an unnecessary requirement for the office. The less that politics are introduced into the department the more efficient will be the service. Mr. Brady, during the past two years, has attended to the duties of door-keeper of the United States Senate at Washington, and with this added experience is likely to develop into a politician of no mean calibre.

CHAPTER IV.

THE DEPARTMENT OF TO-DAY.—CHIEF FARLEY.—1889-1890.

It were quite just to regard a compiler, chronicler or commentator on any subject, whatsoever it might be, as presumptuous in assuming a task for which his knowledge and field of observation did not, at least in some degree, qualify him.

The writer, in his vocation as a journalist, has come into somewhat closer contact and relations with various metropolitan and municipal police departments than do men ordinarily, if we except that branch of society which gains an intimate knowledge of the inner workings of the various police systems under protest.

It is maintained by wise and experienced heads that a thoroughly good policeman should be a good man—a man with a large degree of human nature in his make-up. He should also possess extraordinary judgment and be a gentleman. The city of Denver is fortunate in the possession, at present, of a Chief of Police who is essentially a gentleman, as well as a man of excellent judgment and of vast experience as a detective officer. It must be a source of regret that Mr. Farley's usefulness has been greatly handicapped by conditions that ought not to exist in that class of cities among which Denver ranks. The fault-finders and grumblers, who are as numerous here as elsewhere, are encouraged in their favorite pastime by the false and mistaken notions of economy that prevail; for instance, the secret service, which is an important adjunct of every well regulated police force, is stinted to such a degree that this branch is practically useless. There is absolutely not appropriation sufficient to utilize the resources at hand, and when it is considered that this branch exists especially for the purpose of working up intricate criminal cases and that its inability to act is the result of parsimony, it must be confessed that carping criticism is in very bad taste. Our de-

JOHN F. FARLEY, CHIEF OF POLICE.

partment must be sustained and supported with all the moral and financial aid of which this community is capable. When this shall be done, then, and not until then, will the openly expressed dissatisfaction and fault-finding disappear. To estimate our Chief of Police correctly let us review his still young but useful career.

John F. Farley was born in the County Caven, Ireland, in 1849 and is therefor but forty-one years of age. He came to America with his parents at the age of four. The family settled in Norwich, Connecticut, where the lad received a public school education and remained until he was seventeen, at which age, in the year 1867, he went west to Chicago, where he enlisted in the regular army. He was assigned to company K, Third Regiment Cavalry, Regulars, stationed at Fort Seldon, New Mexico, and here he remained until 1870, when his regiment relieved the Eighth Cavalry in Arizona which in turn took the place of the former.

During his term of enlistment, Mr. Farley rose to the rank of first sergeant of his company and was honorably discharged as such at the expiration of his term of service in 1872. While in service Mr. Farley won an enviable reputation as an Indian fighter. He was in a number of engagements with the redskins, of which the first was a fight with the Mescallero Apaches in the Guadalupe Mountains in western Texas. Besides this Mr. Farley had an experience, which few men have lived through and which attests to his remarkable courage, fearlessness and tact. It was during the now famous battle of Apache Pass, Arizona, on the 19th of July, 1871. He and a first lieutenant were in command of a posse of five mounted men. Mr. Farley was, in consequence of his experience in Indian warfare, given equal command with the lieutenant. This posse was sent out in pursuit of a band of Indians who had been depredating and had been successful in stampeding the post herd of cattle, about half a mile from the post. The garrison consisted of but two companies, one of cavalry and one of infantry. The cavalry company had departed on a scouting expedition, a few days before, with the exception of twelve of their number, who had been left in post for the purpose of escort and other duties, and who were in charge of the first sergeant. The Indians, evidently aware of this, attacked the herd within the very limits of the post, and were especially emboldened as it happened that six of the twelve cavalrymen had departed from the post about an hour before as escort to the United States mail wagon. When Sergeant Farley received his order to pursue the marauding band of savages there were, therefore, but four men besides himself and the lieutenant with whom to give pursuit. The exceeding smallness of the force did not, however, interfere with the ardor of these few brave men and the order had scarcely been given when all were in their saddles and off after the thieving redskins. After pursuing them a half mile the trail was struck and followed for another half mile. Here it divided and the larger of the two trails was chosen by the party. The object of the commanding officer, in sending so inadequate a force after so large a one of the Indians was to temporarily engage and hold them in check until such time as the re-inforcements from the infantry company could come up with them. From this time on the party kept in hot pursuit for a distance of three miles, where the trail led up-hill over quite a rise in the country. Sergeant Farley was in advance and following his usual system of Indian fighting, dismounted at the base of the hill, which at the same time gave his horse an opportunity for rest. While he was ascending the hill and leading his horse, a shot suddenly resounded through the stillness and Mr. Farley immediately realized that he was hit, and, as he at the time supposed, fatally. However, before he fully realized this, there came an entire volley from the Indians, and a ball struck his horse; the animal plunged and got away. Surely, a desperate situation for a wounded man, for at that moment a large body of Indians appeared pouring down from the top of the hill, on both sides of the small party, with the evident purpose of cutting off their retreat to the post. Happily the men were all armed with the latest improved firearms and what still more improved the situation, strange as this may seem, was the fact that three of the party besides Sergeant Farley had also lost their horses. Had they retained possession of their animals, they would have endeavored to escape and becoming separated would have fallen a sure prey to the enemy. The other two in making good their escape to the post, for a moment attracted the attention of the redskins, especially those who were mounted, which was very fortunate for the four men without horses, who were thus enabled to reach the foot of the hill together and there entrench themselves in a strong position without further accident. However, before accomplishing this, Mr. Farley had a very "close call." In his endeavor to reach the point of safety which already sheltered his companions he was exposed to the fire of the foe upon all sides. He was moving along as best he could, with his shattered hip, in a dry arroya at the foot of the slope. This was thickly covered with underbrush. Exhausted from the loss of blood and separated from his companions, he crawled into a thick clump of bushes, hoping thus to be secure for a time at least. He had been there less than half a minute when a volley of shots started the very ground upon which he lay, and covered him with dust and gravel which nearly blinded him. It was evident that he was not so secure as he had deemed himself. He quickly changed his position, hoping to thus better conceal himself. He now took a survey of the situation, and looking up the hill, he espied the head of an Indian slowly making its appearance above the crest, endeavoring to locate his enemy. From the sudden disappearance of this head, Sergeant Farley concluded that he was discovered and the certainty of his death in case of attempting to reach his friends flashed upon him, as in so doing he would have to run in a straight line from the Indian and this would have made him a sure target. Watching his opportunity, the very next time the head appeared, he drew a bead on it and fired. From the sudden and entire disappearance of the gentleman's top-knot it may be safely concluded that the shot told but too well. Farley now made a sudden and determined break and fortune favoring him, he reached his party in safety.

He now concluded that, as they were entirely surrounded, it would be the last fight they would ever make and he besought his friends to make a determined and brave stand for their lives, which they promised to do, he assuring them that he himself would not run from the spot, as he was badly wounded —to the death, he thought. In order to impress upon his comrades his determination and despair, he unbuckled his pistol belt and laying it on the grouud beside him, he prepared to sell his life as dearly as possible. Less than thirty minutes later the mounted Indians returned from their pursuit of the two men, who had succeeded in eluding them, and had reached the post in safety. From this time on until darkness the Indians made assault after assault, but to no purpose. The four hard-driven men repulsed them each time. We read of the heroism of the Spartans at Thermopylæ and the "Charge of the Six Hundred," but think of four American soldiers, one of them wounded and practically disabled, holding off for hours a band of fierce and blood-thirsty Apaches numbering at least twenty-five, firing volley after volley, and not a man hit with the exception of the shot received by Farley in the beginning of the fight. Who can doubt the decrees of Providence, or question the heroism of our little frontier armies?

At night-fall the Indians desisted from further harassing our party of heroes. It is a well-known fact to those familiar with the Apache, that he will not fight after dark, a superstitious custom which prevails among them. This was an intense relief to the brave but exhausted little band and this alone saved them, as neither ammunition nor courage could hold out forever. Darkness was also followed by a heavy thunder shower, much to the relief of the party in general, and to the wounded man in particular, who had lain for three hours under the scorching and tropical July sun in the desert of Arizona. About an hour after dark a rider on a white horse appeared at a distance. He was taken for an enemy by one of the party, who fired a shot at him. The shot was followed by a challenge from Farley and the welcome response "a friend!" cheered the hearts of the forlorn little band. The speaker proved to be in charge of a rescuing party, which had brought with them an ambulance for the purpose of taking back four dead bodies; but much to their surprise they found a very lively set of boys, one with a fractured hip to be sure, but better than a regiment of dead men.

Mr. Farley spent four months in the hospital and on recovering from his wound he was again assigned to active duty.

At the expiration of his period of service he was honorably discharged at Camp Bowie, Arizona, March 1st, 1872.

Four months later, in 1873, Mr. Farley associated himself with Mr. Thiel, who was an old acquaintance, and who at that time established the now famous Thiel's Detective Service, in St. Louis, Mo. Mr. Farley remained in St. Louis about fifteen months and when the agency was enlarged and a New York office opened, he was transferred to the metropolis to aid in the establishing of the agency there. He remained in New York about three years, in charge of the office and was then transferred to St. Paul, Minn., where he opened an office and built up the service to a high degree of efficiency. He remained in charge there about four years and in 1885 came to Denver where he repeated his former good work for the Thiel Detective Service, opening an office and remaining in charge until his appointment as Chief of Police by Mayor Londoner in May, 1889. Mr. Farley had practically become an integral part of the Thiel agency, which is to-day one of the leading detective services of the world, and the establishment of the most of its branch offices is due to his activity. Mr. Thiel always regarded Mr. Farley as his right hand, so to speak, and when he left the agency the former was not inconsiderably annoyed.

Mr. Farley's schooling in detective work is of an exceptionally high order and with the necessary support from the city government he would undoubtedly give to Denver a most excellent police service, but if he is to carry out his ideas to the advantage of the city, the city must at least do what Mr. Thiel did: make a sufficient appropriation to enable him to do so. The appreciation on the part of the citizens of Denver of Mr. Farley's appointment as Chief of Police was gracefully demonstrated by the presentation of an elegant and costly gold star, richly embellished with brilliant setting and appropriate inscription. The people knew what they would gain in Mr. Farley's appointment and manifested their gratification early in his administration. Mr. Farley has recently, after the development of the troubles in the Detective Department, taken personal charge thereof, and that he will properly and efficiently administer it, is beyond the shadow of a doubt.

He knows how. It is only to be hoped that our city government will quickly recognize the necessities of its Police Department and take steps in freeing it from of its crippled condition and thus utilize the good material it possesses and augment this with what it lacks.

CHAS. A. HAWLEY, INSPECTOR.

CHAPTER V.

INSPECTOR OF POLICE, CHAS. A. HAWLEY.

A typical soldier, a thorough disciplinarian and an excellent police officer: what more could be said of any man holding the responsible position of Inspector of Police, a position, second only to that of Chief? Such is Captain Hawley, the subject of this sketch.

Chas. A. Hawley was born in Cleveland, Ohio, in 1848, and is just forty-two years of age. His parents removed to New York City while he was still a child, but he had scarcely reached his seventh year when he left the city for the western part of the state. This section of country, however, was too dull for the lad and in a few months he was back in New York City, whence he went to sea. For four years he was a seafarer, at the expiration of which time he again landed in New York. On the third of June, 1862, he enlisted in the Eleventh United States Infantry Regiment, of which he was bugler for three years. After Appomatox he was among those who entered Richmond, where he was mustered out on June 3, 1865, when he returned to his parents in Philadelphia. He subsequently followed railroading until the year 1878, when he came to Denver.

It was in the special service of the Chicago, Burlington and Quincy railroad that Captain Hawley gained his first experience as a police officer. Once located in Denver, he joined the Merchants' Police, and in the year 1879 General D. J. Cook employed him as a criminal Deputy Sheriff, in which capacity he served until 1880. During this period he made a splendid record, which was much enhanced by his remarkably clever work in the celebrated Hayward murder case, when he captured the criminals after a two months' search.

A brief recalling of this tragic occurrence and the accompanying thrilling episodes, through which Captain Hawley passed, may prove of interest, more especially, as it attests to Hawley's undaunted courage, perspicacity and determination.

On September 11, 1879, two men came over the mountains towards Denver, on their way from Laramie, Wyoming, where they had just been released from imprisonment in the territorial penitentiary. Their names were Sam Woodruff and Joel Seminole. The former was three-fourths white and one-fourth Cherokee Indian; the latter was a half-breed Cheyenne. Arriving at the Hayward ranch, above Mt. Vernon, which is situated in the mountains several miles back of Morrison, they stopped and asked to be driven down to their alleged cattle camp near the Cold Spring ranch in the vicinity of Golden. Hayward accommodated them. When they neared the hog-back they choked Mr. Hayward, and in throwing him out of his wagon broke his neck. The body was disposed of in a box-culvert about five miles out of town. They then drove on to Denver, where they sold the team. On the morning of the 13th the missing of Hayward was reported to the Denver police authorities. Meanwhile the murderers were enjoying the fruits of their crime and were also evidently enjoying supposed security.

Not long after the murder of Mr. Hayward, two men stole a livery rig from Brown's stables, in this city. Captain Hawley took charge of the case and tracked the thieves into Nebraska. He took with him an assistant by the name of Ayres, and the two followed the trail some sixty-five miles along the Niobrara river. It seems that Ayres was hardly of any assistance to Hawley, but on the contrary, came near ruining his plans, by drinking and blabbing. At this point the track of one of the thieves was lost and the other, Hawley discovered, led to Dakota, and he immediately set out to follow it up. He went as far as Pine Ridge and succeeded in capturing Seminole whom he brought safely back to Denver. Captain Hawley, without loss of time, set forth again for Nebraska after the other man, upon whose capture he was bent. Arrived at the point he had reached on his first trip, the indications pointed to a fellow, who kept dodging him and who, when arrested by Captain Hawley, proved none other than the notorious mail robber, "Bill" Johnson, who was wanted in Nebraska. This was an important arrest. Captain Hawley soon found out that Sam Woodruff was the accomplice of Seminole and that these two worthies were the slayers of Hayward. It appears that blood found upon the clothes of Seminole, led to a close investigation which resulted in the confession of the half-breed to the murder and the disclosure of the identity of his companion in crime. When Captain Hawley ascertained the true nature of the scoundrel he had determined to bring to justice, he started back to Nebraska with re-doubled zeal. He struck his trail at North Platte Station. Following this down, meanwhile stopping at all intermediate points between North Platte and Omaha, he reached the latter city. Here Captain Hawley received a letter from Jeff. Carr, then Sheriff of Laramie County, Wyoming, which contained the information that Woodruff's people lived in one of the border counties of Iowa. At Council Bluffs Hawley discovered that a brother of the murderer lived in the eastern part of Pottawatomie county, whither he at once proceeded. Arrived there he disguised himself as a farm hand and hired out as a corn-husker, at three cents per bushel and board. On the same evening, November 23, Captain Hawley went down to a village called Big Grove where he found his man Sam Woodruff assisting his brother Jim who kept a butcher shop. They were killing beef for a railroad construction gang. Being tired and worn out from his long ride of the previous day, Captain Hawley now returned to the farm and rested during the following day, but that same night he again returned to Big Grove and striking up an acquaintance with his man he stood and chatted with him awhile. The next day, however, he returned to Council Bluffs and telegraphed to General D. J. Cook for requisition papers. Then he swore out a warrant for fugitive from justice against Sam Woodruff. After obtaining this he started back for his man, and took with him a constable, in the shape of a little Frenchman, who furnished Captain Hawley considerable amusement because of his timidity and total unfitness for the task about to be undertaken, and of which, for the time being, the constable had been kept in total ignorance. The night was dark and stormy. Leaving Council Bluffs at 9:30 P. M., after riding for six hours through the rain, our friends arrived at Big Grove at three A. M., drenched and cold, when they put up their horses and lay down for a short rest in the stable. At five o'clock they awoke and after an early breakfast Hawley prepared for work, taking every possible precaution to effectually carry out the purposes of his plan. It was only now that the Frenchman learned the true purport of their errand and he was frightened almost out of his wits. Armed with a thirty-eight calibre Colt's revolver, a shot gun, and the necessary official documents, Hawley and his trembling companion went to the store of the village and awaited the right opportunity. Meanwhile Captain Hawley had made his true identity known to the store-keeper, who had on the previous day offered him a job to cut cord wood at two dollars a day, telling him at the same time that he looked too strong and too respectable for a cornhusker, who earned but a pittance at best.

It was not long before Sam and his brother Jim came sauntering down the street, the latter with an ax across his shoulder. When they arrived opposite the doorway in which Hawley stood, he quickly threw his gun up to his left shoulder and leveled his revolver with his right hand and shouted:

"Sam Woodruff, stop! You are my prisoner; throw up your hands!" Sam did stop, but made a move with his right hand toward his hip pocket.

"Take your hand from behind you and throw up both hands or you are a dead man," came from Hawley. By this time Woodruff began to realize that he was face to face with a daring and determined man, and up went his hands high into the air.

"Who are you and what do you want of me?" said Sam.

"I'm a detective from Denver, where you are wanted for the murder of old man Hayward," was the prompt reply.

By this time Jim, the brother, had sidled over toward Hawley's left, ax in hand, but he was not fast enough. Keeping his shotgun leveled at Sam, Captain Hawley threw his revolver over his left arm, thus covering both men, and addressing the brother, he said: "Stop right where you are, Jim Woodruff, or I'll fill you full of cold lead!"

This had the desired effect. Hawley then commanded the trembling constable to take the ax away from Jim and, giving the gun to the Frenchman, he walked up to Sam, quickly took away his revolver, and snapped the handcuffs upon him. With trembling voice the constable read the warrant, after which Hawley told Sam Woodruff that he must go with him; that he might go as a gentleman, or he would take him like a dog. Sam concluded that the former was more preferable, and he went willingly enough to all appearances, after giving his brother Jim some ten dollars, with the remark: "You take this, Jim; it belongs to you anyway."

Captain Hawley proceeded with his prize to Omaha, where they arrived on the night of the 26th, and where requisition papers were awaiting his return. He had shackles riveted upon Woodruff, so as to make absolutely sure of him, and left Omaha with him on the noon train, November 28th, arriving in Denver on the night of the 30th. Here Woodruff was kept until December 10th, when he was delivered to the authorities of Jefferson county. On the evening of December 30th a body of about one hundred men marched to the jail in Golden, took out the two murderers and hanged them from a railway bridge. Seminole, in making his confession, had divulged all the details of the atrocious crime.

The Rocky Mouutain Detective Agency was at this time organized by General Cook. Captain Hawley joined it and remained with it three years. Subsequently he was made Deputy United States Marshal under P. P. Wilcox, by whom Hawley was held in highest esteem. In August 1883 he accepted the position of special agent with the Denver and Rio Grande Western railroad, and served as such until the railway company abandoned this department, when he entered the detective service in the City Police under Mayor Bates. Here he served four months and then went into the Sheriff's office, under Geo. B. Graham. Then for two years he worked as a private detective and again entered the City Police Force on January 7, 1887, under Mayor Lee. He was re-appointed by Mr. Lee's successor, the present Mayor, and on July 31, 1889, he was promoted to First Sergeant. During the following fall on September 14th, he was commissioned Police Inspector on the recommendation of Chief Farley.

Inspector Hawley's duties are as follows: Supervision of all police drills; inspection of uniforms, arms and ammunition; and the sanitary care of the force. He is the purchasing agent, through the City Treasurer, and has charge of the live and rolling stock of the city. In fact, he is to the Police Force what the adjutant is to a regiment. Of him Chief Farley has said: "He is an exemplary officer and comes as near to the standard of a West Point graduate in discipline as any man I ever met outside of the regular service." Captain Hawley earned his military title in 1880, when he raised and commanded the first Zouaves organized west of the Missouri river. He was also the first colonel of the Colorado National Guards, in command of the First Regiment. Captain Hawley stands six feet one and one-half inches, weighs 190 pounds and is a splendid specimen of a man and an exemplary police officer.

JOHN E. PHILLIPS, FIRST LIEUTENANT.

CHAPTER VI.

LIEUTENANTS AND SERGEANTS.

JOHN E. PHILLIPS, FIRST LIEUTENANT.

John E. Phillips was born in New York City, November 23, 1848. After passing through the various grades in the public schools, he attended the business college of Bryant and Stratton, in which he holds a life membership. Mr. Phillips is a carpenter and builder by trade. He joined the Denver Police Force June 1, 1879, and remained in its service until May 1, 1885, under Chiefs Hickey, Cook, Lomery and Smith. He was patrolman about one year and was then appointed license collector, the first one in Denver, by Mayor Sopris. When in 1881 the force was increased the office of Sergeant of Police was created and Mr. Phillips was advanced to this rank. This position he held until 1885 when he resigned from the force.

He again entered into the service of the department and was appointed Second Lieutenant by Mayor Londoner July 1, 1889, and was promoted to the position of First Lieutenant on February 10th, the following year. Mr. Phillips is the man who arrested Clay Wilson, the "killer" of the notorious Jim Moon.

Those who lived in Denver in '79, '80 and '81, well remember how this man Moon terrorized the entire community. He kept a gambling house which was located in the alley behind the Good Block and which was then a gathering place for all the sporting element in and around Denver. Moon was not a bad fellow when sober, but when in his cups woe to the man who crossed him. The affair which terminated his career was owing to a jealous row, between himself and wife. Upon Wilson, the mutual friend of the pair, fell Moon's suspicion and he uttered the threat of killing Wilson the first time the two should meet. The meeting took place in the old Arcade on

Larimer street adjoining the present State National Bank, then the quarters of the First National Bank. About the time that the two men met, Chief Cook and Sergeant Phillips, who had been in Police Justice Whittemore's Court, were walking along on the west side of Larimer street, and had just crossed over to Charpiot's Hotel when the first shot was fired. Phillips ran toward the Arcade, whence he supposed the shot to have come, and General Cook followed. He had just reached the doorway when Clay Wilson issued therefrom, with his revolver, still smoking, in his hand. Mr. Phillips stopped Wilson and asked him what was the matter. "I guess I've killed Jim Moon," he responded coolly. General Cook having also arrived, Mr. Phillips stepped into the Arcade saloon, and there saw Moon lying on the floor near the bar, flat on his back, a corpse. Mr. Phillips turned and went out, and taking charge of Wilson, walked him up to police headquarters, then on Lawrence street, near Fifteenth. The affair created great excitement and when it transpired who had been killed, a sense almost of relief went up from the city, for Moon had really been a menace to the peace of the community. The man was not altogether bad, it was only his wild and ungovernable nature, when under the influence of liquor, that made him the dread and fear of the peaceable portion of the community. When sober he was quiet and generous, and of undaunted courage; this he demonstrated during the Chinese riot, when he faced a crazed mob of a thousand or more, and liberated, at the risk of his own life, a Chinaman who was almost dead from fright. At another time, when a warrant had been issued for the arrest of himself and partner, the two, with their wives upon their arms, and with revolvers in hand, marched undauntedly through a phalanx of police officers to a carriage and drove away. But all this courage only made the man the more dangerous and when therefore the news spread through the city that Clay Wilson had killed Jim Moon every one felt like exonerating the slayer without further questioning into the details of the affair. Wilson was the hero of the hour. Public opinion rendered the verdict and this was "justifiable homicide," and was so sustained by the court.

Another famous arrest made by Lieutenant Phillips was that of Mattie Lemmon, a denizen of a notorious house kept by Belle Warden. The proprietress and inmates were all colored. A barber from Leadville, on his way East, with considerable money in his possession, accompanied the Lemmon woman to a dance held at City Hall. He returned to the Warden house with her where he was murdered. A man, Berry Gates by name, did the killing and was condemned to the penitentiary for life. The other man implicated, was a white man, the paramour of Belle Warden, and known by the sobriquet of "Nigger Charley." His right name was Charles Smith and he was a hack-driver. He, Belle Warden and Mattie got ten years each. Mattie has since died at State's Prison, but before dying made a full confession. The leading up to the arrest of the parties implicated, was brought about by the finding of a bundle in the Platte near the 31st street bridge. This contained a bear robe and a quilt stained with blood. Soon after another discovery of a more horrible nature was made by some children playing in the basin of Cherry Creek, near the Broadway bridge. It was the body of a man, face downward, buried there, and the encroaching waters had exposed portions of it. Lieutenant Phillips devoted his time and attention to the matter and by cleverly connecting the various links brought the murderers to justice.

Mr. Phillips is both intelligent and agreeable, and of a cool, imperturbable temperament: admirable traits in a police officer. The confidence reposed in him, and the esteem in which he is held by the members of the force is best exemplified in his selection to the office of treasurer of the Police Mutual Aid Association.

Lieutenant Phillips, it may be stated, like many of his colleagues, served his country in the days of its severest test. In the year 1864, when the clouds of war darkened the American sky, he, though but a boy in years, was seized with the ardor of patriotism. He offered his services to his country and served in the 44th Volunteer Regiment of Wisconsin Infantry, of which the colonel was the Hon. G. G. Symes, ex-member of congress from Colorado. He passed through the entire war and was honorably discharged from service. He has been a member of Lincoln Post, G. A. R. since its organization.

HENRY NEWMEYER, SECOND LIEUTENANT.

Henry Newmeyer was born in the State of Wisconsin in the year 1846. His father, who was one of the pioneers of that State, arrived there, from Germany, in 1832. Mr. Newmeyer crossed the plains in 1862 and came to Colorado from Montana in 1867. Prior to coming to this State he was engaged in mining in Idaho Territory and was among the first at the Salmon river excitement. Mr. Newmeyer is a pioneer of the plains, having crossed these a number of times to Salt Lake City and Idaho. He was also one of a party which was among the first to make the journey from Walla Walla to Boise Basin, Idaho. In 1866 Mr. Newmeyer came to Denver and later on drifted to the mining district in Gilpin county. He located in Central City and was there married. In 1871 he left Central City for Kansas City, Missouri, but returned to Denver only six months later and has lived here ever since. Mr. Newmeyer has been prominently known here in commercial pursuits. He was a member of the firm of Newmeyer & Co., which did an extensive business in hides and wool. On the second day of August, 1887, Mr. Newmeyer became a member of the Denver Police Force under Mayor Lee, and after serving one year and a half as patrolman, he was made Sergeant on the patrol wagon. Under the present administration he was assigned to the street and on February 19, 1889, was appointed, in spite of considerable competition, Second Lieutenant, in consequence of his steady and faithful services. Mr. Newmeyer possesses the confidence of his superior officers to the fullest degree. He is a magnificent specimen of a man, standing five feet eleven inches in height. He is of courteous and quiet demeanor and a thoroughly efficient and capable officer.

SERGEANTS.

M. B. NORKETT, FIRST SERGEANT.

Mr. Norkett was born at Lake Forrest, in the State of Illinois, in the year 1857, and came to Denver in May, 1881. Shortly after his arrival in this city he entered the employ of

HENRY NEWMEYER, SECOND LIEUTENANT.

the Union Depot Company. He worked in the baggage room for nineteen months and then became a member of the Depot Police. On January 15, 1884, under Mayor Routt, Mr. Norkett entered the City Police as patrolman and under Mayor Lee's administration he was made Second Sergeant, and later on was advanced to First Sergeant, in which position he was confirmed under the the present regime. Mr. Norkett has always been regarded as as excellent officer and enjoys general popularity.

WILLIAM BOHANNA, SECOND SERGEANT.

Mr. Bohanna was born in the State of Massachusetts thirty-four years ago. His business was that of a teamster. He came to Denver in 1877 and entered the Police Department as patrolman in 1880 and in 1889 he was appointed Second Sergeant.

JOHN W. MCNEIL, THIRD SERGEANT.

Mr. McNeil was born in Adams county, Ohio, in the year 1845. He is of Scotch origin and his ancestors were among the first settlers of Ohio. Mr. McNeil was brought up on a farm and received a common school education. He is a carpenter by trade and came to Colorado, settling in Denver, in 1870. He served as Deputy Sheriff under General D. J. Cook during 1877 and 1878. His appointment as roundsman in the City Police Force occurred in 1880. On May 1, 1890, Mr. NcNeil was appointed Third Sergeant.

W. M. TEETER, FOURTH SERGEANT.

Mr. Teeter was born in the State of Ohio in 1848. After going through the course in the public schools he joined the great army of laborers. In 1871 he came west and settled in Denver. Mr. Teeter first joined the Police Force in 1882 and served until 1887 when he left the force. He again entered its service as patrolman in May, 1889, and received his appointment as Fourth Sergeant on the 18th of February, 1890. Mr. Teeter is a good citizen and an efficient officer. He is as well known as any member of the department and generally liked and respected.

PERCY A. CLAY, FIFTH SERGEANT.

Mr. Clay was born in Killbourn City, Wisconsin, June 4, 1859. He attended public school and passed through the Normal University of Illinois. He taught school for two years and then learned telegraphy. He was station agent for the Illinois Central, St. Louis, Iron Mountain and Southern, Union Pacific and Denver and Rio Grande railway companies at various times. Mr. Clay came to Denver in 1882 and became a member of the Police Force on May 1, 1889, serving in the capacity of patrolman until March 1, 1890, when he was appointed as Fifth Sergeant. Mr. Clay is one of the finest looking men in the department, standing six feet one inch and weighing two hundred and fifteen pounds. His popularity among his comrades was testified to by his election to the honorable position of President of the Police Mutual Aid Association of Denver.

GEORGE L. GREEN, SIXTH SERGEANT.

Mr. Green was born in Bradford county, Pennsylvania, in 1845. He received a commercial education, and is a locomotive engineer by profession. He came to Colorado in 1869, located in Denver, and worked at his calling for four years after his arrival here. In January, 1889, Mr. Green was appointed patrolman on the Police Force and on September 1st, the same year, he was promoted to the rank of Sergeant. Mr. Green is another member of the force who is of fine physique, standing six feet one inch in height and weighing two hundred and forty-seven pounds.

R. H. MACDONALD, SEVENTH SERGEANT.

Mr. MacDonald was born at Hazelton, in the State of Pennsylvania, March 4, 1860. He graduated from the high school of that place and then became an iron moulder. In 1881 Mr. MacDonald came to Denver and entered the service

PERCY A. CLAY. GEORGE L GREEN.
WM. BOHANNA. R. H. MACDONALD.
SERGEANTS.

JOHN W. MCNEIL.   M. B. NORKETT.   W. M. TEETER.
SERGEANTS.

of the water department. In June, 1889, he joined the Police Force and was promoted to the rank of Sergeant September 1, 1890. Sergeant MacDonald has the attributes of a good officer and is popular among his comrades.

CHAPTER VII.

THE DETECTIVE DEPARTMENT.

This important adjunct to the Denver Police Force has, of late, been made the subject of much unfavorable comment, not to say adverse criticism. Yet it must be confessed that this was not entirely without cause, and it is but fair to acknowledge that sufficient reason has arisen to justify an expression of dissatisfaction. But even so, there were still extenuating circumstances and these should be taken into consideration before disposing of the subject altogether. Perhaps never in the history of Denver were burglaries and safe-breaking so frequent, or did these follow one another in such rapid succession as during the late summer and fall of 1890. The community was greatly wrought up over them, and the Police Department was particularly incensed at the daring criminals, who defied detection despite the indefatigable perseverance on the part of the detectives, to ferret them out. But a scent was struck and the clue was carefully followed up; and here it would be fitting to refer back to the experience of Chief Farley with a man whose name is not unknown to the public.

Dan Sinks, after his discharge from Canon City, where he had just served a six years' term for implication in burglary and safe-blowing, which occurred at Leadville in 1881, and where he was known under the name of McBride, had returned to Denver. The Chief, in some way had been placed in possession of a bundle of letters belonging to Sinks, among which was one from a lady, the matron of the penitentiary in Canon City, who had taken much interest in the convict, and who was determined to redeem him if it could be done by kind and friendly advice. This letter deplored that he (Sinks) should again have drifted among his old associates and haunts, after the pledges of reformation he had given his friends, who had interested themselves in his case and interceded in his behalf.

Upon gaining this knowledge Chief Farley had Sinks brought before him. He charged him with ingratitude to his friends and told him of his suspicions concerning his supposed connections with the recent burglary. Sinks slyly and doggedly avowed his innocence. As Chief Farley had only moral and not legal evidence against Sinks, he said to him: "Look here, Sinks, I havn't the slightest doubt of your complicity in this affair, but I will give you a chance. If you will tell where the kit of burglars' tools is hidden and promise to leave Denver immediately and stay away from the city as long as I am Chief of Police, I will let you go. On the other hand, if you fail to accept my proposition, the chances are that after persistent work on the part of the officers, they will succeed in obtaining sufficient evidence to connect you with the possession of these burglar tools and this being a penitentiary offense, you will be sent back to Canon City. As the matter now stands I am in possession of moral evidence only, but am pretty sure of getting the necessary legal evidence to convict you." After a little hesitation and thought, Sinks replied:

"All right Chief, I agree."

He led the officers to the place where the tools were hidden and true to his promise left town. But Sinks could neither keep his promise to Chief Farley, nor would he give up his nefarious vocation. A few weeks later several daring burglaries occurred and these bore the ear marks of Sinks' mechanical skill. The blowing up of the safes of the Union Pacific Ticket office and of Pryor & Noah, put the detectives upon their mettle and Sinks, who was suspected by the Chief as the principal in these recent depredations, was apprehended and brought to Police Headquarters where he was subjected to a rigid examination by Detectives Watrous and Crocker, the men engaged in working up the case. The Chief positively declined to see the fellow on this occasion after his previous experience with him. Sinks became defiant, undoubtedly realizing that he had no mercy to expect from the authorities and particularly from the Chief, upon whom he had flagrantly imposed, and whose kindness he had scorned. Sinks not only proved stubborn but indulged in vile and abusive language against the officers, who, exasperated at the prospect of defeat, and seeing the fruits of their labors slipping away from them, more especially after insinuations akin to ridicule on the part of the daily press of this city, forgot themselves and their duties as officers of the peace, and when Sinks became belligerent, they simply struck back and the wiley and audacious criminal got the worst of it. For this they were prosecuted and on their own admissions to the court, of loss of self-control, forfeited their places in the department. The punishment of these offending officers was not too severe and can not fail in its influence for good, but it is nevertheless to be deplored that at their trial the main witness against them and upon whose oath and testimony the men were convicted was a notorious felon, a released convict, who at that very time was under the shadow of recent crimes. His complicity in them was also verified by the admission of one of his confederates, both to Messrs. Pryor & Noah and to Chief Farley. His confederate had been previously in the employ of Pryor & Noah, and was chosen by Sinks on account of his familiarity with the premises.

Even while writing the above, news has reached Denver from Pueblo that Sinks and his gang of safe-blowers have been caught in the act of burglary in that city only the night before (Nov. 28th, 1890) and are in durance vile.

The result of this affair brought about a change in the Department. Chief of Detectives Loar was prompted to resign and the Detective Force was reduced from twelve to nine men, a number altogether inadequate for the demands of the City of Denver.

Prior to the year '83 the City Detective Service of Denver was of a rather desultory character. During that year, however, a permanent and systematic organization of this department was effected. It is now under the personal supervision of Chief Farley with Assistant Chief of Detectives Sam Howe in charge, the latter having absolute control of the office.

The question may be asked, why did not Chief Farley take personal charge of the Detective Force at once, when entering upon his duties as Chief, instead of placing Mr. Loar at its head? The answer to this is easily found. When Mr. Farley

SAMUEL HOWE, ASSISTANT CHIEF OF DETECTIVES.

accepted the office much had to be done in the Police Department and no one man could have superintended both branches with justice to the task. Therefore Mr. Farley selected Mr. Loar, whom he had known as a trustworthy lieutenant in the past. That Mr. Loar lacked the necessary executive ability was as much of a disappointment to the Chief as it was detrimental to the Detective Service. It was the final disagreement between Officers Loar and Howe, which forced the realization upon Mr. Farley that he must give his personal attention to this branch of the Department. As he has consummated many of his plans in the Police Department in the introduction of reforms and improvements, he is now at liberty to look after both. A better state of affairs may be looked forward to and it may be safely predicted that the Detective Service of Denver will be as excellent henceforth as the limited force of men will permit. More men and money are essential for greater efficiency.

SAMUEL HOWE, ASSISTANT CHIEF OF DETECTIVES.

Sam Howe,, as he is familiarly called, was born in Shelby county, Ohio, October 16, 1839, and is, hence, in his fifty-first year, though he looks scarcely more than forty. He received a common school education and learned the trade of a wheelwright. Sometime before the breaking out of the late war for the Union he enlisted in the regular army. He was assigued to the Second Cavalry Regiment, then stationed in Texas. This regiment, after the outbreak of hostilities, was changed to the Fifth United States Cavalry. Mr. Howe served altogether eight years, passing through the entire war, and was honorably discharged from the service in the year 1867 at Atlanta, Georgia. In 1868 he came to Colorado, going to Black Hawk, where he lived for one year and from which place he moved to Denver. In 1873 Mr. Howe joined the Denver Police Force. He served as patrolman ten years and as detective eight years. Under the present administration Mr. Howe, in consequence of his great experience, integrity and ability, was advanced to the responsible position he now fills, which under existing conditions, is paramount to Chief of Detectives. In the famous Fitzgerald murder case (already alluded to as the Belle Warden case) Mr. Howe worked diligently and adroitly and did much toward bringing the parties implicated behind the bars. It was he who broke up a dangerous band of house-burglars, who entered and robbed some fourteen different residences in the city. Mr. Howe captured four of them, each of whom received a thirteen years sentence in State's Prison; and he personally recovered goods to the value of $4,000. Mr. Howe's most recent success in the trapping of the safe-blowers of the West Denver Brewing Company's safe is fresh in the minds of the people. He has been closely identified with nearly every important capture of burglars made in Denver during the eighteen years of his continued service. He has ever enjoyed the confidence of his superior officers. He started the rogues' gallery, now containing nearly thirteen hundred portraits and collected and arranged the curious display of burglar's tools and instruments of crime on exhibition at the office of the Detective Department. Beside these interesting and valuable features Mr. Howe has a series of very valuable and carefully arranged scrap books containing criminal events of the past twenty years and a list of all the murders committed in and about Denver during this period, with the disposition of the perpetrators.

Tried, true and rarely mistaken in his judgment of men and estimate of events, Mr. Howe is one of the members of our department whose services are and have been of great benefit to the community. He and Detective John Holland ore the oldest serving members in the Denver Police Department, each having now served some eighteen years.

CHAPTER VIII.

THE ROUTINE OF OUR POLICE SYSTEM OF TO-DAY.

The first uniformed police was introduced in Denver by Chief McCallin in 1875. The force then numbered but thirteen men, including the Chief. To-day the force by ordinance should number one hundred but for lack of appropriation on the part of the city there are but eighty-three, exclusive of the Police Matron. These are as follows: Chief, 1 Inspector, 2 Lieutenants, 7 Sergeants, 53 Patrolman, 1 Assistant Chief of Dectectives, 8 Detectives, 1 Clerk, 1 Assistant Clerk, 3 Operators, 1 Jailer, 3 Assistant Jailers, and 1 Turnkey.

There are three reliefs known respectively as First, Second and Third Patrol, and these are divided as follows:

First, 10 men on duty from five A. M. until twelve M.

Second, 13 men on duty from 12 M. to 8 P. M.; and two mounted officers on duty from 12 M. to 12 P. M.

Third, 28 men (night relief), of whom four are mounted, from 8 P. M. to 5 A. M.

These reliefs go out in charge of a Sergeant, whose duty it is to visit them while on their beats and report time of visit. The men are also under instructions to report to headquarters every half hour, by means of the patrol-box system, and each report is recorded by the police operator.

During the day the Chief, the Inspector and one Lieutenant are at the Central Station. At night this is in charge of a Lieutenant, from 8 P. M. to 8 A. M.

Of the three operators there is one to each patrol.

The Police Clerk and Assistant are on duty twelve hours each; one by day and one by night. The Police Clerk, James Collins, is another pioneer who came to Colorado in 1861, locating in Gilpin county where he followed a miner's occupation for some years. From 1885 to 1889 Mr. Collins was Under Sheriff of Gilpin county, and in 1889 he came to Denver where he was soon appointed to the position which he now holds. Mr. Collins is a Canadian and was born in Port Stanley, Ontario, in the year 1843. He came to the States in 1854, located in Chicago and during the war enlisted in the First Iowa Infantry Regiment. After serving for two years and a half he was honorably discharged.

The patrol-wagons are stationed, one at the Central Station, City Hall, the other at the station known as Division No. 2, situated at Arapahoe and Thirty-third streets. This latter station is in charge of a Sergeant. The patrol-wagons are manned by a driver and a patrol consisting of a Sergeant in charge and a private who are on duty 12 hours each relief.

The Jailer is on day duty, the Assistant Jailers and Turnkey on night duty, 12 hours each.

The Police Matron, who has her rooms at City Hall, has charge of female prisoners, lost children, etc.

Lieutenants, Night and Day Jailers and patrols change from day to night and *vice versa* once each month.

Aside from the above there are three special assignments of one man each, viz: one at the post-office, one at the intersection of Sixteenth and Larimer streets and one at the Union Depot.

The Detective Office is at present in charge of the Assistant Chief of Detectives, under the supervision of the Chief of Police, and the eight detective officers are at command at all hours, day and night, whenever occasion may require them.

There are two Police Surgeons, one at each station, and these are supposed to be on duty at all hours; in fact, whenever called upon.

There are also two city herders, whose duty it is to look after stray stock, and two hostlers who look after the stock belonging to the department.

Among the most important features introduced by Chief of Police Farley are the following: Duties of Sergeants as roundsmen; their daily reports stating where and when patrolmen are found while on duty; the present patrol-wagon service with reports of Sergeants in charge; Jailer's daily reports; creation of the Inspector's office, and Lieutenants' daily reports.

Prior to the present system, jailers were not required to make daily reports, consequently prisoners might have been incarcerated for weeks at a time without the knowledge of the Chief or Marshal. This is impossible now. Each day informs the Chief of its happenings; who apprehended and upon what grounds. Nothing that concerns the Department can now transpire without the cognizance of the Chief, within the twenty-four hours.

For the various reports, Inspector Hawley has devised and arranged a unique and practical system of blank forms. These forms are all enumerated on the requisition list, a *fac similie* of which appears on page 667.

Thus it will be seen that the machinery must operate with the regularity of clock work and it is but necessary to spend a few hours at Police Headquarters in order to learn of the discipline which exists in the department.

But there still remains something of gravest importance to be done and it can not be done by the department. It must come from the City Council, and it is the introduction into Denver of a WORK-HOUSE. This is perhaps the only city of its size in the world that is without such an institution, the importance of which is hardly to be over-estimated. It is known throughout the length and breadth of the land, among the tramps and "vags," that Denver invites them, is willing to feed and house them and look after their welfare and comforts generally. The result is that our city is the great winter resort for the worthy members of these fraternities. They congregate here and have, to use a modern slang, "a picnic." They commit petty larceny, which means a sentence in the county jail, and this is equivalent to good food, a warm bed and *nothing to do.* In the spring of the year these worthies are set free, looking sleek and fat and prepared to enjoy the summer season out of doors in their own happy and peculiar way. Build the WORK-HOUSE and you will rid the city of a large element which is both objectionable and expensive.

Prior to 1884 a condition existed which at the present time would be regarded as nothing short of chaotic. But Denver was then only a city in embryo and a frontier town at that. Its police service, though severely taxed by reason of the then existing conditions, was but a primitive organization. All this has changed during the past six years and the city has developed into a metropolis. The department is metropolitan in system and it now remains for a legislative act to make it so in fact and thus increase its capacity for usefulness and free it from the incubus of politics and politicians.

THE REQUISITION FOR BLANK FORMS AS USED IN THE

POLICE DEPARTMENT, CITY OF DENVER, COLORADO.

Form Numbers of Blanks Used in the Department.

Form No.	NAMES OF FORMS.	WANTED.
1	Defendent's Recognizance	
2	Daily Report Wagon Sergeants	
3	City Jailer's Monthly Report	
4	Police Matron's Monthly Report	
5	Chief Detective's " "	
6	Chief Herder's " "	
7	Charges and Specifications	
8	Pound Master's Order to Deliver	
9	Property Tag	
10	Requisition on Inspector of Police	
11	Patrol Sergeant's Daily Report	
12	Operator's Monthly Report	
13	Telephone and Signal Service Daily Report	
14	Jailer's Daily Report	
15	Ruled Letter Heads	
16	Unruled " "	
17	Printed Envelopes (small)	
18	Printed Envelopes (large)	
19	Book Record of Gaming and Houses of Prostitution	
20	Pawnbroker's Daily Report	
21	Patrolman's Arrest Book	
22	Form Number of Blanks	
23	Police Uniform Specifications	
24	Large Envelopes for Prisoners' Effects, Detective	
25	Small Envelopes for Prisoners' Effects, Detective	
26	Prisoners' Property Tag	
27	Second Div. Wagon Service Sheet and Opr. Daily Report	
28	Police Record (book for monthly report)	
29	Detectives' Daily Report	
30	Detectives' Daily Record Pocket Memoranda	
31	Second Division Jailer's Daily Report	
32	Description Card	
33	Lieutenants' Daily Report	
34	City Jailer's Register	
35	Vicious Dog Notice	

[SEE PAGE 665.]

CHAPTER IX.

A BOLD PIECE OF WORK IN SAFE BLOWING.—THE TRAP.—THE HAUL.

On Saturday morning, November 15th, 1890, the good people of Denver, after arising from their night's rest, were startled by highly sensational headlines in the newspapers, announcing that the Denver Brewing Company's offices, in West Denver, had been entered by burglars the night previous, the safes blown open and the collector, Charles Narath, who sleeps on the premises, nearly beaten to death by the desperadoes. One thousand and sixty-five dollars in cash, belonging to the company, one hundred and ten dollars and a gold watch and chain, valued at one hundred and fifty more, belonging to Louis Killbach, an employe, who left them there for safe keeping, were gone with the thieves. Three hours later, Mr. Narath, whom the burglars had gagged and bound, after beating him mercilessly, finally managed, by superhuman effort, to release himself and give the alarm. The police were notified, but all trace of the thieves seemed absolutely wiped out. However, the case was not abandoned and a clue was obtained less than twenty-four hours later, which resulted in the most important capture recorded for some years in the United States.

How the department got its first information, which brought about the capture of the safe-burglars, is still a mystery, and one of those secrets which may, perhaps, never transpire, but this much is known: Chief Farley got the clue and immediately detailed several detectives to a certain point on Broadway, opposite the base ball ground. The sidewalk here is in the form of a plank platform, leading over a slope in the ground which marks the delimitation between the street and the bottom along Cherry Creek. The bridging is high enough to admit a man beneath it and is several hundred feet in length. At one end of this walk, hidden beneath it, was found a cloth casing, containing a collection of the finest and most complete

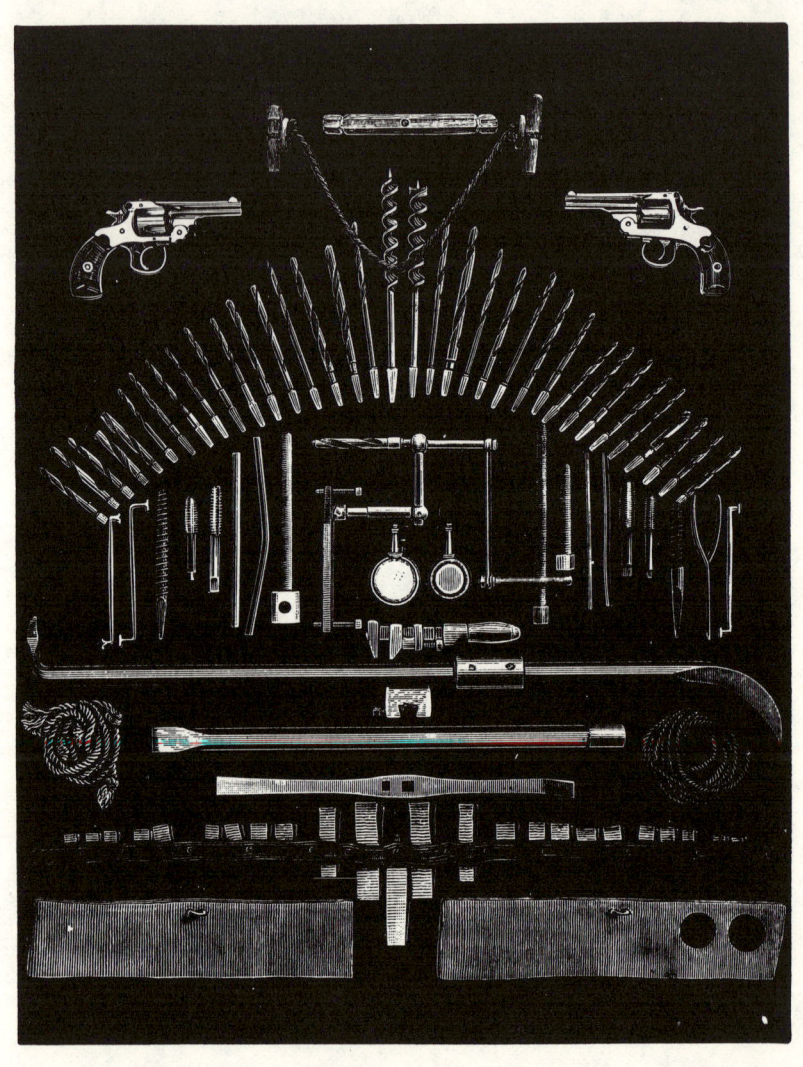

THE FAMOUS KIT OF SAFE-BREAKING AND BURGLARS' TOOLS,
CAPTURED BY THE DENVER POLICE, NOV. 18, 1890.

set of burglars' tools ever made. A description of the find in detail may not be uninteresting.

There are one set of machine drills, numbering thirty pieces; two sectional jimmies with oilcloth casings, so arranged that they may be slung over the shoulders and carried beneath the coat, without fear of detection; twenty assorted drills; one sectional hand drill; three wedges, so fine that they will enter the smallest possible crevice; two oil cans; coil of fuse; three double skeleton keys; one pair of door nippers; three punches; one screw punch; two screw drivers; one monkey wrench; two sets of combination tools.

There is also a diagram, upon the edge of which there is "M" which evidently stands for Mosler, the name of the make of one of the safes used by the Denver Brewing Company and the drawing is a diagram of the combination lock, exact in lines and measurements. All these are now in the detective office carefully and artistically arranged in a glass case, including the revolvers taken from the burglars later on. The exact reproduction, on the next page, will give an accurate idea of the "kit," the sight of which would make the bosom of an expert safe-blower heave with envy.

The capture of these tools, including the stolen watch and chain which were wrapped up in the same bundle, had leaked out in some manner to the knowledge of other members of the force. Chief Farley fearing that this might spread and reach the ears of the burglars and thus thwart his plans for their capture, assembled the twelve men who had the secret and placed them under a solemn oath not to divulge what they knew until he should see fit to release them from their oath. Every man proved faithful to his oath.

Three at a time, did the detectives do watch duty and relieve each other when rest was necessary, and thus the entire force of detectives served in turn, lying in wait and watching for their prey. At last, on the third night, Detectives McAndrews, Ustick and Clark stationed themselves under the board walk, where no passers-by might see them. The weather was cold and the officers, in anticipation of another long night of watching and waiting had wrapped themselves up as warmly as possible; but it was destined to be the hoped-for and eventful night. Everything was still; all was silent. McAndrews' hands rested on his shot-gun and Clark and Ustick had their revolvers convenient.

The hour was about eight when they saw three men stealthily creeping down the embankment and under the platform walk, where they apparently searched for something. They did not find what they sought and seemed at a loss. No wonder; the tools were safely at Police Headquarters. One step brought them sufficiently near to discover to them the men in ambush. One glance was sufficient. Simulating entire indifference they turned and walked away. They had taken but a few steps, landing on the side-walk, when the voice of Officer McAndrews commanded them to stop: "Gentlemen, we are officers. We want to talk to you." Instead of stopping the three men broke into a run. One of them had a revolver in his hand and Detective McAndrews, realizing that the men would escape, drew a bead upon this one and fired.

The man dropped. He had received the charge in his left leg between the knee and the thigh; another of the three endeavored to get behind a telegraph pole. But here he encountered Detective Clark, who placed his revolver at his breast with the injunction to throw up his hands or he would be a dead man. He did not hesitate to do as he was ordered and the officer ran his hand back of him and took from his hip pocket a 44-calibre Smith & Wesson revolver. The third man, having gained an advantage, ran up the street pursued by Messrs. Clark and Ustick, but as there were pedestrians along the street they feared to fire lest they might hit an innocent person; consequently the fellow escaped. A patrol-wagon was summoned and the victors and their captives were rapidly driven to the police station. Dr. Smith examined the wounded man and pronounced him badly hurt. The bone above the knee was shattered and he was taken to the county hospital where he still lies strongly guarded.' The other man, after being searched, was locked up. The men were evidently after the tools, and it is thought that preparations had been made to break into a bank on that same night. It has since transpired that the two men captured are among the most noted, expert and dangerous burglars in America. They gave their names as McDevitt and West. The wounded man is McDevitt. Who the third man was is not known. He doubtlessly got far away on that same night.

RECORD OF THE CAPTIVES.

Under the fire of Chief Farley the prisoners made some very doubtful and improbable statements regarding themselves. One thing, however, was apparent to the Department from the first; that they had succeeded in bagging a brace of very precious birds and the sequel has corroborated the accuracy of the premise. In the endeavor to place the men, Chief Farley has received the following communications by wire and mail:

LETTER FROM M. V. BORGMAN, CHIEF OF POLICE OF DETROIT.

DETROIT, Nov. 23, 1890.

J. F. FARLEY, ESQ.,
    Sup't of Police, Denver, Colo.

Dear Sir:—The man Frank West, whose picture you enclose to me, is recognized by a number of our people as Jim Maguire, alias Cap Roach, an all-around thief and desperate burglar, whose home is in Windsor, Ontario, where he is well known to everybody. Some three years ago he married at Windsor, the wife of Tom Bigelow, the burglar, who is better known by the *nom de plume* of Little Louise. This is not by any means his first trip to Denver, as he was in Denver at the time that Tom Gallagher, the Chicago pick-pocket, was shot and killed by Dan Hunt, in a variety theatre in your city, about two years ago, and was one of a mob of thieves who came there to operate at that time. The killing of Gallagher by Hunt led to the breaking up of the mob, and they left Denver, first securing Hunt's release from prison, and coming back east Maguire went to his home in Windsor. * * * In Windsor Maguire opened a restaurant, which soon became the headquarters for all the traveling thieves in the country, and many drinking bouts and carousals were carried on in the place, until it became notorious. At that time his Denver friend, Dan Hunt, made a headquarters at this place. Maguire, while on a drinking spree, committed an indecent assault on a French boy who lived in Windsor. The boy was scarcely more than half-witted. The thing got out to the public and created a great deal of excitement and Maguire was arrested and sent five years to the Kingston penitentiary on account of it. This was in March, 1890, and on the 16th of October, in company with another convict named John Leslie Cook, he escaped from the prison hospital, and the receipt of his picture is the first that has been heard of him since then. He is described by Warden M. Lovell of Kingston penitentiary, as five feet six and three-quarters inches high, fair complexion, blue eyes, brown hair, face covered with red blotches about the size of peas, first finger on left hand gone, weighed in March, 1890, one hundred and eighty pounds, but lost much during his confinement in prison. This man is as desperate a burglar as there is on the road, and a man of considerable skill and ability. I will write you further particulars regarding the other man, and I wish you would send me an accurate description of him and let me know whether he compares with the description enclosed of—— * * *

Yours Truly,
M. V. Borgman.

[There are omissions which are designated by the stars, this being private matter, and not for publication.—Ed.]

LETTER FROM DONALD MACKAY, ESQ.

Vermilye & Co.,
    Bankers,
16 & 18 Nassau St.,
New York City.

New York, Nov. 29, 1890.

To the Chief of Police,
    Denver, Colorado.

Dear Sir:—I am this morning informed by Inspector Byrnes of this city that you have arrested one known to us as "Milky McDonald," who escaped some months since from Hackensack jail at Hackensack, N. J. He was charged by us with burglary in the first degree, and breaking and entering a safe. The testimony is such that had we the man we could give him at least fifteen years. I understand that he is wounded. Will you please inform me as soon as possible how much of a case you have against him and if not able to hold him and give him as long time as we will here, would it not be better to surrender him to us as he is under indictment for that charge? If so, we will send and get him. Please give me full information. I refer you with pleasure to Inspector Byrnes of New York as to the statement of facts. Yours truly,

Donald Mackay,
President of Englewood Protective
Society, Englewood, N. J.

And of Firm of Vermilye & Co.,
    of New York City.

TELEGRAMS.

December. 1, 1890.

Dated Portsmouth, Ont.
    To J. F. Farley,
        Chief of Police, Denver.

Identified photo as Maguire easily. Facts are as you state. Will write you particulars at once.   M. Lovell, Warden.

December 1, 1890.

Dated St. Paul, Minn.
    To Jas. McParland,
        Opera House Block, Denver, Colo.

Tell Farley Robert identifies burglar McDermott as James, alias Milky McDonald, noted New York burglar, wanted at Hackensack, N. J., for burglary committed at Englewood. Broke jail at Hackensack, is desperate character. Will have to be closely guarded or will break jail in Denver. See Byrnes' book, page 129. W. A. PINKERTON.

DECEMBER 2, 1890.

Dated Boston, Mass.
  To CHIEF OF POLICE FARLEY,
    Denver, Colorado.

Your burglar West is Cap Roach of Windsor, Ont., an escape from Kingston penitentiary. His pal is Milky McDonald, wanted at Englewood, N. J., where he broke jail. A. W. COOKE,
Editor Police News.

From the *Police News* of Dec. 15, 1888, we learn that James McDonald alias "Milky" McDonald is one of the most notorious bank thieves and burglars in this country. He was connected with Joel Dollard, Geo. Feyth and Kid McMannus in the Fairchild burglary of Bridgeport, Conn. He, Clark and Connors did all the safe work in Boston, about six years ago. McDonald's age is about thirty-one,—he is five feet nine and one-half inches in height, weighs one hundred and fifty pounds, has light hair and blue eyes, of medium build and light complexion. He has tatooed on his left arm the initials "J. McD." and an anchor. Has a dot on left hand between thumb and forefinger. He has done some of the neatest jobs in England. He is also charged with the murder of police officer Albert W. Thayer, Detroit, Nov. 26, 1888.

All this information corresponds with the men West and McDermott alias McDevitt and it will be seen that the capture of these dangerous and notorious criminals is of utmost importance. That our police should have succeeded in their capture is a victory to be proud of and will add not a little to the enviable reputation already enjoyed by the Denver Police Department.

CHAPTER X.

THE DENVER POLICE MUTUAL AID ASSOCIATION.

Most of the large cities of the United States, and many of the smaller ones, have either a Police Pension Fund or a Mutual Aid Fund. Some cities have both these funds. It is most fitting that there should be such organizations. Recently, in an interview in one of the Denver newspapers, one of our leading citizens, Mr. Donald Fletcher, is quoted as saying that between the citizens and danger to life and property stands the police officer, ready at a moment's notice to imperil or sacrifice his life, and that there should be a relief fund to assist the widows and children, where an officer gives up his life in the protection of life and property. Mr. Fletcher's humane statements will be voiced by the public at large. No citizen knows but what at any moment, in the protection of his interests, the life of an officer may be sacrificed. Within a short time two brave officers, Wanless and Phillips, have been killed while in the discharge of their duties, the former in the protection and, in all probability, the saving of life, the latter in the protection of both life and property. In such misfortunes, the Mutual Aid steps forward to assist the families of the deceased officers, and the larger the fund may grow, of course the more good it may have in its power to do.

The Denver Police Mutual Aid Association was organized in March, 1890. The desirability of such an association in the Denver Police Department was recognized by Chief Farley, who in connection with Inspector Hawley and Lieutenant Phillips submitted the matter to the force. The proposition met with favor and from suggestion to realization consumed only as much time as was required to perfect the organization. Sergeant P. A. Clay is President and Lieutenant John E. Phillips, Treasurer. The other officers are members of the Department. There is a board of trustees and an investigating committee. Only members of the Police Force are eligible to membership in the Association. The organization of this Association is one of the many things that reflect much credit on the present Department.

A last word may be said for our Police Force. The City of Denver has grown to be a metropolis of nearly one hundred and fifty thousand population. The city covers a great deal of ground. A large floating population is always here, and there comes to us the refuse of the worst elements of eastern cities, that drifts westward to the confines of the country, and what part of it does not make its home here, remains long enough to do its utmost to accomplish the worst possible ends. Considering these matters, and the comparatively small number of Police Officers that we have, the work accomplished by our Police Department compares most favorably with other departments. Each officer has very much too large a beat to patrol, and it is to be hoped that the day is at hand when Denver will show the same progress that exists in her commercial pursuits, in the organization of a metropolitan force of men adequate to the demands.

[THE END.]

ROSTER
OF THE
Denver Police Department.

OFFICERS.

NAME.	RANK.
JOHN F. FARLEY,	Chief.
C. A. HAWLEY,	Inspector.
JOHN E. PHILLIPS,	First Lieutenant.
HENRY NEWMEYER,	Second Lieutenant.
M. B. NORKETT,	First Sergeant.
WM. BOHANNA,	Second Sergeant.
J. W. MCNEIL,	Third Sergeant.
W. M. TEETER,	Fourth Sergeant.
P. A. CLAY,	Fifth Sergeant.
GEORGE GREEN,	Sixth Sergeant.
R. H. MACDONALD,	Seventh Sergeant.
JAMES COLLINS,	Clerk.
GEORGE DAVISON,	Clerk.
WM. FOWLER,	Jailer.
ISAAC LANGAN,	Assistant Jailer.
R. M. MURPHY,	Assistant Jailer.
L. H. WYGANT,	Turnkey.

PRIVATES.

NAME.	RANK.
JOSEPH BARR,	Patrolman.
JOHN BAUGH,	"
P. F. LEGERE,	"
JOHN SWANSAY,	"
E. V. WILLIAMS,	"
JOHN O'DONNELL,	"
PATRICK DONNELLY,	"
J. A. SCRIVNER,	"
JOHN MCDERMOTT,	"
F. T. BRUCE,	"

OF THE DENVER POLICE.

NAME.	RANK.
T. J. RILEY,	Patrolman.
W. P. DUNNINGTON,	"
W. W. JACKSON,	"
A. F. PETERSON,	"
JOHN HOLMES,	"
A. E. HUNT,	"
M. J. GOLDEN,	"
PERCY SMITH,	"
W. W. LOY,	"
S. T. SABIN,	"
O. D. JACKSON,	"
H. SHREVE,	"
WM. A. MORRISON,	"
Z. T. COLE,	"
JOHN BRADY,	"
H. C. SMITH,	"
H. R. RAMSEY,	"
O. P. WIGGINS,	"
JOHN HUNSBERGER,	"
JAMES WALKER,	"
WM. SMITH,	"
H. T. BENSON,	"
A. M. PETERS,	"
G. H. PETERSON,	"
C. M. ALEXANDER,	"
J. P. ANDERSON,	"
J. C. REED,	"
A. J. NORRIS,	"
PATRICK LEWIS,	"
JAMES RAFFERTY,	"
M. M. BURNETT,	"
J. D. BUTTON,	"
GEO. W. KELLOGG,	"
W. F. HENDRICKS,	"
CHARLES OLSEN,	"
BART. SULLIVAN,	"
J. J. KEANE,	"
P. J. DALEY,	"
GEORGE PATTON,	"
W. C. BAKER,	"
A. E. NORTON,	"
J. H. WILCOX,	"
E. P. SMITH,	"
JAMES DEKEATOR,	"
H. L. PALMER,	"

HISTORIC SUPPLEMENT

NAME.	RANK.
T. E. CAMPBELL,	Patrolman.
H. H. ISETT,	"
O. L. HAMSHER,	"
A. RORRISON,	"
M. SHAUGHNESSY,	"
OLAF SWANSON,	"
H. A. MEINART,	"
I. G. GILMORE,	"
FRED. LINDGUIST,	"
J. C. JONES,	City Herder.
GEORGE W. SEFTON,	Assistant City Herder.
MRS. SADIE M. LIKENS,	Police Matron.
R. L. TAYLOR,	Signal Operator.
GEORGE IVERS,	Signal Operator.
H. R. WILLIAMS,	Signal Operator.
M. F. LYON,	Bailiff.
AL. LEACH,	Lineman.

DETECTIVES.

SAMUEL HOWE,	Ass't Chief of Detectives.
WM. INGERSOLL,	Detective.
C. E. CLARK,	"
J. J. MCANDREWS,	"
HOWARD THOMPSON,	"
JOHN HOLLAND,	"
JOHN J. LEYDEN,	"
W. H. RENO,	"
WM. USTICK,	"

INDEX

abortionists, 434-42
Academy of Music, 491, 492
Ackerman, Capt., 57
Adams, Charles Francis, 462-3
Adams, Monro, 355-6
Adams, Samuel, 26
Adams Express Co., 220
adultery, 318, 509-10
aliases, 241
Allaire, Anthony J., 101
Allen, J., 457
Allen, James, 630
Allen, Theodore, 488
Allen, Mrs. "Wes," 293-4
Alton (Ill.) Penitentiary, 562
Ambrose, James, 40, 41, 374
American Exchange Bank, 338
American Fire Insurance Co., 562
American Mabille (dance-hall), 488-9
Anderson, John, 26
Arapahoe County (Colo.) jail, 631
Armory Hall (dance-hall), 489-91
Arnold, Constable & Co., 313, 356
arrests
  modus operandi of, 184, 186-7
  on suspicion, 194-6, 219, 387
Arrowsmith, Capt., 214
Ascher, Dr., 440-1
Ashley, Benjamin, 354-5
Ashley, Benjamin (imposture), 351-5
Associated Press, 94
Astor Place riots, 43-7
Atlantic Mutual Insurance Co., 337-8
Auburn (N.Y.) State Prison, 149, 254

Austin, William, 325
Australian voting system, 605

Bagnicki, Ernst de, 443-8
Bagnicki, Marie de, 444, 445, 447
Bailey, Joseph L., 625-6
Baker, John E., 66
Baker, Lewis, 49, 51
Baker, Mary Ann, 66
Balch, W. R., 415
Baltimore, 68-9, 72
Bank of California (San Francisco), 110, 112
Bank of England, 172, 175, 563, 564
Bank of Nevada, 348
Bank of the Republic (N. Y. City), 343
bank robbers, 236-78
Barber, A. D., 591
Barker, Anselm H., 615
Barker, W. J., 618, 632, 633
Barnard, Judge George G., 328
Barnard, Dr. James W., 176-7
Barnes, Harry, 355
Barnum's Museum, 93, 94-9
Barrett, Judge George C., 374
Barron, James W., 244-6, 274
Bartlett, Frances Amelia, 61
Bartlett, Lieut. W. A., 61
Bates, Joseph E., 618-19, 635, 637, 649
Baxter, Charles, 138
Becker, Charles, 339-41, 510, 512
Beekman, B. F., 443
beggars, 449-52
Bellevue Hospital, 53
Bennett, James, 529
Bennett, James Gordon, 97

Bennett, Mrs. James Gordon, 62
Benson, Egbert, 33
Bernard, Canon Leon J., 476-8
Berry, Jacob, 573-4
Bidwell, Austin, 175
Bidwell, Biron, 175
Bigelow, Tom, 671
Billings, Mrs. J. H., 457
Bird, Sgt. Isaac, 189
Black-and-Tan (dance-hall), 485-8
blackmail
   cases of, 99-100, 318-19, 359, 581-4
   and police officers, 581-4, 602-3
Blackwell's Island, 79, 398, 490, 507
Blaine, James G., 502
Blatchford, Richard Milford, 563
Blatchford, Judge Samuel, 563
Bliss, Col. George, 344
Bodine, Maria, 436
Bohanna, William, 655
Booth, Edwin, 105
"Border Ruffian War," 625
Borgman, M. V., 671-2
Boston Herald, 415
Boudinot, Capt. Tobias, 33
Bowie, Bill, 359
Bowlsby, Alice Augusta, 440
Brady, Judge, 573
Brady, Denny, 148, 149
Brady, Henry, 636-7
Brady, James
   and burglary of Manhattan Savings Institution, 261-2, 267
   downfall of, 473, 475
   escape of from Sing Sing, 300, 302
   and John D. Grady, 473
   and Dan Noble, 254
   suspected by Walling, 386
Brady, Mayor William V., 33
Brendlinger, Hiram J., 617, 626
Brennan, John, jewellery store of, 273

bribery
   of jurors, 26, 268
   political, 161-3
Brockway, Charles O. *Alias of* Vanderpool, Charles O., *q.v.*
Brockway, William E. *Error for* Brockway, Charles O., 342
brokers, 127-31. *See also* gambling, Wall Street
Brooklyn, 543, 551
Brooks, Orson, 630
Brower, Charles, 99
"Brower, Vieve," 99
Brown, Hall, & Vanderpoel, 58
Bryan (warden), 298
Buckingham, R. G., 618, 633
"bunco steerers," 329-30, 574
"Buntline, Ned," 46, 623
Burdell, Dr. Harvey, 52
Burden, Capt. Henry, 117
Bureau of Elections, 605-6
Burger, Capt., 624
Burger, Bertha, 441, 442
burglars. *See also* thieves
   tools of, 240, 668-9
burglary. *See* safe-breaking
Burke, Mrs. B. F., 356
Burke, Joseph, 356
Burns, James, 242
Burr, Capt., 61
Burton, Jesse, 630
Butchers' School, London, 344
Butler, Judge, 561
Byers, William N., 616
Byrnes, Inspector Thomas
   apprehension of a servant girl by, 210-11
   and apprehension of various criminals, 266, 356, 370, 477
   consequences of appointment of, 179
   method of interrogation of, 189-90

Caffrey, Capt. Charles W., 468
Caldwell & Co., 108-10
Calhoun, Mrs. L. G., 105

INDEX. 683

Campbell (detective), 362, 366, 367
Campbell, Supt. Patrick, 543-4, 548-51
"Canada Mac." *See* McKay, William
Canon City, penitentiary at. *See* Colorado State Penitentiary
Cantlan, Phillip, 574
Cardozo, Judge Albert, 120
Carleton House mystery, 405-7
Carpenter, Clark, 673
Carpenter, Inspector Daniel, 153
Carr, T. J., 647
Case, Francis M., 618, 632
Casey, Jim, 272
Cassidy, James, 562
Castleton, Kate, 341
Centre, James D., 159
Cercle Française de l'Harmonie, 491-6
Chadwick, George W., 108, 110
Chapman, Joseph W., 340, 341
Chapman, Mary, 341
Charity Organization Society, 449
Charlestown (Mass.) State Prison. *See* Massachusetts State Prison (Charlestown)
Charlton Street gang, 534
Cherry, Capt. Thomas, 253, 254
Chicago, Burlington & Quincy Railroad, 645
child abuse, 500-2
Chinese, in New York
 and American women, 428-9
 characteristics of, 418-19, 432-3
 festivals of, 431-2
 gambling among, 422-7
 habits of, 419
 joss house of, 429-30
 numbers and habitations of, 419
 prostitution among, 427-8
 restaurants of, 430-1
 smoking of opium by, 419-22
 superstitions of, 427

Chinese riots, 628, 652
chloroform, 463-6
City Hall, 30
City Prison. *See* Tombs, the
Civil War. *See also* draft riots of *1863*
 causation of, 625
 W. T. De Voe and, 69-77
 Austin W. Hogle in, 636
 James W. Lomery in, 635
 Daniel W. Mays in, 633
 John C. Moore in, 617
 Thomas Sampson and, 69-77
 Charles B. Stone in, 634
 tension in period preceding, 68-9
Clapp, Hawley D., 408
Clapp, Mortimer R. and Robert C., 408-9
Clapp, Nellie, 408, 411
Clark (burglar). *See* Carpenter, Clark
Clark, Cyrus G., 108
Clark, E. E., 669-70
Clarke, George T., 617, 626
Clay, Percy A., 656, 674
Clayton, William M., 618, 627
"clergyman's garb" swindle, 134-5
Cleveland, Mrs. John F., 104
clues, used in catching thieves, 35-40, 210
Coakley, Abe, 246-7, 262, 264, 268
Coakley, T. A., 457
coal-cart thieves, 462
Coath, Mary Henrietta, 263, 271, 273-4, 277, 278
Coffin, Judge, 328
Collins, James, 663-4
Colorado Cattle Growers' Association, 626
Colorado State Penitentiary (Canon City), 631, 658, 659, 662
Colored Orphan Asylum, 79
Colt, John C., 26
Columbia Opera House, 573

Commissioner of Charities and Corrections, 394
Comstock, Anthony, 438
Condert Brothers, 476-7
confidence men, 329-30, 462, 574. *See also* swindlers; MacDonnell, George; Miller, Charles P.; Nephegyi, Dr. Gabor; Sheridan, Walter; swindlers; swindles; White, Plymouth
Conkling, George W., 411-13
Conkling, Jonas, 48
Connauton, T. H., 149-50
Connolly, Michael, 160
Connor, Billy, 242, 243
Connor, D. D., 58
Connor, Washington E., 369-70, 372
Connors, Tommy, 673
Consolidation Act, 178
Contre-Guerrillas, 617
Cook, Charles A., 617, 623, 625
Cook, D. J., 348
Cook, Gen. David J., 627-9, 632, 645, 649, 652
Cook, John Leslie, 671
Cook, Joseph C., 436
Cooke, A. W., 673
corruption in government. *See* municipal government
Cosgrove, Frank, 442
counterfeit money, 126-7, 166, 170, 256, 357-8
counterfeiters, 126-30, 164-77, 510, 520. *See also* Robinson, William H.; swindlers; swindles; Vanderpool, Charles O.
Cowing, Judge Rufus B., 574
Cowley, Rev. Edward, 500-2
Cox, Chastine, 414-17
cranks, 507-9, 552-5
Crawford, Charles, 359
Cremorne (dance-hall), 482-4
crime, causation of, 331-2, 596-7
criminals
  description of, 566-7
  life-expectation of, 241
  photographs and photographing of, 191-3, 566
Crocker (detective), 659-60
Crosby, Col. J. Schuyler, 510
Culkin, Peter, 499
Cummings, Dave, 537
Cunard line, 215, 216
Cunningham, Mrs., 52-3
Custer, Gen. George A., 634
"Custom House racket," 461-2
Cutler, Bill, 558
Cutting, Francis B., 528-9

Dana, E. L., 622
dance-halls, 479-96
Danser, Ann Louise, 385, 386
Danser, Matthias, 383-6
Davenport, John I., 344
Davis, Judge, 573
Davis, Theodore M., 247, 250
Davis-Holland murder case, 127
debtors, 393
De Lacey, Peter, 574-5
DeLano, Milton M., 617-18, 627
Delmonico, Charles, 506
Democrats, 160-1, 597, 604
Dempsey, Arthur, 456, 458
Denning, Frank, 537, 539
Denver, City of
  charter of, 616, 618
  Fire Department of, 618
  origins of, 615-16
  population of in *1890*, 615
  sheep farming and, 633
Denver Brewing Company, 668, 669
Denver Police Department. *See* police, Denver
Denver Police Mutual Aid Association, 674-5
De Peyster, Gen. J. Watts, 456
detectives in N. Y. City
  blackmail by, 581-4
  characteristics of, 517-18
  compared with French and English, 519
  duties of, 517

INDEX. 685

detectives in N. Y. City *(cont'd)*
   methods of operation of, 519-20
   popular concept of, 517
detention of complainant, 575
Devlin, William, 356
De Voe, W. T., 69-77
Dexter (Maine) Savings Bank, 244, 274, 275
diet of prisoners, 391, 392, 397-8
Dilks, George, 153, 228, 247, 473
Disbecker, Abraham, 591-2
"dives," 479-96
divorces, fraudulent, 355-6
Dix, Gen. John A., 93
Dix, Rev. Morgan, 306-20
Dobbs, Johnny, 246, 262, 272, 275, 278
Dolan, James, 404
Dolan, Patrick, 122, 268
Dollard, Joel, 673
Donaldson, John, 378
Donohue, Justice, 501
Donovan, Charles A.
   and apprehension of Mike Shannon's gang, 534-7
   and attempted robbery of Thomas J. Smith, 533
   position of, 531
   and William Scott's jail-escape attempt, 537-9
Doolittle, J. K., 631
Dorcey, Joseph M., 402, 404, 477-8
Douglas, Joseph, 200, 202-8
Doyan, Dorcas, 25-6
Doyle, Thomas, 573
Draft riots of *1863*, 78-86
Drake, John, 471-2
Draper, "Shang"
   and Dexter Savings Bank robbery, 275
   and George Howard, 274, 275
   and Manhattan Savings Institution robbery, 262-3
   and Northampton Bank robbery, 242, 243
   saloon of, 274, 299, 399, 400

Dreyfus (thief), 529, 530
drunkenness, arrests for, 196, 387, 388, 506
Duboise, W. C., 630
Dumont, Bishop, 476
Dunlap, Thomas, 242, 243, 539
Dunn, Jerry, 51
Dunn, Robert S., 292
Duryea, Nicholas W., 467-8
duties of police superintendent, 180-4
Duval, Madame, 154
Duykinck, Mary G., 456
Dwyer, Dan, 378
"dynamite scare," 570-1

Earl, James H., 99
Eastern Penitentiary (Phila.), 561, 564
Eberman, "Big Jack," 558
Eckel, John J., 53
Edson, Mayor, 374
Edson, William D., 242-4
Ehrich, Moses, 222
Elbert, Samuel J., 628
Elder, George, 526-7
Elder, William G., 236-7, 239, 247
elections
   desirability of new attitudes towards, 604
   threats of violence at, 375
Elliot, "Little Joe," 339-41
Elliott, Joseph, 51-2
Ellis, George, 122
eloping couples, 567-8
embezzlement, 99
Emerson, Pete, 262, 264, 268, 533
Engleman (thief), 148
Ennis, Horace, 459, 460, 461
escapes from prisons, 243, 292-305, 341, 539, 561
Excise Commissioners, 515
excise laws, violations of, 514-15, 572-4, 601-2
executions, public, 30, 64-6

686 INDEX.

Farley, John F.
  appointment of, 619, 643
  apprehension of burglars by, 658-61, 668-73
  early life of, 639
  in fighting with Indians, 639-43
  innovations of in police department, 664
  and Thiel Detective Agency, 643
Farley, Philip, 247, 301, 302
Farragut, Admiral David G., 93
Farrell, Edward, 533-4
"fences," 40, 143, 279-80, 453-4. *See also* Mandelbaum, Frances
Feyth, George, 673
Field, David Dudley, 60
Field, Kate, 516
Fields, Philo, 124
Fields, Tom, 162
financial panic of *1857*, 67
Fink, Charles, 443-8
fires
  Barnum's Museum destroyed by, 94-9
  plot to destroy New York by, 93
First National Bank of Maryland, 256
first offenses, sentences for, 333
Fish, Hamilton, Jr., 510
Fish, James D., 390-1
Fiske, Col. James, Jr., 158-9, 162, 492
Fitzsimmons, Bernard, 303, 304
Flanagan (coroner), 441
Fletcher, Donald, 674
Flood, John, 378
Florence (Italy), 510
Floswell, Walker F., 347
forgers. *See also* counterfeiters; Elliot, "Little Joe"; Gilman, William C.; Griffis, William; MacDonnell, George; Morey letter; Nephegyi, Dr. Gabor; Sheridan, Walter; Vanderpool, Charles O.; Van Eeten, Louis M.; Wilkes, George W.
  Florentine forgeries, 510
  personality and methods of, 337
Forrest, Edwin, 43, 48-9
Foster, Mary Ann, 328, 329
Foster, William, 154
"Four-fingered Jack." *See* Wright, Jack
Fox, Richard K., 373
Francis, Edward, 498
fraud. *See* swindlers
French Masquerade ball, 491-6
Fuchs, Andrew, 544-7

Gale (keeper), 302
Gallagher, Tom, 671
gallows, 29
gambling. *See also* Danser, Matthias; prize-fighting; Rowe, Johnny
  attempts to enforce laws against, 379-80, 577
  as cause of criminal acts, 382
  among Chinese, 422-7
  dishonesty of professionals at, 575-6
  nonenforcement of laws against, 180, 380-2, 574-5, 577
  participants in, 382-3
  types of, 379, 383
  Wall Street and, 382, 576-7
gangs, 48
Garfield, James A., 343-4, 502
Garvin, Samuel B., 107, 468
Gastlin, Capt. George W., 151, 152
Gates, Berry, 653
Gayles, Joseph, 146
Gaylor, Supt., 318, 319
Gearing, Edward, 276, 499
"Gentleman Joe." *See* Williamson, Eugene Fairfax
German News, 365

INDEX. 687

Germs, Louise, 443-8
Gerry, Elbridge T., 107, 501
Gilkinson (detective), 571
Gilman, William C., 337-9
Gilmore, J. J., 252-4
Glenn, Harry, 272
gold, discovery of in California, 42
gold rush, Pike's Peak area, 622, 625, 627
gold swindles, 127-31
Goodie, Ed. *Alias of* Gearing, Edward, *q.v.*
Goodrich, Charles, 547-9
"Gopher Bill." *See* Robinson, William H.
Gordon, Jim, 624
Gordon, Nathaniel, 64-6
Gordon, Steve, 159-60
Gorman, George, 630
Goss, Joe, 378
Gould, Jay, 368-72
Gould, Tom, 484
Grady, John D., 262, 291, 472-6, 535-6
Graham, Gen. B., 649
Graham, John, 107
Graham, Dr. R. H., 52
Grant, Gov. J. B., 623
Grant, Maxwell, 630
Grant, Ulysses S., 618, 636
grave robbers, 224-35
Gray, Samuel S., 407
Greeley, Horace, 33, 72, 108, 635
Green, George L., 656
Green, Col. Martin E., 633
Greenfield (prize-fighter), 374, 379
Greenwich Saving Bank, 259
Greimet, Louise. *Alias of* Germs, Louise, *q.v.*
Griffis, William, 344-9
Guiteau, Charles, 502-5
Gunner, John, 362, 364, 366
Gunsenhauser & Co. (Chicago), 527-8

Gutermuth, Louis W., 407-9, 411

Hackensack, N.J., 87-93, 672-3
Hackett, Recorder, 108, 448, 573
Haddock, Rev., and impostor, 557-8
Haley, Catherine Maria, 327, 329
Hall, Major, 586-7
Hall, Mayor A. Oakey, 154-6, 160, 222
Hallgarten & Co., 108-10
Hamill, Sexton, 224-8
Handley, Mary, 548-50
hangings, 61-2, 66
harbor police, 144, 145, 151-2, 534
Hardy, John, 85-6
Harper, John, 618
Harrington, Bill, 374-5
Harris family, 332
Hart, Emanuel B., 120
Hatters' Bank, Bethel, Conn., 236, 238, 239
Haurey, Daniel, 220, 222-3
Havemeyer, Mayor William F., 591-2
Haverstick, Wilbur H., 411-13
Hawk, Henry, 297
Hawkes, B. Shafton, 410-11
Hawkes, Josephine, 407-11
Hawley, Charles A., 645-9, 650, 665, 674
Hawley, Seth C., 180
Hayes, Thomas, 146
Haymarket (dance-hall), 480-2
Hays, Capt., 71
Hayward murder case, 645-9
Hearing, "Old Man," 339, 341
Hedden, Capt. Henry, 200, 202
Heidelburg, Charles, 444
Heins, Capt. William R., 200, 202-4
Heron, Matilda, 326
Heubsch, Dr., 363, 368
Hewitt, Abram S., 496
Hickey (detective), 400

688 INDEX.

Hickey, William R., 634-5, 651
Hicks, Albert E., 61-2
Hicks, Charles, 562
Higgins, Alexander, 456, 457
Hill, Harry, 484-5
Hilton, Judge Henry, 225-31, 233
Hoffman, John, 58, 156, 258
Hogan, John, 499
Hogle, Austin W., 635-6
Holland, John, 662
Holly, Edgar E., 251
Hook gang, 148
Hooper, J. S. and Lucy H., 516
Hope, Harry, 399
Hope, Jimmy
  and Dexter Savings Bank robbery, 246
  escape of from Sing Sing, 300
  and Manhattan Savings Institution robbery, 262, 264, 268
  mentioned, 272
  and Dan Noble, 254
Hope, John, 267, 268
Hopkins, G. M., 629-31
horse swindle, 135-7
"hot water" scheme, 132-4
House of Detention, 574, 575
Howard, George
  and Dexter Savings Bank robbery, 246
  life and career of, 269-75, 278
  and Manhattan Savings Institution robbery, 261-2, 263, 264
  murder of, 269, 275-8, 287, 401
  and Northampton Bank robbery, 242
Howard, Harry, 460, 461
Howard, Joe, Jr., 94
Howe, Samuel, 660, 661-2
Howe, William F., 281, 510
Howlett, Nicholas, 138, 143, 144, 148
Hubbard, Albert L., 560-1
Hubbell, George B., 301

Hudson County (N.J.) jail, 215, 537
Hughes, Archbishop John, 61, 436
Hull, Dr. Alonzo G., 414
Hull, Mrs. Jane Lawrence De Forrest, 413-17
Hummel, Abraham, 281, 510
"Hungry Joe." *See* Lewis, Joseph
Hunt, A. C., 626
Hunt, Dan, 671
Hutchinson, William, 325
Hutton, Rev. Mancius C., 456
Hyer, Tom, 40-2, 374, 583-4
"Hyer, Tom," 166-7

Iddesleigh, Lord, 570-1
Imley, John K., 408, 409
Indians, campaigns against, 632, 634, 639-42
Ingalls, Judge, 573
insurance company, fraud on, 443-8
Invalid Corps, 80
Irishmen, 46, 154-8
Irving, "Jim," 160
Irving, Johnny
  death of, 299, 399-401
  escape of from Raymond Street jail, 298-9
  mentioned, 274
  and murder of George Howard, 275, 278, 401
Irving, Washington, 32

jails, 187, 188-93, 390-8. *See also under specific institutions*
Jameson, Inspector William, 156
Japanese embassy, 62, 216
Jefferson Territory, 616
Jenkins, Henry B., 99-100
Jersey City (N.J.) National Bank, 537
Jesup, Paton & Co., 347
Jewellers' Association of New York, 564

INDEX.

Jewett, Helen. *Alias of* Doyan, Dorcas, *q.v.*
Johnson, Andrew, 343
Johnson, "Bill," 646
Johnson, Oliver, 106, 108
Johnson, William, 138
Jones, Becky, 390-1
Jones, Charles, 562
Jones, Gen. Patrick H., 230-1, 232-3
joss house, 429-30
Jourdan, Supt. John
  and apprehension of Hyer, 584
  and murder of Benjamin Nathan, 117-18, 122, 124-5
  and Ocean National Bank robbery, 250
  picture, 123
  position of, 154
Jourdan, Maggie, 292-4, 296
Journal of Commerce, 94
judiciary of N.Y., 606
Judson, Edward Z. C., 46, 623
junk dealers, 143
juries, 26, 268, 574
Jurors, office of Commissioner of, 603

Kansas City Mail, 617
Kansas City Times, 617
Kealy, Capt. James, 230, 343
Keenan, Patsy, 468
Kehler, John H., 623
Keith, W. M., 623
Kelly, Francis R., 555-6, 557-60, 562, 564-6, 569-71
Kelly, William, 264, 268
Kelsey, Lizzie, 346
Kelso, Supt. James J., 117-18, 125, 154, 156, 247
Keneally, Patrick, 251
Kennedy, Supt. John A.
  and cases of blackmail by detectives, 581-4
  and draft riots of *1863*, 78
  and investigation of anti-Lincoln feeling in Baltimore, 68, 69, 71, 77, 78
  period of office of, 153-4
  and robbery of Greenwich Savings Bank messenger, 260
  and robbery of Rufus L. Lord, 460
Kensington bank robbery. *See* South Kensington National Bank
kidnapping, 198-208
Killbach, Louis, 668
King, Charles, 251-2
King, Richard, 220, 247, 343, 457
Kingston (Ontario) Penitentiary, 671, 673
Kirby (thief), 556
Kirkpatrick, Thomas, 347, 349
Klineschmidt, Lena, 87-93
Knox, E. M., 336
Kohler, Julius, 574
Kranowitch, Dr., 445
Kurtz, Dr., 445
Kurtz, Michael, 286

laws. *See also* excise laws, violations of
  absence of against adultery, 509
  governing appearance before police magistrates, 222-3
Lawson, Thomas D., 527-9
lawyers, 193
Leary, John "Red," 242, 243, 262, 302-5, 400
"Leatherheads," 32
Lee, William Scott, 619, 636, 649, 654, 655
Lees, Isaiah W., 348
Lemmon, Mattie, 653
Leo XIII, 476
Leonard, George, 456-7
Leonard, James, 153
Leslie, George Leonidas. *Alias of* Howard, George, *q.v.*
Leslie, Mrs. George Leonidas. *See* Coath, Mary Henrietta
Lessoffsky, Admiral, 93
Lewis, Joseph, 351-5, 360

licenses
  for dance-halls, 484, 601
  for sale of liquor, 601-2
Lincoln, Abraham, 68, 69, 77
Lind, Jenny, 49
Livingstone, John R. *Alias of*
  Van Eeten, Louis M., *q.v.*
Loar, Chief, 660-1
Lock, James, 559-60
Logan, Mary, 384
Lohman, Ann, 434-41
Lohman, Charles R., 436
Lomery, James M., 635, 651
Londoner, Wolfe, 619, 643, 651
Lord, Capt. Bowen G., 583
Lord, Rufus L., 458-61
Lord & Taylor, 313
Loring, Col. Charles, 52
lotteries, 180
Lovell, Michael, 671, 672
Lowrie, Bill, 144, 149
Ludlow Street Jail, 243, 302-5, 389-93
Lycoming Insurance Co., Muncy, Pa., 273
Lyons (detective), 457

McAndrews, J. J., 669-70
McAuley, Jerry, 482-3
McCallin, John C., 632-3, 663
McCarthy, Sam, 144
McClosky, Joe, 563-4
McClosky, John "Country," 374
McClure, W. P., 616
McCord, John, 167, 236-7, 239
McCormick, Tom, 272
McCoy, Frank, 561
McCoy, James, 272
McDonald, James "Milky" *(alias* McDevitt), 671, 672-3
MacDonald, R. H., 656-7
MacDonnell, George, 172-7
Macé, Gustave, 516
McElrath, Thomas, 33
McFarland, Abby and Daniel, 101-8
McGlory, Billy, 489-91

McGonigal, Kate, 328
McGonigal, Mary, 328-9
Mackay, Donald, 672
McKay, William, 251-2, 256
McMannus, "Kid," 673
McNamara, John, 504-5
McNeil, John W., 655
McParland, James, 672
Macready, William Charles, 43-4
Madison Square Garden, 374
Maguire, Jim, 671-3
mail coach, robbery of, 630-1
Mali (Belgian consul-general), 476
Mandelbaum, "Mother" Frances
  activities and life of, 280-91
  and John D. Grady, 473
  and George Howard and his gang, 269, 277, 278
  and Lena Klineschmidt, 87
  and Manhattan Savings Institution robbery, 262
Mandelbaum, Julius, 287
Mandelbaum, William, 280
Mangam, John, 115-17, 119, 120
Manhattan Magazine, 356
Manhattan Savings Institution, robbery of, 261-8, 270
Manning, F. C., 457
Manny, David, 302
Mansfield, Josephine, 492
Mapleson, Col. J. H., 124
Marine National Bank, 391
Marks & Son, 402
Marmaduke, Gen., 617
Martin, D. R., 250, 251
Massachusetts State Prison (Charlestown), 243, 539
Matsell, George W.
  and the Astor Place riots, 46
  and a Jersey City warehouse robbery, 215
  and a Maiden Lane burglary, 35, 36, 39, 40
  and police conflict of *1857,* 56, 60
  as president of Police Board, 178

INDEX. 691

Matsell, George W. *(cont'd)*
  and Thomas Smith, 525
  and suppression of gambling-houses, 382
  and Uling's insurance fraud, 443
Matthews, James, 196, 515
Maxwell, George L., 339-40
Maxwell, Dr. William H., 328
mayor, duties of, 29
Mays, Daniel W., 633-4
Meakim, Sgt. William, 441
Mechanics' Bank, Scranton, Pa., 563
Mendicity Society, 449
Merchants' Life Insurance Co., 443
Merchants' Police, 645
Messerschmidt, Charles, 500
Metropolitan police, 54-61
Mexican War, 622
Mexico City, 336
Middleford Press, 636
Milford (N.H.) National Bank, 273
Miller, Charles P., 359-61
Miller, Charley, 562
Miller, John G., 336
Miller, Lilly, 299-300, 302
Miller, "Shang," 558
Miller, W. A., 300, 302
Mint, Phila., 569-70
missing persons, 505-6, 521-2
Mitchell, Charley, 378
mobs, 153
"mock auction" swindles, 131-2
Monahan, John, 214, 215
Montgomery County Prison, Norristown, Pa., 271
Moon, Jim, 651-2
Moon, Mary, 301
Mooney, Jemmy, 275
Moore, John C., 616, 617, 622
Moore, Tommy, 343
Moran, Joseph, 562
Morey letter, 343-4
Morgan (bank director), 247

Morgan, Gen. J. B., 617
Morgan, William, 254
Morris, George, 630
Morris, Robert, 618, 635
Morrissey, John, 375-6, 382
Mosher, "Gill," 201-2
Mosher, William, 200-8
Muchler (counterfeiter), 357-8
municipal government, 160, 597-600, 604-6
Municipal police, 54-60
murders
  of Samuel Adams, 26
  of Dr. Harvey Burdell, 52-3
  at Carleton House, 405-7
  of Nevaciante Ciampi, 568-9
  committers of, 520-1
  of Dorcas Doyan, 25-6
  of Nicholas W. Duryea, 467-8
  of crew of the "E. A. Johnson," 61-2
  of Joseph Elliott, 51
  of Charles Goodrich, 547-51
  of Louis W. Gutermuth, 407-11
  of W. H. Haverstick, 411-13
  of George Howard, 269, 275-8
  of Mrs. J. L. De F. Hull, 413-17
  of John Irving, 399-401
  of Charles P. Miller, 359, 361
  motives for, 520-1
  of Benjamin Nathan, 115-24
  of James H. Noe, 402-4
  of a patrolman, 100
  of "Bill" Poole, 49-51
  of Avery D. Putnam, 154
  of Albert D. Richardson, 101-3
  by river pirates, 138-41, 145-6
  of Charles M. Rogers, 404-5
  of Mary Rogers, 26-9
  of William W. Simmons, 543-7
  of Henry J. Wagstaff, 66-7
  of Thomas Walker, 100
  of John Walsh, 399-401
Murphy, Michael, 456-7
Murphy, Capt. Michael J., 149
Murray, Robert, 256, 582-3

INDEX

Murray, Inspector William, 180, 228, 374, 384-5, 441
Musgrove gang, 629

Narath, Charles, 668
Nathan, Benjamin, 113-24
Nathan, Frederick, 113-17, 119, 120
Nathan, Washington, 113-15, 120-1, 122, 124
National Bank of Springfield, Ill., 562
"Native American" party, 47, 51
negroes, 79, 80, 487, 653
Nephegyi, Dr. Gabor, 335-7
Newcastle, Duke of, 196
Newcastle (Del.) Jail, 561
Newgate Prison, London, 320
Newmeyer, Henry, 654
newspapers. *See also* press, coverage of crime by
   Boston (Mass.) *Herald*, 415
   German News (N.Y.), 365
   Journal of Commerce (N.Y.), 94
   Kansas City (Mo.) *Mail*, 617
   Kansas City (Mo.) *Times*, 617
   Middleford (Ill.) *Press*, 636
   New York Times, 160
   New York Tribune, 33, 79, 94-9, 101, 105, 108
   New York World, 94
   Police Gazette (N.Y.), 373
   Police News (Boston), 673
   Pueblo (Colo.) *Press*, 617
   Rocky Mountain Herald (Denver), 635
   St. Louis (Mo.) *Times*, 617
   Staats Zeitung (N.Y.), 364, 365
   Truth (N.Y.), 343-4
   Wilkes-Barre (Pa.) *Advocate*, 622
New York (State) Assembly, 160-3
New York Herald, 97, 232, 233, 313, 370
New York Life Insurance Co., 340, 341

New York Times, 160
New York Tombs. *See* Tombs, the
New York Tribune
   and Thomas McElrath, 33
   offices of, 79, 101
   quoted, 94-9
   and Albert D. Richardson, 101, 105
   and Samuel Sinclair, 108
New York World, 94
nihilists, Russian, 362, 365-6, 368
Nims, Theodore S., 66
Noble, Dan, 254-5
Noe, James H., 402-4
Norkett, M. B., 654-5
Norris, "Ede," 379-80
North German Lloyd Steamship Co., 534
Northampton (Mass.) Bank, 241-4, 539
Northcote, Sir Stafford, 570-1
Norton, H. P., 336
Noyes, Edwin, 175
Nugent, John
   and attempted robbery of Thomas J. Smith, 531, 533-4
   and Manhattan Savings Institution robbery, 264, 266, 267, 268
Nye, James W., 56

Oakley, H. Cruger, 472
O'Brien, Sgt. Edwin, 142-3
O'Brien, James, 160
Ocean National Bank, N.Y., 247-54
O'Connor, Charles, 60
O'Farrell, Ann and Michael, 384-5
Ogle, William, 341-3
O'Kell, William, 252
Old Bailey, London, Central Criminal Court at, 175
O'Leary, Cornelius, 356
Olney, Peter B., 287

opium, 413, 418, 419-22, 464, 491
Oporto (Portugal), 564
Orange riots, 154-9
Orcutt (sheriff), 498
Osgood, S. S., 42
Outhouse, John, 302

Packer, Asa, 336
parcel thieves, 462
Patchen Avenue gang, 299
Pearson, Phil, 562
Peck, Dr., 472
Pedder, Henry C., 356
Penal Code, N. Y. State, 373
perjured testimony, 361
Perris, Sam, 246, 262, 275, 278
Perry (coroner), 58
Perry, Ned, 146
Pettengill, Ed, 459-60, 461
Petty, Capt. Joseph, 156
Phelps, Benjamin K., 573, 575
Philadelphia
  corruption in police force of, 272
  kidnapping at, 198-208
Phillips, Sgt., 247, 251
Phillips, Harry, 341
Phillips, John E., 651-4, 674
Philp, Kenward, 344
Phoenix Bank (N.Y.), 99, 343
photographs and photographing of criminals, 191-3, 566
pickpockets, 196, 197, 216-20, 330
Pike's Peak gold rush, 622, 625, 627
pillory, 29, 31
Pinkerton, William A., 562, 673
Pinkerton's National Detective Agency, 203, 287, 362
pirates, 61
Pitkin, Gov. F. W., 623, 628
Poe, Edgar Allan, 28-9, 518
Police, Board of (N. Y. City), 178

police, Denver
  brutality within, case of, 660
  composition and organization of, 663-4
  Detective Department of, 643, 658-62, 664
  discipline of, 636
  inadequate resources of, 620, 638-9
  institution of daily reports to, 664-5
  introduction of uniform in, 663
  memorabilia of, 662
  rogues' gallery of, 662
  roster of, 677-9
  size of, 663
police, English, methods of compared, 194, 196, 519, 601
police, French, methods of compared, 519
police, N. Y. City. See also harbor police
  administration of, 54-61, 178-80, 577-8
  appointments in, 33-4, 48, 592
  attitude of public towards, 600
  authorities' noncooperation with, 600-1
  cooperation of with other police forces, 182
  corruption within, 258, 581-4
  origin of, 29, 31-2
  quality of, 194, 592
  remuneration of, 32, 34, 178
  size of, 178
  suggestions for improvement of, 592-5
  uniform of, 29, 32, 375
police districts, 153
Police Gazette (N. Y. City), 373
Police Mutual Aid Association, Denver, 674-5
Police News (Boston, Mass.), 673
police riot, 58
politics in New York administration, 597-600

694 INDEX.

Pontez, Charles W., 340-1
Poole, Bill, 49, 51
poor-debtor law, 393
Porter, Billy, 275, 278, 298-9, 400, 401-2
presidential campaign of *1880*, 343
presidential election of *1884*, 183
press. *See also* newspapers
　coverage of crime by, 589-91
Price, Gen. Sterling, 617, 633
prisoners, interrogation and subsequent treatment of, 189-93
prisons, 389-98. *See also under specific institutions*
prize-fighting, 373-9
Proctor, Bill, 537, 539
prostitution
　among Chinese, 427-8
　at dance-halls, 481-2, 489-91
　method of eliminating from a neighborhood, 579-80
　in N.Y. compared with abroad, 196, 602
　proposals for control of, 602-3
Pryor & Noah, 659, 660
public executions, 30, 64-6
Pueblo Press, 617
punishment, intention, nature, and effect of, 333-4
Purvis (patrolman), 514
Putnam, Avery D., 154

quarantine laws, 143

raids on gambling-houses, 380
railroad riots, 628
Rand, Councillor F., 573
Rand, Jack, 459, 460, 461
Raymond Street Jail, Brooklyn, 298-9, 401
receivers of stolen goods. *See* "fences"
Reed, John, 35, 38
Republicans, 160-1, 597, 604
Restell, Madam. *Alias of* Lohman, Ann, *q.v.*

Rhinelander, William C., 471-2
Rhodes, Halsey, 635
Richardson, Albert D., 101, 105, 106-7
Ricord, Dr., 446
Ridgeway, Kate, 325-6
Riley (sheriff), 298, 299
Riley, Phil, 189, 372
Riolon, Dr., 501
riots
　at Astor Place, 43-7
　against Chinese in Denver, 628, 652
　against the draft, 78-86
　between Irish Roman Catholics and Protestants, 154-9
　between Metropolitan and Municipal police, 58
river thieves. *See* thieves — harbor thieves
robberies. *See* thieves
Robertson, Judge, 165
Robinson, Gov. Lucius, 573
Robinson, Richard P., 25-6
Robinson, William H., 558-62
Rocky Mountain Detective Agency, 347-8, 627, 629, 649
Rocky Mountain Herald (Denver), 635
Rogers, Charles M., 404-5
Rogers, Mary, 26-9
Rollins (coroner), 121
Romaine, Henry G., 232-3
Rooke, George, 378
Roosevelt, Nicholas, 30
Roosevelt committee (Theodore Roosevelt), 515
Rosenzweig, Dr. Jakob. *Alias of* Ascher, Dr., *q.v.*
Ross, Charley, 198-208, 234
Ross, Christian K., 198-200
Ross, Joseph, 200, 202
Ross, Walter, 198, 208
Rousseaux, Bishop, 476
Routt, John L., 618, 623, 628, 632, 655

INDEX. 695

Rowe, Johnny, 539-42
Rowland, Theodore, 117
Royal Insurance Company, 254
Ruppert, Jacob, 500
Ryan (prize-fighter), 378
Ryan, Capt. Thomas, 470
Rylance, Rev., 228, 231
Rynders, Isaiah, 47

safe-breaking, 658-60, 662, 668-9, 673
Sagart, Edward Herman Johannes, 368
St. Louis Times, 617
St. Luke's Hospital, 500, 501
St. Mark's Church, 224
Sammis, Cora, 441-2
Sampson, Thomas
 apprehension by of Dreyfus, 529
 and apprehension of counterfeiters, 164-5, 168-70
 investigation by of escapes from Sing Sing, 301
 and investigation of anti-Lincoln feeling in Baltimore, 69-77
 and Louis M. Van Eeten, 110-12
Saner, Major J. W., 573
Sanford, Gen., 60, 80
Santa Cruz de Oviedo, Esteban, 61
Saratoga County Bank, Waterford, N.Y., 273
Satterlee, Dr. F. LeRoy, 468
Saul, William, 138, 143, 144, 148
Saville, Georgetta, 347, 348
Saville, John J., 622
"sawdust" swindle, 126-7
Schafflinberg, Mark A., 630
Schultz, Capt. William, 152, 534-5, 536
Schuyler, Philip, 324-5
Scotland Yard, 516
Scott, William, 242, 243, 539

Scott, Gen. Winfield, 622
Seabring, Capt. Jacob, 58
secessionists, 69, 75
Seminole, Joel, 646-9
Seymour, Gov. Horatio, 85-6
Shadbolt, Theodore, 35-9
shanghai, case of, 564-5
Shannon, Mike, 534-7
Sharkey, William J., 251-2, 292-6
Shay, "Si," 43
Shelby, Gen., 617
"Shepherd's Fold," 500-2
Sheridan, John J., 456, 458
Sheridan, Walter, 562-4
Shevlin, Patrick, 264, 267-8, 535
Shinburn, Max, 252, 255, 256-8
Shipman, Judge, 64
shop-lifters, 330-1, 463
Siebert, Capt. Jacob, 151
Silleck (detective), 208
Simmons, John E., 467-8
Simmons, William W., 543-7
Simpson, John, 254
Sinclair, Samuel, 105, 106, 108
Sing Sing State Prison (Ossining, N.Y.), 111, 300-1, 473
Singer, Isaac, 327-9
Singer, Isabella Eugenia, 329
Singer Manufacturing Co., 327
Sinks, Dan, 658-60
Sisty, Wilson E., 616, 622-3
Slade, the "Maori," 378
slave trader, trial and execution of, 64-6
slaves, 30
Slevin, Edward, 384
Sloane, George H., 470-1
Smith, Charles, 653
Smith, Conrad, 297
Smith, Henry, 299-300, 302
Smith, James M., 57-8
Smith, Theodore, 630
Smith, Thomas, 522-5
Smith, Thomas J., 531-4
Smith, William A., 631-2, 651

INDEX.

smuggling, 143
Smythe, Frederick, 502
snuff, 465
Snyder, Andrew J., 625
social evil. *See* prostitution
Society for the Prevention of Cruelty to Children, 501
Sopris, Richard
  in the Civil War, 632
  and George Gorman, 630
  as mayor of Denver, 618, 628
  police appointments of, 635, 651
  and provisional government of Colorado, 616
soubriquets, 241
South Kensington National Bank (Phila.) 149, 272-3
Speckhardt, George, 289
Spencer, Charles S., 107
Spicer, Bob, 324
Spicer, John, 324-5
Spinola, Gen. Frank, 255-6
Spousle, Mary Ann, 327, 328-9
Staats Zeitung, 364, 365
"Stadt Huys," 29
Stagg, "Con," 410
station-houses, 387-9. *See also* jails
Steck, Amos, 617, 626
Stedman, Edmund Clarence, 61
Steele, Gen., 636
Steers, Henry V., 211-12
Steid, Herman, 269, 283, 287
Stephenson, Frank, 486
Stern Bros., 313
Steurer, John, 301-2
Stewart, A. T., & Co., 230, 313
Stewart, Alexander T., 224-35
Stewart, Gen. James, Jr., 552-5
Stiles, B. B., 618, 630, 634
Stoddard, Kate, 548, 549-50, 551
Stoeckel, Baron, 93
Stokes, Edward S., 159
Stone, Charles B., 634
Strasburger, Louis, 362-8

Strasburger, Rosa, 362-8
street-lighting ordinance, 29
Strute, George, 624
Stuart, Gen. "Jeb," 635
"Stuttering John." *See* Monahan, John
Stuyvesant, Gov. Peter, 29
suicide, 66, 112
Sullivan, Dennis, 297-8
Sullivan, James "Yankee." *Ring name of* Ambrose, James, *q.v.*
Sullivan, John L., 374, 376, 378-9
Sunday law, 514-15. *See also* excise law
superintendent of police
  duties of, 180-4
  position of, 178-80
Sweeney, John, 222
Sweeney, Peter B., 160, 161
swindlers, 151, 176-7, 527-8. *See also* confidence men; counterfeiters; forgers
swindles, 126-37, 461-3
sword-cane, 52

Taggart, Joshua, 272, 273
Talmadge, Henry, & Co., 337-8
Talmage, Frederick A., 44
Tammany "Ring," 160
Tansey, Frank, 564-5
taxation, 598-9, 604-5
Taylor, Steve, 378
Teeter, W. M., 655-6
temperance, 29
Thayer, Albert W., 673
Thiel Detective Agency, 643
thieves. *See also* bank robbers; shop-lifters; train robbers
  "butcher-cart" thieves, 497-500
  harbor thieves, 139-44, 146-52, 214-15, 531
  house breakers, 209, 454-5, 521
  methods of, 209-10, 453-6
  reasons for becoming, 331-2

INDEX. 697

thieves *(cont'd)*
  at riots, 85
  servant-girl confederates,
    310-11
  types of, 453-66
Third National Bank, N.Y. City,
  338
Third National Bank of Baltimore, 273
Thompson, George, 456, 458
Thorne, Inspector Thomas W.,
  149, 374
Thornton, George E., 623-5
Tiffany's, 356-7
Tilley (detective), 444
Titterington, James R., 499
Tombs, the (New York city
  prison)
  design and construction of,
    393-7, 398
  escapes from, 26, 292-8
  executions in, 66, 404, 415-17
  life at, 396-8
tools of burglars, 240, 668-9
Tracy, Billy, 359, 361
train robbers, 531
tramps, 449, 665
Trenton (N.J.) State Prison,
  407, 536
Trinity Church, 306
Troy (N.Y.) Prison, 402
Truth, 343-4
Tucker, W. E., 630
Tully (detective), 473
Tutton, Alexander, 556-7, 558
Tweed, William M. ("Boss"),
  160, 161, 162, 389-91, 606
Tyler (city marshal), 241

Uhl, Dr., 53
Uhler, Emma and J. Clement,
  411-13
Uling, Dr. Ernst. *Alias of* Bagnicki, Ernst de, *q.v.*
Umneck, Frederick, 559-60
uniforms, 29, 32, 375, 663
Union Bank of London, 346

Union Depot Co., 655
Union Pacific ticket office, 659
Union Trust Company, 340, 510
United States Sub-Treasury,
  556-8
Ustick, William, 669-70
Utica (N.Y.) State Asylum, 551

Van Brunt, Judge, 205
Van Brunt, Albert, 206
Van Brunt, J. H., 205-6
Vanderbilt, Comm. Cornelius,
  88, 201, 229, 526
Vanderbilt, Comm. Cornelius
  (imposture), 526-7
Vanderbilt, William H., 201
Vanderhoff, George, 104
Vanderpool, Charles O., 170,
  341-3
Van Eeten, Louis M., 110-12
Varien, Gen., 156
Vogel, Felix, 368
Vogel, Moses, 537, 539
Vosburgh, William, 399, 400

Wade, John, 35, 38
Wagstaff, Henry J., 66-7
Wales, Prince of, 62-4, 196
Walker, Gen., 516
Walker, Perry, 630
Walker, Thomas, 100
Wall murder case, 631
Wall Street, 576-7
Walling, Daniel (grandfather), 23
Walling, George W.
  in Europe, 515-16
  experience of as rookie policeman, 33-4
  family and early life of, 23-5
  promoted, 48, 153, 178
Walling, Leonard (brother), 78-80
Walling, Leonard (father), 23-5
Walsh, John, 299, 399, 400, 401
Walters, Lola, 346
Ward, Ferdinand, 390-1
Ward, John, 100
Ward, Sam, 42

Warden, Belle, 653, 662
War of the Rebellion. *See* Civil War
Washington, D.C., 68, 71, 72
watchmen, 29, 31-2
Watrous (detective), 659-60
Webb, Mary, 193, 506, 522
Webster, Tim, 74-5, 77
Weed, Capt., 246
Weed, Smith, 160
Welles, Col. J. Howard, 368, 372
Wells, Fargo & Co., 108
Wellsboro (Pa.) Bank, 273
Werckle, Louis, 264, 266
West, Frank. *Alias of* Maguire, Jim, *q.v.*
West, Louise, 326
Westervelt (sheriff), 58
Westervelt, William, 202, 203-4, 208
whipping-post, 29, 31
White, George Miles, 252
White, Plymouth, 584-8
Wiggin (detective), 277
Wilcox, P. P., 649
Wilde, Oscar, 462
Wilkes, George W., 510-14, 563
Wilkes-Barre Advocate, 622
Williams, Alex S., 374, 400, 401, 414

Williamson, Supt., 516
Williamson, Eugene Fairfax, 306-20
Willis, Nathaniel P., 48-9
wills, contested, 325-7
Wilson, Capt., 156
Wilson, Clay, 651-2
Wilson, "Tug," 378
Winans (state assemblyman), 161-3
Witherell, George, 631
Woglom, Capt., 544, 545-6
Wood, Albertis, 372, 415
Wood, Coal, 624
Wood, Mayor Fernando, 54, 56-7, 58-60, 380
Woodruff, Jim, 647-9
Woods, "Cockey," 378
work-house, need for in Denver, 665
Worth, Thomas, 525-6, 527
Wright, Jack, 236-9, 241

Yost, Gilbert, 271, 275
Young, Capt. John F., 255-6, 460, 461, 583

Zouaves, 82, 85, 650

PATTERSON SMITH REPRINT SERIES IN CRIMINOLOGY, LAW ENFORCEMENT, AND SOCIAL PROBLEMS

1. *Lewis: *The Development of American Prisons and Prison Customs, 1776-1845*
2. Carpenter: *Reformatory Prison Discipline*
3. Brace: *The Dangerous Classes of New York*
4. *Dix: *Remarks on Prisons and Prison Discipline in the United States*
5. Bruce et al.: *The Workings of the Indeterminate-Sentence Law and the Parole System in Illinois*
6. *Wickersham Commission: *Complete Reports, Including the Mooney-Billings Report.* 14 vols.
7. Livingston: *Complete Works on Criminal Jurisprudence.* 2 vols.
8. Cleveland Foundation: *Criminal Justice in Cleveland*
9. Illinois Association for Criminal Justice: *The Illinois Crime Survey*
10. Missouri Association for Criminal Justice: *The Missouri Crime Survey*
11. Aschaffenburg: *Crime and Its Repression*
12. Garofalo: *Criminology*
13. Gross: *Criminal Psychology*
14. Lombroso: *Crime, Its Causes and Remedies*
15. Saleilles: *The Individualization of Punishment*
16. Tarde: *Penal Philosophy*
17. McKelvey: *American Prisons*
18. Sanders: *Negro Child Welfare in North Carolina*
19. Pike: *A History of Crime in England.* 2 vols.
20. Herring: *Welfare Work in Mill Villages*
21. Barnes: *The Evolution of Penology in Pennsylvania*
22. Puckett: *Folk Beliefs of the Southern Negro*
23. Fernald et al.: *A Study of Women Delinquents in New York State*
24. Wines: *The State of Prisons and of Child-Saving Institutions*
25. *Raper: *The Tragedy of Lynching*
26. Thomas: *The Unadjusted Girl*
27. Jorns: *The Quakers as Pioneers in Social Work*
28. Owings: *Women Police*
29. Woolston: *Prostitution in the United States*
30. Flexner: *Prostitution in Europe*
31. Kelso: *The History of Public Poor Relief in Massachusetts, 1820-1920*
32. Spivak: *Georgia Nigger*
33. Earle: *Curious Punishments of Bygone Days*
34. Bonger: *Race and Crime*
35. Fishman: *Crucibles of Crime*
36. Brearley: *Homicide in the United States*
37. *Graper: *American Police Administration*
38. Hichborn: *"The System"*
39. Steiner & Brown: *The North Carolina Chain Gang*
40. Cherrington: *The Evolution of Prohibition in the United States of America*
41. Colquhoun: *A Treatise on the Commerce and Police of the River Thames*
42. Colquhoun: *A Treatise on the Police of the Metropolis*
43. Abrahamsen: *Crime and the Human Mind*
44. Schneider: *The History of Public Welfare in New York State, 1609-1866*
45. Schneider & Deutsch: *The History of Public Welfare in New York State, 1867-1940*
46. Crapsey: *The Nether Side of New York*
47. Young: *Social Treatment in Probation and Delinquency*
48. Quinn: *Gambling and Gambling Devices*
49. McCord & McCord: *Origins of Crime*
50. Worthington & Topping: *Specialized Courts Dealing with Sex Delinquency*
51. Asbury: *Sucker's Progress*
52. Kneeland: *Commercialized Prostitution in New York City*

* new material added

PATTERSON SMITH REPRINT SERIES IN CRIMINOLOGY, LAW ENFORCEMENT, AND SOCIAL PROBLEMS

53. *Fosdick: *American Police Systems*
54. *Fosdick: *European Police Systems*
55. *Shay: *Judge Lynch: His First Hundred Years*
56. Barnes: *The Repression of Crime*
57. †Cable: *The Silent South*
58. Kammerer: *The Unmarried Mother*
59. Doshay: *The Boy Sex Offender and His Later Career*
60. Spaulding: *An Experimental Study of Psychopathic Delinquent Women*
61. Brockway: *Fifty Years of Prison Service*
62. Lawes: *Man's Judgment of Death*
63. Healy & Healy: *Pathological Lying, Accusation, and Swindling*
64. Smith: *The State Police*
65. Adams: *Interracial Marriage in Hawaii*
66. *Halpern: *A Decade of Probation*
67. Tappan: *Delinquent Girls in Court*
68. Alexander & Healy: *Roots of Crime*
69. *Healy & Bronner: *Delinquents and Criminals*
70. Cutler: *Lynch-Law*
71. Gillin: *Taming the Criminal*
72. Osborne: *Within Prison Walls*
73. Ashton: *The History of Gambling in England*
74. Whitlock: *On the Enforcement of Law in Cities*
75. Goldberg: *Child Offenders*
76. *Cressey: *The Taxi-Dance Hall*
77. Riis: *The Battle with the Slum*
78. Larson: *Lying and Its Detection*
79. Comstock: *Frauds Exposed*
80. Carpenter: *Our Convicts. 2 vols. in one*
81. †Horn: *Invisible Empire: The Story of the Ku Klux Klan, 1866–1871*
82. Faris et al.: *Intelligent Philanthropy*
83. Robinson: *History and Organization of Criminal Statistics in the U. S.*
84. Reckless: *Vice in Chicago*
85. Healy: *The Individual Delinquent*
86. *Bogen: *Jewish Philanthropy*
87. *Clinard: *The Black Market: A Study of White Collar Crime*
88. Healy: *Mental Conflicts and Misconduct*
89. Citizens' Police Committee: *Chicago Police Problems*
90. *Clay: *The Prison Chaplain*
91. *Peirce: *A Half Century with Juvenile Delinquents*
92. *Richmond: *Friendly Visiting Among the Poor*
93. Brasol: *Elements of Crime*
94. Strong: *Public Welfare Administration in Canada*
95. Beard: *Juvenile Probation*
96. Steinmetz: *The Gaming Table. 2 vols.*
97. *Crawford: *Report on the Penitentiaries of the United States*
98. *Kuhlman: *A Guide to Material on Crime and Criminal Justice*
99. Culver: *Bibliography of Crime and Criminal Justice, 1927–1931*
100. Culver: *Bibliography of Crime and Criminal Justice, 1932–1937*
101. Tompkins: *Administration of Criminal Justice, 1938–1948*
102. Tompkins: *Administration of Criminal Justice, 1949–1956*
103. Cumming: *Bibliography Dealing with Crime and Cognate Subjects*
104. *Addams et al.: *Philanthropy and Social Progress*
105. *Powell: *The American Siberia*
106. *Carpenter: *Reformatory Schools*
107. *Carpenter: *Juvenile Delinquents*
108. *Montague: *Sixty Years in Waifdom*

* new material added   † new edition, revised or enlarged

PATTERSON SMITH REPRINT SERIES IN
CRIMINOLOGY, LAW ENFORCEMENT, AND SOCIAL PROBLEMS

- 109. *Mannheim: *Juvenile Delinquency in an English Middletown*
- 110. Semmes: *Crime and Punishment in Early Maryland*
- 111. *National Conference of Charities & Correction: *History of Child Saving in the United States*
- 112. †Barnes: *The Story of Punishment*
- 113. Phillipson: *Three Criminal Law Reformers*
- 114. *Drähms: *The Criminal*
- 115. *Terry & Pellens: *The Opium Problem*
- 116. *Ewing: *The Morality of Punishment*
- 117. †Mannheim: *Group Problems in Crime and Punishment*
- 118. *Michael & Adler: *Crime, Law and Social Science*
- 119. *Lee: *A History of Police in England*
- 120. †Schafer: *Compensation and Restitution to Victims of Crime*
- 121. †Mannheim: *Pioneers in Criminology*
- 122. Goebel & Naughton: *Law Enforcement in Colonial New York*
- 123. *Savage: *Police Records and Recollections*
- 124. Ives: *A History of Penal Methods*
- 125. *Bernard (ed.): *Americanization Studies.* 10 vols.:
    - Thompson: *Schooling of the Immigrant*
    - Daniels: *America via the Neighborhood*
    - Thomas: *Old World Traits Transplanted*
    - Speek: *A Stake in the Land*
    - Davis: *Immigrant Health and the Community*
    - Breckinridge: *New Homes for Old*
    - Park: *The Immigrant Press and Its Control*
    - Gavit: *Americans by Choice*
    - Claghorn: *The Immigrant's Day in Court*
    - Leiserson: *Adjusting Immigrant and Industry*
- 126. *Dai: *Opium Addiction in Chicago*
- 127. *Costello: *Our Police Protectors*
- 128. *Wade: *A Treatise on the Police and Crimes of the Metropolis*
- 129. *Robison: *Can Delinquency Be Measured?*
- 130. *Augustus: *John Augustus, First Probation Officer*
- 131. *Vollmer: *The Police and Modern Society*
- 132. Jessel & Horr: *Bibliographies of Works on Playing Cards and Gaming*
- 133. *Walling: *Recollections of a New York Chief of Police;* & Kaufmann: *Supplement on the Denver Police*
- 134. *Lombroso-Ferrero: *Criminal Man*
- 135. *Howard: *Prisons and Lazarettos.* 2 vols.:
    - *The State of the Prisons in England and Wales*
    - *An Account of the Principal Lazarettos in Europe*
- 136. *Fitzgerald: *Chronicles of Bow Street Police-Office.* 2 vols. in one
- 137. *Goring: *The English Convict*
- 138. Ribton-Turner: *A History of Vagrants and Vagrancy*
- 139. *Smith: *Justice and the Poor*
- 140. *Willard: *Tramping with Tramps*
- 141. *Fuld: *Police Administration*
- 142. *Booth: *In Darkest England and the Way Out*
- 143. *Darrow: *Crime, Its Cause and Treatment*
- 144. *Henderson (ed.): *Correction and Prevention.* 4 vols.:
    - Henderson (ed.): *Prison Reform;* & Smith: *Criminal Law in the U. S.*
    - Henderson (ed.): *Penal and Reformatory Institutions*
    - Henderson: *Preventive Agencies and Methods*
    - Hart: *Preventive Treatment of Neglected Children*
- 145. *Carpenter: *The Life and Work of Mary Carpenter*
- 146. *Proal: *Political Crime*

* new material added   † new edition, revised or enlarged

PATTERSON SMITH REPRINT SERIES IN CRIMINOLOGY, LAW ENFORCEMENT, AND SOCIAL PROBLEMS

147. *von Hentig: *Punishment*
148. *Darrow: *Resist Not Evil*
149. Grünhut: *Penal Reform*
150. *Guthrie: *Seed-Time and Harvest of Ragged Schools*
151. *Sproglе: *The Philadelphia Police*
152. †Blumer & Hauser: *Movies, Delinquency, and Crime*
153. *Calvert: *Capital Punishment in the Twentieth Century* & *The Death Penalty Enquiry*
154. *Pinkerton: *Thirty Years a Detective*
155. *Prison Discipline Society [Boston] Reports 1826–1854.* 4 vols.
156. *Woods (ed.): *The City Wilderness*
157. *Woods (ed.): *Americans in Process*
158. *Woods: *The Neighborhood in Nation-Building*
159. Powers & Witmer: *An Experiment in the Prevention of Delinquency*
160. *Andrews: *Bygone Punishments*
161. *Debs: *Walls and Bars*
162. *Hill: *Children of the State*
163. Stewart: *The Philanthropic Work of Josephine Shaw Lowell*
164. *Flinn: *History of the Chicago Police*
165. *Constabulary Force Commissioners: *First Report*
166. *Eldridge & Watts: *Our Rival the Rascal*
167. *Oppenheimer: *The Rationale of Punishment*
168. *Fenner: *Raising the Veil*
169. *Hill: *Suggestions for the Repression of Crime*
170. *Bleackley: *The Hangmen of England*
171. *Altgeld: *Complete Works*
172. *Watson: *The Charity Organization Movement in the United States*
173. *Woods et al.: *The Poor in Great Cities*
174. *Sampson: *Rationale of Crime*
175. *Folsom: *Our Police [Baltimore]*
176. Schmidt: *A Hangman's Diary*
177. *Osborne: *Society and Prisons*
178. *Sutton: *The New York Tombs*
179. *Morrison: *Juvenile Offenders*
180. *Parry: *The History of Torture in England*
181. Henderson: *Modern Methods of Charity*
182. Larned: *The Life and Work of William Pryor Letchworth*
183. *Coleman: *Humane Society Leaders in America*
184. *Duke: *Celebrated Criminal Cases of America*
185. *George: *The Junior Republic*
186. *Hackwood: *The Good Old Times*
187. *Fry & Cresswell: *Memoir of the Life of Elizabeth Fry.* 2 vols. in one
188. *McAdoo: *Guarding a Great City*
189. *Gray: *Prison Discipline in America*
190. *Robinson: *Should Prisoners Work?*
191. *Mayo: *Justice to All*
192. *Winter: *The New York State Reformatory in Elmira*
193. *Green: *Gambling Exposed*
194. *Woods: *Policeman and Public*
195. *Johnson: *Adventures in Social Welfare*
196. *Wines & Dwight: *Report on the Prisons and Reformatories of the United States and Canada*
197. *Salt: *The Flogging Craze*
198. *MacDonald: *Abnormal Man*
199. *Shalloo: *Private Police*
200. *Ellis: *The Criminal*

* new material added   † new edition, revised or enlarged